The Private Side of American History

READINGS IN EVERYDAY LIFE
VOLUME I TO 1877

FOURTH EDITION

Edited by
Gary B. Nash
University of California, Los Angeles

Cynthia J. Shelton

CENGAGE
Learning

Australia • Brazil • Japan • Korea • Mexico • Singapore • Spain • United Kingdom • United States

The Private Side of American History: Readings in Everyday Life - Volume I to 1877, Fourth Edition

Edited by Gary B. Nash
Cynthia J. Shelton

Executive Editors:
Michele Baird

Maureen Staudt

Michael Stranz

Project Development Manager:
Linda deStefano

Senior Marketing Coordinators:
Sara Mecurio

Lindsay Shapiro

Production/Manufacturing Manager:
Donna M. Brown

PreMedia Services Supervisor:
Rebecca A. Walker

Rights & Permissions Specialist:
Kalina Hintz

Cover Image:
Getty Images*

* Unless otherwise noted, all cover images used by Custom Solutions, a part of Cengage Learning, have been supplied courtesy of Getty Images with the exception of the Earthview cover image, which has been supplied by the National Aeronautics and Space Administration (NASA).

For product information and technology assistance, contact us at **Cengage Learning Customer & Sales Support, 1-800-354-9706**

For permission to use material from this text or product, submit all requests online at **cengage.com/permissions** Further permissions questions can be emailed to **permissionrequest@cengage.com**

ISBN-13: 978-0-534-14249-0

ISBN-10: 0-534-14249-4

Cengage Learning

5191 Natorp Boulevard
Mason, Ohio 45040
USA

Cengage Learning is a leading provider of customized learning solutions with office locations around the globe, including Singapore, the United Kingdom, Australia, Mexico, Brazil, and Japan. Locate your local office at: **international.cengage.com/region**

Cengage Learning products are represented in Canada by Nelson Education, Ltd.

For your lifelong learning solutions, visit **custom.cengage.com**

Visit our corporate website at **cengage.com**

Printed in the United States of America

Preface

The Private Side of American History, Volume I, is designed to supplement traditional textbooks that emphasize the political and intellectual aspects of history. This collection of reading offers a vivid description of everyday life in rural and urban America, from the colonial period through the third quarter of the nineteenth century. The selections provide a fresh perspective from which to view such vital but often neglected aspects of American history as work; family life, childbirth, child rearing, and sex; education and entertainment; religion; health, disease, and death; and conflicts created by encounters between diverse population groups—Native Americans and colonists, blacks and whites, and immigrants and established residents.

Arranged in roughly chronological order, the twenty selections are grouped into four sections, each of which concludes with an annotated bibliography. The headnotes place the subject of each selection in its historical context. A brief introduction to the volume describes the major areas that should be considered in a historical study of everyday life.

For assistance in the preparation of this Fourth Edition we would like to thank Nancy Crawford and our former editors at Harcourt Brace Jovanovich, William J. Wisneski and Thomas A. Williamson, who originally suggested the approach to American history reflected in this volume. Special thanks go to the reviewers of the Fourth Edition: Elliott Barkan, California State University, San Bernardino; Rodger Biles, Oklahoma State University; Richard D. Brown, University of Connecticut; Edward M. Cook, Jr., University of Chicago; Robert M. Crunden, University of Texas, Austin; John W. Jeffries, University of Maryland, Baltimore County; Peter Levine, Michigan State University; Ellen Skinner, Pace University–Westchester; Reed Ueda, Tufts University.

Gary B. Nash
Cynthia J. Shelton

Contents

1740–1800
Creating a Nation

1800–1840
The Early Republic

1840–1877
The Expanding Nation

Topical Table of
Contents

Work: Conditions, Attitudes, and Organization

Education and Entertainment

Sex, the Home, and the Family

Religion, Thought, and Values

Health, Disease, and Death

Violence, War, and Social Control

Protest and the Development of Political Consciousness

FOURTH EDITION

The Private Side of American History

Readings in Everyday Life

VOLUME **I** TO 1877

Introduction

History has traditionally been written as a record of public rather than private events. The growth of institutions, the election of officeholders, the passage of laws, the conduct of diplomacy and war, the expansion of scientific knowledge, and the process of economic development—these are the major categories employed by historians to reveal the past, as the table of contents of most history textbooks will indicate. Of course any history that did not investigate these topics would be incomplete. But American historians are recognizing that the public aspects of our past reveal far less than we would like to know about how our society and culture developed. For example, though we may understand the forms of government under which the colonies were founded, or the commercial relations between England and its New World colonies, or the rise of schools and colleges in the eighteenth century, we will still comprehend little about the feelings, motivations, and behavior of the great mass of colonizers. In the nineteenth century we may profitably study the Bank War, the building of canals and railroads, the abolitionist crusade, or the evolution of the Whig party. But the past still will not have come alive because we will know virtually nothing about how people lived, felt, and interacted behind the curtain of public events.

For two reasons, then, the history of public events is lifeless and limited, often unable to move us or re-create a feeling of the past. First, it deals primarily with public figures—the important politicians, business leaders, intellectuals, and military commanders. As many recent critics have noted, that kind of historical writing is elitist. It concentrates on the few and ignores the many, assuming that it was the "dynamic," successful handful who led the "passive," ordinary masses. By narrowing our vision in this way, historians indulge in a dangerous assumption about how events and movements occur. They bury from sight the fascinating and important story of all those who lived, worked, and died without leaving a footprint on the public record. Second, the history of public events is as narrow in its understanding of human motivation and behavior as it is in its choice of subjects. It tells us little about the hidden sources of human action and the intimate experiences of life that play such a vital role in public action. The actions of public figures, even the most powerful, have been influenced by their private lives. So to ignore the private side of American history is to cut ourselves off from sources rich in explanatory potential.

The historian-novelist Leo Tolstoy understood both these failings of traditional history when he wrote *War and Peace*, his great epic of the Russian people during the Napoleonic Wars. "To study the laws of history," he argued, "we must completely change the subject of our observation, must leave aside kings, ministers, and generals, and study the common infinitesimally small elements by which the masses are moved. No one can say how far it is possible for man to advance in this way toward an understanding of the laws of history; but it is evident that only along that path does the possibility of discovering the laws of history lie." Many would doubt that historical "laws" can be discovered at all. But Tolstoy had hit upon an understanding of how a people or a nation may better be studied. A century later we have begun to follow his advice. His concern was not only to study "the masses" but also to find the "infinitesimally small elements" that moved all people, whether they numbered among the elite or among the peasantry.

It is primarily to the second question—by what small elements of life are people moved?—that this collection of readings is addressed. Many other books in American history direct our attention to the "forgotten" or "historically voiceless" people of our past—Native Americans, Afro-Americans, Chicanos, women, the poor, the deviant, and so forth. Some of these groups figure prominently in the selections that follow simply because they made up the vast majority of the population. However, the readings have not been selected for this reason, but rather because they deal with the "private side" of American history. They are concerned with the experience of living and the daily aspects of life that mattered most to individual Americans of the past.

What are the "infinitesimally small elements" that are so important to the experience of a society? Very roughly, they are those aspects of life that occupy most of our waking hours today just as they did the daily rounds of people in the past: *work*—the performance of tasks, whether for pay or not, that consumes the greatest portion of our time; *learning*—whether transmitted formally in schools or inculcated informally through everyday contact with family, peers, strangers around us, the media, or other sources; *family and sexual relations*—through which the most intimate desires and emotions are expressed and basic needs are fulfilled; *reflection*—whether in the form of religious worship, political or social commitment, or merely daydreaming; *physical preservation*—the simple but vital concern for health and the perpetual struggle against sickness and death; *social relations*—interaction with the world around us, which most often involves no more than conforming to the rules of the community but sometimes involves violence and war against our fellow beings; *public involvement and political action*—by which we express support for or dissatisfaction with elected and appointed officials, institutions and policies, and even forces beyond our ken or control. If studied with care, these areas of human experience, taken together, are profoundly revealing of the life of a society in the past. They apply to rich and poor, the mighty and the humble, male and female, black and white. And though they vary in importance, depending on the era under consideration, all have played important roles at every stage of human history.

It is well to keep in mind that the boundaries between the private dimensions of American life and the better-known history of public events are usually blurred. For example, when men and women took to the streets in pre-Revolutionary Boston they were expressing a private need to be heard in public matters. We can read much about the effects of their actions on English policy and colonial politics but still understand little about how their private lives were touched by participation in violent protests. Similarly, the private and public aspects of history overlap in war. Historians have traditionally told us much about how wars began, how they were fought, and how diplomats drew up treaties to end conflict. But war involves personal trauma and transforms the lives of its participants. Conversely, what individuals bring to war in terms of their private makeup affects the outcome. Private and public life mingle everywhere, and only by adding studies of everyday life to the public record can we fully appreciate the richness and complexity of the past.

History is the record of change, so we must be attentive to how the private aspects of American life became transformed on the road from early Jamestown to the present. Careful comparison of articles dealing with the same aspect of everyday life in different eras should make that clear. Attitudes toward work among English colonists in the seventeenth century, for example, played an important role in the way society evolved on the Chesapeake, as Edmund Morgan's essay demonstrates. By the early nineteenth century the work attitudes of Americans were strikingly different, as the essays by Paul Johnson and Robert Gross reveal. Similarly, the daily reality of women's lives in the seventeenth and the nineteenth centuries can be compared in the selection by Laura Ulrich and the essay by Julie Roy Jeffrey. How public events changed the private side of life and, conversely, how changes in everyday life molded larger social and political movements are questions students will want to keep in mind as they ponder these essays.

One other reflection on the nature of social change may be useful here. While the same aspects of everyday life can be studied in different eras in many cases, life itself was changing in America as one generation succeeded another. The controlling elements of daily life were replaced or modified, dramatically in some instances, as American society moved from the earliest colonial beginnings to the turbulent nineteenth century. For the first colonists, relations with native inhabitants of eastern North America constituted a new and frightening experience. Invasion of an already inhabited land involved a fearsome contact with a "different" people; it produced violence on a massive scale; and it preoccupied the private thoughts of many men and women whose religiosity compelled them to seek a moral justification for this confrontation of cultures. In the late eighteenth century, as most Native American peoples withdrew to the west, this aspect of daily existence diminished except on the frontier. Another dominant concern of everyday life in the colonial period was illness and death. Infant mortality was high, the average lifespan was short, and epidemic diseases were common. Everyone had seen death, and few were the families that had not buried several children before they reached adolescence. But intimacy with death waned in the nineteenth century. Medical science conquered many epidemic diseases, the average lifespan increased, and hospitals were created for the sick and dying. The sight and sound of mortal illness and death gradually slipped beyond the experience of most people. While these aspects of private life became less important, others rose in significance. Entertainment assumed far greater importance with the reduction of working hours. Political involvement, only an occasional activity for the widely dispersed agricultural population of the eighteenth century, began to pervade the lives of an industrializing, urbanizing nineteenth-century people. Other examples could be provided. But students will want to make their own calculations of when and how the "infinitesimally small elements" of American society changed, for taking part in the process of exploration is both the surest and the most exciting way of gaining a fuller understanding of the past.

The Colonizers and the Colonized

1600–1740

The building of Jamestown, Virginia

The First American Boom: Virginia 1618 to 1630

EDMUND S. MORGAN

Land and labor are indispensable elements in the development of all new societies. In North America it was the land of Native Americans and the labor performed by indentured servants and slaves upon which most colonial wealth was built. As many as half of the Europeans who arrived in North America in the seventeenth and eighteenth centuries may have come as indentured servants. As such, they were not free to move where they wanted, to marry, or to work for themselves. They had "bound out" their labor and their lives for four to seven years to somebody in the colonies whom they had never seen.

Exploitation of indentured labor became the central reality of life in early Virginia. Once the cultivation of tobacco as an export product was successfully established, the colony quickly became an extraordinarily oppressive society. While a few entrepreneurs and plantation owners reaped handsome profits, thousands of indentured servants, most of them men living without women, worked year after year without adequate food or shelter, debilitated by disease and malnutrition, and able to blot out their despair only with alcohol. The wretched lives of ordinary people in Virginia during and after the first tobacco boom proved that inherited ideas about work and social relationships could rapidly disintegrate under harsh and isolated conditions. In the absence of the restraining institutions of government and morality that applied in England, the exploiter was rebuked, if at all, only by his own inner murmurings.

One of the most important comparisons the student may wish to make while reading this selection is between the quality of life of the white indentured servant and that of the black slave. Both servant and slave endured a debilitating and disorienting Atlantic passage; both faced not only physical acclimatization to a new land but psychological adjustment to a new condition; and both were locked into an intimate and oppressive contact with a hitherto unknown master. Of course there were major differences between servitude and slavery. The slave was bound for life and the servant for a limited period. The children of slaves inherited their parents' status, whereas the children of servants were born free. And the slave, if freed, faced many more obstacles than did the indentured servant who had served his or her time. But the large number of servants who ran away or committed suicide suggests that the conditions of life during the period of bondage may not have been so different for the servant and the slave.

The importance of Virginia far transcended the numbers who went there or the territory they occupied. In their relations with the native inhabitants of the region, in their manner of exploiting labor, and in their redefinition of liberty and authority, Virginians left their mark on all that followed. The Virginians were the first English immigrants to set down permanent roots on the continent, and they provided both models and antimodels for all later colonists. Their imprint, of course, was strongest on the colonial South, but it was not limited to that area.

A merican historians have always taken delight in the success that followed the introduction of private enterprise in England's first American colonies. Ralph Hamor recorded the spectacular change that came over Virginia with Gov. Thomas Dale's assignment of private gardens to settlers in 1614: "When our people were fedde out of the common store and laboured jointly in the manuring of the ground, and planting corne, glad was the man that could slippe from his labour, nay the most honest of them in a generall businesse, would not take so much faithfull and true paines, in a weeke, as now he will doe in a day, neither cared they for the increase, presuming that howsoever their harvest prospered, the generall store must maintain them, by which meanes we reaped not so much corne from the labours of 30 men, as three men have done for themselves." To which A. L. Rowse adds the comment that comes naturally to all of us: "Well, of course."

Governor Dale's assignment of private gardens in 1614 amounted to only three acres a man, and he gave no one title to the land. But by 1617 a substantial number of colonists had fulfilled their obligations to the Virginia Company and worked entirely for themselves. In the following year the "old planters," those who had come to Virginia before 1616, paying their own way, acquired a hundred acres of land in fee simple. Later settlers paying their own way were to get fifty acres apiece and another fifty for every other person whose way they paid. The

THE FIRST AMERICAN BOOM   From *William and Mary Quarterly*, vol. 28 (1971). Reprinted by permission of the author.

Company reached for a new source of profit from the labors of tenants who would be transported to Virginia at Company expense. In seven years, while they lived and worked on Company lands, they would pay rent on a half-and-half, sharecropping basis. And further to encourage immigration and financial investment the Company authorized groups or individual members of the Company to set up "particular plantations" of their own and man them either with servants or with tenants who, like the Company tenants, would work for themselves but give part of their proceeds for a term of years to the men who paid their passage. With the introduction of these new measures in 1618, private enterprise triumphed over the semi-military work gangs that had kept Virginia going, but barely going, in its first years.

In the six years that followed the triumph of private enterprise, Virginia killed off between three and four thousand Englishmen. An estimated thirty-five hundred to four thousand immigrants increased the population of the colony from about one thousand in 1618 to probably no more than fifteen hundred in 1624. In that year the Virginia Company—itself a private enterprise—was dissolved in disgrace. The royal officials who then took over the government of the colony did not revert to any communal system of work for the colonists. Private enterprise was there to stay. Nevertheless, the failure of the Virginia Company and the staggering death rate suggest that our "Well, of course" to the first successes of private enterprise in the colony is perhaps a little hasty. We need not and should not conclude that allowing men to work for themselves was responsible for the disasters that struck Virginia in the years after 1618. Still, it may be worth inquiring into the way that the incentives of private enterprise operated in the colony during those years, and how those incentives affected the fate of the Company and the later history of the colony.

Modern scholarship has placed the blame for the failure of the Virginia Company on the shoulders of Sir Edwin Sandys, who poured men into Virginia faster than the colony could absorb and support them. Without the capital to equip them properly, Sandys concentrated on getting men across the ocean, not only tenants for the Company's lands but artisans of various kinds to set up production of iron, glass, silk, and ships. Moreover, he encouraged dozens of private investors to establish particular plantations. Ship captains crowded men aboard and dumped them in the colony by hundreds, half dead and without provisions. Most of them died soon after, from malnutrition or from disease aggravated by malnutrition. When the king found out what was happening, he dissolved the Company.

There were of course other well-known reasons for Virginia's troubles, particularly the quarreling among different factions within the Company, the king's desire to maximize his revenues from customs duties on Virginia tobacco, and the Indian massacre of 1622, which alone accounted for 347 deaths. But there can be no doubt that the big mistake was the transportation to Virginia of such masses of unprepared and unprovisioned settlers, for whom the colonists already there had neither food nor housing. Admitting this much, we may nevertheless press the question why a colony that had been in existence for eleven years in 1618 was unable to provide a welcome for so many helping hands. And since the answer commonly given has centered on the lack of food supplies, it will be appropriate to begin by examining what people who lived at the time said about the scarcity of provisions, considering their statements from the harvest of one year to the harvest of the next.

1619–1620. When George Yeardley arrived as governor in April 1619 to inaugurate the Company's new program, he took over a colony in which the supplies of cattle and corn had been depleted. Yeardley reported that he would devote himself in the coming year to getting a good crop of corn. During that summer, in spite of an epidemic that weakened and killed large numbers, the colony reaped unprecedented harvests, and by the end of September the settlers enjoyed, according to John Pory (no friend of Yeardley), "a marvelous plenty, suche as hath not bene seen since our first coming into the lande." In January 1620 John Rolfe too reported the abundance of corn, and of fish brought from Newfoundland and sturgeon caught in Virginia. According to these leaders of the settlement, Virginians were apparently well fed in the winter of 1619–1620.

1620–1621. I have found no surviving reports about the amount of corn grown in the summer of 1620, but in November Sir Edwin Sandys informed the Company that the settlers no longer wanted English meal sent them. Instead they preferred beads for trade with the Indians. It is evident from other sources too that the colonists were getting corn from the Indians. In December, long after harvest time, George Thorpe observed that "this countrey meandes [i.e., mends, improves] in plentie of victuall everie daie," and he probably meant in supplies obtained from the Indians. By May 1621 Capt. Thomas Nuce, a newcomer, observed that the men sent under his charge lived "very barely for the most part: havinge no other foode but bread and water and such manner of meate as they make of the Mayze: which I would to God I Could say they had in any reasonable plenty." They would have been distressed, he said, if one of their ships had not brought in corn from Chesapeake Bay, where the colony now had "good and free trade" (with the Indians). The winter of 1620–1621 was apparently not a plentiful one, but there was no talk of starvation. In June George Thorpe reported that people were blessed with good health and good hope of a plentiful harvest of all kinds.

1621–1622. Again there is no specific report of the harvest. On December 15, 1621, Peter Arondelle, another newcomer, complained of his family's lean diet of one and one-half pints of musty meal a day per man. But the governor and Council reported in January that in the nine ships which had arrived during the autumn, none of the passengers died on the way and all continued in health. A ship from Ireland in November came "soe well furnished with all sortes of provisione, aswell as with Cattle, as wee could wishe all men would follow theire example." If Arondelle's complaint represents a general scarcity in the colony it was not serious enough to lower his enthusiasm for Virginia, because just two weeks later he was writing home about the abundance of cattle and hogs both wild and domestic and observing that "any laborious honest man may in a shorte time become ritche in this Country." The winter of 1621–1622 produced no other surviving complaints of scarcity. There was even some boasting that new immigrants no longer need fear danger from "wars, or famine, or want of convenient lodging and looking to."

Then, on March 22, the Indians struck, killing not only settlers but also much needed cattle. The outlying plantations had to be abandoned. Planting operations had to be curtailed, for corn furnished shelter to lurking Indians. There was no choice but to seek relief from the Indians themselves, not those who had participated in the massacre, but those to the north or south. Various captains were commissioned to get corn from them, by trade if they could, by force if they could not. There was not even a remote possibility that the harvest might be sufficient.

1622–1623. The corn obtained from the Indians and from the settlers' meager crops fell far short of the need, and most Virginians went hungry, as the prices of whatever provisions there were skyrocketed. On July 2, 1623, Delphebus Canne, recently arrived in Virginia from England, regretted not having brought more meal, oatmeal, and peas for sale to the settlers, because "now the land is destitute of food." But he noted that the weather had been good and that people anticipated a large harvest of both corn and tobacco. Moreover, ships were expected daily from Canada and Newfoundland, with enough fish for the whole ensuing year.

1623–1624. Whether the corn crop and the awaited cargoes from the north fulfilled expectations is not clear. In January the governor and Council reported that "the scarsitie this foreruninge yeere hath been greate, and who could expect less, after such a massacre, yett none to our knowledg hath Perished through wante, many seasoned men goinge through theire labours, beside harde marches, which endured the same Comone scarasitie." By April enough provisions had been obtained from the Indians so that the crisis was over.

The reports all reflect some scarcity of food between 1618 and 1624. But only during the year following the massacre was the scarcity acute, and in the winter and spring after the bumper harvest of 1619 there seems to have been no scarcity at all. Yet it is precisely from this winter and spring that we have the most explicit complaints from Virginia about people arriving without adequate provisions. On November 4, 1619, when a hundred Company tenants arrived "lusty and well" on the *Bona Nova*, the governor and Council calculated that the 544 bushels of meal sent with them would last only five and one-half months at two pounds a man per day. Fifty men were therefore parcelled out for a year to private planters. Yet two or three months earlier, when a Dutch ship put in at the colony, the governor and cape merchant, in a famous transaction, bartered Virginia provisions for twenty-odd Negroes, who certainly came ashore unsupplied with anything. It is not recorded that the Negroes were put to work for the Company. The following June, after some four hundred more settlers arrived, Governor Yeardley wrote plaintively to the Company, urging them to send subsequent ships with more provisions, adding that "yf such nombers of people come upon me unexpected, and that at an unhealthfull season and to late to sett Corne I cannott then be able to feed them owt of others labors." In the future, he begged them, they should send men before Christmas (by November 4 perhaps?) with six months' provisions (instead of five and one-half?).

Yeardley's complaints, his purchase of the Negroes, and his disposal of the men from the *Bona Nova* at a time when the colony was reporting an unprecedented abundance, suggest that the problem was not altogether one of whether supplies existed. It was a question of who had them and of who could pay for them. In a year of plenty the governor and Council were unable or unwilling to make use of fifty men without supplies when other Virginians *were* able and willing to do so. The great shortage of supplies, to which we attribute the failure of the Sandys program, was not an absolute shortage in which all Virginians shared and suffered alike. It was a shortage that severely afflicted the Company and its dependents, but it furnished large opportunities for private entrepreneurs, and larger ones for Company officials who knew how to turn public distress to private profit.

Throughout the period when too many men were arriving with too few supplies, the established settlers were so eager for more workers that they paid premium wages for them, even when they had to feed as well as pay them. In 1621 the governor and Council set maximum wage rates at three shillings a day for ordinary laborers and four shillings for most skilled craftsmen (joiners got five). If the workman was furnished with food for the day, the rate was only a shilling a day less. These figures amount to three or four times the maximum wages of day labor established by county justices in England, where a man who was fed by his employer generally received about half the wage of one who furnished his own food. Food was comparatively less valuable in Virginia than in England.

Daily wage earners were only one part of Virginia's labor force. An increasing number of workers were servants bound for a period of years. These came at a lower rate, and these were what the planters wanted. It had been common in England for farmers to hire servants by the year, and employers in many trades were required by law to hire their labor by the year. But servants who wanted to go to Virginia were willing to pledge several years' work, usually four to seven years, in return for transportation and maintenance. If a Virginia planter could import a man from England, the cost of his passage to the colony was about six pounds; his provisions and clothes for the voyage and to start him out in the New World might run another four to six pounds. At this rate the cost per year for a servant in Virginia was not much more, and might be less, than in England; for in England too masters had to provide food and shelter and sometimes clothing for their bound servants, and a year's pay for an agricultural worker ran from thirty to fifty shillings in the first decades of the seventeenth century.

Although the planter or enterpreneur who brought a servant to the New World ran the risk of losing his investment through death, Virginia planters evidently shared Edwin Sandys's belief that the rewards outweighed the risks. Despite the fact that bound servants had to be fed, clothed, and housed, Virginians could not get enough of them. Everybody wanted servants. Even tenants who had been unable to pay their own passage to the colony wanted servants. Richard Berkeley and John Smyth of Nibley received from the tenants at their particular plantation a request for two servants apiece "for their owne pryvate benefit and imploymentes." Indeed, as John Pory put it, "our principall wealth . . . consisteth in servants." And after the Virginia Company had been dissolved, former Governor Yeardley, now representing the interests of the colonists, urged the royal commission in charge of the colony "to advance the Plantacion for the future by sending great number of people."

From what little can be discovered about the value of a man's labor in the soil of Virginia between 1618 and 1624, it is not hard to see why the demand for servants was so high, even in the face of a food scarcity. At the time when Sandys took over the Company and began pouring men into the colony, Virginia had just begun to ship tobacco in quantity to the English market. The prices it brought were considerably lower than those for Spanish tobacco, but high enough to excite the cupidity of every settler. In the colony in 1619 the best grade sold for export at three shillings a pound. In 1623 what reached England was worth no more than half that, and in bartering within the colony it was said to have passed at less than a shilling a pound. In a lawsuit recorded in 1624, it was reckoned at two shillings a pound and in 1625 at three shillings again. The boom lasted until 1629 or 1630 when the price tumbled to a penny a pound. Though it recovered somewhat in ensuing years, it never again reached the dizzy heights of the 1620s. During that decade the profits from tobacco growing were enough to keep everybody scrambling for servants in order to grow as many plants as possible.

The amount of tobacco one man could produce in a year by his own labor varied from place to place, from year to year, and from man to man. In 1619 John Rolfe, who introduced tobacco cultivation in Virginia, estimated that a man could tend four acres of corn and one thousand plants of tobacco. Four years later William Capps, an "old planter," said that a man could tend two thousand plants and that this would make five hundred "weight" (presumably five hundred pounds) of tobacco. He also maintained that in 1623 three of his boys, whom he calculated as equal to a man and a half, had produced 3,000 weight of tobacco and 110 barrels (550 bushels) of corn. Richard Brewster, working with three men, was said to have grown 2,800 weight of tobacco and 100 bushels of corn. In 1626 William Spencer testified in court that in 1620 he had overseen the labor of six or seven men who had produced three or four thousand weight. The figures differ, perhaps because some of the authors were boasting, because some men worked harder than others, and because tobacco harvests varied sharply from year to year for reasons beyond human control. But by any calculation the returns from labor invested in growing tobacco were high. John Pory, after the exceptionally good harvest of 1619, said that one man had cleared £200 sterling by his own labor and another with six servants had cleared £1,000 sterling. These, he admitted, were "rare examples, yet possible to be done by others."

Because of the chances of such profits, Jamestown in the last years of the Virginia Company, while a charnel house, was also the first American boom town. There was no gold or silver. A man could not make a fortune by himself. But if he could stay alive and somehow get control of a few servants and keep them alive, he could make more in a year than he was likely to make in several in England. And if he could get a large number of servants, he might indeed make a fortune.

In a boom town not everyone strikes it rich; and even those who come in from the hills with a pocketful of gold generally give it up in a hurry—for drink, for women, even for food and clothing at bonanza prices. Life is cheap, but nothing else is. Those who have what gold will buy get the gold a good deal easier and faster than the miners who dig it. And the pleasures and comforts of normal human relationships, the things that gold will not buy, are not to be had at all. Men have come there not to settle down, but to make their pile and move on. But the easy-come, easy-go miner generally carries away as little as he carries in.

So it was in Virginia, where tobacco took the place of gold. Virginia's counterpart of the easy-come, easy-go miner was the small planter

who squandered his small crop on the liquor and luxuries that show
up in boom towns. "Our Cowe-keeper here of James Citty," wrote
John Pory in 1618, "on Sundayes goes acowterd all in freshe flaming
silkes and a wife of one that in England had professed the black arte
not of a scholler but of a collier of Croydon, wears her rought bever
hatt with a faire perle hattband, and a silken suite therto correspondent." The first legislative assembly in Virginia in 1619 felt obliged to
pass acts against excess in apparel and also against drunkenness. For
it was drink more than clothes that the planters craved. The thirst of
Virginians became notorious in England, and the ships that sailed up
the James River were heavily freighted with sack and strong waters,
even if they neglected to bring more solid fare.

Virginians needed drink, if for nothing else, to solace them for losing the comforts of a settled life. Few were able, like the collier from
Croydon, to enjoy the company of a wife. Women were scarcer than
corn or liquor in Virginia and fetched a higher price. Seeking to overcome the shortage, the Company dispatched shiploads of maids (for
whom prospective husbands were expected to pay), but the numbers
were not large enough to alter the atmosphere of transience that pervaded the boom town. The lonely men who pressed aboard every ship
in the James River to drown their cares in drink looked on Virginia
"not as a place of Habitacion but onely of a short sojourninge." They
would marry and settle down later somewhere else.

The whole appearance of the settlements, a mere collection of ram-
shackle hovels, argued that this was only a stopping place. It was a
time when Englishmen of all classes were putting up larger and more
substantial buildings throughout their own country; and an Englishman's idea of a house was something solid, preferably of brick or stone.
If it had to be made of wood, the walls at least should be plastered.
Visitors to Virginia rightly judged the intentions of the settlers from
the way they were content to live: "Their houses stands scattered one
from another, and are onlie made of wood, few or none of them beeing
framed houses but punches [posts] sett into the Ground And covered
with Boardes so as a firebrand is sufficient to consume them all." In
fact, it did not even take a firebrand. Virginia "houses" could be kept
standing only with difficulty. At Charles City, where the settlers had
considered themselves fortunate to be released earlier than others from
the Company's service, they went on building "such houses as before
and in them lived with continual repairs, and buildinge new where the
old failed." There was no point in putting up more than a temporary
shelter if you did not intend to stay; and as late as 1626 the governing
council admitted that what people looked for in Virginia was only "a
present Cropp, and theire hastie retourne."

The present crop stood in the way of everything else. Although
the government required everyone to plant a certain amount of corn,

men would risk both prosecution and hunger in order to put their time into tobacco. Even self-preservation came second. After the massacre, when the government adopted a policy of continuous attack against the Indians, it was difficult to get men to leave their crops in order to carry on the war for a few days. When the governor commanded them to go, they would "Crye out of the loss of Tyme," and when a campaign lasted as long as two weeks, they would demand "that they might have leave to retourne, lest it should prove their utter undoinge." When William Capps, who had had some experience in Indian fighting, volunteered to lead an expedition of forty men, he found that even the governing council was unwilling to spare them. Capps, whose speech comes through vividly in his letters, had his own explanation of the reasons for the Council's refusal: "take away one of my men," he pictures them saying to themselves, "there's 2000 Plantes gone, thates 500 waight of Tobacco, yea and what shall this man doe, runne after the Indians? soft, I have perhaps 10, perhaps 15, perhaps 20 men and am able to secure my owne Plantation; how will they doe that are fewer? let them first be Crusht alitle, and then perhaps they will themselves make up the Nomber for their owne safetie. Theis I doubt are the Cogitacions of some of our worthier men."

As in other boom towns, a large share of the winnings was carried away by those who supplied the flaming silks and strong waters, by men who had even less intention of settling down than the planters. The ships that anchored in Virginia's great rivers every summer were, as one settler observed, moving taverns, whose masters, usually private traders, got the greater part of the tobacco that should have been enriching the colonists and the shareholders of the Company. Since the Company had never been able to satisfy the needs of the colonists, it was helpless to prevent them from trading with outsiders, and by 1620 it gave up trying. Thereafter, the most it could do was to invest its dwindling funds in the subcorporations, known as "magazines," through which still hopeful members tried to recoup some of their losses.

A magazine was supposed to turn a profit by exchanging supplies for tobacco or other commodities or for the promise of tobacco when the next crop was in. But somehow the promises were not kept. The floating taverns got the tobacco before it could reach the "cape merchant," as the man in charge of a magazine was known, and all magazines seem to have ended with a loss to the investors in England. There were sometimes as many as seventeen sail of ships to be seen at one time in the James River, and the Virginians swarmed aboard them to drink and carouse and squander their tobacco. Anything that smelled of alcohol would sell, and the governor and Council complained bitterly of the "rates which unconscionable marchantes and maryners doe impose uppon our necessities . . . especyally of rotten Wynes which destroy our bodies and empty our purses." One trader even "boasted that the only sale of fower buttes of wyne would be Sufficyent to clere the whole Vioage."

The private traders from aboard were not the only ones who seized the commercial opportunities of the boom. Complaints reached England against Virginians who got to the ships first and engrossed the commodities most in demand, to resell at monopoly prices. And after the massacre, when corn was at its scarcest, those who had boats and could get a commission from the governor were able to bring back hundreds of bushels from the Chesapeake region, some of it bought, some of it stolen, some of it taken by force from the Indians there. At the price of corn then prevailing in Jamestown, these voyages to the Chesapeake must have been highly profitable, and there were charges that the chief men of the colony were only too willing to prolong the scarcity by discouraging or forbidding the planting of corn. As long as the shortage lasted, "they onely haveinge the means in these extremities to Trade for Corne with the Natives doe hereby engrosse all into their hands and soe sell itt aboard att their owne prizes. . . ." In the winter of 1622–1623 English meal was selling at thirty shillings the bushel and Indian corn at ten to fifteen shillings. By April even Indian corn was at twenty to thirty shillings "and non to bee had but with great men." If thirty shillings a bushel in Virginia meant, as the officers of the colony claimed, only ten pounds of tobacco and therefore only ten or fifteen shillings, nevertheless a man who accumulated a thousand bushels of corn on a short trip to the Chesapeake region would be able to trade it for ten thousand pounds of tobacco, worth from five hundred to a thousand pounds sterling.

Although Sir Edwin Sandys had been bent on profit for the Company's investors, profiteering, whether by residents or transients, had been no part of his plans for Virginia. He had hoped to offer a refuge for the underpaid English laborer and at the same time build a community without want and without oppression. Ironically, Virginia suffered both want and oppression, as Sandys's concentration on getting men across the water unwittingly played into the hands of local profiteers who engrossed not only goods but men. Virginia differed from later American boom towns in that success depended not on acquiring the right piece of land but on acquiring men. Land that would grow tobacco was everywhere, so abundant that people frequently did not bother at first to secure patents for the amounts they were entitled to. Instead, men rushed to stake out claims to men, stole them, lured them, fought over them—and bought and sold them, bidding up the prices to four, five, and six times the initial cost. The Company's program obligingly poured men into Virginia for the scramble.

Since the number of older, seasoned servants was limited not only by the high death rate but also by completion of their terms of servitude, it was mainly the newcomers under the Sandys program whose labor enriched the aggressive and enterprising traders and planters. At first sight it might seem that the death rate among the new arrivals (even higher than among men who had survived their first year in the country) was so great as to nullify any advantages to those who sought to exploit them. But the records show that enough of them survived to make up almost the whole labor force and also the vast majority of the population of Virginia by 1625. The muster of inhabitants taken in January and February of that year gives the date of arrival in the colony for 740 of the 1,210 living persons listed. Of the 740, only 110 had come to Virginia before 1618. The muster list also reveals that among the fifteen planters who held ten or more servants or "men" in 1625, only two servants out of 199 whose arrival dates are known had come before 1618.

The bondage of the men sent under the Sandys program was of several kinds. The time and produce of the ordinary bound servant belonged completely to his master. Tenants might live and work independently on the land of the Company or of some other master, but they had to surrender half of what they earned. There were also "apprentices," often known as "*Duty* boys" from the name of the ship (the *Duty*) on which some of them were transported. They were bound to serve for seven years under any planters who would pay ten pounds apiece for them. After their seven years' service, they were to be tenants bound for another seven years. If, however, a *Duty* boy committed a crime at any time during the first seven years, his term as a servant was to begin again for another seven years. Sandys doubtless envisaged the transportation of these children, taken from the streets of London and sent without their own consent, as a favor both to them and to those they served: he would rescue the boys from vice and idleness and at the same time reward the servant-starved planters, who were to make Virginia prosper.

The role of the *Duty* boys reveals, in fact, the main thrust of Sandys's plans for Virginia. Sandys was a champion of the rights of Englishmen against the impositions of the Stuart monarchy. In Virginia he would enable men to live without the heavy burdens of taxation that the expenses of government imposed on Englishmen, with or without their consent. But his way of doing it was to enlist, with or without consent, the surplus labor of England. Send men and boys to Virginia, and let them work there, both for the planters and for the officers of government. Eventually they would have their freedom and a more prosperous life than they could have looked forward to in England. Meanwhile they would enrich everybody else and make possible a government without heavy taxes, whose officers "should not need to prey upon the people."

For the support of each office of government Sandys persuaded the Company to allot a tract of land and a quota of tenants to work it for the incumbent. When a man left an office, he was supposed to turn over both the land and its tenants to his successor. The amounts were generous. The governor got three thousand acres and one hundred tenants, the treasurer and the marshall fifteen hundred acres and fifty tenants apiece, the vice admiral three hundred acres and twelve tenants. Whenever a new office was created or when the Company wished to reward someone for especially meritorious service, the way to do it was to give him land and tenants. When the secretary was found to be taking high fees for issuing land grants, he was forbidden to charge for his services and given land and tenants instead.

The result of this beneficence was to lay open every surviving tenant sent by the Company to exploitation by any officer who claimed him as part of his quota of tenants. And if an officer did not commandeer him, someone else would. Whether a man came as a servant, as an apprentice, as a tenant, or on his own, he was vulnerable. If death disposed of the master who could rightly claim his labor, an heir, real or fraudulent, would quickly lay hold of him. Or if, having paid his own transportation, he arrived in Virginia with no master but also with no provisions, he was easy prey for anyone who could feed and shelter him. Even if he came sufficiently supplied to set himself up independently, a bad harvest, insurmountable debts, or Indian depredations might force him into the service of a bigger operator. This was particularly true after the massacre, when it was reported that ordinary men who had made a start on their own were obliged, for fear of the Indians, "to forsake their houses (which were very farre scattered) and to joyne themselves to some great mans plantation."

Some planters were not above ransoming captives from the Indians in order to claim their labor. Jane Dickenson and her husband Ralph were tenants of Nicholas Hide when Ralph was killed in the massacre of 1622 and Jane was carried into captivity. After some time Dr. John Pott, the physician who had been sent to Virginia at Company expense, ransomed Jane for two pounds of glass beads. Ten months after her deliverance she complained to the governor and Council that she was held in a servitude that "differeth not from her slavery with the Indians," Dr. Pott alleging that she was "linked to his servitude with a towefold Chaine the one of her late husbands obligation [to Hide] and thother for her ransome, of both which shee hopeth that in Conscience shee ought to be discharged, of the first by her widowhood, of the second by the law of nations, Considering shee hath already served teen months, tow much for two pounds of beades." Other complaints reached London that "divers old Planters and others did allure and beguile divers younge persons and others (ignorant and unskillful in such matters) to serve them upon intollerable and unchristianlike conditions upon promises of such rewardes and recompense, as they were no wayes able to performe nor ever meant."

Among the worst offenders were the Company's own officials in the colony. In Sandys's shipments of men bound to the Company they had perceived an opportunity for exploiting not only the tenants but the Company itself. The fact that the men arrived without adequate provisions furnished an excuse for treating tenants as servants. Instead of being seated on Company lands where they could build houses of their own (as the Company's instructions required), the tenants were hired out to private planters, like the fifty men who arrived "lusty and well" on the *Bona Nova*. Although the officers reported that they hired out the sickly rather than the able-bodied, the Company got word that it was the other way round: the strongest men, who might have benefited the Company most, were put to work on private plantations. And "where it is pretended this placinge them with old planters is for theire health, they are so unmercifully used that it is the greatest cause of our Tenntes discontent. . . ." Thus while Company men labored unhappily on the lands of private planters, Company land went uncleared, unfenced, and unplanted. It would be difficult to believe that the Company officials perceived no personal advantage in this situation.

The hiring out of some tenants should have meant more food for those who remained in the Company's care. Apparently, however, the hired men's share of provisions was converted to private uses; and the men who continued as Company tenants were deprived even of the supplies intended for them. Whatever the Company sent, the officers appropriated, and gave the tenants only Indian corn and water, a diet not calculated to speed the recovery of men weakened by a long voyage. But malnutrition and the diseases consequent upon it were not the only reasons for the low productivity of the Company men. According to one dissatisfied London investor, the reason the Company tenants accomplished so little was because "the officers Tenantes were cheifely reguarded and the generall Companies Tenantes the more neglected." By which he probably meant that the officers made it their business to get a day's work out of their own assigned tenants but not out of the rest. Moreover, John Pory reported to the Company in 1624, the officers were seating the men assigned to their offices "on their private Lands, not upon that [that] belongeth to their office," so that the crop produced on these private lands of the officers "alwaies exceeds yours"; and since the land set aside for officers lay "unmanured [i.e., uncultivated] to any purpose," it would yield little profit to the succeeding officers. The existing ones, Pory added, used the Company's tenants "to row them up and downe, whereby both you and they lose more then halfe."

It is only fair to add that what the Company wanted for Virginia probably could not have been achieved by even the most faithful and assiduous of officers. The Company wanted a stable, diversified society, where men would make reasonable profits and live ordinary, reasonable lives. It was Virginia's misfortune in the last years of the Company to offer opportunities for profit that were much more than reasonable.

The men who seized the opportunities and captured the labor of Virginia's perishing immigrants are not difficult to identify. In January and February 1625 a muster of the inhabitants indicated the names and numbers of every man's "men" or servants, including both tenants and genuine servants. The fifteen who had ten or more may be taken as the winners in the servant sweepstakes:

Ralph Hamor	10
John Pott	12
Edward Bennett	12
William Epps	13
William Peirce	13
Roger Smith	14
William Barry	15
Francis Wyatt	17
Edward Blaney	17
William Tucker	17
Daniel Gookin	20
Samuel Mathews	23
George Sandys	37
George Yeardley	39
Abraham Peirsey	39

Some of these men may have won fair and square; about several of them we know very little. But the careers of the others make it a question whether we should call them labor barons or robber barons. It would be tedious to pile up the evidence about each of them, but a few simple facts may be suggestive.

The frontrunner, Abraham Peirsey, with 39 servants, had been "a verie poore man" when he came to Virginia in 1616 as the cape merchant in charge of the Company's magazine. Although he sold goods at two or three times the prices set by the investors, the magazine under his direction showed a loss, and in 1626 he had not yet paid the investors for the goods sold. But when he died two years later, he "left the best Estate that was ever yett knowen in Virginia." Edward Blaney succeeded Peirsey as cape merchant in 1620. At his death in 1626 he too had not paid for the goods he sold, but he had acquired seventeen servants. He had also succeeded in embezzling a fair amount by marrying a widow and successfully claiming an estate left by a man with the same surname as his wife's first husband, a trick played by a number of quick-witted Virginians at the death of a stranger who happened to bear the same surname. George Sandys, treasurer of the colony, having failed to receive the full quota of tenants assigned to his office, simply appropriated sixteen Company tenants as his servants. Although for some time before his departure for England in 1625 he refused to execute his office (the commission having expired), he continued to hold the tenants in bondage. One of them, listed in the muster as a freeman, wrote to a friend, "he maketh us serve him whether wee will or noe and how to helpe yt we doe not knowe for hee beareth all the sway."

William Tucker, who may originally have been a ship captain, probably came to Virginia between 1617 and 1619. Some time before 1622 he was entrusted by John Ferrar and associates with £900 worth of goods to sell in Virginia, for which, like other Virginia factors, he failed to deliver either cash or accounts. He was one of the men commissioned to trade with the Indians for corn in 1622–1623 and was also empowered to negotiate peace with the Pamunkeys of the Potomac River area. His methods of dealing may be judged by his success in poisoning two hundred Pamunkeys with wine brought for that purpose, which he gave them to drink in celebration of the peace treaty he pretended to conclude with them. By 1632 the House of Burgesses was finding his attitude toward his fellow Virginians unsatisfactory and objected to the Privy Council about merchants "who have by needlesse and unprofitable Commodities . . . ingaged the inhabitants in debts of Tobacco, to the value almost of theire ensuinge croppe . . . amonge whome we have good cause to complayne of Captayne *Tucker*, who hath farr exceeded all other marchaunts in the prizes of theire goods. . . ."

Ralph Hamor, though he wrote one of the most effective pamphlets in praise of Virginia, got off to a slow start or else lost heavily in the massacre. In 1623, when other men were already getting rich, George Sandys observed that "Captain Hamor is miserablie poore and necessitie will inforce him to shiftes." The shifts to which he resorted included trading with the Indians and selling English goods at prices that brought accusations of extortion. By 1625, with ten men growing tobacco for him, he was far from poor.

Dr. John Pott seems to have been more assiduous in pursuit of cattle and servants than of his duties as physician. In 1623 George Sandys dismissed him as a mere cipher, but by 1628 he was acting governor. According to his successor, Gov. John Harvey, he took advantage of the position to advance his private interest "by foule and coveteous ways," in particular "by cuting out the markes of other mens neate cattell and markinge them for himselfe with his owne handes, whereby he hath gotten into a greate stock of cattell." Harvey pardoned him because of the colony's need for his services as a physician and because Harvey found his delinquencies to have been in imitation of "the example of a former governor who passed unquestioned for many notable oppressions."

The former governor to whom Harvey referred was probably George Yeardley, who had found Virginia a rewarding environment from the beginning. According to John Pory, when Yeardley arrived there in 1610, he carried with him nothing more valuable than a sword. But when he visited London in 1617, after his first term as governor of Virginia, he was able "out of his meer gettings here" to spend "very near three thousand poundes." Before returning to the colony he got himself knighted, and Londoners observed that "he flaunts it up and down the streets in extraordinary bravery, with fourteen or fifteen fair liveries after him."

Yeardley, when appointed governor in 1618, was assigned three thousand acres of land and one hundred tenants plus thirty more in 1620 to make up for deaths among the first group. When Yeardley gave up the governorship in 1621, he turned over only forty-six tenants. The governor's Council, which now included Yeardley, wrote to the Company in London that "as for the rest of the Tenantes Sir George yardley denieth to make them good, And sayeth that havinge made noe strong Agrement with you at any tyme he holdeth nott him selfe tyed unto yt, And therfore should take it for a matter of great Injustice to bee Compelled therunto." Yeardley, whom William Capps characterized as a "right worthie Statesman, for his own profit," did not give up his tenants, and the records contain accusations against him of detaining servants belonging to other planters and of keeping as a servant a young man whose relatives had paid his way. He remained nevertheless a member of the Council and was again serving as governor when he died in 1627. He was one of those commissioned to trade for corn after the massacre of 1622 and was accused by one settler of discouraging the planting of corn, the word being "that Sir G. Yardlie should provide them Corne if they would provide Tobacco." He did, in fact, provide the corn, one thousand bushels in January 1623 alone. At his death Yeardley's estate was apparently valued at only about £10,000. But it is not unlikely that he had already transferred much of what he owned to his wife and children in order to circumvent the litigation that a substantial will often produced.

It seems evident that while the Virginia Company was failing in London a number of its officers in the colony were succeeding. In order to do so they not only rendered less than faithful service to their employers; they also reduced other Virginians to a condition which, while short of slavery, was also some distance from the freedom that Englishmen liked to consider as their birthright. The Company in 1618 had inaugurated a popularly elected representative assembly, but the effective power for at least ten or fifteen years longer remained in the governor and his Council. By no coincidence, the Council consisted almost entirely of the men holding large numbers of servants. Between 1619 and 1627 Hamor, Pott, Smyth, Sandys, Tucker, Mathews, and

Yeardley sat on it, while Wyatt and Yeardley took turns in the governor's chair. These men, with a more than average interest in controlling the labor force, were thus enabled to maintain their personal ascendancy not only over their servants but over all lesser men. Whether operating under the Company or, after 1625, under the king, they met every challenge to their authority with a rigor not exceeded by what we know of the earlier absolute government of John Smith or Thomas Dale.

In May 1624, when they discovered that Richard Barnes had uttered "base and detracting" speeches against the governor, they ordered that he "be disarmed, and have his armes broken and his tongue bored through with a awl. shall pass through a guard of 40 men and shalbe butted by every one of them, and att the head of the troope kicked downe and footed out of the fort: that he shalbe banished out of *James Cittye* and Iland, that he shall not be capable of any privilege of freedome of the countrey, and that (before he goe out of the Iland) he shall put in suretyes of £200 bond for the good behaviour." When John Heny was reprimanded by Captain Tucker for going aboard a ship contrary to the governor's command, Heny made the mistake of saying, after Tucker had left, that Tucker "would be the death of him as he was of *Robert leyster*." For these words, reported to the Council, Heny got sixty stripes and had to beg forgiveness of Tucker, pay him one hundred pounds of tobacco, and be imprisoned until he could give bond for good behavior.

Heny's offense came at a time when the Council had also heard of murmurs against their execution of Richard Cornish, a ship master, for sodomy. There is no record of the execution, but some of the testimony in the case was recorded, and there can be no doubt that the execution took place. Afterwards, on a voyage to Canada, one Edward Nevell met up with Cornish's brother, and upon the latter's inquiry as to how the execution came about, Nevell replied "he was put to death through a scurvie boys meanes, and no other came against him." For this statement, made aboard ship off Canada where the governing council of Virginia could scarcely claim jurisdiction, Nevell upon his return to Virginia was required to "stand one the pillory with a paper one his head shewinge the cause of his offence in the markett place, and to loose both his Ears and to serve the Colony for A yeere, And forever to be incapable to be A ffreeman of the Countrey." A month later Thomas Hatch was heard to say in a private house in James City "that in his consyence he thought the said Cornishe was put to death wrongfully." Hatch had the misfortune to be a *Duty* boy, and his seven-year period of service was nearly up. The court therefore ordered that *"Thomas Hatch* for his offence shalbe whipt from the forte to the gallows and from thence to be whipt back againe, and be sett uppon the Pillory and there to loose one of his eares, And that his service to Sir *George Yeardley* for seaven yeers Shallbegan [again] from the present dye."

The councillors not only guarded their authority jealously, and perhaps unconstitutionally, but not infrequently they wielded it on their own behalf, participating in decisions that favored their interests. Sandys sat at a meeting in which Luke Eden was seeking payment of twenty bushels of corn due him from Sandys. Whether Eden got the corn is not recorded, but he did get himself fined two hundred pounds of tobacco and laid neck and heels "for his lewd behavior and unreverent speche" towrd Sandys in the council chamber. Wyatt participated in a judgment that awarded him a Negro servant "notwithstandinge, any sale by Capt. *Jonnes* to Capt. *Bass,* or any other chaleng by the ships company" (Captain Jones had brought a privateer into the James for provisions and apparently considered the servant part of the ship's booty). Abraham Peirsey sat at a meeting that had Richard Crocker put in the pillory with his ears nailed for saying that Peirsey and Hamor were not fit to sit on the Council because "they deale uppon nothing but extortion." Yeardley sat at a meeting that ordered the execution of a man for killing a calf of Yeardley's and at another meeting that awarded him as tenants all the *Duty* boys who had finished their terms as servants. He also participated in sentencing John Radish to lie neck and heels because Radish "Caryed over Sir *George Yardley* his servants to his house at unsesonable tyme of the night and there gave them Entertainment and made them drunke."

It was apparently not without reason that ordinary men grumbled at the government. In the words of William Tyler, "neither the Governor nor Counsell could or would doe any poore men right, but that they would shew favor to great men and wronge the poore."

It may be contended that severe discipline was necessary in a colony consisting predominantly of lusty young men who had just shaken loose the fetters of home and country. And it must be acknowledged that the men entrusted with government did protect some of the rights of servants. When a master failed to teach an indentured apprentice his trade or when he sought to hold a servant beyond the term of his indenture, the Council might interfere. Dr. Pott was ordered by a meeting at which he was himself present either to teach his apprentice the art of an apothecary (which he was neglecting to do) or else pay him wages.

Nevertheless serious differences made servitude in Virginia more onerous than servitude in England. The ordinary term of service that a man agreed to work in Virginia was not a year but several years; and the wages to which he was entitled had been paid in advance in the form of transportation across the ocean. Almost all servants were therefore in a condition resembling that of the least privileged type of English servant, the parish apprentice, a child who (to relieve the community of supporting him) was bound to service by court order until he was twenty-one or twenty-four, with no obligation on his appointed master's part to teach him a trade or to pay him. In Virginia a master had little reason to treat his servant well in order to obtain a renewal of his services at the expiration of his term, and a servant had little reason to work hard in order to assure being rehired, because men would not bind themselves out for a second long term when they could make more by working for themselves. There was accordingly the more reason for a master to assert his authority in order to get what he considered a full quota of work from his servants. Not surprisingly it was reported in England that Virginians "abuse their servantes there with intollerable oppression and hard usage."

The records are not sufficiently complete to show how extensive the abuse of servants may have been, but there is some evidence that the Council in Virginia (until 1634 the only court) supported masters in severities that would not have been allowed in England. The most extreme example is the case of John and Alice Proctor and their servants Elizabeth Abbott and Elias Hinton, both of whom died after a series of beatings inflicted by the Proctors and by other servants acting under orders from the Proctors. Thomas Gates testified that he counted five hundred lashes inflicted on the girl at one time and warned Proctor that he might as well kill her and be done with it. Alice Bennett, who examined her, "fownd she had been sore beaten and her body full of sores and holes very dangerously raunckled and putrified both above her wast and uppon her hips and thighes." Other witnesses testified that Proctor beat Hinton with a rake. Yet there is no indication that the Proctors were punished. By contrast we find English courts undertaking the work of correcting unruly servants themselves (as the statues required) and even on occasion forbidding masters to do it. In Virginia, servants who found themselves in the hands of brutal masters like the Proctors had no way out. Some ran away to the Indians and went native, or escaped to the Dutch settlements or to New England. But a Virginian who harbored another man's servant was liable to prosecution, and the records speak often of runaways apprehended and returned to their masters. Even the compassionate witnesses who testified against the Proctors indicated that when the maid came to them for shelter they had instead returned her to her master and mistress in her half-dead condition, with entreaties that *they* pardon *her!*

But whether physically abused or not, Englishmen found servitude in Virginia more degrading than servitude in England. In England the hiring of workers was dignified by laws and customs that gave a servant some control over his own life. He had to give his master three months' notice if he intended to leave at the end of his term, and in order to move from one place to another, he had to have a testimonial that his term of service was finished. But by the same token, a master could not turn away a servant before his term was up and had to give him three months' advance notice that his contract would not be renewed. Once a year, in the petty sessions held by the constables, servants could renew their contracts or make new ones, with the constables recording the transaction. These sessions, usually held in a churchyard, came to be known as hiring fairs and constituted a kind of open labor market where workmen sold their annual services. But in Virginia it was the masters who sold the workmen, and there was no annual hiring fair. Masters bought and sold servants at any time for any period of years covered by their transportation contracts; and during that period a servant might find himself sold without his consent from one master to another. In 1633 a Dutch sea captain found the planters gambling at cards with their servants as stakes. Virginians dealt in servants the way Englishmen dealt in land or chattels.

This development was a simple outgrowth of the extreme demand for labor in combination with the long terms of service that were exacted for transportation to Virginia. In England itself, after labor became more valuable, the demand produced a certain amount of buying and selling of industrial apprentices. When a man had more apprentices than he needed, he might with the permission of his guild sell an apprentice to another master of the guild. But industrial apprentices were a special case, and the idea of a large-scale market in men, or at least in English men, was shocking to Englishmen. "My Master Atkins," wrote Thomas Best from Virginia in 1623, "hath sold me for a £150 sterling like a damnd slave." This "buying and selling men and boies" had already become a scandal by 1619, when John Rolfe noted that it "was held in *England* a thing most intolerable." Capt. John Smith denounced the "pride, covetousnesse, extortion, and oppression" of men who sold "even men, women and children for who will give most." It would be better, he said, that these profiteers be "made such merchandize themselves, then suffered any longer to use that trade." And in 1625 Thomas Weston refused to carry servants in his ship from Canada to Virginia because "servants were sold heere upp and downe like horses, and therfore he held it not lawfull to carie any."

Other shipmasters were not so scrupulous, and the dissolution of the Virginia Company brought no end to the market in men or to their importation. So much did the planters count on continued importations that the Council during the 1620s awarded as yet unarrived, unknown, and unnamed servants to the victors in lawsuits. A servant, by going to Virginia, became for a number of years a thing, a commodity with a price. Although the government might protect him against continuation in the status beyond the time agreed upon, it was not likely to shorten his term or give him his freedom, even if his master's crimes against him were serious enough to warrant the death penalty. The servant who was the victim of Richard Cornish's homosexual attack did not win his freedom by his master's execution. Even though no other man had a legal claim to his service, the court decreed that he must choose another master, who in return was to compensate the government for the costs of prosecuting Cornish. A servant in Virginia, as long as his term had not expired, was a machine to make tobacco for somebody else.

"Like a damnd slave," said Thomas Best. To buy and sell servants for a brief period of years was not the same as buying and selling men for life and their unborn children with them. But it was a step in that direction. We can perhaps see, then, in boom-time Virginia not only the fleeting ugliness of private enterprise operating temporarily without check, not only greed magnified by opportunity, producing fortunes for a few and misery for many. We may also see Virginians beginning to move toward a system of labor that treated men as things.

A
TREATY

HELD WITH THE

CATAWBA and CHEROKEE INDIANS,

AT THE

CATAWBA-TOWN *and* BROAD-RIVER,

IN THE

Months of *February* and *March* 1756.

By Virtue of a Commiffion granted by the Honorable *ROBERT DINWIDDIE*, Efquire, His Majefty's Lieutenant-Governor, and Commander in Chief of the Colony and Dominion of VIRGINIA, to the Honorable PETER RANDOLPH and WILLIAM BYRD, Efquires, Members of His Majefty's Council of the faid Colony.

Publifhed by Order of the GOVERNOR.

WILLIAMSBURG: Printed by W. HUNTER.   M.DCC.LVI.

The Indians' New World:
The Catawba Experience

JAMES H. MERRELL

The arrival of European colonists and African slaves to America's Atlantic shore in the early seventeenth century began a new and fateful era for the American Indian. For centuries prior to 1492, native societies had inhabited the woodlands, plains, and deserts of the North American continent. On the eve of English colonization of the eastern seaboard, hundreds of different Indian societies carried on their everyday lives within established political, economic, and cultural systems. A central fact of our colonial period is that the colonists were in constant and intimate contact with these native societies. Indeed, our early history is the history of the convergence of America's native inhabitants, African slaves, and European immigrants, each from a different continent but linked by circumstances and design.

As James Merrell argues in the following essay, Indians, as well as the settlers and slaves with whom they interacted, lived in a "New World" after European colonization began. Merrell explores how the patterns of everyday existence of the Indians of what is today North and South Carolina and Virginia were transformed by European contact. European diseases, technologies, and desire for land in turn transformed the material and cultural lives of the Catawbas. Rather than becoming passive victims of this process, they responded in creative ways, altering their lifeways to coexist with the invaders from across the Atlantic.

In studying our early history, one of the myths to overcome is that the course of Indian-white relations was simply a matter of white military conquest and the consequent cultural obliteration of Native American culture. It is true that European colonizers ultimately triumphed after serveral centuries of armed clashes, that the Indians lost most of their land, and that by the late nineteenth century the reservation had become the home of most surviving Indian people. But, as Merrell shows, the Catawba persisted through decades of contact with European-Americans, continuously adapting in a struggle for cultural as well as physical survival.

What does the Catawba's experience tell us about the impact of European colonization on native societies? After you read this selection and that by Peter H. Wood on blacks in colonial South Carolina, make some comparisons between the nature of Indian-Euroamerican interaction and African-Euroamerican interaction.

In August 1608 John Smith and his band of explorers captured an Indian named Amoroleck during a skirmish along the Rappahannock River. Asked why his men—a hunting party from towns upstream—had attacked the English, Amoroleck replied that they had heard the strangers "were a people come from under the world, to take their world from them." Smith's prisoner grasped a simple yet important truth that students of colonial America have overlooked: after 1492 native Americans lived in a world every bit as new as that confronting transplanted Africans or Europeans.

The failure to explore the Indians' new world helps explain why, despite many excellent studies of the native American past, colonial history often remains "a history of those men and women—English, European, and African—who transformed America from a geographical expression into a new nation." One reason Indians generally are left out may be the apparent inability to fit them into the new world theme, a theme that exerts a powerful hold on our historical imagination and runs throughout our efforts to interpret American development. From Frederick Jackson Turner to David Grayson Allen, from Melville J. Herskovits to Daniel C. Littlefield, scholars have analyzed encounters between peoples from the Old World and conditions in the New, studying the complex interplay between Europeans or African cultural patterns and the American environment. Indians crossed no ocean, peopled no faraway land. It might seem logical to exclude them.

The natives' segregation persists, in no small degree, because historians still tend to think only of the new world as the New World, a geographic entity bounded by the Atlantic Ocean on the one side and the Pacific on the other. Recent research suggests that process was as important as place. Many settlers in New England recreated familiar forms with such success that they did not really face an alien environment until long after their arrival. Africans, on the other hand, were struck by the shock of the new at the moment of the enslavement, well

THE INDIANS' NEW WORLD   *William and Mary Quarterly*, vol. 41 (Oct. 1984). Reprinted by permission of the author.

before they stepped on board ship or set foot on American soil. If the Atlantic was not a barrier between one world and another, if what happened to people was more a matter of subtle cultural processes than mere physical displacements, perhaps we should set aside the maps and think instead of a "world" as the physical and cultural milieu within which people live and a "new world" as a dramatically different milieu demanding basic changes in ways of life. Considered in these terms, the experience of natives was more closely akin to that of immigrants and slaves, and the idea of an encounter between worlds can—indeed, must—include the aboriginal inhabitants of America.

For American Indians a new order arrived in three distinct yet overlapping stages. First, alien microbes killed vast numbers of natives, sometimes before the victims had seen a white or black face. Next came traders who exchanged European technology for Indian products and brought natives into the developing world market. In time traders gave way to settlers eager to develop the land according to their own lights. These three intrusions combined to transform native existence, disrupting established cultural habits and requiring creative responses to drastically altered conditions. Like their new neighbors, then, Indians were forced to blend old and new in ways that would permit them to survive in the present without forsaking their past. By the close of the colonial era, native Americans as well as whites and blacks had created new societies, each similar to, yet very different from, its parent culture.

The range of native societies produced by this mingling of ingredients probably exceeded the variety of social forms Europeans and Africans developed. Rather than survey the broad spectrum of Indian adaptations, this article considers in some depth the response of natives in one area, the southern piedmont. Avoiding extinction and eschewing retreat, the Indians of the piedmont have been in continuous contact with the invaders from across the sea almost since the beginning of the colonial period, thus permitting a thorough analysis of cultural intercourse. Moreover, a regional approach embracing groups from South Carolina to Virginia can transcend narrow (and still poorly understood) ethnic or "tribal" boundaries without sacrificing the richness of detail a focused study provides.

Indeed, piedmont peoples had so much in common that a regional perspective is almost imperative. No formal political ties bound them at the onset of European contact, but a similar environment shaped their lives, and their adjustment to this environment fostered cultural uniformity. Perhaps even more important, these groups shared a single history once Europeans and Africans arrived on the scene. Drawn together by their cultural affinities and their common plight, after 1700 they migrated to the Catawba Nation, a cluster of villages along the border between the Carolinas that became the focus of native life in the region. Tracing the experience of these upland communities both before and after they joined the Catawbas can illustrate the consequences of contact and illuminate the process by which natives learned to survive in their own new world.

For centuries, ancestors of the Catawbas had lived astride important aboriginal trade routes and straddled the boundary between two cultural traditions, a position that involved them in a far-flung network of contacts and affected everything from potting techniques to burial practices. Nonetheless, Africans and Europeans were utterly unlike any earlier foreign visitors to the piedmont. Their arrival meant more than merely another encounter with outsiders; it marked an important turning point in Indian history. Once these newcomers disembarked and began to feel their way across the continent, they forever altered the course and pace of native development.

Bacteria brought the most profound disturbances to upcountry villages. When Hernando de Soto led the first Europeans into the area in 1540, he found large towns already "grown up in grass" because "there had been a pest in the land" two years before, a malady probably brought inland by natives who had visited distant Spanish posts. The sources are silent about other "pests" over the next century, but soon after the English began colonizing Carolina in 1670 the disease pattern became all too clear. Major epidemics struck the region at least once every generation—in 1698, 1718, 1738, and 1759—and a variety of less virulent illnesses almost never left native settlements.

Indians were not the only inhabitants of colonial America living—and dying—in a new disease environment. The swamps and lowlands of the Chesapeake were a deathtrap for Europeans, and sickness obliged colonists to discard or rearrange many of the social forms brought from England. Among native peoples long isolated from the rest of the world and therefore lacking immunity to pathogens introduced by the intruders, the devastation was even more severe. John Lawson, who visited the Carolina upcountry in 1701, when perhaps ten thousand Indians were still there, estimated that "there is not the sixth Savage living within two hundred Miles of all our Settlements, as there were fifty Years ago." The recent smallpox epidemic "destroy'd whole Towns," he remarked," without leaving one *Indian* alive in the Village." Resistance to disease developed with painful slowness; colonists reported that the outbreak of smallpox in 1759 wiped out 60 percent of the natives, and, according to one source, "the woods were offensive with the dead bodies of the Indians; and dogs, wolves, and vultures were . . . busy for months in banqueting on them."

Survivors of these horrors were thrust into a situation no less alien than what European immigrants and African slaves found. The collected wisdom of generations could vanish in a matter of days if sickness struck older members of a community who kept sacred traditions and taught special skills. When many of the elders succumbed at once, the deep pools of collective memory grew shallow, and some dried up altogether. In 1710, Indians near Charleston told a settler that "they have forgot most of their traditions since the Establishment of this Colony, they keep their Festivals and can tell but little of the reasons: their Old Men are dead." Impoverishment of a rich cultural heritage followed the spread of disease. Nearly a century later, a South Carolinian exaggerated but captured the general trend when he noted that Catawbas "have forgotten their antient rites, ceremonies, and manufactures."

The same diseases that robbed a piedmont town of some of its most precious resources also stripped it of the population necessary to maintain an independent existence. In order to survive, groups were compelled to construct new societies from the splintered remnants of the old. The result was a kaleidoscopic array of migrations from ancient territories and mergers with nearby peoples. While such behavior was not unheard of in aboriginal times, population levels fell so precipitously after contact that survivors endured disruptions unlike anything previously known.

The dislocations of the Saponi Indians illustrate the common course of events. In 1670 they lived on the Staunton River in Virginia and were closely affiliated with a group called Nahyssans. A decade later Saponis moved toward the coast and built a town near the Occaneechees. When John Lawson came upon them along the Yadkin River in 1701, they were on the verge of banding together in a single village with Tutelos and Keyauwees. Soon thereafter Saponis applied to Virginia officials for permission to move to the Meherrin River, where Occaneechees, Tutelos, and others joined them. In 1714, at the urging of Virginia's Lt. Gov. Alexander Spotswood, these groups settled at Fort Christanna farther up the Meherrin. Their friendship with Virginia soured during the 1720s, and most of the "Christanna Indians" moved to the Catawba Nation. For some reason this arrangement did not satisfy them, and many returned to Virginia in 1732, remaining there for a decade before choosing to migrate north and accept the protection of the Iroquois.

Saponis were unusual only in their decision to leave the Catawbas. Enos, Occaneechees, Waterees, Keyauwees, Cheraws, and others have their own stories to tell, similar in outline if not in detail. With the exception of the towns near the confluence of Sugar Creek and the Catawba River that composed the heart of the Catawba Nation, piedmont communities decimated by disease lived through a common round of catastrophes, shifting from place to place and group to group in search of a safe haven. Most eventually ended up in the Nation, and during the opening decades of the eighteenth century the villages scattered across the southern upcountry were abandoned as people drifted into the Catawba orbit.

No mere catalog of migrations and mergers can begin to convey how profoundly unsettling this experience was for those swept up in it. While upcountry Indians did not sail away to some distant land, they, too, were among the uprooted, leaving their ancestral homes to try to make a new life elsewhere. The peripatetic existence of Saponis and others proved deeply disruptive. A village and its surrounding territory were important elements of personal and collective identity, physical links in a chain binding a group to its past and making a locality sacred. Colonists, convinced that Indians were by nature "a shifting, wandring People," were oblivious to this, but Lawson offered a glimpse of the reasons for native attachment to a particular locale. "In our way," he wrote on leaving an Eno-Shakori town in 1701, "there stood a great Stone about the Size of a large Oven, and hollow; this the *Indians* took great Notice of, putting some Tobacco into the Concavity, and spitting after it. I ask'd them the Reason of their so doing, but they made me no Answer." Natives throughout the interior honored similar places—graves of ancestors, monuments of stones commemorating important events—that could not be left behind without some cost.

The toll could be physical as well as spiritual, for even the most uneventful of moves interrupted the established cycle of subsistence. Belongings had to be packed and unpacked, dwellings constructed, palisades raised. Once migrants had completed the business of settling in, the still more arduous task of exploiting new terrain awaited them. Living in one place year after year endowed a people with intimate knowledge of the area. The richest soils, the best hunting grounds, the choicest sites for gathering nuts or berries—none could be learned without years of experience, tested by time and passed down from one generation to the next. Small wonder that Carolina Indians worried about being "driven to some unknown Country, to live, hunt, and get our Bread in."

Some displaced groups tried to leave "unknown Country" behind and make their way back home. In 1716 Enos asked Virginia's permission to settle at "Enoe Town" on the North Carolina frontier, their location in Lawson's day. Seventeen years later William Byrd II came upon an abandoned Cheraw village on a tributary of the upper Roanoke River and remarked how "it must have been a great misfortune to them to be obliged to abandon so beautiful a dwelling." The Indians apparently agreed: in 1717 the Virginia Council received "Divers applications" from the Cheraws (now living along the Pee Dee River) "for Liberty to Seat themselves on the head of Roanoke River." Few natives managed to return permanently to their homelands. But their efforts to retrace their steps hint at a profound sense of loss and testify to the powerful hold of ancient sites.

Compounding the trauma of leaving familiar territories was the necessity of abandoning customary relationships. Casting their lot with others traditionally considered foreign compelled Indians to rearrange basic ways of ordering their existence. Despite frequent contacts among peoples, native life had always centered in kin and town. The consequences of this deep-seated localism were evident even to a newcomer like John Lawson, who in 1701 found striking differences in language, dress, and physical appearance among Carolina Indians living only a few miles apart. Rules governing behavior also drew sharp distinctions between outsiders and one's own "Country-Folks." Indians were "very kind, and charitable to one another," Lawson reported, "but more especially to those of their own Nation." A visitor desiring a liaison with a local woman was required to approach her relatives and the village headman. On the other hand, "if it be an *Indian* of their own Town or Neighbourhood, that wants a Mistress, he comes to none but the Girl." Lawson seemed unperturbed by this barrier until he discovered that a "Thief [is] held in Disgrace, that steals from any of his Country-Folks," "but to steal from the *English* [or any other foreigners] they reckon no Harm."

Communities unable to continue on their own had to revise these rules and reweave the social fabric into new designs. What language would be spoken? How would fields be laid out, hunting territories divided, houses built? How would decisions be reached, offenders punished, ceremonies performed? When Lawson remarked that "now adays" the Indians must seek mates "amongst Strangers," he unwittingly characterized life in native Carolina. Those who managed to withstand the ravages of disease had to redefine the meaning of the term *stranger* and transform outsiders into insiders.

The need to harmonize discordant peoples, an unpleasant fact of life for all native Americans, was no less common among black and white inhabitants of America during these years. Africans from a host of different groups were thrown into slavery together and forced to seek some common cultural ground, to blend or set aside clashing habits and beliefs. Europeans who came to America also met unexpected and unwelcome ethnic, religious, and linguistic diversity. The roots of the problem were quite different; the problem itself was much the same. In each case people from different backgrounds had to forge a common culture and a common future.

Indians in the southern uplands customarily combined with others like themselves in an attempt to solve the dilemma. Following the "principle of least effort," shattered communities cushioned the blows inflicted by disease and depopulation by joining a kindred society known through generations of trade and alliances. Thus Saponis coalesced with Occaneechees and Tutelos—nearby groups "speaking much the same language"—and Catawbas became a sanctuary for culturally related refugees from throughout the region. Even after moving in with friends and neighbors, however, natives tended to cling to ethnic boundaries in order to ease the transition. In 1715 Spotswood noticed that the Saponis and others gathered at Fort Christanna were "confederated together, tho' still preserving their different Rules." Indians entering the Catawba Nation were equally conservative. As late as 1743 a visitor could hear more than twenty different dialects spoken by peoples living there, and some bands continued to reside in separate towns under their own leaders.

Time inevitably sapped the strength of ethnic feeling, allowing a more unified Nation to emerge from the collection of Indian communities that occupied the valleys of the Catawba River and its tributaries. By the mid-eighteenth century, the authority of village headmen was waning and leaders from the host population had begun to take responsibility for the actions of constituent groups. The babel of different tongues fell silent as *"Kàtahba,"* the Nation's "standard, or court-dialect," slowly drowned out all others. Eventually, entire peoples followed their languages and their leaders into oblivion, leaving only personal names like Santee Jemmy, Cheraw George, Congaree Jamie, Saponey Johnny, and Eno Jemmy as reminders of the Nation's diverse heritage.

No European observer recorded the means by which nations became mere names and a congeries of groups forged itself into one people. No doubt the colonists' habit of ignoring ethnic distinctions and lumping confederated entities together under the Catawba rubric encouraged amalgamation. But Anglo-American efforts to create a society by proclamation were invariably unsuccessful; consolidation had to come from within. In the absence of evidence, it seems reasonable to conclude that years of contacts paved the way for a closer relationship. Once a group moved to the Nation, intermarriages blurred ancient kinship networks, joint war parties or hunting expeditions brought young men together, and elders met in a council that gave everyone some say by including "all the Indian Chiefs or Head Men of that [Catawba] Nation and the several Tribes amongst them together." The concentration of settlements within a day's walk of one another facilitated contact and communication. From their close proximity, common experience, and shared concerns, people developed ceremonies and myths that compensated for those lost to disease and gave the Nation a stronger collective consciousness. Associations evolved that balanced traditional narrow ethnic allegiance with a new, broader, "national" identity, a balance that tilted steadily toward the latter. Ethnic differences died hard, but the peoples of the Catawba Nation learned to speak with a single voice.

Muskets and kettles came to the piedmont more slowly than smallpox and measles. Spanish explorers distributed a few gifts to local headmen, but inhabitants of the interior did not enjoy their first real taste of the fruits of European technology until Englishmen began venturing inland after 1650. Indians these traders met in upcountry towns were glad to barter for the more efficient tools, more lethal weapons, and more durable clothing that colonists offered. Spurred on by eager natives, men from Virginia and Carolina quickly flooded the region with the material trappings of European culture. In 1701 John Lawson considered the Wateree Chickanees "very poor in *English* Effects" because a few of them lacked muskets.

Slower to arrive, trade goods were also less obvious agents of change. The Indians' ability to absorb foreign artifacts into established modes of existence hid the revolutionary consequences of trade for some time. Natives leaped the technological gulf with ease in part because they were discriminating shoppers. If hoes were too small, beads too large, or cloth the wrong color, Indian traders refused them. Items they did select fit smoothly into existing ways. Waxhaws tied horse bells around their ankles at ceremonial dances, and some of the traditional stone pipes passed among the spectators at these dances had been shaped by metal files. Those who could not afford a European weapon fashioned arrows from broken glass. Those who could went to great lengths to "set [a new musket] streight, sometimes shooting away above 100 Loads of Ammunition, before they bring the Gun to shoot according to their Mind."

Not every piece of merchandise hauled into the upcountry on a trader's packhorse could be "set streight" so easily. Liquor, for example, proved both impossible to resist and extraordinarily destructive. Indians "have no Power to refrain this Enemy," Larson observed, "though sensible how many of them (are by it) hurry'd into the other World before their Time." And yet even here, natives aware of the risks sought to control alcohol by incorporating it into their ceremonial life as a device for achieving a different level of consciousness. Consumption was usually restricted to men, who "go as solemnly about it, as if it were part of their Religion," preferring to drink only at night and only in quantities sufficient to stupefy them. When ritual could not confine liquor to safe channels, Indians went still further and excused the excesses of overindulgence by refusing to hold an intoxicated person responsible for his actions. "They never call any Man to account for what he did, when he was drunk," wrote Lawson, "but say, it was the Drink that caused his Misbehaviour, therefore he ought to be forgiven."

Working to absorb even the most dangerous commodities acquired from their new neighbors, aboriginal inhabitants of the uplands, like African slaves in the lowlands, made themselves at home in a different technological environment. Indians became convinced that "Guns, and Ammunition, besides a great many other Necessaries, . . . are helpful to Man" and eagerly searched for the key that would unlock the secret of their production. At first many were confident that the *"Quera*, or good Spirit," would teach them to make these commodities "when that good Spirit sees fit." Later they decided to help their deity along by approaching the colonists. In 1757, Catawbas asked Gov. Arthur Dobbs of North Carolina "to send us Smiths and other Tradesmen to teach our Children."

It was not the new products themselves but the Indians' failure to learn the mysteries of manufacture from either Dobbs or the *Quera* that marked the real revolution wrought by trade. During the seventeenth and eighteenth centuries, everyone in eastern North America—masters and slaves, farmers near the coast and Indians near the mountains—became producers of raw materials for foreign markets and found themselves caught up in an international economic network. Piedmont natives were part of this larger process, but their adjustment was more difficult because the contrast with previous ways was so pronounced. Before European contact, the localism characteristic of life in the uplands had been sustained by a remarkable degree of self-sufficiency. Trade among peoples, while common, was conducted primarily in commodities such as copper, mica, and shells, items that, exchanged with the appropriate ceremony, initiated or confirmed friendships among groups. Few, if any, villages relied on outsiders for goods essential to daily life.

Intercultural exchange eroded this traditional independence and entangled natives in a web of commercial relations few of them understood and none controlled. In 1670 the explorer John Lederer observed a striking disparity in the trading habits of Indians living near Virginia and those deep in the interior. The "remoter Indians," still operating within a precontact framework, were content with ornamental items such as mirrors, beads, "and all manner of gaudy toys and knacks for children." "Neighbour-Indians," on the other hand, habitually traded with colonists for cloth, metal tools, and weapons. Before long, towns near and far were demanding the entire range of European wares and were growing accustomed—even addicted—to them. "They say we English are fools for . . . not always going with a gun," one Virginia colonist familiar with piedmont Indians wrote in the early 1690s, "for they think themselves undrest and not fit to walk abroad, unless they have their gun on their shoulder, and their shot-bag by their side." Such an enthusiastic conversion to the new technology eroded ancient craft skills and hastened complete dependence on substitutes only colonists could supply.

By forcing Indians to look beyond their own territories for certain indispensable products, Anglo-American traders inserted new variables into the aboriginal equation of exchange. Colonists sought two commodities from Indians—human beings and deerskins—and both undermined established relationships among native groups. While the demand for slaves encouraged piedmont peoples to expand their traditional warfare, the demand for peltry may have fostered conflicts over hunting territories. Those who did not fight each other for slaves or deerskins fought each other for the European products these could bring. As firearms, cloth, and other items became increasingly important to native existence, competition replaced comity at the foundation of trade encounters as villages scrambled for the cargoes of merchandise. Some were in a better position to profit than others. In the early 1670s Occaneechees living on an island in the Roanoke River enjoyed power out of all proportion to their numbers because they controlled an important ford on the trading path from Virginia to the interior, and they resorted to threats, and even to force, to retain their advantage. In Lawson's day Tuscaroras did the same, "hating that any of these Westward *Indians* should have any Commerce with the *English,* which would prove a Hinderance to their Gains."

Competition among native groups was only the beginning of the transformation brought about by new forms of exchange. Inhabitants of the piedmont might bypass the native middleman, but they could not break free from a perilous dependence on colonial sources of supply. The danger may not have been immediately apparent to Indians caught up in the excitement of acquiring new and wonderful things. For years they managed to dictate the terms of trade, compelling visitors from Carolina and Virginia to abide by aboriginal codes of conduct and playing one colony's traders against the other to ensure an abundance of goods at favorable rates. But the natives' influence over the protocol of exchange combined with their skill at incorporating alien products to mask a loss of control over their own destiny. The mask came off when, in 1715, the traders—and the trade goods—suddenly disappeared during the Yamassee War.

The conflict's origins lay in a growing colonial awareness of the Indians' need for regular supplies of European merchandise. In 1701 Lawson pronounced the Santees "very tractable" because of their close connections with South Carolina. Eight years later he was convinced that the colonial officials in Charleston "are absolute Masters over the *Indians* . . . within the Circle of their Trade." Carolina traders who shared this conviction quite naturally felt less and less constrained to obey native rules governing proper behavior. Abuses against Indians mounted until some men were literally getting away with murder. When repeated appeals to colonial officials failed, natives throughout Carolina began to consider war. Persuaded by Yamassee ambassadors that the conspiracy was widespread and convinced by years of ruthless commercial competition between Virginia and Carolina that an attack on one colony would not affect relations with the other, in the spring of 1715 Catawbas and their neighbors joined the invasion of South Carolina.

The decision to fight was disastrous. Colonists everywhere shut off the flow of goods to the interior, and after some initial successes Carolina's native enemies soon plumbed the depths of their dependence. In a matter of months, refugees holed up in Charleston noticed that "the Indians want ammunition and are not able to mend their Arms." The peace negotiations that ensued revealed a desperate thirst for fresh supplies of European wares. Ambassadors from piedmont towns invariably spoke in a single breath of restoring "a Peace and a free Trade," and one delegation even admitted that its people "cannot live without the assistance of the English."

Natives unable to live without the English henceforth tried to live with them. No upcountry group mounted a direct challenge to Anglo-American after 1715. Trade quickly resumed, and the piedmont Indians, now concentrated almost exclusively in the Catawba valley, briefly enjoyed a regular supply of necessary products sold by men willing once again to deal according to the old rules. By mid-century, however, deer were scarce and fresh sources of slaves almost impossible to find. Anglo-American traders took their business elsewhere, leaving inhabitants of the Nation with another material crisis of different but equally dangerous dimensions.

Indians casting about for an alternative means of procuring the commodities they craved looked to imperial officials. During the 1740s and 1750s native dependence shifted from colonial traders to colonial authorities as Catawba leaders repeatedly visited provincial capitals to request goods. These delegations came not to beg but to bargain. Catawbas were still of enormous value to the English as allies and frontier guards, especially at a time when Anglo-America felt threatened by the French and their Indian auxiliaries. The Nation's position within reach of Virginia and both Carolinas enhanced its value by enabling headmen to approach all three colonies and offer their people's services to the highest bidder.

The strategy yielded Indians an arsenal of ammunition and a variety of other merchandise that helped offset the declining trade. Crown officials were especially generous when the Nation managed to play one colony off against another. In 1746 a rumor that the Catawbas were about to move to Virginia was enough to garner them a large shipment of powder and lead from officials in Charleston concerned about losing this "valuable people." A decade later, while the two Carolinas fought for the honor of constructing a fort in the Nation, the Indians encouraged (and received) gifts symbolizing good will from both colonies without reaching an agreement with either. Surveying the tangled thicket of promises and presents, the Crown's superintendent of Indian affairs, Edmond Atkin, ruefully admitted that "the People of both Provinces . . . have I beleive [sic] tampered too much on both sides with those Indians, who seem to understand well how to make their Advantage of it."

By the end of the colonial period delicate negotiations across cultural boundaries were as familiar to Catawbas as the strouds they wore and the muskets they carried. But no matter how shrewdly the headmen loosened provincial purse strings to extract vital merchandise, they could not escape the simple fact that they no longer held the purse containing everything needed for their daily existence. In the space of a century the Indians had become thoroughly embedded in an alien economy, denizens of a new material world. The ancient self-sufficiency was only a dim memory in the minds of the Nation's elders.

The Catawba peoples were veterans of countless campaigns against disease and masters of the arts of trade long before the third major element of their new world, white planters, became an integral part of their life. Settlement of the Carolina uplands did not begin until the 1730s, but once underway it spread with frightening speed. In November 1752, concerned Catawbas reminded South Carolina governor James Glen how they had "complained already . . . that the white People were settled too near us." Two years later five hundred families lived within thirty miles of the Nation and surveyors were running their lines into the middle of native towns. "[T]hose Indians are now in a fair way to be surrounded by White People," one observer concluded.

Settlers' attitudes were as alarming as their numbers. Unlike traders who profited from them or colonial officials who deployed them as allies, ordinary colonists had little use for Indians. Natives made poor servants and worse slaves; they obstructed settlement; they attracted enemy warriors to the area. Even men who respected Indians and earned a living by trading with them admitted that they made unpleasant neighbors. "We may observe of them as of the fire," wrote the South Carolina trader James Adair after considering the Catawbas' situation on the eve of the American Revolution, " 'it is safe and useful, cherished at proper distance; but if too near us, it becomes dangerous, and will scorch if not consume us.' "

A common fondness for alcohol increased the likelihood of intercultural hostilities. Catawba leaders acknowledged that the Indians "get very Drunk with [liquor] this is the Very Cause that they oftentimes Commit those Crimes that is offencive to You and us." Colonists were equally prone to bouts of drunkenness. In the 1760s the itinerant Anglican minister, Charles Woodmason, was shocked to find the citizens of one South Carolina upcountry community "continually drunk." More appalling still, after attending church services "one half of them got drunk before they went home." Indians sometimes suffered at the hands of intoxicated farmers. In 1760 a Catawba woman was murdered when she happened by a tavern shortly after four of its patrons "swore they would kill the first Indian they should meet with."

Even when sober, natives and newcomers found many reasons to quarrel. Catawbas were outraged if colonists built farms on the Indians' doorstep or tramped across ancient burial grounds. Planters, ignorant of (or indifferent to) native rules of hospitality, considered Indians who requested food nothing more than beggars and angrily drove them away. Other disputes arose when the Nation's young men went looking for trouble. As hunting, warfare, and other traditional avenues for achieving status narrowed, Catawba youths transferred older patterns of behavior into a new arena by raiding nearby farms and hunting cattle or horses.

Contrasting images of the piedmont landscape quite unintentionally generated still more friction. Colonists determined to tame what they considered a wilderness were in fact erasing a native signature on the land and scrawling their own. Bridges, buildings, fences, roads, crops, and other "improvements" made the area comfortable and familiar to colonists but uncomfortable and unfamiliar to Indians. "The Country side wear[s] a New face," proclaimed Woodmason proudly; to the original inhabitants, it was a grim face indeed. "His Land was spoiled," one Catawba headman told British officials in 1763. "They have spoiled him 100 Miles every way." Under these circumstances, even a settler with no wish to fight Indians met opposition to his fences, his outbuildings, his very presence. Similarly, a Catawba on a routine foray into traditional hunting territories had his weapon destroyed, his goods confiscated, his life threatened by men with different notions of the proper use of the land.

To make matters worse, the importance both cultures attached to personal independence hampered efforts by authorities on either side to resolve conflicts. Piedmont settlers along the border between the Carolinas were "people of desperate fortune," a frightened North Carolina official reported after visiting the area. "[N]o officer of Justice from either Province dare meddle with them." Woodmason, who spent even more time in the region, came to the same conclusion. "We are without any Law, or Order," he complained; the inhabitants' "Impudence is so very high, as to be past bearing." Catawba leaders could have sympathized. Headmen informed colonists that the Nation's people "are oftentimes Cautioned from . . . ill Doings altho' to no purpose for we Cannot be present at all times to Look after them." "What they have done I could not prevent," one chief explained.

Unruly, angry, intoxicated—Catawbas and Carolinians were constantly at odds during the middle decades of the eighteenth century. Planters who considered Indians "proud and deveilish" were themselves accused by natives of being "very bad and quarrelsome." Warriors made a habit of "going into the Settlements, robbing and stealing where ever they get an Oppertunity." Complaints generally brought no satisfaction—"they laugh and makes their Game of it, and says it is what they will"—leading some settlers to "whip [Indians] about the head, beat and abuse them." "The white People . . . and the Cuttahbaws, are Continually at varience," a visitor to the Nation fretted in June 1759, "and Dayly New Animositys Doth a rise Between them which In my Humble oppion will be of Bad Consequence In a Short time, Both Partys Being obstinate."

The litany of intercultural crimes committed by each side disguised a fundamental shift in the balance of physical and cultural power. In the early years of colonization of the interior the least disturbance by Indians sent scattered planters into a panic. Soon, however, Catawbas were few, colonists many, and it was the natives who now lived in fear. "[T]he white men [who] Lives Near the Neation is Contenuely asembleing and goes In the [Indian] towns In Bodys," worried another observer during the tense summer of 1759. "[T]he[y] tretton the[y] will Kill all the Cattabues."

The Indians would have to find some way to get along with these unpleasant neighbors if the Nation was to survive. As Catawba population fell below five hundred after the smallpox epidemic of 1759 and the number of colonists continued to climb, natives gradually came to recognize the futility of violent resistance. During the last decades of the eighteenth century they drew on years of experience in dealing with Europeans at a distance and sought to overturn the common conviction that Indian neighbors were frightening and useless.

This process was not the result of some clever plan; Catawbas had no strategy for survival. A headman could warn them that "the White people were now seated all round them and by that means had them entirely in their power." He could not command them to submit peacefully to the invasion of their homeland. The Nation's continued existence required countless individual decisions, made in a host of diverse circumstances, to complain rather than retaliate, to accept a subordinate place in a land that once was theirs. Few of the choices made survive in the record. But it is clear that, like the response to disease and to technology, the adaptation to white settlement was both painful and prolonged.

Catawbas took one of the first steps along the road to accommodation in the early 1760s, when they used their influence with colonial officials to acquire a reservation encompassing the heart of their ancient territories. This grant gave the Indians a land base, grounded in Anglo-American law, that prevented farmers from shouldering them aside. Equally important, Catawbas now had a commodity to exchange with nearby settlers. These men wanted land, the natives had plenty, and shortly before the Revolution the Nation was renting tracts to planters for cash, livestock, and manufactured goods.

Important as it was, land was not the only item Catawbas began trading to their neighbors. Some Indians put their skills as hunters and woodsmen to a different use, picking up stray horses and escaped slaves for a reward. Others bartered their pottery, baskets, and table mats. Still others traveled through the upcountry, demonstrating their prowess with the bow and arrow before appreciative audiences. The exchange of these goods and services for European merchandise marked an important adjustment to the settlers' arrival. In the past, natives had acquired essential items by trading peltry and slaves or requesting gifts from representatives of the Crown. But piedmont planters frowned on hunting and warfare, while provincial authorities—finding Catawbas less useful as the Nation's population declined and the French threat disappeared—discouraged formal visits and handed out fewer presents. Hence the Indians had to develop new avenues of exchange that would enable them to obtain goods in ways less objectionable to their neighbors. Pots, baskets, and acres proved harmless substitutes for earlier methods of earning an income.

Quite apart from its economic benefits, trade had a profound impact on the character of Catawba-settler relations. Through countless repetitions of the same simple procedure at homesteads scattered across the Carolinas, a new form of intercourse arose, based not on suspicion and an expectation of conflict but on trust and a measure of friendship. When a farmer looked out his window and saw Indians approaching, his reaction more commonly became to pick up money or a jug of whiskey rather than a musket or an axe. The natives now appeared, the settler knew, not to plunder or kill but to peddle their wares or collect their rents.

The development of new trade forms could not bury all of the differences between Catawba and colonist overnight. But in the latter half of the eighteenth century the beleaguered Indians learned to rely on peaceful means of resolving intercultural conflicts that did arise. Drawing a sharp distinction between "the good men that have rented lands from us" and "the bad People [who] has frequently imposed upon us," Catawbas called on the former to protect the Nation from the latter. In 1771 they met with the prominent Camden storekeeper, Joseph Kershaw, to request that he "represent us when [we are] a grieved." After the Revolution the position became more formal. Catawbas informed the South Carolina government that, being "destitute of a man to take care of, and assist us in our affairs," they had chosen one Robert Patten "to take charge of our affairs, and to act and do for us."

Neither Patten nor any other intermediary could have protected the Nation had it not joined the patriot side during the Revolutionary

War. Though one scholar has termed the Indians' contribution to the cause "rather negligible," they fought in battles throughout the southeast and supplied rebel forces with food from time to time. These actions made the Catawbas heroes and laid a foundation for their popular renown as staunch patriots. In 1781 their old friend Kershaw told Catawba leaders how he welcomed the end of "this Long and Bloody War, in which You have taken so Noble a part and have fought and Bled with your white Brothers of America." Grateful Carolinians would not soon forget the Nation's service. Shortly after the Civil War an elderly settler whose father had served with the Indians in the Revolution echoed Kershaw's sentiments, recalling that "his father never communicated much to him [about the Catawbas], except that all the tribe served the entire war and fought most heroically."

Catawbas rose even higher in their neighbors' esteem when they began calling their chiefs "General" instead of "King" and stressed that these men were elected by the people. The change reflected little if any real shift in the Nation's political forms, but it delighted the victorious Revolutionaries. In 1794 the Charleston *City Gazette* reported that during the war "King" Frow had abdicated and the Indians chose "General" New River in his stead. "What a pity," the paper concluded, "certain people on a certain island have not as good optics as the Catawbas!" In the same year the citizens of Camden celebrated the anniversary of the fall of the Bastille by raising their glasses to toast "King Prow [*sic*]—may all kings who will not follow his example follow that of Louis XVI." Like tales of Indian patriots, the story proved durable. Nearly a century after the Revolution one nearby planter wrote that "the Catawbas, emulating the examples of their white brethren, threw off regal government."

The Indians' new image as republicans and patriots, added to their trade with whites and their willingness to resolve conflicts peacefully, brought settlers to view Catawbas in a different light. By 1800 the natives were no longer violent and dangerous strangers but what one visitor termed an "inoffensive" people and one group of planters called "harmless and friendly" neighbors. They had become traders of pottery but not deerskins, experts with a bow and arrow but not hunters, ferocious warriors against runaway slaves or tories but not against settlers. In these ways Catawbas could be distinctively Indian yet reassuringly harmless at the same time.

The Nation's separate identity rested on such obvious aboriginal traits. But its survival ultimately depended on a more general conformity with the surrounding society. During the nineteenth century both settlers and Indians owned or rented land. Both spoke proudly of their Revolutionary heritage and their republican forms of government. Both drank to excess. Even the fact that Catawbas were not Christians failed to differentiate them sharply from nearby white settlements, where, one visitor noted in 1822, "little attention is paid to the sabbath, or religeon."

In retrospect it is clear that these similarities were as superficial as they were essential. For all the changes generated by contacts with vital Euro-American and Afro-American cultures, the Nation was never torn loose from its cultural moorings. Well after the Revolution, Indians maintained a distinctive way of life rich in tradition and meaningful to those it embraced. Ceremonies conducted by headmen and folk tales told by relatives continued to transmit traditional values and skills from one generation to the next. Catawba children grew up speaking the native language, making bows and arrows or pottery, and otherwise following patterns of belief and behavior derived from the past. The Indians' physical appearance and the meandering paths that set Catawba settlements off from neighboring communities served to reinforce this cultural isolation.

The natives' utter indifference to missionary efforts after 1800 testified to the enduring power of established ways. Several clergymen stopped at the reservation in the first years of the nineteenth century; some stayed a year or two; none enjoyed any success. As one white South Carolinian noted in 1826, Catawbas were "Indians still." Outward conformity made it easier for them to blend into the changed landscape. Beneath the surface lay a more complex story.

Those few outsiders who tried to piece together that story generally found it difficult to learn much from the Indians. A people shrewd enough to discard the title of "King" was shrewd enough to understand that some things were better left unsaid and unseen. Catawbas kept their Indian names, and sometimes their language, a secret from prying visitors. They echoed the racist attitudes of their white neighbors and even owned a few slaves, all the time trading with blacks and hiring them to work in the Nation, where the laborers "enjoyed considerable freedom" among the natives. Like Afro-Americans on the plantation who adopted a happy, childlike demeanor to placate suspicious whites, Indians on the reservation learned that a "harmless and friendly" posture revealing little of life in the Nation was best suited to conditions in post-Revolutionary South Carolina.

Success in clinging to their cultural identity and at least a fraction of their ancient lands cannot obscure the cost Catawba peoples paid. From the time the first European arrived, the deck was stacked against them. They played the hand dealt well enough to survive, but they could never win. An incident that took place at the end of the eighteenth century helps shed light on the consequences of compromise. When the Catawba headman, General New River, accidentally injured the horse he had borrowed from a nearby planter named Thomas Spratt, Spratt responded by "banging old New River with a pole all over the yard." This episode provided the settler with a colorful tale for his grandchildren; its effect on New River and his descendants can only be imagined. Catawbas did succeed in the sense that they adjusted to a hostile and different world, becoming trusted friends instead of feared enemies. Had they been any less successful they would not have survived the eighteenth century. But poverty and oppression have plagued the Nation from New River's day to our own. For a people who had once been proprietors of the piedmont, the pain of learning new rules was very great, the price of success very high.

On that August day in 1608 when Amoroleck feared the loss of his world, John Smith assured him that the English "came to them in peace, and to seeke their loves." Events soon proved Amoroleck right and his captor wrong. Over the course of the next three centuries not only Amoroleck and other piedmont Indians but natives throughout North America had their world stolen and another put in its place. Though this occurred at different times and in different ways, no Indians escaped the explosive mixture of deadly bacteria, material riches, and alien peoples that was the invasion of America. Those in the southern piedmont who survived the onslaught were ensconced in their new world by the end of the eighteenth century. Population levels stabilized as the Catawba peoples developed immunities to once-lethal diseases. Rents, sales of pottery, and other economic activities proved adequate to support the Nation at a stable (if low) level of material life. Finally, the Indian's image as "inoffensive" neighbors gave them a place in South Carolina society and continues to sustain them today.

Vast differences separated Catawbas and other natives from their colonial contemporaries. Europeans were the colonizers, Africans the enslaved, Indians the dispossessed: from these distinct positions came distinct histories. Yet once we acknowledge the differences, instructive similarities remain that help to integrate natives more thoroughly into the story of early America. By carving a niche for themselves in response to drastically different conditions, the peoples who composed the Catawba Nation shared in the most fundamental of American experiences. Like Afro-Americans, these Indians were compelled to accept a subordinate position in American life yet did not altogether lose their cultural integrity. Like settlers of the Chesapeake, aboriginal inhabitants of the uplands adjusted to appalling mortality rates and wrestled with the difficult task of "living with death." Like inhabitants of the Middle Colonies, piedmont groups learned to cope with unprecedented ethnic diversity by balancing the pull of traditional loyalties with the demands of a new social order. Like Puritans in New England, Catawbas found that a new world did not arrive all at once and that localism, self-sufficiency, and the power of old ways were only gradually eroded by conditions in colonial America. More hints of a comparable heritage could be added to this list, but by now it should be clear that Indians belong on the colonial stage as important actors in the unfolding American drama rather than bit players, props, or spectators. For they, too, lived in a new world.

Witches Apprehended, Examined and Executed, for notable villanies by them committed both by Land and Water.

With a strange and most true triall how to know whether a woman be a Witch or not.

Printed at London for *Edward Marchant*, and are to be fold at his fhop ouer againft the Croffe in Pauls Church-yard. 1613.

"Swimming a witch" in seventeenth-century England.

A World of Wonders: The Mentality of the Supernatural in Seventeenth-Century New England

DAVID D. HALL

In 1630 the great Puritan migration to New England began populating the early northern colonies with men and women intent on building a godly New Zion in the wilderness. The Puritan settlers were religious reformers, committed to creating a model society of Christian purity and practice. Every aspect of daily life was to be integrated into the quest for utopia—economic activity, political activity, intellectual activity, and religious activity. Intensely dedicated male authorities were expected to head the township governments, preside in the churches, and mold their families to meet God's ends.

In the selection that follows, David Hall examines an unusual part of the everyday experience of the New England Puritans—the phenomenon of wonders and supernatural events. Witchcraft, apparitions, strange voices, inexplicable sounds, monstrous growths and deformed births, and the work of the devil were the stuff of daily life. Deaths caused by what today we call natural catastrophes—lightning bolts, earthquakes, hailstorms—were understood as the punishment of evildoers by an inscrutable God. Meteors and thundershowers portended the wrath of God. Both the learned and the unlearned of early New England society observed these phenomena, told and retold their occurrences in private conversations around the hearth, and recorded them in diaries and almanacs.

As David Hall argues, we must go beyond the doctrines of Puritanism to understand the sources and significance of the belief in the supernatural in seventeenth-century New England. What intellectual traditions underlay the mental "world of wonders" of these colonists? How does Hall's account of the everyday observations of supernatural events help us to understand the Puritan mind?

T he people of seventeenth-century New England lived in an enchanted universe. Theirs was a world of wonders. Ghosts came to people in the night, and trumpets blared, though no one saw from where the sound emerged. Nor could people see the lines of force that made a "long staff dance up and down in the chimney" of William Morse's house. In this enchanted world, the sky on a "clear day" could fill with "many companies of armed men in the air, clothed in light-colored garments, and the commander in sad [somber]." Many of the townsfolk of New Haven had seen a phantom ship sail regally into the harbor. An old man in Lynn had espied

> a strange black cloud in which after some space he saw a man in arms complete standing with his legs straddling and having a pike in his hands which he held across his breast . . . ; after a while the man vanished in whose room appeared a spacious ship seeming under sail though she kept the same station.

Voices spoke from heaven, and little children uttered warnings. Bending over his son Joseph's cradle one evening, an astonished Samuel Sewall heard him say, "The French are coming."

All of these events were "wonders" to the colonists, events betokening the presence of superhuman or supernatural forces. In seventeenth-century New England it was common to speak of the providence of God as "wonder-working." Some wonders were like miracles in being demonstrations of God's power to suspend or interrupt the laws of nature. Others were natural events that God employed as portents or signals of impending change. The events that Cotton Mather described in *Wonders of the Invisible World* were the handiwork of Satan and his minions. A wonder could also be something unexpected or extraordinary, like a sudden death or freak coincidence.

In the course of the seventeenth century, many of the colonists would experience a wonder and many others tell stories of them. Either way, these events aroused strong feelings. An earthquake in New England in 1638 had caused

> divers men (that had never known an Earthquake before) being at work in the fields, to cast down their working tools, and run with ghastly terrified looks, to the next company they could meet withall.

Almost a century later, as an earthquake rocked Boston, the "young people" in Samuel Sewall's house "were quickly frighted out of the shaking clattering kitchen, and fled with weeping cries into" their fa-

A WORLD OF WONDERS   From David D. Hall, ed., *Seventeenth-Century New England* (Charlottesville: University Press of Virginia, 1984). Reprinted by permission of the publisher.

ther's bedroom, "where they made a fire, and abode there till morning." In responding to such "marvellous" events, people used words like "awful," "terrible" and "amazing" to describe what had happened. Every wonder made visible and real the immense forces that impinged upon the order of the world. A wonder reaffirmed the insecurity of existence and the majesty of a supreme God.

This essay is about the wonder as the colonists would know and tell of it. At the outset, we may dispose of one false issue: the people in New England who heard voices and saw apparitions were not deluded fanatics or "primitive" in their mentality. The possibility of these experiences was widely affirmed as credible in the best science and religion of the early seventeenth century. We can never answer with complete satisfaction the question as to why some persons do see ghosts or witness apparitions. But for the people of seventeenth-century Europe and America, these were ordinary events that many persons encountered, and many more believed in.

This is an essay, therefore, about phenomena that occurred on both sides of the Atlantic, and among both Protestants and Catholics. We may speak of a lore of wonders, an accumulation of stock references and literary conventions that descended to the colonists from Scripture, antiquity, the early Church and the Middle Ages. People in the seventeenth century inherited a lore that stretched back to the Greeks and Romans. Chaucer had told of portents and prodigies in *The Canterbury Tales*, as had the author of *The Golden Legend*, a medieval collection of saints' lives. Whenever the colonists spoke or wrote of wonders, they drew freely on this lore; theirs was a borrowed language.

To speak of continuity is to raise two other questions: how did this lore pass to the colonists, and how did it consort with their doctrinal understanding of the universe? The key intermediaries in transmitting an old language to the colonists were the English printer-booksellers who published great quantities of wonder tales in the sixteenth and seventeenth centuries. They had allies in certain writers who put together collections of this lore to suit new purposes, like the emergence of Protestantism. Protestants drew freely on the lore of wonders, adapting it to indicate the merits of their cause. To this end Luther had retold the story of a "monster" fish found in the River Tiber, interpreting it as a portent of Rome's mistakes. And the wonder could serve to reinforce the concept of God's providence, a doctrine of importance to the early Reformers.

But what of all the "superstitions" that this lore reiterated? The language of the wonder was rich in motifs and assumptions that seem at odds with the mentality of the Puritans who colonized New England. In breaking with the past, and especially with Catholicism, the

Puritan movement had turned against the "magic" of the sacraments and holy relics, of sacred places and saints' days. The religion of the colonists seems, in retrospect, to have forecast and initiated a "disenchantment" of the world. The Puritan God was a God of order and reason, interpreted by learned men in the form of systematic theology. In such statements, Puritanism assumed the shape of a coherent world view, intellectually neat and tidy and swept clean of superstition.

Such, at least, is how we characteristically understand the religion of the colonists. But the lore of wonders as repeated and developed by the colonists cannot be reconciled with so static or so modernist an understanding. We may come instead to recognize that contradiction, or a kind of intellectual pluralism, was truer of the colonists than a uniform and systematic mode of thought. So too, we may come to recognize that these people were not hostile to a folklore that had roots in paganism. Indeed, the wonder tale would introduce them to a popular culture that drew on many sources and traditions. In reiterating these tales, the colonists would affirm their own participation in this wider, older culture.

The lore of wonders was popular culture in the sense of being accessible to everyone; it was a language that all groups in society shared, known not only to the "learned" but to ordinary folk as well. It was popular in being so pervasive, and in being tolerant of contradictions. A full history of this culture and its absorption into Protestantism would lead in several directions, including that of witchcraft. My purpose is more limited, to begin upon a history of this lore as it was received by the colonists, and to trace how it provided them with a mentality of the supernatural.

Portents and prodigies were routine events in English printed broadsides of the seventeenth century. "Strange news from Brotherton," announced a broadside ballad of 1648 that told of wheat that rained down from the sky. "A wonder of wonders" of 1663 concerned a drummer boy who moved invisibly about the town of Tidworth. In "Strange and true news from Westmoreland," a murder story ends with the devil pointing out the guilty person. Hundreds of such broadside ballads, stories told in verse and printed on a single sheet of paper, circulated in the England of Cromwell and the Stuarts. Newsheets, which began appearing with some regularity in the 1640's, carried tales of other marvels. Pamphlets of no more than eight or sixteen pages contained reports of children speaking preternaturally and offered *Strange and wonderful News . . . of certain dreadfull Apparitions*. The yearly almanacs weighed in with their accounts of mystic forces emanating from the stars and planets.

The same prodigies and portents would recur again and again in broadside ballads, newsheets, chapbooks, and almanacs. Tales of witchcraft and the devil, of comets, hailstorms, monster births and apparitions—these were some of the most commonplace. "Murder will out," as supernatural forces intervened to indicate the guilty. The earth could open up and swallow persons who tell lies. "Many are the wonders which have lately happened," declared the anonymous author of *A miracle, of miracles,*

> as of sodaine and strange death upon perjured persons, strange sights in the Ayre, strange births on the Earth, Earthquakes, Commets, and fierie Impressions, with the execution of God himself from his holy fire in heaven, on the wretched man and his wife, at Holnhurst. . . .

A single ballad spoke of blazing stars, monstrous births, a rainstorm of blood, lightning, rainbows, and the sound of great guns. Others told of dreams and prophecies that bore upon the future of kings and countries. Almanacs and other astrological compendia reported similar events: comets, eclipses, joined foetuses, infants speaking.

All of these were cheap forms of print. Hawked by peddlars and hung up in stalls for everyone to see and gape at, they reached the barely literate and the lower orders as well as readers of more means and schooling. The stories they contained would also turn up in a very different kind of book that ran to several hundred pages. Big books— perhaps in the grand format of the folio—were too expensive to circulate in quantity and had authors who announced themselves as of the "learned." But these differences in form and audience did not extend into the contents. The lore of portents and prodigies appeared in books like Thomas Beard's *The Theatre of Gods Judgements* as well as in the cheapest pamphlet.

Thomas Beard was a learned man, a graduate of Cambridge who practiced schoolteaching and received ordination as a minister. Born in the early years of Elizabeth's reign, he published *The Theatre of Gods Judgements* in 1597. Three more editions followed, the last of these in 1648. That same year, Samuel Clarke, like Beard a graduate of Cambridge and a minister, brought out a rival collection: *A Mirrour or Looking-Glasse both for Saints and Sinners, Held forth in about two thousand Examples: Wherein is presented, as Gods Wonderful Mercies to the one, so his severe Judgments against the other.* Clarke's *Examples* (to call it by the title the colonists would use) went through five editions, the final one appearing in 1671. Clarke was a non-conformist after 1662, ejected from the Church of England because he would not recant his presbyterianism. The sequel of his book was William Turner's folio *Compleat History of the Most Remarkable Providences, Both of Judgement and Mercy, which have hapned in this Present Age* (1697). To this series should be added another Elizabethan work, Stephen Batman's *The Doome warning all men to Judgmente: Wherein are contayned for the most parte all the straunge Prodigies hapned in the Worlde* (1581). Ministers all, Batman, Beard, Clarke, and Turner had a secular competitor in the hack writer Nathaniel Crouch. His *Wonderful Prodigies of Judgment and Mercy, discovered in above Three Hundred Memorable Histories* (1682) was one of a string of works on prodigies and strange wonders that Crouch would publish in the 1680's under his pen name of Robert Burton.

As in the ballads and chapbooks, so in these books nature offered up innumerable signs of supernatural intervention:

> Now according to the variety and diversity of mens offences, the Lord in his most just and admirable judgment, useth diversity of punishments: sometimes correcting them by storms and tempests, both by sea and land; other times by lightning, haile, and deluge of waters and not seldome by remedilesse and sudden fires, heaven and earth, and all the elements being armed with an invincible force, to take vengeance upon such as traytors and rebels against God.

Earthquakes, multiple suns, strange lights in the sky, rainbows, sudden deaths, monstrous births—these were other frequent signs or signals.

Like the ballad writers, Beard and Batman reported esoteric, even violent, events: rats that ate a man, a crow whose dung struck someone dead, the agonies of martyrs. In one or another of these books, we hear of dreams and prophecies, of crimes detected by some form of sympathetic magic, of thieves who rot away, and of armed men in the sky. Much too was made of Satan. He offered compacts to young men in need of money, while sometimes serving as God's agent for inflicting vengeance. Many tales revolved around the curse, "the devil take you," and its surprising consequences:

> Not long since a Cavalier in Salisbury in the middest of his health-drinking and carousing in a Tavern, drank a health to the Devil, saying, That if the devil would not come, and pledge him, he would not believe that there was either God or devil: whereupon his companions strucken with horror, hastened out of the room, and presently after hearing a hideous noise, and smelling a stinking savour, the Vintner ran up into the Chamber: and coming in, he missed his guest, and found the window broken, the Iron barre in it bowed, and all bloody, but the man was never heard of afterwards.

The devil might appear in several guises. Black bears, a favorite of the ballad writers, turned up again in stories told by Beard and Batman, as did black dogs.

In telling of these wonders, the men who organized the great collections borrowed from the broadside and the chapbook; a ballad tale of a woman who sank into the ground was reported in Clarke's *Examples*, in Crouch's *Wonderful Prodigies*, and again in Turner's *Compleat History*. This flow of stories meant that "learned" men accorded credibility to wonders as readily as any ballad writer. In this regard, the great folios were no more critical or selective than the cheapest forms of print. The one format was the work of learned men, the other of printers and their literary hacks. But the two shared a popular culture of portents and prodigies, a common lore that linked small books and great, the reader of the ballad and the reader of the folio.

This was a lore that other Europeans were collecting and reporting in the sixteenth and seventeenth centuries. Sixteenth-century German broadsides told of comets, multiple suns, monster births and armies in the air. A Lutheran who wrote an introduction to an encyclopedia of portents "attempted to define the spectrum of such 'wonder works,' " listing "signs, miracles, visions, prophecies, dreams, oracles, predictions, prodigies, divinations, omens, wonders, portents, presages, presentiments, monsters, impressions, marvels, spells, charms and incantations." In Catholic France the *livrets bleus*, those inexpensive books that circulated widely in the seventeenth century, were dominated by accounts of apparitions, miracles, witchcraft, and possession. Some of these continental stories would reappear in England. Certain ballads were translated or adapted from a foreign source. Thomas Beard described *The Theatre* as "translated from the French," and though his source remains unspecified, his book was parallelled by Simon Goulart's *Histories admirables et memorables de nostre temps*, of which there was an English translation in 1607. On the Continent, as in the England of Beard and Clarke, the distinction between reading matter that was "learned" and reading that was "popular" did not apply to tales of wonders. Nor was this lore of more appeal to Catholics than to Protestants. Indeed it seemed to cut across the line between the pagan and the Christian worlds.

No better demonstration of this blending exists than the eclectic sources on which Beard, Clarke and their contemporaries drew. Aside from newsheets and ballads, whether English or imported, most of their material was culled from printed books that subsumed the sweep of western culture. The classical and early Christian sources included Vergil, Pliny, Plutarch, Seneca, Cicero, Josephus (a favorite), Gildas, Eusebius, and Bede. Then came the historians and chroniclers of the Middle Ages: Geoffrey of Monmouth, Voragine's *The Golden Legend*. The sixteenth and seventeenth centuries supplied a host of chronicles and encyclopedias: *The Mirrour of Magistrates*, the *Magdeburg Centuries*, and others by such writers as Hollingshead, Polydore Vergil, Conrad Lycosthenes, Sleiden, Camden, and Heylin. No source was more important to the English writers than John Foxe's *Acts and Monuments*, itself a résumé of narratives and chronicles extending back to Eusebius. A final source was that great wonder book, the Bible. Its narratives of visions, voices, strange deaths, and witches lent credence to such stories of a later date.

In plundering this great mass of materials, Beard, Batman, and their successors made modest efforts to be critical. As Protestants, they followed Foxe's lead in dropping from their histories most of the visions, cures, and other miracles associated with the legends of the saints. But otherwise the English writers were willing to reprint the stories that descended to them from the Middle Ages and antiquity. No one questioned the legitimacy of Pliny's *Natural History* and its kin, to which, indeed, these writers conceded an unusual authority. The parting of the ways between the "ancients" and the "moderns" lay in the future. In conceding so much to their sources, whether classical or of the early Church or even of the Middle Ages, Beard and Clarke admitted to their pages a strange mixture of ideas and themes. This was a mixture that requires closer scrutiny, for the stories in these books were charged with several meanings.

Wonder stories were interesting in and of themselves; even now, events that seem to defy nature attract our curiosity. But in the seventeenth century, each portent carried a large burden of meaning. Much of this burden was compounded out of three main systems or traditions of ideas—apocalypticism, astrology, and the meteorology of the Greeks. Each of these systems was in decay or disrepute by the middle of the century, under challenge either from an alternative, more up-to-date science or from a growing disenchantment with prophetic visionaries. But even in decay these systems continued to give meaning to the wonder tales.

The most widely used of these traditions was the meteorology of the Greeks and Romans. In Aristotle's physics, meteorology referred to everything occurring in the region of the universe between the earth and moon. As a science it encompassed blazing stars, comets (deemed to circle earth below the moon), rainbows, lightning, and thunder as well as fanciful or misinterpreted phenomena like apparitions in the sky. After Aristotle, the key commentator on meteorology was Pliny, whose *Natural History* "embellished Aristotle's rational theory with many elements of wonder and even superstition." Pliny had become available in translation by the 1560's, and most other major Roman writers who spoke of meteors—Seneca, Plutarch, Vergil—had been made available in English by the early seventeenth century. But English readers learned of blazing stars and comets chiefly from translated versions of a dozen medieval and Renaissance encyclopedias, or from poetic versions such as *La Sepmaine* (1578), the work of a French Huguenot and poet du Bartas. His long poem, which proved immensely popular in English translation, melded Protestant didacticism with the lore of meteors as "prodigious signs."

No less commonplace to most Elizabethans was astrology, the science of celestial bodies. Elizabethans learned their astrology from a medley of medieval and renaissance handbooks. These books taught a Christian version of the science, affirming, for example, that the stars and planets had no independent power but depended on the will of God. Astrology reached a wide audience via almanacs and their "prognostications" as keyed to planetary oppositions and conjunctions. Weather lore was another common vehicle of astrological ideas and images.

A third intellectual tradition was apocalypticism. Several different strands converged to form this one tradition. The Scripture offered up a vision of the end in the Apocalypse. The Old and New Testaments told of persons who could prophesy the future on the basis of some vision, or perhaps by hearing voices: "If there be a prophet among you, I the Lord will make myself known unto him in a vision, and will speak to him in a dream" (Numbers 12:6). The legends of the saints were rich in visions, as were the lives of martyrs in Eusebius. Geoffrey of Monmouth, a thirteenth-century English writer, invented prophecies that he ascribed to Merlin. These would survive into the seventeenth century in the company of other legendary sayings—of "Mother Shipton," of the Sybilline oracles, or of obscure Germans whose manuscript predictions were always being rediscovered. With the coming of the Reformation, apocalypticism gained new vigor as Protestants connected their own movement to the cryptic references in Revelation. The feeling was pervasive that contemporary history manifested the great struggle between Christ and Antichrist, and that some cataclysmic alternation was impending. In his influential explication of the Book of Revelation, Joseph Mede reaffirmed the prophetic significance of voices, thunder, lightning, hail, eclipses, blazing stars, and the rise and fall of kings. Mede regarded all the seals and trumpets in Revelation as forecasting real historical events, and in working out the parallels he made it seem that the Apocalypse would not be long postponed.

But the more crucial contribution of the Reformation was the doctrine of God's providence. The doctrine antedated Luther and Calvin. Chaucer's Knight had spoken of "Destiny, that Minister-General / Who executed on earth and over all / That providence which God has long foreseen," and the Psalmist sang of a God who stretched out his protection to the ends of the earth. Nonetheless, the doctrine had a fresh importance in the sixteenth century. In reaffirming the sovereignty of God, the Reformers also wished to understand their own emergence as prefigured in God's grand providential design. John Foxe, the martyrologist, made providence the animating principle of his great book. In its wake, Thomas Beard would reassure his readers that God was

immediately and actively present in the world, the ultimate force behind everything that happened: "Is there any substance in this world
that hath no cause of his subsisting? . . . Doth not every thunderclap
constraine you to tremble at the blast of his voyce?" Nothing in this
world occurred according to contingency or "blind chance." All of nature, all of history, displayed a regularity that men must marvel at, a
regularity that witnessed to the "all-surpassing power of God's will."
From time to time this "marvellous" order was interrupted by other
acts of providence, for God had the power to suspend the laws of nature and work wonders that were even more impressive than the routine harmony of things. The providence of God was as manifest in the
swift and unexpected as in the "constant" order of the world.

Beard, Clarke, and Turner were aggressively Protestant in pointing
out the significance of God's providence, especially as it affected evil-
doers, papists, and persecutors of the Church. In doing so, they continued to rely on astrology, apocalypticism, and meteorology for motifs
and evidence. No one viewed these systems as in contradiction with
each other. Indeed they seemed to reinforce the patterns of a providential universe. Astrology taught men to regard the heavens as infused
with law and order. The meteorology of the ancients rested on assumptions about natural law. Science, whether old or new, was still
allied with religion, and the synthesis of Christianity and classical culture remained intact. Then too, the sciences of Greece and Rome were
rich in possibilities for disruption and disorder. The conjunction of two
planets could send shock waves through the universe. Stars could
wander out of their ordained paths, and storms arise as nature fell into
imbalance. The world as pictured by astrologers and scientists was prone
to violent eruptions. This sense of things was echoed in apocalypticism, and writers on the Apocalypse would cite comets and eclipses as
signs of the portending end. Meanwhile Satan raged incessantly against
God's kingdom, leading many into sin and tormenting seekers after
truth. Sin, injustice, persecution—these disorders of the moral universe were mirrored in the conflict and disorder of the heavens. An
angry God was the supreme agent of disruption. Astrologers, the He-
brew prophets, the oracles of Greece and Rome, all spoke alike of doom
portended in the turmoil of the heavens and the earth. A teleological
universe yielded incessant signals of God's providential plan and his
impending judgments.

As emblem of God's providence in all of its variety, the wonder
had a rich significance. Still more possibilities for meaning were provided by a set of themes that circulated widely in Elizabethan England.
One of these was the theme of decay or dissolution. It was a commonplace assumption among Elizabethans that the world was running down
and soon would be exhausted. Portents never seemed to hint at progress or improvement but at impending chaos. Another theme was *De*

Causibus, or the rise and fall of great men. In Beard as in books like the *Mirrour of Magistrates,* Elizabethans read of kings and princes, of men of greed and overreaching ambition, who seemed propelled by some inevitable force to fall from their high rank. A third theme concerned evil as a power operating almost on its own. Evil was not distant or abstract but something always present in the flow of daily life. A book like Beard's, with its grand metaphor of "theatre," made good and evil the main actors in the drama of existence. Yet another motif was fortune, its symbol a great wheel that swept some people up and others down. A final theme was the interpenetration of the moral and the natural orders. Disruptions of the moral order had their echo in nature, and vice versa. This sympathy or correspondence was why Elizabethans assumed that corpses bled when touched by guilty persons. Hence too this correspondence meant that ills of the body, like sickness and death, betokened spiritual corruption. All of the natural world was permeated by forces of the spirit, be they forces working for good or for evil.

The wonder books incorporated all these themes without concern for how they might seem contradictory. Fortune and providence were, after all, competing if not antithetical interpretations. But the wonder books were remarkably tolerant. They made room for decayed systems of belief; in their pages the pagan coexisted with the Christian, the old science of the Greeks with the new Protestant emphasis on providence. The "learned" may have preferred more distinctions, and a man like Thomas Hobbes found the whole body of this lore distasteful. But in the first half of the seventeenth century, the lore of wonders remained generously eclectic both in its themes and in its audience. Everyone in Elizabethan England had some access to this lore. Writers such as Shakespeare and Milton availed themselves of references and motifs that also were the stock of ballad writers. Conventional, familiar, tolerant and open-ended, the lore of wonders was a language that everyone could speak and understand.

To trace the uses of this language for two or three examples is to trace them for the whole repertory of signs and signals. For Beard and his contemporaries, comets were perhaps the most widely publicized of all the meteors described in ancient science. It was a commonplace of Renaissance discussions to view comets as portending drastic change if not disaster—"drought, the pestilence, hunger, battels, the alteration of kingdomes, and common weales, and the traditions of men. Also windes, earthquakes, dearth, landflouds, and great heate to follow." Du Bartas summed up this wisdom in his *La Sepmaine:*

> There, with long bloody Hair, a Blazing Star
> Threatens the World with Famine, Plague & War:
> To Princes, death; to Kingdomes many crosses:
> To all Estates, Inevitable Losses. . . .

His idiom came straight from Pliny, who, in viewing comets as "a very terrible portent," had noted their appearance "during the civil disorder in the consulship of Octavius, and again during the war between Pompey and Caesar."

Thunder and lightning were other portents that drew on ancient sources for their meaning. In Scripture, they were repeatedly the instruments of an avenging God: "Cast forth lightning, and scatter them: Shoot out thine arrows, and destroy them" (Psalm 144:6). The prophecies of St. John in Revelation evoked the "voice" of thunder, lightning, and earthquakes (8:5; 10:4). Pliny had viewed thunder bolts as "direful and accursed," associating them with many kinds of wonders such as prophecy. To writers of the Renaissance, lightning seemed especially to betoken destructive violence. But the prophetic context could be invoked in plays like Marlowe's *Tamburlaine*, where the hero saw himself as the scourge of "a God full of revenging wrath, From whom the thunder and the lightning breaks."

As for apparitions in the sky, the would-be scientific description in writers such as Pliny yielded to interpretation of such sights as portents of impending conflict or defeat. Among Beard, Clarke, and their contemporaries, a much repeated apparition story concerned the fall of Jerusalem. Recounting the destruction of Jerusalem, Josephus had described at length "the strange signes and tokens that appeared" before the city's fall. "One while there was a comet in form of a fiery sword, which for a year together did hang over the city." There were voices, and a man who cried out, "Wo, wo unto Jerusalem." Iron chariots flew through the air, and an army became visible in the clouds. All of this seemed credible to Elizabethans, and no less so, as we shall see, to the people of New England.

Apparitions were credible on the authority of Josephus and Pliny, but they also figured in the folk belief of the English people. Folk belief is not easily distinguished from popular culture in an age when both could circulate by word-of-mouth. Where such beliefs arose and how they were transmitted—and whether they were fragments of some "primitive" mentality—are questions that are difficult to answer. What remains clear is that the wonder books made room for folklore also: stories of the devil as black dog or bear, the legends of the saints and their "white magic," tales of fairies, ghosts, and apparitions, of "murder will out," of curses and their consequences.

So many sources; so many possibilities for meaning! In their tolerance, the great collections ended up without a unifying order of their own. Clarke verged off into sensationalism. Ballads recounted fables of serpents and dragons. Writers such as Crouch felt free to invent stories—as if most ballads were not fiction to begin with. This playfulness was nowhere more amusingly revealed than in a chapbook of the 1640's that mated the prediction of the legendary "Mother Shipton" with the prophecies of a radical Puritan. The new and the old lay side-by-side without apparent contradiction.

But were the colonists this tolerant, or did they order and discriminate in keeping with their Puritanism?

The same wonder tales that Englishmen were buying circulated in the colonies, often via books imported from the London book trade. As a student at Harvard in the 1670's, Edward Taylor had access to a copy of Samuel Clarke's *Examples*, out of which he copied "An Account of ante-mortem visions of Mr. John Holland." In sermons of the 1670's, Increase Mather quoted frequently from Clarke and Beard. Imported broadsides made some of Beard's stories familiar to New England readers; the Boston printer, John Foster, published in 1679 a facsimile of a London broadside, *Divine Examples of Gods Severe Judgments against Sabbath-Breakers*, a set of warning tales drawn mostly from *A Theatre of Gods Judgements*. Hezekiah Usher, a Boston bookseller, was importing copies of Nathaniel Crouch's *Wonderful Prodigies of Judgment and Mercy* in the 1680's, and another of Crouch's books, *Delights for the Ingenious*, came into the hands of the children of the Goodwin family. Many more such books and broadsides must have crossed the Atlantic in the seventeenth century, though leaving no specific trace of their presence.

In the absence of such evidence we may turn to books and pamphlets that the colonists were writing. Almanacs appeared each year as soon as the colonists had established a printing press. As in England, these local products included references to portents and wonders. The almanac for 1649 offered its readers a lengthy "prognostication" that played on the theme of earthquakes as a portent of impending catastrophe:

> Great Earthquakes frequently (as one relates)
> Forerun strange plagues, dearths, wars and change of states,
> Earths shaking fits by venemous vapours here,
> How is it that they hurt not, as elsewhere!

Like its European counterpart, the New England almanac contained cryptic clues to what the future held:

> The morning Kings may next ensuing year,
> With mighty Armies in the aire appear,
> By one mans means there shall be hither sent
> The Army, City, King and Parliament . . .
> A Child but newly born, shall then foretell
> Great changes in a winding-sheet; Farewell.

The almanac for 1648 tucked portents and prodigies into a "Chronologicall Table" that later almanacs would update:

> Mr. Stoughton and all the souldiers returned home, none being slain.
>
> Mrs. Dier brought forth her horned-foure-talented monster.
>
> The great and general Earth-quake.

Soon enough, moreover, the colonists were writing commentaries on meteors. The first to appear was Samuel Danforth's *An Astronomical Description of the late Comet or Blazing Star . . . Together with a brief Theological Application thereof* (1665). The comets of 1680 and 1682 stirred the Reverend Increase Mather to publish *Heavens Alarm to the World . . . Wherein Is Shewed, That fearful Sights and Signs in Heaven are the Presages of great Calamities at hand* and *Kometographia or A Discourse Concerning Comets*. In 1684, Mather undertook a more ambitious project, a compendium that resembled Clarke's *Examples*. *An Essay for the Recording of Illustrious Providences* was at once a collection of wonder tales and a plea for greater efforts among the colonists to preserve such stories.

Reiterating the commonplace of a literary tradition, these books—the almanacs, the works of meteorology—are proof of the transfer of culture. It should be noted that Danforth and Mather were learned men who had become aware of scientific challenges to Aristotle's meteorology, challenges that jeopardized some aspects of the portent lore. Yet the two men put aside these alternatives to address a general audience, using an old language and familiar references, and insisting that "blazing stars" remained portents of God's providence.

This message had wide credibility in seventeenth-century New England. We have some measure of its popularity in the record-keeping that went on. Certain public bodies, like the churches in Dorchester and Roxbury, incorporated references to "remarkable providences"—fires, storms, eclipses, victories, sudden deaths—into their records. Each of the Puritan colonies summoned their people repeatedly to days of fasting and thanksgiving, and the calling of these days was cued to the perception of God's providence. Early on, William Bradford, Edward Johnson, and John Winthrop wrote works of history that were richly providential in their narratives of how the colonists had overcome adversity and conflict. These books noted the usual array of signs and portents—eclipses, monster births, strange deaths and storms, miraculous deliverances and reversals—while telling also of more puzzling events, like the lights in the form of a man that were seen in Boston harbor, followed by a voice "calling out in a most dreadful manner, boy, boy, come away, come away." Second- and third-generation historians would reiterate many of these stories, notably in Cotton Mather's *Magnalia Christi Americana* (1702).

All of this public record-keeping or public history was paralleled in private journals that functioned as individual "memorials" of "remarkable providences." The most extensive of these diaries were kept by John Hull, a Boston merchant and the mint master for Massachusetts Bay, and the magistrate Samuel Sewall, who was Hull's son-in-law. Hull seemed almost overwhelmed at times by the flow of prophetic signals, as in his entry for a year—1666—itself accorded apocalyptic significance because 666 was the mark of the beast (Revelation 13:18).

> At New Haven was distinctly and plainly heard the noise of guns, two, three, five at a time, a great part of the day, being only such noises in the air. The same day, at evening, a house at Northampton [was] fired by lightning; a part of the timber split; a man in it killed. . . . At Narriganset, in Mr. Edward Hutchinson's flock of sheep, were several monsters. In July were very many noises heard by several towns on Long Island, from the sea, distinctly, of great guns and small, and drums.

Early on in Samuel Sewall's record-keeping, he responded strongly to an eclipse: "Morning proper fair, the weather exceedingly benign, but (to me) metaphoric, dismal, dark and portentous, some prodigie appearing in every corner of the skies." For more than fifty years he kept track of many kinds of portents, from thunder storms and rainbows to sudden deaths and disturbing sounds. A faithful buyer of each year's almanac, he inserted notes on deaths and weather portents in each monthly calendar.

Hull and Sewall had witnessed many of the portents they took note of in their diaries; news of many others reached them second-hand. Travellers dropped by to tell of strange events, and Sewall heard of more from correspondents. A fierce hail storm that struck while he was having dinner with Cotton Mather led to an exchange of stories; Sewall remembered that a hail storm coincided with the Duke of Monmouth's ill-fated invasion of England in 1685, and Mather knew of other houses that had been struck by hail or lightning. The stories that reached Hull and Sewall were being told and listened to all over New England.

This trade in stories is revealed with unique vividness in two places, a notebook Edward Taylor kept at Harvard and the correspondence passing in and out of Increase Mather's household. In his notebook Taylor recorded the story of "magical performances by a juggler." He had heard the story from Jonathan Mitchel, the minister in Cambridge, who in turn had learned it from Henry Dunster, the president of Harvard, "during recitation." Dunster had it from the Reverend John Wilson—and here the chain is interrupted. In his notebook Taylor wrote down the essence of another story passed along by word of mouth. A minister and Harvard president, Urian Oakes, had done the telling:

> A child that was born at Norwich last Bartholomew-Day . . . being in the nurses arms last Easterday . . . being about 30 weeks old spake these words (This is an hard world): the nurse when she had recovered herselfe a little from her trembling, & amazement at the Extraordinariness of the thing, said Why dear child! thou hast not known it: the child after a pause, replied, But it will be an hard world & you shall know it.

To this same notebook Taylor added his extracts out of Clarke's *Examples* and, from some other printed source, the prophetic scaffold speech of an Englishman executed in 1651.

The traffic in wonder stories was crucial to the making of Increase Mather's *Essay for the Recording of Illustrious Providences*. In the early 1680's Mather was soliciting his fellow ministers for contributions to his impending book. John Higginson of Salem, an older man who came to Boston as a student in the 1630's, responded to this call for stories by sending him word of the Reverend Joshua Moodey's collection of annotated almanacs, "so that I doubt not but besides those [stories] he hath sent you, you may have many more from him. For instance,—he speaks of 26 men thereabouts, dying or cast away in their drunkennes which calls to mind some such case here."

The following year, having learned from Mather that he did not "confine" himself "to things done in N.E.," Higginson wrote out and dispatched two wonder stories attributed to "persons credible," and of events "I believe . . . to be certain." Both concerned the devil, the one a story of a book that acted strangely on its readers, the other of a man who covenanted with the devil to insinuate "that there was neither God nor Devil, no Heaven nor Hell." The informant who told Higginson of the magical book, a man no longer living, had been a ruling elder of the church in Salem. Long after the experience—it happened back in England—he could still remember that,

> as he read in [the book], he was seized on by a strange kind [of] Horror, both of Body & minde, the hair of his head standing up, & c. Finding these effects severall times, he acquainted his master with it, who observing the same effects, they concluding it was a Conjuring Book, resolved to burn it, which they did. He that brought it, in the shape of a man, never coming to call for it, they concluded it was the Devil.

The other story Higginson had collected in his days as minister at Guilford "from a godly old man yet living."

As Higginson predicted, Joshua Moodey had stories to pass on. One was of a house inhabited by evil spirits, as told by the man who lived there. All was relatively quiet now; "the last sight I have heard of," Moodey added, "was the carrying away of severall Axes in the night, notwithstanding they were layed up, yea, lockt up very safe."

From a "sober woman" Moodey also had a story of a "monstrous birth" that he described at length, concluding with an offer to "goe up and discourse with the midwife" if Mather wanted more details.

Meanwhile Mather had heard from several informants in Connecticut. The minister in Stamford, John Bishop, had written him some years earlier to answer his inquiries about "the noise of a great gun in the air." In his new letter, Bishop poured out a flood of stories:

> We have had of late, great stormes of rain & wind, & sometimes of thunder & lightning, whereby some execution hath been done by the Lord's holy Hand, though with sparing mercy to mankind. Mr. Jones his house at N[ew] H[aven] broken into, & strange work made in one room thereof especially, wherein one of his daughters had been a little before; & no hurt to any of the family, but the house only . . . A little after which, at Norwalk, there were nine working oxen smitten dead in the woods, in a few rods space of ground, & after that, at Greenwich (a small town neer us, on the west side) on the 5 mo. 13, (when we had great thunder & lightning), there were seven swine & a dog smitten all dead, & so found the next morning, very near the dwelling house, where a family of children were alone (their parents not then at home) & no hurt to any of them, more then amazing fear.

More such stories came to Mather from other hands—a narrative of Ann Cole's bewitchment, together with the story of a man who drank too much and died, accounts of providential rainstorms and remarkable deliverances, and of "two terrible strokes by thunder and lightning" that struck Marshfield in Plymouth Colony.

From his brother, finally, came a letter of encouragement. Nathaniel Mather had moved to England in the early 1650's and remained there. But he remembered many of the stories he had listened to while growing up in Dorchester, or as a Harvard student:

> Mrs. Hibbons witchcrafts, & the discovery thereof, as also of H. Lake's wife, of Dorchester, whom, as I have heard, the devil drew in by appearing to her in the likeness, & acting the part of a child of hers then lately dead, on whom her heart was much set: as also another of a girl in Connecticut who was judged to dye a reall convert, tho she dyed for the same crime: Stories, as I heard them, as remarkable for some circumstances as most I have read. Mrs. Dyer's and Mrs. Hutchinson's monstrous births, & the remarkable death of the latter, with Mr. Wilson's prediction or threatening thereof, which, I remember, I heard of in New England.

Flowing from the memories of a man long since departed from New England, these stories reveal how much was passed along in conversation, and how rapidly a stock of native wonder tales had been accumulated.

Most of these local stories had counterparts in stories told by Clarke and Beard or by the ballad writers. Many of these older stories passed

among the colonists as well, enriching and legitimizing their own testimonies of the supernatural. We may speak again of all this lore as
constituting a form of popular culture. Everyone knew this lore. Its
circulation was not limited to print, as the Mather correspondence indicates so clearly. Nor was it something the rude multitude but not the
learned could appreciate. When presidents of Harvard told wonder tales
in class, when ministers retold stories of "magical" books and freakish
bolts of lightning, we can be sure that we are dealing with a culture
shared, with few exceptions, by all of the colonists. One other aspect
of this culture deserves emphasis. Its cast was thoroughly traditional,
employing the same mix of intellectual traditions, the same references
and conventions, as the lore in Beard, Clarke, and the ballad writers.

Consider Danforth and Mather's descriptions of the comets they
had witnessed. Like so many other commentators before them, Danforth and Mather relied on the meteorology of the ancients, as mediated via medieval and Renaissance encyclopedias. In proving that
comets were "Portentous and Signal of great and notable Changes,"
Danforth drew upon du Bartas while citing, as parallels, events such
as the death of Julius Caesar, which, according to tradition, had been
prefigured by a comet. Mather cited Josephus, Cicero, du Bartas, Mede,
and Scripture as authorities when preaching on the comet of 1680. The
description he gave of a comet that appeared in 1527 was entirely
derivative:

> On the eleventh day of August, a most terrifying Comet was seen,
> of an immense longitude, and bloody colour. The form of it, was
> like a mans arm holding an huge Sword in his hand with which he
> was ready to strike. Such terrour and horrour surprized the Spec-
> tators of this Prodigy, as that some died away with dread & amaze-
> ment.

So, too, the references in diaries and in histories to lightning and
the phenomenon of three suns repeated elements of an old code of
reference. All of the traditional associations between lightning, disorder and prophecy lay in the background of Sewall's frequent diary entries on thunder and lightning, Cotton Mather's *Brontologia Sacra: The
Voice of the Glorious God in the Thunder*, and Samuel Arnold's description
of a storm that struck the town of Marshfield, in which "the most dismal black cloud . . . that ever" anyone had seen had passed overhead,
shooting forth its "arrows." The phenomenon of three suns, remarked
on in Shakespeare's works and by medieval chronicles as signalling the
overthrow of kings, remained a "wonder" to Edward Johnson, who
linked the "unwonted sights" of "two Parlii, or images of the Sun, and
some other strange apparitions," with the "desperate opinion" of persons who in New England "would overthrow all the Ordinances
of Christ."

From medieval handbooks the colonists also borrowed the language of astrology. For them it was a Christian science; the stars were signs not causes. New England almanacs retained the old combination of weather lore and astrological prediction, as in an essay Israel Chauncey inserted in his almanac for 1663 on "The Natural Portents of Eclipses, according to Approved Authors." Just as commonplace were the allusions to the consequences of certain planetary motions: "On October the third will be celebrated a famous conjunction of Saturn and Mars, and wherein they are deemed the two Malevolent and Infortunate Planets, the conjunction thereof (say Astrologers) Imports no good." The mixture of astrology and political prediction that had flourished amid civil war in England also reached the colonies in 1690, when a printer newly disembarked from London published an abridged edition of John Holwell's fiercely anti-Tory, anti-Catholic *Catastrophe Mundi: or, Europe's Many Mutations Until the Year 1701.*

Even more appealing to the colonists was the apocalyptic tradition. Visions, dreams, unseen voices—all these were almost everyday experiences, talked about in private and, remarkably, in books. Little children who spoke preternaturally were, as in the ballad literature, accorded special notice, as Taylor indicated by preserving the story of the child who told his nurse it was "an hard world." Nathaniel Morton reported an unseen "voice" that had alerted the beleaguered colonists at Plymouth to arson in their storehouse. The Reverend Noadiah Russell

> heard of a man in Connecticut . . . who was taken with a sudden shivering after which he heard a voice saying that four dreadful judgments should come speedily upon the whole world viz: sword, famine, fire and sickness which should, without speedy reformation prevented, begin at New England.

To interpret dreams as prophecy was to participate in a long-established tradition. John Winthrop, to whom a minister had told a dream of his, responded with another of his own:

> coming into his chamber, he found his wife . . . in bed, and three or four of their children lying by her, with most sweet and smiling countenances, with crowns upon their heads, and blue ribbons about their eyes. When he awaked, he told his wife his dream, and made this interpretation of it, that God would take of her children to make them fellow heirs with Christ in his kingdom.

The *Magnalia Christi Americana*, a veritable encyclopedia of New England wonder tales, included many dreams and other acts of prophecying. The Reverend John Wilson had prophetic dreams as well as a "certain prophetical afflatus" that made his prayers affect or forecast the future. Another minister, John Eliot, was gifted with "forebodings of things that were to come," and a third, John Brock of Marblehead, could predict success for fishermen and locate missing boats!

Here we sense ourselves approaching folk belief. The wonder tales that passed among the colonists were openly folkloric in certain of their themes and motifs. Stephen Batman had incorporated the folk tradition of spectral, shape-shifting black dogs into *The Doome warning to Iudgemente*. A century later, people in New England testified that they had seen the devil in the shape of a black dog. William Barker, Jr., a confessing witch at Salem in 1692, had seen "the Shape of a black dog which looked Very fercly Upon him" as "he was Goeing into the Woods one Evening" in search of cows. Sarah Carrier, enticed into witchcraft by members of her family, was promised "a black dog." Many of the witnesses at Salem had been visited at night by apparitions of persons crying out for vengeance on their murderers. Such stories were a staple of folk legend and also of the ballad literature. Another folk belief expressed at Salem was the power of white—or in this case, black—magic to keep persons dry in rainstorms. A witness had become suspicious of a visitor whose clothes showed no signs of passing through a storm on muddy roads. Many centuries before Salem witchcraft, the legend had grown up of a saint who remained dry in spite of rain. His was the power of white magic. In some fashion that defies analysis, the colonists were able to repeat this story, though modifying its details and making it a devil story.

Where many of these strands converge—folklore, apocalypticism, white magic, the meteorology of Pliny and Aristotle—is in Increase Mather's *Essay for the Recording of Illustrious Providences*. Because it built upon the wonder tales that people told as stories, the *Essay* has something of the quality of a folk narrative. Yet it is also a "learned" book. Between his own books—he owned the largest private library in New England—and those he found at Harvard, Mather could pillage most of western culture for his lore of portents. In keeping with its bookish sources, the *Essay* borrowed widely from the ancients and their mediators of the Renaissance. It borrowed also from the English collectors, especially Samuel Clarke and his *Examples*. And since Mather was committed to the mystery of the supernatural, he spent portions of the *Essay* arguing the validity of wonders against contemporary Europeans who were growing skeptical. As proof of the reality of witchcraft, he would repeat the story of the invisible drummer boy of Tidworth, taking it as true on the authority of the English minister and proto-scientist Joseph Glanville, though knowing that the story was denounced by others as a fable.

The man on the receiving end of stories from his fellow clergy made use of some of them but not of others. The book bears signs of haste, as though his printer were impatient and his own control of what he wished to do imperfect. Chapter one told of "sea-deliverances," some of them native, others taken from an English book. In chapter two, a potpourri of stories, Mather reached back to King Philip's War for a captivity narrative and two related episodes; after telling of another "sea-deliverance," he opened up his Clarke's *Examples* and began to copy from it. In chapter three, on "Thunder and Lightning," he quoted from John Bishop's letter and added several other stories of lightning in New England. But the chapter ended with two German stories, some references to Scripture and several bits of pedantry. Chapters four, six, seven, and eight were meditations and general arguments on providence, using European sources. Chapter nine demonstrated how thin the line was between the wonder and the curiosity, for here he told of persons who were deaf and dumb but learned to speak. Chapter ten, "Of remarkable tempests," covered hurricanes, whirlwinds, earthquakes, and floods; chapter eleven, "concerning remarkable judgements," related how the enemies of God—Quakers, drunkards, and other enemies of New England—had been punished. Mather added a letter from Connecticut as chapter twelve, and in chapter five drew together several stories of "things preternatural"—demons, apparitions, and evil spirits.

The many layers of the *Essay* included the esoteric. Like Beard and Clarke before him, Mather had an eye for the unusual event. Some of his stranger stories were borrowed from a manuscript, presumably of English origin, that he had inherited from John Davenport, the longtime minister of New Haven. From it he drew a Faust-type story of a young student who contracted with the devil for money. But the black magic of the devil yielded to the higher powers of a group of faithful ministers, whose prayers forced Satan

> to give up that contract; after some hours continuance in prayer, a cloud was seen to spread itself over them, and out of it the very contract signed with the poor creatures blood was dropped down amongst them.

From this manuscript Mather drew an even more sensational story of a minister who drank too much, went to a cockfight on the Lord's Day, and who, while "curses . . . were between his lips, God smote him dead in the twinkle of an eye. And though Juxon were but young . . . his carcase was immediately so corrupted as that the stench of it was insufferable."

From the same collection, finally, Mather copied out a "strange passage" concerning a man suspected of stealing sheep who swore his innocence and

> wished, that if he had stollen it, God would cause the horns of the sheep to grow upon him. This man was seen within these few days by a minister of great repute for piety, who saith, that the man has a horn growing out of one corner of his mouth, just like that of a

sheep; from which he hath cut seventeen inches, and is forced to keep it tyed by a string to his ear, to prevent its growing up to his eye.

Here again we sense ourselves confronting folk belief. This story of the sheep's horn had its parallel or antecedent in a medieval legend of a man who stole and ate a sheep, and then found a sheep's ear growing out of his mouth. The story of a student who compacted with the devil had roots in legends of the saints and, more remotely, in lore of eastern cultures.

How like it was for wonder tales to build on folk or pagan legends! With its mixture of motifs and sources, *An Essay for the Recording of Illustrious Providences* reaffirmed the traditional tolerance of the genre. The tolerance of the *Essay* was mirrored in broader patterns of response. As readers and book buyers, the colonists were caught up in the wonder tale as it appeared in Beard and Clarke. As storytellers, they repeated to each other a growing stock of local wonders. And in their almanacs and diaries they recorded the prodigies and portents that were the stuff of everyday experience—the voices and strange sounds, monster births and lightning bolts, apparitions in the sky and doings of the devil. In confirming the validity and significance of all of these phenomena, Mather's *Essay* summed up a popular culture that the colonists shared in common with most other Europeans. His book epitomized the transfer of old ways of thinking to the New World.

But still we need to ask what kind of world view was it that accepted the reality of evil spirits and of sheep's horns growing out of someone's mouth? The answer to this question lies elsewhere than in the theology of John Calvin or William Perkins. We are so accustomed to inflating the significance of Puritanism that we easily forget how much else impinged upon the making of beliefs among the colonists. Indeed, the historians who have commented on Mather's *Essay* have actively resisted its complexity. A century ago, the rational-minded Moses Coit Tyler was irritated by Mather's "palpable eagerness . . . to welcome, from any quarter of the earth or sea or sky, any messenger whatever, who may be seen hurrying toward Boston with his mouth full of marvels." Tyler deemed the stories in the book variously "tragic, or amusing, or disgusting, now and then merely stupid," and in one sweeping statement he condemned the book as "at once a laughable and an instructive memorial of the mental habits" of the colonists. Fifty years later, Kenneth Murdock tried to rescue the *Essay*, and, by implication, Puritanism, by insisting that Mather was up-to-date in his science and in his efforts to weigh and judge the evidence for marvels. Dismissing this interpretation, Perry Miller politicized the book, while

admitting that it "seems a collection of old-wives tales and atrocity stories, at best hilariously funny and at worst a parade of gullibility." This
indifference to the texture of the *Essay*—Miller did acknowledge that
its roots lay "in a venerable tradition, stretching back to the medieval
exempla"—was symptomatic of a larger indifference to traditional belief
and popular culture in early New England. Center stage was wholly
occupied by the complexities of Puritanism as an intellectual system,
and if certain other beliefs, like witchcraft, lingered in the wings, they
could safely be ignored since they were headed for extinction.

But the mental world of the colonists was not really fashioned in
this manner. High or low, learned or unlearned, these people had absorbed a host of older beliefs. A modern critic who has written on
Milton and science remarks that everyone in the early seventeenth century relied on a body of common knowledge that stemmed from Pliny,
Aristotle, and the encyclopedists. This old lore was being challenged
by new theories of the planets; yet like Mather and the colonists, Milton "was not ever seriously interested in a contest of cosmological theories." As a Christian and a Puritan, Milton believed that the universe
was theocentric and teleological. He was also quite at home with a
"popular science" that included astrology, finding "no incompatibility
between" this science and the doctrines of free will and providence.
This eclectic synthesis supported a view of the everyday world as hovering between anarchy and order. Decay and corruption were constant, and disorder in the moral sphere of things was echoed in the
disorder of nature. Such a mixture of science and religion in Milton
was formed out of intellectual, or popular, traditions that long antedated Puritanism. It is not important to give dates or exact boundaries
to these traditions. The point is rather that certain deeper layers of
belief—call them folklore, call them "popular"—flowed into Milton's
world view as into Increase Mather's.

Armed with this insight, we come finally to understand that the
mentality of the supernatural in seventeenth-century New England encompassed themes and motifs that owed little to formal theology or to
Puritanism. The people of New England viewed the world about them
as demonstrating pattern and order. This was the order of God's providence; their world, like Milton's was theocentric. It was also teleological, its structure the grand scheme laid out in the Apocalypse, the war
of Antichrist against the godly. The forces of evil were immensely strong
and cunning, in such sort that the providential order could seem to be
"overthrown and turned upside down, men speak[ing] evill of good,
and good of evil, accounting darknesse light, and light darknesse."
Disorder was profound in other ways. The world was rife with violence—with wars and persecution, pestilence and famine, pride, greed
and envy. A righteous God could strike with terrible swiftness, disrupting natural law to punish evil-doers or afflict the godly. The devil

too had powers to wreak havoc. Each kind of violence was attuned to every other, as were the forms of order. This correspondence enriched the meaning of portents and prodigies, making them more terrifying. The plan and order of the universe was, after all, not always visible or readily deciphered. If there were purpose and plan, there were also the marvellous, the inexplicable, and the wonderful:

> One providence seems to look this way, another providence seems to look that way, quite contrary one to another. Hence these works are marveilous. Yea, and that which does add to the wonderment, is, in that the works of God sometimes seem to run counter with his word: so that there is dark and amazing intricacie in the ways of providence.

There was mystery at the heart of things. Death could strike at any moment, the devil could mislead, the earth begin to tremble. In dramatizing all these possibilities, the wonder tale evoked the radical contingency of a world so thoroughly infused with invisible forces.

This mentality of the supernatural reflects the syncreticism of the Christian tradition. Early in its history Christianity had come to terms with the pagan notion of the prodigy and with such systems as astrology. The mixture that resulted cannot arbitrarily be separated into distinct spheres, one "magical" or pagan, the other orthodox or Christian. As one modern historian has noted, the early modern European was receptive to the wonder tale because he "believed that every body, living or inanimate, was composed of matter and a spirit. This idea was shared by eminent minds right up to the scientific revolution in the seventeenth century; it underlay the neo-Platonic belief of the Renaissance in the souls of stars and justified the persistence of astrology." In this same period no one could "make a clear distinction between nature and supernature" or view the world as simply "ruled . . . by laws" and not "caprice." This way of thinking made its way across the Atlantic with the colonists. Theirs too was a syncretic Christianity. In tolerating the wonder tale and all its underlying themes, the colonists demonstrated the capacity to abide contradiction and ambiguity. So too they demonstrated their attachment to an old mentality, a popular culture transmitted through the lore of wonders

Before the century ended, this mentality began to fall apart. Witchcraft, prophecy, and portents came under attack from a coalition of scientists, freethinkers, and clergy (especially Anglicans) who wanted to discredit them as "superstitions." The world lost its enchantment as the realm of nature became separate from the realm of spirit. Comets lost their role as portents; a Harvard graduate of another generation spurned this old belief in an essay published in 1719. Wonder tales, and the mentality embedded in them, lived on but now more clearly in the form of fringe or lower-class beliefs. No learned man dared take the point of view that Increase Mather had assumed in 1684. In its own day, the wonder tale united what became sundered in the eighteenth century. Living as we do on the further side of disenchantment, it is not easy to reenter a world where matter and spirit were interlinked, where "superstitions" remained credible. But therein lies the challenge of the wonder.

This picture of a poor fugitive is from one of the stereotype cuts manufactured in this city for the southern market, and used on handbills offering rewards for runaway slaves.

THE RUNAWAY.

A runaway Southern slave.

Runaways: Slaves Who Stole Themselves

PETER H. WOOD

Knowing that slavery in early America was a brutal and dehumanizing system, we can easily assume that enslaved Africans were simply fitted into a closed system of forced labor under which they lived out their lives, cowed and abject, as best they could. As the seventeenth century gave way to the eighteenth, their descendants faced an increasingly elaborate body of colonial laws whose end was to ensure that a master's slaves would be legally protected as property and subordinated and debased as human beings. In spite of a system that defined them as chattel property, however, enslaved men and women actively participated in the creation of an Afro-American culture. Studies of everyday slave existence in the colonial South show that early American slaves formed nurturing family and kin systems, adapted traditional African spiritual beliefs and practices to the plantation environment, took steps to achieve small degrees of economic independence, and resisted their enslavement in hundreds of subtle and covert ways.

As more historians probe the daily lives of slaves in eighteenth-century America, it becomes clear that, though kept in bondage, slaves were far from passive. They participated in a dynamic relationship with their owners that allowed them, despite the starkly uneven distribution of power, to find a variety of ways of setting limits on the master's ability to coerce them. However brutal the master's power, slaves were actively and continuously involved in carving out physical and psychological "space" for themselves.

One of the most common forms of resistance and self-assertion was to run away. Daily life on the plantation was routinely marked by this overt act of men and women who defied their masters and the very viability of the slave system by "stealing themselves." As Peter H. Wood describes in the following study of runaways in colonial South Carolina, slaves who ran away were prompted by a variety of motives, adopted various strategies, and had many destinations and goals in mind. Motives and strategies changed in the eighteenth century as the black population became a mixture of African and American-born slaves and as the master class forged an increasingly coercive system of controls over its enslaved majority. It is important to understand the significance that running away held for both blacks and whites in South Carolina, and how this highly personal act of resistance helped to define the relationship of master and slave in the colonial South.

No single act of self-assertion was more significant among slaves or more disconcerting among whites than that of running away. This common practice, which has often been oversimplified by historians and novelists, offers insights into the tensions that were building up within the South Carolina colony after 1720. While the number and percentage of blacks in the colony were growing, individual Negroes were finding it increasingly difficult to exercise even the rudimentary aspects of independence and autonomy which had been possible during earlier decades. Personal and social initiatives among slaves were gradually being checked by the evolving economic patterns and legal codes imposed by the European settlers. Changing circumstances prompted an increasing number of runaways. In a society where slaves were defined as property and where blacks were becoming artful in appropriating things they were denied, these were the people who, in a real sense, elected to "steal themselves."

Runaways, of course, had existed in the colony from the start. As early as 1688 the governor had sent an envoy to St. Augustine to negotiate the return of Negroes "that roned away from Carolina." At first, notices of slaves lost or taken up were posted at the guard house in Charlestown, but as the settlement spread and the number of absentees increased, such notification proved inadequate. By 1714 it had already become standard for the provost marshal to give notice in writing of any runaways brought to Charlestown "by sending up the names, ages, and sexes, to the several parish churches, and the most notorious marks belonging to . . . slaves . . . in his custody." In the spring of 1734 the marshal placed a notice in the *South Carolina Gazette* "of what Negroes or Slaves are brought to the Common Gaol," and the Assembly ordered that he continue this list every week. Moreover, from the founding of the newspaper in 1732, subscribers began to advertise some of their own slave losses, and these advertisements for runaways, taken

RUNAWAYS: SLAVES WHO STOLE THEMSELVES   From *Black Majority: Negroes in Colonial South Carolina from 1670 Through the Stone Rebellion*, by Peter H. Wood. Copyright © 1974 by Peter H. Wood. Reprinted by permission of Alfred A. Knopf, Inc.

in conjunction with other sources, provide an important category of historical evidence. An initial survey of all such ads from the *Gazette*, simply through the mid-1740s, offers detailed and revealing information.

The runaways found in this survey number well over three hundred, yet this group must represent little more than the top of an ill-defined iceberg. In the first place, the time lag which often existed between date of disappearance and date of advertisement suggests that newspaper notices were only a last resort. Many slaves must have been caught before any ad was necessary, and others, as will be suggested, returned from short absences on their own initiative. Some slaves may have escaped so completely that advertising seemed futile. Nor could all masters afford to advertise in the *Gazette*, and one would expect a bias within the notices toward owners who were wealthy town-dwellers and toward slaves who were highly valued. Nevertheless, an examination of this newspaper evidence can suggest a great deal not only about those who ran away but about the tensions faced by all slaves, whether or not they ever chose to take flight.

Historians have only recently recognized the need and the opportunity for quantifying such data, yet already the analysis of runaway ads by date and region is beginning to reflect the variation of the American slave experience at different times in different places. For example, in colonial Virginia, young men, frequently mulattoes who knew a trade, figured disproportionately in the runaway ads, but in South Carolina the absentees of the 1730s and 1740s appear to have approached a cross section of the colony's slave population. Only 6 percent of the runaways cited in the *South Carolina Gazette* during the 1730s were identified as artisans, and an equally small percentage were described as house servants or personal slaves. Not surprisingly, there is evidence that skilled craftsmen who had been born in America and possessed a thorough command of English stood the best chance of obtaining permanent freedom and were the most determined in seeking it, but the vast majority of the Carolina slaves who disappeared for any length of time seem to have been a representative sampling of field hands with no single distinguishing attribute.

Seventy-seven percent of the runaways advertised during the 1730s were males, and the ratio of more than three men for every woman persisted in later decades. The overall sex ratio among Carolina slaves was not unbalanced to the same extent, so it is safe to say that men ran away somewhat more frequently than women. On the other hand, statistics show that women runaways were more likely than men to visit other slaves and then return of their own accord in a pattern less likely to prompt public advertising, so the imbalance by sex among all runaways may not have been great. The distribution by age also seems to have been roughly representative. Babes in arms were among those listed as missing, and adolescents sometimes ran away on their own. A boy named London was "about 12 or 14 Years of Age" when he left his master, and an Angolan girl who spoke "pretty good English" was "about 14" when she deserted her mistress. Young adults predominated among the runaways as they did among the black populace as a whole. For slaves who survived past their forties, increased age by no means precluded the urge to run away. A number of slaves described as "old" and "aged" were still considered worth advertising for when they disappeared.

So diverse an assortment of runaways could only be prompted by a variety of motives. Quite often the immediate act hinged upon the slave's relation to a single European: a stranger, a fellow renegade, or a master. Some slaves actually departed against their will, for incidents were common in which Negroes were stolen away by whites. As early as 1673 two white men ran away from Charlestown with a Negro belonging to Nathaniel Sayle. They were overtaken and condemned to death but obtained reprieves because of their "extraordinary penitency" and the need for labor; the fate of the slave is unknown. The Negro Act of 1722 imposed a £25 fine on any "evil and ill-disposed" white person who "attempted to steal away negroes or other slaves, by specious pretences of promising them their freedom in another country." Any person caught and convicted of attempting to "actually convey away" slaves from the province was to "suffer death as a felon." Blacks who had already set out on their own could still be subject to exploitation by white strangers. In 1741, for example, two young Negro men named Bob and Isaac, who had been absent from a Winyaw plantation for some time, "were taken up by white Men near Bond's Ferry," according to the report of a fellow deserter, but their whereabouts was not made known to officials.

No servant could avoid altogether the thought of absconding, and it is important to keep in mind that white runaways were commonplace. For this reason black and white fugitives, with distinct but overlapping interests, were occasionally thrown together as fellow renegades to assist and exploit one another briefly in relationships reminiscent of Huck Finn and Jim. In such instances it is difficult to say where kidnaping ends and willing complicity on the part of blacks begins. When an Irish soldier deserted the garrison at Port Royal in 1734, it was believed that he had "taken with him two Negroes belonging to Ensign Farrington," and the next year the following ad appeared in the Gazette:

Run away from Mr. Bryan Reily and Mr. John CarMichael, two Irishmen Servants, both talking broad Scotch. . . . They stole from the said Masters a new yellow stocked trading Gun. . . . Run away likewise from the said Masters two Negro Men (which we suspect they have taken with them) one this Country born, named George, he speaks good English, a short thick well set sensible fellow, the other named Derry, a tall likely young Ibo Negro branded on the breast I.C.

Two months later Lt. Gov. Thomas Broughton "received Information that several White persons and Blacks, have Committed many Outrages and Robbery, and lye in the Swamp at the Head of Wando River, where they bid defiance to the Chief Justices Warrant." Broughton ordered that the nearest militia company be sent to "apprehend those disturbers of the Peace by taking them alive, . . . or in case of resistance from them to Exercise Military discipline, either by shooting them or otherwise." Later that same summer, when a sandy-haired young felon escaped from the constable in Georgetown and stole a horse, he "enticed with him a short lusty well set Negro Wench, she speaks plain English, is very well Cloathed and about 30 Years old, supposed to be in Man's Cloaths." Similarly, the following year a white servant boy who had worked in a tavern and was renowned as a thief ran away from Edisto Island and artfully obtained a pass from the local justice. The *Gazette* reported that "he has enticed an Angola Negro to go along with him, named Dick, speaks good English, a middling Stature, has on a homespun Jacket and breeches."

The association between black and white deserters was too dangerous to be frequent, however, and most often if any white person figured in a slave's disappearance it was his own master. A decision on the owner's part to change a Negro's location or line of work could provide the final impetus for running away. For example, three Negro sawyers named Primus, Venture, and Syphax were employed making cypress shingles for Mrs. Catherine Bettison. In the spring of 1733, when Col. Bull led a group from Charlestown to assist Oglethorpe's newly arrived Georgian contingent, the three men were hired out "for the service of Georgia," but before Bull's party could transport them they gathered up their clothes and blankets and disappeared in the night.

Perhaps more important than any specific assignment was the general quality of the master's treatment. Already by this period slaveowners had begun to debate the degree to which kindness and leniency were inducements to resistance rather than deterrents against it. There is no way to judge whether the many runaways whose masters considered them well used disappeared because of benevolent treatment, such as it was, or in spite of it. Tokens of generosity within an overwhelmingly hostile system may well have engendered further bitterness, although it seems more likely that few acts of kindness were significant enough to be determinative. Acts of particular cruelty, on the other hand, may well have tipped the balance for individual slaves, and it is interesting to notice, even in the terse columns of the *Gazette,* how the names of certain owners stand out. Several seem to advertise for runaways with peculiar frequency and in vindictive tones which may suggest their deeper feelings.

A Goose Creek planter named Alexander Vander Dussen, for example, appears repeatedly in these pages. In 1733 he offered a £10 reward for "a Negro Man named Thomas Butler, the famous Pushing and Dancing Master . . . [said to be] lurking at Ashley River Ferry." In June 1735 he put a similar price on Guan, a "Spanish Negro Man . . . supposed to lurk about Town," and six months later he was advertising the disappearance of two Negro men: "the one a tall elderly Fellow named Guan, a Taylor by Trade, has on a blew livery Coat trimm'd with red, the other a short thick Fellow, named Steven, had on a white Negro Cloath jacket & breeches." That same year a single issue of the *Gazette* carried an ad for a new Negro who had run away from Vander Dussen after being branded and an ad for a rented slave who had been missing from Vander Dussen's plantation for three months. In 1738, after advertising fruitlessly for a runaway Angolan field hand, he went so far as to insert an italicized paragraph in the newspaper stating, *"I am inform'd that there are certain Persons, who entertain Run aways, and in Time send them out of the Settlements."* He offered a reward of £50 to *"any Person that can inform me . . . in order that such Persons may be prosecuted according to Law."*

But no slaves could have felt a greater urge to escape from a vindictive master than those belonging to Francis Le Brasseur. Not long after this man opened a general store on Elliott Street, he announced in the *Gazette* that his Negro named Parris had "absented himself . . . to avoid punishment," adding: "The Boy is about 16 Years of Age, well-set, qualified for any plantation Work, provided it be far off from Charlestown. The Owner is willing to Hire, or sell him." By the following week the slave had reappeared, but a year later Le Brasseur gave sharp notice that

> whosoever at any time finds a young lusty Negro, named *Parris,* without a Ticket from myself (which he never shall have,) . . . [is] desired to take him up as a Runaway. . . .
> N.B. If he do refuse to surrender, knock him down, or shoot him with small shot about his Breech to make him stand.
> Mr. B-------s Advertisement continued.
> *Against my Negro man nam'd Parris*
> *From this day forth denounced War is:*
> *For now the Dog is grown so wicked*
> *He's run away without a Ticket.*
> *Which he shall never have, I tell ye,*
> *Nor maigre soup to fill his belly.*

If he don't halt at your command,
Pray knock him down to make him stand,
Or pepper him well about the A--e
Be gar, dis make one pretty farce.

There was nothing farcical in the situation for Parris, who managed to return in the middle of the night at one point and depart again before day despite "a Chaine and 3 Spurrs on each of his legs." His endurance finally prompted an anonymous outburst of frustration and hatred in the *Gazette* which could only have come from Le Brasseur:

> Whereas a stately *Baboon* hath lately slipp'd his Collar and run away: He is big-bon'd, full in Flesh, and has learn'd to walk very erect on his two Hind-Legs, he grins and chatters much, but will not bite, he plays Tricks impudently well, and is mightily given to clambering, whereby he often shews his A---. If any one finds him, or will send any news of him to ----- Office, in ----- street, shall be rewarded proportionally to the Merit of the Creature.

In the spring of 1735 Le Brasseur advertised vigorously for a Negro woman named Filledy, and he successfully prosecuted a slave named Peter River for having harbored her. The next year he gave notice that a man, a woman, and three boys had been gone from his Habshaw plantation on Wando River for three months. Le Brasseur died not long after this, but in 1737 his widow saw fit to run her own threatening notice in the *Gazette* concerning "an old Negro Woman" who had run away.

In many cases, therefore, immediate provocation from the master in terms of punishment or abuse must have prompted a slave's disappearance. Olaudah Equiano recalls in his autobiography how, as a young slave in Africa at about this time, he once hid from his master through fear of being punished, and the same response was common among slaves in Carolina. Such a reaction to immediate circumstance cannot in the least be seen as a reflection of unreasoned and spontaneous behavior in a childlike people; instead it is an appropriate if desperate response to a vicious circle of fear and reprisal. Fettered runaways testify to the degree to which harsh punishments could prompt fresh resistance: Hercules "had on when he went away 2 Irons on his Feet"; Tom had "one Leg galded by wearing a Spurr"; Billy "has a Chain & Pad lock on his Neck."

Several notices concerning a slave belonging to Lewis Timothy, the printer of the *Gazette*, illustrate the early stages of this brutal spiral. A youth named London, purchased by Timothy from a local vintner, had his head shaved by his new master as a means of punishment or humiliation. That must have been one reason for his running away in the fall of 1735, with a red silk handkerchief over his head. He was apparently apprehended, but the following spring Timothy gave notice in his paper that London had disappeared again, this time "with an iron head-piece on his Head." John Brickell observed that in North Carolina at this time servants and slaves who persisted in running away despite increasingly harsh laws were often made to wear cumbersome neck-yokes as a punishment and deterrent.

But dwelling at length upon aspects of white involvement seriously distorts the actual experience of black runaways. It lends misleading support to the traditional assumption of white interpreters that slaves, stripped of initiative in so many ways, were incapable of independent thought and action. Even in the act of running away, when they quite literally and obviously took their lives in their own hands, these individuals have been misrepresented as passive objects, "forced," "urged," "allowed," or "provoked" to escape by various whites. This bias began among the early slaveowners themselves, who refused to acknowledge among runaways signs of rationality, emotion, and independence, which they hoped to both ignore and suppress. The furthest they could go in recognizing any Negro initiative in these matters was to accept a perverse obstinacy as motivating numerous slaves. In 1783, for example, the legislature on the island of Antigua complained about "the late frequent running away of their Slaves who generally without any other Reason, than the Dictates of their own Vicious Inclinations, absent themselves from their Duty, and till they are apprehended and Compelled will not return thereto." Such begrudging statements, if the following evidence from South Carolina sources earlier in the eighteenth century offers any indication, do little justice to the complex and personal motives of the Negro runaway. Within the varied web of reasons which could prompt a slave to run away, at lease three patterns emerge which are worth examining more closely. One grouping involves slaves with obvious family ties; another contains newly arrived Africans; a third includes Negroes who have recently changed masters.

The drive to sustain family connections was a significant motivation of which white owners were only occasionally aware. Olaudah Equiano relates from personal experience how this concern could take hold with captivity in Africa and persist in the face of overwhelming odds. Equiano's regard for his sister seems paralleled by the case of Ben, a pockmarked young Negro who disappeared from Edward Thomas' lowland plantation in 1735. According to the *Gazette*, this slave had been "waiting man to Mr. John Wright deceased, when he was in England," so it was suspected that he might be near the Wrights' plantation at James Island, but the advertisement also mentioned as a hint to Ben's whereabouts that "he has a Sister at Dorchester at Mr. Tidmarsh's." A slave named Jack, who had gone to a new master and then disappeared for six months, was "suppos'd to be lurking about

Mr. Maybank's Plantation, with his Wife." A similar notice appeared for a young Negro carpenter named Primus, who had also changed owners recently: "He pass'd over Combahee Ferry about 6 Weeks ago, and is suspected to be at Port-Royal Island, having a Wife at or near Mr. Hazard's Plantation." But the most extreme example of the way in which a black family bond could be severed by a white owner comes from the letterbook of Robert Pringle. In the fall of 1740 this Charlestown merchant placed a Negro girl named Esther aboard the snow *Dorsett*, bound for Lisbon, Portugal. "She is a Very Likely Young Wench," he wrote to his contacts there, "& can doe any House Work, such as Makeing Beds, Cleaning Rooms, Washing, Attending at Table &c. & talks good English being this Province Born, & is not given to any Vice." Pringle stated he had "always found her honest" and added: "—The only Reason of my sending her off the Province, is that she had a practice of goeing frequently to her Father and Mother, who Live at a Plantation I am Concern'd in, about Twenty Miles from Town." Since "there was no Refraining her from Running away there, & Staying every now & then," Pringle had decided to ship her away and hoped his colleagues in Lisbon might "sell her to good Advantage."

For every province-born slave deported during these years, hundreds of newcomers were arriving from Africa. Though it is sometimes stated that acculturated slaves were most likely to run away, a striking number of "salt-water" slaves managed to disappear. Some of these slaves were from the Caribbean—"Francisco a Spanish Negro"; "Tony, Barbadian born, about 30 years of age"; "John, West-India born, aged about 40"—but most of them were from Africa. More than a quarter of all runaways advertised during the 1730s were cited as having been born in Africa, and nearly half of these were indicated as recent imports. Where specific origins were given during the colonial period, the proportion of runaways from Gambia, Guinea, and Angola correlated fairly directly with the proportion of the slave population arriving from each region. The only marked exception was among Ibo tribesmen from the Bight of Biafra, who represented only several per cent of the incoming slaves but who constituted more than one tenth of the colonial runaways whose African origins are known, a fact which may explain in part why Carolina merchants avoided dealing in Ibo slaves.

The ads for newcomers who ran away provide insight into the initial shock of debarkation and sale which all imported Negroes shared. A sense of bewilderment was inevitable for every immigrant. At times it must have grown overwhelming, and some new arrivals, like the old man brought to the workhouse from Ashley Ferry in 1742, sound more lost than escaped: "speaks very bad English, says his name is Bendar and that his Country is Mundingo, but cannot tell his Master's Name." An ad placed in the *Gazette* by Henry Laurens suggests the real or pretended innocence of another Mandingan newcomer:

STROLLED away from my house, about midnight . . . , a tall well-
made new negro man (of the Mindinga country) of a yellowish
complexion, can speak no English, had on a new osnaburg shirt,
and long trowsers, and a new romall handkerchief about his head.
The hair of his forehead, about two or three inches up toward the
crown of his head, was lately cut with scissars, and will appear as
a mark for some time to come. His name is John, but he will more
readily answer to the name of FOOTBEA, which he went by in his
own country. He is supposed to have been decoyed away by some
other negro. . . .

But some slaves did a great deal more than "stroll away." There
were instances reported in Virginia of Africans striking out overland,
"being persuaded that they could find the Way back to their Country."
Smug Europeans may have overlooked the fact that the exertions of
newcomers were less likely to be simplistic attempts to return to Africa
than herculean efforts to retain contact with families and countrymen,
despite the weakness which followed their ocean crossing. Juno, a girl
of scarcely fifteen who was "slender and strait Limb'd, and of the blackest
Colour," arrived at Charlestown aboard the ship *Speaker* in June 1733
and was sold in Joseph Wragg's auction yard to an owner from Dorchester. But in two weeks she disappeared, still carrying "a large Scar on
her right Knee" which may have been a mark of her voyage. An Ibo
boy of similar age was taken up in Charlestown in June 1735 by a local
hatter scarcely a month after he arrived in port aboard the galley *Rain-
bow* from Africa. During the same spring a man with "one sore eye,"
who arrived among 318 slaves from Angola aboard the *Morning Star*,
took his blanket and departed at the end of his first week of work on
a rice plantation. Such fugitives did not even have recognized names
when they disappeared, as was also the case with four slaves taken up
in Charlestown early in 1737. They had been among 350 slaves imported from Angola aboard the *Shepherd* the previous fall and sold at
auction by Joseph Wragg. They spoke no English and did not know
their master's name, but they had managed to make their way back to
Wragg's slave pen in a vain search for relatives and shipmates.

The odds for such strangers remaining at large were slim, but some
managed to avoid starvation and capture for months at a time. In 1734
a planter took up two Negroes swimming across the Combahee River;
they had been branded and wore long white frocks after the African
fashion. He reported that "they can't speak English (or will not) but I
understand by one of my Negroes, who is of their Country, they have
been out for Months." While many of these runaways must have depended upon seasoned slaves for clandestine assistance, some newcomers appear to have helped and encouraged each other. Three of the
slaves imported from the River Gambia aboard the *Princess Carolina* and

auctioned in August 1736 disappeared from their new home in St. John's Parish within ten days, and from another ad a month later it appears as though two of their shipmates soon left the same plantation to join them. It is natural that recent arrivals sought out shipmates from the same passage, with whom they shared not only the experience of the voyage but perhaps a common origin, a common language, or even blood ties as well. Yet it is also worth noting that slaves from separate parts of Africa occasionally joined in running away (usually after mastering a common pidgin language), for such associations suggest the failure of the owners' conscious strategy to put Africans from different regions together so as to minimize their chances to conspire.

If the odds were heavily against such newcomers, the desperation driving them was often great. This is seen both in the distances they traveled and in the obstacles they overcame. One new Angola man, being led to his master's Willtown plantation with his arms pinioned, managed to escape and avoid discovery for at least six months. "A big belly'd run away Negro Woman," apparently well along in pregnancy, was taken up beyond Ashley Ferry by another slave and brought to the workhouse; she spoke no English and bore African markings on her cheeks and breast. But the best index of the frenzy to escape which could consume a new arrival can be found in the instances where Africans were no sooner captured and punished than they broke away again. In 1734 planters took into custody at Santee "a Negro Man, about 30 Years of Age, a very large strong Fellow, speaks no English at all." They reported that the slave had been "sent several times to Charles Town, in order to put him in Gaol, but always has made his Escape, and return'd back." The next year a new Negro named Flanders escaped from Edisto Island in February 1735 and was taken up on a neighboring island a month later "but made off again" immediately. Harry, an Ibo man, was picked up near Cooper River and confined to the jail in November 1740; in less than four weeks he was at large again, only to be apprehended on Charlestown Neck and reconfined.

If newcomers were prompted to escape by a sense of bewilderment and desperation, another group of runaways defected for a different set of motives. Slaves who ran away upon confronting the prospect of a new owner were moved by a more calculated awareness of their present and future. The fact that so many absent slaves are described as "formerly the property of" someone else is in part simply a reflection of the fact that few Negroes belonged to one master for an entire lifetime. But the personal dislocations caused by a change of ownership in which the slave had no say could be catastrophic enough in their own right to spur escape. Often such changes came without warning in accordance with the shifting economic status of the master, for his financial losses, as well as his financial gains, generally occurred at the expense of his slaves. As the economy expanded, an ever-increasing number of Negroes were exchanged as payment on mortgages and other debts.

When death came to a master, it made a change in ownership automatic, and a planter's will often had greater import for residents of the slave quarters than for anyone else. Sometimes an owner bequeathed slaves by name; other times their distribution was left to executors. In either case, for those Negroes who had been waiting their chance, the interregnum which followed the passing of a master could provide the breakdown of authority necessary for escape. A document from the turn of the century illustrates this point: Richard Baker died early in 1698 while his slaves were planting a crop, and his widow drew up an agreement with her sons for the year, "the better to manage and Govern the s^d Slaves and . . . for the Management of ye s^d Cropp and to Prevent any Disorder and Disobedience that may happen to Arrise by the Unrulyiness of the s^d Slaves." The inventory of an estate from 1737 is not unique in listing among the slaves of the deceased several "in the woods" and one "disputed in ye Estate."

The uncertainty and fear connected with such transitions are obvious enough to explain any increase in disappearances, but one other factor may have had an important bearing upon these early generations of American Negroes: the West African tradition of slavery frequently frowned upon the sale of members of an estate. Francis Moore, who was living in Senegambia at this time, reported:

> Several of the Natives have many Slaves born in their Families. . . . And tho' in some Parts of Africa they sell their Slaves born in the Family, yet in the River Gambia they think it a very wicked thing; and I never heard of but one that ever sold a Family-Slave, except for such Crimes as would have made them to be sold had they been free. If there are many Family-Slaves, and one of them commits a Crime, the Master cannot sell him without the joint Consent of the rest; for if he does, they will all run away, and be protected by the next kingdom, to which they fly.

What the runaways took with them gives some indication of their various situations and intents. A few slaves brought into the Charlestown jail scarcely had clothes to cover themselves: several were wrapped in Negro blankets when apprehended; one man had on "only an Arsecloth"; still another was entirely naked. Pierro, or Peter, the twenty-five-year-old man who delivered *Gazettes* for the printer and who had been wearing his black leather printer's breeches, along with a white shirt and woolen cap, when he ran away in 1740, was located late one Friday night in a home outside Charlestown. According to the paper,

"In making his Escape he left his Breeches and Hat in the House, so that 'tis uncertain whether he has any on, he having been since seen without them in the Swamp there." In contrast, some runaways wore their best clothes and many took extra garments with them so as to belie their newspaper description. Sue, a dark-haired mustee woman who disappeared in 1734, "carried all her cloaths with her, but being this Country born, and having many Relations, it is supposed she has changed them to prevent being discovered."

Often the extra clothes were worn, as in the case of Peter and Bristoll, two Charlestown slaves who set out toward Santee one night wearing "new blue Plains Jackets and Breeches, and their old white cotton cloaths over them." In 1742, Hampshire, a highly valued mustee slave, ignored a severely swollen foot and ankle to run away from the man in Morton Town who had purchased him off the estate of his deceased master. The new owner reported that the man had probably returned to Charlestown or James Island, "and had on when he went away white Negro Cloth Jacket and Trowsers, an Oznaburgh Shirt, and a Gown of white Plains." Clothes could also provide a full-fledged disguise: an Indian slave named Sarah who disappeared from John's Island wearing "a strip'd flannel Gown" was thought ten months later to have "gone over to Hobkoy in Men's Apparel."

Some runaways gathered up money or valuables: an eighteen-year-old named Phyllis "broke open her Master's Box and took from thence £110 and some other Money" before departing. Other slaves took along weapons or were able to acquire them later. It was claimed in an act of 1751 that "slaves which run away and lie out for a considerable space of time, at length become desperate, and stand upon their defence with knives, weapons or arms." When two Angolan brothers left a plantation on Wando Neck in 1734 in a stolen canoe, they "carried with them their Axes and Howes." Another Angolan named Tim possessed a gun when taken up at Stono in 1742. The following year word reached Boston from South Carolina that "30 of their sensible Negroes, 15 of whom had Fire Arms," had run away in a group and were heading for St. Augustine. In the 1750s the *South Carolina Gazette* illustrated its ads for runaways with a woodcut of a Negro (branded with an R on the chest and wearing a skirt-like garment) who was carrying a lance.

As for transportation, some slaves who were good riders and hoped to cover a broad distance dared take horses, even though this inevitably raised the owner's wrath and also increased the possibilities of being spotted. In 1732 a slave named Owen took the bay horse of his new master, tied some clothes and a white blanket behind the saddle, and rode away under the pretense of going to see his wife on a nearby plantation. About the time of the Stono slave uprising in 1739 an "old Negro Man named England, And a young slim Mustee Fellow, named

Prosper (his Son) about 19 Years of Age" disappeared suddenly from Joseph Wragg's Goose Creek plantation. The notice in the *Gazette* reported that several weeks later there departed

> another young Mustee Fellow, named Prince, about 22 Years of Age (also Son of England) with an Iron round one Leg, he took with him out of the Stable, a large Bay natural pacing Stallion. . . .
>
> It is supposed they are together near Dorchester, or about the Plantation of Bethal Dewes to whom they did belong, the old Fellow England is well known, having worked at the Bricklayer's Trade at several Plantations in this Province and his Sons with him.

Taking a boat was more commonplace than taking a horse, especially when several slaves departed together. Shortly after William Webb moved his slaves from James Island to Maggot's Island in 1732, three men and two women, "being very clever Negroes," disappeared in his twenty-five-foot poplar canoe. Two women, one nursing a baby, stole a cypress canoe and escaped from their master several months later. Such incidents continued to be as frequent as they had been in the earliest years when overland trails had been minimal, but as the colony spread out, an increasing majority of those who disappeared seem to have made off on foot.

By no means all runaways were bent upon quitting the colony altogether, but for those who had such extreme ambitions, whether they left via water or over land depended upon their intended destination. These destinations varied widely, and the old stereotype, not even thoroughly valid for the nineteenth century, of the slave who follows the Drinking Gourd toward freedom in the North has little applicability in colonial Carolina. When runaways did navigate by the stars, and many were capable of doing so, they only occasionally headed due north, for in this period each point of the compass offered a different prospect of escape. The paths of some slaves were naturally determined by misinformation or ignorance about local geography, but a far greater number had a clear sense about where they were heading and why, having weighed at least to some degree the comparative dangers and prospects associated with each direction.

To the east the open ocean was an inevitable lure, and Charlestown harbor became a common locale for runaways. In 1725 well over one hundred local merchants and freeholders signed a petition which commended the captain of Johnson's Fort on the south side of the bay, for "the many good Services done . . . in Apprehending run away Servants & Negroes" and assured him sufficient men and boats to continue. If a few newcomers entertained fancies of recrossing the Atlantic to Africa, most of those who hoped to depart illegally by sea had gained a clearer sense of their actual prospects through observation or experience. For example, a young Charlestown runaway named Harry, who was suspected of putting to sea in 1732, had no doubt seen and heard a great deal during the years he was the attendant in the "Physick and Surgery" shop of Daniel Gibson and Thomas Stitsmith beside the bay. When he vanished from Stitsmith's house on Broad Street, readers of the *Gazette* were warned: "Be it at the Peril of any Captain to take him off." A similar warning was issued for Sampson, a well-known painter and glazier in Charlestown, who disappeared in the uneasy fall of 1739. Since he had been raised in the West Indies, his owner advertised that "He is likely to be hid on Board of Vessels, therefore I desire all Commanders to make enquiry on board their respective Vessels."

Some of these runaways had prior experience at sea which they hoped would assist their efforts to escape. In 1743 Toney, a slave who had once belonged to Capt. Ebenezar Simmons of Charlestown, ran away from a purchaser who had taken him north to a rice plantation along the Peedee; he was described as "a lusty tall Gambia Fellow, . . . about 35 Years of Age, speaks pretty good English, . . . and affects to dress like a Sailor." Less knowledgeable runaways who frequented the docksides may have been trying to assess the sea as a possible avenue of escape. In 1737, for example, the *Gazette* reported that "a young Negro Fellow named Peter," who had already had four owners including an Indian trader, "has been lately seen with the fishing Negroes, at the Markett Place." Slaves escaping to the north or south could also travel by water, and Lt. Gov. Bull reminded the Assembly in 1741 that the maintenance of scout boats at Hilton Head and Dawfuskee Islands was crucial to "prevent the Desertion of our Negroes, who might (perhaps) make frequent Attempts if those Places were left unguarded."

As official vigilance and commercial traffic grew, the numerous coastal passages became more difficult avenues for escape, and runaways were obliged to test more thoroughly the colony's inland borders. North Carolina, thinly populated and rarely on good terms with its southern neighbor, had served as a refuge since the seventeenth century, and in 1722 South Carolina's agents in London were instructed to argue for the annexation of that region "by Shewing how much this Province Suffers by the Inhabitants and Slaves running away there where they are Succour'd." Some of the runaways who headed north were undoubtedly slaves brought from that direction who desired to return. When Toney, "a Virginian middle sized yellowish Negro Fellow," ran away from a plantation in Christ Church Parish he may well have hoped to reach Virginia again, although in fact he was brought to the workhouse in Charlestown within ten days. Other slaves traveling in the lowland region claimed with varying degrees of honesty and success that they were "born free in Virginia."

Exodus toward the south retained an even greater attraction for South Carolina slaves because of the continuing Spanish presence in Florida. Just as Negroes from the Virgin Islands would later defect to Puerto Rico and work on Spanish fortifications there in exchange for a plot of land, so Carolina slaves of this period were drawn toward St. Augustine by the thought of protection and freedom among enemies of the English. The establishment of Georgia as a nonslave settlement created new difficulties for black deserters, for as Capt. Massey told that colony's trustees in 1740: "Georgia is a fine Barrier for the Northern Provinces, and especially for Carolina; And is also a great Security against the running away of Negroes from Carolina to Augustine, because Every Negroe at his first Appearance in Georgia must be immediately known to be a Run away, since there are no Negroes in Georgia." But after slavery was allowed (or imposed) there in 1750, the situation changed, and some of those Negroes heading south in the following years had actually started in Georgia. In 1758, for example, Austin and Laurens offered a £20 reward for "a slim sprightly sensible yellow Negro Boy, named Harry, lately sent from Georgia to be sold, and imagined to be returned to that Province."

As for those slaves who escaped toward the west into Indian country, the prospect of total absorption into a compatible culture had to be balanced against the risk of betrayal, captivity, or death. Decades of considerable contact must have made these contrasting possibilities broadly known, but the tensions of wilderness diplomacy kept red–white–black relations in a state of considerable doubt. Occasionally, the familiar issue of runaways taking refuge with the Indians gained prominence among whites, as in 1735 when the Assembly announced "that Several Slaves have made their Escape from this Province and very probably are sheltered & protected by the Tuskerora Indians." The assemblymen charged that tribe with killing cattle and abducting slaves and undertook "to expel those Tuskeroras out of this Government" by offering a bounty to freemen or slaves who killed or captured any Tuscaroras, warning that as "the next step on the like Provocation we shall endeavour to extirpate them."

For Negroes disappearing westward, Indians consistently played a major role, stealing some slaves away and helping others escape, but relations were always ambiguous. Upon occasion redmen killed blacks with no clear provocation, as in 1721 when a member of the Cussoe Nation named Toby shot a valuable Negro sawyer named Bram as he was working on his master's plantation. Months later a Negro runaway "was Shott by a Slave Indian by nobody's Order." White colonists encouraged such animosity. Sensing that the interests of these two groups often overlapped, they did all that they could to insure separation and promote hostility between black and red. An early move of the first royal governor in 1721 was to negotiate a pact of "Friendship and Commerce" with the Upper and Lower Creeks, whose head men promised "to apprehend and secure any Negro or other Slave which shall run away from any English Settlements to our Nation," in return for four blankets or two guns if taken up beyond the Oconoy River, one gun if returned a shorter distance. "And in Case we or our People should kill any such Slaves for their Resistance, or running away from us in apprehending them," continued the article, "then we are to be paid one Blanket for his Head by any Trader we shall carry such Slave's Head unto."

The Creeks may have been one of the tribes to steal and redeem slaves simultaneously, for in February 1728 an English agent charged that for several years they had been "Robbing and Plundering us of our Slaves and Goods and laying the blame on the Yamasees." Later that same month a committee appointed to consider ways to make the neighboring tribes "more Serviceable" to the interests of the colony suggested the appointment of Indian Commissioners whose duties would include distributing rewards to Indians who killed or captured runaways. At the same time it was recommended that such officials should be empowered to punish any Negroes who tried to intimidate local Indians from carrying out white orders. It was also hoped that they would "Discourage any Trade or Traffick being carryed on between the Indians and Negroes and likewise prevent any Negroe from takeing a Wife among the Free Indians, or Free Indians from takeing a Slave a Wife."

By this time reports of "an outlying Negro being shot" by Indians had become a regular occurrence, and their frequency increased as slave numbers and Indian desperation grew. In 1730 seven Cherokee chiefs traveled to London for an audience with the English king. There they signed an agreement similar to that struck with the Creeks nine years before, promising among other things to return Negro runaways for the somewhat reduced payment of a musket and a match coat per slave, alive or dead.

Experience gradually taught the English that runaways who reached the hinterlands were not easily returned to the low country alive, even when spared by the Indians. In 1723 a band of warriors brought two half-starved runaways to a trading post on the Ochese River and settled down to await payment. Though uncertain the slaves could survive the trip or that their ransom would be paid, the trader felt obliged to ship them to Charlestown in a pettiauger and pay off their captors. In 1726 the Assembly granted a trader £50 in restitution for "a wound he received of a Negro bringing him down prison^r: from the Indians." During the following winter an English captain returning from the Creek tribes ran up a bill of £25 "for men employ'd to pursue a Negro that was taken & made his escape."

In 1728 another English agent, sent among the Cowetaws, reported that "They have now a Negro belonging to a Man at Pon Pon who has run away from his Master and has been catch'd several times and still gets away. I desire your Order about him," the agent told officials; "I believe it as much as he is worth to bring him down. I believe it would be better to set his head up for an example." An item from the *Gazette* in 1737 told how seven Upper Creeks had come upon an outlaw band composed of a Spaniard, an Indian, a Negro and a mulatto, known to have made forays against whites and Indians alike. The Creeks promptly killed the brigands and sold their stolen Spanish horses to the English. Among the Cherokee, and perhaps among other nations as well, patrolling for runaways became such an accepted occupation that by the middle of the eighteenth century the term "slave catcher" was applied to a certain class of braves.

Whether slaves departed singly or together, by sea or land, armed or unarmed, toward north or south, their chances of successful escape became increasingly slight. This did not preclude desperate slaves from undertaking such escapes, as the events surrounding the Stono Uprising will make clear. But it meant that Negroes who actually took flight from South Carolina in various directions were only a minority of the entire runaway population. Many more slaves seem to have succeeded in going "underground," intermittently or for good, without leaving the colony. It is hard to estimate how many people simply disappeared temporarily and endured a set punishment upon return. For practical purposes they were "absent without leave," and one would not expect such individuals to show up proportionally in the printed ads. Even so, where specific motives can be discerned from notices in the colony's newspaper, South Carolina Negroes were more likely to disappear in order to visit and to maintain contact with other slaves than for any other single reason. Such short-term absences became acknowledged as an effective "coping" process within the system, and both blacks and whites realized that these brief departures could represent a means of relieving tension and avoiding more dangerous confrontations or desertions.

Even the shortest disappearance was by no means a carefree gesture and demanded constant ingenuity and vigilance toward other Negroes, as well as toward Englishmen and Indians. Harboring escaped slaves could draw severe penalties, and although many blacks ran the risk gladly, there were others who would reveal the whereabouts of a runaway to settle a grudge, curry favor with their owner, or lay claim to a small reward. In 1737 the disappearance of a Negro man named Tom prompted his new owner, Thomas Gadsden, to give notice in the *Gazette* that "If any one will bring him to me, I will pay 5 *l.* reward, and I shall be oblig'd to those that will acquaint their Negroes of this, he being known by many." When a sixteen-year-old named Lucy ("formerly bělonging to Jonathan Fitch, by whom she is supposed to be harboured") ran away in 1742, her current master advertised: "Ten

Pounds reward will be given to any white Person, giving such Intelligence of the abovesaid Girl that she may be had again, and to any Negro Five Pounds for the like Intelligence."

There were always slaves to respond to such inducements, as shown by the weekly lists of runaways brought to Charlestown jail. In late April 1735 a slave boy from Ponpon was "taken up at Wappow at Mr. Harvey's Plantation by one of his Negro Men named Dubb." The next day a new African was turned in by a slave named Tony, and several weeks later a man named Bristol took up another newcomer on his owner's plantation. If the fugitives were very young or old, if they could not make themselves understood, or if they had been mutilated for previous offenses, they fell easy victims to "loyal" slaves. But to threaten the freedom of strong men entailed considerable risk. On the night of March 22, 1743, a runaway named Hannibal appeared near the slave quarters on John Paggett's plantation. Two resident Negroes tried to apprehend him, "but he being armed with a Knife stabbed one . . . (named Harry) in the Heart of which he instantly died, and maiming the other very much made his Escape." Paggett was reimbursed liberally for the loss of Harry, in accordance with the Negro Act, but Hannibal remained at large. Even strong men fully armed, however, often could not avoid eventual betrayal, and more than one found himself being shot at by a fellow slave.

Fugitives were not even safe among other absentees. In 1742 several ordinary runaways, encountering a surviving ringleader of the Stono Uprising, captured him in Cocaw Swamp and collected a reward for turning him over to the hangman. In encouraging slaves for capturing slaves, white colonists went so far as to accept the logic that a Negro who "recovered" himself could be eligible for a reward. In 1721 the government voted £5 to Harry, "a Negroe Man belonging to the Widdow Perry, . . . for his faithfulness in returning from St Augustine to this Government." Seven years later "a Negroe Man named Cuffee belonging to Mr. Jones who had been serviceable, in makeing his Escape from the Spaniards and giveing Information to this Province" was granted £10 by the Assembly. However, these incidents in which a reappearing slave was paid for returning stolen property—himself—were highly exceptional. Whatever the pyschological benefits of disappearing for a time and then surrendering, no Negro could engineer a financial profit through running away.

If anything, the incentives for departed slaves to remain "underground" increased as their absence lengthened. Negroes who continued to stay away, because with the passage of time they had become increasingly fond of their autonomous status or fearful of added reprisals, were designated by authorities as "notorious fugitive slaves" after a year at large. Such persons who were prompted in their absence by family ties undoubtedly gained refuge from a relative within the colony. Other runaways sought out friends from whom they had been separated. An ad in the *Gazette,* August 8, 1743, suggests that this practice was acknowledged by both black and white:

> RUN away about January last, from John Fenwicke's Plantation at Ashepoo, a short well set Mustee Fellow, named Cadjoe, formerly belonging to Mrs. Beamer on Charles Town Neck; He is a sensible Fellow, about 28 Years old, born in the Province; and not being heard of, about Ashepoo or elsewhere, for above these three Months, it's supposed, that he is harboured by some Negroes of his old Acquaintance, especially those formerly belonging to said Beamer.

Sometimes the whereabouts of an absent slave could only be guessed by a master, but often the knowledge of a runaway's location seems strikingly specific. The *Gazette* contains numerous references to absentees who continued to elude authorities, even after they had been seen at a distance or located by a reliable source. In 1738 Roger Saunders noted that an Indian slave named Peter, who had worked for Thomas Elliott as a carpenter and wheelwright,

> has eloped from me several Times, and generally has been taken up on the Town Neck. Also run away about two Years since, a Negro Man, named Abram, who is a good Sawyer, middle sized and middle aged, and speaks broken English, he formerly belonged to Major Tobias Fitch, I have a good deal of Reason to think that he is harboured sometimes about Four hole Swamp, sometimes about Mr. Baccots at Goose Creek, and sometimes on the Town Neck, he having been frequently seen about them Places, and not long since on the latter.

Phillis, "a pretty tall young Negro Wench . . . well known in Charlestown," had been absent less than a week when her master placed a notice in the *Gazette,* but she had already "been seen often about Town at Work, and Friday Evening last was seen going up the Road with Capt. Gadsden's Negroes."

Although hiding in Charlestown was the opposite of hiding in the woods, the crowded anonymity of the city attracted numerous runaways, especially those who had been there before. Franke, "a young Molatto House-Wench . . . known by most People in Charlestown," was sold to a John's Island planter by the executors of an estate in 1734. She soon absconded and was seen in the town by several people, "without doubt harbour'd by some free Negroes or Slaves." Fear of being recognized apparently did not deter these runaways, who knew the safety of Charlestown's numbers and had learned to rely on their own shrewdness. The ad for one Negro who deserted his new master reads: "well known about Charles Town but not for his goodness." A slave named Minos who ran off from Mr. Wragg's plantation in 1734 was also "well known in Charles Town, having liv'd there several Years." His master supposed him "to be lurking in or about the Town" and warned readers of the *Gazette:* "He is a very crafty subtil Fellow, and if taken, without great Care, will get away again."

Slaves seeking refuge in Charlestown must occasionally have crossed paths with Negroes running away from the city. In the fall of 1734, for example, the *Gazette* not only carried ads for "a Negro Wench named Flora," who had disappeared from James Island and been seen in town, but also for Hanna, the absent slave of a Charlestown bricklayer. When this woman first left the city in June she was "seen at Capt. Gadsden's and Mad. Guyle's Plantations"; in October she was still at large and said to keep "between Mr. Edward's and Capt. Gadsden's Plantations." Some Negroes who disappeared into the countryside must have sought out enslaved relatives or friends while others went into solitary hiding. A Negro who escaped from James Kerr lived for a considerable time on Otter Island before being hunted down. A few found safety on the remote fringes of the colony. London, for example, an Angolan who had been brought to Carolina in 1730 had lived in St. John's Parish for ten years, ran away from his new master near Pine Tree Creek. Two years later, an ad in the *Gazette* stated that he was "supposed to be harbour'd in some of the Out Settlements."

Therefore, from the center of the port city to the edge of settlement and beyond, the presence—or nonpresence—of absentee Negroes was a fact of colonial existence. As agricultural production intensified during the first half of the eighteenth century, the pressure on Negroes to run away increased, but at the same time the machinery for their containment multiplied: tickets were required, patrols were strengthened, punishments were enforced. Perhaps hardest of all, rewards were offered to buy the loyalty of slaves. Individually and collectively, therefore, Negroes felt their situation becoming more desperate. As the incentives grew higher on the one hand to rebel or escape, the inducements mounted on the other hand to submit and even to inform. For slaves caught in such a vicious circle, running away represented a personal and partial kind of resistance which at one moment seemed too bold and at another moment did not seem bold enough. If the majority of slaves never actually broke out of the circle and ran away, even for a short time, it was due not to any ignorance of the variables involved but to an acute awareness of them. And these specific considerations weighed by every potential runaway were in many ways emblematic of the larger ongoing dilemma which enslavement posed for all black people.

But their masters too were confronting a circular dilemma. Although no single runaway posed a threat to the slave system, scores of absentees constituted not simply a minor nuisance and ominous reminder but a potential nucleus for more concerted acts of rebellion. And the harder the hammer fell, the more likely it was to create further sparks. A subtle spiral of fear and repression had begun to generate around the inner anxieties of the white community.

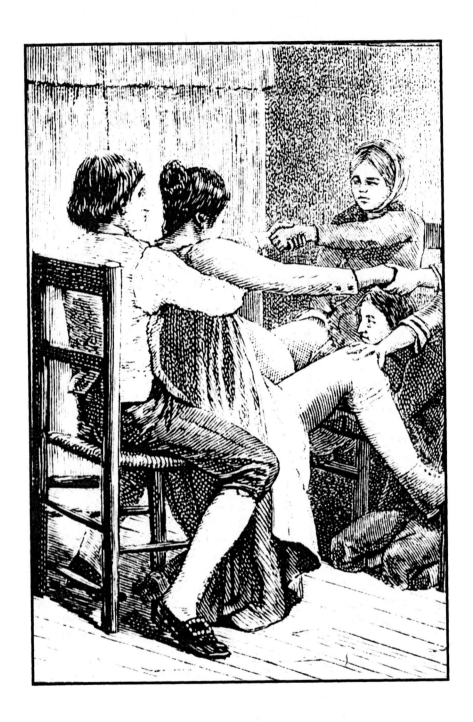

*Husband holds wife as neighbors and midwife assist
in childbirth.*

Travail: Childbirth in Colonial New England

LAUREL THATCHER ULRICH

The basic unit of society in colonial New England was the household. The vast majority of New England inhabitants formed families, lived in small rural villages, and re-created the traditional English world on the small farms that dotted the New England landscape. Limited by the harshness of the environment and traditional English world views, their expectations and daily lives revolved around the maintenance of the family economy. Typically, both men and women could expect to marry young, spend most of their lives raising children, bury at least one of their offspring, and labor long days to support their families.

In all New England communities, husbands and wives lived in an unequal world. Women were denied political rights, were legally subordinate to their husbands, were excluded from positions of authority in the church, and were isolated from the public life of the community. Hence, the lives of women revolved around the household economy and family life, where their responsibilities were very large. Farm wives were responsible for the daily operations of the rural household—food preparation, the making of clothes, soap, and candles, cultivation of the garden, and care of farm animals. While presiding over these household operations, married women were also preoccupied with childbearing and child rearing.

In this selection, Laurel Thatcher Ulrich describes the central place that childbirth held in the lives of rural colonial women. After marriage, women's existence was bound by the cycles of pregnancy, birth and lactation. The birthrate was much higher than today, so that a woman could expect to raise six to eight children. At the same time, there were few parents in early America who did not see at least one of their offspring die in birth or in infancy, and it was not uncommon for parents to bury many or most of their children. As Ulrich describes in the following selection, childbearing in early America shows little likeness to today's practice and experience. Men were completely excluded from the event, and midwives, not male physicians, attended the birth. The father was not allowed in the birthing room, which was often filled with female friends and acquaintances.

Modern writers sometimes state rather glibly that the only difference between the sexes is that women can bear children while men cannot. In the premodern world this simple fact had enormous consequences. Reproduction was the axis of female life. A fortunate bride not only brought into marriage the pots and sheep and kettles provided by her father, but also a set of "childbed linen" inherited from her mother, a mysterious collection of bedding and apparel which was as much ceremonial as practical. The finest childbed linen was embellished with embroidery or lace, like a best petticoat or pillowcase. The rituals of childbirth testified not only to the separateness and the subjection, but to the mysterious power of womankind.

Labor and delivery were central events not only for the mother and baby but for the community of women. Depositions in an Essex County case of 1657 reported a dozen women present at a Gloucester birth. A hundred years later Matthew Patten of Bedford, New Hampshire, recorded the names of seven women gathered in the middle of the night when his wife's travail grew "smart." An eighth neighbor arrived in the morning. But Sarah Smith, the wife of the first minister of Portland, Maine, may have set the record for neighborly participation in birth. According to family tradition, all of the married women living in the tiny settlement on Falmouth Neck in June of 1731 were present when she gave birth to her second son.

It would be helpful to know the rules which governed these assemblies. Were there particular tasks assigned according to consanguinity or status? Who, for example, supported the mother in delivery position? Who changed the linen? Did the midwife, the nurse, or the grandmother receive and wash the child? In this same-sex environment, were there procedures to preserve modesty? Could newlywed women or unmarried girls observe the actual process of birth before they experienced it themselves? On such questions the records are silent. Childbirth in early America was almost exclusively in the hands of women, which is another way of saying that its interior history has been lost. Yet in male diaries and in court depositions for the period there are shards of evidence which occasionally allow the historian to penetrate the silence and to make connections with the experience of women in other centuries and with the ragbag of English folk practice preserved in medical-advice books of the period.

In the nineteenth and twentieth centuries childbirth in America became a private ordeal undergone in the antiseptic sanctity of a hospital. The mother's safety—and presumably her dignity—were ensured by the professional anonymity of the attendants. In the past twenty years this medical sanctuary has gradually been undermined. Today the home-birth movement welcomes not only lay midwives but sometimes children, friends, and neighbors as well, making birth the semi-public event which it was in the traditional world. But there is an important difference. In the past the badge of entry was sex. A shared gender identity shaped each detail of the drama of delivery.

For many women, the first stage of labor probably took on something of the character of a party. One of the mother's responsibilities was to provide refreshments for her attendants. The very names *groaning beer* and *groaning cakes* suggest that at least some of this food was consumed during labor itself. Midwifery manuals encouraged the mother to eat light but nourishing foods—broth, poached eggs, or toasted bread in wine—during labor and immediately after birth. They told her to walk about rather than lie down at this stage.

To relieve discomfort, the women used herbs gathered earlier from the field and garden. Most families had a supply of medicinal and culinary herbs; husbands as well as wives might be involved in their preparation. When Nicholas Gilman of Exeter, New Hampshire, went into the woods to gather betony in May of 1740, he was consciously or unconsciously following the instructions of an English midwifery manual of the seventeenth century, which recommended picking the plant "in its prime, which is in May." Mary Gilman may have processed the herb which her husband gathered, crushing it, clarifying the juice, then making it into a syrup with double its weight of sugar. When she went into labor four months later, she was prepared.

Remedies came from the barnyard as well as the forest. When Cotton Mather's wife was suffering in her last illness, she dreamed that a "grave person" appeared to her and told her that the pain in her breast could be relieved by cutting "the warm Wool from a living Sheep" and applying it "warm unto the grieved Pain." She confided the mystical remedy to her physician, who encouraged the family to try it. The remedy which so amazed Mistress Mather's husband was actually an ancient device for relieving labor pain. It had probably existed in oral tradition long before it appeared either in an English medical treatise of the seventeenth century or in Mrs. Mather's dream. She had perhaps heard it talked about, if not seen it used, at a long-since-forgotten birth.

There is symbolic fitness in the use of new-laid eggs. They were not only served to the mother as food but soon after birth were applied externally, first having been stirred over hot embers in an earthen pipkin, then plastered on a dressing. Most of the midwife's supplies were probably as ordinary. Matthew Patten purchased or borrowed butter immediately before each of his wife's deliveries. This may have been coincidental, but probably was not. Fresh butter, with less savory emollients like hog's grease, was used to lubricate the midwife's hands and to anoint the vagina and perineum to facilitate stretching during labor. For the parturient woman, there was comfort as well as reassurance in familiar things.

But an even more important source of aid came from the attendants themselves. Recent studies of the psychology of birth have shown the significance of emotional support during labor. An informed and empathetic coach is an effective analgesic in helping a woman surmount fear and pain. In delivery there was physical as well as emotional intimacy among the women. A mother might give birth held in another woman's lap or leaning against her attendants as she squatted on the low, open-seated "midwife's stool." In cases of extreme difficulty a draught of another mother's milk was considered a sure remedy. The presence in the room of a lactating woman was useful for another reason as well. A friend or neighbor was probably the baby's first nurse, since the mother's own milk (or colostrum) was presumed impure for several days owing to the "commotions" of birth.

Because the attending women would watch the child grow to maturity, they also represented a kind of insurance that nothing would go wrong in delivery that might result in trouble after. A whole collection of superstitions surrounded the handling of the umbilical cord. It must not touch the floor lest the child grow up unable to hold water. It must not be cut too short for a boy, lest he prove "insufficient in encounters with Venus," nor too long for a girl, lest she become immodest. Delivery was characterized by a succession of gender-infused rituals.

Childbearing in seventeenth- and early eighteenth-century New England differed from today's community-centered home birth not only in the exclusion of males and in the intimacy with the natural world, but in the attitude toward suffering. "Natural" birth in the premodern world was presumed to be both painful and dangerous—as God intended. Pious women like Anne Bradstreet of Andover or Sarah Goodhue of Ipswich wrote spiritual testaments as they faced childbirth, just as men of the same class and time signed wills before embarking on a long sea journey or military expedition. A manuscript record kept by

John Cotton of Hampton, New Hampshire, and passed on to his son-in-law, Nathaniel Gookin, shows this theme in two generations of Anne Bradstreet's descendants.

Anne Lake Cotton gave birth to nine children in the twenty years between September 1687 and January 1707. Although she lost her first baby two months before the birth of her second, the next five children survived infancy. Then in quick succession she lost three babies at or soon after delivery. The first of these three children was born on Tuesday and died on Saturday before his expected christening on Sunday. "The name design'd was Samuel," his father wrote, "in remembrance of Gods hearing prayers for his mother, who was wonderfully delivered of him after 11 convulsion fits. . . . God grant his Mercy herein may never be forgotten, tho Samuel be gone to the land of Forgetfullness!"

Mrs. Cotton was apparently suffering from eclampsia, a severe form of toxemia characterized by dangerous elevation of blood pressure. With modern prenatal care this condition seldom develops to the state of convulsions today, but should it do so, the danger is extreme. Although mothers have been known to recover after as many as two hundred "fits," the prognosis for the infant is grim. Even in relatively recent times perinatal mortality has been as high as forty-five percent. Little Samuel's death is not surprising.

Dorothy, the oldest Cotton daughter, was ten years old when the first of three doomed siblings was born. When the last dead fetus was buried in the garden behind the house, she was thirteen. Just four years later she married Nathaniel Gookin and within nine months was delivered of her own first son. By any statistical standard her childbearing record was remarkable. In twenty-three years she gave birth to thirteen children, losing only one premature baby at birth. But she must have carried into her childbearing years the memory of her mother's suffering. Ten of the twelve entries in her husband's handwriting record some variant of the proverbial "long and dangerous travail."

According to the family record, Dorothy Gookin experienced "exceeding hard & Dangerous Travail," "very long Travail," "very sharp (tho' not long) Travail," "hard Travail," "very hard Travail," and "very hard & dangerous travail." With her ninth child she "fell in Travail and was under very Dangerous Circumstances But it pleased God [in] his Great Mercy to Spare her." Despite these recurrent crises, she outlived her husband, who died the very month their last child was born. The thirteenth entry is in the handwriting of their oldest son: "Saturday Aug. 10, 1734 between 9 & 10 in the Morning after a long & dangerous travail My Mother was delivered of a son."

In historical documents the nature of "travail" is almost always a subjective impression reported by women and recorded by men. Childbirth was not only an emblem of the suffering of Eve—it was a moment of supreme drama. One need not diminish in any way the actual suffering of woman to recognize that the expected pain and trial were also a source of attention and sympathy. In the drama of childbirth, husbands were twice removed from the scene. Their sex excluded them not only from direct participation but in a very real sense from active support. In the early stages they ran errands, summoning the midwife and getting supplies, but at the height of the crisis their only real calling was to wait. This is apparent in the diary of Nicholas Gilman of Exeter, New Hampshire, who recorded the events surrounding the birth of his fifth child in September of 1740.

> After the Women had been Some time assembled I went out to get a little Briony Water—Upon My return My Wives mother came to me with tears in her Eyes, O, says she, I dont know how it will fare with your poor wife, hinting withal her extreme danger.

Not only the birth itself but the husband's very awareness of the progress of the birth was controlled by the women in the delivery room.

The diary of Matthew Patten, a farmer of Bedford, New Hampshire, is much more matter-of-fact than Gilman's, yet even his laconic entries reveal a similar management of events. "My wife was Delivered Safe of a Daughter precisely at 12 o Clock at noon after abundance of hard Labor and a great deal of Discouragement and fear of Deficulaty," he wrote, adding, "My Wife and the Women were all a great Deal Discouraged." Momentarily at least, childbirth reversed the positions of the sexes, thrusting women into center stage, casting men in supporting roles.

Christ had likened his own death and resurrection to the sorrow and deliverance of a woman whose "time had come." Travail, the curse visited by God upon the daughters of Eve, was not only an emblem of weakness and sin but a means of redemption. Joy permeated the birth record of Mary Cleaveland of Chebacco Parish in Ipswich, who recorded the birth of each child in her own shaky and unformed hand. "[T]he Lord apeard for me and maid me the liveing mother of another liveing Child," she wrote in October of 1751. For her the entry was formulaic. After the birth of her seventh child she wrote, "The Lord was better to me than my fears." So he must have been to more than one woman in northern New England. Bolstered by scriptures and sustained by their sisters, they labored and overcame.

In no other experience in the premodern world were women so completely in control or so firmly bonded. But it would be a mistake to see early American childbirth as entirely independent of male authority. Two men—the minister and the physician—were at least potential intruders into this female milieu. By the end of the eighteenth century, medical involvement in childbirth would be common in cities, foretelling the "modernization" which would eventually banish the midwife. Before 1750 the authority of the women was secure, though there are telling glimpses of what would come in the activities of two northern New England ministers, men who combined scientific and religious authority.

The most dramatic example of ministerial interest in childbirth comes from the period just after the Antinomian controversy in Massachusetts. In the 1640s, when the two chief female dissenters in the colony, Anne Hutchinson and Mary Dyer, both gave birth to "monsters," ministers and public officials were quick to see the judging hand of God. Little wonder that a scientifically curious minister like John Fiske of Wenham would want to examine an "unnatural birth" reported to him. In 1647, in the presence of three women, he performed a partial autopsy on the body of a stillborn infant, a process which he carefully described in his journal, detailing the opening of the skull and the examination of the "brains, fibres, and blood." He decided that the fetus was basically normal but had been damaged in birth. What had brought him to this home? The fears of the mother? The suspicions of the attending women? Or simply neighborhood gossip? In this case the reason for his visit is less important than the authority which he carried. Learning—the formal book-learning which was denied to women—brought him to the home of the mother. His role here was not to officiate at a birth but to interpret it.

Hugh Adams, physician and minister in Durham, New Hampshire, three-quarters of a century later, went further. Adams, an eccentric who was eventually ousted from his parish, wrote a self-serving memoir after his dismissal in which he claimed to have assisted at the birth of Mary Glitten's first child in December of 1724. According to Adams' account, the woman had been in labor three and one-half days when the midwife, Madame Hilton, summoned him. He rode the seven miles to Exeter, carrying both medicine and the authority of Christ. He began with a prayer, pleading the promise of I Timothy "that the woman shall be saved in child bearing." He then gave her "some of the most strong Hysterick medicines to recall and quicken her labour pains; and Dilated the passage of nature with Unguentum Aperitivum meipsum." That failing, he cried unto Christ and then "proceeded by manual operation" to "move the Babe into a capable posture." Within a minute it was born. Having facilitated the child's first birth, Adams then officiated at its second, baptizing it with the name of Benjamin.

It is astonishing to think of the Reverend Mr. Adams, whose obstetrical knowledge consisted of reading a few English treatises, walking into the midwife's house in Exeter and working a medical miracle, especially one which involved complex manipulation of the fetus, a procedure hardly mastered without practice. There is no way of knowing exactly what happened, but is clear from the minister's own account that he considered his efforts on behalf of Mrs. Glitten one with the other "remarkable providences" described in his memoir. These included calling down the vengeance of the Lord upon the Jesuit missionary Father Rale, as well as protecting his own sons' lives in battle by the ritual blowing of animal horns. Adams believed that melodious psalm-singing (an eighteenth-century innovation opposed by conservatives) was a direct cause of the success of New Hampshire troops against the Indians! It is difficult to know whether his mind-set was that of an eighteenth-century man of science or a seventeenth-century wizard. According to his own account, Adams delivered one other baby. Although the mother survived, the child did not.

Two deliveries hardly constitute an obstetrical practice, and we might dismiss Adams' story if it were not so instructive. His success in the case of Mary Glitten can probably be credited to the encouragement of English medical treatises, his own authority as a man of God, a remarkably inflated ego, and luck. But it is also a reminder of the power of the "learned man" in this society. In a moment of extreme peril the traditional experience of the midwife gave way to the book-learning and professional aura of the minister-physician.

In the development of obstetrics in northern New England, Hugh Adams of Durham stands midway between a scientifically curious minister like John Fiske and a professional physician like Edward Augustus Holyoke of Salem, who by 1755 was regularly consulted in cases of "hard labor." The rapid development of forceps in the second half of the eighteenth century gave the physician a technological advantage he had not had before. By 1800 "male science" had diverged dramatically from "female tradition" and midwifery was under strenuous attack.

But the decline of the midwives in the nineteenth century cannot be attributed solely to the development of obstetrical science. It was also a consequence of the undermining of traditional social relations and the increasing privatization of the family. Midwives were "experienced," whereas physicians were "learned." Because the base of the midwives' experience was shared by all women, their authority was communal as well as personal. In attacking the midwives, nineteenth-century physicians were attacking a system more than a profession. The very intensity of their disdain for "old wives' tales" suggests the continuing authority of the women even in this period of dramatic change.

The diary of Mary Holyoke . . . gives some glimpses of childbearing customs in Augustus Holyoke's own family. Holyoke's long interest in obstetrics may well have been stimulated by the death of his first wife in childbed. The recurring trauma of his second marriage was not "hard labor," however, but infant death. Mary Holyoke gave birth to twelve children in twenty-two years, only four of whom survived infancy. Her first little Polly lived four years, her second ten months, and her third, christened for her older sisters on the fifth of September

1767, died four days later. Five other infants died in the first weeks or months of life. One after another, the "dear babies" came and went, while Mary continued to garden, write in her journal, sew cravats for the doctor, and take tea with friends.

She summarized each delivery in the simple phrase "brought to bed," seldom adding any other details. On September 12, 1771, she was "Brought to Bed quite alone 11 A.M. of a Daughter." Was she literally alone in her house, without the assistance of her husband, a maid, or a midwife? Or was she simply implying that no one from outside the family had arrived in time for the birth? For five of the twelve deliveries she did list the names of two or three women who were with her. "Mrs. Jones" was present at four births, "Mrs. Mascarene" (who was Augustus' sister Peggy) at three, and "Mrs. Carwick" at two. No assemblage of the neighborhood is implied here, just an intimate circle of relatives and friends. There are two explicit references to her husband's ministration near the time of birth. Three days before one baby arrived, "the Doctor" bled her. Two months after the birth of another, when she developed a breast infection, he lanced it. Medical assistance did not banish traditional comforts, however. When Mary developed a "knot" in her breast a few days after the birth of her ninth child, "Nurse annointed it with Parsley, wormwood & Camomel Stewed in Butter."

The diary suggests that in urban Salem, as elsewhere in New England, childbirth remained a central event in the community of women. Mary noted in her diary when her friends were "brought to bed," but among these women a formal "sitting up week" seems to have replaced the hasty gathering in the night still characteristic of rural neighborhoods. On March 3 Mary herself "kept chamber" and the next day was "Brought to bed of Peggy." Two weeks later, when she was ready to sit in a chair and chat, the visits began. On Sunday one friend came, on Monday five, on Thursday two, and during the following week eight more. These women sipped tea and admired each other's gifts, including perhaps a fancy pincushion stuck with the baby's initials or the motto "Welcome Little Stranger." The circle of female support had begun to shrink as the intimate ritual of birth gave way to a more distant ceremony of welcome.

For most women, life in the childbearing years was less firmly bound by the agricultural seasons than by personal seasons of pregnancy and lactation, twenty-to-thirty-month cycles which stretched from the birth of one baby to the birth of the next. The "travail" of birth was preceded by the "travail" of pregnancy.

Twentieth-century women would recognize some aspects of seventeenth-century prenatal care. Missing from premodern guides to pregnancy was any reference to weight control, but there were remedies for other common problems. For swelling of feet and ankles, *The Experienced Midwife* offered a lotion of vinegar and rosewater; for pressure pain, it suggested an improvised and probably uncomfortable version of a maternity corset, swathing bands looped around the abdomen and tied at the neck. It had little to say about the most famous of female complaints—morning sickness—though it did note that nausea was a possible sign of pregnancy.

Court records suggest that daily life continued with little interruption for pregnancy. At the same time, they make it clear that pregnant women were endowed with a special status entitling them to deference and protection. The case of Sarah Boynton of Haverhill is instructive. She was probably in her fourth month when Ebenezer Browne came to her yard looking for an ox which her husband had locked up. Sarah ordered Browne off their ground, telling him, "If you will come, you must take what comes, for I will do what I can to hinder you." Browne retorted, "If you were a man as you are a woman I would stave out your braines." Not to be intimidated, she thrust a ladder against the door of the hovel where the animal was kept. When Browne grabbed it and threw it down, the uppermost rung struck her.

In March, Sarah Boynton's husband successfully sued for damages, claiming that his wife, being pregnant, had suffered great pain from her injuries, had been unable to do her work for twenty-six weeks, and had required expensive advice from midwives. Although Sarah Boynton clearly felt it her duty to defend her husband's right to the ox, her pregnancy notwithstanding, her frailness became a key point of the damage claim in court. Ebenezer Browne knew he should not strike a woman, yet he did. His taunt, "If you were a man as you are a woman," implied that Sarah had stepped beyond the bounds which he would tolerate in a male, as though in abandoning feminine weakness she had invited attack. The court, in this case, did not agree.

But what were the limits of male protectiveness? And what was the responsibility of the woman herself for her own health and that of her child? Margaret Prince of Gloucester said she "was as lusty as any woman in town" before William Browne began to trouble her, dropping veiled threats, calling her "one of Goodwife Jackson's imps," and warning her that the formal complaint she had lodged in court would be the dearest day's work she ever made. She had a difficult delivery and her child was stillborn. In her mind the case was clear: Browne was responsible for the death of her child. She probably implied witchcraft, though not necessarily. Midwifery manuals warned newly pregnant women to avoid all unusual worries and anxieties for the good of the child. In attacking the psychological health of the mother, Browne attacked the baby.

Yet two neighbors, Goody and Goodman Kettle, argued in Browne's defense that there were much more apparent reasons for Margaret

Prince's troubles. Not three weeks before her travail they had seen her carrying clay to her house in a bucket on her head. What is more, she had "reached up over the door to daub with clay." They were undoubtedly referring to a folk belief (still held by some women in the middle of the twentieth century) that reaching over one's head in the last months of pregnancy would result in a tangled umbilical cord and the possible death of the child. Goody Kettle said that she had walked home with her neighbor and told her "she did wrong in carrying clay at such a time, but Goody Prince replied that she had to, her husband would not, and her house lay open. She had carried three pails and had three more to carry."

Here was a woman caught between two imperatives—to preserve the safety of her unborn child and to finish her house. Perhaps her behavior was a kind of demonstration of desperation, an appeal for help. She apparently got none. Goody Kettle could offer advice, but, without ignoring her own precepts, she could not offer physical assistance because she herself was pregnant. Angry at her husband, Margaret Prince violated folk wisdom, then turned her anguish at the loss of her child toward William Browne, a troublesome and disrespectful neighbor. Although her husband (perhaps experiencing some guilt of his own) concurred in the accusation, the court was not convinced and the Princes lost their suit.

Because such cases are isolated, they admit only tentative impressions. Yet the kind of conflict Margaret Prince and Sarah Boynton exemplify may have been frequent among women of ordinary status and small means. Folk proscriptions on lifting helped to curb what might have become a dangerous workload in this labor-poor society. Yet, regardless of status, a woman could afford to be pampered only in proportion to the number of other persons available to do her work.

For a gentlewoman, like Mary Gilman of Exeter, relatives and servants might prove as much an added burden as a help. In the spring of 1740 the Gilman family included four children ranging in age from eighteen months to eight years. Mary's mother lived with them, as did a teen-aged cousin, Molly Little. Nicholas' parents and several unmarried sisters lived nearby. Despite all this potential help, it is doubtful if Mary Gilman had much time to put up her feet during the last five months of her fifth pregnancy. One after the other, over a two-month period all four children contracted measles, followed by Molly Little herself. Meanwhile Mary's mother was called away to Newbury to the bedside of a dying father, and Nicholas' mother was totally absorbed in nursing one daughter who was dying and another who was chronically ill. Mary herself took a turn watching her sisters-in-law at night. Nicholas was absorbed with his own spiritual and professional problems. Between bouts of headache and toothache he prepared sermons, spending two to three days a week in his new pastorate of Durham, fifteen miles away. Except for one brief entry noting that Mary herself had broken out with a rash, he never mentions her health in the diary. The first evidence of her pregnancy is the announcement of the birth of a son in September.

Through such records we can barely glimpse the routines, shared anxieties, and supporting female lore which characterized the "nine months travail" which preceded the birth of each child.

"Daughter begins to suckle her little Molly; God make her a good nurse," Benjamin Lynde of Salem wrote in his diary four days after the birth of his first grandchild. Lynde reflected a common attitude in New England—nursing one's own children was both a blessing and a duty. An ordinary woman had no choice, of course, since the only alternative was to hire another mother to do it for her. For all classes in northern New England, maternal breast-feeding was the norm.

Mothers nursed in public as well as in private, sitting on the ground outside the village church as well as at home in their own beds—with or without the presence of visitors. Young mothers learned by observation as well as by explicit instruction how to deal with cracked nipples, sleepy infants, and insistent toddlers. They probably also learned a medley of techniques lost to their more fastidious descendants, including the use of puppies to relieve engorged breasts. At some point they discovered that suckling "suppressed the terms." Whether or not they consciously relied upon this ancient method of contraception, they tuned their lives to the natural rhythms of the reproductive cycle.

That those rhythms did indeed shape female life becomes apparent if we look closely at the reproductive histories of three eighteenth-century women as reflected in their husbands' diaries. Although male diarists seldom wrote about their wives, they did consistently record those female activities which disrupted or affected their own. Simply by correlating the two events most consistently mentioned—births and overnight journeys—one can derive circumstantial, though impressive, evidence of the personal meaning of fertility.

The diaries of Zaccheus Collins, Matthew Patten, and Joseph Green cover large portions of the years of childbearing for each of their wives—fifteen out of seventeen years for Mrs. Green, eighteen out of twenty-one years for Mrs. Patten, and twenty out of twenty-two years for Mrs. Collins. The three families were not only prolific but unusually healthy, exemplifying premodern reproductive patterns in an almost ideal form, with birth intervals average twenty-two, twenty-three, and twenty-five months. Elizabeth Collins and Elizabeth Patten each gave birth to eleven children. Elizabeth Green was expecting her ninth child at the time of her husband's death.

The diary of Joseph Green begins in 1700, soon after his call to the ministry in Salem Village, now Danvers, Massachusetts. That of Zaccheus Collins, a Quaker farmer of Lynn, Massachusetts, opens in 1725, while that of Matthew Patten, a founder of the Scotch-Irish community of Bedford, New Hampshire, begins in 1754. In comparison to their husbands, all three wives led sheltered and narrow lives, though each traveled—in her own way and according to her own seasons. As might be expected, Elizabeth Collins, the Quaker, traveled most frequently, sometimes accompanying itinerant Friends who were passing through Lynn on their way to nearby meetings. Mrs. Patten, who lived in an isolated and, in its early stages, frontier community, traveled least. Yet the journeys of all three women fall into a remarkably consistent pattern when keyed to their reproductive histories.

For purposes of analysis, the overnight journeys of the three wives can be divided into three periods: a period of "Pregnancy," beginning 280 days before the birth of each child; a period of "Infancy," from birth to ten months; and an "Interim" period, a variable span from ten months after the birth of the last child to 280 days before the birth of the next. (See table.) For all three women, the greatest frequency of travel was in the so-called "Interim" period. For two of the three women, "Infancy" was clearly a more serious restraint than "Pregnancy." To grasp the significance of these rather limited facts, we must look at each period in greater detail.

It is hardly surprising that pregnancy restrained travel. What is surprising is the number of times all three women undertook journeys in the middle trimester. The most adventuresome trip Elizabeth Patten ever took was during the fifth month of her tenth pregnancy when she went by horseback alone the more than eighty miles to Boston to sell cloth and thread. Matthew, who was usually responsible for such ventures, was heavily involved in harvesting at the time. Elizabeth Collins took a number of journeys early in the sixth month of pregnancy. In March of 1731 she spent almost two weeks in Haverhill and Newbury, presumably visiting relatives. In April of 1741 Zaccheus took her and her sister-in-law to Boston, returning for them three days later. Elizabeth Green completed two journeys in the seventh month, both of them to nearby Wenham, where her parents lived. Joseph's diary entry for June 8, 1710, is quite explicit about the fact that they shared a horse.

All three women, however, remained close to their homes during the last two months of each pregnancy. This seems to have been true even when unusual circumstances might have impelled them to travel.

Incidence of Travel During Pregnancy and Lactation

	Pregnancy	Infancy	Interim	All
Elizabeth Collins	.185	.044	.229	.142
Elizabeth Green	.105	.016	.225	.102
Elizabeth Patten	.11	.071	.266	.129

Late in September of 1755 Elizabeth Patten remained in Bedford while her husband attended her own father's funeral in nearby Londonderry. She was just one month away from the delivery of her fourth child. Pregnancy may have been a "nine month sickness" as the midwifery manual said, but these women were slow to succumb. A more dramatic restraint on travel is apparent in the next period—the first ten months of each baby's life. This is undoubtedly related to lactation, which in many ways placed more demands on the mother than pregnancy. Although a woman might leave her infant for a short while, perhaps relying for an occasional feeding upon a neighbor who was also nursing, she could not travel far or long without taking the child with her. Mrs. Green and Mrs. Patten occasionally traveled with infants (James Patten was baptized in Londonderry, New Hampshire, at the age of seven months while his parents were visiting there). But all three mothers avoided traveling during the third quarter of their child's first year. One reason is obvious. Compared with a newborn infant, a baby seven or eight months old is simply not very portable, being both heavier and more active. If he or she were still dependent upon mother's milk, the only practical solution was to stay home.

But for all three women, the most significant pattern is not the restraint on travel during pregnancy and infancy but the sudden jump in activity after the tenth month of each baby's life. For Elizabeth Collins, this is especially dramatic. For six of the nine babies mentioned in the diary, her first journey after birth was between ten and fifteen months. For the other babies, the second journey after birth fell into this same crucial period. A similar pattern is discernible for Mrs. Green. The timing suggests some connections with weaning, a possibility confirmed in Joseph Green's diary entry for April 12, 1702. Green noted that on this day he took his wife to her parents' home in Wenham, then "came home to wean John," who was then seventeen months old.

There is supporting evidence in less-detailed diaries of the period for the idea of the "weaning journey." From January 1740, when Nicholas Gilman began his daily diary, until late in August of 1741, his wife, Mary, apparently never left Exeter, New Hampshire, where they lived. This period included the last eight months of her fifth pregnancy and the first year of their son Josiah's life. But just before Josiah's first birthday she took an unexplained three-day journey alone to her grandmother's home in Newbury, Massachusetts. There is a similar example in the almanac diary of Edward Holyoke of Salem. In January of 1730 his wife made a two-week visit to her parents' home in Ipswich. Their child was then sixteen months old. The evidence is circumstantial but suggestive.

Supposing New England mothers did leave home to wean their babies, what might this mean? Did maternal absence mean abrupt and traumatic weaning? Was it a manifestation of a repressive and potentially pathological approach to child care? Some historians might argue that it did. Noting the pervasiveness of oral themes and anxieties in the historical record of New England witchcraft, John Demos has speculated that "many New England children were faced with some unspecified but extremely difficult psychic tasks in the first year or so of life." James Axtell has pointed to John Winthrop's simile for his own conversion: "I became as a weaned child. I knew I was worthy of nothing for I knew I could doe nothing for my self." Certainly the sudden disappearance not only of the breast but of the mother herself might present severe difficulties for the infant.

Yet the Winthrop quotation cuts in two directions. It documents the child's sense of loss, but it does so from the parent's point of view. Discounting the unlikely possibility that John Winthrop remembered his own weaning, we find him describing the feelings of the child as he perceived them from the outside. The situation he described may indeed document parental harshness, but the *description* of the situation suggests considerable empathy. Winthrop did not focus upon the behavior of the child, its crying or its demands for its mother, but upon his perception of its interior state, its feeling of helplessness.

Now, the really crucial problem for our purposes is the response of parents to this perceived state. How can parents who understand and sympathize with a child's need deliberately deny it? As the scripture says, "What man is there of you, whom if his son ask bread, will he give him a stone?" Setting aside for the moment unconscious motives, we can say that loving parents will deny a child's need for only two reasons: either they lack the ability to satisfy it or they believe that denial will result in long-term good. In the crisis of weaning, mothers and fathers were obviously in quite different positions because one could supply the demand, one could not. Assuming that in colonial America both parents believed that rather sudden weaning was for the ultimate benefit of the child, the withdrawal of the mother made perfectly good sense.

This would be especially so if the parent who *could* supply the need might be tempted to do so. In the words of an eighteenth-century Maine minister, the converted Christian learned that Christ was "as willing to feed him with his Flesh and Blood; as ever Tender Mother was to draw out her full & asking Breast to her hungry, crying child." Abrupt or sudden weaning would be as painful for the mother as it was difficult for the child. The discomfort would be both physical and psychological, as the mother thwarted both the impulse to relieve her breasts and the desire to nurture her crying child. This denial of the maternal role may well have reduced *her* to the state of psychic helplessness characteristic of a weaned child. Hence her own trip home to mother.

The facts fit together neatly—rather too neatly perhaps. Although there is circumstantial evidence for a more widespread practice, there is only one fully documented example of a "weaning journey" in the diaries under investigation—that of Elizabeth Green, who remained at her parents' home in Wenham in the spring of 1702 while her husband returned home to wean sixteen-month-old John. Even this event can have more than one interpretation. On the one hand, the mother's journey can be seen as a drastic measure, an abrupt and psychologically disturbing end to infancy. On the other hand, at sixteen months little John might already have shown clear independence and a loss of interest in the breast. Nursing may have been confined to one or two brief feedings, perhaps at night or in the early morning when it was easier for the mother to bring him to bed than get up and prepare other food. The journey of the mother may have been simply the ritual termination of an already waning stage, an experience made more pleasant for both mother and child by the active interest and involvement of the father.

Yet disturbing questions remain. If the stage of weaning was not marked with anxiety and potential conflict, why did the mother find it necessary to leave? Was she in fact acting counter to her own instincts? Did Joseph Green's diary entry mark the eventual triumph of a husband over the prolonged, and to him perhaps disturbing, intimacy of mother and child? Or was it that Mrs. Green simply did not trust her own resolve? Did she believe herself incapable of surmounting that "softness," that excessiveness of maternal affection so mistrusted by ministers? Was her dependence on John perhaps an even greater issue than his dependence on her? Little matter, perhaps, for within a few months there would be another infant in the house and the whole cycle would begin again.

Pregnancy, birth, lactation—these three stages in the female reproductive cycle established the parameters of life in the childbearing years. One need not exaggerate their importance or describe women in bondage to the curse of Eve to recognize that these personal seasons might shape the smallest details of daily life—when to lift a heavy wash kettle or daub the chinks of a house, how far to go from home in quest of butter or yarn, whether to travel to Newbury meeting, mount a neighbor's horse for a trip to Boston, or stay at home and brew beer. Each cycle of reproduction was marked by epicycles, recurring patterns of restraint and release, pain and deliverance, sorrow and celebration. All of these were summarized in the word *travail*, a term which connoted not simply pain but *effort*, especially strenuous or self-sacrificing effort.

"O my children all, which in pains and care have cost me dear," Sarah Goodhue began a long passage of advice to her offspring. In *The Four Ages of Man* Anne Bradstreet put a more detailed description of maternal effort into the mouth of a child.

With tears into the world I did arrive,
My mother still did waste as I did thrive,
Who yet with love and all alacrity,
Spending, was willing to be spent for me.

With wayward cryes I did disturb her rest,
Who sought still to appease me with the breast:
With weary arms she danc'd and *By By* sung,
When wretched I ingrate had done the wrong.

Eve's badge of sorrow might reinforce cultural notions of the weakness or vulnerability of women, but it might also become an instrument of female power. Suffering in childbirth could arouse the sympathy and protective instincts of husbands, but, even more profoundly perhaps, the prolonged sacrifices of pregnancy, birth, and lactation might convince religious children of their mother's claims upon them.

In 1701 Samuel Sewall of Boston stood in tearful elegy beside the grave of his mother, one of the first settlers of Newbury, Massachusetts. "My honoured and beloved Friends and Neighbours!" he exclaimed. "My dear Mother never thought much of doing the most frequent and homely offices of Love for me; and lavish'd away many Thousands of Words upon me, before I could return one word in Answer." Sewall spoke of his mother's piety and her industry, but the focus of emotion for this grown man was clearly his own infancy. Spending herself in childbearing, Mistress Sewall had earned the devotion of her son.

Suggestions for Further Reading

The everyday lives of colonizing Europeans in the seventeenth century are disclosed in a variety of recent work. For ideas about the New World and what immigrants might have expected to find, see Howard Mumford Jones, *O Strange New World: American Culture, the Formative Years** (New York, 1964); Richard Slotkin, *Regeneration Through Violence: The Mythology of the American Frontier, 1600–1860** (Middletown, Conn., 1973); and Karen Ordahl Kupperman, *Settling with the Indians: The Meeting of English and Indian Cultures in America, 1580–1640* (Totowa, N.J., 1980).

Attitudes toward work are discussed in Keith Thomas, "Work and Leisure in Pre-Industrial Society," *Past and Present*, 29 (1964): 50–66; David Bertelson, *The Lazy South* (New York, 1967); and Stephen Innes, *Labor in a New Land: Economy and Society in Seventeenth-Century Springfield* (Princeton, N.J., 1983).

For a general introduction to the Indian cultures of eastern North America at the time of European arrival consult Gary B. Nash, *Red, White, and Black: The Peoples of Early America*, 2d ed.* (Englewood Cliffs, N.J., 1982). Also valuable are William Cronon, *Changes in the Land: Indians, Colonists, and the Ecology of New England** (New York, 1983); and Neal Salisbury, *Manitou and Providence: Indians, Europeans, and the Making of New England** (New York, 1982).

The mental world of early colonists is explored in John Demos, *Entertaining Satan: Witchcraft and Culture in Early New England** (New York, 1982); Richard Weisman, *Witchcraft, Magic, and Religion in 17th Century Massachusetts* (Amherst, Mass., 1984); Ann Kibbey, "Mutations of the Supernatural: Witchcraft, Remarkable Providences, and the Power of Puritan Men," *American Quarterly*, 34 (1982): 125–48; and Howard Kerr and Charles L. Crow, eds., *The Occult in America* (Urbana, Ill., 1983).

The interior lives of slaves can be studied in Gerald W. Mullin, *Flight and Rebellion: Slave Resistance in Eighteenth-Century Virginia** (New York, 1972); Allan Kulikoff, "The Origins of Afro-American Society in Tidewater Maryland and Virginia, 1700–1790," *William and Mary Quarterly*, 35 (1978): 226–59; and Philip Morgan, "Black

*Available in paperback edition.

Society in the Lowcountry, 1760–1810," in Ira Berlin and Ronald Hoffman, eds., *Slavery and Freedom in the Age of the American Revolution** (Charlottesville, Va., 1982).

Family relations, including attitudes toward sex, love, marriage, child rearing, and familial rights and responsibilities, are discussed in J. William Frost, *The Quaker Family in Colonial America* (New York, 1973); Edmund S. Morgan, *The Puritan Family: Religion and Domestic Relations in Seventeenth-Century New England** (New York, 1966) and *Virginians at Home: Family Life in the Eighteenth Century** (Williamsburg, Va., 1952); Philip J. Greven, Jr., *Four Generations: Population, Land, and Family in Colonial Andover, Massachusetts** (Ithaca, N.Y., 1970) and *The Protestant Temperament: Patterns of Child-rearing, Religious Experiences, and the Self in Early America** (New York, 1977); and Peter G. Slater, *Children in the New England Mind in Death and Life* (Hamden, Conn., 1977).

The daily lives of colonial women are discussed in Lyle Koehler, *A Search for Power: The "Weaker Sex" in Seventeenth-Century New England* (Urbana, Ill., 1980); Ben Barker-Benfield, "Anne Hutchinson and the Puritan Attitude toward Women," *Feminist Studies*, 1 (1972): 65–96; Julia C. Spruill, *Women's Life and Work in the Southern Colonies** (Chapel Hill, N.C., 1938); and Peter C. Hoffer and N. E. H. Hull, *Murdering Mothers: Infanticide in England and New England, 1558–1803* (New York, 1981).

Other insights into the daily lives of the earliest colonists can be gleaned from David E. Stannard, *The Puritan Way of Death* (New York, 1977); David H. Flaherty, *Privacy in Colonial New England* (Charlottesville, Va., 1972); Darrett B. Rutman, *Husbandmen of Plymouth: Farms and Villages of the Old Colony, 1620–1692* (Boston, 1967); Rose Ann Lockwood, "Birth, Illness, and Death in 18th-Century New England," *Journal of Social History*, 12 (1978): 111–28; the essays in Thad W. Tate and David Ammerman, eds., *The Chesapeake in the Seventeenth Century: Essays on Anglo-American Society and Politics* (Chapel Hill, N.C., 1981); and from John Barth's marvelously revealing novel about early life on the Chesapeake, *The Sot-Weed Factor** (Garden City, N.Y., 1960).

Creating a Nation

1740–1800

Mt. Vernon on the Potomac River.

Domestic Tranquillity and the Management of Emotion Among the Gentry of Pre-Revolutionary Virginia

JAN LEWIS

Migration patterns, modes of settlement, and individual expectations and goals produced patterns of household life in the early seventeenth-century Chesapeake that contrasted sharply with those in early colonial New England. For reasons that Morgan has made clear in the first essay in these readings, males far outnumbered females, mortality rates were unusually high, a ruling ideology was missing, and many fewer adults and children lived in the traditional family unit perpetuated by New Englanders. By the mid-eighteenth century, however, the demographic characteristics of white southerners and northerners had much in common. Nevertheless, the daily lives and personal expectations of the white planter families in a slave society differed markedly from those of families on the small subsistence farms of the Northeast.

In the following selection, Jan Lewis explores the private relations among family members of the gentry class in eighteenth-century Virginia. Diaries and letters kept by both men and women serve as a window into the nature of affection and the expressing of emotions among husbands and wives and parents and children of the upper class in the pre-Revolutionary South. In general, family members sought to keep emotion in check, to suppress open expressions of affection, and to maintain a controlled domestic environment. In matters of love or grief it was expected that emotions would be strictly managed. Lewis links this private behavior of family members to the wider cultural and social context of eighteenth century Virginia. Compare what Ulrich's essay told you about family life in early New England with that in pre-Revolutionary Virginia as described here. Can you make some generalizations about how the private and domestic experiences of white women differed in colonial New England and the South? What experiences did they share?

When Frederick Jones of Virginia visited his North Carolina kin in 1757, he fell in love. He married, made his home with his wife's folks (his cousins), and several years later reflected that except for his separation from his own family, "in every other circumstance of life, I have the greatest reason to be vastly happy & thankful to the wise disposer of all things & upon the whole submit & agree . . . that whatever is is right." The story is in many ways unexceptional, for by the early decades of the eighteenth century the Virginia gentry had cause for the complacency reflected in Jones's evocation of Alexander Pope. After a tumultuous first century, Virginia's planter elite had come to preside over a society that was demographically secure and socially at peace.

Recent studies of the character, temperament, and values of the gentry have given us pictures of its members at horse races and at worship, astride their favorite mounts and in the front rows of their parish churches, always proving their prowess and displaying their persons, always on top or in front. Self-confident and extroverted, the gentry exuded self-assurance on the public stage. We know both the impression that they wanted to make on others and the importance to them of making an impression. Less clear is the nature of the gentry's private life. What values directed their behavior at home? Of what did their emotional life consist?

Historians have recently suggested that the eighteenth-century Chesapeake gentry, like their English counterparts, nurtured and cherished an intimate and harmonious household. The affectionate domestic circle embraced fathers and mothers, daughters and sons, inspiring their love for one another; it encouraged appreciation of the individual, expression of emotion, and exploration of feeling. The gentry family, it is argued, fostered love and self-expression, warmth and individuality—the lineaments, if not the flesh, of a recognizably "modern" family. The private writings of the pre-Revolutionary Virginia gentry, men and women alike, disclose, however, that for them neither affection nor self-expression was yet an unqualified value; both were managed and restrained in the service of a higher good, domestic tranquillity.

Let us begin with Frederick Jones and his vast happiness. Such satisfaction was typical of the gentry, but it was at least as much a statement of faith as of fact, shaping their prayers as much as their

DOMESTIC TRANQUILLITY AND THE MANAGEMENT OF EMOTION From *William and Mary Quarterly*, vol. 39 (Jan. 1982). Reprinted by permission of the author. Footnotes omitted by permission.

praise. So ardently did Virginians desire peace at home that they struck a posture of complacency, as if a mask of composure might pass for the real thing. Surely that was the case with Jones, whose studied self-satisfaction hid an abiding bitterness he was unwilling to reveal.

When the young man fell in love with his cousin Jane Swann, their parents entered into the negotiations that regularly preceded gentry marriages. The girl's mother approvingly observed that the couple "had enough to Enable them on their first coming together to set out in the world in a way to live comfortably, and Provide for a Family," so that neither set of parents was under immediate necessity of contributing more. Although the children were free to live with them until her husband could "set them out in the world," Mrs. Swann hoped that her Virginia cousins could help, for "young people . . . are impatiently fond of having something seperate [sic] of their own to improve & manage." Samuel Swann's letter to Jones's father was more explicit. He could give his daughter no dowry, for he had suffered from a bad harvest and a failed investment and had heavy current expenses, including the costs of educating his only other child, a son, in England. At Samuel's death, however, Jane would receive a share equal to her brother's, "which will be sufficient to make [the couple's] circumstances Easy in the world." Swann made clear that he expected young Jones to receive an equal share with his brothers and sisters in his father's estate.

Such negotiations reveal widely shared expectations about family relationships. Prospering parents felt an unquestioned obligation to "launch" their children "out into some happy subsistence in this world." So well understood was this responsibility that one planter could invoke it in cutting off trade with a London merchant who refused to extend further credit: "You must know that I have a large family, & that the chiefest of my estates entailed on a few of my children so that I [am?] under a necessity of purchasing lands for the others which I can now do to advantage under the present condition of our country." Pre-marital negotiations thus consisted in actualizing and making specific the general obligation. Typically, Henry Fitzhugh advised Francis Thornton that he was "well pleased with your son and what you have given him. . . . I will give them three hundred and seventy five pounds currentlcy [sic], the one half of which I oblige myself to pay this market as soon as my Rents can be collected and disposed off [sic] and the other half to be paid next year, also three slaves." Children, knowing what they might receive from their parents, accepted these commitments as their due.

How such expectations could shape family relations is well illustrated by Frederick Jones. He and his cousin were married in North Carolina and early the next summer were making plans to return to Virginia. The young husband wrote his father (who, unbeknown to the son, had recently died) requesting a pole chair; his wife's pregnancy made it impossible for her to ride horseback. "Was there any such thing to be had here, my Father in Law would not allow me giving you this Trouble," Frederick explained. A chair ordered from England could not arrive in time; "besides I would choose to avoid it; indeed I think it is more than I expect from him, as he has acted so generously by me, since my Marriage as well as before." His father-in-law hoped to sell land for Virginia currency so that Frederick could buy slaves when he returned to Virginia. Frederick implored his father for the chair, asking that its value be deducted from his inheritance and promising that he would be accountable for it to his brothers and sisters. "Your complying," he suggested, "will be a particular Instance of yours and my Mother[']s Love and Affection to me, as it will be advancing so much for me toward my Share or Part, which I have no reason to expect 'till your Death to share with the rest." Young Jones asked no more than his due. Two months later, thinking that his brothers and sisters might be anxious, he explained to one brother why he preferred not to ask the chair of Samuel Swann: "I should choose to avoid being under obligations of this Nature, so soon to my Father in Law, tho' his unbounded Generosity & Goodness has already layn me under greater obligation, I doubt I shall ever be able to compensate."

Frederick Jones used the language of an almost mechanical reciprocity in explaining his dilemma. As a son he felt entitled to a share of his parents' estate. He was reluctant to accept such aid from his wife's father, knowing that he would ultimately be called on to balance the accounts in some way. The young man, however, never received the pole chair from his parents, and so he and his wife remained in North Carolina, no doubt increasing their already large debt of gratitude to Samuel Swann. The Swanns must have been delighted with the arrangement, for Mrs. Swann had borne only two children and dreaded an empty house; as his daughter's family began to grow, Samuel Swann boasted that she was "likely to make up for the deficits of her Mother." Frederick Jones might still have preferred to live in his native Virginia. When informed of his mother's death and the plans for the disposition of her estate, he did not hide his bitterness from his brother. The estate was to be portioned among the four brothers and four sisters. "Had my father thought proper to have divided [his estate] between his four Sons," Jones complained, "it might have been the means of our spending our days happily near each other, and have afforded pretty Settlements,—but as he ordered it otherwise, it deprives us from ever hoping to have so great a blessing."

His brothers and sisters established their families in Virginia, and Frederick Jones remained in North Carolina. A number of years later, Frederick's brother Thomas explained that he would not be able to pay the debt he owed Frederick resulting from the sale of their parents' estate. Frederick was "in much pain to be informed your Circumstances are not so easy and clear as I very sincerly [sic] wish they were," but he could not forgive the debt, for "the present Situation of my affairs, undoubtedly calls very pressingly for it; & it is no small disappointment & obstacle to my advancing & improving my Estate for my increasing family, as I might otherwise do." Jones had a young family; providing for them was his greatest obligation, a responsibility he had assumed the moment he married. He would demonstrate his love and affection for his children by establishing them in the world. He knew from experience that a father who defaulted would surrender his claim to companionship and affection from his offspring.

Parents, then, owed their children a settlement. The obligation was both material and measurable. More striking than the formal style of Frederick Jones's letter to his parents is that he demanded, and then intended to provide for his own children, something tangible as "a particular Instance of . . . Love and Affection." Emotions were presented formally; the manner of expression in a young man's letter to his parents was appropriate to the sentiment: the style was precise, restrained, mannered; the emotion clear, explicit, external. When Jones later spoke of his vast happiness, his thankfulness to God, and his conviction that whatever is is right, these sentiments covered his feelings of disappointment in his parents and antagonism toward his siblings. Clearly, the manner of expression and the emotional style sought to check and control human feelings.

That the aim was restraint emerges in the correspondence of other Virginians in the pre-Revolutionary period. Several examples, once again from the Jones family but typical of the gentry, should serve to make the point. After the death of their father, Thomas Jones became guardian of his younger brother Walter. When the latter went to Edinburgh to study medicine, he came to depend on his brother as a son on a father. Anxious at not having received funds from home for over a year, he reasoned that "some unexpected event has obliged you to withhold the Testimonies of that Kindness & affection, which I have always Experienced & which Love & gratitude have as constantly prompted me to deserve." This is the language of Frederick Jones: reciprocating love was the right of a dutiful and loving son, and parental affection should be demonstrated materially. How did a young man acquire such a mechanical and external notion of love? Consider that seven years earlier, when Walter Jones in a letter had misspelled "write" as "right," his older brother had lectured him: "This is the Consequence of being thoughtless, and Passionate, which follies, I hope you will endeavour for the Future to Conquer." If such a trifle could seem so heinous, surely passion was feared. Consider also the proud letter Thomas Jones drafted to his brother in 1770 when he received his medical degree: "It caused such an emotion in me that obliges me to leave the room, I can imagine you have no conception of the feeling & know not what I mean. . . . [H]owever let it suffice that I love you." In the final copy, Jones omitted that last clause; an explicit declaration of love was not appropriate.

Strong emotions, even of love, were thus to be blunted and curbed. To be sure, this restraint was partly a matter of style, but it was more than that when an earlier Thomas Jones (in fact mourning the death of his horse) proclaimed, "It is my opinion we ought not to have any immoderate concern for any thing that happens to us in this world." And the style became the substance when young men schooled in emotional restraint were able to think of family relationships as formal contracts.

Several historians have viewed the eighteenth-century Virginia gentry family as particularly affectionate, shaped by that "surge of sentiment" that would distinguish so-called "modern" families from their more traditional European antecedents. Surely, if a young man could and did demand from his family "testimonies of . . . kindness and affection," love was one of the bases of family life; yet pre-Revolutionary gentry relationships lacked—or, more precisely, stifled—emotional intensity. Put another way, love was important, but it was not central. Both within and without the family, other ideals—such as peace and moderation—prevailed, creating the context within which emotion might safely be displayed.

If parents had clear material obligations to their children, so also had children duties to their parents. They showed their love by their deportment. Even when grown they were expected to be cheerful and obedient—in the language of the time, a "comfort" to their parents in their old age. Thus, when the planter William Fitzhugh heard that his mother had experienced misfortune, he released money to his brother in England to aid her. "I . . . do think it both our dutys . . . not to suffer one to want, who gave us our being, nor suffer her to struggle to live, who (under God) gave us life here," he explained. "Nature, duty, the Laws of God and Man . . . command . . . to give the utmost help to a distressed Parent." Fitzhugh was doing no more than adopting for himself a standard he held for others. The sentiment and language were similarly stilted when Fitzhugh hoped that a cousin's son would as "he grows in years . . . grow in grace to serve his God, & then without question you his Parents will find him abound with all dutiful observance, & due Obedience." Repaying, literally, a parent was one way of discharging the child's debt, but men and women whose parents were materially secure could lighten the burdens of old age and discharge their debts in other ways. When he completed his college education, John Clopton hoped he would "cease to be so expensive" to his father. He appreciated the older man's "paternal kindness . . . for which may I ever retain a grateful Sense, study to be an Honour to your old Age by diffusing thro' the world the Fruits of that liberal Education you have been so careful to give me." The language is mannered, but, significantly, Fitzhugh and Clopton felt that by sending money or a noble sentiment they were playing the part of the dutiful son.

The language was stilted because the role was scripted and most children learned their lines. In the wider world the gentry were bound to assert themselves, prove their prowess, leave their mark. They were trained to act with more restraint and less individuality at home: the goal was a family life that was at once simple and affectionate. So long as a son or daughter was obedient and appreciative, most parents felt amply repaid for the expense and care of rearing them. Where expectations were thus clear and simple, children could be confident that they had discharged their duties. An exception that helps prove the rule of reciprocity comes from the agitated domestic experiences of Landon Carter, an unusually bitter and bad-humored man, who found his children a continual disappointment. Carter contrasted their disobedience to his devotion to his own father. When his father was declining, Carter used to sleep at his head, to comfort and divert him. "I did it with both duty and pleasure," Carter boasted to his diary; "but I fancy not a child of mine but would refuse even their duty." In fact, Carter kept the diary in the hope that his offspring would one day read it and recall how they had failed him; in it he recorded his frequent quarrels with his children, one daughter-in-law, and his son-in-law.

The most serious confrontations were with his eldest son, Robert Wormeley Carter, who lived with his wife and children in his father's home. The younger Carter, a notorious gambler, was as relaxed as his father was rigid, and the great difference in temperaments made arguments inevitable. The two men could not refrain from goading one another; their disputes revealed deep tensions. During an afternoon tea Landon remarked "in a joke" that his son probably thought they should drink tea, an expensive commodity, only once a week. As the father told the story, his son's "replye was neither ought you to use it any more than we." The father retorted, "What Sir, can't I spend my own money[?]" Robert answered, "By God You will have none to spend soon. I replyed I might owe about £1000. His [sic] answered . . . that [he] would not pay it. I then indeed grew outrageous and said it was a damned infamous lie etc. For which I do suppose Mr. Carter leaves the house. . . . Indeed he said abundance more and I replyed as tauntingly . . . he had been my dayly curse." When he cooled, the son told the father that although it would be inappropriate to instruct a stranger how to spend his money, a man might take such a liberty with his father, for the son would be obliged to pay the debts the father left at death. The elder Carter concluded that "Sons are determined against the least indulgence to the Grey hour of a Parent."

Landon Carter was extremely proud of the skill with which he had worked his plantation, established all his children, and, contrary to his gibe, avoided debt. He was outraged that Robert could not so manage his share as to make money rather than draw from his father. The estate he had given his son was worth £300 a year if directed properly. "I have tried every way to be better treated, but cannot even Purchase it of him; many are the Pounds that I have paid out of my Pocket for him; but nothing will do." Carter would never understand why the obedience he believed he had bought from his son was not forthcoming; after all, he had paid his own father what he owed him.

Robert thought his father's demands were excessive, and with good reason, for Landon was a self-styled patriarch in whose home a subservient role was difficult, especially for a son whose temperament was so different. After Landon disrupted one of Robert's card parties, removing the table and cards, the father and son argued. The father recorded, "I was told by the 40 year old man he was not a child to be controuled; but 40 ought to hear reasons." A month after the outburst over the tea, ten years before the interrupted card game, Robert had determined to move from the house in order "to avoid the frequent quar[rels between?] Father and me." He changed his plans when he learned that such an action would cause his father to "take away the maids that tended my Children, & that he would not aid me but distress me." This threat made the son "bid adieu to all Satisfaction, being compelled to live with him who told me I was his daily curse; & who [imp]uted to me his Negroes running away. . . . [B]ut he is still my Father & I must [torn] bear with every thing from him; in order [to lead a?] quiet life." To protect his own children's interests, Robert resolved to remain in his father's house, to refrain from criticizing his management, to renounce all interest in "domestic affairs," and to endure insult and humiliation. All this he attempted for twelve years, until Landon died. Despite the acrimony, he was constrained both by his sense of obligation to his own children and by his belief that sons ought to be obedient and domestic life quiet.

The ideal was peace. Another planter, exasperated by a fifty-year-old brother who was exhausting both his funds and his patience, lectured him on the proper conduct of domestic life. "You were heartily welcome to the best accommodations my house afforded," Catesby Cocke assured his brother William, "and should always have been so, if you could have been contented." William's financial "Extravagancies," however, were more than Catesby could support. "As my only Study in life is to make my Self and every one about me easy," he explained, "your manners . . . are a bar to my peaceable Scheme." Therefore, he wrote, "compose your Self, preserve sobriety, forbear being troublesome, particularly borrowing. Stay quietly at your home, wherever you make it, and resolve to spend no faster than it comes in." When William Cocke interfered with his brother's "peaceable Scheme," he exhausted his welcome.

It is a commonplace of southern history that the family was of overriding importance, that the family line took precedence over the individual. True, family obligations were taken seriously, but it is easy to oversimplify, for notions of family responsibility were neither vague nor overarching. More important was a particular vision of domestic happiness. The premium was placed not on honor (as those who emphasize the traditional nature of southern culture would expect), nor on affection (as those impressed by its modernity believe), but on peace.

As a result, Virginians of the gentry class were neither introspective nor self-critical. They masked and moderated their feelings; consequently, they did not expect or demand intimacy with others. Thus in 1769 one man could inform a good friend of his recent marriage in these words: "Last Tuesday Miss Kendall gave me her hand, and I am happy in having all the reason in the world to believe that her heart also gave me the preference to every other person." To be sure, the language is in some measure conventional, but the convention itself is revealing, for it dissociates the heart from the hand; and once again, behavior—here, the act of marrying—serves as a sufficient index of love. Edmund Randolph voiced the belief on which the convention was based. At the time of his wedding he did not believe that marital happiness "depended upon an exclusive preference being given to [the husband] before all other men, and I desired nothing more than that she should sincerely persuade herself, that she could be happy with me." If he did not expect his bride to know and love him deeply, neither did he stare into her soul. Writing three-and-a-half decades after his marriage, Randolph noted that he had not at that time "reflected much upon that range of qualities which I afterwards found to be constituents of marital happiness." Virginians did not like to reflect on matters of feeling.

Emotional intensity between husband and wife, as between parent and child, was avoided. Landon Carter, for example, found a Mrs. Foy "more fond of her husband Perhaps than the politeness of the day allows of." There is the suggestion that good manners or even happiness required the curbing of instinct and its expression. Thus one young bride, pregnant for the first time and distressed by her husband's sudden departure on an extended business trip, thought she could "bear the disap[p]ointment better at any time than this as I expect within these two months to stand in need of some such a comforter as you but I will not make you uneasy with complaints & will summon all my small stock of philosophy to wait with patience till that mercifull director of all things . . . Shall think fitt to bless me with meeting you again." The only acceptable way in which Margaret Parker could reveal her anxiety was by saying that she would hide her true feelings for fear of disturbing her husband's peace: in baring her emotions, she feared she did wrong.

Of all experiences, the death of loved ones might have shattered the mask of composure, yet Virginians kept their descriptions of death and their letters of consolation brief, fully aware that dwelling on the subject might stimulate the emotional excess they found so threatening. Thus one young woman told a friend about the unexpected death of another young woman: "Who would have thought when last we saw Miss Brown so blooming, her Fate was so near a Crisis? but hold! we'll quit this gloomy subject." The obvious lesson, that death comes without warning, would not be drawn; rather, it would be defended against. Virginians refused to dwell on even the deaths of those dearest to them. When his infant daughter died, one man wrote to his brother, "Providence has been pleased to handle us lately very Severely. . . . [E]nough of that melancholy Subject." The melancholy thought occurs but is stifled: men and women told each other that death was not to be discussed, grief not to be indulged. Did the gentry perhaps mourn in private, revealing to themselves more than convention let them show to the world? In fact, the style was the substance: death was no more the subject of pre-Revolutionary diaries than of letters. For example, on his tenth wedding anniversary Robert Wormeley Carter wrote tersely: "I have now living two Sons & a Daughter my Wife has miscarried five times; brought a dead Child & lost a fine little Boy about 18 months." The facts noted, no more was to be said. Consider William Byrd II's reaction to the death of his ten-month-old son: "God gives and God takes away; blessed be the name of God." He compared his stoicism favorably to his wife's grief. She "was much afflicted but I submitted to His judgment better, not withstanding I was very sensible of my loss, but God's will be done." Proud of his ability to check his emotions, Byrd scrutinized his wife, finding signs of grief, evidence of weakness, up to twelve days after their son died. By the standards of the nineteenth century, Virginians mourned visibly hardly at all.

Such emotions were not to be explored; instead, Virginians summoned reason to control feeling. Thus Thomas Jones informed his brother that the death of their elderly mother "could not be of any great Stock to you, it being no more than you might hourly expect to hear. . . . [Y]our Grief must have ceased as soon as your reflection took place." Similarly, Frances Randolph was told by her brother when their sister died, leaving several young daughters, "Alas Fanny tis in vain for us to grieve at Misfortunes." That was also the message she in turn conveyed to her sister, who shared her grief, "but as you say . . . it is of little use to dwell on Melancholy Subjects." The Virginian temperament—active and external—saw in mourning no practical benefit.

As in other realms of life, the gentry strove for balance when confronted by death. The bereaved were advised to count their remaining blessings, weighing them against the loss. A young woman sorrowed when "a sweet little girl of my brother's died" but found some consolation in the reflection that "my brother & Sister Hansford will soon be blest with a pledge of their mutual affection which will in some measure compensate for the loss of their other dear little Angel." It is not that such men and women were lacking in feeling, for the characterization of a baby as a "dear little Angel" certainly betokens affection, albeit a studied affection.

The complexity of feelings about love and death is illustrated by the letter of consolation William Ronald wrote to two friends, a married couple, when he learned that one of their two young sons had died. He was relieved that they had lost the infant rather than the older child: "I could not help being a good [deal] pleased at finding your loss so small in comparison to what [it might have been]. However tender the heart may be, and whatever the attachment a parent may have to his offspring, the heart can be but little affected with their loss in comparison with what we feel when deprived of those whose infant prattle and dawning reason . . . has deeply impressed their image in our breasts, and fancy long after paints to us what the little innocent would have been in their riper years had not Death untimely cut them off." Once again, there is something in Virginian thought that is detached and jarring; here it is the juxtaposition of a sentimental view of infancy with a matter-of-fact stance toward infant mortality. Childhood is rhapsodized, but not the child. Lest one think that children were treasured only after they had passed through the first perilous months, consider Peter Fontaine's thoughts about the death of his grown niece. Fontaine agreed that his "brother's loss is great in being deprived of his only daughter, in the bloom of her years." He reminded his brother and sister-in-law, however, that "your two precious lives . . . are of much more consequence towards directing and providing for the four hopeful boys under your management, who as yet are but young, and beginning to launch out into the world." As much as parents loved their children, the death of a child was not considered irreparable. Fearing grief, striving for equanimity, Virginians looked to the brighter side.

Virginians seemed to grieve most when, through death, the reciprocal bonds, the mutual expectations and responsibilities, between family members were broken. Fontaine, after all, hoped that his brother and sister-in-law would live to establish their sons in the world. An orphaned girl "labour'd under many disadvantages" because of her guardians' 'incapacity for doing any essential services." A child without a protector was at a great loss. Although consoled by the good life his daughter had led, Landon Carter considered her death a "Severe stroke indeed to A Man bereft of a Wife and in the decline of life because at such periods 'tis natural to look out for such Connections that may be reasonably expected to be the support of Greyhairs and such an one I had promised myself in this child in Particular."

The gentry sought a family life that was composed and balanced, reciprocal and restrained. It is no coincidence that all these adjectives could be used to describe the religion to which they subscribed. True, the Anglican church was unobtrusive, which is merely one way of saying that it voiced the values of its parishioners. As Henry F. May has written, "A good many Virginians simply took the Church for granted as a familiar source of comfort and instruction, with words and actions appropriate to the daily rounds of life and also to its great emergencies." It held forth order, moderation, decency, and a reasoned optimism, while discouraging "too much speculation about predestination and eternal punishment." Virginians were taught that an all-wise Dispenser planned things for the best. Belief in a divine order mitigated anxiety about the unknown and despair over the uncontrollable.

By and large the gentry accepted the doctrines of the church without question, for they found reflection itself discomforting. Thus Landon Carter observed, "I see it is a good thing to have some business to keep our thoughts employed for the man who cannot divert the present moment falls naturally into a disponding [sic] way and makes even the common cares of life a very heavy weight upon himself." If anything, religion was used to ward off disturbing thoughts and feelings. Finding himself sinking into a melancholy mood, Carter took action: "I shook myself and roused into a religeous [sic] mood of doing all I could." Religion meant self-exertion rather than self-examination. The gentry tried not to think too hard about perplexing matters; they "did not wish to have their feelings touched deeply." One's duty was to do one's best and trust in God. Religion was thus part of the dominant mode, external and active. It aided Virginians in their search for tranquillity.

The gentry's self-assurance, geniality, and careful good manners almost obscure the fact that the appearance of ease, at home as well as abroad, depended on those manners. Ease was achieved not effortlessly, as they wished, but intentionally, as they needed. Philip Greven, in his discussion of the "genteel" temperament, has noted that the gentry used "politeness"—that is, convention—to protect themselves against "unpleasantness, discomfort . . . and intimacy." Beneath their manners lay a fear of unpleasant thoughts and disturbing feelings. Within the family, these men and women tried to avoid unpleasantness by encouraging affection on the one hand, yet by stifling intimacy on the other. Family life was to be warm: not cold, and certainly not hot. Emotions were to be managed: the proper ones expressed and the others squelched. Neither self-expression nor individuality was a goal, for each might disrupt the tranquillity the gentry so prized. The "intimate distance" (Greven's phrase) with and from those they loved could be secured only in a world in which domestic relations were regarded as simple and individuals were seen as similar in their emotional constitutions. The gentry family indeed sought a domestic life that was simple, predictable, and secure. Yet as affection was encouraged at home, domestic life would inevitably inspire the kinds of intense emotions it was intended to restrain. "Intimate distance" is, after all, an oxymoron, and Virginians on the eve of the Revolution were repressing those very passions that the new modes of familial intimacy were creating. The sweet peace of domestic tranquillity could be purchased only by chaining the individual's emotions.

*George Whitefield, the greatest of the revivalist
preachers of the Great Awakening.*

Evangelical Revolt in Virginia

RHYS ISAAC

Sparks of religious revival began to appear in the mid-Atlantic colonies in the late 1720s and a decade later in New England. Then, in 1739, a man appeared in America whose religious passion was so great and whose exhortatory abilities so sharply honed that he altered the social landscape from Georgia to New Hampshire. It was George Whitefield, only twenty-five years old, who began a barnstorming trip that evoked a mass religious response of dimensions never before witnessed in America. Now, more than two centuries later, we still lack an adequate sociological and psychological model for interpreting this outpouring of religious fervor called the Great Awakening.

This essay by Rhys Isaac captures the feeling of how profoundly the evangelical preachers affected the lives of thousands of colonial Americans, in this case in Virginia, where the Awakening occurred much later than in the North. Isaac shows that the Awakening cannot be understood solely in religious terms—as simply a return to the religion-centered life of the seventeenth century. At its core it challenged established sources of authority and spread the message that ordinary people should cast aside deference to those above them and participate in the revitalization of their communities. In its religious content the Awakening foresaw a second coming of Christ, a rebirth of godly communities. In its social forms it often pitted plebeian against patrician. Drawing upon anthropologists' exploration of ritual interaction, Isaac shows how the Baptist "evangelical revolt" mobilized masses of lower-class Virginians and taught them lessons that paved the road to revolution. Perhaps more than any other change in the colonial period, this resurgence of piety altered the everyday values and attitudes of common folk and thereby energized them for public activity when colonial society, after the Seven Years' War, moved from protest to resistance to rebellion.

An intense struggle for allegiance had developed in the Virginia countryside during the decade before the Revolution. Two eyewitness accounts may open to us the nature of the conflict.

First, a scene vividly remembered and described by the Reverend James Ireland etches in sharp profile the postures of the forces in contest. As a young man Ireland, who was a propertyless schoolmaster of genteel origin, had cut a considerable figure in Frederick County society. His success had arisen largely from his prowess at dancing and his gay facility as a satiric wit. Then, like many other young men at this time (ca. 1768), he came deeply "under conviction of sin" and withdrew from the convivialities of gentry society. When an older friend and patron of Ireland heard that his young protégé could not be expected at a forthcoming assembly, this gentleman, a leader in county society, sensed the challenge to his way of life that was implicit in Ireland's withdrawal. He swore instantly that "there could not be a dance in the settlement without [Ireland] being there, and if they would leave it to him, he would convert [him], and that to the dance, on Monday; and they would see [Ireland] lead the ball that day." Frederick County, for all its geographical spread, was a close community. Young James learned that his patron would call, and dreaded the coming test of strength:

> When I viewed him riding up, I never beheld such a display of pride arising from his deportment, attitude and jesture; he rode a lofty elegant horse, . . . his countenance appeared to me as bold and daring as satan himself, and with a commanding authority [he] called upon me, if I were there to come out, which I accordingly did, with a fearful and timorous heart. But O! how quickly can God level pride. . . . For no sooner did he behold my disconsolate looks, emaciated countenance and solemn aspect, than he . . . was riveted to the beast he rode on. . . . And soon as he could articulate a little his eyes fixed upon me, and his first address was this; "In the name of the Lord, what is the matter with you?"

The evident overdramatization in this account is its most revealing feature for its is eloquent concerning the tormented convert's heightened awareness of the contrast between the social world he was leaving and the one he was entering.

The struggle for allegiance between these social worlds had begun with the Great Awakening in the 1740s, but entered into its most fierce and bitter phase with the incursions of the "New Light" Separate Bap-

EVANGELICAL REVOLT IN VIRGINIA   From *William and Mary Quarterly*, vol. 31 (1974). Reprinted by permission of the author.

tists into the older parts of Virginia in the years after 1765. The social conflict was not over the distribution of political power or of economic wealth, but over the ways of men and the ways of God. By the figures in the encounter described we may begin to know the sides drawn: on the one hand, a mounted gentleman of the world with "commanding authority" responding to challenge; on the other, a guilt-humbled, God-possessed youth with "disconsolate looks . . . and solemn aspect."

A second scene—this time in the Tidewater—reveals through actions some characteristic responses of the forces arrayed. From a diary entry of 1771 we have a description of the disruption of a Baptist meeting by some gentlemen and their followers, intent on upholding the cause of the established Church:

> Brother Waller informed us . . . [that] about two weeks ago on the Sabbath Day down in Caroline County he introduced the worship of God by singing. . . . The Parson of the Parish [who had ridden up with his clerk, the sheriff, and some others] would keep running the end of his horsewhip in [Waller's] mouth, laying his whip across the hymn book, etc. When done singing [Waller] proceeded to prayer. In it he was violently jerked off the stage; they caught him by the back part of his neck, beat his head against the ground, sometimes up, sometimes down, they carried him through a gate that stood some considerable distance, where a gentleman [the sheriff] gave him . . . twenty lashes with his horsewhip. . . . Then Bro. Waller was released, went back singing praise to God, mounted the stage and preached with a great deal of liberty.

Violence of this kind had become a recurrent feature of social-religious life in Tidewater and Piedmont. We must ask: What kind of conflict was this? What was it that aroused such antagonism? What manner of man, what manner of movement, was it that found liberty in endurance under the lash?

The continuation of the account gives fuller understanding of the meaning of this "liberty" and of the true character of this encounter. Asked "if his nature did not interfere in the time of violent persecution, when whipped, etc.," Waller "answered that the Lord stood by him . . . and poured his love into his soul without measure, and the brethren and sisters about him singing praises . . . so that he could scarcely feel the stripes . . . rejoicing . . . that he was worthy to suffer for his dear Lord and Master."

Again we see contrasted postures: on the one hand, a forceful, indeed brutal, response to the implicit challenge of religious dissidence; on the other, an acceptance of suffering sustained by shared emotions that gave release—"liberty." Both sides were, of course, engaged in combat, yet their modes of conducting themselves were diametrically opposite. If we are to understand the struggle that had developed, we must look as deeply as possible into the divergent styles of life, at the conflicting visions of what life should be like, that are reflected in this episode.

Opposites are intimately linked not only by the societal context in which they occur but also by the very antagonism that orients them to each other. The strength of the fascination that existed in this case is evident from the recurrent accounts of men drawn to Baptist meetings to make violent opposition, who, at the time or later, came "under conviction" and experienced conversion. The study of a polarity such as we find in the Virginia pre-Revolutionary religious scene should illuminate not only the conflict but also some of the fundamental structures of the society in which it occurred. A profile of the style of the gentry, and of those for whom they were a pattern, must be attempted. Their values, and the system by which these values were maintained, must be sketched. A somewhat fuller contrasting picture of the less familiar Virginia Baptist culture must then be offered, so that its character as a radical social movement is indicated.

The gentry style, of which we have seen glimpses in the confrontation with Baptists, is best understood in relation to the concept of honor—the proving of prowess. A formality of manners barely concealed adversary relationships; the essence of social exchange was overt self-assertion.

Display and bearing were important aspects of this system. We can best get a sense of the self-images that underlay it from the symbolic importance of horses. The figure of the gentleman who came to call Ireland back to society was etched on his memory as mounted on a "lofty . . . elegant horse." It was noted repeatedly in the eighteenth century that Virginians would "go five miles to catch a horse, to ride only one mile upon afterwards." This apparent absurdity had its logic in the necessity of being mounted when making an entrance on the social scene. The role of the steed as a valuable part of proud self-presentation is suggested by the intimate identification of the gentry with their horses that was constantly manifested through their conversation. Philip Fithian, the New Jersey tutor, sometimes felt that he heard nothing but "Loud disputes concerning the Excellence of each others Colts . . . their Fathers, Mothers (for so they call the Dams) Brothers, Sisters, Uncles, Aunts, Nephews, Nieces, and Cousins to the fourth Degree!"

Where did the essential display and self-assertion take place? There were few towns in Virginia; the outstanding characteristic of settlement was its diffuseness. Population was rather thinly scattered in very small groupings throughout a forested, river-dissected landscape. If there is to be larger community in such circumstances, there must be centers of action and communication. Insofar as cohesion is important in such an agrarian society, considerable significance must attach to the occasions when, coming together for certain purposes, the community realizes itself. The principal public centers in traditional Virginia were the parish churches and the county courthouses, with lesser foci established in a scatter of inns or "ordinaries." The principal general gatherings apart from these centers were for gala events such as horse race meetings and cockfights. Although lacking a specifically community character, the great estate house was also undoubtedly a very significant locus of action. By the operation of mimetic process and by the reinforcement of expectations concerning conduct and relationships, such centers and occasions were integral parts of the system of social control.

The most frequently held public gatherings at generally distributed centers were those for Sunday worship in the Anglican churches and chapels. An ideal identification of parish and community had been expressed in the law making persistent absence from church punishable. The continuance of this ideal is indicated by the fact that prosecutions under the law occurred right up to the time of the Revolution.

Philip Fithian has left us a number of vivid sketches of the typical Sunday scene at a parish church, sketches that illuminate the social nature and function of this institution. It was an important center of communication, especially among the elite, for it was "a general custom on Sundays here, with Gentlemen to invite one another home to dine, after Church; and to consult about, determine their common business, either before or after Service," when they would engage in discussing "the price of Tobacco, Grain, etc. and settling either the lineage, Age, or qualities of favourite Horses." The occasion also served to demonstrate to the community, by visual representation, the rank structure of society. Fithian's further description evokes a dramatic image of haughty squires trampling past seated hoi polloi to their pews in the front. He noted that it was "not the Custom for Gentlemen to go into Church til Service is beginning, when they enter in a Body, in the same manner as they come out."

Similarly, vestry records show that fifty miles to the south of Fithian's Westmoreland County the front pews of a King and Queen County church were allocated to the gentry, but the pressure for place and precedence was such that only the greatest dignitaries (like the Corbins) could be accommodated together with their families; lesser gentlemen represented the honor of their houses in single places while their wives were seated farther back.

The size and composition of the ordinary congregations in the midst of which these representations of social style and status took place is as yet uncertain, but Fithian's description of a high festival is very suggestive on two counts: "This being Easter-Sunday, all the Parish seem'd to meet together High, Low, black, White all come out." We learn both that such general attendance was unusual, and that at least once a year full expression of ritual community was achieved. The whole society was then led to see itself in order.

The county courthouse was a most important center of social action. Monthly court days were attended by great numbers, for these were also the times for markets and fairs. The facts of social dominance were there visibly represented by the bearing of the "gentlemen justices" and the respect they commanded. On court days economic exchange was openly merged with social exchange (both plentifully sealed by the taking of liquor) and also expressed in conventional forms of aggression—in banter, swearing, and fighting.

The ruling gentry, who set the tone in this society, lived scattered across broad counties in the midst of concentrations of slaves that often amounted to black villages. Clearly the great houses that they erected in these settings were important statements: they expressed a style, they asserted a claim to dominance. The lavish entertainments, often lasting days, which were held in these houses performed equally important social functions in maintaining this claim, and in establishing communication and control within the elite itself. Here the convivial contests that were so essential to traditional Virginia social culture would issue in their most elaborate and stylish performances.

The importance of sporting occasions such as horse racing meets and cockfights for the maintenance of the values of self-assertion, in challenge and response, is strongly suggested by the comments of the marquis de Chastellux concerning cockfighting. His observations, dating from 1782, were that "when the principal promoters of this diversion [who were certainly gentry] propose to [match] their champions, they take great care to announce it to the public; and although there are neither posts, nor regular conveyances, this important news spreads with such facility, that the planters for thirty or forty miles round, attend, some with cocks, but all with money for betting, which is sometimes very considerable." An intensely shared interest of this kind, crossing but not leveling social distinctions, has powerful effects in transmitting style and reinforcing the leadership of the elite that controls proceedings and excels in the display.

Discussion so far has focused on the gentry, for *there* was established in dominant form the way of life the Baptists appeared to challenge. Yet this way was diffused throughout the society. All the forms of communication and exchange noted already had their popular acceptances with variations appropriate to the context, as can be seen in the recollections of the young Devereaux Jarratt. The son of a middling farmer-artisan, Jarratt grew up totally intimidated by the proximity of gentlemen, yet his marked preference for engagement "in keeping and exercising race-horses for the turf . . . in taking care of and preparing game-cocks for a match and main" served to bind him nonetheless into the gentry social world, and would, had he persisted, have brought him into contact—gratifying contact—with gentlemen. The remembered images of his upbringing among the small farmers of Tidewater New Kent County are strongly evocative of the cultural continuum between his humble social world and that of the gentry. In addition to the absorbing contest pastimes mentioned, there were the card play, the gathering at farmhouses for drinking (cider not wine), violin playing, and dancing.

The importance of pastime as a channel of communication, and even as a bond, between the ranks of a society such as this can hardly be too much stressed. People were drawn together by occasions such as horse races, cockfights, and dancing as by no other, because here men would become "known" to each other—"known" in the ways which the culture defined as "real." Skill and daring in that violent duel, the "quarter race"; coolness in the "deep play" of the betting that necessarily went with racing, cockfighting, and cards—these were means whereby Virginia males could prove themselves. Conviviality was an essential part of the social exchange, but through its soft coating pressed a harder structure of contest, or "emulation" as the contemporary phrase had it. Even in dancing this was so. Observers noted not only the passion for dancing—"*Virginians* are of genuine Blood—They will dance or die!"—but also the marked preference for the jig—in effect solo performances by partners of each sex, which were closely watched and were evidently competitive. In such activities, in social contexts high or low, enhanced eligibility for marriage was established by young persons who emerged as virtuosos of the dominant style. Situations where so much could happen presented powerful images of the "good life" to traditional Virginians, especially young ones. It was probably true, as alleged, that religious piety was generally considered appropriate only for the aged.

When one turns to the social world of the Baptists, the picture that emerges is so striking a negative of the one that has just been sketched that it must be considered to have been structured to an important extent by processes of reaction to the dominant culture.

Contemporaries were struck by the contrast between the challenging gaiety of traditional Virginia formal exchange and the solemn fellowship of the Baptists, who addressed each other as "Brother" and "Sister" and were perceived as "the most melancholy people in the world"—people who "cannot meet a man upon the road, but they must ram a text of Scripture down his throat." The finery of a gentleman who might ride forth in a gold-laced hat, sporting a gleaming Masonic medal, must be contrasted with the strict dress of the Separate Baptist, his hair "cut off" and such "superfluous forms and Modes of Dressing . . . as cock't hatts" explicitly renounced.

The appearance was austere, to be sure, but we shall not understand the deep appeal of the evangelical movement, or the nature and full extent of its challenging contrast to the style and vision of the gentry-oriented social world, unless we look into the rich offerings beneath this somber exterior. The converts were proffered some escape from the harsh realities of disease, debt, overindulgence and deprivation, violence and sudden death, which were the common lot of small farmers. They could seek refuge in a close, supportive, orderly community, "a congregation of faithful persons, called out of the world by divine grace, who mutually agree to live together, and execute gospel discipline among them." Entrance into this community was attained by the relation of a personal experience of profound importance to the candidates, who would certainly be heard with respect, however humble their station. There was a community resonance for deep feelings, since, despite their sober face to the outside world, the Baptists encouraged in their religious practice a sharing of emotion to an extent far beyond that which would elicit crushing ridicule in gentry-oriented society. Personal testimonies of the experiences of simple folk have not come down to us from that time, but the central importance of the ritual of admission and its role in renewing the common experience of ecstatic conversion is powerfully evoked by such recurrent phrases in the church books as "and a dore was opened to experience." This search for deep fellow-feeling must be set in contrast to the formal distance and rivalry in the social exchanges of the traditional system.

The warm supportive relationship that fellowship in faith and experience could engender appears to have played an important part in the spread of the movement. For example, about the year 1760 Peter Cornwell of Fauquier County sought out in the backcountry one Hays of pious repute, and settled him on his own land for the sake of godly companionship. "Interviews between these two families were frequent . . . their conversation religious . . . in so much that it began to be talked of abroad as a very strange thing. Many came to see them, to whom they related what God did for their souls . . . to the spreading of seriousness through the whole neighborhood."

A concomitant of fellowship in deep emotions was comparative equality. Democracy is an ideal, and there are no indications that the pre-Revolutionary Baptists espoused it as such, yet there can be no doubt that these men, calling each other brothers, who believed that the only authority in their church was the meeting of those in fellowship together, conducted their affairs on a footing of equality in sharp contrast to the explicit preoccupation with rank and precedence that characterized the world from which they had been called. Important Baptist church elections generally required unanimity and might be held up by the doubts of a few. The number of preachers who were raised from obscurity to play an epic role in the Virginia of their day is a clear indication of the opportunities for fulfillment that the movement opened up to men who would have found no other avenue for public achievement. There is no reason to doubt the contemporary reputation of the early Virginia Baptist movement as one of the poor and unlearned. Only isolated converts were made among the gentry, but many among the slaves.

The tight cohesive brotherhood of the Baptists must be understood as an explicit rejection of the formalism of traditional community organization. The antithesis is apparent in the contrast between Fithian's account of a parish congregation that dispersed without any act of worship when a storm prevented the attendance of both parson and clerk, and the report of the Baptist David Thomas that "when no minister . . . is expected, our people meet notwithstanding; and spend . . . time in praying, singing, reading, and in religious conversation."

The popular style and appeal of the Baptist Church found its most powerful and visible expression in the richness of its rituals, again a total contrast to the "prayrs read over in haste" of the colonial Church of England, where even congregational singing appears to have been a rarity. The most prominent and moving rite practiced by the sect was adult baptism, in which the candidates were publicly sealed into fellowship. A scrap of Daniel Fristoe's journal for June 15–16, 1771, survives as a unique contemporary description by a participant:

> (Being sunday) about 2000 people came together; after preaching [I] heard others that proposed to be baptized. . . . Then went to the water where I preached and baptized 29 persons. . . . When I had finished we went to a field and making a circle in the center, there laid hands on the persons baptized. The multitude stood round weeping, but when we sang *Come we that love the lord* and they were so affected that they lifted up their hand and faces towards heaven and discovered such chearful countenances in the midst of flowing tears as I had never seen before.

The warm emotional appeal at a popular level can even now be felt in that account, but it must be noted that the scene was also a vivid enactment of *a* community within and apart from *the* community. We must try to see that closed circle for the laying on of hands through the eyes of those who had been raised in Tidewater or Piedmont Virginia with the expectation that they would always have a monistic parish community encompassing all the inhabitants within its measured liturgical celebrations. The antagonism and violence that the Baptists aroused then also become intelligible.

The celebration of the Lord's Supper frequently followed baptism, in which circumstances it was a further open enactment of closed community. We have some idea of the importance attached to this public display from David Thomas's justification:

> . . . should we forbid even the worst of men, from viewing the solemn representation of his [the LORD JESUS CHRIST's] dying

agonies? May not the sight of this mournful tragedy, have a tendency to alarm stupid creatures . . . when GOD himself is held
forth . . . trembling, falling, bleeding, yea, expiring under the intollerable pressure of that wrath due to [sin]. . . . And therefore,
this ordinance should not be put under a bushel, but on a candle-
stick, that all may enjoy the illumination.

We may see the potency attributed to the ordinances starkly through
the eyes of the abashed young John Taylor who, hanging back from
baptism, heard the professions of seven candidates surreptitiously,
judged them not saved, and then watched them go "into the water,
and from thence, as I thought, seal their own damnation at the Lord's
table. I left the meeting with awful horror of mind."

More intimate, yet evidently important for the close community,
were the rites of fellowship. The forms are elusive, but an abundance
of ritual is suggested by the simple entry of Morgan Edwards concerning Falls Creek: "In this church are admitted, Evangelists, Ruling Elders, deaconesses, laying on of hands, feasts of charity, anointing the
sick, kiss of charity, washing feet, right hand of fellowship, and devoting children." Far from being mere formal observances, these and other
rites, such as the ordaining of "apostles" to "pervade" the churches,
were keenly experimented with to determine their efficacy.

Aspects of preaching also ought to be understood as ritual rather
than as formal instruction. It was common for persons to come under
conviction or to obtain ecstatic release "under preaching," and this established a special relationship between the neophyte and his or her
"father in the gospel." Nowhere was the ritual character of the preaching more apparent than in the great meetings of the Virginia Separate
Baptist Association. The messengers would preach to the people along
the way to the meeting place and back; thousands would gather for
the Sunday specially set aside for worship and preaching. There the
close independent congregational communities found themselves merged
in a great and swelling collective. The varieties of physical manifesta-
tions such as crying out and falling down, which were frequently brought
on by the ritualized emotionalism of such preaching, are too well known
to require description.

Virginia Baptist sermons from the 1770s have not survived, perhaps another indication that their purely verbal content was not considered of the first importance. Ireland's account of his early ministry
(he was ordained in 1769) reveals the ritual recurrence of the dominant
themes expected to lead into repentance those who were not hardened:
"I began first to preach . . . our awful apostacy by the fall; the necessity of repentance unto life, and of faith in the Lord Jesus Christ . . .
our helpless incapacity to extricate ourselves therefrom I stated and
urged."

As "seriousness" spread, with fear of hell-fire and concern for salvation, it was small wonder that a gentleman of Loudoun County should find to his alarm "that the *Anabaptists* . . . growing very numerous . . . seem to be increasing in afluence [influence?]; and . . . quite destroying pleasure in the Country; for they encourage ardent Pray'r; strong and constant faith, and an intire Banishment of *Gaming, Dancing,* and Sabbath-Day Diversions." That the Baptists were drawing away increasing numbers from the dominant to the insurgent culture was radical enough, but the implications of solemnity, austerity, and stern sobriety were more radical still, for they called into question the validity—indeed the propriety—of the occasions and modes of display and association so important in maintaining the bonds of Virginia's geographically diffuse society. Against the system in which proud men were joined in rivalry and convivial excess was set a reproachful model of an order in which God-humbled men would seek a deep sharing of emotion while repudiating indulgence of the flesh. Yet the Baptist movement, although it must be understood as a revolt against the traditional system, was not primarily negative. Behind it can be discerned an impulse toward a tighter, more effective system of values and of exemplary conduct to be established and maintained within the ranks of the common folk.

In this aspect evangelicalism must be seen as a popular response to mounting social disorder. It would be difficult—perhaps even impossible—to establish an objective scale for measuring disorder in Virginia. What can be established is that during the 1760s and 1770s disorder was perceived by many as increasing. This has been argued for the gentry by Jack P. Greene and Gordon S. Wood, and need not be elaborated here. What does need to be reemphasized is that the gentry's growing perception of disorder was focused on those forms of activity which the Baptists denounced and which provided the main arenas for the challenge and response essential to the traditional "good life." It was coming to be felt that horse racing, cockfighting, and card play, with their concomitants of gambling and drinking, rather than serving to maintain the gentry's prowess, were destructive of it and of social order generally. Display might now be negatively perceived as "luxury."

Given the absence of the restraints imposed by tight village community in traditional Virginia, disorder was probably an even more acute problem in the lower than in the upper echelons of society— more acute because it was compounded by the harshness and brutality of everyday life, and most acute in proportion to the social proximity of the lowest stratum, the enslaved. The last named sector of society, lacking sanctioned marriage and legitimated familial authority, was certainly disorderly by English Protestant standards, and must therefore have had a disturbing effect on the consciousness of the whole community.

As the conversion experience was at the heart of the popular evangelical movement, so a sense of a great burden of guilt was at the heart of the conversion experience. An explanation in terms of social process must be sought for the sudden widespread intensification and vocal expression of such feelings, especially when this is found in areas of the Virginia Piedmont and Tidewater where no cultural tradition existed as preconditioning for the communal confession, remorse, and expiation that characterized the spread of the Baptist movement. The hypothesis here advanced is that the social process was one in which popular perceptions of disorder in society—and hence by individuals in themselves—came to be expressed in the metaphor of "sin." It is clear that the movement was largely spread by revolt from within, not by "agitators" from without. Commonly the first visit of itinerant preachers to a neighborhood was made by invitation of a group of penitents already formed and actively meeting together. Thus the "spread of seriousness" and alarm at the sinful disorder of the traditional world tended to precede the creation of an emotional mass movement "under preaching." A further indication of the importance of order-disorder preoccupations for the spread of the new vision with its contrasted life style was the insistence on "works." Conversion could ultimately be validated among church members only by a radical reform of conduct. The Baptist church books reveal the close concern for the disciplinary supervision of such changes.

Drunkenness was a persistent problem in Virginia society. There were frequent cases in the Baptist records where censure, ritual excommunication, and moving penitence were unable to effect a lasting cure. Quarreling, slandering, and disputes over property were other endemic disorders that the churches sought patiently and endlessly to control within their own communities. With its base in slavery, this was a society in which contests readily turned into disorderly violence. Accounts of the occasion, manner, and frequency of wrestling furnish a horrifying testimony to the effects of combining a code of honor with the coarseness of life in the lower echelons of society. Hearing that "by appointment is to be fought this Day . . . two fist Battles between four young Fellows," Fithian noted the common causes of such conflicts, listing numbers of trivial affronts such as that one "has in a merry hour call'd [another] a *Lubber*, . . . or a *Buckskin,* or a *Scotchman, . . .* or offered him a dram without wiping the mouth of the Bottle." He noted also the savagery of the fighting, including "Kicking, Scratching, Biting, . . . Throtling, Gouging [the eyes], Dismembring [the private parts]. . . . This spectacle . . . generally is attended with a crowd of People!" Such practices prevailed throughout the province. An episode in the life of one of the great Baptist preachers, John, formerly "swearing-

Jack," Waller, illustrates both prevailing violence and something of the relationship between classes. Waller and some gentry companions were riding on the road when a drunken butcher addressed them in a manner they considered insolent. One of the gentlemen had a horse trained to rear and "paw what was before him," which he then had it do to frighten the butcher. The man was struck by the hooves and died soon after. Tried for manslaughter, the company of gentlemen were acquitted on a doubt as to whether the injury had indeed caused the butcher's death. The episode may have helped prepare Waller for conversion into a radically opposed social world.

Nowhere does the radicalism of the evangelical reaction to the dominant values of self-assertion, challenge, and response of the gentry-oriented society reveal itself so clearly as in the treatment of physical aggression. In the Baptist community a man might come forward by way of confession with an accusation against himself for "Geting angry Tho in Just Defense of himself in Despute." The meeting of another church was informed that its clerk, Rawley Hazard, had been approached on his own land and addressed in "Very scurrilous language" and then assaulted, and that he then "did defend himself against this sd Violence, that both the Assailant and Defendent was much hurt." The members voted that the minister "do Admonish Brother Rawley . . . in the presents of the Church . . . saying that his defence was Irregular."

A further mark of their radicalism, and without doubt the most significant aspect of the quest for a system of social control centered in the people, was the inclusion of slaves as "brothers" and "sisters" in their close community. When the Baptists sealed the slaves unto eternal life, leading them in white robes into the water and then back to receive the bread and wine, they were also laying upon them responsibility for godly conduct, demanding an internalization of strict Protestant Christian values and norms. They were seeking to create an orderly moral community where hitherto there had seemed to be none.

The slaves were members and therefore subject to church discipline. The incidence of excommunication of slaves, especially for the sin of adultery, points to the desire of the Baptists to introduce their own standards of conduct, including stable marital relationships, among slaves. A revealing indication of the perception of the problem in this area is found in the recurrent phrase that was sometimes given as the sole reason for excommunication: "walking disorderly." Discipline was also clearly directed toward inculcating a sense of duty in the slaves, who could be excommunicated for "disobedience and Aggrevation to [a] master."

The recurrent use of the words "order," "orderly," "disorderly" in the Baptist records reveals a preoccupation that lends further support to the hypothesis that concern for the establishment of a securer system of social control was a powerful impulse for the movement. "Is it orderly?" is the usual introduction to the queries concerning right conduct that were frequently brought forward for resolution at monthly meetings.

With alarm at perceived disorder must also be associated the deep concern for Sabbath-day observance that is so strongly manifested in autobiographies, apologetics, and church books. It appears that the Virginia method of keeping the Sabbath "with sport, merriment, and dissipation" readily served to symbolize the disorder perceived in society. It was his observation of this that gave Ireland his first recorded shock. Conversely, cosmic order was affirmed and held up as a model for society in the setting aside on the Lord's Day of worldly pursuits, while men expressed their reverence for their Maker and Redeemer.

When the Baptist movement is understood as a rejection of the style of life for which the gentry set the pattern and as a search for more powerful popular models of proper conduct, it can be seen why the ground on which the battle was mainly fought was not the estate or the great house, but the neighborhood, the farmstead, and the slave quarter. This was a contemporary perception, for it was generally charged that the Baptists were "continual fomenters of discord" who "not only divided good neighbors, but slaves and their masters; children and their parents . . . wives and their husbands." The only reported complaint against the first preachers to be imprisoned was of "their running into private houses and making dissensions." The struggle for allegiance in the homesteads between a style of life modeled on that of the leisured gentry and that embodied in evangelicalism was intense. In humbler, more straitened circumstances a popular culture based on the code of honor and almost hedonist values was necessarily less securely established than among the more affluent gentry. Hence the anxious aggressiveness of popular anti-New Light feeling and action.

The Baptists did not make a bid for control of the political system—still less did they seek a leveling or redistribution of worldly wealth. It was clearly a mark of the strength of gentry hegemony and of the rigidities of a social hierarchy with slavery at its base that the evangelical revolt should have been so closely restricted in scope. Yet the Baptists' salvationism and sabbatarianism effectively redefined morality and human relationships; their church leaders and organization established new and more popular foci of authority, and sought to impose a radically different and more inclusive model for the maintenance of order in society. Within the context of the traditional monistic, face-to-face, deferential society such a regrouping necessarily constituted a powerful challenge.

The beginnings of a cultural disjunction between gentry and sections of the lower orders, where hitherto there had been a continuum, posed a serious threat to the traditional leaders of the community; their response was characteristic. The popular emotional style, the encouragement given to men of little learning to "exercise their gifts" in preaching, and the preponderance of humble folk in the movement gave to the proud gentry their readiest defense—contempt and ridicule. The stereotype of the Baptists as "an ignorant . . . set . . . of . . . the contemptible class of the people," a "poor and illiterate sect" which "none of the rich or learned ever join," became generally established. References in the *Virginia Gazette* to "ignorant enthusiasts" were common, and there could appear in its columns without challenge a heartless satire detailing "A Receipt to make an Anabaptist Preacher": "Take the Herbes of Hypocrisy and Ambition, . . . of the Seed of Dissention and Discord one Ounce, . . . one Pint of the Spirit of Self-Conceitedness."

An encounter with some gentlemen at an inn in Goochland County is recorded by Morgan Edwards, a college-educated Pennsylvania Baptist minister. He noted the moderation of the gentry in this area, yet their arrogant scorn for dissenters in general, and for Baptists in particular, is unmistakable from the dialogue reported. Since Edwards had just come from Georgia, they began with ribald jests about "mr Whitefield's children . . . by the squaw" and continued as follows:

> Esq[uire] U: Pray are you not a clergyman? . . .
> Capt. L: Of the church of England I presume?
> N[orthern] M[inister]: No, Sir; I am a clergyman of a better church than that; for she is a persecutor.
> Omnes: Ha! Ha! Ha! . . .
> Esq. U: Then you are one of the fleabitten clergy?
> N.M.: Are there fleas in this bed, Sir?
> Esq. U: I ask, if you are a clergyman of the itchy true blue kirk of Scotland? . . .
> Capt. L. (whispers): He is ashamed to own her for fear you should scratch him 'Squire.' . . .
> [When they have discovered that this educated man, who shows such address in fencing with words, is a Baptist minister, they discuss the subject bibulously among themselves.]
> Esq. U: He is no baptist . . . I take him to be one of the Georgia law[ye]rs.
> Mr. G: For my part I believe him to be a baptist minister. There are some clever fellows among them. . . .
> Major W: I confess they have often confounded me with their arguments and texts of Scripture; and if any other people but the baptists professed their religion I would make it my religion before tomorrow.

The class of folk who filled the Baptist churches were a great obstacle to gentry participation. Behind the ridicule and contempt, of course, lay incomprehension, and behind that, fear of this menacing, unintelligible movement. The only firsthand account we have of a meeting broken up by the arrest of the preachers tells how they "were carried before the magistrate," who had them taken "one by one into a room and examined our pockets and wallets for firearms." He accused them of "carrying on a mutiny against the authority of the land." This sort of dark suspicion impelled David Thomas, in his printed defense of the Baptists, to reiterate several times that "We concern not ourselves with the government . . . we form no intrigues . . . nor make any attempts to alter the constitution of the kingdom to which as men we belong."

Fear breeds fantasy. So it was that alarmed observers put a very crude interpretation on the emotional and even physical intimacy of this intrusive new society. Its members were associated with German Anabaptists, and a "historical" account of the erotic indulgences of that sect was published on the front page of the *Virginia Gazette*.

Driven by uneasiness, although toughened by their instinctive contempt, some members of the establishment made direct moves to assert proper social authority and to outface the upstarts. Denunciations from parish pulpits were frequent. Debates were not uncommon, being sought on both sides. Ireland recalled vividly an encounter that reveals the pride and presumption of the gentlemen who came forward in defense of the Church of England. Captain M'Clanagan's place was thronged with people, some of whom had come forty miles to hear John Pickett, a Baptist preacher of Fauquier County. The rector of a neighboring parish attended with some leading parishioners "who were as much prejudiced . . . as he was." "The parson had a chair brought for himself, which he placed three or four yards in front of Mr. Pickett . . . taking out his pen, ink and paper, to take down notes of what he conceived to be false doctrine." When Pickett had finished, "the Parson called him a schismatick, a broacher of false doctrines . . . [who] held up damnable errors that day." Pickett answered adequately (it appeared to Ireland), but "when contradicted it would in a measure confuse him." So Ireland, who had been raised a gentleman, took it on himself to sustain the Baptist cause. The parson immediately "wheeled about on his chair . . . and let out a broadside of his eloquence, with an expectation, no doubt, that he would confound me with the first fire." However, Ireland, "gently laid hold of a chair, and placed . . . it close by him, determined to argue." The contest was long, and "both gentlemen and ladies," who had evidently seated themselves near the parson, "would repeatedly help him to scripture, in order to support his arguments." When the debate ended (as the narrator recalled) in the refutation of the clergyman, Ireland "addressed one of the gentlemen who had been so officious in helping his teacher; he was a magistrate . . . 'Sir, as the dispute between the Parson and myself is ended, if you are disposed to argue the subject over again, I am willing to enter upon it with you.' He stretched out his arm straight before him, at that instant, and declared that I should not come nigher than that length." Ireland "concluded what the consequence would be, therefore made a peaceable retreat." Such scenes of action are the stuff of social structure, as of social conflict, and require no further comment.

Great popular movements are not quelled, however, by outfacing, nor are they stemmed by the ridicule, scorn, or scurrility of incomprehension. Moreover, they draw into themselves members of all sections of society. Although the social worlds most open to proselytizing by the Baptists were the neighborhoods and the slave quarters, there were converts from the great houses too. Some of the defectors, such as Samuel Harris, played a leading role in the movement. The squirearchy was disturbed by the realization that the contemptible sect was reaching among themselves. The exchanges between Morgan Edwards and the gentlemen in the Goochland inn were confused by the breakdown of the stereotype of ignorance and poverty. Edwards's cultured facility reminded the squires that "there are some clever fellows among [the Baptists]. I heard one Jery Walker support a petition of theirs at the assembly in such a manner as surprised us all, and [made] our witts draw in their horns." The pride and assurance of the gentry could be engaged by awareness that their own members might withdraw from their ranks and choose the other way. The vigorous response of Ireland's patron to the challenge implicit in his defection provides a striking example.

The intensity of the conflict for allegiance among the people and, increasingly, among the gentry, makes intelligible the growing frequency of violent clashes of the kind illustrated at the beginning of this article. The violence was, however, one-sided and self-defeating. The episode of April 1771 in which the parson brutally interfered with the devotions of the preacher, who was then horsewhipped by the sheriff, must have produced a shock of revulsion in many quarters. Those who engaged in such actions were not typical of either the Anglican clergy or the country gentlemen. The extreme responses of some, however, show the anxieties to which all were subject, and the excesses in question could only heighten the tension.

Disquiet was further exacerbated by the fact that the law governing dissent, under which the repressive county benches were intent on acting, was of doubtful validity, and became the subject of public controversy in the fall of 1771. This controversy, combined with the appalling scenes of disorder and the growing numbers of Separate Baptists, led the House of Burgesses to attempt action in its spring 1772 session. The Separates had shown renewed tendencies to intransigence as recently as May 1771, when a move was strongly supported to deny fellowship to all ministers who submitted to the secular authority by applying for permission to preach. The fact that eight months later the House of Burgesses received a petition for easier licensing conditions was a sign that a compromise was at last being sought. Nevertheless, prejudices were so strong that the bill that the Burgesses approved was considerably more restrictive than the English act that had hitherto been deemed law in the colony.

The crisis of self-confidence which the evangelical challenges and the failure of forceful responses were inducing in the Virginia gentry was subtly revealed in March 1772 by the unprecedented decision of the House, ordinarily assertive of its authority, not to send the engrossed bill to the Council, but to have it printed and referred to the public for discussion. Nearly two years later, in January 1774, the young James Madison, exultant about the progress of the American cause in the aftermath of the Boston Tea Party, despaired of Virginia on account of religious intolerance. He wrote that he had "nothing to brag of as to the State and Liberty" of his "Country," where "Poverty and Luxury prevail among all sorts" and "that diabolical Hell conceived principle of persecution rages." In April of the same year he still had little hope that a bill would pass to ease the situation of dissenters. In the previous session "such incredible and extravagant stories" had been "told in the House of the monstrous effects of the Enthusiasm prevalent among the Sectaries and so greedily swallowed by their Enemies that . . . they lost footing by it." Burgesses "who pretend too much contempt to examine into their principles . . . and are too much devoted to the ecclesiastical establishment to hear of the Toleration of Dissentients" were likely to prevail once again. Madison's foreboding was correct inasmuch as the old regime in Virginia never accomplished a legal resolution of the toleration problem.

The Revolution ultimately enshrined religious pluralism as a fundamental principle in Virginia. It rendered illegitimate the assumptions concerning the nature of community religious corporateness that underlay aggressive defense against the Baptists. It legitimated new forms of conflict, so that by the end of the century the popular evangelists were able to counterattack and symbolize social revolution in many localities by having the Episcopal Church's lands and even communion plate sold at auction. But to seek the conclusion to this study in such political-constitutional developments would be a deflection, for it has focused on a brief period of intense, yet deadlocked conflict in order to search out the social-cultural configurations of the forces that confronted each other. The diametrical opposition of the swelling Baptist movement to traditional mores shows it to have been indeed a radical social revolt, indicative of real strains within society.

Challenging questions remain. Can some of the appeal of the Revolution's republican ideology be understood in terms of its capacity to command the allegiance of both self-humbled evangelicals and honor-upholding gentry? What different meanings did the republican ideology assume within the mutually opposed systems of values and belief? And, looking forward to the post-Revolutionary period, what was the configuration—what the balance between antagonistic cultural elements—when confrontation within a monistic framework had given way to accommodation in a more pluralist republican society? These questions are closely related to the subject that this study has endeavored to illuminate—the forms and sources of popular culture in Virginia, and the relationship of popular culture to that of the gentry elite.

The young George Robert Twelves Hewes witnessed the
Boston Massacre, here depicted in an engraving copied
closely from one by Paul Revere.

George Robert Twelves Hewes: Shoemaker and Patriot

ALFRED F. YOUNG

Although historians have lavished attention on political events in our history, they have seldom studied how politics affected the lives of common people and, conversely, how common people affected politics. Yet political events were a part of the everyday lives of most colonists. This was especially true in New England, where the town meeting gave common folk an opportunity to make their opinions heard, and where most men in their lifetime were likely to occupy at least a minor office, such as "fence viewer" or "hogreeve."

At no time are common people more important in politics than when change occurs swiftly, for rapid political alterations are almost always associated with challenges to established authority. These challenges are usually accompanied by violence. In most historical writing only the leaders of political movements appear before our view. Behind the scenes operates the "mob"—a term that itself is loaded with emotional meaning. But who made up the mob, or "crowd," as we might better label a collection of individuals massed for political purposes? How did they come together? What did its members intend? How did they impose their collective will on those who held political power? Until we answer questions of this kind the political lives of ordinary people will be obscured, and those beneath the elite will remain historically voiceless.

Insofar as they have studied the political "crowd," American historians have employed several explanatory models. In the eighteenth century, upper-class targets of the crowd's wrath frequently described the mob as "frenzied," "mad," or "unthinking." This is the model of crowd behavior that historians have most often used, especially since the invention of the term "mass hysteria" by social psychologists. In this view the crowd is made up of lower-class individuals inspired by passion rather than reason. The "mob" surges through a town willy-nilly, feeding on its own emotions and striking out recklessly and wantonly at anything in its way. A second model of crowd behavior, equally condescending, presumes that most crowds are led and controlled by middle-class or upper-class individuals who manipulate ordinary people for their own purposes. The Tory Peter Oliver, one of the targets of the crowd's wrath in Boston in 1765, wrote: "As for the People in general, they were like the Mobility of all Countries, perfect Machines, wound up by any Hand who might first take the Winch."

The third model of crowd dynamics; formulated by historians only recently, sees most eighteenth-century mobs in a far different way. The urban mob is not emotionally out of control. It does not strike out indiscriminately. Instead it pursues specific interests related to the lives of its members, who are often skilled artisans and small shopkeepers. Its targets are selected in advance, and its goals are carefully calculated.

In part this theory has only lately received attention from American historians because violent mass action has not been widely recognized in modern America as a legitimate form of protest. Such was not the case in the eighteenth century. Popular expression of grievances, often accompanied by violence, was accepted as a proper antidote to unresponsive holders of political power. Moreover, mass disobedience often brought quick results, for in colonial America those in authority, as yet unshielded from the people by urban police forces, maintained only a frail grip on their offices. Rather than being "irrational" or manipulated, crowds acted in self-conscious and self-activating ways.

Alfred Young, the author of this selection, is a pioneer in studying the political consciousness of ordinary laboring people in pre-industrial America. Of special concern to him have been the artisans of this pre-factory world. In this essay he takes us into the private world of an obscure shoemaker of Boston—into his struggles to carve out a niche for himself in the workplace, into his family relations, into his awakening political consciousness, and into his later religious commitment. The essay makes clear that even at the lowest level of society people were in the habit of dealing creatively with the social circumstances that surrounded them rather than passively accepting their lot. Though they did not succeed in conventional terms, their personal dramas influenced, changed, and sometimes even dictated the course of public events. Ordinary people like George Robert Twelves Hewes, and thousands of others like him, were the true motivators of social change because they were the producers, consumers, taxpayers, tax collectors, law abiders, law deriders, factors, transactors, complainers, maintainers, cobblers of shoes, cultivators of fields, drivers of oxen, and schemers of schemes. When laws were made or wars declared or ideas enunciated or merchandise put up for sale, it was the active and largely undocumented response of the mass of people that made these abstractions reality.

Late in 1762 or early in 1763, George Robert Twelves Hewes, a Boston shoemaker in the last year or so of his apprenticeship, repaired a shoe for John Hancock and delivered it to him in Dock Square. Hancock was pleased and invited the young man to "come and see him on New Year's day, and bid him a happy New-Year," according to the custom of the day, a ritual of noblesse oblige on the part of the gentry. On New Year's Day, after some urging by his master,

> George washed his face, and put his best jacket on, and proceeded straightaway to the Hancock House (as it is still called). His heart was in his mouth, but assuming a cheerful courage, he knocked at the front door, and took his hat off. The servant came:
> "Is 'Squire Hancock at home, Sir?" enquired Hewes, making a bow.
> He was introduced directly to the *kitchen,* and requested to seat himself, while report should be made above stairs. The man came down directly, with a new varnish of civility suddenly spread over his face. He ushered him into the 'Squire's sitting-room, and left him to make his obeisance. Hancock remembered him, and addressed him kindly. George was anxious to get through, and he commenced a desperate speech—"as pretty a one," he says, "as he any way knew how,"—intended to announce the purpose of his visit, and to accomplish it, in the same breath.
> "Very well, my lad," said the 'Squire—"now take a chair, my lad."
> He sat down, scared all the while (as he now confesses) "almost to death," while Hancock put his hand into his breeches-pocket and pulled out a crown-piece, which he placed softly in his hand, thanking him at the same time for his punctual attendance, and his compliments. He then invited his young friend to drink his health—called for wine—poured it out for him—and ticked glasses with him,—a feat in which Hewes, though he had never seen it performed before, having acquitted himself with a creditable dexterity, hastened to make his bow again, and secure his retreat, though not till the 'Squire had extorted a sort of half promise from him to come the next New-Year's—which, for a rarity, he never discharged.

The episode is a demonstration of what the eighteenth century called deference.

Another episode catches the point at which Hewes had arrived a decade and a half later. In 1778 or 1779, after one stint in the war on board a privateer and another in the militia, he was ready to ship out again, from Boston. "Here he enlisted, or engaged to enlist, on board

GEORGE ROBERT TWELVES HEWES From *William and Mary Quarterly,* vol. 38 (Oct. 1981). Reprinted by permission of the author.

the Hancock, a twenty-gun ship, but not liking the manners of the Lieutenant very well, who ordered him one day in the streets to take his hat off to him—which he refused to do for any man,—he went aboard the 'Defence,' Captain Smedley, of Fairfield Connecticut." This, with a vengeance, is the casting off of deference.

What had happened in the intervening years? What had turned the young shoemaker tongue-tied in the face of his betters into the defiant person who would not take his hat off for any man? And why should stories like this have stayed in his memory sixty and seventy years later?

George Robert Twelves Hewes was born in Boston in 1742 and died in Richfield Springs, New York, in 1840. He participated in several of the principal political events of the American Revolution in Boston, among them the Massacre and the Tea Party, and during the war he served as a privateersman and militiaman. A shoemaker all his life, and intermittently or concurrently a fisherman, sailor, and farmer, he remained a poor man. He never made it, not before the war in Boston, not at sea, not after the war in Wrentham and Attleborough, Massachusetts, not in Otsego County, New York. He was a nobody who briefly became a somebody in the Revolution and, for a moment near the end of his life, a hero.

Hewes might have been unknown to posterity save for his longevity and a shift in the historical mood that rekindled the "spirit of '76." To Americans of the 1830s the Boston Tea Party had become a leading symbol of the Revolution, and Hewes lived long enough to be thought of as one of the last surviving participants, perhaps the very last. In 1833, when James Hawkes "discovered" him in the "obscurity" of upstate New York, Hewes was ninety-one but thought he was ninety-eight, a claim Hawkes accepted when he published the first memoir of Hewes that year. Thus in 1835 when Hewes was invited to Boston, people thought that this survivor of one of the greatest moments of the Revolution was approaching his one hundredth birthday and on "the verge of eternity," as a Fourth of July orator put it. He became a celebrity, the guest of honor on Independence Day, the subject of a second biography by Benjamin Thatcher and of an oil portrait by Joseph Cole, which hangs today in Boston's Old State House.

To Thatcher, Hewes was one of the "humble classes" that made the success of the Revolution possible. How typical he was we can only suggest at this point in our limited knowledge of the "humble classes." Probably he was as representative a member of the "lower trades" of the cities and as much a rank-and-file participant in the political events and the war as historians have found. The two biographies, which come close to being oral histories, provide an unusually rich cumulative record, over a very long period of time, of his thoughts, attitudes, and values. Consequently, we can answer, with varying degrees of satisfaction, a number of questions about one man of the "humble classes." About the "lower trades": why did a boy enter a craft with such bleak prospects as shoemaking? what was the life of an apprentice? what did it mean to be a shoemaker and a poor man in Boston? About the Revolution: what moved such a rank-and-file person to action? what action did he take? may we speak of his "ideology"? does the evidence of his loss of deference permit us to speak of change in his consciousness? About the war: how did a poor man, an older man, a man with a family exercise his patriotism? what choices did he make? About the results of the Revolution: how did the war affect him? to what extent did he achieve his life goals? why did he go west? what did it mean to be an aged veteran of the Revolution? What, in sum, after more than half a century had passed, was the meaning of the Revolution to someone still in the "humble classes"?

I

Hewes's recollections, as recorded in the biographies by Hawkes and Thatcher, had strengths and weaknesses. He was, to begin with, in remarkable physical condition. In 1833 Hawkes found his "physical and intellectual" powers "of no ordinary character." "I have generally enjoyed sound health," Hewes said. He showed few signs of his advanced age. His hair was light brown, salted with gray, and he had most of it. He was not bent down by his years but was "so perfectly erect" and moved "with so much agility and firmness . . . that he might be taken for a man in all the vigour of youth." He regularly walked two or three miles each day, and was of such an "active disposition" that Hawkes found he would hardly stay put long enough to be interviewed. When Hewes became excited, his "dark blue eyes" would "sparkle with a glow of lustre." Thatcher was impressed with "a strength and clearness in his faculties" often not present in men twenty years younger. "Both his mental and bodily faculties are wonderfully hale. He converses with almost the promptness of middle life." His mind did not wander. He answered questions directly, and "he can seldom be detected in any redundancy or deficiency of expression." He was not garrulous.

Both men were amazed at Hewes's memory. Thatcher found it "so extraordinary" that at times it "absolutely astonished" him. Hewes recounted details from many stages of his life: from his childhood, youth, and young adulthood, from the years leading up to the Revolution, from seven years of war. While he told next to nothing about the next half-century of his life, his memory of recent events was clear. He graphically recalled a trip to Boston in 1821. He remembered names and how things looked; he even seemed to recall how things tasted. Most important, he remembered his own emotions, evoking them once again. He seems to have kept no diary or journal, and by his own claim he had not read any accounts of the Tea Party or by implication any other events of the Revolution.

His memory also displayed common weaknesses. He had trouble with his age, which was not unusual at a time when birthdays were not much celebrated and birth certificates not issued. He had trouble with sequences of events and with the intervals of time between events. He was somewhat confused, for example, about his military tours of duty, something common in other veterans' narratives. He also got political events in Boston somewhat out of order, telescoping what for him had become one emotionally. Or he told his good stories first, following up with the less interesting ones. All this is harmless enough. He remembered, understandably, experiences that were pleasant, and while he did well with painful experiences that had been seared into him—like childhood punishments and the Boston Massacre—he "forgot" other experiences that were humiliating.

On balance, Hewes's memory was strong, yet what he remembered, as well as the meaning he attached to it, inevitably was shaped by his values, attitudes, and temperament. First, he had a stake, both monetary and psychic, in his contribution to the Revolution. He had applied for a pension in October 1832; by the summer of 1833, when he talked to Hawkes, it had been granted. He had also become a personage of sorts in his own locale, at least on the Fourth of July. And when he talked with Thatcher he was bathed in Boston's recognition. Thus though he did not have to prove himself, he had spent many years trying to do just that. Moreover, he had to live up to his reputation and had the possibility of enhancing it.

Secondly, he may have imposed an overlay of his current religious values on the younger man. He had generally been "of a cheerful mind," he told Hawkes, and Thatcher spoke of the "cheerfulness and evenness of his temper." There is evidence for such traits earlier in his life. In his old age, however, he became a practicing Methodist—composed in the assurance of his own salvation, confident of his record of good deeds, and forgiving to his enemies. As a consequence he may well have blotted out some contrary feelings he had once held. One suspects he had been a much more angry and aggressive younger man than he or his biographers convey.

Finally, in the 1830s he lived in a society that no longer bestowed the deference once reserved for old age and had never granted much respect to poor old shoemakers. In the Revolution for a time it had been different; the shoemaker won recognition as a citizen; his betters sought his support and seemingly deferred to him. This contributed to a tendency, as he remembered the Revolution, not so much to exaggerate what he had done—he was consistently modest in his claims for himself—as to place himself closer to some of the great men of the time than is susceptible to proof. For a moment he was on a level with his betters. So he thought at the time, and so it grew in his memory as it disappeared in his life. And in this memory of an awakening to citizenship and recognition from his betters we shall argue—a memory with both substance and shadow—lay the meaning of the Revolution to George Hewes.

II

In 1756, when Hewes was fourteen, he was apprenticed to a shoemaker. Why did a boy become a shoemaker in mid-eighteenth-century Boston? The town's shoemakers were generally poor and their prospects were worsening. From 1756 to 1775, eight out of thirteen shoemakers who died and left wills at probate did not even own their own homes. In 1790, shoemakers ranked thirty-eighth among forty-four occupations in mean tax assessments.

It was not a trade in which boys were eager to be apprentices. Few sons continued in their fathers' footsteps, as they did, for example, in prosperous trades like silversmithing or shipbuilding. Leatherworkers, after mariners, headed the list of artisans who got their apprentices from the orphans, illegitimate children, and boys put out to apprenticeship by Boston's Overseers of the Poor. In England, shoemaking was a trade with proud traditions, symbolized by St. Crispin's Day, a shoemakers' holiday, a trade with a reputation for producing poets, philosophers, and politicians, celebrated by Elizabethan playwrights as "the gentle craft." But there were few signs of a flourishing shoemaker culture in Boston before the Revolution. In children's lore shoemakers were proverbially poor, like the cobbler in a Boston chapbook who "labored hard and took a great deal of pains for a small livelihood." Shoemakers, moreover, were low in status. John Adams spoke of shoemaking as "too mean and dimi[nu]tive an Occupation" to hold a client of his who wanted to "rise in the World."

Where one ended up in life depended very much on where one started out. George was born under the sign of the Bulls Head and Horns on Water Street near the docks in the South End. His father—also named George—was a tallow chandler and tanner. Hewes drew the connections between his class origins and his life chances as he began his narrative for Hawkes:

> My father, said he, was born in Wrentham in the state of Massachusetts, about twenty-eight miles from Boston. My grandfather having made no provision for his support, and being unable to give him an education, apprenticed him at Boston to learn a mechanical trade. . . .

In my childhood, my advantages for education were very limited, much more so than children enjoy at the present time in my native state. My whole education which my opportunities permitted me to acquire, consisted only of a moderate knowledge of reading and writing; my father's circumstances being confined to such humble means as he was enabled to acquire by his mechanical employment, I was kept running of errands, and exposed of course to all the mischiefs to which children are liable in populous cities.

Hewes's family on his father's side was "no better off than what is called in New England *moderate,* and probably not as good." The American progenitor of the line seems to have come from Wales. Solomon Hewes, George Robert's grandfather, was born in New Hampshire in 1674, became a joiner, and moved his family to Wrentham, Massachusetts. There he became a landholder; most of his brothers were farmers; two became doctors, one of whom prospered. His son—our George's father—was born in 1701. On the side of his mother, Abigail Seaver, Hewes's family was a shade different. They had lived for four generations in Roxbury, a small farming town immediately south of Boston. Abigail's ancestors seem to have been farmers, but one was a minister. Her father, Shubael, was a country cordwainer who owned a house, barn, and two acres. She was born in 1711 and married in 1728.

George Robert Twelves Hewes, born August 25, 1742, was the sixth of nine children, the fourth of seven sons. Five of the nine survived childhood—his three older brothers, Samuel, Shubael, and Solomon, and a younger brother, Daniel. He was named George after his father, Robert after a paternal uncle, and the unlikely Twelves for his mother's mother, also Abigail, whose maiden name was Twelves.

The family heritage to George, it might be argued, was more genetic than economic. He inherited a chance to live long: the men in the Seaver line were all long-lived. And he inherited his size. He was unusually short—five feet, one inch. "I have never acquired the ordinary weight or size of other men," Hewes told Hawkes, who wrote that "his whole person is of a slight and slender texture." In old age he was known as "the little old man." Anatomy is not destiny, but Hewes's short size and long name helped shape his personality. It was a big name for a small boy to carry. He was the butt of endless teasing jibes—George Robert what?—that Thatcher turned into anecdotes the humor of which masked the pain Hewes may have felt.

"Moderate" as it was, Hewes had a sense of family. Wrentham, town of his grandfather and uncles, was a place he would be sent as a boy, a place of refuge in the war, and after the war his home. He would receive an inheritance three times in his life, each one a reminder of the importance or potential importance of relatives.

His father's life in Boston had been an endless, futile struggle to succeed as a tanner. Capital was the problem. In 1729 he bought a one-third ownership in a tannery for £600 in bills of credit. Two years later, he sold half of his third to his brother Robert, who became a working partner. The two brothers turned to a rich merchant, Nathaniel Cunningham, who put up £3500 in return for half the profits. The investment was huge: pits, a yard, workshops, hides, bark, two horses, four slaves, journeymen. For a time the tannery flourished. Then there was a disastrous falling out with Cunningham: furious fights, a raid on the yards, debtors' jail twice for George, suits and countersuits that dragged on in the courts for years. The Hewes brothers saw themselves as "very laborious" artisans who "managed their trade with good skill," only to be ruined by a wealthy, arrogant merchant. To Cunningham, they were incompetent and defaulters. Several years before George Robert was born, his father had fallen back to "butchering, tallow chandlering, hog killing, soap boiling &c."

The family was not impoverished. George had a memory as a little boy of boarding a ship with his mother to buy a small slave girl "at the rate of two dollars a pound." And there was enough money to pay the fees for his early schooling. But beginning in 1748, when he was six, there was a series of family tragedies. In 1748 an infant brother, Joseph, died, followed later in the year by his sister Abigail, age thirteen, and brother Ebenezer, age two. In 1749 his father died suddenly of a stroke, leaving the family nothing it would seem, his estate tangled in debt and litigation. George's mother would have joined the more than one thousand widows in Boston, most of whom were on poor relief. Sometime before 1755 she died. In 1756 Grandfather Seaver died, leaving less than £15 to be divided among George and his four surviving brothers. Thus in 1756, at the age of fourteen, when boys were customarily put out to apprenticeship, George was an orphan, the ward of his uncle Robert, as was his brother Daniel, age twelve, each with a legacy of £2 17s. 4d. Uncle Robert, though warmly recollected by Hewes, could not do much to help him: a gluemaker, he was struggling to set up his own manufactory. Nor could George's three older brothers, whom he also remembered fondly. In 1756 they were all in the "lower" trades. Samuel, age twenty-six, and Solomon, twenty-two, were fishermen; Shubael, twenty-four, was a butcher.

The reason why George was put to shoemaking becomes clearer: no one in the family had the indenture fee to enable him to enter one of the more lucrative "higher" trades. Josiah Franklin, also a tallow chandler, could not make his son Benjamin a cutler because he lacked the fee. But in shoemaking the prospects were so poor that some masters would pay to get an apprentice. In addition, George was too small to enter trades that demanded brawn; he could hardly have become a ropewalk worker, a housewright, or a shipwright. The trade was a sort of dumping ground for poor boys who could not handle heavy work. Boston's Overseers of the Poor acted on this assumption in 1770; so did recruiting officers for the American navy forty years later. The same was true in Europe. Getting into a good trade required "connections"; the family connections were in the leather trades, through Uncle Robert, the gluemaker, or brother Shubael, the butcher. Finally, there was family tradition. Grandfather Shubael had been a cordwainer, and on his death in 1756 there might even have been a prospect of acquiring his tools and lasts. In any case, the capital that would be needed to set up a shop of one's own was relatively small. And so the boy became a shoemaker—because he had very little choice.

III

Josiah Franklin had known how important it was to place a boy in a trade that was to his liking. Otherwise there was the threat that Benjamin made explicit: he would run away to sea. Hawkes saw the same thrust in Hewes's life: Shoemaking "was never an occupation of his choice," he "being inclined to more active pursuits." George was the wrong boy to put in a sedentary trade that was not to his liking. He was what Bostonians called "saucy". The memories of his childhood and youth that Thatcher elicited were almost all of defying authority— his mother, his teachers, at dame school, his schoolmaster, his aunt, his shoemaker master, a farmer, a doctor.

Hewes spoke of his mother only as a figure who inflicted punishment for disobedience. The earliest incident he remembered could have happened only to a poor family living near the waterfront. When George was about six, Abigail Hewes sent him off to the nearby shipyards with a basket to gather chips for the fire. At the water's edge George put the basket aside, straddled some floating planks to watch the fish, fell in, and sank to the bottom. He was saved only when some ship carpenters saw the basket without the boy, "found him motionless on the bottom, hooked him out with a boat hook, and rolled him on a tar barrel until signs of life were discovered." His mother nursed him back to health. Then she flogged him.

The lesson did not take, nor did others in school. First there was a dame school with Miss Tinkum, wife of the town crier. He ran away. She put him in a dark closet. He dug his way out. The next day she put him in again. This time he discovered a jar of quince marmalade and devoured it. A new dame school with "mother McLeod" followed. Then school with "our famous Master Holyoke," which Hewes remembered as "little more than a series of escapes made or attempted from the reign of the birch."

Abigail Hewes must have been desperate to control George. She sent him back after one truancy with a note requesting Holyoke to give him a good whipping. Uncle Robert took pity and sent a substitute note. Abigail threatened, "If you run away again I shall go to school with you myself." When George was about ten, she took the final step: she sent him to Wrentham to live with one of his paternal uncles. Here, George recalled, "he spent several years of his boyhood . . . in the monotonous routine of his Uncle's farm." The only incident he recounted was of defying his aunt. His five-year-old cousin hit him in the face with a stick "without any provocation." George cursed the boy out, for which his aunt whipped him, and when she refused to do the same with her son, George undertook to "chastise" him himself. "I caught my cousin at the barn" and applied the rod. The aunt locked him up but his uncle let him go, responsive to his plea for "equal justice."

Thus when George entered his apprenticeship, if he was not quite the young whig his biographers made him out to be, he was not a youth who would suffer arbitrary authority easily. His master, Downing, had an irascible side and was willing to use a cowhide. Hewes lived in Downing's attic with a fellow apprentice, John Gilbert. All the incidents Hewes recalled from this period had two motifs: petty defiance and a quest for food. There was an escapade on a Saturday night when the two apprentices made off for Gilbert's house and bought a loaf of bread, a pound of butter, and some coffee. They returned after curfew to encounter an enraged Downing, whom they foiled by setting pans and tubs to trip over when he came to the door. There was an excursion to Roxbury on Training Day, the traditional apprentices' holiday in Boston, with fellow apprentices and his younger brother. Caught stealing apples, they were taken before the farmer, who was also justice of the peace and who laughed uproariously at Hewes's name and let him go. There was an incident with a doctor who inoculated Hewes and a fellow worker for smallpox and warned them to abstain from food. Sick, fearful of death, Hewes and his friend consumed a dish of venison in melted butter and a mug of flip—and lived to tell the tale.

These memories of youthful defiance and youthful hunger lingered on for seventy years: a loaf of bread and a pound of butter, a parcel of apples, a dish of venison. This shoemaker's apprentice could hardly have been well fed or treated with affection.

The proof is that Hewes tried to end his apprenticeship by the only way he saw possible: escape to the military. "After finding that my depressed condition would probably render it impracticable for me to acquire that education requisite for civil employments," he told Hawkes, "I had resolved to engage in the military service of my country, should an opportunity present." Late in the 1750s, possibly in 1760, as the fourth and last of England's great colonial wars with France ground on and his majesty's army recruiters beat their drums through Boston's streets, Hewes and Gilbert tried to enlist. Gilbert was accepted, but Hewes was not. Recruiting captains were under orders to "enlist no Roman-Catholic, nor any under five feet two inches high without their shoes." "I could not pass muster," Hewes told Hawkes, "because I was not tall enough." As Thatcher embroiders Hawkes's story, Hewes then "went to the shoe shop of several of his acquaintances and heightened his heels by several taps[;] then stuffing his stocking with paper and rags," he returned. The examining captain saw through the trick and rejected him again. Frustrated, humiliated, vowing he would never return to Downing, he took an even more desperate step: he went down to the wharf and tried to enlist on a British ship of war. "His brothers, however, soon heard of it and interfered," and "he was compelled to abandon that plan." Bostonians like Solomon and Samuel Hewes, who made their living on the waterfront, did not need long memories to remember the city's massive resistance to the impressment sweeps of 1747 and to know that the British navy would be, not escape, but another prison.

About this time, shoemaker Downing failed after fire swept his shop. This would have freed Hewes of his indenture, but he was not qualified to be a shoemaker until he had completed apprenticeship. He therefore apprenticed himself "for the remainder of his minority," that is, until he turned twenty-one. In 1835 he could tell Thatcher how much time he then had left to serve, down to the month and day. Of the rest of his "time" he had no bad memories.

Apprenticeship had a lighter side. Hewes's anecdotes give tantalizing glimpses into an embryonic apprentice culture in Boston to which other sources attest—glimpses of pranks played on masters, of revelry after curfew, of Training Day, when the militia displayed its maneuvers and there was drink, food, and "frolicking" on the Common. One may speculate that George also took part in the annual Pope's Day festival, November 5, when apprentices, servants, artisans in the lower trades, and young people of all classes took over the town, parading effigies of Pope, Devil, and Pretender, exacting tribute from the better sort, and engaging in a battle royal between North End and South End Pope's Day "companies."

Hewes's stories of his youth hint at his winning a place for himself as the small schoolboy who got the better of his elders, the apprentice who defied his master, perhaps even a leader among his peers. There are also hints of the adult personality. Hewes was punished often, but if childhood punishment inured some to pain, it made Hewes reluctant to inflict pain on others. He developed a generous streak that led him to reach out to others in trouble. When Downing, a broken man, was on the verge of leaving for Nova Scotia to start anew, Hewes went down to his ship and gave him half of the apprentice fee he had received. Downing broke into tears. The story smacks of the Good Samaritan, of the Methodist of the 1830s counting his good deeds; and yet the memory was so vivid, wrote Thatcher, that "his features light up even now with a gleam of rejoicing pride." Hewes spoke later of the "tender sympathies of my nature." He did not want to be, but he was a fit candidate for the "gentle craft" he was about to enter.

IV

In Boston from 1763, when he entered his majority, until 1775, when he went off to war, Hewes never made a go of it as a shoemaker. He remembered these years more fondly than he had lived them. As Hawkes took down his story, shifting from the third to the first person:

> Hewes said he cheerfully submitted to the course of life to which his destinies directed.
>
> He built him a shop and pursued the private avocation of his trade for a considerable length of time, until on the application of his brother he was induced to go with him on two fishing voyages to the banks of New Foundland, which occupied his time for two years.
>
> After the conclusion of the French war . . . he continued at Boston, except the two years absence with his brother.
>
> During that period, said Hewes, when I was at the age of twenty-six, I married the daughter of Benjamin Sumner, of Boston. At the time of our intermarriage, the age of my wife was seventeen. We lived together very happily seventy years. She died at the age of eighty-seven.
>
> At the time when the British troops were first stationed at Boston, we had several children, the exact number I do not recollect. By our industry and mutual efforts we were improving our condition.

Thatcher added a few bits to this narrative, some illuminating. Benjamin Sumner, "if we mistake not," was a "sexton of one of the principal churches in town." His wife was a "washer-woman" near the Mill Pond, assisted by her five daughters. Hewes courted one of the girls when he "used to go to the house regularly every Saturday night to pay Sally for the week's washing." The father was stern, the swain persistent, and after a couple of years George and Sally were married. "The business was good, and growing better," Thatcher wrote, "especially as it became more and more fashionable to encourage our own manufactures."

The reality was more harsh. What kind of shoemaker was Hewes? He had his own shop—this much is clear, but the rest is surmise. There were at that time in Boston about sixty to seventy shoemakers, most of whom seem to have catered to the local market. If Hewes was typical, he would have made shoes to order, "bespoke" work; this would have made him a cordwainer. And he would have repaired shoes; this would have made him a cobbler. Who were his customers? No business records survive. A shoemaker probably drew his customers from his immediate neighborhood. Located as he was near the waterfront and the ropewalks, Hewes might well have had customers of the "meaner" sort. In a ward inhabited by the "middling" sort he may also have drawn on them. When the British troops occupied Boston, he did some work for them. Nothing suggests that he catered to the "carriage trade."

Was his business "improving" or "growing better"? Probably it was never very good and grew worse. From his own words we know that he took off two years on fishing voyages with his brothers. He did not mention that during this period he lived for a short time in Roxbury. His prospects were thus not good enough to keep him in Boston. His marriage is another clue to his low fortune. Sally (or Sarah) Sumner's father was a sexton so poor that his wife and daughters had to take in washing. The couple was married by the Reverend Samuel Stillman of the First Baptist Church, which suggests that this was the church that Benjamin Sumner served. Though Stillman was respected, First Baptist was not "one of the principal churches in town," as Thatcher guessed, but one of the poorest and smallest, with a congregation heavy with laboring people, sailors, and blacks. Marriage, one of the few potential sources of capital for an aspiring tradesman, as Benjamin Franklin made clear in his autobiography, did not lift Hewes up.

Other sources fill in what Hewes forgot. He married in January 1768. In September 1770 he landed in debtors' prison. In 1767 he had contracted a debt of £6 8s. 3d. to Thomas Courtney, a merchant tailor, for "making a sappled coat & breeches of fine cloth." The shoemaker bought this extravagant outfit when he was courting. What other way was there to persuade Sally's parents that he had good prospects? Over the three years since, he had neither earned enough to pay the debt nor accumulated £9 property that might be confiscated to satisfy it. "For want of Goods or Estate of the within named George Robt Twelve Hewes, I have taken his bodey & committed him to his majesty's goal [sic] in Boston," wrote Constable Thomas Rice on the back of the writ. Who got Hewes out of jail? Perhaps his uncle Robert, perhaps a brother.

Once out of jail, Hewes stayed poor. The Boston tax records of 1771 show him living as a lodger in the house of Christopher Ranks, a watchmaker, in the old North End. He was not taxed for any property. In 1773 he and his family, which now included three children, were apparently living with his uncle Robert in the South End; at some time during these years before the war they also lived with a brother. After almost a decade on his own, Hewes could not afford his own place. In January 1774 he inadvertently summed up his condition and reputation in the course of a violent street encounter. Damned as "a rascal" and "a vagabond" who had no right to "speak to a gentleman in the street," Hewes retorted that he was neither "and though a poor man, in as good credit in town" as his well-to-do antagonist.

The economic odds were against a Boston shoemaker thriving these years. Even the movement "to encourage our manufactures" may have worked against him. The patriot boycott would have raised his hopes; the Boston town meeting of 1767 put men's and women's shoes on the list of items Bostonians were encouraged to buy from American craftsmen. But if this meant shoes made in Lynn—the manufacturing town ten miles to the north that produced 80,000 shoes in 1767 alone—it might well have put Hewes at a competitive disadvantage. And if Hewes was caught up in the system whereby Lynn masters were already "putting out" shoes in Boston, he would have made even less. Whatever the reason, the early 1770s were hard times for shoemakers; Ebenezer McIntosh also landed in debtors' jail in 1770.

As a struggling shoemaker, what would have been Hewes's aspirations? He does not tell us in so many words, but "the course of his life," Hawkes was convinced, was marked "by habits of industry, integrity, temperance and economy"; in other words, he practiced the virtues set down by "another soap boiler and tallow chandler's son" (Thatcher's phrase for Benjamin Franklin). "From childhood," Hewes told Hawkes, "he has been accustomed to rise very early and expose himself to the morning air; that his father compelled him to do this from his infancy." ("Early to bed, Early to rise, makes a man healthy, wealthy and wise.") "I was often . . . admonished," said Hewes, "of the importance of faithfulness in executing the commands of my parents, or others who had a right to my services." Thatcher also reported that "he makes it a rule to rise from the table with an appetite, and another to partake of but a single dish at a meal." ("A Fat kitchen makes a lean will, as Poor Richard says.")

Poor Richard spoke to and for artisans at every level—masters, journeymen, and apprentices—whose goal was "independence" or "a competency" in their trade. What he advocated, we need remind ourselves, "was not unlimited acquisition but rather prosperity, which was the midpoint between the ruin of extravagance and the want of poverty. The living he envisaged was a decent middling wealth, which could only be attained through unremitting labor and self-control." Hewes's likely goal, then, was to keep his shop so that his shop would keep him.

But he could no more live by Poor Richard's precepts than could Franklin. "Industry" must have come hard. He was in an occupation "never of his choice." How could he "stick to his last" when he was "inclined towards more active pursuits"? "Avoid, above all else, debt," counselled Poor Richard, warning that "fond pride of dress is sure a very curse; E'er Fancy you consult, consult your purse." But Hewes surrendered to pride and as a consequence to the warden of the debtors' jail. "Economy"—that is, saving—produced no surplus. And so he would succumb, when war presented the opportunity, to the gamble for sudden wealth. He was as much the object as the exemplar of Poor Richard's advice, as indeed was Franklin himself.

If Hewes's memories softened such realities, in other ways his silences spoke. He said nothing about being part of any of Boston's traditional institutions—church, town meeting, or private associations. He was baptized in Old South, a Congregational church, and married by the minister of the First Baptist Church; there is no evidence that he took part in either. In his old age a convert to Methodism, a churchgoer, and Bible reader, he reminisced to neither biographer about the religion of youth.

Nor does he seem to have taken a part in town government. He was not a taxpayer in 1771. He probably did not own enough property to qualify as a voter for either provincial offices (£40 sterling) or town offices (£20 sterling). Recollecting the political events of the Revolution, he did not speak of attending town meetings until they became what patriots called meetings of "the whole body of the people," without regard to property. The town had to fill some two hundred minor positions; it was customary to stick artisans with the menial jobs. Hewes's father was hogreeve and measurer of boards. Hewes was appointed to nothing.

He does not seem to have belonged to any associations such as a fire company or the Masons, which enrolled other artisans. It was not that he was a loner. There was simply not much for a poor artisan to belong to. There was no shoemakers' society or general society of mechanics. Shoemakers had a long tradition of taking ad hoc collective actions, as did other Boston craftsmen, and Hewes may have participated in such occasional informal activities of the trade. Very likely he drilled in the militia with other artisans on Training Day (size would not have barred him). He seems to have known many artisans and recalled their names in describing events. So it is not hard to imagine him at a South End tavern enjoying a mug of flip with a leatherworker or a breechesmaker. Nor is it difficult to imagine him in the streets on November 5, in the South End Pope's Day company captained by McIntosh. But there was little else in respectable Boston for him to belong to. Though he lived in Boston proper, he was not part of proper Boston—not until the events of the Revolution.

V

Between 1768 and 1775, the shoemaker became a citizen—an active participant in the events that led to the Revolution, an angry, assertive man who won recognition as a patriot. What explains the transformation? We have enough evidence to take stock of Hewes's role in three major events of the decade: the Massacre (1770), the Tea Party (1773), and the tarring and feathering of John Malcolm (1774).

Thatcher began the story of Hewes in the Revolution at the Stamp Act Riots of 1765, when he was a bystander at the famous effigy-hanging at the Liberty Tree that launched Boston's protest. "The town's-people left their work—and Hewes, his hammer among the rest—to swell the multitude." If Hewes was a member of the South End Pope's Day company, he may have joined the crowd actions of August 14 and 26, the massive processions of the united North and South End companies on November 1 and 5, and the forced resignation of stampmaster Andrew Oliver in December. But he may well have been off on fishing voyages in 1765. Hewes himself remembered seventy years later only the celebration of the repeal of the Stamp Act in May 1766, at which he drank from the pipe of madeira that John Hancock set out on the Common. "Such a day has not been seen in Boston before or since," wrote his biographer.

On the night of the Boston Massacre, March 5, 1770, Hewes was in the thick of the action. What he tells us about what brought him to King Street, what brought others there, and what he did during and after this tumultuous event gives us the perspective of a man in the street.

The presence of British troops in Boston beginning in the summer of 1768—four thousand soldiers in a town of fewer than sixteen thousand inhabitants—touched Hewes personally. Anecdotes about soldiers flowed from him. He had seen them march off the transports at the Long Wharf; he had seen them every day occupying civilian buildings on Griffin's Wharf near his shop. He knew how irritating it was to be challenged by British sentries after curfew (his solution was to offer a swig of rum from the bottle he carried).

More important, he was personally cheated by a soldier who ordered shoes allegedly for Captain Thomas Preston, picked them up, but never paid for them. Hewes complained to Preston, who made good and suggested he bring a complaint. A military hearing ensued, at which Hewes testified. The soldier, to Hewes's horror, was sentenced to three hundred fifty lashes. He "remarked to the court that if he had thought the fellow was to be punished so severely for such an offense, bad as he was, he would have said nothing about it." And he saw others victimized by soldiers. He witnessed an incident in which a soldier sneaked up behind a woman, felled her with his fist, and "stripped her of her bonnet, cardinal muff and tippet." He followed the man to his barracks, identified him (Hewes remembered him as Private Kilroy, who would appear later at the Massacre), and got him to give up the stolen goods, but decided this time not to press charges. Hewes was also keenly aware of grievances felt by the laboring men and youths who formed the bulk of the crowd—and the principal victims—at the Massacre.

First in time, and vividly recalled by Hewes, was the murder of eleven-year-old Christopher Seider on February 23, ten days before the Massacre. Seider was one of a large crowd of schoolboys and apprentices picketing the shop of a merchant violating the anti-import resolutions. A paid customs informer shot into the throng and killed Seider and would have been tarred and feathered, or worse, had not whig leaders intervened to hustle him off to jail. At Seider's funeral, only a week before the Massacre, five hundred boys marched two by two behind the coffin, followed by two thousand or more adults, "the largest [funeral] perhaps ever known in America," Thomas Hutchinson thought.

Second, Hewes emphasized the bitter fight two days before the Massacre between soldiers and workers at Gray's ropewalk down the block from Hewes's shop. Off-duty soldiers were allowed to moonlight, taking work from civilians. On Friday, March 3, when one of them asked for work at Gray's, a battle ensued between a few score soldiers and ropewalk workers joined by others in the maritime trades. The soldiers were beaten and sought revenge. Consequently, "quite a number of soldiers, in a word, were determined to have a row on the night of the 5th."

Third, the precipitating events on the night of the Massacre, by Hewes's account, were an attempt by a barber's apprentice to collect an overdue bill from a British officer, the sentry's abuse of the boy, and the subsequent harassment of the sentry by a small band of boys that led to the calling of the guard commanded by Captain Preston.

Hewes viewed the civilians as essentially defensive. On the evening of the Massacre he appeared early on the scene at King Street, attracted by the clamor over the apprentice. "I was soon on the ground among them," he said, as if it were only natural that he should turn out in defense of fellow townsmen against what was assumed to be the danger of aggressive action by soldiers. He was not part of a conspiracy; neither was he there out of curiosity. He was unarmed, carrying neither club nor stave as some others did. He saw snow, ice, and "missiles" thrown at the soldiers. When the main guard rushed out in support of the sentry, Private Kilroy dealt Hewes a blow on his shoulder with his gun. Preston ordered the townspeople to disperse. Hewes believed they had a legal basis to refuse: "they were in the king's highway, and had as good a right to be there" as Preston.

The five men killed were all workingmen. Hewes claimed to know four: Samuel Gray, a ropewalk worker; Samuel Maverick, age seventeen, an apprentice to an ivory turner; Patrick Carr, an apprentice to a leather breeches worker; and James Caldwell, second mate on a ship—all but Christopher Attucks. Caldwell, "who was shot in the back was standing by the side of Hewes, and the latter caught him in his arms as he fell," helped carry him to Dr. Thomas Young in Prison Lane, then ran to Caldwell's ship captain on Cold Lane.

More than horror was burned into Hewes's memory. He remembered the political confrontation that followed the slaughter, when thousands of angry townspeople faced hundreds of British troops massed with ready rifles. "The people," Hewes recounted, "then immediately chose a committee to report to the governor the result of Captain Preston's conduct, and to demand of him satisfaction." In the dark hours after the Massacre a self-appointed group of patriot leaders met with officials and forced Lt. Governor Hutchinson to commit Preston and the soldiers to jail. The town meeting the next day was so huge that it had to adjourn from Fanueil Hall, the traditional meeting place that held only twelve hundred, to Old South Church, which had room for five to six thousand. This was one of the meetings at which property bars were let down and it accepted an offer from the Lt. Governor to remove two regiments from the city.

What Hewes did not recount, but what he had promptly put down in a deposition the next day, was how militant he was after the Massacre. At 1:00 A.M., like many other enraged Bostonians, he went home to arm himself. On his way back to the Town House with a cane he had a defiant exchange with Sergeant Chambers of the 29th Regiment and eight or nine soldiers, "all with very large clubs or cutlasses." A soldier, Dobson, "ask'd him how he far'd; he told him very badly to see his townsmen shot in such a manner, and asked him if he did not think it was a dreadful thing." Dobson swore "it was a fine thing" and "you shall see more of it." Chambers "seized and forced" the cane from Hewes, "saying I had no right to carry it. I told him I had as good a right to carry a cane as they had to carry clubs."

The Massacre had stirred Hewes to political action. He was one of 99 Bostonians who gave depositions for the prosecution that were published by the town in a pamphlet. Undoubtedly, he marched in the great funeral procession for the victims that brought the city to a standstill. He attended the tempestuous trials of Seider's slayer and Capt. Preston, and he later claimed to have given testimony at Preston's trial, at which his loyalist brother Shubael was a witness for the defense:

> I was called as one of the witnesses, on the part of the government, and testified, that I believed it was the same man, Captain Preston, that ordered his soldiers to make ready, who also ordered them to fire. Mr. John Adams . . . was advocate for the prisoners, and denied the fact, that Captain Preston gave orders to his men to fire; and on his cross examination of me asked whether my position was such, that I could see the captain's lips in motion when the order to fire was given; to which I answered, that I could not.

There is no proof that Hewes testified. In one sense, it does not matter. When he was remembering was that he had become involved. He turned out because of a sense of kinship with "his townsmen" in danger; he stood his ground in defense of his "rights"; he was among the "people" who delegated a committee to act on their behalf; he took part in the legal process by given a deposition, by attending the trials, and, as he remembered it, by testifying. In sum, he had become a citizen, a political man.

Four years later, at the Tea Party on the night of December 16, 1773, the citizen "volunteered" and became the kind of leader for whom most historians have never found a place. The Tea Party, unlike the Massacre, was organized by the radical whig leaders of Boston. They mapped the strategy, organized the public meetings, appointed the companies to guard the tea ships at Griffin's Wharf (among them Daniel Hewes, George's brother), and planned the official boarding parties. As in 1770, they converted the town meetings into meetings of "the whole body of the people," which Hutchinson found "consisted principally of the Lower ranks of the People & even Journeymen Tradesmen were brought in to increase the number & the Rabble were not excluded yet there were divers Gentlemen of Good Fortunes among them."

The boarding parties showed this same combination of "ranks."

A journeyman blacksmith later recalled that "It was proposed that young men, not much known in town and not liable to be easily recognized should lead in the business"; hence "most of the persons selected for the occasion were apprentices and journeymen." Those in the officially designated parties, about thirty men better known, appeared in well-prepared Indian disguises. As nobodies, the volunteers—anywhere from fifty to one hundred men—could get away with hastily improvised disguises. Hewes said he got himself up as an Indian and daubed his "face and hands with coal dust in the shop of a blacksmith." In the streets "I fell in with many who were dressed, equipped and painted as I was, and who fell in with me and marched in order to the place of our destination."

At Griffin's Wharf the volunteers were orderly, self-disciplined, and ready to accept leadership.

> When we arrived at the wharf, there were three of our number who assumed an authority to direct our operations, to which we readily submitted. They divided us into three parties, for the purpose of boarding the three ships which contained the tea at the same time. . . . We were immediately ordered by the respective commanders to board all the ships at the same time, which we promptly obeyed.

But for Hewes there was something new: he was singled out of the rank and file and made an officer in the field.

> The commander of the division to which I belonged, as soon as we were on board the ship, appointed me boatswain, and ordered me

to go to the captain and demand of him the keys to the hatches and a dozen candles. I made the demand accordingly, and the captain promptly replied, and delivered the articles; but requested me at the same time to do no damage to the ship or rigging. We then were ordered by our commander to open the hatches, and take out all the chests of tea and throw them overboard, and we immediately proceeded to execute his orders; first cutting and splitting the chests with our tomahawks, so as thoroughly to expose them to the effects of the water. In about three hours from the time we went on board, we had thus broken and thrown overboard every tea chest to be found in the ship; while those in the other ships were disposing of the tea in the same way, at the same time. We were surrounded by British armed ships, but no attempt was made to resist us. We then quietly retired to our several places of residence, without having any conversation with each other, or taking any measures to discover who were our associates.

This was Hewes's story, via Hawkes. Thatcher reported a new anecdote, that Hewes worked alongside John Hancock throwing tea overboard. And he added that Hewes, "whose whistling talent was a matter of public notoriety, acted as a boatswain," that is, as the officer whose duty it was to summon men with a whistle. That Hewes was a leader was confirmed by the reminiscence of a teamster from a neighboring town who made a delivery to Hancock the day of the event and was asked by him to go to Griffin's Wharf. "I went accordingly, joined the band under one Captain Hewes; we mounted the ships and made tea in a trice; this done I took my team and went home as any honest man should."

As the Tea Party ended, Hewes was stirred to further action on his own initiative, just as he had been in the hours after the Massacre. While the crews were throwing the tea overboard, a few other men tried to smuggle off some of the tea scattered on the decks. "One Captain O'Connor whom I well knew," said Hewes, "came on board for that purpose, and when he supposed he was not noticed, filled his pockets, and also the lining of his coat. But I had detected him, and gave information to the captain of what he was doing. We were ordered to take him into custody, and just as he was stepping from the vessel, I seized him by the skirt of his coat, and in attempting to pull him back, I tore it off." They scuffled. O'Connor recognized him and "threatened to 'complain to the Governor.' 'You had better make your will first,' quoth Hewes, doubling his fist expressively," and O'Connor escaped, running the gauntlet of the crowd on the wharf. "The next day we nailed the skirt of his coat, which I had pulled off, to the whipping post in Charlestown, the place of his residence, with a label upon it," to shame O'Connor by "popular indignation."

A month later, at the third event for which we have full evidence, Hewes won public recognition for an act of courage that almost cost his life and precipitated the most publicized tarring and feathering of the Revolution. The incident that set it off would have been trivial at any other time. On Tuesday, January 25, 1774, at about two in the afternoon, the shoemaker was making his way back to his shop after his dinner. According to the very full account in the *Massachusetts Gazette,*

> Mr. George-Robert-Twelves Hewes was coming along Fore-Street, near Captain Ridgway's, and found the redoubted John Malcolm, standing over a small boy, who was pushing a little sled before him, cursing, damning, threatening and shaking a very large cane with a very heavy ferril on it over his head. The boy at that time was perfectly quiet, notwithstanding which Malcolm continued his threats of striking him, which Mr. Hewes conceiving if he struck him with that weapon he must have killed him out-right, came up to him, and said to him, Mr. Malcolm I hope you are not going to strike this boy with that stick.

Malcolm had already acquired an odious reputation with patriots of the lower sort. A Bostonian, he had been a sea captain, an army officer, and recently an employee of the customs service. He was a strong supporter of royal authority and had a fiery temper. As a customs informer he was known to have turned in a vessel to punish sailors for petty smuggling, a custom of the sea. In November 1773, near Portsmouth, New Hampshire, a crowd of thirty sailors had "genteely tarr'd and feather'd" him, as the *Boston Gazette* put it: they did the job over his clothes. Back in Boston he made "frequent complaints" to Hutchinson of "being hooted at in the streets" for this by "tradesmen"; and the lieutenant governor cautioned him, "being a passionate man," not to reply in kind.

The exchange between Malcolm and Hewes resonated with class as well as political differences:

> Malcolm returned, you are an impertinent rascal, it is none of your business. Mr. Hewes then asked him, what had the child done to him. Malcolm damned him and asked him if he was going to take his part? Mr. Hewes answered no further than this, that he thought it was a shame for him to strike the child with such a club as that, if he intended to strike him. Malcolm on that damned Mr. Hewes, called him a vagabond, and said he would let him know he should not speak to a gentleman on the street. Mr. Hewes returned to that, he was neither a rascal nor vagabond, and though a poor man was in as good credit in town as he was. Malcolm called him a liar, and said he was not, nor ever would be. Mr. Hewes retorted, be that as it will, I never was tarred nor feathered any how. On this Malcolm struck him, and wounded him deeply on the forehead, so that Mr. Hewes for some time lost his senses. Capt. Godfrey, then present, interposed, and after some altercation, Malcolm went home.

Hewes was rushed to Joseph Warren, the patriot doctor, his distant relative. Malcolm's cane had almost penetrated his skull. Thatcher and Hawkes found "the indentation as plainly perceptible as it was sixty years ago." Warren dressed the wound, and Hewes was able to make his way to a magistrate to swear out a warrant for Malcolm's arrest. Malcolm, meanwhile, had retreated to his house, where he responded in white heat to taunts about the half-way tarring and feathering in Portsmouth with "damn you let me see the man that dare do it better."

In the evening a crowd took Malcolm from his house and dragged him on a sled into King Street "amidst the huzzas of thousands." At this point "several gentlemen endeavoured to divert the populace from their intention." The ensuing dialogue laid bare the clash of conceptions of justice between the sailors and laboring people heading the action and Sons of Liberty leaders. The "gentlemen" argued that Malcolm was "open to the laws of the land which would undoubtedly award a reasonable satisfaction to the parties he had abused," that is, the child and Hewes. The answer was political. Malcolm "had been an old impudent and mischievious [sic] offender—he had seized vessels on account of sailors having a bottle or two of gin on board—he had in other words behaved in the most capricious, insulting and daringly abusive manner." He could not be trusted to justice. "When they were told the law would have its course with him, they asked what course had the law taken" with the Seider boy's killer (convicted but later pardoned by the Crown) or with Preston or his soldiers, who had been let off with token punishment? "For their parts they had seen so much partiality to the soldiers and customhouse officers by the present Judges, that while things remained as they were, they would, on all such occasions, take satisfaction their own way, and let them take it off."

The crowd won and proceeded to a ritualized tarring and feathering, the purpose of which was to punish Malcolm, force a recantation, and ostracize him.

> With these and such like arguments, together with a gentle crouding of persons not of their way of thinking out of the ring they proceeded to elevate Mr. Malcolm from his sled into a cart, and stripping him to buff and breeches, gave him a modern jacket [a coat of tar and feathers] and hied him away to liberty-tree, where they proposed to him to renounce his present commission, and swear that he would never hold another inconsistent with the liberties of his country; but this he obstinately refusing, they then carted him to the gallows, passed a rope round his neck, and threw the other end over the beam as if they intended to hang him: But this manoeuvre he set at defiance. They then basted him for some time with a rope's end, and threatened to cut his ears off, and on this he complied, and they then brought him home.

Hewes had precipitated an electrifying event. It was part of the upsurge of spontaneous action in the wake of the Tea Party that prompted the whig leaders to promote a "Committee for Tarring and Feathering" as an instrument of crowd control. The "Committee" made its appearance in broadsides signed by "Captain Joyce, Jun.," a sobriquet meant to invoke the bold cornet who had captured King Charles in 1647. The event was reported in the English newspapers, popularized in three or four satirical prints, and dramatized still further when Malcolm went to England, where he campaigned for a pension and ran for Parliament (without success) against John Wilkes, the leading champion of America. The event confirmed the British ministry in its punitive effort to bring rebellious Boston to heel.

What was lost to the public was that Hewes was at odds with the crowd. He wanted justice from the courts, not a mob; after all, he had sworn out a warrant against Malcolm. And he could not bear to see cruel punishment inflicted on a man, any more than on a boy. As he told the story to Thatcher, when he returned and saw Malcolm being carted away in tar and feathers, "his instant impulse was to push after the procession as fast as he could, with a blanket to put over his shoulders. He overtook them [the crowd] at his brother's [Shubael's] house and made an effort to relieve him; but the ruffians who now had the charge of him about the cart, pushed him aside, and warned him to keep off." This may have been the Good Samaritan of 1835, but the story rings true. While "the very excitement which the affront must have wrought upon him began to rekindle," Hewes conveyed no hatred for Malcolm.

The denouement of the affair was an incident of several weeks later. "Malcolm recovered from his wounds and went about as usual. 'How do you do, Mr. Malcolm?' said Hewes, very civilly, the next time he met him. 'Your humble servant, Mr. George Robert Twelves Hewes,' quoth he,—touching his hat genteely as he passed by. 'Thank ye,' thought Hewes, 'and I am glad you have learned *better manners at last.'* " Hewes's mood was one of triumph. Malcolm had been taught a lesson. The issue was respect for Hewes, a patriot, a poor man, an honest citizen, a decent man standing up for a child against an unspeakably arrogant "gentleman" who was an enemy of his country.

Hewes's role in these three events fits few of the categories that historians have applied to the participation of ordinary men in the Revolution. He was not a member of any organized committee, caucus, or club. He did not attend the expensive public dinners of the Sons of Liberty. He was capable of acting on his own volition without being summoned by any leaders (as in the Massacre). He could volunteer and assume leadership (as in the Tea Party). He was at home on the streets in crowds but he could also reject a crowd (as in the tarring and feathering of Malcolm). He was at home in the other places where ordinary Bostonians turned out to express their convictions: at funeral processions, at meetings of the "whole body of the people," in courtrooms at public trials. He recoiled from violence to persons if not to property. The man who could remember the whippings of his own boyhood did not want to be the source of pain to others, whether a soldier who had tried to cheat him over a pair of shoes, or John Malcolm, who almost killed him. It is in keeping with his character that he should have come to the aid of a little boy facing a beating.

Nevertheless, Hewes was more of a militant than he conveyed or his biographers recognized in 1833 and 1835. He was capable of acting on his own initiative in the wake of collective action at both the Massacre and the Tea Party. He had "public notoriety," Thatcher tells us, for his "whistling talent"; whistling was the customary way of assembling a crowd. According to Malcolm, Hewes was among the "tradesmen" who had "several times before affronted him" by "hooting" at him in the streets.

What moved Hewes to action? It was not the written word; indeed there is no sign he was much of a reader until old age, and then it was the Bible he read. "My whole education," he told Hawkes, "consisted of only a moderate knowledge of reading and writing." He seems to have read one of the most sensational pamphlets of 1773, which he prized enough to hold onto for more than fifty years.

Hewes was moved to act by personal experiences that he shared with large numbers of other plebeian Bostonians. He seems to have been politicized, if not by the Stamp Act, then by the coming of the troops after 1768, and then by things that happened to him, that he saw, or that happened to people he knew. Once aroused, he took action with others of his own rank and condition—the laboring classes who formed the bulk of the actors of the Massacre, the Tea Party, and the Malcolm affair—and with other members of his family: his uncle Robert, "known for a staunch Liberty Boy," and his brother Daniel, a guard at the tea ship. Shubael, alone among his brothers, became a tory. These shared experiences were interpreted and focused more likely by the spoken than the written word and as much by his peers at taverns and crowd actions as by leaders in huge public meetings.

As he became active politically he may have had a growing awareness of his worth as a shoemaker. McIntosh was clearly the man of the year in 1765; indeed, whigs were no less fearful than loyalists that "the Captain General of the Liberty Tree" might become the Masaniello of Boston. After a shoemaker made the boot to hang in the Liberty Tree as an effigy of Lord Bute, "Jack Cobler" served notice that "whenever the Public Good requires my services, I shall be ready to distinguish myself." In 1772, "Crispin" began an anti-loyalist diatribe by saying, "I am a shoemaker, a citizen, a free man and a freeholder." The editor added a postscript justifying "Crispin's performance" and explaining that "it should be known what common people, even *coblers* think and feel under the present administration." In city after city, "coblers" were singled out for derision by conservatives for leaving their lasts to engage in the body politic. Hewes could not have been unaware of all this; he was part of it.

He may also have been responding to the rising demand among artisans for support of American manufacturers, whether or not it brought him immediate benefit. He most certainly subscribed to the secularized Puritan ethic—self-denial, industry, frugality—that made artisans take to the nonimportation agreement with its crusade against foreign luxury and its vision of American manufactures. And he could easily have identified with the appeal of the Massachusetts Provincial Congress of 1774 that equated the political need "to encourage agriculture, manufacturers and economy so as to render this state as independent of every other state as the nature of our country will admit" with the "happiness of particular families" in being "independent."

But what ideas did Hewes articulate? He spoke of what he did but very little of what he thought. In the brief statement he offered Hawkes about why he went off to war in 1776, he expressed a commitment to general principles as they had been brought home to him by his experiences. "I was continually reflecting upon the unwarrantable sufferings inflicted on the citizens of Boston by the usurpation and tyranny of Great Britain, and my mind was excited with an unextinguishable desire to aid in chastising them." When Hawkes expressed a doubt "as to the correctness of his conduct in absenting himself from his family," Hewes "emphatically reiterated" the same phrases, adding to a "desire to aid in chastising them" the phrase "and securing our independence." This was clearly not an afterthought; it probably reflected the way many others moved toward the goal of Independence, not as a matter of original intent, but as a step made necessary when all other resorts failed. Ideology thus did not set George Hewes apart from Samuel Adams or John Hancock. The difference lies in what the Revolution did to him as a person. His experiences transformed him, giving him a sense of citizenship and personal worth. Adams and Hancock began with both; Hewes had to arrive there, and in arriving he cast off the constraints of deference.

The two incidents with which we introduced Hewes's life measure the distance he had come: from the young man tongue-tied in the presence of John Hancock to the man who would not take his hat off to the officer of the ship named *Hancock*. Did he cast off his deference to Hancock? Hewes's affirmation of his worth as a human being was a form of class consciousness. Implicit in the idea, "I am as good as any man regardless of rank or wealth," was the idea that any poor man might be as good as any rich man. This did not mean that all rich men were bad. On the contrary, in Boston, more than any other major co-

lonial seaport, a majority of the merchants were part of the patriot coalition; "divers Gentelmen of Good Fortunes," as Hutchinson put it,
were with the "Rabble." This blunted class consciousness. Boston's
mechanics, unlike New York's or Philadelphia's, did not develop mechanic committees or a mechanic consciousness before the Revolution.
Yet in Boston the rich were forced to defer to the people in order to
obtain or retain their support. Indeed, the entire public career of Hancock from 1765 on—distributing largesse, buying uniforms for Pope's
Day marchers, building ships to employ artisans—can be understood
as an exercise of this kind of deference, proving his civic virtue and
patriotism.

This gives meaning to Hewes's tale of working beside Hancock at
the Tea Party where as Thatcher said

> Mr. Hewes, however, positively affirms, as of his own observation,
> that *Samuel Adams and John Hancock were both actively engaged in the
> process of destruction.* Of the latter he speaks more particularly, being
> entirely confident that he was himself at one time engaged with
> him in the demolition of the same chest of tea. He recognized him
> not only by his *ruffles* making their appearance in the heat of the
> work, from under the disguise which pretty thoroughly covered
> him,—and by his figure, and gait;—but by his features, which nei-
> ther his paint nor his loosened club of hair behind wholly con-
> cealed from a close view;—and by his voice also, for he exchanged
> with him an Indian *grunt*, and the expression *"me know you,"* which
> was a good deal used on that occasion for a countersign.

In fact, it is very unlikely that Hancock was there. Participants swore
themselves to secrecy; their identity was one of the best-kept secrets of
the Revolution, but it was not part of the patriot plan for the well-
known leaders to be present. When the all-day meeting that sanctioned
the action adjourned, the leaders, including Hancock, stayed behind
conspicuously in Old South. Still, there can be little question that Hewes
was convinced at the time that Hancock was on the ship: some gentlemen were indeed present; it was reasonable to assume that Hancock,
who had been so conspicuous on the tea issue, was there; Hewes knew
what Hancock looked like; he was too insistent about details for his
testimony to be dismissed as made up. And the way he recorded it in
his mind at the time was the way he stored it in his memory.

Hewes in effect had brought Hancock down to his own level. The
poor shoemaker had not toppled the wealthy merchant; he was no
"leveller." But the rich and powerful—the men in "ruffles"—had become, in his revealing word, his "associates." John Hancock and George
Hewes breaking open the same chest at the Tea Party remained for
Hewes a symbol of a moment of equality. To the shoemaker, one suspects, this above all was what the Revolutionary events of Boston meant,
as did the war that followed.

VI

Hewes's decisions from 1775 to 1783—his choice of services and the timing and sequence of his military activities—suggest a pattern of patriotism mingled with a hope to strike it rich and a pressing need to provide for his family.

After the outbreak of hostilities at Lexington and Concord in April 1775, Boston became a garrison town; patriot civilians streamed out—perhaps ten thousand of them—Tory refugees moved in, and the number of British troops grew to 13,500 by July. Hewes sent his wife and children to Wrentham—his father's native town—where they would be safe with relatives. His brother Daniel did the same; Solomon went elsewhere; Shubael alone stayed with the British, as butcher-general to General Gage. George himself remained—"imprisoned," as he remembered it—prevented like other able-bodied men from leaving the city. He made a living as a fisherman; the British allowed him to pass in and out of the harbor in exchange for the pick of the day's catch. He was in Boston nine weeks, was harassed by soldiers on the street, witnessed the Battle of Bunker Hill from a neck of land far out in the bay (he "saw" [Joseph Warren] fall"), and saw the corpses of British soldiers "chucked" into an open pit at one end of the Common. One morning he bade good-bye to Shubael, hid his shoemaker's tools under the deck of a small boat borrowed from a tory, and, after a narrow scrape with British guards, made good an escape with two friends to nearby Lynn. The Committee of Safety took him to Cambridge, where General Washington plied him with questions about conditions in Boston. Then he made his way south to join his family in Wrentham.

After some months, very likely in the fall of 1776, he enlisted on a privateer at Providence for a voyage north that lasted about three months. He returned to Wrentham and a year later, in the fall of 1777, served in the militia from one to three months. In late August 1778 he served again, most likely for one month. In February 1779 he made a second privateering voyage, this time out of Boston, an eventful seven-and-a-half-month trip to the South and the West Indies. In 1780 he very likely was in the militia again from late July to late October, and in 1781 he definitely was in the militia at the same time of year. That was his final tour of duty: in the closing years of the war, to avoid the Massachusetts draft, he hired a substitute. All these enlistments were as a private; he did not rise in the ranks.

Several things stand out in this record. Hewes did not go at once, not until he provided for his family. He remembered that he did not make his first enlistment until "about two years after the battle of Bunker Hill," although actually it was closer to a year or fifteen months. He served often, twice at sea, at least four and possibly five times in the militia, but not at all in the Continental army, which would have meant longer periods away from home. For almost all of these stints he volunteered; once he was drafted; once he sent a substitute; he drew these distinctions carefully.

This record, put alongside what we know about other Massachusetts men in the war, places Hewes a good cut above the average. He served at least nine months in the militia and ten-and-a-half months at sea—about twenty months in all. Hewes served less than the thirty-three months of the average man in the Continental army, but perhaps twice as long altogether as most militia volunteers. Like others who put in this much time, he was poor. Hewes was in his mid-thirties; he and Sarah had four children by 1776, six by 1781. He spent most of the years of war at home providing for them, doing what, he did not say, but possibly making shoes for the army like other country cordwainers. His patriotism was thus tempered by the need for survival.

Going to war was a wrenching experience. When Hewes told his wife he intended to "take a privateering cruise," she "was greatly afflicted at the prospect of our separation, and my absence from a numerous family of children, who needed a father's parental care." Taught from boyhood to repress his emotions, Hewes cut the pain of parting by a ruse.

> On the day which I had appointed to take my departure, I came into the room where my wife was, and inquired if all was ready? She pointed in silence to my knapsack. I observed, that I would put it on and walk with it a few rods, to see if it was rightly fitted to carry with ease. I went out, to return no more until the end of my cruise. The manly fortitude which becomes the soldier, could not overcome the tender sympathies of my nature. I had not courage to encounter the trial of taking a formal leave. When I had arrived at a solitary place on my way, I sat down for a few moments, and sought to allay the keenness of my grief by giving vent to a profusion of tears.

Why was privateering Hewes's first choice? Privateering was legalized piracy with a share of the booty for each pirate. Under a state or Continental letter of marque, a privately owned ship was authorized to take enemy vessels as prizes. The government received a share, as did the owners and crew, prorated by rank. During the seven years of war, the United States commissioned 2,000 privateers, 626 in Massachusetts alone, which itself issued 1,524 commissions.

War for Hewes meant opportunity: a chance to escape from a humdrum occupation never to his liking; to be at thirty-five what had been denied at sixteen—a fighting man; above all, a chance to accumulate the capital that could mean a house, a new shop, apprentices and journeymen, perhaps a start in something altogether new. He was following a path trod by tens of thousands of poor New Englanders ever since the wars against the French in the 1740s and 1750s. As an economic flyer, however, privateering ultimately proved disastrous for Hewes.

His first voyage went well. He sailed on the *Diamond* out of Providence, attracted possibly by an advertisement that promised fortune and adventure. They captured three vessels, the last of which Hewes brought back to Providence as a member of the prize crew. He said nothing about his share; by inference he got enough to whet his appetite but not enough to boast about. He also nearly drowned off Newfoundland when a line he and two shipmates were standing on broke.

His second voyage was shattering. He went on the Connecticut ship of war *Defence*, sailing from Boston with the *Oliver Cromwell*. The *Defence* and the *Cromwell* captured two richly laden vessels and later, after a layover in Charleston, South Carolina, two British privateers; on the way home, the *Defence* stopped a ship and relieved the tory passengers of their money. The prize money from the two privateers alone was $80,000. But Hewes got nothing. His share was supposed to be $250, "but some pretext was always offered for withholding my share from me; so that I never received one cent of it." When he asked for his wages, the captain "told me he was about fitting out an expedition to the West Indies, and could not, without great inconvenience, spare the money then; but said he would call on his way to Providence . . . and would pay me; but I never saw him afterwards. Neither have I, at any time since, received a farthing, either of my share of prize money or wages."

There was an adventurous side to privateering. His stories stress the thrill of the chase, the intrepid maneuvering of his ship in battle, the excitement of a boarding party. They also deal with the prosaic. He remembered manning the pumps on the leaking *Defence* "for eight days and eight nights to keep us from sinking." He remembered before battle that "we sat up all night . . . we made bandages, scraped lint, so that we might be prepared to dress wounds as we expected to have a hard time of it." The man of tender sympathies did not become a bloodthirsty buccaneer.

Most important of all was the memory that at sea he had participated in making decisions and that the captains had shown deference to their crews. On his first voyage, the initial agreement was for a cruise of seven weeks. "When that term had expired," said Hewes, "and we had seen no enemy during the time, we were discouraged, and threatened to mutiny, unless he would return." The captain asked for one more week, after which he promised to sail home if they saw nothing, "to which we assented." On the second voyage, when the *Defence* sighted enemy ships and the captain "asked us if we were willing to give chase to them, we assented, we were all ready to go and risk our lives with him." In Charleston, their tour of duty legally over, the captain proposed a five-day extension when the British privateers were

sighted. "Our Captain put it to a vote, and it was found we were unanimously agreed to make the cruise." One hesitates to call this process
democratic: even the captain of a pirate ship could not function without the support of his crew. What Hewes remembered was that the
captains deferred to him and his mates, not the other way around.

This is the motif of his encounter with George Washington in 1775.
When Hewes and his fellow escapees from Boston were taken to
Washington's headquarters in Cambridge, he was recognized as the
nephew of the "staunch Liberty Man" Robert Hewes. Washington invited Hewes into his parlor—"with him, alone. There he told him his
story, every word of it, from beginning to end, and answered all his
questions besides." Washington, in Hewes's words, "didn't *laugh*, to
be sure, but *looked amazing good-natured* you may depend." Washington
then treated him and his companions to punch and invited them to a
meal. All this is entirely possible. Washington was considering an invasion of Boston; he would have welcomed intelligence from a street-
wise man just out of the town, and as a Virginia planter he knew the
importance of the gesture of hospitality.

In military duty on land there was no recognition of this sort from
his betters, though he was in the militia, by reputation the most democratic branch of service. Even his adventures were humdrum. The
"general destination" of his units was "to guard the coasts." He saw
action perhaps twice. He remembered rowing through the darkness in
silence in an attack on a British fort that had to be aborted when one
of the rowers talked. On duty at West Point in 1781 he went out on
forays against the "cowboys," lawless bands pillaging Westchester
County. In all this activity he claimed no moment of glory; there was
a lot of marching; a lot of sentry duty; much drudgery. If he mended
shoes for soldiers, as did other shoemakers in the ranks, he did not
speak of it. And military service did not kindle in him an ambition to
rise, as it did in a number of other shoemakers who became officers.

After all this service it hurt to be subjected to an inequitable draft
when in 1781 Massachusetts required all men of military age to serve
"or to form themselves into classes of nine men, and each class to hire
an able bodied man, on such terms as they could, and pay him for his
services, while they were to receive their pay of the state." Why did
Hewes refuse to go? He said later that the "extreme exigencies" of his
family and the "pressure of his circumstances" forced him to "withdraw his services from the army." The decision was painful, and it was
costly. Hewes's substitute "demanded . . . specie while we received
nothing of the government but paper money, of very little value, and
continually depreciating."

Hewes's service was "poorly rewarded." He was one of "the mass
of people, at large; such as had little property to fight for, or to lose,
on one hand, and could reasonably expect to gain still less, either in

the way of emolument or distinction on the other." Instead, the inequities of civilian life were repeated on an even crasser scale. The rich could easily afford a substitute; the men who had already fought paid through the nose for one. The ship's officers got their share of the prize; the poor sailor got neither prize money nor wages.

But the war meant more than this to Hewes. It left a memory of rights asserted (by a threat of mutiny) and rights respected by captains who put decisions to a vote of the crew, and of the crew giving assent. It was a memory, above all, of respect from his betters: from General Washington at Cambridge, from captains at sea, from John Hancock in Boston. For a moment, it had been a world that marched to the tune of the old English nursery rhyme supposedly played at Cornwallis's surrender, "The World Turned Upside Down." Then "in a trice" Hewes's world came right side up—but little, if any, better than before.

VII

For thirty-three years, from 1783 to about 1815, George Hewes almost eludes us. We know that at the end of the war he did not return to Boston but stayed in Wrentham; that he produced a large family; that after the War of 1812 he moved to Otsego County, New York. But we hardly know what he did these years. His biographers were uninterested. Hawkes said he was in "laborious pursuits either in some agricultural or mechanical employment." Later lore had it that he returned to the sea and "for many years" was "a mate on merchant vessels in the West Indies trade." Legal documents refer to him in 1796–1797 as a "yeoman" and in 1810 as a "cordwainer." These clues are not inconsistent. Wrentham in those years was a small inland farming town of about 2,000 people, no more than a good day's walk to the port of Providence. If Hewes was a cordwainer, he would have had to be a farmer too, as were most country shoemakers. If he went to sea, he would have had to fall back on landlubber pursuits, especially in his later years. There were few "old salts" in their fifties or sixties.

All we may say with certainty is that he came out of the war poor and stayed poor. By 1783, he had turned forty, and had very little to show for it. That he did not go back to Boston, that he did not visit there more than a few times until 1821, tells us how small a stake he had in his native city. In this he was like at least a thousand other Bostonians—for the most part "the poorest and least successful"—who migrated elsewhere. "The shop which I had built in Boston, I lost," he told Hawkes. British troops "appropriated it for the purpose of a wash and lumber house, and eventually pulled it down and burnt it up." He owned no real estate. After seven years of war he could hardly count on customers waiting at his door. There was really nothing to go back to. Uncle Robert had died. His brothers were still there: Solomon was a fisherman and Daniel a mason, but Shubael could list himself as a gentleman. Hewes bore his loyalist brother no ill will; he named a son Shubael in 1781. But his own low estate, compared to his brother's success, must have rankled.

There is no evidence that he acquired land in Wrentham. The census names him; the records of real estate bought and sold do not. The town's tax records of the 1790s list him only as a "poll rateable," owning neither real nor personal taxable property. In 1796, at the age of fifty-four, he was assessed thirty-three cents for his Massachusetts poll tax, seven cents for his county tax, fifty cents for his town tax. He may possibly have been joint owner of a property listed in someone else's name; more likely he rented or lived on a relative's land. His uncle Joseph, a Providence physician who died in 1796, willed George and Sarah one thirty-sixth share of the estate—$580.25. The windfall helped keep him going. In 1810 he finally became a property holder in nearby Attleborough: a co-owner, with eighteen others, of "a burying yard."

That Hewes stayed poor is also suggested by what little we know about his children. Sarah Hewes gave birth to fifteen, it would seem, of whom we have the names of eleven, three girls and eight boys, possibly all who survived birth. Six were born by 1781, the rest by 1796 at the latest. The naming pattern suggests the strength of family attachments: Sally for her mother; Mary and Elizabeth for aunts, Hewes's father's sisters; Solomon, Daniel, and Shubael after his brothers. One son was named Eleven, and the last-born, George Robert Twelves Fifteen. What can we make of this? A mischievous sense of humor? His own long name, the subject of teasing in his youth, after all had been a way of getting attention. Perhaps the only inheritance a poor shoemaker-farmer-seaman could guarantee—especially to his eleventh and fifteenth children—was a name that would be a badge of distinction as his had been.

Hewes could do little for this brood. Solomon, the first-born, became a shoemaker—undoubtedly trained by his father. Robert became a blacksmith. For the other sons we know no occupations. Of the daughters, two of the three married late—Elizabeth at twenty-two but Sarah (also Sally) in her mid-thirties and Mary at thirty-two—understandable when a father could not provide a suitor with dowry, position, or a sought-after craft skill.

For opportunity the family would have to move much farther away. And so they did, like tens of thousands of families who left New England in the 1790s and early 1800s, and like a large number of New England veterans. Robert, Sally who married William Morrison, and Elizabeth who married Preserved Whipple moved to Otsego County, New York. George Fifteen went first to Connecticut, then to Richfield Springs, finally to Michigan. Solomon also moved to Otsego County for a while, then went down east to Maine, where he acquired twenty-eight acres. Eleven went to Kentucky.

What had become these years of George Hewes, the citizen? We have only one thing to go on. According to family tradition, during the War of 1812 he tried to enlist in the navy as a boatswain but was turned down; tried to ship out on the frigate *Constitution;* then tried to join Commodore Perry's fleet fighting against the British on Lake Erie. Two sons we know saw service, Eleven in the Kentucky militia and George Fifteen in Connecticut. Such patriotism in Wrentham, where there was "no rush of men" to arms, would have been extraordinary. It meant that the War of 1812 was a second War of Independence to Hewes; and to have sons who responded meant that the father had passed on well the heritage of the Revolution.

At the end of the war, perhaps before, George and Sarah Hewes went west to Richfield Springs. George was seventy-four, Sarah sixty-five. His family was dispersed, but three or four children were already in Otsego County or accompanied him there. Did he mean to spend his declining years in retirement with his family? He was still vigorous. One suspects he went in search of the "living," the "independence," that had eluded the artisan and the recognition that had eluded the citizen. He had gone from city to sea to small town; now he would try again in a place where at the least he would be with sons and daughters. And so he left Wrentham about 1815, as he had left Boston in 1775, probably with not much more than the tools of his trade. Only this time he had an old soldier's uniform as well.

VIII

In New York, Hewes did not find independence either for himself or through his children. For the last decade of his life he did not even have the haven of family. He did find recognition.

Richfield Springs, west of Albany, was no longer frontier country after 1815. The area had been opened up to homesteaders in the 1790s by Judge William Cooper, the novelist's father, who boasted of settling 50,000 families. The pioneers were already moving away to find more fertile land on better terms in western New York or the Old Northwest. Richfield Springs was located in a beautiful area of rolling hills and low mountain peaks, of streams and lakes. In the 1820s, after mineral waters were discovered, it became a resort town. But its prosperity was uneven.

What did Hewes do these years? We have more to go on for the last twenty-five years of his life than for the three decades before because a visiting historian collected some fascinating reminiscences by

Hewes's contemporaries collected in 1896. According to "an old jesting rhyme attributed to James Fenimore Cooper who knew honest Hewes,"

> Old Father Hewes, he makes good shoes,
> And sews them well together
> It has no heels but those he steals
> And begs his upper leather.

Hewes, then, was once again a poor shoemaker.

He and Sally lived in "a small house which his son Robert had built for him" on Robert's land. Sarah Morrison was nine miles away in German Flats and Elizabeth Whipple was also in the area, each with a large and growing family. Fifteen lived nearby for a time, a property holder; so did Solomon. As before, their father had no house or land of his own.

He can hardly have prospered. The clue is that when Daniel, his last surviving brother, died in 1821, Hewes travelled with Robert to Boston for five days in a one-horse wagon to secure their legacy, a third share in an estate of $2,900 and a windfall when there were no other prospects of accumulation. Hewes considered his share "a considerable sum," but it could not have stretched very far. "For some years," Hawkes wrote in 1833, Robert had "contributed what was necessary" to support his father and mother.

Sarah died in 1828, aged 77. It is difficult to bring Sarah out from her husband's shadow. He spoke of her with affection: "we lived together very happily," he told Hawkes; he expected to see her in heaven. He had hardly married her for money; he had courted her for two years. He was grief-stricken when he left her in wartime. He called her Sally, not Sarah. What was her role? A washerwoman before she was married, she labored a lifetime as a housewife, without servants. She bore, it seems, fifteen children and raised eleven of them. She was illiterate; unlike her husband, she signed her name with a mark. A daughter of a sexton, she may well have been religious. Certainly, she was apolitical. When George got home from the Tea Party, and told her his story, " 'Well George,' she said, at the end of it, *did you bring me home a lot of it?*' " "We shouldn't wonder," Thatcher added, "if Mrs. Hewes was more of a tea-drinker than a Whig." Or, we might add, more of a woman struggling to make ends meet on a shoemaker's income.

After she died, it was all downhill. George moved from one child to another, each so poor they could not long provide for him. At first, he lived with Robert, who soon after, "having met with some misfortune, was obliged to sell his house" and move farther west. For a while he was "a sojourner among friends." Then he moved in with his daughter and son-in-law, the Morrisons, but stayed only a year. "Morrison and his wife had several children," wrote Hawkes, "and were, as they are now very poor . . . Morrison not being able by his manuel [sic] services to provide for his family but a mere subsistence." Hewes had a "severe sickness." Next he took up "a short residence with a son who resides near Richfield Springs," very likely George, Jr. Soon after, he "fell down a stairway on some iron ware," severely lacerating both legs. He healed with remarkable speed for a man his age, but a son with eight children to feed could not provide "for his comfortable support." Finally, a "worthy gentleman" in the neighborhood took the old man in, and it was there that Hawkes found him in 1833, "pressed down by the iron hand of poverty" and "supported by the charity of his friends." His children had failed and, in the classic style of poor pioneers, were moving on to greener fields. They and his grandchildren would scatter, most to the Midwest, some to California, some still in mechanic trades in Boston.

In the fall of 1832 Hewes applied successfully for a veteran's pension. His application, in the hand of the county clerk to which a local judge and county official attested, gives minute details of his service. A clerk in Washington disallowed three of the months he claimed at sea, listing him for seven months', fifteen days' service as a seaman and nine months in the militia. It added up to sixteen months, fifteen days, or less than the two years required for a full pension; he was therefore prorated down to $60 a year, with $150 in arrears retroactive to 1831. It was a "miserable pittance of a soldier's pension."

Meanwhile, Hewes was winning recognition of a sort. A "venerable lady" interviewed in 1896 said she had first met Hewes in 1820 at a "house raising" where she saw "an alert and little old man with the cocked hat and faded uniform of a continental soldier, who charmed the young people with the account of the destruction of the tea in Boston in December 1773, and his stories of battles on land and sea." Another woman remembered that as a girl she had always been delighted to listen to the old soldier's stories and to see him on the Fourth of July, "when he would put on his ancient uniform, shoulder his crutch, . . . and show how fields were won." By the late 1820s, possibly earlier, Hewes had become a figure at Fourth of July observances. In 1829 the local paper reported that he "walked three miles on foot to join in the festivities," and "after mingling in the enjoyments of the occasion, with a fine flow of spirits returned in the same manner thro' the wet to home." In 1833 the celebrants toasted him as "the last survivor of the tea party," and he toasted them in turn.

The "venerable lady" also claimed to have seen "the old soldier in conversation with James Fenimore Cooper who invited Hewes to his home in Cooperstown where he was quite a lion at the author's table." This is entirely possible. The novelist, who returned to his family home at intervals, was always mining old timers for the lore of the sea and the Revolution.

This recognition, it can be argued, had a price. The old man had to dress up in his uniform and tell stories. He was trotted out once a year on Independence Day. He had to play a role; perhaps this may have contributed to his "remembering" himself almost ten years older than he was. And the already-quoted "jesting rhyme," whether Cooper's or not, suggests that if children sat at his feet to hear his tales, they also poked fun at "Old Father Hewes."

Hawkes captured a mood in Hewes that bordered on alienation, especially as he talked about his reactions to Boston in 1821, when he went there to receive his legacy. Hewes spoke on the experience in haunting, poetic language. As he walked around town, he looked for old friends.

> But, alas! I looked in vain. They were gone. Neither were those who once knew them as I did, to be found. The place where I drew my first breath and formed my most endearing attachments, had to me become a land of strangers.

He looked for familiar places.

> Not only had my former companions and friends disappeared, but the places of their habitations were occupied by those who could give no account of them. The house in which I was born was not to be found, and the spot where it stood could not be ascertained by any visible object.

The physical city of 1775 was gone.

> The whole scenery about me seemed like the work of enchantment. Beacon hill was levelled, and a pond on which had stood three mills, was filled up with its contents; over which two spacious streets had been laid and many elegant fabrics erected. The whole street, from Boston Neck to the Long Wharf, had been built up. It was to me almost as a new town, a strange city; I could hardly realize that I was in the place of my nativity.

As he stood in the market, an "aged man" stared at him, then asked,

> Was you not a citizen of Boston at the time the British tea was destroyed in Boston harbour? I replied that I was, and was one of those who aided in throwing it into the water. He then inquired who commanded the division to which I belonged in that affair; I told him one Leonard Pitt. So he did mine, said he; and I had believed there was a man by the name of Hewes aboard the same ship with me, and I think you must be that man.

They had a "social glass," reminisced, parted. "I found he as well as myself had outlived the associates of his youthful days." Hewes did his legal business, saw his nephews and nieces, and after three days headed home.

Sometime in his declining years Hewes became a Methodist. He was known to the children of the village as "The Old Saturday Man," Wilson reported, because "every Saturday for several years he walked into Richfield Springs for the purpose of being present at the services of the Methodist Church of which he was a member." This lore seems trustworthy. He had become a Bible reader ("he can still read his Bible without glasses," a grandson wrote in 1836), and Hawkes found that he "often expresses his gratitude to a kind providence, for the many favours with which he has been indulged." He was also known for his temperance, a badge of Methodists. It stuck in the memory of the "venerable lady" that at the house-raising Hewes was "perhaps the only man present who did not drink the blackstrap (a mixture of whiskey and molasses) provided for the occasion."

Hewes had not been a member of any other church in Richfield Springs and could hardly have been a Methodist before moving there. But it is not surprising that he became one. Methodism had a growing appeal to poor, hard-working people low in status, whether among shoemakers, or rural folk in the west. Richfield Springs had no fewer than three Methodist chapels scattered around the township, none of which could sustain a minister; circuit riders or laymen served them. Many things about the Methodists would have attracted Hewes: a warm atmosphere of Christian fellowship; a stress on sobriety and indus- triousness, the Franklinian virtues he had been raised on; the promise of salvation without regard to rank or wealth. This was also a church that stressed lay leadership; shoemakers could serve as stewards, "class" leaders, and lay preachers. Hewes's Methodism seems late blooming; he may have found in the fellowship of the chapel the wholehearted acceptance of himself as a person that was missing in the Fourth of July kind of recognition from the village.

IX

For Hewes, the publication of James Hawkes's *Retrospect* in 1834 led to recognition in New England, paving the way for the return of one of the "last surviving members" of the Tea Party. Hewes's attraction was his age, supposedly almost one hundred, combined with his role in a symbolic moment of the Revolution. In 1821 Hewes had been ignored. By 1835 a change in historical mood made Boston ready for him. Work- ingmen demonstrated a special identification with the artisan republi- canism of the Revolution. In May 1835, when Boston journeymen house carpenters, masons, and stone cutters went on strike, they claimed "by the blood of our fathers shed on our battle fields on the War of the Revolution, the rights of American Freeman."

In 1835 Hewes returned to New England on a triumphal tour of sorts accompanied by his youngest son, Fifteen. At Providence he was interviewed by the local newspaper, and the merchant patriarch Moses Brown called on him. On the way to Boston he stopped at Wrentham, perhaps to visit, perhaps to crow a bit. In Boston the papers noted his arrival, printing an excerpt from Hawkes's book. He was a celebrity. He stayed with his nephew Richard Brooke Hewes, Shubael's son, a politician who doubtless made the arrangements for his uncle's visit. Thatcher interviewed him for his biography, reliving his life in Boston. He sat for a portrait by Joseph G. Cole, Boston's rising young painter, entitled "The Centenarian." A group of ladies presented him with a snuffbox.

The highlight, of course, was the Fourth of July. He was the featured guest at South Boston's observance. "In a conspicuous part of the procession," according to the newspaper, "was the venerable Mr. Hewes, in a barouche, drawn by four splendid greys," accompanied by the lieutenant governor and his entourage. There was a church service and a dinner. When the orator of the day reached the Tea Party and "alluded to the venerable patriot," Hewes "arose and received the united and enthusiastic congratulations of the audience." He was supported on one side by Major Benjamin Rusell, for forty years a leader of the mechanic interest as printer and publisher, and on the other by Colonel Henry Purkitt, who had been a cooper's apprentice and, like Hewes, a Tea Party volunteer. The orator was fulsome in his tribute to Hewes, "formerly a citizen of Boston," now "on the verge of eternity": "Though you come to the land of your childhood, leaning upon a staff and feeling your dependence on the charities of a selfish world, you are surrounded by friends who feel that their prosperity is referable to the privations sacrifices and personal labors of you and your brave associates in arms." At the dinner after the toasts it was Hewes's turn. "Under the influence of strong emotion he gave the following toast, 'Those I leave behind me, May God Bless them.' "

When the celebrations ended, Hewes made his way to Augusta, Maine. Solomon, his eldest, had died there the year before, and his wife had just died, but there were grandchildren to visit. He also went to Portland, perhaps for more family. From Maine, back to Boston, and thence home to Richfield Springs.

Several things struck those who saw Hewes. The first, of course, was his great age. The second was his remarkable physical condition. Third was his wonderful mood. A correspondent of the *Boston Courier* who rode the stagecoach to Augusta was astonished that "he bore the ride of fifty-eight miles with very little apparent fatigue, amusing himself and his fellow passengers occasionally upon the route, with snatches of revolutionary songs, and by the recital of anecdotes of the days which tried mens souls." He was in his glory. And lastly, there was his demeanor. Hewes's Providence interviewer found him "even at this age, a brave, high spirited, warm hearted man, whose tongue was never controlled by ceremony, and whose manners have not been moulded by the fashion of any day. His etiquette may be tea party etiquette, but it was not acquired at tea parties in Beacon Street or Broadway." Hewes, in short, was still not taking his hat off for any man.

The remaining five years in Richfield Springs were no different than the previous twenty. "The Old Saturday Man" continued to walk to church. The veteran continued to be a guest on the Fourth of July. His family was dispersed; there were more than fifty grandchildren, and occasionally one visited him. In 1836 George Whipple, Elizabeth's son, found him "pretty well, and very jovial. He sang for me many old songs and told over all the incidents of the 'scrape' in Boston Harbor. His memory is uncommonly good for one of his age. He jumped about so when I made myself known to him he liked to have lost his drumsticks." The old man clearly was starved for company. A visit from a grandchild only underscored his isolation. In 1836 he sat for a portrait by a local artist, commissioned by a grandson. He looked smaller, shrunken.

On July 4, 1840, as Hewes was getting into a carriage to go to the annual observance, the horses bolted and he was seriously injured. He died on November 5, Pope's Day, once the "grand gala day" of Boston's apprentices. He was buried in what became the Presbyterian cemetery, where his wife already lay. There seem to have been no obituary notices, no public memorial services.

The only portrait of Hewes that survives was, in the opinion of contemporaries, "an admirable likeness." It shows a happy man of ninety-three in his moment of triumph in Boston. He wears Sunday clothes, nineteenth-century style, and leans forward in a chair, his hands firmly gripping a cane. His face is wrinkled but not ravaged; his features are full, his eyes alert. He has most of his hair. There is a twinkle in his eyes, a slightly bemused smile on his lips. The mood is one of pride. It is not a picture of a man as a shoemaker, but we can understand it only if we know the man was a shoemaker. It shows the pride of a man the world had counted as a nobody at a moment in his life when he was a somebody, when he had won recognition from a town that had never granted it before. It is the pride of a citizen, of one who "would not take his hat off to any man." The apprentice who had once deferred to John Hancock lived with the memory that Hancock had toiled side by side with him, throwing tea chests into Boston harbor. The man who had to defer to British officers, royal officials, and colonial gentry had lived to see General Washington, ship captains, and now lieutenant governors, educated lawyers, and writers defer to him.

It is the pride of a survivor. His enemies had all passed on. His "associates," the patriots, had all gone to their graves. He had outlived them all. Fortified by his religion, the old man could rejoice that he would soon join them, but as their equal. "May we meet hereafter," he told his Independence Day well-wishers, "where the wicked will cease from troubling and the true sons of Liberty be forever at rest."

Graduation ceremony at an early nineteenth-century female seminary.

Vindicating the Equality of Female Intellect

MARY BETH NORTON

In colonial America education was the concern not of schools and universities but of the family. The family and, to a lesser degree, the church were the primary means for transmitting skills, knowledge, and moral precepts. Most children learned little more than the rudimentary ABCs, taught by parents or older siblings from a Bible or almanac. A few fortunate male offspring might be sent to a formal grammar school and then, in their midteens, attend one of the colonial colleges to prepare for the ministry. Daughters were usually not educated beyond the basics. At the time of the Revolution only 50 percent of adult women in New England could sign their names, whereas the literacy rate among men stood at 80 to 90 percent.

The Revolution and the creation of a new nation, however, transformed attitudes toward schooling and the significance of education. The 1780s and 1790s became a time of major educational reform because of the widely shared notion that only an educated and informed citizenry could preserve the new republic. Although the movement for tax-supported public schools was still a generation away, this early era of educational reform proved particularly significant for women as the post-Revolutionary reformers took the first steps to provide for the formal schooling of girls. In the following selection, Mary Beth Norton looks at the changing world of female education in the decades following the Revolution. She examines how attitudes toward the female intellect changed and the value of the new girls' academies came to be appreciated. As you read this selection, note how the formal training of young women and young men differed. What do you think were the significant changes made in female educational theory and practices? How closely were the changes connected to the American Revolution?

Prior to the Revolution, Americans had paid little attention to the formal education of women. If a girl knew the rudiments of learning, that was thought to be more than sufficient for her limited needs. The education of all colonial children was haphazard at best, depending upon local and familial circumstances, but even less care was taken with girls than with boys. In the new republic, by contrast, the importance of female education was repeatedly emphasized. The Americans' vision of the ideal woman—an independent thinker and patriot, a virtuous wife, competent household manager, and knowledgeable mother—required formal instruction in a way that the earlier paragon, the notable housewife, did not. Moreover, Americans' wartime experiences convinced them that women needed broader training to prepare them for unforeseen contingencies.

These motives combined to lead to widespread changes in the education of white American girls during the postwar decades. Public education at the elementary level was opened to female as well as male children, and private academies founded in the 1780s and 1790s greatly expanded the curriculum previously offered to girls. Whereas their mothers, if they were fortunate, had had advanced training only in such ornamental accomplishments as music, dancing, French, and fancy needlework, republican girls from middling and well-to-do families could attend schools at which they were taught grammar, rhetoric, history, geography, mathematics, and some of the natural sciences. These women composed the first generation of educated female Americans; among them were teachers, missionaries, authors, and the early leaders of such nineteenth-century reform movements as abolitionism and women's rights.

The education of American children began at home. In addition to teaching youngsters behavior and manners, literate parents or older siblings instructed them in basic reading and writing. The firstborn children in any family were usually taught by their mother or perhaps by another resident adult. Later-born children often, though not always, learned the rudiments from their siblings. In neither case was the instruction entirely satisfactory; those who were cast in the role of teacher frequently complained of their inadequacies. Thus, for example, Nelly Custis Lewis remarked in 1806 that she was "not well calculated for an instructress" and that she did not know the best method

VINDICATING THE QUALITY OF FEMALE INTELLECT   From *Liberty's Daughters: The Revolutionary Experience of American Women 1750–1800* by Mary Beth Norton. Copyright © 1980 by Mary Beth Norton. By permission of Little, Brown and Company.

of teaching her daughter to read and write. But Mrs. Lewis and other parents had no alternatives: even such primary schools as existed (both public and private) would not admit pupils who did not already know the basics.

Mary Palmer Tyler's account of the educational history of her family illustrates the changes that would occur in instructional patterns over the course of a family's life cycle. Mary herself was taught to read by an unmarried aunt, but her mother heard her recite lessons in later years. When she and her sister Betsy were teenagers, they did the housework so their mother could instruct the smaller children. But Sophia, the baby of the family, was born while the senior Palmers were "so harassed with trials and afflictions they could not train their little ones as they wished to," so Mary and Betsy undertook to instruct her. Yet Mary revealed, "[W]e . . . had not been properly taught ourselves," and their efforts were not very successful. Eventually, the cycle began again after Mary's wedding to Royall Tyler, for her younger sister Amelia came to live with her in order to teach the Tyler youngsters to read.

In some households instruction began very early. At the age of twenty-two months Charles Cotesworth Pinckney, Eliza's son, could "tell all his letters in any book without hesitation and begins to spell." The farm wife Sarah Snell Bryant taught her sons Austin and Cullen to read when they were only two. Austin, who was born in April 1793, "began to read in words of two syllables" in early February 1796 and started the Bible only six weeks later. Before his third birthday, he had "read Genesis through," and by the time he was four he had completed both Old and New Testaments. Cullen, in turn, knew his alphabet at the age of sixteen months. Yet other parents were less certain that encouraging such precocity was wise. A Georgian informed her husband in 1784 that she did not plan to begin teaching their three-year-old son to read for another year. "Many sensible people will tell you," she wrote, " 'tis not right to stuff a child with learning before his mind has had time to expand." And as an adult Charles Cotesworth Pinckney urged friends not to follow his parents' example, declaring that the elderly Pinckneys' "over anxiety to make him a clever fellow" had nearly been ruinous.

Reading was taught first, then writing. Whereas the children of literate households generally knew how to read by the time they were five or six, instruction in writing did not begin until they had reached at least seven or eight. Thus, when Philip Vickers Fithian became the tutor of Robert Carter's children in 1773, he discovered that the seven-year-old was learning to spell, the ten-year-old was reading, and the thirteen-year-old was starting to write. But all three were female, and Carter may well have wanted his sons to acquire literacy skills somewhat sooner. In any event, five years later Carter himself began to teach his youngest son to write when the boy was only six and a half.

In rare instances black children learned to read and write. Both Eliza Lucas Pinckney and Elizabeth Foote Washington instructed some of their slaves in the rudiments of literacy. Thomas Jefferson's house servant Hannah, a member of the large Hubbard clan, could write with some facility, although it is not clear how she acquired that skill. But when in the 1760s Dr. Bray's Associates, an English missionary organization, attempted to open schools in Virginia and North Carolina for the instruction of black children, especially girls, they met with both indifference and resistance from the children's masters and mistresses. One discouraged emissary of the group reported in 1767 that he could attract no more than eight or nine pupils to a school he had planned for a minimum of fifteen. "I had agreed with the Mistress to teach the girls to Sew, knit and Mark, thinking that wou'd excite people to send young negroe girls, but I find they wou'd rather their Slaves shou'd remain Ignorant as brutes," he explained to his superiors in London.

As an alternative or supplement to home education, white children who lived in towns or cities could be sent to dame schools. Such schools . . . were usually established by women who needed a means of support. Few instructors were as well qualified as Sarah Osborn, who had briefly attended a female academy in England before her parents emigrated to the colonies. In fact, many of the so-called schools seem to have been little more than baby-sitting establishments. Certainly some mothers used them that way: a Nova Scotian explained, for instance, that she sent her young son to school "merely that he may be kept from Mischief, for he has no idea of learning as yet." Similarly, Mary and Betsy Palmer first attended dame school on a day when company was coming to dinner and their mother wanted them out of the house. A Virginian who attended such an establishment in Norfolk in the 1750s described her teacher, "a poor old dame by the name of Mrs. Drudge, and, to be sure, she did drudge to teach me my letters—spelling and reading after a fashion."

A girl in prerevolutionary America could progress beyond these bare rudiments only through some combination of her own initiative, the inclination of her parents, and the proximity of one of the "adventure schools" that, before the 1780s, constituted the sole means through which girls could gain access to advanced training. Boys could attend private or public grammar schools and eventually colleges like Harvard, Yale, William and Mary, or Princeton, but their sisters' formal education was effectively halted at the primary level. Like dame schools, adventure schools catering to girls were usually run by women or perhaps by married couples. Located in the homes of the instructors, they were short-lived, with no staff other than the owners, and their course of study stressed ornamental accomplishments. By the 1760s, adventure schools teaching music, dancing, drawing and painting, fancy neeedlework, and handicrafts flourished in every colonial city along with other similar establishments offering some instruction in advanced writing, grammar, and arithmetic. But as late as 1782 a New Englander complained about Boston: "[W]e don't pretend to teach ye female part of ye town anything more than dancing, or a little music perhaps. . . . I will venture to say that a lady is a rarity among us who can write a page of commonplace sentiment, the words being well spelt, & ye style & language kept up with purity & elegance."

One of the best known of these schools, and perhaps the one with the most rigorous curriculum, was that founded in Philadelphia by Anthony Benezet. First established in 1754, it continued for some years under his direction. Among Benezet's pupils was Elizabeth Sandwith Drinker, whose diary entries in the 1780s and 1790s recalling her school days testify to his lasting impact on his students. But Benezet's school was clearly anomalous, even in forward-looking Philadelphia. More common were the several establishments like those attended by the Philadelphian Sally Powel between 1759 and 1766. The accounts for her education detail outlays for crewel work, "fraims Glasses, & Matirials for wax Work & painting," a French language teacher, prints to be copied with "several sorts of paint Gum & Brushes," and a "Master for Learning Artificial Fruits."

Girls would often attend a number of such establishments simultaneously. In 1771–1772, for example, the Bostonian Anna Winslow went to one school for sewing and another for writing. Elizabeth Murray, who herself had taught needlework, sent her niece Dolly to separate schools for sewing, dancing, writing, reading, and fancywork. "I tried her to sew att home," Elizabeth told Dolly's father in 1756, "but people coming out & in so much to the shop took her of[f] so much she made nothing of it." During the winter Dolly received instruction only in reading and sewing, for, Elizabeth explained, "she cannot attend so many schools in the cold wether to advantage." The chance for even such a limited education as this was denied to northern farm girls, though, for the schools rarely made provisions for boarding their pupils. Only wealthy or middling urban residents could attend them.

In the plantation South the pattern differed considerably, since well-to-do girls were taught by tutors hired chiefly for their brothers, and poor girls had no instructors other than members of their own families. The Carter sisters, pupils of Philip Fithian, learned basic reading, writing, and arithmetic from him while their brothers were being taught advanced grammar, Latin, and Greek. Fithian's attempts to keep his female charges at their studies were continually frustrated by frequent interruptions for music lessons, dancing schools, and visits to neighbors with their mother. Both the Carters and their daughters, in other words, saw academic instruction as less important to the girls than training in ornamental skills. Judging by wealthy southerners' lack of attention to their daughters' advancement in learning—as distinct from domestic accomplishments and musical training—southern girls were even less likely to receive an advanced education than were their northern counterparts.

A notable exception was Eliza Lucas, whose father sent her to school in England because he believed that a stress on education in needle-work alone left girls' minds "vacant and uninformed." Eliza early established a habit of reading voraciously in French as well as English, and just before her marriage to Charles Pinckney she thanked her father "[for] the pains and mony you laid out in my Education which I esteem a more valuable fortune than any you could now have given me." The contrast to John Hunt, a Harvard graduate, could not have been sharper. According to his granddaughter Mary Palmer Tyler, Hunt adhered "tenaciously" to the principle that boys should go to college, "but girls knew quite enough if they could make a shirt and a pudding." Mary further recalled that her grandmother Hunt "often lectured me and others on our waste of time because we would read while tending baby brothers and sisters," for she thought they should be sewing instead. Thus Mary's mother, Betsy Hunt, had to be educated largely by her husband, Joseph Palmer, who systematically introduced her to literature, history, geography, and arithmetic, as well as overseeing her practice in writing. Betsy's sister Catherine was not so fortunate: because she never learned to write, she was unable to respond when an infatuated suitor began to court her by mail.

Since most colonial parents resembled the Hunts rather than George Lucas, much depended on a girl's own initiative. Accounts of prominent women who reached adulthood before the Revolution uniformly stress their precocity and love of learning. Sarah Franklin Bache insisted on studying French, although her mother "had no desire of her larning that Language." Ann Eliza Bleecker, the poet from upstate New York, was so "passionately fond of books" as a child that she had already read many "long before the time that children in common pass their Spelling-Books." Elizabeth Graeme Fergusson, according to her admirer Benjamin Rush, "discovered, in early life, signs of uncommon talents and virtues." And Harriott Pinckney Horry, whose mother Eliza had early noted and "indulge[d]" her fondness for learning, studied Latin as a girl, in later years teaching herself algebra and geometry by using textbooks borrowed from her younger brother.

Women with less initiative keenly felt their lack of education when they reached adulthood. For the most part, their distress centered upon their inability to spell, write, and "indite" (compose) letters properly. In the eighteenth century the ability to write a good letter was the mark of an educated person. "To be greatly deficient in this matter is almost inexcusable in one of our Sex" who has any social standing, Eliza Lucas Pinckney once explained. Consequently, colonial women referred repeatedly in their letters to their shame at their lack of writing skills. Those who had reached maturity by the middle years of the century, and who had therefore been educated much earlier, were especially sensitive on the subject. "Pray excuse my bat riting and inditing," wrote Abiah Franklin, mother of Jane and Benjamin, in 1751. Thirteen years later Joseph Reed's embarrassed grandmother told him, "I have but one ours warning to rite this in and you will i am sur mack allowins for the shortnis of time and bad riting and wors spalling." The next generation of female Americans labored under the same handicap, and a number of them confessed to being "very avers" to writing. "Nothing would have induced me to set pen to paper but righting to so Dear a friend who I know will Escuse all Erors in righting & Endighing," said Deborah Cushing of Massachusetts to her husband in 1774.

For such women, writing even a "few lins" was "a great undertaken," as a Virginian told a male relative in 1801. "The employment of the pen is of all others the most fatiguing to me," the elderly New Yorker Joyce Myers disclosed to her daughter Rebecca Mordecai, as she explained why she did not write more frequently. A common lament of these older women was the fact that they had had little writing practice in girlhood. Consequently, they repeatedly urged their younger female relatives to improve their handwriting. "Tho I write a bad hand yours shou'd be better," Grace Galloway informed her daughter Betsy in 1780; five years later Abigail Adams acknowledged the deficiencies of her own untutored writing, then revealed to a niece, "[I]t is from feeling the disadvantages of it myself, that I am the more solicitous that my young acquaintance should excel me."

Mrs. Adams's keen sense of deprivation led her to criticize the "trifling narrow contracted Education of the Females" in America during her wartime correspondence with her husband. "If you complain of neglect of Education in sons, What shall I say with regard to daughters?" she asked him rhetorically in 1776. Yet it was to John's protégé John Thaxter that Abigail Adams spoke most vehemently on the subject. It is "mortifying," she told him in early 1778, to see "the difference of Education betweeen the male and female Sex, even in those families where Education is attended too." Perhaps, she hypothesized darkly, men sought to deprive their "companions and associates" of schooling because of "an ungenerous jealo[u]sy of rivals near the Throne."

Apart from Mrs. Adams's letters, there is little evidence that American women before the 1780s perceived their lack of educational opportunity as a circumstance that called for a societal remedy. By failing to complain about the poor instruction they received in other than personal terms, female colonists demonstrated how restricted were their self-conceptions and aspirations. The very idea that their access to education could (or should) be improved was so alien that it never occurred to them. They may have decried their rudimentary literacy, but few of them took the further step of suggesting that the situation could be corrected. Only during the postwar years did American women begin to argue systematically that members of their sex should be better educated.

Reformers seeking to improve female education in the United States during the 1780s and 1790s had to confront a major problem: the traditional argument that excessive learning would "unsex" women. Since it was commonly contended that men and women had different natures, corresponding to their divergent roles in life, most persons believed that woman's intellect, though equal to man's, had quite different qualities. "Nature appears to have formed the faculties of your sex for the most part with less vigour than those of ours," the Reverend James Fordyce told his female readers, pointing out women's "defect in point of depth and force," a failing offset by their "sentiment" and "uncommon penetration in what relates to characters." He recommended that women concentrate on "refined" rather than "profound" subjects, and that they avoid studies irrelevant to the "milder modes of life." The Reverend John Bennett, another popular English author, revealed the reason why females should shun such topics as "politics, philosophy, mathematics, or metaphysics": "They would render you unwomanly indeed. They would damp that vivacity, and destroy that disengaged ease and softness, which are the very essence of your graces."

An improper education, in short, could threaten woman's sexual identity itself. So Dr. Bennet suggested, "[L]et your knowledge be feminine, as well as your person," and Alphonzo, the American essayist, proclaimed in 1788, "[T]o be *lovely* then you must be content to be *women*; to be mild, social and sentimental—to be acquainted with all that belongs to your department—and leave the masculine virtues, and the profound researches of study to the province of the other sex." Neither Bennet nor Alphonzo proposed to deny all education to women; quite the contrary, Alphonzo wrote, "[L]earning or an acquaintance with books may be a very agreeable . . . accomplishment" in a woman. The difficulty was caused when a female tried to go beyond the knowledge appropriate to her sex, for then she risked becoming that universal object of ridicule and reproach, a "learned lady," a "female pedant." An American poet put it this way: if women felt advanced learning's "strict embrace,"

> Farewell to ev'ry winning grace;
> Farewell to ev'ry pleasing art,
> That binds in chains the yielding heart; . . .

At her approach the roses fade,
Each charm forsakes th' astonish'd maid;
And o'er her face, of sickly pale,
Thought slowly draws its loathsome veil.

The educational reformers had to find an effective means of countering such conservative arguments. They fervently believed that the United States had to improve the academic training available to its female citizens, for the survival of the republic required it, yet traditional attitudes seemed to place an insurmountable barrier in their path. In order to circumvent the conventional objections to advanced education for women, then, the reformers developed three separate but intertwined arguments. The first insisted that education would not "unsex" women but would instead make them better wives, mothers, and mistresses of households. The second stressed the "feminine" nature of the instruction proposed for girls by carefully delineating the curriculum and emphasizing the cultivation of proper behavior. Neither of these first two contentions challenged the traditional ends of female education, but the third, which was based upon the novel circumstances of the republic, turned the requirements of republican citizenship into a justification for changing educational goals. In the hands of the conservative Benjamin Rush, the latter tack led to an emphasis on a strictly utilitarian course of study; in the hands of the more radical Judith Sargent Murray, it implied a sharp break with the past and an attempt to give women an education truly comparable to men's.

Eliza Southgate adopted the first approach in 1801, when a male cousin berated her for advocating improved academic training for women. "You ask if this plan of education will render one a more dutiful child, a more affectionate wife, etc, etc, surely it will," she asserted. "A sense of duty, and a mind sufficiently strengthened not to yield implicitly to every impulse, will give a degree of uniformity, of stability to the female character, which it evidently at present does not possess." Abigail Adams, too, found this argument persuasive. "It is very certain, that a well-informed woman, conscious of her nature and dignity, is more capable of performing the relative duties of life, and of engaging and retaining the affections of a man of understanding, than one whose intellectual endowments rise not above the common level," she declared in 1814.

But simple assertions that a broader education for girls would not create the despised "learned ladies" were obviously insufficient to convince the doubtful, and so, paradoxically, the reformers stressed the need to restrict female education at the same time they were arguing for its expansion. By emphasizing the behavioral goals they sought, they downplayed the importance of purely intellectual accomplishments, and by devising their curriculum solely on the basis of its utility for future wives and mothers, they eliminated its more threatening aspects.

Thus Noah Webster, for instance, defined a good education as that which "renders the ladies correct in their manners, respectable in their families, and agreeable in society," making no mention of fostering their intellectual development. A woman's "real merit," he declared, lay in her "domestic worth." Other republican authors echoed the same themes. In 1793, a contributor to the *Lady's Magazine* proclaimed, "[L]et them be taught that domestic usefulness is before modern refinement, and that to manage a family with economy, is far beyond touching a harpsichord." It was not that women should be trained only in domestic occupations, for that was the stance the reformers rejected; rather, the goals of female education were viewed as behavioral and utilitarian instead of intellectual or ornamental. "Lavinia" made this clear in an essay printed in Caleb Bingham's *American Preceptor*. No woman should pursue a subject to the point at which it would "interrupt or supersede domestic employments," she observed, "for these require attention in a greater or less degree from every woman; and unless she understand and discharge them according to her circumstances, she is contemptible and useless."

The dilemma confronting these educators is nowhere more fully apparent than in the Reverend Penuel Bowen's "Upon Virtue in general, and female Education & manners in particular," the address he delivered on November 26, 1786, as he opened his "English Academy for young Ladies & Misses" in Savannah, Georgia. The New England cleric stressed the equality of the sexes, while still pointing out that woman has "her proper station, & her part to act; partly common w[i]th man, & partly peculiar to herself." He went on to discuss female virtue in great detail, embarking upon a series of complex philosophical digressions that must have mystified his audience of prospective pupils and their parents. At least Bowen's conclusion was unambiguous: "[T]he great polar object of female education" was "to nurture & fix the principles of virtue; the Virtues especially proper to the sex: such as are best calculated to render you most accomplished for your department in life."

No goal could have been more traditional, but Bowen, like other reformers, proposed to achieve his end by improving the curriculum. He accordingly told his students, "[Y]our ideas should not be compressed, or shut up within a small circle or particular place, but so open & expanded to comprehend more general & generous sentiments & opinions." Nevertheless, he observed, "[T]o become *much* learned is not an essential requisite in a female. The professions are not proper to the sex, it is not looked for in you to be doctresses, teachers of the arts & sciences, politicks or laws." Yet Bowen had the honesty to admit, "[I]t strikes me as wrongly timeing & placing *here,* anything against Books & reading," because if there was a problem with female learning in America, particularly in the South, it was a "deficiency' rather than a "superabundance." After such intricate waffling, Bowen ultimately resolved his confusion conventionally, by arguing that girls should receive a basic, practical education which attended to their moral development as well as to their academic achievement.

Penuel Bowen's contradictory statements starkly exposed the conceptual problems that lay behind the more conservative reformers' position on female education. They understood that the instruction of girls had to be improved, that keeping the female population in ignorance of higher learning could no longer be justified, yet on the other hand they did not want to change the end product. The better-educated woman was to resemble her ideal predecessor in all important respects. What then could be the rationale for altering the mode of female education, and, in particular, alerting it in the manner they proposed, by increasing the academic content of the curriculum? Bowen's floundering was ultimately caused by the fact that he was in effect prescribing an irrelevant remedy for a disease he did not believe existed.

Benjamin Rush avoided these difficulties through the use of a more consistently utilitarian framework in his "Thoughts upon Female Education," an address delivered to the Philadelphia Young Ladies Academy—which he had helped to found—in 1787. Rush's proposed curriculum was based upon his assumption that "female education should be accommodated to the state of society, manners, and government" in the United States. Therefore, he said, it had to be "conducted upon principles very different from what it is in Great Britain, and in some respects different from what it was when we were part of a monarchical empire." American women, he declared, should be trained in bookkeeping and writing so they could assist their husbands or eventually administer their estates; should be acquainted with history, geography, natural philosophy, and religion so they could teach their children more effectively; and should not concentrate their attention on such frivolous and distracting accomplishments as drawing, French, and instrumental music. He did, on the other hand, find vocal music and dancing acceptable, because singing would enable a woman "to soothe the cares of a domestic life" and dancing "promotes health and renders the figure and motions of the body easy and agreeable."

Rush's formula constituted a genuine step forward. By justifying his suggested reforms through reference to the demands of a republican society, he linked women's private development to political imperatives. His emphasis on utility led him to make a much stronger case for the improvement of female education than had the Reverend Mr. Bowen, who was mired in traditional ways of thinking. Unlike Bowen,

Rush did want to change the end product; he did want to create a new type of American woman. Yet even so his conception was severely limited. The shortcomings of his approach—and of that taken by the other educators connected with the Philadelphia Young Ladies Academy—can be seen in the contrast between two addresses by the Reverend Samuel Magaw, one to the academy in 1787 and the other at the University of Pennsylvania five years earlier.

At the Young Ladies Academy Magaw was careful to note that he did not advocate "excessive refinement, or deep erudition" for young women, nor was it necessary for a female to have "a classical education, even with respect to her own tongue." He stressed that "all should be formed to the habits of obedience, and a placid graceful attention to whatever duty they may be concerned in." Although he then outlined a broad course of study, Magaw's aim was conservative: the creation of "sensible, virtuous, sweet-tempered women." The contrast to his prescription for the education of the girls' male contemporaries was remarkable. To them he recommended the perusal of Latin and Greek "with critical exactness," because a superficial knowledge would be insufficient. To them he spoke of the "higher exercise of the mind," the development of speculative and rational powers, the study of metaphysics, logic, and rhetoric, in addition to the history, geography, and other topics also suggested for girls. At the university, Magaw described the need "to trim and brighten the golden lamp of learning"; at the academy, he talked of the need to protect the young ladies' "innocence and delicacy."

Magaw and Rush accordingly took a restricted view of even a reformed female education, but some of their republican contemporaries adopted a more enlightened approach. A few men and a larger number of women were convinced that domestic excellence alone was not an adequate goal for females; that women should be able to participate in all areas of study; and that, above all else, like their male counterparts, women students should learn how to reason. Together, these authors advocated a radical departure from past practice.

"Reflections on What is Called Amiable Weakness in Woman," an anonymous essay that appeared in the *Lady and Gentleman's Pocket Magazine of Literature and Polite Amusement* in 1796, stressed the first of these three contentions. Significantly, the author declared that girls should aspire to be more than "*mere* notable women." He would have agreed with the "American Lady" who published "A Second Vindication of the Rights of Women" five years later that "a good kitchen woman, very seldom makes a desirable wife, to a man of any refinement." Can a woman believe that "she was only made to submit to man, her equal?" he inquired. "Can she be content to be occupied merely to please him . . . ? And can she rest supinely dependent on man for reason, when she ought to mount with him the arduous steeps of knowledge?" The "American Lady" concurred. Although females should acquire domestic skills, she argued, yet ought they "therefore to be necessarily excluded from a participation in those improvements that tend to dignify human nature"? The "greatest and most exalted prerogative" of man, "granted from his Creator," was *"freedom of thought, will, and action.* Woman is indisputably included in this grant." But females could not fully realize their potential, she observed, as long as men compelled them "to act inconsistently with their better knowledge and experience, to effect ignorance for fear of giving offence by evincing a superior judgement," or made them "believe that they can best please by prattling incoherent smalltalk." Men had to accept women as equals, and to afford them equal access to knowledge, in order to complete "women's emancipation from injustice and oppression."

Those who believed with this "American Lady" that the key to progress lay in opening learning of all sorts to women refused to accept the sorts of curricular limitations outlined by more conservative thinkers. "Since we have the same natural abilities as themselves," asked a female author in the *New York Magazine* in 1794, "why should we not have the same opportunity of polishing and displaying them by the principles of an independent and virtuous education?" Drawing an intriguing, if inexact, analogy between women's quest for learning and the male rebels' fight for independence, she declared, "[S]ince the Americans have bravely established their liberties, (notwithstanding the vain efforts of tyranny) we hope their modesty will keep them from exercising that despotism over us, which they so openly despised in their masters." She then expressed the hope that men would soon place "the fair sex on an equal footing with themselves, enjoying all the blessings of freedom." Two essayists in the *Massachusetts Magazine* in 1789 developed similar themes. "The Speculator" urged his readers, "[L]et merit and not sex, be the criterion by which we shall determine the most proper subjects [i.e., pupils] for the culturing hand of science to polish," and "Sophronia," in recounting the address delivered by the preceptress general of the mythical Massachusetts Publick Female Academy, stated her belief that men and women should have equivalent educational opportunities.

The final step in this chain of reasoning was taken only by a few. More persons were willing to criticize the restricted schooling offered to women and to advocate its improvement in general terms than wished to hold out to them the identical educational goal ultimately placed before men: training in the exercise of their rational faculties. One of the rare males to do so was one of the Harvard students who contributed to "The Competitor" series in the *Boston Magazine*. "Anaximander" complained that the education currently available to girls was "highly derogatory to their dignity." He accordingly outlined a curriculum that included the study not only of music and geography but also of the sciences, especially astronomy. Rejecting contentions that well-educated women would be "self sufficient, vain and pedantic," he declared unhesitatingly that "the great aim in all their pursuits, should be to obtain, upon a liberal, unbiassed plan, the art of thinking." Sarah Pierce, the Litchfield, Connecticut, educator, adopted this as her primary goal. In an address to her students at the close of the 1818 school year, she revealed the aims her academy had sought since its inception in 1792. In order to "vindicate the equality of female intellect," she had tried to cultivate three faculties of the mind in particular: memory, imagination, and reason. The latter was by far the most important, she noted, for formal instruction would simply place students "on the threshold of improvement." Thereafter, they would have to rely upon "the acuteness of excellent reasoning" to guide them through life.

Judith Sargent Murray, in accord with her innovative approach to women's status and role in the early republic, also placed great stress upon rational thinking as the chief aim of female education. Girls should be taught "to reason, investigate, and compare, and to invigorate their understandings by a comprehension, and a consequent adoption of those arguments which result from sound sense, and are recognized by truth," she asserted. And so she described for the readers of *The Gleaner* her vision of the ideal female: "a sensible and informed woman—companionable and serious—possessing also a facility of temper, and united to a congenial mind—blest with competency—and rearing to maturity a promising family of children."

Although they differed significantly among themselves, Murray, Rush, Pierce, and the other republican reformers all advocated educational opportunities for American girls more advanced than those available to their English and European contemporaries. In Britain the last decades of the eighteenth century witnessed no comparable upsurge in reformist impulses concerning female education, no vast expansion in the number of female academies. The most advanced thinkers of the day in England—Hannah More, Erasmus Darwin, and Thomas Gisborne—continued to emphasize ornamental accomplishments rather than the practical necessities of domesticity and motherhood. They were even more concerned about inculcating properly feminine behavior than were Webster, Bowen, and Rush, and they failed to stress the cultivation of woman's intellectual powers with the same fervor that moved Murray. Darwin, perhaps the most radical of all (with the notable exception of Mary Wollstonecraft), sounded more like American conservatives than like Judith Sargent Murray or Sarah Pierce, writing in 1797 of the necessity for women to be "pliant," to display "the mild and retiring virtues," and to avoid demonstrating "great apparent strength of character," lest men be alarmed. The more advanced American thinkers had long since abandoned such restrictive modes of discourse.

The fact that the English approach to female education diverged so sharply from that taken in the United States underscores the revolutionary origins of American ideas. To their developing national ideology, American girls owed the stress in their education on domesticity and motherhood; to wartime disruptions, the emphasis on creation of independent, rational female adults. Neither concern was evident in the thinking of foreign educational theorists.

The aims of the Americans were thus distinctive for their time. But most of the founders of academies sought the limited goals outlined by Rush and Webster rather than the more radical ones promulgated by Judith Sargent Murray and Sarah Pierce. Were the new republican academies, then, little more than a continuation of the adventure-school tradition, albeit with a new emphasis on practical achievement, or were they indeed a new creation? What sort of training did their pupils receive, and what eventually became of those students? No examination of postwar education would be complete without attention to these questions.

As the Reverend Ezra Stiles observed in 1786, during the postwar years "the Spirit for Academy making" was "vigorous." The event that elicited Stiles's comment was Timothy Dwight's announcement that he had opened his school in Greenfield Hill, Connecticut, to girls as well as boys, "promis[in]g to carry them thro' a Course of belles Lettres, Geography, Philosophy, & Astronomy." In addition to institutions like Dwight's, once restricted to boys but now encompassing girls, a number of academies were founded solely for the instruction of females. In Philadelphia, there was John Poor's school and its successor, the Young Ladies Academy, and in New York City Isabella Graham, a Scottish immigrant, established a school with the assistance of her daughter, Joanna Bethune. During the same decade Caleb Bingham and Jedidiah Morse started girls' schools in Boston and New Haven, respectively; and William Woodbridge, who later claimed the distinction of having run "the first female school . . . that ever was attempted in New England, above the district schools" because he had taught evening classes to a group of girls while he was a Yale undergraduate in 1779, opened his academy for young ladies in Medford, Massachusetts. The 1790s brought the founding of Susanna Rowson's academy, also in Medford, and Sarah Pierce's school in Litchfield. These were but the best known of a large number of similar establishments that, within the space of two decades, suddenly made higher education available to young American women from middling and well-to-do families.

The academies shared four characteristics that distinguished them from the adventure schools of the colonial years. Although they usually offered instruction in some ornamental accomplishments, needle-work, music, and dancing played a relatively small role in their overall curricula. At the same time, they stressed the study of such academic subjects as composition, history, and geography, thus helping to close the gap that had traditionally separated the education of girls from that of their brothers. Further, instead of being concentrated in major cities and serving only urban residents, many of the academies were located in small towns and drew boarding pupils from throughout the nation. Among the students at Sarah Pierce's school in 1802, for example, were thirteen from Litchfield, nine from other Connecticut towns, six from Georgia, five from New York, two from Massachusetts, two from New Hampshire, and three from the West Indies. Third, the academies often developed more of an institutional base than had the adventure schools, which had normally been run by a single woman. They acquired permanent buildings, hired additional teachers as their student bodies increased, and relied upon financial support from the communities in which they were based. Consequently, they exhibited a fourth attribute that differentiated them from their predecessors: they tended to be longer lived. Whereas the adventure schools rarely continued for more than two or three years at most, some of the academies survived well into the nineteenth century and a few even have lineal descendants in operation today.

Significantly, the South lagged behind the North in the founding of such academies, and so planter families who wanted their daughters to receive advanced instruction had to send them to northern institutions. In 1785, Judith Randolph, envious of Patsy Jefferson's experiences in a French convent school, lamented to her future sister-in-law, "[M]y prospect for a tolerable education, is but a bad one, which in my opinion is one of the greatest disadvantages which the Virginia Girls, are attended with." As late as 1801, Sarah Pierce's nephew Timothy found the situation no better. On a visit to South Carolina, he recorded his disappointment that "little attention is paid to the cultivation of the mind" of Charleston girls.

The reasons for the South's belated conversion to the cause of advanced female education—its first school on the northern model was that founded by Jacob Mordecai in Warrenton, North Carolina, in 1809—lay in what one foreign visitor in 1799 termed "the baleful effects of the revolutionary war." The South in general suffered far greater war-time losses than did the North, and those losses were concentrated in the later years of the conflict. By the mid-1780s Philadelphia, Boston, and even New York City had largely recovered from the impact of the war, but the same was not true of the South. When the Reverend Penuel Bowen arrived in Savannah in 1786, for instance, he found the public buildings "going to rack & ruin." The Georgians "were distressed & torn to pieces by the war in this place & neighborhood," he told a relative; "the common observation among them is, they have not had time yet to gain the ground they lost." Other visitors to the South from the mid-1780s to the mid-1790s likewise noted seeing "the ravages of war wherever [they] went" or described in detail "the many charred ruins that still remain." As late as 1790, a Georgian predicted that few planters "can expect to live long enough to see them[selves] recover their former Situation."

Under such circumstances, David Ramsay later wrote, "[T]o reproduce a state of things favorable to social happiness, required all the energies of the well disposed inhabitants." Instead of devoting their resources to such frills as better education for their daughters (and sons), white southerners, recalled a Carolina boy born in 1785, strained "every nerve . . . to repair the broken fortunes of the Planters by the severest thrift and patient industry." To that end, all the money they could spare was allocated to the purchase of slaves to replace those lost during the war. In early 1784, a Georgia merchant commented accurately, "[T]he Negro business is a great object with us. . . . The Planter will as far as in his power sacrifice every thing to attain Negroes." So the Carolinian observed that in his youth "schools, churches, with all the requisites of refinements and amenities of life were sadly neglected."

If southern girls were to acquire an advanced education during the immediate postwar decades, then, they had to be sent far from home. Indeed, the same could have been said of northern girls as well, for they too had to leave their families in order to attend school, unless they were fortunate enough to reside in one of the towns that also housed an academy. Since female whites had usually lived at home until marriage, those enrolled at boarding schools constituted the first generation of well-to-do American girls who lived away from home and relatives for lengthy periods. The novelty of the experience seems to have made the pain of parting especially intense. Indeed, the sense of loss evident in the correspondence of students and their families makes it clear that only the strongest of motives could have prompted their separation. In 1807, after a conversation with her daughter Bess, a boarding-school pupil, the New Yorker Elizabeth Kent told her husband, James, "I almost regret we ever agreed to send her, she takes it so very hard, she Cries very much & says she shall never be reconciled to live there a year—she likes the school & likes her Boarding place exceedingly but the being away from home almost kills her." The only thing that sustained parents and their daughters through such difficult times was a recognition of the significance of the enterprise upon which they had embarked.

The contents of their letters reveal the extent of the change that had occurred in Americans' attitude toward female education. "I consider it a duty I owe you to send you from me and trust you will improve much more then you would at Home," a New Yorker told her daughter in 1806. Admitting ruefully that she had "burst into tears" from homesickness when she first arrived at Wyman's academy in Medford, Eliza Southgate promised her parents in 1797 "[to] think of the duty that now attends me, to think that here I may drink freely of the fountain of knowledge."

In the republic, in short, the education of girls had become a "duty"—a duty their parents owed them, a duty they owed themselves. Whereas parents had once referred only to the need for their daughters to acquire good work habits, they now spoke of improvement, advancement, emulation. Their words conveyed a very different message from the common colonial injunction to girls to be industrious and simultaneously exposed a major shift in attitudes. For the first time, American daughters as well as sons were being told that they could "improve."

"Let your Studies call your first Attention they will lay the Ground Work for Pleasures hereafter," a Rhode Islander instructed her daughter in 1786, when the girl was in school in Boston; "[N]ow is your Goalden Age for the Acquirement of the best and Most Sellibrated Education of the Sex, pray let me Intreet your best Exertions," her father added. In 1801, a Virginia woman reminded her daughter, "[Y]ou know how anxious I am, that you shou'd be Clever as well as good," urging, "be studious, & . . . take every advantage to improve your mind that falls in your way." Significantly, parents urged their daughters to learn to think for themselves, to study subjects in depth, and to prepare for future usefulness. A New Yorker in 1794 advised, "[W]hatever you learn remember that you will receive no Benefit form it without making yourself Mistress of it." Studying with "a great deal of reflection," he explained, "will enable you to form sentiments of your own which is more useful than those you borrow." That same year Sarah Jay told her oldest daughter, Maria, then a student at the Moravian Seminary for Young Ladies in Bethlehem, Pennsylvania, "[I]f you reflect that on your present endeavors, may hereafter depend the satisfaction of rearing a family agreeably to your wishes, it will I'm sure stimulate you to improve every advantage."

Mothers' remarks on their daughters' education occasionally contained special overtones. In Atkinson, New Hampshire, Elizabeth Smith Peabody, who had long complained, "[M]y Sex have been cruelly injured, in the unjust niggardly distructive mode of Education," took great pains to ensure that her daughter could attend a nearby academy and expressed her delight at the fact that a woman was no longer "considered a Pheonix" if she could merely "write *intelligbly*." "Oh my sister," she exclaimed to Mary Cranch, "what an advantage the youth of the present day have, compared with former times." Similarly, a Virginian whose mother had refused to allow her to attend an adventure school in the 1760s saw to it that her daughter went to a boarding school twenty years later. And when in the 1820s Cornelia Boardman, the daughter of Mary Anna Whiting Boardman, expressed the hope that her school days would soon be over, her mother decisively rebuked her. Mary Anna had been educated at Jedidiah Morse's New Haven school in the mid-1780s, and so she had had better academic training than many of the women of her generation. She valued that education, yet still regretted that she had not had the opportunities her daughter now did. "I am covetous of your school-days," she told Cornelia, "and I do not like you to lose *one* of them." Obviously recalling her own experience, Mary Anna asked her, "[W]hy do you speak with exultation of leaving school? I am much mistaken, if you do not say, twenty years hence, if you live so long, that your school days were the happiest of your life." Her chief fear was, she revealed, "[Y]ou do not improve as fast as you might, because you do not love study as you ought."

But if Cornelia Boardman did not in fact "love study," she appears to have been an exception. Many republican girls hardly needed parental injunctions to encourage them to be studious. Like Eliza Southgate, young women understood that they had the chance for a better education than that available to any previous generation of female Americans, and they were determined to take full advantage of their favored position.

Nelly Curtis Lewis's daughter Parke, for example, attended a Philadelphia school at her own "earnest wish," though her mother (who had been a pupil of Isabella Graham) had vowed not to send her away from home to an academy. Kitty Duane, another of Graham's students, worked "to the utmost of her capacity, making the most of her time & opportunities" in 1795–1796. Describing Kitty as "indefatigable," Mrs. Graham reported to her father, James Duane, the New York politician, that the girl had decided to forgo instruction in drawing and embroidery, "finding all her time necessary to accomplish that degree of perfection in her studies that she wished, & has chosen those branches which are likely to give her most enjoyment through life," namely reading, grammar, and geography. Eliza Southgate likewise informed her family in the summer of 1797, "I fear that the time allotted for my stay here will be too short for me to go so far as I wish" in arithmetic. She accordingly asked to remain in school for several additional months, explaining, "[Because of] a strong desire to possess more useful knowledge than I at present do, I can dispense with the pleasure a little longer of beholding my friends."

The same desire to learn also infected girls who were unable to attend the academies, or who had graduated from them but wished to continue their education. Patty Hitchcock, a tavernkeeper's daughter from Brookfield, Massachusetts, felt "mortified" that since she was necessarily "a slave to business" she had "very inferior" chances "for cultivating both mind & manners." Consequently, her brother sought the advice of their uncle Enos, the child-rearing theorist, as to how she could educate herself. Some years later another New Englander took similar action. "[I] am not satisfied with remaining ignorant as I am of much important knowledge," she told her schoolteacher brother-in-law, asking him to recommend a "future course of reading." In North Carolina, Anne Iredell "entankled [her]self in a course of modern history" and also read the works of Lord Kames, through which she was introduced to Aristotle's logic. In Massachusetts, Ann Jean Robbins, a great-niece of Elizabeth Murray Inman, read a number of leading works in the fields of metaphysics and ethics in the four years after she left school.

The examples could be multiplied endlessly, but the point has been made: advanced learning, so long forbidden to women in America, had become a goal to which they could legitimately aspire. Indeed, as William Woodbridge later remarked, "[T]he love of reading and habits of application became fashionable, and *fashion* we know is the mistress of the world." Part of that new fashion was evident in women's comments on the intellectual capacities of the other females they encountered. Whereas they had once remarked solely upon the "softness" and "delicacy" of new acquaintances, they now began to assess their friends' mental abilities: she "posses[ses] a mind naturely strong, which is intirely improved and cultivated"; she is (or is not) "well informed"; she has "an excellent understanding, a cultivated mind, & a lively imagination." When Gertrude Ogden Meredith, a Philadelphia intellectual and author, visited Baltimore in 1804, she complained to her husband, "I really never have viewed my own sex with so little interest as in this place, they possess not the most common information, less reflexion, and very little understanding." Clearly, times had changed: the criteria upon which women judged each other now encompassed the qualities of the mind as well as beauty and personality.

As a means of illustrating the remarkable nature of the transition, it is useful to compare the instruction received by Elizabeth Murray Inman's nieces in the 1750s and 1760s with that given to two of her grandnieces in the 1790s. Mrs. Inman had educated her nieces Dolly and Betsy Murray and Anne Clark to the best of her ability. She had sent them to adventure schools and had herself supervised their training in business methods. Consequently, they were among the best-educated American women of their generation, and the many admiring comments they elicited indicated as much. Yet the contrast to the education of Harriet and Anne Eliza Clark, the daughters of Anne's brother John, could not have been sharper. Because their mother, Lydia, was ill for an extended period, the girls were placed in a boarding school earlier than usual, at the ages of six and nine. In other respects, the Clarks' experience was similar to that of other daughters of middling and well-to-do republican families.

The girls spent the years from 1788 to 1791 at Mr. and Mrs. Usher's school in Bristol, Rhode Island. There Harriet learned to write, practiced reading, and began the study of grammar, while Eliza worked on grammar and arithmetic, read such books as *The Ladies Library*, and sewed extensively for her family. Both girls had their "babies" with them and reported to their parents on the dolls' activities. "I have the pleasure to tell you my babies are all recover'd of their illness," Harriet told her mother in 1791, "but are in want of clothes, having but one suit, must certainly lie in bed all day, when those are wash'd." Mrs. Usher paid close attention to the girls' behavior, preparing rules of conduct for Harriet in June 1789 and assuring the elder Clarks that same month that their daughters' "spiritual duties" were being attended to. When the Ushers began to teach male pupils in the fall of 1789, Eliza informed her parents, "Mrs. Usher will take the utmost care tha[t] they [*sic*] [will] be no indecencies acted or spoke in the house that we shall be by ourselves and the boys by themselves except in Schooltime and meal times."

The Clark girls left the Ushers' school in the spring of 1791. The following fall Anne Eliza was enrolled in William Woodbridge's academy in Medford, while Harriet was placed in a day school near her parents' home in Providence. Early in 1792 Eliza described her daily routine for her sister. She arose about half an hour before dawn, washing, participating in prayers, and reciting a geography lesson before breakfast. After the meal and some chores, she wrote, "we then go to school spell two pages write & copy read in the bible and then read in another book and if we have any time we work [i.e., sew]." After dinner, the schedule was repeated, and following tea they studied geography until 8:30. "We then read some novel aloud," Eliza recounted; "we are now reading Evelina." Bedtime was 9:45 or 10 P.M. In other letters she carefully explained to her mother that her schoolwork was so demanding she could no longer do as much sewing for the family. Among Eliza's fellow students at Woodbridge's academy that year were her cousin Julia Bowen, whom she cheerfully described as a *"numskull"* because "she cannot learn her grammer well nor has not learnt a piece perfect since she has been here," and Penuel Bowen's daughter Frances.

After a two-year break in Eliza's boarding-school education, she was next enrolled in Mehetabel Higginson's academy in Salem, Massachusetts. Then fifteen, she had advanced to the study of French and history in addition to geography. She worked hard at her writing and arithmetic, informing her mother in November 1794, "I have kept a constant account of my expences since I have been here and shall forward them to you once in a while[.] I know it is extremely necessary to be acquainted with accounts I shall therefore pay great attention to my cyphering." She purchased Hester Chapone's *Letters on the Improvement of the Mind* on Mrs. Higginson's recommendation, and she asked her parents to send her a copy of Madame de Sévigné's letters in French. Eliza explained to her parents that she liked Mrs. Higginson's school because she "attends to the health and morals of her scholars which is . . . more than any one else does at least there are but few." The Clarks must have been satisfied with Mehetabel Higginson's efforts with Eliza, for the following year Harriet followed her older sister to the Salem school. She too studied French, in addition to writing, arithmetic (including geometry), geography, and even astronomy.

When John Clark visited his sister Anne and brother-in-law William Hooper in North Carolina in late 1792, he informed his wife that their relatives had made "many inquiries" about Harriet and Eliza, "about their abelities and accomplishments, all expecting from the opportunities they have had, to hear of their being something extraordinary." Certainly the Clark girls had had an unusually good education, but even so their parents had explicitly decided not to send them to the largest and best-known of the republican academies, the Moravian Young Ladies Seminary in Bethlehem, Pennsylvania. Since the daughters of many prominent families were educated there, it is important to take a close look at that preeminent republican institution.

From its founding in 1742 until 1785, the Moravian Seminary served only the daughters of members of the small German sect. But congressmen and army officers who visited the school during the Revolution were impressed by what they saw, and they asked the seminary's trustees to open it to non-Moravians. When the trustees complied in 1785, they announced that they would teach girls "reading and writing in both the German and English languages, also arithmetic, sewing, knitting, and other feminine crafts. Likewise they will be instructed in history, geography, and music, with great care and faithfulness."

The leading families of the young republic eagerly took advantage of the opportunity to send their daughters to the Moravian Seminary. The North Carolina congressman John Steele explained to his daughter Ann in mid-1799 that he had enrolled her in the academy because he was "really of opinion that Bethlehem is unrivalled in the United States as a place for female education." When he sent his eleven-year-old daughter Fanny to the school two years earlier, Ephraim Kirby of Connecticut stressed that he wanted her "to be made perfect" in the academic subjects, while the acquisition of ornamental accomplishments was of "secondary" importance. But he also wanted Fanny to learn "the government of the passions" and to develop "habits of industry, economy and neatness." Undoubtedly, the belief that the Moravians would foster moral growth and self-discipline in addition to intellectual development was what led such Americans as Nathanael and Catherine Green, John and Sarah Jay, and Helena Kortwright Brasher to enroll their daughters at the Bethlehem, Pennsylvania, institution.

In the case of Maria Jay, it is evident that she herself made the decision to attend the highly regarded seminary. Maria's mother, Sarah, had carefully supervised her early education and had entered her in Isabella Graham's school in 1791. Yet in October 1794 Maria surprised her mother by telling her that she "wished to make a greater profi-ciency in her studies than in her present situation she was able" and that she had "a long time had a great inclination to go to Bethlehem." Mrs. Jay understandably hesitated to accede to Maria's request, since her daughter was only twelve and the school was hundreds of miles away from their New York City home. But relatives who were traveling west offered to escort her, and, Sarah later commented, "[H]er little heart was so much engaged in it that I could not resolve to disappoint her." Less than a month later the academy had accepted Maria's application and she was on her way, her display of independence having gained her "great eclat" among her schoolmates while it simultaneously earned the disapproval of their mothers.

But although Sarah Jay's friends might not have concurred in her decision to allow Maria to choose her own school, they could hardly have objected to the course of instruction at the Moravian academy. Everyone connected with the school—parents, students, and teachers alike—expressed satisfaction with the education girls received there. Elizabeth Chester, whose daughter Elizabeth attended the seminary in 1789, is a case in point. In response to a question from Lydia Bowen Clark, Mrs. Chester gave the school an enthusiastic recommendation in late 1790. "The people of the Society appear very amiable in their manners; an honest simplicity, void of affectation characterizes them. The government is a government of persuasion, calculated more to attach the affections than pain the body." Mrs. Chester emphasized that the site of the academy was "*very* pleasant & healthy," that the "Tuteresses are well bred & educated," and that girls did not acquire "any rusticity" during their stay. "As to the morals of a Child," she added, "the Parent may repose entire confidence in the directors, who pay the strictest attention to check every deviation from delicacy & decorum." In short, Mrs. Chester concluded, "I wish all my daughters might have the advantage of that school for one or two years," and she acted accordingly by enrolling another of them at Bethlehem in 1793.

The students appeared equally pleased with their experiences at the seminary. In a letter published in the *American Magazine* in 1788, a Baltimore girl, probably Amelia Blakely, described her daily schedule and then observed, "I could not be more happily situated than I am.—I have every possible attention paid both to my person and education." Three years later, upon leaving the academy, a young woman (again probably Amelia) gratefully thanked her teachers for providing her with "such examples of domestic economy, purity of morals, and reverence for religion." Speaking directly to her fellow pupils, she declared, "[W]e are not here prepared to ride the whirlwind of thoughtless dissipation: but in these calm retreats, we are taught lessons which dignify the character of our sex—entitle us to respect in society—and, if duly attended to, will have a happy influence in rendering us accomplished and agreeable companions."

Private comments coincided with the published ones. In 1790 Mary Anna Boardman told a friend that her sister Fanny Whiting, then a student at Bethlehem, was "too happy in her situation, to feel the least inclination to leave it." On a visit to the school in July 1797 Ephraim Kirby found his daughter Fanny to be "apparently very happy." For her part, Ann Steele left Bethlehem reluctantly after having studied there less than a year, simply because her mother wanted her to return home. Maria Jay told her family in late 1794, "I felt a little strange at first but now I like it much," and before her exams the following spring she wrote, "I hope I shall be able to give satisfaction to my dear tutoresses who take much pains with me[.] I shall indeed try all in my power to improve myself in all my studies while I am here[. I] hope when I return again to my beloved parents that they may not be disappointed in my improvements."

Given the breadth of the seminary's curriculum and the rigor of its requirements, it is unlikely that, upon her return home, the Jays were disappointed with Maria's "improvements." On a typical day in 1788, for example, classes began at eight o'clock (after prayers and breakfast) with cyphering, followed by German reading and English grammar before lunch. Afterwards the pupils turned their attention to history and geography, and late in the afternoon they could learn music, drawing, painting, or tambour (a type of needlework) if they and their parents wished. In 1796, in the midst of preparing for the annual examinations, the New Yorker Margaretta Akerly wrote distractedly to her older sister Catherine, who had also been a student at Bethlehem, "I have so much to learn I dont know what to do with myself I hardly know what I write I think of nothing only what I have to learn; this morning I was up at 4 oClock sitting by the Lamp studying & every night I have 3 or 4 books under my head."

Detailed records of the year-end public examinations reveal why Margaretta was so worried. In 1791, for instance, the examination took five days. On the first morning, the girls were tested on their knowledge of the Bible. That afternoon the subject was German. The following day they were examined in grammar and arithmetic, and on the third the topic was history, with afternoon recitations of memorized pieces. The fourth day was devoted to geography and astronomy in the morning, French in the afternoon. On the final day the students demonstrated their musical ability and showed the audience examples of their writing, drawing, painting, embroidery, and tambour work.

The fact that even the Moravian Seminary, which stressed simplicity, offered instruction in ornamental skills suggests that it is important not to accept unquestioningly the utilitarian reformers' negative judgment of such accomplishments. Jane Nylander, who has studied the paintings and needlework done by young women in this period, has accurately observed that only through such work could girls gain proficiency in the fine arts. Some of the instruction in the republican academies was excellent, and the better teachers did much to develop the artistic talents of their students. Like boys who studied painting, the girls copied well-known prints, often reproducing them in stitchery. Surviving examples of their handiwork show the exquisite care with which they worked and sometimes demonstrate great talent and sensitivity. Most of the students must have learned enough to help them decorate their homes after marriage, and a few became artists of some renown.

The founders of the academies sought to train republican wives and mothers, and this task they unquestionably accomplished. The graduates of the Moravian Seminary, the Philadelphia Young Ladies Academy, Miss Pierce's school, and other similar institutions were well qualified to instruct their sons in the principles of patriotism, to make their homes well-run havens of efficiency, to converse knowledgeably with their husbands on a variety of subjects, and to understand familial finances. But an academy education had unanticipated consequences as well, for some of the graduates of such schools showed in their adulthood a desire to go beyond the standard roles of wife and mother and to widen the boundaries of the feminine sphere.

The Slater Mill in Pawtucket, Rhode Island.

The Modernization of Mayo Greenleaf Patch: Land, Family, and Marginality in New England, 1766–1818

PAUL E. JOHNSON

The climactic political events of the late eighteenth century—the Revolution, the great constitutional debates, and the turbulence of national politics in the first federal administration—tend to dominate the historical landscape as the century closed. Ordinary people, however, were affected more profoundly by the economic and social circumstances of their daily lives. As the nineteenth century opened, southern blacks still lived and labored in slavery, Native Americans faced the ongoing struggle for political sovereignty and survival, and the majority of northern families confronted major changes in their rural economies.

This was the era when Americans in the northeast began to make the transition from the farm to the factory. The process began in the longest settled and most developed areas of the northeast. In this selection, Paul Johnson reconstructs the fascinating life story of a New England man and his family who faced hard choices in the declining rural economy of their forebears. The chronicle of Mayo Greenleaf Patch and his wife, Abigail McIntire, touches on many of the fundamental changes and choices confronted by ordinary people in rural New England. A growing population and the continuing division of farm property left many New England sons without land by the end of the eighteenth century. Much of the land that was left had been robbed of its fertility by decades of unscientific cultivation. Without access to productive land to farm, New England's farm families became more transient and migratory. Many who did not stand to inherit land headed for the more fertile frontier of New York. Other families, like the Patches, eventually sought jobs in the new textile mills being established on scores of small rivers throughout New England. Over their lifetimes, Mayo and Abigail Patch and their children confronted a number of personal and family crises that signaled the decline of the traditional agrarian lifeways in New England. As you

read this piece, note the particular developments that unsettled the Patches'
way of life. You may want to compare these developments with the changes
that overcame a New England rural community, as described by Robert Gross
in an essay later in this book.

This is the story of Mayo Greenleaf Patch and Abigail McIntire Patch,
ordinary people who helped write a decisive chapter in American history: they were among the first New Englanders to abandon farming
and take up factory labor. They did so because rural society had no
room for them, and their history is a tale of progressive exclusion from
an agrarian world governed by family, kinship, and inherited land.
Mayo Greenleaf Patch was the youngest son of a man who owned a
small farm. He inherited nothing, and in his early and middle years he
improvised a living at the edges of the family economy. He grew up
with an uncle and brother, combined farming and shoemaking with
dependence on his wife's family in the 1790s, recruited a half-sister
into schemes against his in-laws' property, then lived briefly off an
inheritance from a distant relative. Finally, having used up his exploit-
able kin connections, he left the countryside and moved to a mill town
in which his wife and children could support the family.

That is how Greenleaf and Abigail Patch made the journey from
farm to factory. But they experienced their troubles most intimately as
members of a family; their story can be comprehended only as family
history. Greenleaf Patch was a failed patriarch. His marriage to Abigail
McIntire began with an early pregnancy, was punctuated by indebtedness and frequent moves, and ended in alcoholism and a divorce.
Along the way, a previously submissive Abigail began making decisions for the family, decisions that were shaped by an economic situation in which she but not her husband found work and by her midlife
conversion into a Baptist church.

The outlines of the Patch family history are familiar, for recent
scholarship on New England in the century following 1750 centers on
its principal themes: the crisis of the rural social order in the eighteenth
century, the beginnings of commercial and industrial society in the
nineteenth, and transformations in personal and family life that occurred in transit between the two. The Patches shared even the partic-
ulars of their story—disinheritance, premarital pregnancy, alcoholism,
transiency, indebtedness, divorce, female religious conversion—with

THE MODERNIZATION OF MAYO GREENLEAF PATCH   From *New England Quarterly*, vol. 55
(Dec. 1982). Reprinted by permission of *New England Quarterly* and the author.

many of their neighbors. In short, Abigail and Greenleaf Patch lived at the center of a decisive social transformation and experienced many of its defining events.

The story of the Patches throws light on the process whereby farmers in post-Revolutionary New England became "available" for work outside of agriculture. That light, however, is dim and oblique, and we must confront two qualifications at the outset. First, the Patches were obscure people who left incomplete traces of their lives. Neither Greenleaf nor Abigail kept a diary or wrote an autobiography, their names never appeared in newspapers, and no one bothered to save their mail. Apart from one rambling and inaccurate family reminiscence, their story must be reconstructed from distant, impersonal, and fragmentary sources: wills and deeds, church records, tax lists, censuses, the minutes of town governments, court records, and histories of the towns in which they lived and the shoe and textile industries in which they worked. The results are not perfect. The broad outlines of the story can be drawn with confidence, and a few episodes emerge in fine-grained detail. But some crucial points must rest on controlled inference, others on inferences that are a little less controlled, still others on outright guesswork. Scholars who demand certainty should stay away from people like Greenleaf and Abigail Patch. But historians of ordinary individuals must learn to work with the evidence that they left behind. In part, this essay is an exploration of the possibilities and limits of such evidence.

A second qualification concerns the problem of generalizing from a single case. It must be stated strongly that the Patches were not typical. No one really is. The Patches, moreover, can claim uniqueness, for they were the parents of Sam Patch, a millworker who earned national notoriety in the 1820s as a professional daredevil. The younger Patch's life was an elaborate exercise in self-destruction, and we might question the normality of the household in which he grew up. Indeed the history of the Patch family is shot through with brutality and eccentricity and with a consistent sadness that is all its own. The Patches were not typical but marginal, and that is the point: it was persons who were marginal to rural society who sought jobs outside of agriculture. The number of such persons grew rapidly in post-Revolutionary New England. This is the story of two of them.

New England men of Greenleaf Patch's generation grew up confronting two uncomfortable facts. The first was the immense value that their culture placed on the ownership of land. Freehold tenure conferred not only economic security but personal and moral independence, the ability to support and govern a family, political rights, and the respect of one's neighbors and oneself. New Englanders trusted the man who owned land; they feared and despised the man who did not. The second fact was that in the late eighteenth century increasing numbers of men owned no land. Greenleaf Patch was among them.

Like nearly everyone else in Revolutionary Massachusetts, Patch was descended from yeoman stock. His family had come to Salem in 1636, and they operated a farm in nearby Wenham for more than a century. The Patches were church members and farm owners, and their men served regularly in the militia and in town offices. Greenleaf's father, grandfather, and great-grandfather all served terms as selectmen of Wenham; his great-grandfather was that community's representative to the Massachusetts General Court; his older brother was a militiaman who fought on the first day of the American Revolution.

The Patches commanded respect among their neighbors, but in the eighteenth century their future was uncertain. Like thousands of New England families, they owned small farms and had many children; by mid-century it was clear that young Patch men would not inherit the material standards enjoyed by their fathers. The farm on which Greenleaf Patch was born was an artifact of that problem. His father, Timothy Patch, Jr., had inherited a house, an eighteen-acre farm, and eleven acres of outlying meadow and woodland upon his own father's death in 1751. Next door, Timothy's younger brother Samuel farmed the remaining nine acres of what had been their father's homestead. The father had known that neither Timothy nor Samuel could make a farm of what he had, and he required that they share resources. His will granted Timothy access to a shop and cider mill that lay on Samuel's land and drew the boundary between the two farms through the only barn on the property. It was the end of the line: further subdivision would make both farms unworkable.

Timothy Patch's situation was precarious, and he made it worse by overextending himself, both as a landholder and as a father. Timothy was forty-three years old when he inherited his farm, and he was busy buying pieces of woodland, upland, and meadow all over Wenham. Evidently he speculated in marginal land and/or shifted from farming to livestock raising. He financed his schemes on credit, and he bought on a fairly large scale. By the early 1760s Timothy Patch held title to 114 acres, nearly all of it in small plots of poor land.

Timothy Patch may have engaged in speculation in order to provide for an impossibly large number of heirs. Timothy was the father of ten children when he inherited his farm. In succeeding years he was widowed, remarried, and sired two more daughters and a son. In all, he fathered ten children who survived to adulthood. The youngest was a son born in 1766. Timothy named him Mayo Greenleaf.

Greenleaf Patch's life began badly: his father went bankrupt in the year of his birth. Timothy had transferred the house and farm to his two oldest sons in the early 1760s, possibly to keep the property out of the hands of creditors. Then, in 1766, the creditors began making trouble. In September Timothy relinquished twenty acres of his outlying land to satisfy a debt. By March 1767, having lost five court cases and sold all of his remaining land to pay debts and court costs, he was preparing to leave Wenham. Timothy's first two sons stayed on, but both left Wenham before their deaths, and none of the other children established households in the community. After a century as substantial farmers and local leaders, the Patch family abandoned their hometown.

Greenleaf Patch was taken from his home village as an infant, and his family's wanderings after that can be traced only through his father's appearances in court. By 1770 the family had moved a few miles north and west to Andover, where Timothy was sued by yet another creditor. Nine years later Timothy Patch was in Danvers, where he went to court seven times in three years. The court cases suggest that the family experienced drastic ups and downs. Some cases involved substantial amounts of money, but in the last, Timothy was accused of stealing firewood. He then left Danvers and moved to Nottingham West, New Hampshire. There Timothy seems to have recouped his fortunes once again, for in 1782 he was a gambler-investor in an American Revolutionary privateer.

That is all we know about the Patch family during the childhood of Mayo Greenleaf Patch. About the childhood itself we know nothing. Doubtless Greenleaf shared his parents' frequent moves and their bouts of good and bad luck, and from his subsequent behavior we might conclude that he inherited his father's penchant for economic adventurism. He may also have spent parts of his childhood and youth in other households. Since he later named his own children after relatives in Wenham, he probably lived there in the families of his brother and uncle. We know also that during his youth he learned how to make shoes, and since his first independent appearance in the record came when he was twenty-one, we might guess that he served a formal, live-in apprenticeship. Even these points, however, rest on speculation. Only this is certain: Greenleaf Patch was the tenth and youngest child of a family that broke and scattered in the year of his birth, and he entered adulthood alone and without visible resources.

In 1787 Mayo Greenleaf Patch appeared in the Second (North) Parish of Reading, Massachusetts—fifteen miles due north of Boston. He was twenty-one years old and unmarried, and he owned almost nothing. He had no relatives in Reading; indeed no one named Patch had ever lived in that town. In a world where property was inherited and where kinfolk were essential social and economic assets, young Greenleaf Patch inherited nothing and lived alone.

Greenleaf's prospects in 1787 were not promising. But he soon took steps to improve them. In July 1788 he married Abigail McIntire in Reading. He was twenty-two years old; she was seventeen and pregnant. This early marriage is most easily explained as an unfortunate accident. But from the viewpoint of Greenleaf Patch it was not unfortunate at all, for it put him into a family that possessed resources that his own family had lost. For the next twelve years, Patch's livelihood and ambitions would center on the McIntires and their land.

The McIntires were Scots, descendants of highlanders who had been exiled to Maine after the Battle of Dunbar. Some had walked south, and Philip McIntire was among those who pioneered the North Parish in the 1650s. By the 1780s McIntire households were scattered throughout the parish. Archelaus McIntire, Abigail's father, headed the most prosperous of those households. Archelaus had been the eldest son of a man who died without a will, and he inherited the family farm intact. He added to the farm and by 1791 owned ninety-seven acres in Reading and patches of meadowland in two neighboring townships, a flock of seventeen sheep as well as cattle and oxen and other animals, and personal property that indicates comfort and material decency if not wealth. Of 122 taxable estates in the North Parish in 1792, Archelaus McIntire's ranked twenty-third.

In 1788 Archelaus McIntire learned that his youngest daughter was pregnant and would marry Mayo Greenleaf Patch. No doubt he was angry, but he had seen such things before. One in three Massachusetts women of Abigail's generation was pregnant on her wedding day, a statistic to which the McIntires had contributed amply. Archelaus himself had been born three months after his parents' marriage in 1729. One of his older daughters had conceived a child at the age of fourteen, and his only son would marry a pregnant lover in 1795.

Faced with yet another early pregnancy, Archelaus McIntire determined to make the best of a bad situation. In the winter of 1789/90, he built a shoemaker's shop and a small house for Greenleaf Patch and granted him use of the land on which they sat. At a stroke, Patch was endowed with family connections and economic independence.

Greenleaf Patch took his place among the farmer-shoemakers of northeastern Massachusetts in 1790. The region had been exporting shoes since before the Revolution, for it possessed the prerequisites of cottage industry in abundance: it was poor and overcrowded and had access to markets through Boston and the port towns of Essex County. With the Revolution and the protection of footwear under the first national tariffs, with the expansion of the maritime economy of which the shoe trade was a part, and with the continuing growth of rural poverty, thousands of farm families turned to making shoes in the 1790s.

Their workshops were not entrepreneurial ventures. Neither, if we listen to the complaints of merchants and skilled artisans about "slop work" coming out of the countryside, were they likely sources of craft traditions or occupational pride. The trade was simply the means by which farmers on small plots of worn-out land maintained their independence.

The journal of Isaac Weston, a Reading shoemaker during the 1790s, suggests something of the cottage shoemaker's way of life. Weston was first and last a farmer. He spent his time worrying about the weather, working his farm, repairing his house and outbuildings, and trading farm labor with his neighbors and relatives. His tasks accomplished, he went hunting with his brothers-in-law, took frequent fishing trips to the coast at Lynn, and made an endless round of social calls in the neighborhood. The little shop at the back of Weston's house supplemented his earnings, and he spent extended periods of time in it only during the winter months. With his bags of finished shoes, he made regular trips to Boston, often in company with other Reading shoemakers. The larger merchants did not yet dominate the trade in country shoes, and Weston and his neighbors went from buyer to buyer bargaining as a group and came home with enough money to purchase leather, pay debts and taxes, and subsist for another year as farmers.

Isaac Weston's workshop enabled him to survive as an independent proprietor. At the same time, it fostered relations of neighborly cooperation with other men. He was the head of a self-supporting household and an equal participant in neighborhood affairs; in eighteenth-century Massachusetts, those criteria constituted the definition of manhood. Mayo Greenleaf Patch received that status as a wedding present.

Greenleaf and Abigail occupied the new house and shop early in 1790, and their tax listings over the next few years reveal a rise from poverty to self-sufficiency with perhaps a little extra. In 1790, for the first time, Greenleaf paid the tax on a small piece of land. Two years later he ranked fifty-sixth among the 122 taxpayers in the North Parish. Patch was not getting rich, but he enjoyed a secure place in the economy of his neighborhood. That alone was a remarkable achievement for a young stranger who had come to town with almost nothing.

With marriage and proprietorship came authority over a complex and growing household. Few rural shoemakers in the 1790s worked alone; they hired outside help and put their wives and children to work binding shoes. Isaac Weston brought in apprentices and journeymen, and Greenleaf Patch seems to have done the same. In 1790 the Patch family included Greenleaf and Abigail and their infant daughter, along with a boy under the age of sixteen and an unidentified adult male. In 1792 Patch paid the tax on two polls, suggesting that again the household included an adult male dependent. It seems clear that Greenleaf hired outsiders and (assuming Abigail helped) regularly headed a family work team that numbered at least four persons.

During the same years, Patch won the respect of the McIntires and their neighbors. When Archelaus McIntire died in 1791, his will named Patch executor of the estate. Greenleaf spent considerable effort, including two successful appearances in court, ordering his father-in-law's affairs. In 1794, he witnessed a land transaction involving his brother-in-law, again indicating that he was a trusted member of the McIntire family. That trust was shared by the neighbors. In 1793 the town built a schoolhouse near the Patch home, and in 1794 and 1795 the parish paid Greenleaf Patch for boarding the schoolmistress and for escorting her home at the end of the term. Those were duties that could only have gone to a trusted neighbor who ran an orderly house.

Greenleaf Patch's marriage to Abigail McIntire rescued him from the shiftless and uncertain life that had been dealt to him at birth. In 1787 he was a propertyless wanderer. By the early 1790s, he was the head of a growing family, a useful member of the McIntire clan, and a familiar and trusted neighbor. Greenleaf Patch had found a home. But his gains were precarious, for they rested on the use of land that belonged not to him but his father-in-law. When Archelaus died, the title to the McIntire properties fell to his nineteen-year-old son, Archelaus, Jr. Young Archelaus was bound out to a guardian, and Patch, as executor of the estate, began to prey openly on the resources of Abigail's family. In succeeding years bad luck and moral failings would cost him everything that he had gained.

With Archelaus McIntire dead and his son living with a guardian, the household that the senior Archelaus had headed shrank to two women: his widow and his daughter Deborah. The widow described herself as an invalid, and there may have been something wrong with Deborah as well. In the will that he wrote in 1791, Archelaus ordered that his heir take care of Deborah. His son would repeat that order ten years later, when Deborah, still unmarried and still living at home, was thirty-five years old. Shortly after the death of Archelaus McIntire (and shortly before Patch was to inventory the estate), the widow complained to authorities that "considerable of my household goods & furniture have been given to my children" and begged that she be spared "whatever household furniture that may be left which is but a bare sufficiency to keep household." At that time two of her four daughters were dead, a third lived with her, and her only son was under the care of a guardian. The "children" could have been none other than Greenleaf and Abigail Patch, whose personal property taxes mysteriously doubled between 1791 and 1792. Greenleaf Patch had entered a house occupied by helpless women and walked off with the furniture.

Patch followed this with a second and more treacherous assault on the McIntires and their resources. In November 1793 Archelaus Mc-

Intire, Jr. came of age and assumed control of the estate. Greenleaf's use of McIntire land no longer rested on his relationship with his father-in-law or his role as executor but on the whim of Archelaus, Jr. Patch took steps that would tie him closely to young Archelaus and his land. Those steps involved a woman named Nancy Barker, who moved into Reading sometime in 1795. Mrs. Barker had been widowed twice, the second time, apparently, by a Haverhill shoemaker who left her with his tools and scraps of leather, a few valueless sticks of furniture, and two small children. Nancy Barker, it turns out, was the half-sister of Mayo Greenleaf Patch.

In November 1795 Nancy Barker married Archelaus McIntire, Jr. She was thirty-one years old. He had turned twenty-three the previous day, and his marriage was not a matter of choice: Nancy was four months pregnant. Archelaus and Nancy were an unlikely couple, and we must ask how the match came about. Archelaus had grown up with three older sisters and no brothers; his attraction and/or vulnerability to a woman nearly nine years his senior is not altogether mysterious. Nancy, of course, had sensible reasons for being attracted to Archelaus. She was a destitute widow with two children, and he was young, unmarried, and the owner of substantial property. Finally, Greenleaf Patch, who was the only known link between the two, had a vital interest in creating ties between his family and his in-law's land. It would be plausible—indeed it seems inescapable—to conclude that Nancy Barker, in collusion with her half-brother, had seduced young Archelaus McIntire and forced a marriage.

Of course, that may be nothing more than perverse speculation. Nancy and Archelaus may simply have fallen in love, started a baby, and married. Whatever role Greenleaf Patch played in the affair may have added to his esteem among the McIntires and in the community. That line of reasoning, however, must confront an unhappy fact: in 1795 the neighbors and the McIntires began to dislike Mayo Greenleaf Patch.

The first sign of trouble came in the fall of 1795, when town officials stepped into a boundary dispute between Patch and Deacon John Swain. Massachusetts towns encouraged neighbors to settle arguments among themselves. In all three parishes of Reading in the 1790s, only three disagreements over boundaries came before the town government, and one of those was settled informally. Thus Greenleaf Patch was party to half of Reading's mediated boundary disputes in the 1790s. The list of conflicts grew: after 1795 the schoolmistress was moved out of the Patch household; in 1797 Patch complained that he had been overtaxed (another rare occurrence), demanded a reassessment, and was reimbursed. Then he started going to court. In 1798 Greenleaf Patch sued Thomas Tuttle for nonpayment of a debt and was awarded nearly $100 when Tuttle failed to appear. A few months earlier, Patch had been hauled into court by William Herrick, a carpenter who claimed that Patch owed him $480. Patch denied the charge and hired a lawyer; the court found in his favor, but Herrick appealed the case, and a higher court awarded him $100.52. Six years later, Patch's lawyer was still trying to collect his fee.

There is also a question about land. In the dispute with John Swain, the description of Patch's farm matches none of the properties described in McIntire deeds. We know that Patch no longer occupied McIntire land in 1798, and town records identified him as the "tenant" of his disputed farm in 1795. Perhaps as early as 1795, Patch had been evicted from McIntire land.

Finally, there is clear evidence that the authorities had stopped trusting Mayo Greenleaf Patch. Nancy Barker McIntire died in 1798 at the age of thirty-four. Archelaus remarried a year later, then died suddenly in 1801. His estate—two houses and the ninety-seven-acre farm, sixty acres of upland and meadow in Reading, and fifteen acres in the neighboring town of Lynnfield—was willed to his two children by Nancy Barker. Archelaus's second wife sold her right of dower and left town, and the property fell to girls who were four and five years of age. Their guardian would have use of the land for many years. By this time Greenleaf and Abigail Patch had moved away, but surely authorities knew their whereabouts and that they were the orphan's closest living relatives. Yet the officials passed them over and appointed a farmer from Reading as legal guardian. The court, doubtless with the advice of the neighbors, had decided against placing Greenleaf Patch in a position of trust. For Patch it was a costly decision. It finally cut him off from property that he had occupied and plotted against for many years.

Each of these facts and inferences says little by itself, but together they form an unmistakable pattern: from the date of his marriage through the mid-1790s, Greenleaf Patch accumulated resources and participated in the collective life of Abigail's family and neighborhood; from 1795 onward he entered the record only when he was fighting the neighbors or being shunned by the family. The promising family man of the early 1790s was a contentious and morally bankrupt outcast by 1798.

Late in 1799 or early in 1800 Greenleaf and Abigail and their four children left Reading and resettled in Danvers, a community of farmer-shoemakers on the outskirts of Salem. We cannot know why they selected that town, but their best connection with the place came through Abigail. Danvers was her mother's birthplace, and she had an aunt and uncle, five first cousins, and innumerable distant relatives in the town. Indeed Abigail's father had owned land in Danvers. In 1785 Archelaus McIntire, Sr. had seized seven acres from John Felton, one of his in-laws, in payment of a debt. Archelaus, Jr. sold the land back to the

Feltons in 1794 but did not record the transaction until 1799. Perhaps he made an arrangement whereby the Patches had use of the land. (Doubtless Archelaus was glad to be rid of Greenleaf Patch, but he may have felt some responsibility for his sister.)

Danvers was another shoemaking town, and the Patches probably rented a farm and made shoes. In 1800 the household included Greenleaf and Abigail, their children, and no one else, suggesting that they were no longer able to hire help. But this, like everything else about the family's career in Danvers, rests on inference. We know only that they were in Danvers and that they stayed three years.

Late in 1802 Greenleaf Patch received a final reprieve, again through family channels. His half-brother Job Davis (his mother's son by her first marriage) died in the fishing port of Marblehead and left Patch one-fifth of his estate. The full property included a butcher's shop at the edge of town, an unfinished new house, and what was described as a "mansion house" that needed repairs. The property, however, was mortgaged to the merchants William and Benjamin T. Reid. The survivors of Job Davis inherited the mortgage along with the estate.

The other heirs sold to the Reids without a struggle, but Greenleaf Patch, whether from demented ambition or lack of alternatives, moved his family to Marblehead early in 1803. He finished the new house and moved into it, reopened the butcher's shop, and ran up debts. Some of the debts were old. Patch owed Ebenezer Goodale of Danvers $54. He also owed Porter Sawyer of Reading $92 and paid a part of it by laboring at 75¢ a day. Then there were debts incurred in Marblehead: $70 to the widow Sarah Dolebar; a few dollars for building materials and furnishings bought from the Reids; $50 to a farmer named Benjamin Burnham; $33 to Zachariah King of Danvers; $35 to Joseph Holt of Reading; another $35 to Caleb Totman of Hampshire County. Finally, there was the original mortgage held by the Reids.

Patch's renewed dreams of independence collapsed under the weight of his debts. In March 1803 a creditor repossessed the property up to a value of $150, and a few weeks before Christmas of the same year the sheriff seized the new house. In the following spring, Patch missed a mortgage payment, and the Reids took him to court, seized the remaining property, and sold it at auction. Still, Patch retained the right to reclaim the property by paying his debts. The story ends early in 1805, when the Reids bought Greenleaf Patch's right of redemption for $60. Patch had struggled with the Marblehead property for two years, and all had come to nothing.

With this final failure, the Patches exhausted the family connections on which they had subsisted since their marriage. The long stay in Reading and the moves to Danvers and Marblehead were all determined by the availability of relatives and their resources. In 1807 the Patches resettled in Pawtucket, Rhode Island, the pioneer textile mill-ing town in the United States. It was the climactic event in their history: it marked their passage out of the family economy and into the labor market.

When the family arrived in Pawtucket early in 1807, they found four textile mills surrounding the waterfall at the center of town. The mills were small and limited to the spinning of yarn, and much of the work was done by outworkers. Children picked and cleaned raw cotton in their homes, then sent it to the mills to be carded by other children. The cotton next went to the spinning rooms, where, with the help of water-driven machinery, a few skilled men, and still more children, it was turned into yarn. Millers put the yarn out to women, many of them widows with children, who wove it into cloth. There was thus plenty of work for Abigail and her older children, and it was they who supported the family in Pawtucket. Samuel, the second son, spent his childhood in the mills, and his sisters probably did the same. It is likely that Abigail worked as a weaver; certainly the wool produced on her father's farm suggests that she knew something about that trade.

That leaves only the father. Pawtucket was booming in 1807, and if Greenleaf Patch were willing and physically able, he could have found work. We know, however, that he did not work in that town. He drank, he stole the money earned by his wife and children, and he threatened them frequently with violence. Then, in 1812, he abandoned them. Abigail waited six years and divorced him in 1818. She recounted Greenleaf's drinking and his threats and his refusal to work, then revealed what for her was the determining blow: Greenleaf Patch had drifted back to Massachusetts and had been caught passing counterfeit money. In February 1817 he entered the Massachusetts State Prison at Charlestown. He was released the following August. Patch was fifty-two years old, and that is the last we hear of him.

In a society that located virtue and respectability in the yeoman freeholder, Mayo Greenleaf Patch never owned land. We have seen some public consequences of that fact: his lifelong inability to attain material independence, the troubled relations with in-laws, neighbors, creditors, and legal authorities that resulted when he tried, and the personal and moral disintegration that accompanied unending economic distress.

Now we turn to private troubles, and here the story centers on Abigail McIntire Patch. Recent studies of late eighteenth- and early nineteenth-century family life have documented a decline of patriarchal authority, the creation of a separate and female-dominated domestic sphere, an increase in female religiosity, and, bound up with all three, the elevation of women's status and power within the home. Most of these studies center on middle- and upper-class women, and we are left to wonder whether the conclusions can be extended to women further down the social scale. In the case of Abigail Patch, they can: her story begins with patriarchy and ends with female control. In grotesque miniature, the history of the Patches is a story of the feminization of family life.

Abigail grew up in a family that, judged from available evidence, was ruled by her father. Archelaus McIntire owned a respected family name and a farm that he had inherited from his father and that he would pass on to his son; he was the steward of the family's past and future as well as its present provider. As a McIntire, he conferred status on every member of his household. As a voter he spoke for the family in town affairs; as a father and church member he led the family in daily prayers; and as a proprietor he made decisions about the allocation of family resources, handled relations with outsiders, and performed much of the heavy work.

Archelaus McIntire's wife and daughters were subordinate members of his household. He had married Abigail Felton of Danvers and had brought her to a town where she lived apart from her own family but surrounded by his; her status in Reading derived from her husband's family and not from her own. On the farm, she and her daughters spent long days cooking and cleaning, gardening, tending and milking cows, making cloth and clothing, and caring for the younger children—work that took place in and near the house and not on the farm. That work was essential, but New England men assumed that it would be done and attached no special importance to it. The notion of a separate and cherished domestic sphere was slow to catch on in the countryside, and if we may judge from the spending patterns of the McIntires, it played no role in their house. Archelaus McIntire spent his money on implements of work and male sociability—horses, wagons, well-made cider barrels, a rifle—and not on the china, tea sets, and feather beds that were appearing in the towns and among the rural well-to-do. The McIntires owned a solid table and a Bible and a few other books, and there was a clock and a set of glassware as well. But the most valuable item of furniture in the house was Archelaus's desk. Insofar as the McIntires found time for quiet evenings at home, they probably spent them listening to the father read his Bible (the mother was illiterate) or keeping quiet while he figured his accounts.

As the fourth and youngest of Archelaus McIntire's daughters, Abigail had doubtless traded work and quiet subordination for security, for the status that went with being a female McIntire, perhaps even for peace and affection in the home. As she set up housekeeping with Mayo Greenleaf Patch, she doubtless did not expect things to change. Years later Abigail recalled that in taking a husband she wanted not a partner but "a friend and protector." For her part, Abigail spoke of her "duties" and claimed to have been an "attentive and affectionate wife."

It was the arrangement that she had learned as a child: husbands protected their wives and supported them, wives worked and were attentive to their husbands' needs and wishes. All available evidence suggests that those rules governed the Patch household during the years in Reading.

Abigail and Greenleaf Patch maintained neither the way of life nor the standard of living necessary for the creation of a private sphere in which Abigail could have exercised independent authority. The house was small and there was little money, and the household regularly included persons from outside the immediate family. Greenleaf's apprentices and journeymen were in and out of the house constantly. For two summers the Patches boarded the schoolmistress, and Nancy Barker may have stayed with Greenleaf and Abigail before her marriage. With these persons present in hit-and-miss records, we may assume that outsiders were normal members of the Patch household.

At work, rural shoemakers maintained a rigid division of labor based on sex and age, and Greenleaf's authority was pervasive. Abigail's kitchen, if indeed it was a separate room, was a busy place. There she bound shoes as a semiskilled and subordinate member of her husband's work team, cared for the children (she gave birth five times between 1789 and 1799), did the cooking, cleaning, and laundry for a large household, and stared across the table at apprentices and journeymen who symbolized her own drudgery and her husband's authority at the same time. As Abigail Patch endured her hectic and exhausting days, she may have dreamed of wallpapered parlors and privacy and quiet nights by the fire with her husband. But she must have known that such things were for others and not for her. They had played little role in her father's house, and they were totally absent from her own.

Greenleaf Patch seems to have taken his authority as head of the household seriously. Available evidence suggests that he consistently made family decisions—not just the economic choices that were indisputably his to make but decisions that shaped the texture and meaning of life within the family.

Take the naming of the children. Greenleaf Patch was separated from his own family and dependent on McIntire resources, so when children came along we would expect him and Abigail to have honored McIntire relatives. That is not what happened. The first Patch child was a daughter born in 1789. The baby was named Molly, after a daughter of Greenleaf's brother Isaac. A son came two years later, and the Patches named him Greenleaf. Another daughter, born in 1794, was given the name Nabby, after another of Isaac Patch's daughters. A second son, born in 1798, was named for Greenleaf's uncle Samuel. That child died, and a son born the following year (the daredevil Sam Patch) received the same name. The last child was born in 1803 and was named for Greenleaf's brother Isaac. None of the six children was named for Abigail or a member of her family. Instead, all of the names came from the little world in Wenham—uncle Samuel's nine-acre farm, the shared barn and outbuildings, and the eighteen acres operated by brother Isaac—in which Greenleaf Patch presumably spent much of his childhood.

Religion is a second and more important sphere in which Patch seems to have made choices for the family. Abigail McIntire had grown up in a religious household. Her father had joined the North Parish Congregational Church a few days after the birth of his first child in 1762. Her mother had followed two months later, and the couple baptized each of their five children. The children in their turn became churchgoers. Abigail's sisters Mary and Mehitable joined churches, and her brother Archelaus, Jr. expressed a strong interest in religion as well. Among Abigail's parents and siblings, only the questionable Deborah left no religious traces.

Religious traditions in the Patch family were not as strong. Greenleaf's father and his first wife joined the Congregational church at Wenham during the sixth year of their marriage in 1736, but the family's ties to religion weakened after that. Timothy Patch, Jr. did not baptize any of his thirteen children, either the ten presented him by his first wife or the three born to Thomasine Greenleaf Davis, the non-churchgoing widow whom he married in 1759. None of Greenleaf's brothers or sisters became full members of the church, and only his oldest brother Andrew owned the covenant, thus placing his family under the government of the church.

Among the Wenham Patches, however, there remained pockets of religiosity, and they centered, perhaps significantly, in the homes of Greenleaf's brother Isaac and his uncle Samuel. Uncle Samuel was a communicant of the church, and although Isaac had no formal religious ties, he married a woman who owned the covenant. The churchgoing tradition that Greenleaf Patch carried into marriage was thus ambiguous, but it almost certainly was weaker than that carried by his wife. And from his actions as an adult, we may assume that Greenleaf was not a man who would have been drawn to the religious life.

As Greenleaf and Abigail married and had children, the question of religion could not have been overlooked. The family lived near the church in which Abigail had been baptized and in which her family and her old friends spent Sunday mornings. As the wife of Greenleaf Patch, Abigail had three options: she could lead her husband into church; she could, as many women did, join the church without her husband and take the children with her; finally, she could break with the church and spend Sundays with an irreligious husband. The first two choices would assert Abigail's authority and independent rights within the family. The third would be a capitulation, and it would have painful results. It would cut her off from the religious community in which she had been born, and it would remove her young family from religious influence.

The Patches lived in Reading for twelve years and had five children there. Neither Greenleaf nor Abigail joined the church, and none of the babies was baptized. We cannot retrieve the actions and feelings that produced these facts, but this much is certain: in the crucial area of religious practice, the Patch family bore the stamp of Greenleaf Patch and not of Abigail McIntire. When Greenleaf Patch and Abigail named a baby or chose whether to join a church or baptize a child, the decisions extended his family's history and not hers.

Abigail Patch accepted her husband's dominance in family affairs throughout the years in Reading, years in which he played, however ineptly and dishonestly, his role as "friend and protector." With his final separation from the rural economy and his humiliating failure in Marblehead, he abdicated that role. In Marblehead Abigail began to impose her will upon domestic decisions. The result, within a few years, would be a full-scale female takeover of the family.

In 1803 the sixth—and, perhaps significantly, the last—Patch child was baptized at Second Congregational Church in Marblehead. And in 1807, shortly after the move to Rhode Island, Abigail and her oldest daughter joined the First Baptist Church in Pawtucket. At that date Abigail was thirty-seven years old, had been married nineteen years, and had five living children. Her daughter Molly was eighteen years old and unmarried. Neither followed the customs of the McIntire or Patch families, where women who joined churches did so within a few years after marriage. Abigail and Molly Patch presented themselves for baptism in 1807 not because they had reached points in their life cycles but because they had experienced religion and had decided to join a church.

At the same time (here was feminization with a vengeance) Abigail's daughters dropped their given names and evolved new ones drawn from their mother's and not their father's side of the family. The oldest daughter joined the church not as Molly but as Polly Patch. Two years later the same woman married under the name Mary Patch. Abigail's oldest sister, who had died in the year that Abigail married Greenleaf, had been named Mary. The second Patch daughter, Nabby, joined the Baptist church in 1811. At that time she was calling herself Abby Patch. By 1829 she was known as Abigail. The daughters of Abigail Patch, it seems, were affiliating with their mother and severing symbolic ties with their father. It should be noted that the father remained in the house while they did so.

In Pawtucket Abigail built a new family life that centered on her church and her female relatives. That life constituted a rejection not only of male dominance but of men. For five years Abigail worked and took the children to church while her husband drank, stole her money, and issued sullen threats. He ran off in 1812, and by 1820 Abigail, now officially head of the household, had rented a house and was taking in boarders. Over the next few years the Patch sons left home: Samuel for New Jersey, Isaac for the Northwest, Greenleaf for parts unknown. Abigail's younger daughter married and moved to Pittsburgh. Among the Patch children only Mary (Molly, Polly) stayed in Pawtucket. In 1825 Mary was caught committing adultery. Her husband left town, and Mary began calling herself a widow. Abigail closed the boarding-house and moved into a little house on Main Street with Mary and her children sometime before 1830. She and her daughter and granddaughters would live in that house for the next quarter-century.

The neighbors remembered Abigail Patch as a quiet, steady little woman who attended the Baptist church. She did so with all of the Patch women. Mary had joined with her in 1807, and each of Mary's daughters followed in their turn: Mary and Sarah Anne in 1829, Emily in 1841. First Baptist was a grim and overwhelmingly female Calvinist church, subsidized and governed by the owners of Pawtucket's mills. The Articles of Faith insisted that most of humankind was hopelessly damned, that God chose only a few for eternal life and had in fact chosen them before the beginning of time, "and that in the flesh dwelleth no good thing." It was not a cheerful message. But it struck home among the Patch women.

Apart from the church, the women spent their time in the house on Main Street. Abigail bought the house in 1842—the first land that the Patches owned—and her granddaughters Mary and Emily taught school in the front room for many years. The household was self-supporting, and its membership was made up of women whose relations with men were either troubled or nonexistent. Abigail never remarried. We cannot know what preceded and surrounded the instance of adultery and the breakup of Mary's marriage, but she too remained single for the rest of her life. Sarah Anne Jones, one of the granddaughters, was thirty-six years old and unmarried when called before a church committee in 1853. Although she married a man name Kelley during the investigation, she was excommunicated "because she has given this church reason to believe she is licentious." Sarah Anne's sisters, the schoolteachers Mary and Emily, were spinsters all their lives. The lives of Abigail Patch and her daughter Mary Jones had been blighted by bad relations with men; the women whom they raised either avoided men or got into trouble when they did not. Abigail Patch lived on Main Street with the other women until 1854, when she died at the age of eighty-four.

We know little of what went on in that house. The women lived quietly, and former pupils remembered Abigail's granddaughters with affection. But beyond the schoolroom, in rooms inhabited only by the Patch women, there was a cloistered world. Within that world, Abigail and her daughter Mary reconstructed not only themselves but the history of their family.

Pawtucket celebrated its Cotton Centennial in 1890, and a Providence newspaperman decided to write about the millworker-hero Sam Patch. He asked Emily Jones, one of Abigail's aged granddaughters, about the Patch family history. Emily had been born after 1810, and her knowledge of the family's past was limited to what she had picked up from her mother and grandmother. Her response to the reporter demonstrated the selective amnesia with which any family remembers its history, but in this case the fabrications were sadly revealing.

Miss Jones told the newspaperman that her oldest uncle, Greenleaf Patch, Jr., had gone off to Salem and become a lawyer. That is demonstrably untrue. No one named Greenleaf Patch has ever been licensed to practice law in Massachusetts. About her uncle Sam Patch, Emily said: in the 1820s he operated a spinning mill of his own north of Pawtucket, but failed when his partner ran off with the funds; it was only then that he moved to New Jersey and became a daredevil. That too is a fabrication. What we know about Sam Patch is that he was an alcoholic with powerful suicidal drives, and that he succeeded in killing himself at the age of thirty. Miss Jones remembered that her youngest uncle, Isaac, moved to Illinois and became a farmer. That was true: in 1850 Isaac Patch was farming and raising a family near Peoria. It seems that Abigail Patch and Mary Patch Jones idealized the first two Patch sons by giving them success and / or ambitions that they did not have. The third son was born in 1803 and grew up in a household dominated by Abigail and not by her dissipated husband; he became a family man. By inventing a similar ordinariness for the older sons, Abigail may have erased some of the history created by Mayo Greenleaf Patch.

Emily's memory of her grandfather provokes similar suspicions. We know that Greenleaf Patch lived in Pawtucket until 1812. But Miss Jones remembered that her grandfather had been a farmer in Massachusetts, and that he died before Abigail brought her family to Rhode Island. Greenleaf Patch, it seems, was absent from Abigail's house in more ways than one.

Suggestions for Further Reading

Eighteenth-century gentry life styles and outlooks can be explored in the following: Daniel Blake Smith, *Inside the Great House: Planter Family Life in Eighteenth-Century Chesapeake Society* (Ithaca, N.Y., 1980); Rhys Isaac, *The Transformation of Virginia, 1740–1790** (Chapel Hill, N.C., 1982); T. H. Breen, *Tobacco Culture: The Mentality of the Great Tidewater Planters on the Eve of Revolution* (Princeton, N.J., 1985); and Carl Bridenbaugh, *Rebels and Gentlemen: Philadelphia in the Age of Franklin** (New York, 1942).

Religion has been a primary focus for colonial historians; yet most scholarship in this area deals with doctrinal and institutional aspects of Puritanism, Anglicanism, and other forms of Protestant commitment. A literature is growing, however, on the personal experience of religion. See, for example, Charles Hambrick-Stowe, *The Practice of Piety: Puritan Devotional Disciplines in Seventeenth-Century New England* (Chapel Hill, N.C., 1982); Norman Pettit, *The Heart Prepared: Grace and Conversion in Puritan Spiritual Life* (New Haven, Conn., 1966); and Perry Miller's essays in *Errand into the Wilderness** (Cambridge, Mass., 1956). For the Great Awakening see J. M. Bumsted and John E. Van de Wetering, *What Must I Do to Be Saved: The Great Awakening in Colonial America** (Hinsdale, Ill., 1976); Alan Heimert, *Religion and the American Mind from the Great Awakening to the Revolution* (Cambridge, Mass., 1966); and Harry S. Stout, "Religion, Communications, and the Ideological Origins of the American Revolution," *William and Mary Quarterly* 34 (1977): 519–41; Patricia J. Tracy, *Jonathan Edwards, Pastor; Religion and Society in Eighteenth-Century Northampton** (New York, 1979); David S. Lovejoy, *Religious Enthusiasm in the New World: Heresy to Revolution* (Cambridge, Mass., 1985); and Stephen A. Marini, *Radical Sects of Revolutionary New England* (Cambridge, Mass., 1982).

The role of ordinary people in the colonial wars and then in the American Revolution is addressed in Fred Anderson, *A People's Army: Massachusetts Soldiers and Society in the Seven Years' War* (Chapel Hill, N.C., 1984); Charles Royster, *A Revolutionary People at War: The Continental Army and American Character, 1775–1783* (Chapel

*Available in paperback edition.

Hill, N.C., 1979); Steven Rosswurm, " 'As a Lyen out of His Den': Philadelphia's Popular Movement, 1776–1780," in Margaret Jacob and James Jacob, eds., *The Origins of Anglo-American Radicalism* (London, 1984); Jesse Lemisch, "Jack Tar in the Streets: Merchant Seamen in the Politics of the American Revolution," *William and Mary Quarterly*, 25 (1968): 371–407, and "Listening to the 'Inarticulate': William Widger's Dream and the Loyalties of American Revolutionary Seamen in British Prisons," *Journal of Social History*, 3 (1969–1970): 1–29; Pauline Maier, "Popular Uprisings and Civil Authority in Eighteenth-Century America," *William and Mary Quarterly*, 27 (1970): 3–35; Rhys Isaac, "Dramatizing the Ideology of Revolution: Popular Mobilization in Virginia, 1774 to 1776," *William and Mary Quarterly*, 33 (1976): 357–85; Edward Countryman, *A People in Revolution: The American Revolution and Society in New York, 1760–1790* (Baltimore, 1981); Dirk Hoerder, *Crowd Action in Revolutionary Massachusetts, 1765–1780* (New York, 1977); Gary B. Nash, *The Urban Crucible: Social Change, Political Consciousness, and the Origins of the American Revolution* (Cambridge, Mass., 1979); and Rhys Isaac, *The Transformation of Virginia, 1740–1790* (Chapel Hill, N.C., 1982).

Women in the Revolutionary era may be studied further by reading Joan Hoff Wilson, "The Illusion of Change: Women and the American Revolution," in Alfred F. Young, ed. *The American Revolution: Essays in the History of American Radicalism** (Dekalb, IL, Nov. 1976), 383–445; Nancy F. Cott, "Divorce and the Changing Status of Women in Eighteenth-Century Massachusetts," *William and Mary Quarterly*, 33 (1976): 586–614; Linda K. Kerber, *Women of the Republic: Intellect and Ideology in Revolutionary America** (Chapel Hill, N.C., 1980); Joy Day Buel and Richard Buel, Jr., *The Way of Duty: A Woman and Her Family in Revolutionary America** (New York, 1984); Lynne Withey, *Dearest Friend: A Life of Abigail Adams* (New York, 1981); Charles Akers, *Abigail Adams: An American Woman** (Boston, 1980); and Lester H. Cohen, "Mercy Otis Warren: The Politics of Language and the Aesthetics of Self," *American Quarterly*, 35 (1983): 481–98.

The Early Republic

1800–1840

Absalom Jones, first minister for the African Church of Philadelphia.

Forging Freedom: The Emancipation Experience in the Northern Seaport Cities, 1775–1820

GARY B. NASH

The ideas and events that fueled the movement for independence greatly accelerated the abolition of slavery in the North. Many northern colonists perceived the glaring contradiction, exposed by the increasing number of abolitionists, in denying liberty to Afro-Americans while invoking a host of inalienable rights to justify their war for independence. In the South, thousands of blacks made personal declarations of independence during the war by fleeing from their masters to join the British troops; meanwhile, thousands of northern slaves gained their freedom by private acts of manumission. By 1804 every northern state had either freed its slaves or enacted a plan for gradual emancipation. Thus, two generations before the forces unleashed in the Civil War would end slavery in the South, thousands of northern black men and women had made the transition from bondage to freedom.

What was the emancipation experience like for the first generation of freedmen and freedwomen? What kinds of adjustments did newly freed slaves make in the North? How did personal lives, work, and associational life change for northern blacks in the new republic? These are questions that concern Gary B. Nash in his study of free blacks in the northern seaport capitals. Slavery had been much more of an urban phenomenon in the northern colonies than in the South. In the post-Revolutionary period most northern urban slaves stayed in the cities after gaining their freedom. Joined by former bondspeople from the hinterland and newly manumitted blacks and fugitive slaves from the South, they made the major urban seaports of Boston, New York, and Philadelphia the centers of free black life after the Revolution. Nash focuses on the ways these free Afro-Americans created a life outside of bondage and shows how in doing so they had to cope with social scorn and economic exploitation, which did not disappear with emancipation.

On the eve of the American Revolution some 4,000 slaves and a few hundred free blacks lived in Boston, New York, and Philadelphia, the northern seaport capitals of colonial society. Fifty years later nearly 22,000 free blacks and about 500 slaves resided in these same cities, most of the latter in New York. In two generations a large majority of the northern Afro-American population made the transition from bondage to freedom. Although northern slavemasters had neither constructed a strong moral justification for holding slaves nor manifested a powerful economic need for bonded labor, blacks did not scale the barrier between slavery and freedom easily. Instead, they constructed the economic, institutional, and social scaffolding of freedom slowly, usually in the face of open white hostility. Moreover, the transit from slavery to freedom proceeded unevenly, depending on the nature of slavery and the timing of emancipation, as well as the specific economic and demographic conditions of urban life. But everywhere the coming of freedom marked the transformation of black life, the emergence of new institutions, and the development of a new consciousness.

Once the exhilaration of freedom had been savored, one brute necessity stood above all others for black Americans of the Revolutionary era: finding a livelihood. During the years of actual fighting some blacks solved the problem of maintenance by military service, either with the American or, more typically, the British armies. At war's end, the necessities of life could no longer be procured through membership in a large, white-directed organization; now every freedman was on his own. Standing alone, freed blacks, both men and women, looked to the coastal towns for economic survival. The urban migration that ensued swelled the black population in Boston, New York, and Philadelphia fourfold between the Revolution and 1820.

Rapid postemancipation urbanization increased the urban bias already characteristic of black life in the colonial period. The intensive capitalization of a few industries, demand for laborers by artisans, and the desire of status-conscious gentlefolk for black servants had combined to make pre-Revolutionary bondage a disproportionately urban phenomenon. Thus, New York City, which contained 13 percent of the colony's white population in 1771, was the home of 16 percent of the slave population. Boston, with 6 percent of the white population of Massachusetts in 1765, contained 15 percent of the colony's slaves. Slaves

FORGING FREEDOM   From Ira Berlin and Ronald Hoffman, eds., *Slavery and Freedom in the Age of the American Revolution* (Charlottesville: University Press of Virginia, 1983). Reprinted by permission of the publisher.

in Pennsylvania were twice as likely to live in Philadelphia as were the colony's white inhabitants in the 1760s.

Most urban slaves apparently remained in the cities after gaining their liberty. They were joined there by hundreds of former bondspeople from the countryside who, like their urban counterparts, concluded that the cities offered the best chance for widening their economic opportunities and enriching their social life. In particular they headed for the maritime towns, for black men had long been important on the coasting vessels and overseas ships of colonial commerce, and black women could hope for domestic service in the homes of an increasingly affluent urban upper class. By taking out of the hands of the master class decisions about where blacks lived, emancipation permanently altered the geography of northern black life.

This urban migration was especially pronounced in the first two decades after the Revolution, when a large proportion of northern slaves received their freedom. The percentage of Massachusetts free blacks who lived in Boston rose only slowly in this period, but in both New York and Pennsylvania the proportion of the black populace living in the capital city doubled between the early 1770s and 1800. By 1820 Massachusetts blacks were three times as likely to live in Boston as were Massachusetts whites; in New York and Pennsylvania, Afro-Americans were four times as likely as whites to live in the seaport capital.

Immigrants from the South augmented the expansion of urban black life in the North. Between the Revolution and 1800 Delaware, Maryland, and Virginia masters manumitted thousands of slaves, many of whom, along with hundreds of fugitive bondspeople, headed northward. For the first time the North Star came to symbolize freedom. As the center of American abolitionism, Philadelphia especially became the destination for a generation of southern blacks, mostly from the upper South. Because it adjoined three slave states, Pennsylvania "afforded an asylum for their free blacks and runaway slaves." Indeed, by 1800 the Afro-American population of Philadelphia overtook that of New York City, although on the eve of the Revolution it had been less than a quarter as large.

For freedmen the possibility of maritime work, either on ships at sea or as stevedores along the wharves, provided a large part of the urban pull. Federal protection certificates, issued to merchant seamen beginning in 1796, indicate that by the beginning of the nineteenth century free blacks composed at least one-fifth of some 2,000 merchant seamen in Philadelphia, making this the city's single most important job opportunity for black freedmen. Because they indicate the birthplace of each mariner, these certificates can be used to trace migration into the seaport centers from both the rural North and the upper South. James Phillips, a free black mariner, received his certificate in 1798.

Born outside Philadelphia in 1771 to a free black mother and a white father, he had come to the Delaware River port to make a living at sea. Alexander Giles, another free black Philadelphia seaman, had been born in 1777 in nearby Kent County, Delaware. The son of a black freeman, he too migrated to the Pennsylvania capital. Randall Shepherd, the son of a free black laborer in Nansemond County, Virginia, had trekked north and taken up life as a merchant seaman in Philadelphia, where he obtained a certificate in 1798. Henry Bray had been born in Boston in the year of the Massacre. Like his father, he went to sea to make a living but had resettled in Philadelphia in the 1790s. George Gray had tried all three major maritime capitals. Born in New York City, he moved to Boston and then to Philadelphia. Of the fifteen black mariners who shipped out of Philadelphia in 1798 and applied for certificates, only two had been born in that city. Six had migrated from the upper South, four from the Philadelphia hinterland, two from New England, and one had been born in Africa.

Crew lists also reveal the lure of maritime jobs. From a random selection of thirty-seven ships departing Philadelphia in 1803, the place of birth of forty-one black merchant seamen can be ascertained. Only two of these had been born in Philadelphia. Four black seamen came from elsewhere in Pennsylvania and eight from adjoining areas in New Jersey and Delaware. Three were from New York; four claimed New England birthplaces; thirteen hailed from Maryland, Virginia, or South Carolina; four came from Saint-Domingue; and one each had been born elsewhere in the West Indies, in Guinea, and in Portugal. Young black men freed in the hinterlands after the Revolution could have had only faint hope of carving out a life for themselves as independent farmers and landholders. Facing strong racial prejudice and lacking capital to buy land, tools, and livestock, life in the countryside meant becoming one of a growing number of rural transients or hiring out as a day laborer to farmers, ironmasters, or small-town shopkeepers. More and more black men seized the opportunities available in the maritime centers, where they became part of a literally floating proletariat.

The appeal of the city was not solely economic. Alongside greater opportunities for employment stood the many attractions of black community life. In rural areas freed Afro-Americans lived in relative isolation from other black people and therefore were relatively defenseless against white hostility. But in the cities the concentration of free blacks provided some security against a hostile world and meant greater chances to find an acceptable marriage partner, to establish a family, and to participate in the activities of black churches, schools, fraternal societies, and benevolent organizations. The strength of this urban attraction cannot be quantified, but the possibility of developing a black community doubtless made the city even more appealing to black migrants. Every Afro-American in the post-Revolutionary generation faced the fact that the abolition of slavery tended to augment rather than dissolve white racial hostility, and the animus was no less virulent in the cities than in rural areas. But the dense network of urban black institutions and a rich community life made it easier to confront racism in the cities than in the countryside.

The timing of emancipation shaped the pattern of the black urban migration. Boston reported no slaves in the first federal census, and in Philadelphia, where a gradual abolition law had been in effect for ten years, enumerators counted only 273 bondspeople. By the turn of the century both cities had become havens for free Afro-Americans. New York, on the other hand, did not pass an abolition law until 1799, and this measure offered no immediate freedom; instead it liberated slave-born children only when they reached the age of twenty-five if female, twenty-eight if male. Consequently, the slave population of New York City continued to increase steadily from the end of the Revolution until about 1800. Indeed, as late as 1790 New York had more slaves than any city in the nation except Charleston, South Carolina. As the remaining center of northern slavery in the early nineteenth century, New York at first attracted less than its share of freedpeople. Although that city's slaveowners released or sold their slaves far faster than their rural counterparts in the rest of the state, the free black population nevertheless grew less rapidly in New York City than in Philadelphia from 1780 to 1800. Migrating blacks found "free" cities more attractive than "slave" ones.

Black migration to the cities after the Revolution was disproportionately female, a fact with important ramifications for every aspect of urban black life. It reversed the sexual imbalance of the colonial urban black population, which had usually numbered about three males for every two females. Although the failure of the federal census to distinguish blacks by gender before 1820 makes this development difficult to chart, in that year females represented 55 percent of Boston's black population, 57 percent of Philadelphia's, and 60 percent of New York's. The deficit of males in 1820 applied to all age categories but was particularly pronounced among young adults between fourteen and twenty-five years old. This shortage can be explained partially by forced sales of young slaves to the South and partially by kidnapping, a constant danger in all northern cities. In addition, census takers and other enumerators exaggerated this sexual imbalance by ignoring large numbers of young male transients and mariners who spent much of their time at sea. Still, the deficit of young men cannot be denied. More than eighty years ago W. E. B. Du Bois offered perhaps the most important explanation for this sexual imbalance in the urban black population: "The industrial opportunities of Negro women in cities have been far greater than those of men, through their large employment in domestic service. At the same time the restriction of employments open to Negroes, which perhaps reached a climax in 1830–1840, . . . has served to limit the number of men." Corroboration for his analysis can be found in the sex ratios of free blacks in the rural areas surrounding the port cities. In many such counties in 1820, males outnumbered females in the fourteen to twenty-five age category.

The possibility of maritime work for men and domestic employment for women lay at the root of the free black migration to the cities. But former slaves also availed themselves of a variety of other occupational opportunities. Historians have customarily assumed a degradation of black skills in the emancipation period, as former slave artisans, lacking a master's protection and patronage, were forced as freemen into menial labor. But loss of skill may not in fact have been extensive, since fewer colonial slaves possessed artisan training than historians have sometimes supposed. In any case, it would be a mistake to analyze only the changing occupational status of black men, for the labor of black women was equally important to the survival of black households. Far more than among whites, the black family was an economic partnership in which both husband and wife earned wages in the marketplace economy.

Some indications of the occupational structure of the first generation of free blacks can be derived from the 1795 Philadelphia directory, the first in any of the port cities to designate black heads of household. The directory lists only 105 blacks, 83 men and 22 women, which is only one-sixth as many heads of households as might be expected, given Philadelphia's total black population of about 4,000. Of the men, 41 percent worked in unskilled positions as laborers, sweepers, sawyers, and whitewashers. Those employed in domestic or personal service, mostly as waitingmen and coachmen, composed another 12 percent. Nearly 10 percent were mariners, and this figure should probably be doubled, given what other sources reveal about black participation in the seagoing labor force and the traditional underenumeration of seafarers. But a significant number worked as professionals (5 percent) and artisans (12 percent) or were engaged in retailing or other proprietorial roles as hucksters, carters, bakers, fruiterers, and grocers (21 percent). Among the 22 women, more than a third were retailers and boardinghouse keepers, and half labored as washerwomen. In 1797 a Philadelphia editor confirmed this evidence that a large number of Afro-Americans had found profitable employment and made a satisfactory adjustment to freedom; he found "the most afflictive and accumulated distress amongst the *Irish Emigrants* and the *French Negroes.*"

Twenty-one years after the 1795 enumeration another Philadelphia directory that designated free blacks provided a second snapshot of black occupational structure. The 1816 directory listed nearly 900 blacks with occupations. The male occupations indicate remarkable stability over two decades. There was a slight drift toward retail and proprietorial roles and toward domestic and personal service, and an erosion of professional positions. But mariners and artisans held their own and even increased slightly their proportions among free blacks.

While more than half of Philadelphia's black men held positions as laborers, bootblacks, coachmen, sweep masters, wood sawyers, or waiters, many former slaves had found their way into more remunerative and independent occupations. One in five was a small retailer or proprietor, or, in a few cases, a professional. Philadelphia's forty-five black oystermen dominated that business; fifty other blacks were traders, grocers, shopkeepers, fruiterers, victuallers, and milkmen. One in ten listed in the directory worked as a mariner and another one of every eight as a craftsman. Thirty-two black artisans labored in the building trades, eleven in metal crafts, twenty-seven in leather trades, twelve in shipbuilding, and a dozen more in miscellaneous crafts. The transition from slavery to freedom does not appear to have altered dramatically the occupational structure of black society, and most freedpeople continued to work as day laborers and domestic servants. Still, some improved themselves considerably by plying artisan trades or keeping small shops of their own.

Many black men found employment within the fast-growing black neighborhoods of Philadelphia. To even the least skilled worker this must have provided a satisfaction of its own. And even among those who were no longer permitted to practice an artisan skill acquired under slavery, a life of semiskilled or unskilled work for white employers at least left the black waterman, well digger, or whitewasher free to retire each night to his own residence, free to form a family, free to change his residence, free to worship where he chose, and free to seek the company of his brethren.

In analyzing the occupations of black women, whose wages were indispensable to the household budget, city directories and federal census returns are of little use, for they usually reported only those women who were widowed heads of household. But investigations into black life by the Pennsylvania Abolition Society partially fill the void. In 1795 the Society reported that "the Women generally, both married and single, wash clothes for a living." Half a century later, a far more extensive survey of black households showed that of 4,249 adult women, all but 290 (7 percent) were employed. The vast majority performed domestic labor, mostly for white families, as washerwomen, seamstresses, and "dayworkers"; others were cooks, tradeswomen, ragpickers, and proprietors. In total, employed black women outnumbered employed black men by 3,959 to 3,358, which corresponds roughly to the female-male ratio reported in the 1850 census.

The Society's reports make it evident that a large majority of free black women performed domestic wage labor for white households throughout the early nineteenth century. For the black family this provided the additional income necessary for survival. The laboring experience of the black woman had changed little since bondage, for under slavery she had also worked in the homes of the white upper and middle classes. Emancipation did not lessen white demand for black domestic servants but merely converted slave labor into domestic wage labor. But some black women, perhaps one in twenty, now occupied roles formerly held by no slave women: shopkeeper, fruiterer, baker, boardinghouse keeper, schoolmistress, huckster. If emancipation degraded the work roles of some black men while raising those of others, it elevated the occupations of a few black women, leaving the labor of the vast majority unaltered.

For newly freed blacks, moving to the city was a logical way to prepare for the future and find work, but changing one's name was the most personal and one of the most satisfying aspects of the transition from bondage to freedom. "A new name," writes Ira Berlin, "was both a symbol of personal liberation and an act of political defiance; it reversed the enslavement process and confirmed the free Negro's newly won liberty, just as the loss of an African name had earlier symbolized enslavement."

By analyzing the forenames and surnames of slaves and freed Afro-Americans in the northern cities, two stages in the process of cultural transformation can be observed: first, the creation of a creole culture; second, the symbolic obliteration of the slave past. A generation before the Revolution, when slave importations into the northern ports were at an all-time high, African names or Anglicized versions of African names were common. Twenty-two of the 155 slaves indicted for conspiracy in New York in 1741 had African day names—Cuffee, Cajoe, Quash, Quack, and the like—signifying the day of the week on which they were born. A slightly larger number bore classical names—Pompey, Caesar, and Cato were the most popular—and 28 carried place-names, such as London, York, Hanover, Hereford, and Jamaica. Anglo-American names, usually in a shortened form, were the most common, with 47 slaves named Dick, John, Tom, Toby, or Will. What is striking in this mix of cognomens is the frequency of African names and the relative absence of biblical names, which were attached to only 4 percent of the indicted slaves.

As slaves adjusted to life in the northern cities, formed conjugal relationships, and bore children, they rapidly adopted Anglo-American cultural ways, especially in comparison to slaves in the southern colonies. On large plantations blacks found the preservation of African customs far easier, because the slave quarters furnished Africans with an arena for cultural autonomy. The urban slave, in contrast, almost always lived amidst a white family, and, while a few other slaves sometimes resided in the same domicile, urban blacks constantly intermingled with whites. Strong evidence of rapid northern acculturation before the

Revolution can be found in the forenames given to slave children as they were brought before the Anglican church in Philadelphia for baptism. African, geographical, and classical names were far less common than among the New York slave conspirators of 1741, and biblical and English names appeared far more frequently. No scholar has been able to determine precisely how these forenames were assigned, but historians have presumed that while the master may have had some role in naming slave children, the parents bore most of the responsibility. To the extent that slaves assumed the right to name their own children, the infrequency of classical and geographical names represented their desire to rid themselves of absurd invocations of the classical past and of names that connoted where the master was from or where he traded. By the same token, the increasing frequency of biblical and English names provides evidence of adaptation to the culture into which their children were being born and would presumably spend their lives. Philadelphia's slaves often passed their own names along to their children if their names were Elizabeth, Sarah, Benjamin, Richard, or John. But they rarely perpetuated such names as London, Toss, Sharp, Cato, Othello, and Dirander; and such African names as Quasheba, Quam, and Cuffee also disappeared.

Upon gaining freedom, Afro-Americans took complete possession of the naming process. Aggregate statistics on forenames, compiled from city directories, manumission records, and census returns, demonstrate the psychological importance that blacks attached to affirming freedom and wiping away reminders of the slave past by taking a new name or adding to an old one. Of all the free black men listed in the Philadelphia directory of 1795, only one had retained a place-name (Dublin), and none carried derisive names (such as Mistake, Moody, and Fortune) that had been hung on them by former owners. The frequency of biblical names increased. The same was true of English names but with one significant difference. The diminutive forms that had earlier been so common had been traded in for the full English cognomen: Ben became Benjamin, Will became William, Tom became Thomas.

Within a generation of emancipation the classically derived Cato, Scipio, Caesar, and Pompey had all but disappeared among Philadelphia's free blacks, as had geographical names and names connoting qualities, virtuous or otherwise. African forenames were also rare by 1795, with only an occasional Cuffe or Cuff remaining from the list of old day names. But biblical names were on the rise among blacks, who in many cases had been born free: Abraham, Isaac, Jacob, Daniel, David, and Joseph were common, and black men named Absalom, Aaron, Elijah, Ishmael, or Solomon were scattered throughout the city. However, the most common male forenames in the 1795 listing were John, James, William, and Thomas, and English forenames accounted for three-quarters of all the names of black men in the 1816 directory—striking evidence of the degree of acculturation that had occurred since slave days. In Boston and New York the trend was the same. Slaves freed in New York after the Revolution divested themselves of comical and geographical forenames, African day names died out rapidly, classical names waned, and English and biblical names were increasingly common.

Surnames also provide important evidence of how emancipated Afro-Americans extended the boundaries of psychological space as they pursued a new life in the port cities. In slavery most blacks had no surnames or carried the surname of a master. In freedom they took new surnames or chose one for the first time. In this selection process there was a pronounced effort to make complete the break with the former master. Few of the free blacks listed in the Philadelphia directory of 1795 bore the names of their former owners. The same is true in New York, where the surnames of Dutch slaveowners in manumission records were in use only rarely by 1830. Cognomens such as Alburtus, Brinkerhoff, DePeyster, Schermerhorn, Van der Water, and Van Zandt held no appeal for New York's free blacks, who traded them in for names that bore no reminders of the days of bondage.

Many freed Afro-Americans used the choice of a new name to make manifest their transition from slavery to freedom. Freemans, Newmans, Somersets, and Armsteads were scattered through the census returns of all northern cities. Freeman appears with much greater frequency in New York than in Boston or Philadelphia, which may indicate that since New York's free blacks lived in a society where slavery continued for so long after the Revolution, a number of them wanted to declare their liberation unmistakably through a name announcing their new status. Names suggesting artisan skills were also fairly common—Cooper, Mason, and Carpenter, for example—although sometimes this may have been coincidental. Occasionally a former slave would celebrate freedom with etymological flourish, as did Francis Drake and Hudson Rivers in New York and Julius Caesar in Philadelphia. Others took names commemorating turning points or moments of high drama in their lives. The previous name of the slaveborn West Indian sailor who turned up in Philadelphia during the Revolution and signed aboard John Paul Jones's *Bonhomme Richard* remains unknown. But this Afro-American mariner fought lustily in the epic battle against the *Serapis*, losing a leg during the sanguinary fray, and sometime thereafter renamed himself Paul Jones.

But freed Afro-Americans overwhelmingly chose the most common English surnames, such as Johnson, Brown, Smith, Morris, Williams, Jackson, Thompson, and Thomas. The plainest of English names took an uncommon hold on the black consciousness during the renaming process, to an extent that makes it possible to speak of a homogenization of black surnames during the first and second generations of freedom. Of the 910 surnames of blacks in the 1816 Philadelphia directory, five—Brown, Johnson, Jones, Jackson, and Miller—account for 15 percent of the entries, and the twelve most frequently given surnames make up almost one-quarter of all family names, a far more concentrated naming pattern than among whites.

This selection of common white surnames seems to indicate that free blacks wished to minimize the chance that they would be associated, either within the black community or in the view of whites, with the slave past. To assume the name Johnson or Jones or Jackson was as neutral as one could get, and its full meaning can be appreciated only by observing—to take the Philadelphia case—how studiously blacks avoided the names of prominent slaveowning families such as Cadwalader, Wharton, Shippen, and Dickinson. The clustering of common English surnames among blacks also shows how far acculturation had proceeded and perhaps indicates a growing feeling of racial solidarity among freedpeople. The African past had not been forgotten, but in the names by which they established their individual identities northern urban free blacks strove to show that they were both Afro-American and free of slavery's grip.

In leaving thralldom behind, northern free blacks sought to perpetuate or create a family life. They neither easily nor automatically accomplished this. The great disruption of slave family life during the Revolutionary War, the dislocation in the war's aftermath, the postemancipation migration, and the constraints placed on family formation by the poverty that enshrouded freedmen and freedwomen all made the creation of black households a complex, multifaceted process that occurred not instantly but over a period of years, extending through the first generation in freedom. Consequently, emancipated Afro-Americans first extricated themselves from white households; then often combined households, with relatives, friends, and boarders intermingling; and finally, as they were able, established nuclear households. The process proceeded at different rates in the three cities, depending on when slavery ended, but everywhere black family life grew more secure.

Any discussion of the free black family should be prefaced with a few comments on slave family life in the northern cities. First, a majority of slaveowners in Boston and Philadelphia owned only one adult slave, which greatly reduced the possibilities that two-parent slave families could live, work, and raise children together. Of Philadelphia's 905 slaves aged twelve or older in 1767, one-third lived by themselves in the home of their owner, and another third lived with only one other slave. The hundreds of inventories of slaveowner estates recorded in Boston between 1685 and 1775 indicate that nearly two-thirds of all slaves lived by themselves or with one other slave. Multiple slaveholding was more common in Philadelphia, with one-third of all slaves living alone or with one other slave, and two-thirds living in groups of three or more. In New York, where slaveholding was more extensive, the presence of two adult slaves in the same white household was more common in the colonial era. But slave units declined in size over the course of the eighteenth century. In 1790 six of every ten slaveowners held only one slave and another two had only two slaves, meaning that most slave children did not live in two-parent households.

Despite the barriers to living together, slaves commonly married in all the cities, and fertility rates among black women were similar to those prevailing among white women. In New York, where the best data are available, child-woman ratio among blacks was the same or higher than among whites in three mid-eighteenth-century censuses and was somewhat lower in 1771. The child-woman ratio in Philadelphia cannot be measured, but the steady procession of slaves who came to Christ Church to be married and who brought their children there for christening provides firm evidence of slave family formation. For example, Richard and Dinah brought their son Salisbury before the church early in 1749. William Allen's slaves, Quaco and Hannah, presented their son Joseph for christening in July 1751, returned with another son, James, in the following year, and brought a daughter, Hannah, to the church in 1755. Between 1742 and 1775 several hundred slave children were christened in a church that included one-third to one-half of the city's slaveowners.

Still, enslaved blacks had to struggle to maintain the sanctity of their family life. Masters not only shattered slave families by sale, but they also bound out slave children, sometimes as young as six years of age. For example, William Masters, one of Philadelphia's largest slaveowners, apprenticed eleven of the seventeen slave children, aged four to sixteen, who had been born to his adult slaves. Both of Bellinda's daughters, aged twelve and seven, were bound out until the age of eighteen, the older daughter to a man in Wilmington, Delaware. Scipio and Chloe had their seven-year-old son and four-year-old daughter at their sides, but three older sons were bound out. In sum, before the Revolution slaves in northern cities eagerly sought conjugal relationships, frequently parented children in spite of not living together, but had difficulty in keeping their offspring with them because of the common practices of hiring out and sundering family ties through sale.

With freedom, Afro-Americans began to establish separate households and secure an independent family life. But for many extricating themselves from their master's house proved to be a slow and difficult task. In Boston, where slavery had been completely eradicated by 1790, more than one of every three blacks still resided in a white household at the time of the first federal census, most of them without another black in the same residence. Thirty years later, all but 16 percent of the city's blacks were members of autonomous black households. In Philadelphia, where 13 percent of the city's blacks remained enslaved in 1790, half of the free blacks, many of them emancipated only in the previous few years, still lived in white households. A generation later, at the time of the 1820 census, only one in four did.

Economic necessity, which pressed hard on the newly freed, was doubtless the largest factor in keeping emancipated blacks in the households of former masters or obliging them to take live-in domestic jobs in the homes of other whites. The need was probably greatest when a man or woman had no spouse or relatives and was therefore forced to seek the security that service in a white household could provide. A single black, usually a woman, resided in more than half the white households where former slaves remained. The fact that twice as many black women as men continued to live in white households also indicates the demand for live-in domestic servants.

Comparative data for New York confirm the notion that from one-half to two-thirds of northern blacks were able to establish their own households within a few years of gaining freedom, while for the others the process was much slower. In 1790, when New York still had twice as many slaves as free blacks, about 36 percent of the free blacks were living in white households, almost the same proportion as in Boston. Three decades later, when all but 16 percent of Boston's free blacks and all but 27 percent of Philadelphia's had extricated themselves from white households, 38 percent of New York's free blacks still lived among whites, almost the same as thirty years before. Slavery's longer life explains the difference between New York and the other cities. A gradual abolition law was not passed until 1799, and even then it took almost three decades more to end slavery. In 1810, 1,686 blacks remained enslaved in New York City, and many of those who received their freedom in the next decade were probably among the free blacks continuing to reside in white households at the time of the 1820 census. In Boston and Philadelphia, by contrast, the emancipation, process began earlier and concluded more rapidly. By the time of the 1820 census, almost all Afro-Americans in the two cities had been free for a generation or more.

Though residence in a white household, often under an indenture lasting seven years or more, was the intermediate step between subservient and autonomous existence for many freed blacks, a large majority of urban blacks lived in black households by 1820. The census returns for that year do not indicate exact family relationships within households, so it is impossible to delineate family composition exactly. But this census did for the first time enumerate black residents by age and sex, thus permitting some tentative generalizations about black household and family formation in the early decades of freedom.

In all three cities more than three-quarters of the black households contained at least one adult male and one adult female. This was true of 76 percent of the black households in Boston, 79 percent in Philadelphia, and 81 percent in New York. Single-parent families were even less frequent in black households containing children under the age of fourteen. Such households were overwhelmingly headed by both an adult male and female—in 78 percent of the cases in Boston, 88 percent in Philadelphia, and 82 percent in New York. In a sample of 1,407 black children under fourteen years of age in 1820, 92 percent lived in households that included at least one adult male and one adult female.

Still, blacks achieved the goal of a nuclear household slowly. In the immediate aftermath of slavery, unable to establish their own separate households but unwilling to continue to reside with whites, blacks often joined together to form large extended or augmented household units. Black families boarded relatives and friends newly arrived from the countryside and emerging from slavery with no assets or knowledge of urban life. Strong evidence exists for this pattern in New York, where emancipation came later than in Boston or Philadelphia, although the pattern was probably present in the other seaport cities as well in the immediate aftermath of slavery. Thus in 1820 the average black household was far larger in New York than in Philadelphia or Boston: 6.3 persons as compared with 3.9 in Philadelphia and 4.2 in Boston. This reflected not a larger number of children in New York black families but the greater number of "extra" people in the household. While most Boston and Philadelphia black families lived in nuclear units by the second decade of the nineteenth century, the majority of black households in New York remained augmented or extended, and the nonfamily type of household virtually nonexistent. In Philadelphia and Boston 7 to 8 percent of the black households were made up of a single male or female or several adults of the same sex. But in New York only one of 247 households in Ward Six was of the nonfamily type. This circumstance, combined with the large number of blacks living in white households relative to the other cities, suggests that the distance from slavery was often still too short for an individual free black to maintain a household of his or her own.

Black families generally contained far fewer children than white families. In New York and Boston the number of children per adult woman was more than twice as high for whites as for blacks. In Philadelphia the ratio was 2.7 for whites and 1.6 for blacks. Some of this difference may be accounted for by the extremely high mortality rate among blacks, usually two to three times that of whites. But family limitation was also a factor. In New York, the one city where we have data from the slave period to compare with the 1820 census figures, it appears that the woman-child ratio actually dropped significantly as slaves passed from bondage to freedom.

These various measurements, although crude, make it clear that the stereotypes about the unstable and matrifocal black family after slavery have little basis in fact, at least so far as concerns the seaport cities of the North. In general, these data support Herbert G. Gutman's contention that "black households and family systems were exceedingly complex in the aftermath of emancipaton" but that conjugal and nuclear-family relationships predominated. In all three cities, though the timing differed, freed blacks moved toward the establishment of two-parent nuclear households. Boston, farthest from slavery, had the smallest proportion of blacks living in white households in 1820 (one in six) and a high incidence of nuclear families among black householders (three of five). New York, where 45 percent of the black population remained enslaved in 1800 and 5 percent in 1820, had the largest proportion of free blacks living in white households (nearly two of five) and among black householders a dramatically lower incidence of nuclear families. Philadelphia's free blacks, who were between their counterparts in Boston and New York in terms of distance from slavery, were also between the two extremes in terms of the proportion who lived in white households (one of four) and slightly ahead of Boston in the formation of nuclear families. The effort to create autonomous families was one of the remarkable features of Afro-American life in the early years of freedom.

As they worked themselves free of white households and established households of their own, new patterns of black residence began to emerge. In slave days, of course, Afro-Americans had resided with their masters or with those to whom they had been hired out. Since these masters lived in cities that were only gradually becoming segregated by function and class, slaves lived scattered throughout urban areas. In the first decade of freedom this dispersal continued in some measure, because from one-third to one-half of all manumitted slaves continued to live in white households.

In the 1780s, as blacks began forming their own households, they made independent decisions about where to locate. In Philadelphia, to focus on one case, they began clustering in two areas, one old and one new. The old area, in the northern part of the city, was in North and South Mulberry wards, a relatively poor district of the city with a concentration of Irish and German laboring-class families. Located between Arch and Vine streets west of Fourth, North and South Mulberry wards attracted about 29 of the city's 169 black households by 1790. Another 32 families lived in the Northern Liberties, beyond North Mulberry Ward. The other area was almost entirely new. Located in the southern part of the city, it comprised Cedar and Locust wards and the west part of South Ward. As late as 1785 this had been mostly open land, but within a few years contractors began erecting cheap housing to accommodate the city's growing population. By 1790 some 56 black households had established themselves in the area. They appeared as the advance guard of what would shortly become an enormous movement of black Philadelphians into this southern part of the city. Fifty-two other black families were dispersed throughout the rest of the city.

Because new cheaply constructed tenements rented at a lower rate than older but larger dwellings, black Philadelphians moved steadily into the southern section of the city. But another process, the establishment of African churches and schools, also drew blacks. In 1791, Richard Allen and Absalom Jones were laying plans to build a black church at Sixth and Lombard streets, in some measure because Philadelphia's free blacks had been moving into new housing in this section of Cedar Ward. By 1794 two black churches had opened their doors in the same neighborhood. But if the nascent black neighborhood attracted African churches, the churches, once established, became vital centers of black community life, drawing hundreds of black families as they worked their way out of white households into their own residences. St. Thomas's had a membership of 427 one year after its building was completed; by 1813 it had 560 members, while Bethel Church counted 1,272 communicants.

The lure of the black churches can be seen in the changing residential pattern of blacks in Philadelphia. Black families continued to settle in the northern part of the city, many of them perhaps because they had jobs in that part of town. But the black population in Cedar and Locust wards grew much faster, from 265 free blacks in 1790 to 4,191 in 1820. This "Cedar Street corridor" of black life, as Emma Lapsansky styles it, was no black ghetto. While free blacks established residences there in great numbers, they were never a majority in this period. Neighborhoods remained mixed, both racially and occupationally. Yet the development of racial and class segregation had received a strong impetus as builders constructed primarily cheap housing in new parts of the city and black families sought the security and group consciousness that came through residential consolidation.

To the south of Cedar Ward lay West Southwark and Moyamensing. Still not incorporated into the city at this time, they nonetheless were part of the rapid development of the southern part of Philadelphia. Free blacks moved there by the hundreds after 1790, living in "cabins," "sheds," and "mean low box[es] of wood." Especially in Moyamensing the free black population increased dramatically in thirty years, from 27 in 1790 to 1,174 in 1820. All told, this southern sector of the city, composed of Locust and Cedar wards, West Southwark, and Moyamensing, contained three of every five blacks in Philadelphia by 1820. Moreover, among independent black householders the percentage living in this area was even higher.

Some sense of these emerging neighborhoods, where free black families mixed extensively with laboring-class whites, can be gained from looking at city directories. Gaskill Street, which ran from Third to Fifth between Cedar and Lombard streets, had two black families listed in the 1795 directory and three in the directory of 1811. But five years later, twenty-four black families were spread along Gaskill, all but two of them in the block between Third and Fourth streets. Sometimes families doubled up, as did Richard Bennett, shoemaker, John Bahimy, mariner, and Joseph Reed, laborer, at 62 Gaskill. Charles Brown, porter, and Phillips Exeter, washerwoman, shared 88 Gaskill. By 1816 eighteen black families made their residence on Blackberry Alley, running north and south from the Pennsylvania Hospital. Among the heads of household were a carpenter, painter, carter, porter, plasterer, trader, gardener, waiter, coachman, and laborer. Black families made their homes throughout the Cedar Street corridor, especially in the crowded courts and alleys that builders and landlords were developing in the early nineteenth century.

In the organization of black institutions, closely tied to emerging neighborhoods, free Afro-Americans constructed the social, religious, and emotional ligaments of their communities. The black church, as many historians have noted, stood at the center of this process and marked the strongest tie between the distant African past, the more proximate slave past, and the present and future as free persons. "The Negro church," wrote Du Bois, "is the peculiar and characteristic product of the transplanted African. . . . It has preserved, on the one hand, many functions of tribal organization, and on the other hand, many of the family functions. Its tribal functions are shown in its religious activity, its social authority, and general guiding and co-ordinating work; its family functions are shown by the fact that the church is a centre of social life and intercourse."

Two closely related factors led to the organization of the first black churches in northern cities in the 1790s: discriminatory treatment in white churches and "the gradual rise of a community of interest" among the Afro-Americans drawn into the metropolis after emancipation. This separatist church movement drew much inspiration from the indifference of white churches to the social and political injustices that freed blacks confronted at the end of the eighteenth century. It was also grounded in the desire of Afro-Americans for a more evangelical gospel than white churches proffered and in a determination "to arise out of the dust and shake ourselves, and throw off that servile fear, that the habit of oppression and bondage trained us up in." Similarly, in New York and Boston separate black churches emerged not only because of discrimination but also because of "a growing self-reliance and the rise of individual leaders."

To some extent the rise of the independent black church appears to have been triggered as much by concern for the religious care of the dead as by concern for the living. In both Philadelphia and New York free black churches had their origins in the Free African societies established in the late 1780s and early 1790s. In each case one of the society's first acts was to apply for a separate black burial ground. White churches did not permit the mortal remains of black worshippers to be interred in their cemeteries but instead consigned blacks to the Potter's Field or "Stranger's Burial Ground," as it was tellingly called in Philadelphia. This extension to the dead of the racial inequalities among the living may have been especially grievous to Afro-Americans, whose African religious heritage stressed ancestor reverence and thus emphasized dignifying the dead.

To signify their group identity and to separate themselves from whites, blacks—from the beginning—named their churches, schools, and mutual aid associations and fraternal societies "African." In 1787 Philadelphia free blacks established their first independent organization and called it the Free African Society. From it derived the African Methodist Episcopal Church and the African Episcopal Church of St. Thomas. The African Baptist and African Presbyterian churches would follow. Among the benevolent societies established in this early period were the Angolian Society and the Angola Beneficial Association in 1808, the Sons of Africa in 1810, the African Female Benevolent Society (founding date unknown), and the Male African Benevolent Society in 1819. The Quaker school for blacks, founded in 1770, became known as the Friends African School in the 1790s. The first black insurance company, in existence by 1809, was called the African Insurance Company of Philadelphia. In New York the term *African* was also used for almost all the early churches, the first black school, and the first mutual aid societies. In Boston the African Society, founded in 1797, established the African School in 1798 and the African Meeting House in 1805. The frequency of the term in the names of early churches, schools, and benevolent societies, when considered in conjunction with the rapid Anglicization of black personal names in this period, suggests that while free blacks took on common English names as a way of wiping out the slave past, they simultaneously and self-consciously fostered black solidarity by affixing an adjective to their institutions that would unmistakably differentiate them from parallel white institutions.

Establishing independent institutions took time, and the continued enslavement of a sizable portion of the black population delayed the process, partly because the business of obtaining freedom for those still in bondage absorbed the time, money, and energy of those who were free, and partly because it took a generation of freedom for blacks to extricate themselves from white households and establish residences of their own in neighborhoods where black consciousness could thrive.

This stifling effect of slavery can be seen in the wide disparity in black institutional development in Philadelphia and New York. The two cities had black populations of roughly the same size in the first quarter of the nineteenth century. But whereas nearly all Philadelphia blacks were free by 1790, it took another generation to extinguish slavery in New York City. Thus by 1813, when Philadelphia blacks had created six black churches with a total membership of 2,366, only two existed in New York, with a membership that cannot have exceeded one-third of Philadelphia's. Similarly, New York's first free black school was founded in 1786 and the second not until 1820. Meanwhile, by 1811 nine black schools were operating in Philadelphia. New York blacks founded their first mutual aid society, the New York African Society for Mutual Relief, in 1810, while Philadelphia blacks had organized eleven benevolent societies by 1813. Where slavery had been expunged soon after the Revolution, black institutional life thrived; where it lingered, it had a deadening effect even on those blacks who did escape its clutches.

At different rates, black institutions took form in all northern cities. Created out of the massing of free blacks in the cities and the rise of an independent black consciousness, these churches, schools, fraternal societies, and mutual aid associations in turn became part of the magnetic pull of urban life. By the 1820s Philadelphia Afro-Americans had created an institutional life that was richer and more stable than that of the lower-income whites with whom they shared neighborhoods. Since Afro-Americans were "blocked from upward mobility out of the neighborhood," writes Lapsansky, "they wanted institutions that would provide them with a reasonable future there." For whites, by contrast, these increasingly class-segregated neighborhoods were seen as a "brief stopping place" on the way to something better. White gangs were the institution better suited to "a transient constituency," for they required no large expenditures for permanent structures, no "long-range planned activity," and no regular commitments of time. Hence, white churches and fraternal organizations fared poorly in comparison to black institutions in the lower-class wards of Philadelphia in this period, and black institutions became the envy of whites in racially mixed neighborhoods. Oppressed both as an economic class and a racial caste, urban freedmen and freedwomen drew upon a collective black consciousness to form their own network of thriving institutions.

"Sir," thundered South Carolina's Robert Y. Hayne in the famous nullification debate of 1830, "there does not exist on the face of the earth, a population so poor, so wretched, so vile, so loathsome, so utterly destitute of all the comforts, conveniences, and decencies of life, as the unfortunate blacks of Philadelphia, New York, and Boston.

Liberty has been to them the greatest of calamities, the heaviest of curses." The words were uttered, of course, to shame the North for its treatment of emancipated slaves and to contrast their condition unfavorably with those still held in bondage in the South. Hayne's indictment truthfully acknowledged the wretched effects of northern racism. White urban dwellers in the North, as Leon Litwack has written, "worked free Negroes severely in menial employments, excluded them from the polls, the juries, the churches, and the learned professions, snubbed them in social circles, and finally even barred them from entering some states." Yet this is not the full story, for it focuses on what was done to free blacks rather than on what emancipated Afro-Americans did for themselves. Alongside the history of oppression must be placed the history of people striving to live life as fully, as freely, and as creatively as their inner resources and external circumstances would allow. In the northern capitals of American life after the Revolution, emancipated slaves suffered greatly to be sure, but they also formed communities that would not die and created a viable culture of their own.

*Susan Beverley Randolf, a member of the antebellum
planter class, was mistress of a plantation household.*

The Moral Bind: Women and the Plantation Household

CATHERINE CLINTON

Southern slave society gave rise to a peculiar culture and morality that we identify with the antebellum planter class. In part, it was a product of the attempt of the master class to create an idealized world in a society based on the brutal system of slavery. An important component and justification of this culture was paternalism. The paternalistic planter perceived himself not as an oppressor but as a benevolent and generous guardian of an inferior race. Indeed, a master derived much of his authority from playing the role of responsible father to his slaves.

Paternalism shaped relationships within the planter household as well. In a private world where the husband and father reigned supreme, the southern woman was expected to behave in a prescribed way. In the selection that follows, Catherine Clinton portrays the idealized world and role of the southern plantation mistress that contributed so substantially to defining the peculiar culture of the antebellum South.

Because the system of chattel slavery allowed for the systematic exploitation of black women, slaveholders, Clinton argues, created a fantasy world that sentimentalized and idealized the white woman. Wives and daughters were burdened with perpetuating and guarding the morality and virtues of their race. This is the culture that figuratively elevated women to a pedestal. What does this account of the private side of plantation life reveal about the roles and attitudes of men and women of the planter class? What was peculiar about their paternalistic culture?

T he idealized image of the southern lady had numerous sources. Men were virtually obsessed with female innocence. The notion of white women as virginal precipitated a whole series of associations: delicate as lilies, spotless as doves, polished as alabaster, fragile as porcelain— but above all, pure as the driven snow (with its inherent connotation of coldness). The vocabulary of ideologues and preceptors conveyed sentimentalized yet severe prescriptions for women.

Using this vocabulary, slaveholders created a fantasy world in an attempt to transform the harsher aspects of life around them, to insulate themselves against those elements that would eventually bring about the downfall of the plantation system. The exalted image of the lady, like the portrait of the happy-go-lucky "Sambo," was not merely a figment of planter imaginations but a powerful coercive force within plantation society.

Southern men portrayed white women as unsullied and frail, perhaps as an unconscious counterpoint to their own option of rowdy debauchery. Because the system of slavery could and did allow for the sordid exploitation of black women by white masters, male slaveowners were by implication morally tainted. The ban on sexual relations between white women and black men and the southern lady's elevation to a pedestal were socially enforced and strictly observed to counter male corruption: a balance of requisite evil and hyperbolic good. The character and nature of this double standard will be developed later, but its existence serves to remind us not only that southern slaveowners struggled with ambivalence, but that moral persuasion and economic necessity were in constant and racking conflict within plantation culture.

In the southern plantation system, relief from the burdens of physical labor allegedly offset, for the others, the moral taxation of slaveowning. Whites freed themselves from drudgery by using slaves as manual laborers—so the more indolent their lives appeared, the greater the wealth (in slaves) implied. Elite males in many societies have used women, too, as living proof of their wealth and status, testimonies of their worth. Planters necessarily chose for their women the role that would most flatter the image of plantation life that southern slaveowners were striving to project; hence the formulation of the mythical ideal of the southern lady.

The path to this ideal was long and arduous for planter daughters. The children of slaveowners were taught from an early age that their actions reflected the honor and virtue of the planter patriarchs. South-

THE MORAL BIND   From Catherine Clinton, *The Plantation Mistress: Woman's World in the Old South* (New York: Pantheon, 1982). Copyright © 1982 by Catherine Clinton. Reprinted by permission of Random House, Inc.

ern society prided itself on a rigorous code of behavior. The female preoccupation with the "niceties," a rigid pattern of manners and politeness, contrasted with the obvious indifference of men to much of what they preached. Male authorities subjected everyone but themselves to a strict regimen. Women, children, and slaves followed rules laid down by white men; these rules ostensibly governed male activities as well, but society excused men as long as they conducted their illicit affairs discreetly.

Because a double standard was so completely integrated into southern ethical conduct, men could dedicate themselves to the maintenance of high standards—for women. Female purity became a practical crusade for a society in which the wives and mothers of the ruling class had to be above suspicion. The masters of a biracial slave system were understandably concerned with the sexual continence of those women who bore their heirs and held some sway as keepers of the culture; thus planters required their wives to be living examples of Christian virtue. If plantation mistresses could live above reproach, their husbands, fathers, sons, and brothers could boast of the superiority of their civilization. The vessels to which these men trusted their reproductive potential and cultural values must, of necessity, be unblemished, alabaster representations of the plantation idyll. The sullying influence of slavery must not touch the women of the upper class lest the entire structure crumble.

As cultivators of the land, planters were concerned with the growth and prosperity of all their holdings, human and otherwise. While they carefully supervised both real estate and chattels, nothing surpassed the patriarchs' preoccupation with their offspring. Children were plants to be tended; sons were the sturdy vines and daughters the fragile blossoms in the southern moral garden. Especially during the formative years after infancy, sons and daughters were safeguarded by pious and protective parental guidance. Bolling Hall, an Alabama politician, wrote to his daughter in 1813: "Look at the cedars in the potters' garden, they are the same with those which grow in the forest and would only have assumed their shape and form had it not been for the care and attention of a skillful hand." Hall goes on to describe the evils of temper and vanity and the positive need for pruning, finally counseling his daughter that "as the cedars you will become the ornament of society." David Campbell wrote to his niece Margaret along similar lines in 1831. Concerned with her intellectual cultivation, he advised Margaret to recognize her own ignorance and imperfection, for "the ground is then prepared for the seed and nothing which is sown will be lost."

The moral training of the young was a complex and continuous task for ante-bellum parents, most of whom believed, as a southern gentleman explained in his commonplace book, that "man is a compound creature made up of three distinct parts, viz. the body, which is the earthly or mortal part of him; the soul which is the animal or sensitive part; and the spirit or mind which is the rational and immortal part." They saw individuals as constantly at war with themselves: spirit against flesh, reason battling emotion, mortality at odds with the immortal soul. Christians, in conscience and deed, were called upon to mediate perpetually between these claims. The goal of planter parents was to instill in their children this sense of values, for virtue was "that which can make every station happy, and without which every station must be wretched."

Woman, as a function of her exalted status as guardian of the culture and her isolation from the "outside world," was assigned the role of moral exemplar and counselor. Women's purity and spirituality were believed to be vital assets in assuming the sacred charge of motherhood, which included the burden of religious training. Thus the patriarch imagined his family as a domestic haven sheltered from the pernicious influences of the world and guided by the saintly precepts of his untainted wife.

Not surprisingly, women held different views. Their ideas on moral nature were not philosophical opinions culled from texts, but rather lessons learned from personal contact. Mothers generally conceived of the battle against sin in their offspring as an internal affair, waged against the evil side of human nature, not that of society, which was, after all, merely the magnified reflection of individual nature. The plantation mistress took small comfort from her family circle's seclusion, and believed that evil lay within as well as without.

The practical extension of the household added another dimension. Slaves surrounded the planter family, and their behavior especially preoccupied the majority of plantation mistresses. Most complained constantly of the lying, cheating, and disobedience of their house slaves. The task of supervising black as well as white overwhelmed many mistresses. Few were aware of the irony involved in trying to convince a class held in bondage to follow the moral example of their masters, but all struggled to impose literal, if not Christian, order on every member of the plantation household.

The overt sexual double standard further complicated for plantation mistresses the task of imposing Christian morality on their charges, whether children or slaves. It was next to impossible to enforce ethical precepts while male planters consistently defied them. One concerned mother wrote in her diary: "My children, beloved parts of my being! dear boys, especially, whose life will expose you most, set no wicked thing before you." Plantation life constantly exposed children to illicit sex, venereal diseases, and other harsh aspects of sexuality. Many planter sons ignored their mothers' warnings and explored the forbidden yet beckoning world of interracial sex. Nights in slave cabins were an acceptable adolescent sexual outlet—for males only.

Plantation mistresses attempted to exert an "uplifting" influence on black women—to little avail. One white woman confided in 1829: "I had much solemn talk with our cook Maria, who has now resided with us three years and whose habits in respect to personal purity are a continual violation of the seventh commandment. I hoped an impression was made, but at night she was again absent." This matron interpreted her cook's behavior in typical planter fashion, discounting the idea that Maria might have been exercising her own judgment, doing what she wanted instead of obeying the hypocritical dictates of her racist owners. Instead, this white woman viewed her slave's immorality as a genetic defect: "How truly does it illustrate that the Ethiopian cannot change his skin nor the leopard his spots." Sexual debauchery, interracial or other, was never blamed on men—where surely the guilt partially rested. Planter women pretended—or indeed believed—that the "Ethiopians" were at the root of the problem, not their own husbands, brothers, sons, and fathers.

The very fact of slavery posed an obstacle to the establishment of a sound and integral moral order. Mothers feared for children exposed from so early and impressionable an age to a system ripe for abuse and characterized by tyranny, cruelty, and exploitation. They believed in the negative influence of slavery, but rationalized that this was not inevitable; they cast the issue in terms of contamination and insisted that strict segregation could shield the young by minimizing their opportunities to sin. Virginia Cary warned in her advice book of 1830: "The most deadly of all pernicious habits is that of putting young slaves to be companions of young children. The infant despot enforces his lawless authority over his allotted victim and thus encourages all the most malignant vices of his nature." Although this "lawless" authority was the backbone of the slave system, mothers imagined that this bent should initially be tempered. They believed that adults, but not children, should be allowed such sway; when the individual was old enough, he would somehow rightly assume the responsibilities of the slaveowner's power. The truly Christian mother was powerless against the potent moral imperatives of slavery.

No matter how benevolently protected their childhood had been, most young men eventually succumbed to the arrogance cultivated by a slaveowning society. One girl complained: "You slaveholders have lived so long on your plantations with no one to gainsay or contradict you that you expect to govern everybody and have it all your own way. I can see it in Father—in Brother John—in Brother Patrick." It was at this point that the moral universes of male and female separated; slavery, the most significant economic and political influence in southern society, was in opposition to the central value of the religious and social order, Christian virtue. Although both men and women of the master class resisted the notion that the possession of slaves was the real sin undermining virtue, planters and especially their wives were disturbed by the numerous vices that stemmed from slaveholding. Women, the guardians of virtue, had to achieve a balance between these values, and the deception, self-deception, and contradiction involved imposed considerable strain on their emotional lives.

The tombstone of Milly Jones reads: "In the various characters of wife, mother, sister, friend and mistress she was ever affectionate and truly exemplary." The model woman in the plantation South was able in myriad roles, possessing "sentiments that would do honor to a Roman matron in the best times of that republic." To fulfill these expectations, southern belles not only underwent long and careful tutorship beneath their domestic role-models, but also extensive formal education outside the family circle. Plantation mistresses drew on both British advice literature and American texts, including Virginia Cary's work, *Letters on Female Character*, and Mrs. Taylor's volume, *Practical Hints to Young Females*, which contained such useful chapters as Conduct to the Husband, Domestic Economy, Servants, Education, Sickness, Visitors, Keeping a Home, Recreation, and The Step Mother. The urgent need for this domestic guidance was clear to planters, despite the relative undervaluing of practical training for women. John Campbell wrote to his sister in 1827: "Some men have said that (even in our enlightened day) females need not to be taken as much pains with as to their education as the males; for the Creator has not given them as strong powers for their mind as he has given the males. What a pitiful and unfounded excuse. . . . I am of the opinion that females have equally as strong powers given to their minds as the males and if either have the strongest it is the female." But planters trusted their wives to instill in daughters a sense of feminine values which would counter any "masculine" effects an education might produce.

Without proper supervision, a woman's education could lead her to the unattractive plight which Southerners believed beset the "masculine" Queen Elizabeth I. As a gentleman wrote to his sister, another Elizabeth, regarding the British monarch: "She reigned over her people with distinguished ability, yet perhaps in private life she would have been harsh and unamiable. She might not have professed those tender sensibilities, those soft feminine and engaging manners which throw such a charm around the female character in her intercourse with society." Even a bluestocking like Georgian Mary Telfair wrote to her confidante and fellow spinster, Mary Few: "Superiority of intellect is no safeguard to domestic happiness—Sweetness of temper, ingenuousness, and disinterestedness are the qualities which throw a charm around the domestic circle." "Throwing charm" was the paramount duty of the female sex.

Ante-bellum attitudes toward women reveal deep and pervasive conflicts within plantation culture. The cult of virtue was all the more fervent because men believed that the opposite sex possessed a dual and dangerous essence; femininity was rooted in vice, but women could be raised to a state of virtue. This process of redemption was the sacred duty of planter parents. Daughters were rescued from their sinful natures by stiff doses of discipline and the improving examples of Christian mothers, themselves already "saved." Many of the toasts proposed by planters at celebratory gatherings during this era reveal the ambivalence aroused by the female sex. The exaggerated gallantry of southern chivalry articulated the myth of innocent purity ("Woman at such an hour as this, her spirit comes over us like the sweet South that breathes upon a bank of violets, stealing and giving ardor.") and, alternately, the veiled threat of feminine influence ("The fair sex—without participation in public affairs their dominion is in the hearts of their countrymen"; "The beauty of a fine woman is the only tyranny to which a man should submit"). The following verse, popular in 1814, pinpoints one aspect of sexual attitudes in plantation culture by equating females with dissipation: "Women and wine, game and deceit / Makes the wealth small and the want great." In yet another toast, females are linked with the implicit threat of evil and vice: "Woman—lovely woman; if she brought death into the world, she produced everlasting life through a Saviour."

Women in a sense symbolized regeneration: death and redemption. If man is to be reborn, he must brave the jaws of death—which have psychologically been personified as female. For example, females are subjected to physical and psychic penetration in the process of reproduction, while men are threatened with engulfment. Each sex endures its own psychic vulnerability: the sexual act allows both parties to participate in mutual risk, with the individual submitting to violation in order to gain a genetically everlasting life. Women's suffering historically has been more institutionalized than men's. Patriarchy has translated male vulnerability concerning reproduction into a variety of restrictions upon female behavior from chastity belts to clitoridectomies. In a realm so sensitive as reproduction, men have been throughout history preoccupied with and severe in power over females, and ante-bellum southern planters were no exception.

Chastity was a crucial condition of female purity. Men sought partners in life who were virginal before marriage and would continue to be virtuous in wedlock. A southern planter rationalized in 1827: "The only security a husband has is found in the purity of his wife's character before her marriage. . . . Hence, I am inclined to believe by the appointment of God, a man has a greater horror of sharing the person of the woman he hopes with another man than a woman has of sharing with a woman. . . . Hence incontinence before marriage, by diminishing the security the husband should have of the fidelity of his wife after marriage, sinks her value so much in the society of which she is a member, and is in fact a greater crime in a woman than in a man." Chastity—or a reputation as chaste—was so much a commodity in southern culture that the courts could place a dollar value on it: "A young lady of South Carolina got a verdict of one thousand dollars against a man (of moderate means) for imputation of unchastity." Although crucial to an unmarried female, continence was no less critical for the matron; husbands extolled the value of their wives in terms of purity.

Social gatherings, however, created climates ripe for immodesty. One young girl confessed her horror at the spectacle of a fashionable wedding: "Their backs and bosoms were all uncovered. My heart was indignant at the sight, and as I saw those shameless women, surrounded by their beaux, I shrank yet farther into the recess." Although this sounds like prudery, a proper unmarried female of any age showed puritanical disdain for any but the most circumspect behavior. Wary of temptation and the punishment that might ensue, southern women believed that men and fashion could threaten their own purity—and fashionable men were doubly dangerous. Correspondence between female friends reveals a vigorous strain of moral chastisement; women fortified each other against the potential treachery of men, as in this letter of 1834: "I am almost glad that Robert Walton has gone; for his manners which are certainly fascinating make his society dangerous for any girl." The writer goes on to warn: "How often is a woman's heart, with its spotless purity given in exchange for one whose every thought is wicked." The strongest defense against temptation was not, however, female friendship, but an auxiliary of purity: piety.

Women's personal moral duty went hand in hand with an evangelical mission to safeguard the souls of their society. Although the ministry remained a male bastion, the role of women in the Christian church increased rather than decreased following the American Revolution, and religion was slowly "feminized" during the first half of the nineteenth century. Indeed, the measure of spiritual prosperity in the culture was gauged on an index of female religiosity. One matron wrote in 1825: "In reality, carelessness and impiety on this sacred occasion [public worship] is not less sinful in men than in women, but public sentiment exacts a much more strict observance of decorous and pious conduct from *our* sex than from *yours.*" The "tender and pious" mother was invaluable to the moral tenor of southern culture. Elizabeth Jaquelin Ambler wrote rapturous accounts of her mother's spiritual example: "She considered cheerfulness a Christian virtue and when ever her health would permit, entered into all the innocent gaieties of life provided they did not interfere with religious duties (none of which under any circumstances did she ever omit). It was her meat and drink to do the will of God and never in one instance do I recollect her ever to have shrunk from it. Her whole life was a continual series of practical Christian duty. . . ."

The struggle against impiety was unending; most girls felt that temptations to sin abounded. A woman wrote her sister in 1821: "I earnestly beseech you to beware of vain jesting, light laughing and talking, in short all frivolous conversation. It will draw your attention from study and poison your mind besides disgusting any genteel person you meet with." Another woman, recently converted, confessed to a friend: "There has lately been a dance at Mrs. Jones' but I did not think it would be very consistent in one who had so lately joined the church to go to a dance for although I do not think it wrong to dance, I do not think dancing parties contribute to growth of grace."

The female preoccupation with "growth of grace" was not a peculiarly southern phenomenon. Rural women throughout the country manifested a strain of religious intensity in their personal lives, a pent-up energy that had little or no public outlet; they diverged only in the external form of their crusades. Southern moralists focused on the vices that most commonly plagued planter daughters: temper, vanity, immodesty, and—the greatest threat of all—impropriety. Plantation mistresses considered temper and vanity to be rather benign flaws, requiring a program of personal vigilance and self-control. Immodesty and impropriety, on the other hand, were malignancies, demanding that the individual be put right by her family and friends before disaster rendered her unsalvageable. These four sins, although not interchangeable, were nevertheless interdependent; accordingly, southern mothers waged a war on all fronts.

Temper was a special problem for plantation women, one in which slavery proved a key factor. "But of the consequences arising from slavery, one of the most pernicious and least notified," Virginia Cary wrote in her advice book, "is its effect on the female temper. I acknowledge it is hard to bear with patience, the trials incident to domestic life in Virginia." Planters would not tolerate female temper, however, demanding compliance without complaint. Fathers cautioned their daughters against any departure from a pleasant disposition: "Be watchful over your temper, nothing can be more disgusting than to see the female bosom, the seat of tenderness and virtue, agitated by anger." A girl's education was liberally enhanced with lessons on female character. A teacher wrote in 1812: "I have just read a little work by Miss Edgeworth, entitled 'The Modern Griselda' . . . the heroine has talents, education, beauty, accomplishments, in short almost every requisite to inspire both love and admiration, and yet renders herself, her husband and her friends miserable by a peevish, irascible temper. It would be well, I think for all our young to read 'The Modern Griselda.' " But books were not enough to guard against youthful tantrums. As Martha Richardson confided to her nephew about their mutual relative: "Elizabeth is improving and I think will turn out a fine woman— she promises to be very smart—but we shall have to watch her temper—this will require great care—we must teach her the importance of governing it entirely—and not to suppress it only to suit occasions—it will cost her some pains, but it will be worth the trial—as her own happiness as well as those she may be connected with depends on it—so much do I value an amiable temper that in my opinion no advantages of education can compensate for want of it."

Many of the cautionary tales traded by plantation mistresses involved the ruin of a good woman by her temper. Having learned these supposed lessons, most women wholly subscribed to the theory that contentment could be obtained only through curtailment of their complaints to men and a seeming acceptance of the established order. At the same time, men were not only disturbed but threatened by women's anger; plantation mistresses were necessary components of slaveowning plantations, and planters required cooperation from the women of the ruling class. Myth and manipulation combined to keep females subordinated. The cult of the lady may have been in part a collaboration: southern gentlemen enshrined and adorned their females, while women were willing to exemplify these "ladylike" virtues. Oppression thus was exercised not only through sanctions against rebellion but internally, as women's compliance with the silencing stereotypes determined their own self-censuring behavior.

Another threat to feminine virtue, but a sin less practically irksome to planters, was vanity. William O. Gregory summed up the fears of many planters when he wrote: "Vanity is truly and emphatically the bane of the female heart. It is a monster of exceeding rapid growth, which requires but little food in its youth to make it grow in a short time to be master of the heart, and to expel thence every noble or virtuous feeling." When Gregory's seventeen-year-old sister Martha attended a wedding against his advice, he punished his sibling for her "vanity" by canceling a prearranged holiday visit. He warned her: "Examine nicely and earnestly into the motives which produce every action, which you do or wish to perform; and whenever you discover vanity to be the prompting cause, forbear by all means to do it."

Although they lectured against the vanity of an excessive preoccupation with grooming, fathers demanded a presentable appearance from their daughters. Bolling Hall wrote in 1813 to his daughter Polly at school: "The precepts of religion strongly injoin the duty of living cleanly in our dress and persons—nothing can be more disgusting than to see a person with dirty hands or face, and to see a girl with dirty clothes is truly shocking." Cleanliness and neatness were the foundations for a ladylike appearance. Thomas Jefferson advised his elder daughter, Martha, in 1783: "Nothing is so disgusting to our sex as the want of cleanliness and delicacy in yours. I hope therefore the moment you rise from bed, your first work will be to dress yourself in such stile as that you may be seen by any gentleman without his being able to discover a pin amiss, or any other circumstances of neatness wanting." Jefferson went on to warn that "some ladies think they may be under the privileges of the dishabille be loose and negligent of their dress in the morning. But be you from the moment you rise till you go to bed as cleanly and properly dressed as at the hours of dinner or tea." Because the body was a temple, and cleanliness next to godliness, an unkempt woman displayed impiety; a spotless appearance equaled a spotless heart. Girls scrubbed and attired themselves to reflect both Christian devotion and proper attention to appearance.

The question of dress raised controversial issues for the pious plantation mistress. To be a lady of fashion was socially enviable, but nonetheless wholly reviled by the moral preceptors of southern culture. Fashion, therefore, represented a serious temptation toward impropriety. Virginian Maria Campbell commented to her husband in 1822: "What can be more wretched than a woman of fashion obeying every varying and yet monotonous dictate of her capricious fancy." She continued by lamenting the "woman of fashion" as "a stranger in her family, her children, if children are so unfortunate as to belong to such a mother, committed to the mercy, the inattention, the example of menials without the benefit of a mother's tenderness, instruction and care." David Campbell replied to his wife: "How true is every remark, every word you have written about fashionable life. I see it here [Richmond] daily exemplified, Madam Scott is here this winter. . . . She is daily on the run—after what she does not know—Every night at the theatre or a party." Most plantation mistresses in residence at home could not afford the luxury of fashion; their rural isolation provided little chance to see or emulate new styles, and even those ladies who lived in town found the expense a hindrance. A Charleston woman wrote in 1784: "The last fashion just arrived from London; there are balloon hats arrived, the price 18 and 20 dollars, you may form an idea of the extravagance of fashion from that one article."

In spite of these constraints, southern women remained fascinated, and tried to find an appropriate compromise between the evil of becoming "slaves of fashion" and the grace of dressing in a style reflecting position and wealth. Most ladies forged a network of female friends and relatives, extending outward from the coastal urban centers where European imports and sophisticated tastes dominated women's apparel. A friend in Tennessee pleaded of Maria Campbell in Virginia: "If you have any new fashioned dress or handkerchiefs, please send me the patterns of them by Uncle." Despite the inevitable time lag, planter wives and daughters cherished the notion that they could copy the latest Continental creations, even in their removed circumstances, and women traded advice on every facet of dress, from head to toe.

Fashionable ladies wore corsets throughout most of the ante-bellum era, and considered lacing an indispensable improvement to a woman's figure. A matron wrote her daughter in 1818: "Apropos of dress, Margaret tells me you have made a new set of corsetts and to save you the trouble of unlacing them you have made them large enough to jump out of them when you take them off. If you love me, alter these corsetts before I see you. Endeavour to make your shape look as well as I am sure with a little ingenuity you might do. You are now too old to have any scruples on this subject. A little art in remedying the faults of nature is always allowable. It is unpardonable and untasteful not to do it." Tightlacing, however, became a subject of some controversy after the beginning of the nineteenth century—a conflict stimulated both by the corsetless styles of Napoleonic Europe and by the medical impetus of dress reform. A girl's letter to her father in 1811 reveals an amused objection to the practice: "They were laced up so tight that everyone of the Gentlemen in the room took notice of it. Crawford told S. Heirkeel & myself that he thought that Miss' conscience was in the center of her breast for she always put her hand there whenever she talked but he sayed that he would keep his knife ready to cut their strings."

Constriction by corset was in fact a serious issue. Some parents recognized that whalebone was an actual danger to a girl's health. Many women suffered from respiratory difficulties due to their constrictive clothing. Indeed, some were felled by internal injuries brought on by binding themselves into wasp-waisted corsets. In 1816, a friend opined that one southern girl would have had a fashionable figure "if her father did not make her spoil it by not allowing her to wear a corset bone. This she has given up merely to please him." Such a parental prohibition was not unusual by mid-century, even in the South. As early as the 1840s, southern periodicals reflected the medical wisdom of the dress reform campaign, even if the plantation mistress did not. An 1842 article in *Magnolia* chastised: "Nothing can be more absurd— nothing more detrimental to health and beauty than the system of tightlacing." The magazine went on enthusiastically: "French women are about casting them aside and are beginning to allow nature, not the milliner, to mould their shapes." Despite the impracticality and discomfort, women continued to heed the dictates of fashion rather than medical literature in matters of dress.

Ante-bellum ladies also obeyed strict prohibitions against sunning themselves. Plantation mistresses took precautions against overexposure—some to the degree of no exposure at all—because beauty was measured on a standard of facial pallor. A woman wrote in 1832 of one acquaintance: "Pretty, too, in spite of her freckles." Freckles were viewed as natural blemishes; tanned skin, on the other hand, was an unforgivable and unnatural departure for the southern lady. Not only were there unfavorable racial connotations associated with darker skin, but ladies preserved their complexion as testifying to their pampered status within an agrarian society. Thomas Jefferson wrote to his younger daughter, Maria, in 1786: "Remember too as a constant charge not to go out without your bonnet because it will make you very ugly and then we should not love you so much." Such strong warnings were not uncommon; southern girls were alternately threatened and cajoled into submission on matters of disposition and dress. A matron wrote to her sister in 1820 of a mutual acquaintance: "Jane has grown very much a very *shamefully tanned* and every one telling her of it. I could not help thinking of you all the evening and wondering if you would neglect your bonnet, and treat your friends about you with so much contempt. For it cannot be called anything else when their friendly advice is not attended to. But I will hope better of you until I hear from you."

Purity ruled appearance and piety ruled thought; the measure of a plantation mistress's propriety was thereby reflected in her every deed and word. Correct behavior laid the foundation for social order. Boys and girls alike were expected to observe the rules that parents enforced with strict adherence to form and decorum. Respect rested firmly on propriety, and as one planter confessed to his wife in 1790: "I have thought frequently that if anything could forever destroy my pride it would be to see my children devoid of Reputation." Bolling Hall expressed equally strong feelings in a letter to his daughter Polly in 1813: "It would make my heart bleed within me if I was to hear of your doing anything wrong—the distress which any improper conduct of yours would occasion in the trust of your parents would be indescribable.

Fathers were concerned about their daughters not only for practical reasons but with respect to their capacity as potential mothers, the spiritual advisers of future families. One planter warned his daughter that "because your father on earth cannot see and know you have a Father in Heaven who sees and knows all things and from whose censure and judgment you cannot escape." Thomas Jefferson, ever mindful of his responsibility to his motherless daughters, had strong opinions on this issue, as on most others. He wrote to his elder daughter, Patsy, in 1783: "If ever you are about to say anything amiss or to do anything wrong consider before hand. You will feel something within you which will tell you it is wrong and ought not to be said or done: this is your conscience, and be sure to obey it. Our maker has given us all this faithful internal Monitor, and if you always obey it, you will always be prepared for the end of the world: or for a much more certain event which is death."

Once again, planters revived Roman imagery to bolster their arguments for female virtue. David Campbell advised his niece: "Propriety is to a woman what the great Roman critic says action is to an Orator: it is the first, the second and the third requisite. A woman may be knowing, active, witty and amusing; but without propriety she cannot be amiable. Propriety is the centre in which all the lines of duty and of agreeableness meet." Duty and agreeableness demanded much of the planter daughter. Traveling, visiting, and social events presented girls with opportunities to amuse themselves, but parents and daughters alike feared that such frivolity might foster a climate of impropriety. Although planter families arranged an array of social activities for marriageable girls, the latter were simultaneously burdened with excessive chaperonage and severe restrictions on their behavior. John Steele reminded his daughter Margaret in 1807 that "discretion in a female is not merely commendable but to pass well and happily through the world it is indispensable."

When daughters were away from home, parents tirelessly warned and advised. A planter wrote to his daughter in 1800, during her visit with relatives: "You must conduct yourself with prudence or you cannot expect to have their esteem." On these visits and during girls' attendance at balls, fathers worried about the improper advances of men. Bolling Hall cautioned his daughter Martha in 1829: "If you should be in company with Gentlemen you will be treated with politeness and respect, but if any unwarrantable liberties in actions or conversations are attempted, be on your guard against such a person, and do not for an instant permit anything which modesty or virtue can disapprove." It was to avoid this eventuality that most parents insisted on chaperones. Bolling Hall instructed another daughter, Polly, about ballroom etiquette: "You should never visit such a place without being accompanied by some respectable friend much older than yourself, whose presence alone would protect you from the smallest insult or suspicion, or neglect."

Traveling alone was absolutely forbidden to females. Chaperonage, ostensibly for their protection, created a system in which women became virtual wards; and the price for this "protection" was high, in isolation and limited mobility. Society subjected even married women to the practice of male chaperonage during travel. Matrons might not be as carefully guarded at balls and while on family visits, but they were still subject to the rigid code of propriety. Husbands demanded that their wives afford not even the slightest cause for reproach. John Steele enjoined his wife, Mary, in 1796: "Whilst I am doing my best to make a fortune, and support an honorable character in life, it is only reasonable, my love, that you shou'd treat me with affection and preserve for my sake, for your own sake, and for the sake of our dear little ones, a sootless and unblemished reputation . . . maintain that dignity of character which you know, I and all men adore in the female sex."

Cultural prescriptions concerning behavior clearly divided along gender lines. Morality ruled in the public domain; both sexes subscribed to the same ethical standards. In the private sphere, however, men might bend or break the rules at their own discretion. Such a division resulted in strict regulation of women's activities and correspondingly lax attitudes toward male affairs. Women responded with a pronouncedly pious social posture, but some men at least indulged in a sordid subculture, while striking a pose of concern for honor and reputation. It is difficult now to ascertain which was the shadow and which the substance of southern men's lives. Official southern "morality" is fairly easy to understand, but the reality of behavior is another matter. Planters habitually cloaked their illicit impulses and activities in secrecy; a few men, however, revealed themselves in diaries or private correspondence. In one such exchange, a planter son writing to his confidant referred to women vulgarly as "meat." Another gentleman confided to a friend in 1831 that his thoughts were centering on women; he even contemplated getting married. In this long letter, he relates the following incident: "I met a girl not long since going to plough barefoot riding astraddle barebacked by a crook in the Road. I got up to her before she discovered me. She had a good foot and ankle, a well turned leg up to the knee. She looked to be about 18 years old, had titties as big as your fist, as round as a butter ball and would have weighed a pound." He was obviously not describing a lady—a suitable object for his matrimonial designs—but rather a female about whom he could frankly admit his carnal desires.

Licentiousness, when it came to fact rather than fantasy, was costly. The recipe books of southern plantation mistresses are full of concoctions to cure gonorrhea. Venereal disease plagued plantation society. One southern gentleman reported in distress: "When on my brother's plantation, I was informed that each of his family servants were suffering from a venereal disease, and I ascertained that each of my brother's children, girls and boys had been informed of it and knew how and from whom it had been acquired." But venereal diseases did not flourish exclusively within slave quarters. Maria Bryan's correspondence recorded one incident: "That wretched Holinbec who, you know, went to Columbus as a missionary, has been preaching and administering the ordinances of the church with the venereal disease upon, until it finally became so bad that concealment was impossible." Such considerations made some men careful about their activities. A young man of Petersburg, Virginia, wrote in 1827 to a friend in medical college in Philadelphia: "I am much surprised at your resolution of never getting married, make haste, and get some 'sheep skin' and come to the old Dominion and if you can resist the pouting lips and cherry cheeks of the Girls, I'll be darned and you know there is plenty of them here. There will be no danger getting the Damn's clap that you speak of being so afraid of."

A look behind the doors of the brothel is rare in the annals of the closed society of the ante-bellum South. William D. Valentine offers such a glance in his diary entry for March 26, 1837. Writing in Bethel, North Carolina, Valentine confessed that he had not knowingly visited the place; rather, he was passing by a house "suspected" of ill-repute and wandered in when he overheard a friend within. Valentine recorded his reactions at length:

> Lo, men, women and cards and shocking obsenity. Several of my respectable acquaintance were here and cordially greeted me. Although shocked and indignant (for some were married men) I concealed my emotion—and to make the best of my situation—I apparently (though in reality did not) participated; this is seeming to countenance what was before me. Modesty and morals were here put to blush indeed. Low life, wretched. The head of this seraglio was in every respect a beautiful girl, a splendid girl to look at. Nature has done much for her in giving her an exquisitely beautiful person and a strong mind—but vice has warped her notions of propriety—she was deficient in one quality and that quality is it which renders the fair sex so ethereal, so much the angel—the virtue of woman. . . . to see this fairest specimen of her workmanship prostituted to the lowest, meanest, obscenest practices. . . . my curiosity being satiated with disgust, sorrow and sympathy (for this girl expressed her sensibility of her degradation) I retired.

One presumes that the appalled Mr. Valentine "retired" to his own quarters rather than to one of the chambers of the house. His repeated protestations of innocence are almost comic, although testimony of his earnestness.

The image of southern manhood was probably as significant for plantation culture as that of the lady. Although drunkenness, excessive gambling, or unbridled violence could result in social ostracism, plantation culture maintained an extremely high tolerance for these vices in men—indeed, moderate indulgence in these activities was viewed as conventional masculine recreation. Women not only refrained utterly from such behavior—which would have been seen in them as insupportable—but spent considerable effort counseling their male relatives against these evils. Martha Richardson wrote to her nephew, away at school: "Do not, my dearest James, be lead away by gay* companions to follow the vile and bad habits of men. I have great confidence in you but often fear and tremble for you as you grow and are obliged to enter the world and see all its wicked ways. . . . The more I see and know men the more I dislike them and think they are a vile set of animals." A concerned mother wrote home to her son in Alabama of the evils of Washington, D.C.: "There is much poverty and crime here; yesterday a poor little infant was found under some large stones a short

---

*In this nineteenth-century context "gay" means loose and licentious, with no suggestion of sexual preference.

distance from us and in sight of my chamber window! *Crime* brought it into the world and *shame* no doubt caused it to be murdered and cast out *naked!*" She closed her letter to her son, "Beware of the first step *towards vice* and think not that you can say 'thus and no further shall my passions stray.' "

Many plantation mistress saw sin in terms of increment; they were prepared to cope with small trespasses, yet ever fearful of the uncontrollable momentum of immorality. The journal of Jane Gay Robertson Bernard testifies to her vigilance. In the summer of 1825, her husband became overly fond of card playing. He would often stay up all night playing loo, and sometimes remained away from home two nights in a row at card parties. When Jane Bernard finally demanded that her husband stop this gambling spree, he promised her that he would no longer waste time and money away from his family. Having rescued her husband from his dissipation, she calmed her own fears of his moral disintegration. Some women were not so fortunate in their proposed reforms. One bemoaned the fate of a friend whose husband gambled: "Her heart is bursting to think his love for her was all too feeble to save him from vice, and that his confidence never had been hers. She will be the martyr, he may rise again, from a long, painful probation, to the station he has sunk from, but she will never be able to forget how impotent affection was to save."

Gambling was not as virulent a threat as drinking. Young and unmarried planters frequently drank to excess; drunkenness was almost rite of passage for adolescent males. A man on a visit to Tuscaloosa from his native Maine wrote home to his mother: "There is vastly more dissipation here than in N.E. [New England]. It is no disgrace to get intoxicated at public times. I have seen on public days perhaps an hundred at time all partially intoxicated who would act more like maniacs than men." Another northern visitor wrote home from Milledgeville, Georgia, in 1809: "The manners of the young people in this town are corrupt beyond any idea you or I could form. . . . were I to expose myself as unnecessarily and to the extent that others do, I should lose all my money in a week and die the next." Not only Yankees complained of southern dissipation. Southerner Ellen Mordecai wrote to her brother Solomon in 1823 about her visit to Warrenton, North Carolina: "The old prevailing vice predominates. . . . It is shocking to hear of young men scarcely more than boys reeling intoxicated into manhood."

A drunken husband made it impossible for the wife to maintain domestic harmony. Maria Bryan reported to her sister Julia Cumming of a mutual friend: "Mr. Norton it is said (entre nous) drinks a great deal, and though not unkind is far from being the devoted husband he once was. But what is certain that instead of soothing and consoling his wife and family in their misfortunes, he yields not only to gloom,

but indulges harsh repinings whose profanity is absolutely shocking."
Ann Mordecai wrote to her daughter about a drunkard who had turned
wife-beater: "Old Jos. Hinton has whipped his wife and slapped Miss
Disheel's face. It created a great excitement and young men talked of
riding him on a rail through the streets for it but the old man armed
himself and they thought it best to leave him alone."

Men's violence against men was the commonest by-product of
drinking. A Yankee observer described this aggressive behavior: "At
such times they fight more or less, I saw one short fight musterday
about ten steps from the store. It was excessively muddy, you have
nothing like it at home. The parties grappled, fell and rolled in the
mud some time. . . . In their fights they generally bite, gouge or dirk."
The climate of violence often resulted in death to one or more parties.
Quarrels and brawling were common, as was ambush or assassination.
Rachel O'Connor wrote to her brother, David Weeks, of a local murder: "Tomy Chaney's killed old Mr. Coursey's son with a club. He
slipped up behind him when he was eating his supper and struck him
dead and then took all his own negroes and run off. Tom was drunk
at the time." She also wrote to her sister-in-law, Mary, about another
tragedy in her Louisiana parish: "Mrs. McDermit's second son John
has been at the point of death for two or three weeks caused by getting
into a quarrel at the river with a man that shot him and stabed him
shockingly." John Quitman reported an impromptu duel in Clinton,
Mississippi, to his wife: "This morning there was a dreadful encounter
on the pavement before this house between Gen. Runnels and Jas. B.
Marsh in which seven pistols were discharged, both are wounded. . . ."
Single combat was far from rare, but the format of this duel was atyp-
ical. More commonly, dueling was a serious and ritualized affair.

Francis Bacon once described dueling as "sorcery that enchanteth
young men," but southern gentlemen of all ages seemed bewitched.
Americans rarely dueled in the seventeenth century, but by the mid-
eighteenth century more and more men of the upper class, especially
planters, "defended their honor" with pistols at ten paces. The practice
was imported from England, mainly by southern planters' sons educated abroad, and gained great popularity in the post-Revolutionary
South, especially in Savannah and Charleston. Dueling societies, modeled on London clubs, granted admission only to those who had participated in a duel—a self-perpetuating system in which a man's rank
in the organization was based on the number of his encounters. Southern state legislatures responded to both the frequency and the threat
of this personal combat with anti-dueling laws, but measures passed
in Georgia in 1809 and Virginia in 1810 were generally disregarded,
and duels flourished well into the mid-nineteenth century.

In the popular imagery of the Old South, duels have been mistakenly associated with chivalry. But while medieval jousts were fought

to gain a lady's favor, duels centered exclusively on masculine affairs. As William O. Stevens asserts in his study of the subject: "The duel over a woman was exceedingly rare. Men shot each other for gambling, debts, for a dispute . . . almost never, however, did they fight over a woman." Plantation mistresses concertedly opposed the practice, seeing in the ritual senseless violence leading to needless death. One mother lamented to her son in 1821: "How delighted I would be if duelling was done away with in this country but there has been several fought this year. . . . I hope you my dear will never be placed in a situation where you will have to resort to Pistols, horrid things." Martha Richardson gave the following advice to her nephew: "Every gentleman has it in his power to avoid quarrels—he should never give an affront—there are few men so brutal as to seek an opportunity mearly for the love of shooting or being shot at. . . . Keep guard over your temper and recollect that he is the greatest Hero who has learned to conquer himself."

Planters habitally, however, staked their lives on their reputations—and created reputations for themselves by risking their lives. Reckless behavior was one aspect of comradeship for men in southern culture, as the example of Arthur Middleton illustrates. A planter wrote to his brother in 1807 of Middleton's affair of honor: "He found it necessary to go to Georgia to settle a dispute with a Mr. James Pringle which happened at sea, at a card table. The business was fortunately terminated without bloodshed, though they each fired three times. Arthur and Mr. J. Pringle are upon as good terms as ever, and I have met them several times lately walking arm in arm as if they had never been at variance." But not all duels ended so amicably; often one of the duelists would receive a wound, which sometimes proved fatal. One woman reported an even more tragic encounter: "Have you heard of Mrs. Pearson's misfortune in the Death of her youngest son, he was killed in a Duel—his adversary as soon as he had kill'd him blew his own brains out. . . ." When a gentleman had been challenged on what he felt to be unreasonable or frivolous grounds, he might ignore the challenge and keep his good name, if the challenger dropped his suit. But in general a southern planter was honor-bound to accept the challenge of a duel, if he had no family. A gentleman was routinely excused from participation, however, if he claimed family responsibility. As a woman explained concerning her brother: "He is a husband and a Father and the laws of this much famed Code of Honour does not make it binding on him to accept the challenge of any madman or fool that may envy him, or his happiness." More often than not, a family claimed the gentleman's responsibility to them, rather than the other way around.

The plight of Ann McDonald in November 1828 aptly illustrates the burden imposed by the code of honor on southern women. McDonald and his doctor fell into discord; his wife feared a duel. Ann McDonald wrote to her husband's friend J. L. Lamar, begging him to intercede to prevent bloodshed; dread and despair provoked her "perhaps unwarranted liberty" in addressing him. As a woman, even as McDonald's wife, she was helpless, "for if I introduce the subject, he either avoids answering or leaves me." Her frustration led her to repudiate the code of honor, "which might be said, truly said, to be founded in *Injustice, Revenge, Ambition, Pride*—In short it might be justly defined the opposite of Civic and Divine Law." She went on to call dueling murder, and "although the perpetrator (vainly) strives to consecrate his crime by throwing around it the imposing garb of Honor . . . such argument is only chaff against the wind." She concluded that "to be a brave man one need not be a murderer."

The nature of southern morality forced women into rigid and exacting roles. They were protected, yet at the same time confined, by interlocking systems of patriarchal authority. Men further confounded women with contradictory and often hypocritical challenges: to fulfill the belle ideal, to ensure the spiritual welfare of all plantation dwellers, to turn a blind eye on male transgressions. Myth, ideal, and duty weighed heavily on plantation women.

These women were merely prisoners in disguise. However comfortable their surroundings, however elaborate the rhetoric that celebrated them, however sheltered they were from the market economy and class oppression, plantation mistresses spent much of their lives under constraint and in isolation: fettered nonetheless.

Life and labor changed in important ways or small New England farms like this between 1800 and 1850.

Culture and Cultivation: Agriculture and Society in Thoreau's Concord

ROBERT A. GROSS

In the previous section you read about the family of Mayo Greenleaf Patch as they struggled to adapt to the unsettling experiences of agrarian life at the end of the eighteenth century. In this selection we return to rural New England, in the first half of the nineteenth century, for Robert Gross's description of the changes and adaptations made by farmers participating in the rise of the competitive market economy. In the earlier selection, Paul Johnson followed the personal experiences of a family that could not remain on the land in Massachusetts at the turn of the century. In this one, Gross looks at the opportunities and challenges faced by those residents of Concord, Massachusetts, who did stay in farming through the first half of the new century.

Gross shows how a traditional economy tied to barter, family labor, and communal work customs was giving way to the practices and imperatives of an impersonal, commercialized kind of farming. By the early nineteenth century Concord's farmers were changing the crops they grew in response to the demands of the urban market; and by 1820 hired wage labor had supplanted family labor on many Concord farms. Old communal gatherings such as huskings, apple bees, and country dances were abandoned as wasteful of time and money.

In reading Gross's discussion, identify the particular ways in which the farmer's world changed in the antebellum period. To what extent did Concord's farmers resist changes, and to what extent did they eagerly participate in them or even cause them?

The town of Concord, Massachusetts, is usually thought of as the home of minutemen and transcendentalists—the place where "the embattled farmers" launched America's war for political independence on April 19, 1775, and where Ralph Waldo Emerson and Henry David Thoreau, more than a half-century later, waged their own struggles for intellectual independence, both for themselves as writers and for American culture as a whole. But in the late nineteenth century, Concord acquired a distinction it never possessed in the years when it was seedbed of revolutionary scholars and soldiers. It became a leading center of agricultural improvement. Thanks to the coming of the railroad in 1844, Concord farmers played milkmen to the metropolis and branched out into market gardening and fruit raising as well. Concord was nursery to a popular new variety of grape, developed by a retired mechanic-turned-horticulturist named Ephraim Bull. And to crown its reputation, the town called the cultural capital of antebellum America by Stanley Elkins became the asparagus capital of the Gilded Age. Concord was, in short, a full participant in yet another revolution: the agricultural revolution that transformed the countryside of New England in the middle decades of the nineteenth century.

The progress of that agricultural revolution forms my central theme. The minutemen of 1775 inhabited a radically different world from that of their grandchildren and great-grandchildren on the eve of the Civil War. We know the general outlines of how things changed—that farmers gradually abandoned producing their own food, clothing, and tools and turned to supplying specialized, urban markets for a living. In the process, they rationalized their methods and altered the ways they thought about their work. Theirs was a new world in which modern science was wedded to agricultural capitalism. But the process by which that world came into being is little known. Historians have given their attention chiefly to more dramatic events—to the rise of cities and factories, to the story of Boston and Lowell. No less important was the revolution in the countryside. Without it, the creation of an urban-industrial society would have been impossible.

Together, the city and the country underwent a great transformation. The years from around 1800 and 1860 comprise what Emerson called an "age of Revolution"—a time "when the old and the new stand side by side and admit of being compared; when the energies of all men are searched by fear and by hope; when the historic glories of the old can be compensated by the rich possibilities of the new era." What

CULTURE AND CULTIVATION   From *Journal of American History*, 69 (June 1982), 42–61. Reprinted by permission of the author and the Organization of American Historians.

could be a better time to be alive, Emerson asked. That is essentially the inquiry I am undertaking—an inquiry into what it was like to make and to experience the great transition to modern agricultural capitalism in Concord.

This investigation represents an early effort to gather together the evidence of agricultural change in Concord and to suggest its implications for the lives of farming people in the middle decades of the nineteenth century. The principal sources have been town valuations and assessment lists and the United States agricultural census of 1850. These enumerations of land, livestock, and crops, among other goods, cover more than a century of Concord history, from the mid-eighteenth century to the eve of the Civil War. They allow us to view the agricultural changes of the antebellum era in long perspective—to date the beginning of fundamental breaks in the old way of life, to observe the parallel decay of the old and the rise of the new, and to pinpoint just when the adoption of new practices decisively accelerated and culminated in the triumph of a new agricultural regime. For the agricultural revolution did not come suddenly in an irresistible wave of change. The process was a slow and uneven one, proceeding by fits and starts and sometimes encountering setbacks along the way. Some things never really changed at all, and not until the end of the period, with the coming of the railroad, had a new world truly been born.

All of this, of course, can be said only with the historian's benefit of hindsight. To the participants in the process, who did not know the outcomes, the transition must have been at time a deeply unsettling experience. It challenged old habits and practices, demanded new responses while promising only uncertain rewards, and swept up those who wanted only to be left alone, comfortably carrying on their fathers' ways. Even those farmers and entrepreneurs who successfully rode the tide must have had their doubts. Those who resisted or just plain failed said little about their fate, succumbing to what Thoreau saw as lives of "quiet desperation." In the effort to reconstruct the experience of the transition, Thoreau's observations bear close reading. Thoreau was the most powerful and articulate critic of agricultural capitalism that America produced in the decades before the Civil War.

Had a visitor come to Concord around 1800 and lived through the 1850s, he would certainly have been unprepared for the ways things changed. At the opening of a new century, the agricultural economy was very much tied to the past. In the size of their farms, in the crops and livestock they raised, in the ways they used the land, farmers still carried on as their fathers had.

For one thing, the number of farms was the same in 1800 as it had been in 1750 and 1771: about 200. And the average size of a farm was no bigger in 1800 than it had been before: around sixty acres. These were unchanging facts of life in eighteenth-century Concord; nothing—not even revolution, war, and depression—would alter them in the slightest.

This fundamental stability in the number and size of farms was no accident, no haphazard outcome of social evolution. It was a deliberate creation, a rational adaptation to the conditions of farming and family life in the preindustrial, household economy. This arrangement of farms on the landscape arose in response to a basic dilemma Concord began to encounter as early as the 1720s: there were too many young people in town and not enough land for them all—not enough, at least, for them to support families in the usual way. Markets did not exist to sustain comfortable livings on very small farms. Nor would the farming methods of the day have enabled the yeomen of Concord to produce substantial surpluses had the demand for them suddenly appeared. As a result, so long as families continued to be fruitful and multiply as successfully as they did and so long as death continued to stalk New Englanders less relentlessly than it did people in the Old World, the people of Concord would have to face up to the inevitable outcome. There was a fundamental imbalance between numbers and resources. Something would have to give.

As it turned out, what gave was the aspiration of colonial patriarchs to settle all their sons close-by on family lands. As early as the 1720s, it was becoming clear that some estates in Concord could not be split up "without Spoiling the Whole." Instead, increasingly, one son—often, but not invariably, the eldest—would inherit the homestead intact. The other children would have to go into trade, take portions and dowries in cash, or, in what was commonly the case, move away and settle on frontier lands. In effect, a continuing exodus of young people to new lands underwrote the stability of Concord's farms. Emigration was the key to the future, to insuring that old patterns would go on unchanged. That mechanism worked so successfully that the colonial framework of farming in Concord—some 200 farms of about sixty acres on the average—survived intact not just until 1800 but until the eve of the Civil War. No matter how much things changed, young people growing up on farms in nineteenth-century Concord had in common with their eighteenth-century forebears the expectation that most would move away and make new lives in another town.

For those who stayed behind on the homesteads around 1800, farming went on in traditional ways. In the household economy of Concord the needs of the family and the labor it supplied largely determined what was produced and in what amounts. This does not mean that farms were self-sufficient. Farmers normally strove to obtain a surplus of goods to exchange with neighbors and to enter into the stream of trade. Given the limited markets and the constraints on production in the eighteenth century, surpluses were necessarily small. Most farmers lacked the incentive or the capacity to participate extensively in trade.

Indeed, most farmers even lacked the ability to be fully self-sufficient. Historians have been led astray by the image of the independent yeoman, wholly dependent on his own resources, that eighteenth-century writers like J. Hector St. John Crèvecoeur have handed down to us. What we would think of as the basic necessities of colonial husbandry—plows, oxen, pastures, sheep—were absent on a great many farms. A third of Concord's farmers did not own oxen, and if they were like the farmers in the towns of Groton, Marlborough, and Dedham, whose inventories have been examined by Winifred Rothenberg at Brandeis University, half of them did not possess a plow and three-quarters (72 percent) had no harrow (this was the case down to 1840). Nor were farmers in Concord any more self-sufficient in the production of textiles. Almost half had no sheep in 1771, and in 1750 some 56 percent raised no flax at all.

What did people do, then, for basic necessities? They borrowed from neighbors or kin, exchanged goods or labor with others, or resorted to the store. Perhaps most often, they made do with what they had. This was a world of scarcity in which expectations were modest and always circumscribed. People had to accept the fact that labor and capital were required to supply all one's necessities "from within." It was the rich—the large landholders and the men who combined farming with a profitable trade—who could aspire to independence. It was they who produced most of the flax in Concord in 1750, planting about one-fourth to one-half an acre on the average, which is what the books say the ordinary farmer usually had. And it was they who could provide a wide variety of their own foods. The wealthy were able to take care of these needs precisely because they were engaged in trade, thereby acquiring the resources to hire labor and diversify livestock and crops. Market participation and self-sufficiency were not at opposite ends of a spectrum. Rather, market dependence without facilitated independence within. So when we read about the self-sufficient farmer, we should be skeptical: he was the exceptional man, uniquely favored by fortune. The editor of *Old Farmer's Almanack*, Robert Bailey Thomas, spoke for a good many readers when he remarked that "there is a great satisfaction derived from living as much as possible upon the produce of one's own farm." But it was a satisfaction that only a few farmers ever enjoyed. Although independence was the general ambition, interdependence was the inescapable fact of life.

The world of trade, then, offered a way out of the pervasive dependency of farmers on one another—out of the constant borrowing back and forth, the necessity of exchanging work, the endless keeping of accounts to ascertain one's standing in the community-wide network of credits and debts. And trade in agricultural surpluses played an important role in colonial Concord, shaping the principal uses to which people put their lands. In 1774, not long after he fled the fury of revolution for sanctuary in England, Massachusetts Gov. Thomas Hutchinson was received by George III. One might think that the king would have examined Hutchinson closely about the political situation in the colony. But no; George III was famous not only for losing an empire but also for promoting the cause of agriculture, and he wanted to know about farming in Massachusetts. "To what produce is your climate best adapted?" asked the king. "To grazing, Sir," Hutchinson replied. "Your Majesty has not a finer Colony for grass in all your dominions: and nothing is more profitable in America than pasture, because labour is very dear."

Hutchinson may have misjudged the political temper of the countryside, but he knew the lay of the land. Throughout the second half of the eighteenth century, farmers in Concord and elsewhere in eastern Massachusetts kept most of their improved land in grass. In Ipswich, over 90 percent of the improved land in 1771 was in meadows and pasture; in Concord that year, 80 percent. In a sense, farmers were doing what came naturally; as Hutchinson said, the soil was well suited to raising grass. But it was the pull of urban markets that prompted farmers to emphasize their mowing and grazing lands. Concord was beef country in the late colonial era. The agricultural economy was based on cereals—mainly rye and corn—for home consumption and beef for market.

This was an extensive agricultural regime, where farmers saved on labor by exploiting land. The trouble was that by the eve of the Revolution, the land was losing its capacity to support livestock. Between 1749 and 1771, cattle holdings increased by a fifth, but to feed them farmers had to expand their pasturage by 84 percent, even though sheep raising was declining sharply. Concord was starting to experience a serious agricultural decline. Indeed, so poor was the town's farming reputation that it blighted the marriage prospects of a young cabinet maker and farmer named Joseph Hosmer. It is said that when he asked for the hand of a wealthy farmer's daughter in Marlborough, Massachusetts, in 1759, he was rejected out of hand. "Concord plains are sandy," complained the father. "Concord soil is poor; you have miserable farms there, and no fruit. There is little hope that you will ever do better than your father, for you have both farm and shop to attend to, *and two trades spoil one.* Lucy shall marry her cousin John; he owns the best farm in Marlboro', and you must marry a Concord girl, who cannot tell good land from poor." Joseph Hosmer ultimately won the girl, but he had to pasture his cattle outside of Concord—in Rutland and Princeton, Massachusetts.

By 1801, though still very much bound to the past, Concord was beginning to feel the stirrings of agricultural change. Markets were opening up everywhere for farmers, thanks to the extraordinary prosperity the United States enjoyed during the era of the Napoleonic wars. The port cities—merchants to the world in the 1790s and early 1800s—boomed, and so, in turn, did their hinterland. Concord farmers began to raise substantial surpluses of rye, wood, and hay for the market. They met the needs not only of Boston and Charlestown but also of the rapidly growing nonfarming population at home. Between 1771 and 1801, the share of Concord's population engaged in crafts and trade doubled, from 15 percent to 33 percent.

The agricultural economy remained essentially what it had been: an economy based on cereals, grasses, and cattle. It would stay that way up through 1840. That year 86 percent of the improved land lay in meadows and pasture. But within that framework, farmers steadily devoted more and more of their energies to producing for market. They raised three principal commodities for sale: oats, hay, and wood. The production of oats was clearly geared to city markets; it far outstripped the growth in the numbers of horses in Concord, and it clearly paralleled the periods of most rapid increase for Boston and Lowell. Expanded hay production came as a result of the increasing conversion of pastures and unimproved land to what were called "English and upland meadows," land plowed and seeded with clover, timothy, and herd's-grass. Adoption of English hay was the major agricultural improvement of the era, and Concord farmers took it up with zeal. They cultivated meadowlands for cash, while relying on the natural river meadows of the Concord and Assabet rivers to feed their own livestock. As a result, the average farmer doubled his production of English hay from 4 to 8 tons between 1801 and 1840, while his output of fresh meadow hay barely increased from about 8 to 8.5 tons. For the most part, the land converted to English hay was made available by the clearing of vast woodlands for market.

At the same time as farmers were concentrating on these staples, they also sought out new crops. They experimented with teasels, broomcorn, and silk, none of which worked. They added potatoes for both family use and sale. A few wealthy farmers engaged in commercial wool growing on a large scale, raising flocks of one thousand or so sheep before the entire business collapsed in the 1830s from cheap western competition. Far more typical were the small-scale efforts of men like "Uncle Ben" Hosmer—Joseph's younger brother—to assemble surpluses for sale.

The story is told that in the 1790s, Ben Hosmer began taking butter, eggs, and other goods to Cambridge market. He lacked a wagon, as did most farmers in those days; so he had to sling baskets full of butter and eggs across the "old mare's" back and ride her into town. One day Ben Hosmer, who was notoriously impulsive, suddenly decided to pack up the horse and go to market. He was feeling "grand poorly," he declared, and was almost out of "black-strap." Besides, there was no West India rum in the house to serve if Parson Ripley stopped by. "It was a hot dog-day morning in August," we are told, and by the time Ben Hosmer got going, he was in quite a hurry. He pushed the old mare over the hills to Lexington so fiercely—his cane was four feet long and an inch in diameter—that she was sweating "profusely" by the time they stopped for rest at a brook in East Lexington. He intended only for her to take a cool drink, but once that mare felt the refreshing waters of the brook, she would have nothing less than a bath. With the panniers full of butter and eggs still on, the mare rolled over and over in the brook.

"To say that Uncle Ben was surprised and astonished," it is said, "would be to draw it very mild; nay, he was dumb founded. He had a tremendous voice, and at once opened up the bottom scale." By the time people had rushed to his aid, he was in greater lather than the horse; it was all he could do to sputter curses at her. "Don't you know any better than to lie down in the brook with Dinah's butter and eggs on your condemned back?" The horse had no answer. Soon Ben Hosmer was pounding the poor animal severely. A crowd gathered round, and when he had finally worked off his rage, one latecomer asked him politely if the mare really had lain down in the brook with the butter and eggs. "Don't you see the yolks running all down the ole mare's belly, and the butter is fit for nothing more than grease!"

Ben Hosmer's adventures may seem comical now—they probably did then—but they illustrate the difficulties and risks of carrying foods like butter and eggs to market in the early days of the new republic. By 1840 wagons and roads had so improved that a good deal of butter was being made and sold in Concord. But it was not until the coming of the railroad that large-scale production of milk, eggs, fruits, and garden vegetables became truly profitable in Concord. Before then, small farmers like Ben Hosmer had to concentrate on bulky goods—oats, hay, and wood—supplemented by whatever other surpluses they could get. And note that it was Dinah Hosmer, not Ben, who put up the butter and eggs.

In these circumstances, it is not surprising that farmers continued the effort to supply their own necessities, even as they sought new products for market. To be sure, they were quick to abandon raising their own cloth when cheap textiles started streaming out of the new mills. But a great many farmers never had been able to furnish their own linen or wool. When it came to foodstuffs, they still did as much as they could for themselves. Rye steadily declined in relative importance from 1800 to 1840, but even in 1840 three-quarters of the farmers in town still raised enough for their bread. The same holds true for fodder crops. English hay went to market; the fresh meadows fed livestock at home.

This combination of production for both markets and home use meant, in practice, that farmers were adding greatly to the burdens of their work. One crop was not substituted for another. Farmers simply exploited themselves more intensively than ever. Once they had spread their labor over the land, plowing shallowly, manuring thinly, and cultivating infrequently, with the result that yields were low. That was acceptable when farmers chiefly raised grain crops for family use and the profits came from grazing livestock. But now farmers depended for a living on far more intensive work: chopping wood, reclaiming land for English hay, digging potatoes, making butter, and occasionally even nursing mulberry bushes.

Farmers not only labored more intensively than ever. They did so in a radically new setting. By the mid-1820s, the evidence strongly suggests that hired labor had come to supplant family labor on the farm. Between 1801 and 1826 the ranks of landless men in Concord expanded from around 150 to 250, even as opportunities in crafts and trade stagnated and the number of farms remained unchanged. Those laborers must have been doing something for a living. Since farmers' sons were continuing the exodus out of Concord—but at an earlier age and to lands farther and farther from home—it is likely the laborers were taking their place. The hired hand had become a commonplace figure on the farm as early as 1815. Thomas's "Farmer's Calendar" for May of that year assumed that farmers had already "hired a man for a few months, to help along with your work," and it offered this advice: "If you have a good faithful one, then set store by him and treat him well, and, mind me now, don't you fret.—*Steady, boys, steady*, is the song for a farmer—If you get yourself into a habit of continually fretting, as some do, then it is ten to one if you can get good men to work for you. But some prefer a dull, lazy lubber, because he is cheap! but these *cheap* fellows I never want on my farm."

Thomas's comments suggest that a calculating, even suspicious spirit dominated the relations between farmers and their help. Where once farm boys had labored for their fathers out of duty, love, and an expectation that they would inherit land of their own someday, now it was money—and money alone—that kept help working on the farm. The social relations of production were imbued with the ethos of agricultural capitalism.

The same rationalizing, economizing impulse transformed the work customs of the community. As late as 1840, many farmers still lacked basic resources to do their work, even as they added to the demands on themselves. Nonetheless, they gave up cooperative practices like the huskings and apple bees of old. These were now condemned as uneconomical and wasteful "frolics," given over to heavy drinking and coarse entertainment. When one writer in the *Concord Gazette* of 1825 wistfully lamented the disappearance of bundling, country dances, and "the joyous huskings" of the past, he was roundly denounced by another for peddling immorality in the press. Neighborly sharing and cooperation probably diminished in another way as well. Agricultural reformers urged farmers to be as sparing as possible in "changing works." Again the *Old Farmer's Almanack* tells the changing sentiment. "There are some," Thomas complained in 1821, "who cannot bear to work alone. If they have a yard of cabbages to hoe, they must call in a neighbour to change work. Now this is very pleasant, but it tends to lounging and idleness, and neglect of business; for we cannot always have our neighbours at work with us." Concord farmers likely took such advice; in *Walden*, Thoreau assumes that the farmer characteristically works alone and is starved for company by the time he comes back from the fields. An era had come to an end; farmers now relied on the claims of cash rather than the chain of community to do their work.

Edward Jarvis, a prominent nineteenth-century medical reformer who grew up in Concord, celebrated this development as a positive force in social life. "The people of Concord are none the less kind, sympathetic and generous than their fathers, but they are stronger in body and in beast. They are more self-sustaining, and it is better that each should do his own work, with his own hands or by such aid as he can compensate in the ordinary way. . . . The world's work is now as well and completely done as ever and people both individually and socially are as happy and more prosperous, and are loving, generous and ready to aid in distress, poverty, and sickness, wherever these shall present themselves, in any family or neighborhood."

Jarvis wrote in 1878, at the end of the long transition, and he summarized as progress what small farmers at the time may have experienced as a very mixed blessing. Huskings may have wasted corn; changing works may have been a bother; and the exchange of goods and labor among farmers could sometimes end up in hard feelings and lawsuits on both sides. Still, the farmer who lacked money to hire all the help he needed had no alternative but to depend on his neighbors or exploit himself to the hilt.

It is possible, of course, that improvements in farm tools let people do more work in less time. There were certainly people in Concord who were alert to the latest innovations. One of them was the first to use a cast-iron plow at the annual plowing match in Brighton, sponsored by the Massachusetts Society for Promoting Agriculture. Moreover, about a third of Concord's farmers in the mid-nineteenth century belonged to the Middlesex Agricultural Society. But from the absence of plows and harrows from inventories as late as 1840 and from the fact that 40 percent of Concord farmers still had no oxen even then, it appears that labor-saving inventions did not have widespread impact until after the coming of the railroad.

We may gain some clues, too, from the agricultural reform literature of the day. It is full of complaints that boys no longer want to follow their fathers on the farm. Even more to the point, the central theme of that literature—the overwhelming burden of the many pieces on crop rotations, saving manure, raising turnips, and storing tools, among other subjects—is the absolute necessity for system in farm work. The trouble with farming, complained one observer after another, is that men do everything "by halves"—"half fencing, half tilling, and half manuring"—and without any forethought or plan. They labor hard, far harder than they ought, but "to no kind of good purpose." "Their work hurries them on," a New Hampshire writer observed, "and they have not time to make the necessary retrenchments and improvements: but continue (to use the common expression) 'slashing on, heels over head,' without consideration—zeal without improvement; thus they make perfect slaves of themselves, and never reform, pass through the world without enjoying the sweets of living—they follow their fathers' paths and swerve not."

Even before the railroad era, then, Concord farmers had entered the world of modern capitalism, with its characteristic institutions of money and markets. Producing for market had not, however, wholly displaced traditional activities on the farm; men still tried to furnish their food from within. This attempt to combine new demands with old ones added significantly to the burden of farm work; it amounted to a speed-up: more output in less time.

The intensification of farm work accelerated even more sharply after the railroad linked Concord more tightly and speedily to Boston market. The goods that the city demanded were those that required long hours of unremitting toil. Dairying was probably to become the most important. Between 1800 and 1840, as farmers turned to making butter for sale, the average herd of cows on a farm rose slightly from 4½ to 5. The next decade saw that figure increase again to 6. More dramatically, the proportion of men owning ten cows or more doubled from 11 to 22 percent. It was in the 1840s, too, that farmers began on a large scale to reclaim the many acres of boggy meadow in town for English hay. This was immensely costly and labor-intensive work. Those who could afford it hired Irish laborers to do the job; increasingly, cheap foreign labor displaced native help. Finally, the demand for wood boomed in these years; so vigorously did farmers respond to the market that by 1850 they had reduced the forests of Concord to a mere tenth of the town. Some people were already alarmed at the prospect of timber running out. In short, the steady chopping of the ax; the bustle of men spading up meadows, hauling gravel, and raking hay; the clanging of milk pails—these were the dominant sounds on Concord's farms in the 1840s. These sounds reverberate through *Walden*, and all of them finally were orchestrated to the movements of that locomotive whose piercing whistle as it swept into town announced the triumph of a new order of things.

It was, of course, precisely that new system of agricultural capitalism that Thoreau assailed so incisively, so unrelentingly. We tend to forget that Thoreau addressed *Walden* first of all to his neighbors, in the faint hope of waking them up, and he invariably drew his evidence of the false "economy" of his time from the life immediately around him. It was the farmers of Concord who plowed their manhood into the soil and pushed barns and lands before them as they crept down the road of life. It was they who were the slavemasters of themselves. Behind these strictures lay a deeper critique of what small farmers were doing to themselves as they tried to keep up with the market. Thoreau's attack was remarkably comprehensive. It emphasized:

1. the extending division of labor in society. People were becoming tools of their tools, individuals reduced to functions.
2. the intensification of work, which meant a tight constriction of individual autonomy. People rationalized their work and harnessed their lives to the clock. There was little in the way of true leisure.
3. the commercialization of life and dominance of commodities over men. Things were in the saddle and rode mankind. People spent their lives accumulating goods they would never enjoy.
4. the inequality of the results: the vast disparity in living standards between different levels of society. Luxuries, Thoreau thought, were built on exploitation of the many by the few.
5. most important of all, a decay of the spirit. Farmers treated nature not as a medium of spiritual growth but merely as a commodity, as a means for turning crops and livestock into money. And that narrow materialism extended into all their lives. The farmers and merchants would spend for barns and lands and imposing town halls. But they stinted the lyceum and did too little for the libraries and schools. There was no true culture in Concord.

Yet Thoreau's critique was flawed by his idealization of the preindustrial order. In his travels through Concord he talked to old-timers about what life used to be like and came away romanticizing their picture of independence and self-sufficiency on the farm—a world that hardly ever was. The real world of eighteenth-century farming demanded interdependence and mutual cooperation among households that would never have suited one who marched to a different drummer. Thoreau was too much a part of his own time ever to approve of the more leisurely ways of the eighteenth century. He may have looked suspiciously idle to his neighbors as he wandered off into the woods, but the prescription he offered in *Walden* was close in spirit to the advice of agricultural reformers. People, he said, needed to systematize, to rationalize their lives so that they might cultivate their higher selves in the very process of getting a living. But in giving this counsel and holding up his own experience at Walden Pond, Thoreau inverted the values of the agricultural writers, subjecting them to his highly individualistic, transcendental purposes. By paring back their material needs, providing as much—one might say, as little—as possible for themselves, and keeping their purchases to a minimum, people would be liberated from the grip of economic necessity and into lives of true leisure.

That solution, of course, required enormous self-discipline, parents nearby, and a bachelor's solitary existence. Even then, Thoreau wearied of growing beans and preferred a hunter-gatherer's life. In the end, the critique proved far more powerful than the alternative. There was little the small farmer could do to survive but move to cheaper lands farther west or adapt as best he could to the market, specializing ever more in profitable crops, buying ever more of his necessities at the store, intensifying ever more his exploitation of himself and/or his laborers. Perhaps only those with access to substantial capital or with unenviable capacities for restricting their own wants would come to enjoy the new world of agricultural capitalism. A great many more farming families would be lost in the transition. Theirs was an experience unvarnished with the trappings of a successful middle-class culture. Recovering that experience is the key to understanding what was lost as well as gained in America's "age of Revolution."

Charles G. Finney, evangelical preacher of the Second Great Awakening.

Pentecost: The Second Great Awakening in Rochester

PAUL E. JOHNSON

In 1830–31 a religious awakening swept through the northern United States, climaxing three decades of revivals known as the Second Great Awakening. In one year the number of churches in New England grew by one-third. The waves of evangelical revivals moved through western New York with such intensity that the region became known as the "burned-over" district. In communities throughout this region, including Rochester, New York, church membership doubled in just six months. Lyman Beecher, a prominent evangelist of the period, called the awakening of 1831 "the greatest work of God, and the greatest revival of religion, that the world has ever seen." Beecher was impressed not just by the numbers converted but by the event that marked, in the words of Paul Johnson, "the acceptance of an activist and millennialist evangelicalism as the faith of the northern middle class."

In the selection that follows, Johnson examines the revival as it unfolded in Rochester, New York, in the winter of 1830–31. At the center of the "burned-over" district, Rochester claims a significant place in the history of the Second Great Awakening. It was here that the unrivaled evangelist Charles Grandison Finney, "the father of modern revivalism," claimed his greatest triumph of conversions. In these pages, Johnson recaptures the revivalist messages that Finney brought to the churches of Rochester in the late fall of 1831. He then seeks to explain the social as well as cultural basis for the religious enthusiasm.

Previously in this volume you read two selections, by Johnson and by Robert Gross, about the effects of an expanding market economy on the traditional relations of the family and the community in early nineteenth-century New England. As you read this essay by Johnson, think about how the revivals in Rochester were connected to those larger societal changes. Also, what comparisons can you make between the Second Great Awakening as

discussed here and the Great Awakening of the eighteenth century as described in the selection by Rhys Isaac?

C harles Grandison Finney came to Rochester in September 1830.
For six months he preached in Presbyterian churches nearly every night
and three times on Sunday, and his audience included members of
every sect. During the day he prayed with individuals and led an almost continuous series of prayer meetings. Soon there were simulta-
neous meetings in churches and homes throughout the village. Pious
women went door-to-door praying for troubled souls. The high school
stopped classes and prayed. Businessmen closed their doors early and
prayed with their families. "You could not go upon the streets," recalled one convert, "and hear any conversation, except upon religion."
By early spring the churches faced the world with a militance and unity
that had been unthinkable only months before, and with a boundless
and urgent sense of their ability to change society. In the words of its
closest student, ". . . no more impressive revival has occurred in
American history."

NEW MEASURES

First, a word on the evangelical plan of salvation. Man is innately evil
and can overcome his corrupt nature only through faith in Christ the
redeemer—that much is common to Christianity in all its forms. Institutional and theological differences among Christians trace ultimately
to varying means of attaining that faith. The Reformation abolished
sacred beings, places, and institutions that had eased the path between
the natural and supernatural worlds. Without ritual, without priest-
magicians, without divine immanence in an institutional church, Protestants face God across infinite lonely space. They bridge that space
through prayer—through the state of absolute selflessness and submission known generally as transcendence. The experience of transcend-
ing oneself and this world through prayer is for Protestants direct
experience of the Holy Ghost, and it constitutes assurance of salvation,
sanctification, and new life.

PENTECOST   From Paul E. Johnson, *A Shopkeeper's Millennium: Society and Revivals in Rochester, New York, 1815–1837* (New York: Hill and Wang, 1978). Copyright © 1978 by Paul
E. Johnson. Reprinted by permission of Farrar, Straus & Giroux, Inc.

Prayer, then, is the one means by which a Protestant establishes his relation with God and his assurance that he is one of God's people. Prayer is a personal relationship between God and man, and the decision whether that relationship is established belongs to God. No Protestants dispute that. But they have argued endlessly on man's ability to influence the decision. The evangelical position was phrased (and it was understood by its detractors) as an increase in human ability so great that prayer and individual salvation were ultimately voluntary. Hurried notes to Charles Finney's Rochester sermons insisted: "It should in all cases be required now to repent, now to give themselves up to God, now to say and feel Lord here I am take me, it's all I can do. And when the sinner can do that . . . his conversion is attained." "The truth," he explained, "is employed to influence men, prayer to move God . . . I do not mean that God's mind is changed by prayer . . . But prayer produces such a change *in us* as renders it consistent for him to do otherwise." To hyper-Calvinists who protested that this filled helpless man with false confidence, Finney shouted, "What is that but telling them to hold on to their rebellion against God? . . . as though God was to blame for not converting them." The only thing preventing individual conversion was the individual himself.

This reevaluation of human ability caught the evangelicals in a dilemma. But it was a dilemma they had already solved in practice. Finney and his friends insisted that God granted new life in answer to faithful prayer. But the ability to pray with faith was itself experimental proof of conversion. By definition, the unregenerate could not pray. For Finney there was a clear and obvious way out, a way that he and Rochester Protestants witnessed hundreds of times during the revival winter: "Nothing is more calculated to beget a spirit of prayer, than to unite in social prayer with one who has the spirit himself." That simple mechanism is at the heart of evangelical Protestantism.

Conversion had always ended in prayer and humiliation before God. But ministers had explained the terms of salvation and left terrified sinners to wrestle with it alone. Prayer was transacted in private between a man and his God, and most middle-class Protestants were uncomfortable with public displays of humiliation. As late as 1829, Rochester Presbyterians had scandalized the village when they began to kneel rather than stand at prayer. More than their theological implications, Finney's revival techniques aroused controversy because they transformed conversion from a private to a public and intensely social event. The door-to-door canvass, the intensification of family devotions, prayer meetings that lasted till dawn, the open humiliation of sinners on the anxious bench: all of these transformed prayer and conversion from private communion into spectacular public events.

What gave these events their peculiar force was the immediatist corollary to voluntary conversion. The Reverend Whitehouse of St. Luke's Church (yes, the Episcopalians too) explained it in quiet terms:

Appeals are addressed to the heart and the appeals are in reference to the present time. And each time the unconverted sinner leaves the house of God without having closed with the terms of the Gospel he rejects the offer of mercy. Had some future time been specified as that in which we were to make a decision we might listen time after time to the invitations and reject them. But it is expressly said today and now is the accepted time.

Initially, these pressures fell on the already converted. It was the prayers of Christians that led others to Christ, and it was their failure to pray that sent untold millions into hell. Lay evangelicals seldom explained the terms of salvation in the language of a Reverend Whitehouse—or even of a Charles Finney. But with the fate of their children and neighbors at stake, they carried their awful responsibility to the point of emotional terrorism. Finney tells the story of a woman who prayed while her son-in-law attended an anxious meeting. He came home converted, and she thanked God and fell dead on the spot. Everard Peck reported the death of his wife to an unregenerate father-in-law, and told the old man that his dead daughter's last wish was to see him converted. "We are either marching towards heaven or towards hell," wrote one convert to his sister. "How is it with you?"

The new measures brought sinners into intense and public contact with praying Christians. Conversion hinged not on private prayer, arbitrary grace, or intellectual choice, but on purposive encounters between people. The secret of the Rochester revival and of the attendant transformation of society lay ultimately in the strategy of those encounters.

While Finney led morning prayer meetings, pious women visited families. Reputedly they went door-to-door. But the visits were far from random. Visitors paid special attention to the homes of sinners who had Christian wives, and they arrived in the morning hours when husbands were at work. Finney himself found time to pray with Melania Smith, wife of a young physician. The doctor was anxious for his soul, but sickness in the village kept him busy and he was both unable to pray and unwilling to try. But his wife prayed and tormented him constantly, reminding him of "the woe which is denounced against the families which call not on the Name of the Lord." Soon his pride broke and he joined her as a member of Brick Presbyterian Church. Finney's wife, Lydia, made a bolder intrusion into the home of James Buchan, a merchant-tailor and a Roman Catholic whose wife, Caroline, was a Presbyterian. Buchan, with what must have been enormous self-restraint, apologized for having been out of the house, thanked Finney for the tract, and invited him and his wife to tea. (It is not known whether Finney accepted the invitation, but this was one bit of family meddling which may have backfired. In 1833 Caroline Buchan withdrew from the Presbyterian Church and converted to Catholicism.) In hundreds of cases the strategy of family visits worked. As the first converts fell, the *Observer* announced with satisfaction that the largest group among them was "young heads of families."

Revival enthusiasm began with the rededication of church members and spread to the people closest to them. Inevitably, much of it flowed through family channels. Finney claimed Samuel D. Porter, for instance, as a personal conquest. But clearly he had help. Porter was an infidel, but his sister in Connecticut and his brother-in-law Everard Peck were committed evangelicals. Porter came under a barrage of family exhortation, and in January Peck wrote home that "Samuel is indulging a trembling hope . . ." He remained the object of family prayer for eight more months before hope turned into assurance. Then he joined his sister and brother-in-law in praying for the soul of their freethinking father. The realtor Bradford King left another record of evangelism within and between related households. After weeks of social prayer and private agony, he awoke and heard himself singing, "*I am going to the Kingdom will you come along with me.*" He testified at meeting the next day, but did not gain assurance until he returned home and for the first time prayed with his family. He rose and "decided that as for me & my house we would serve the Lord." Immediately King turned newfound powers on his brother's house in nearby Bloomfield. After two months of visiting and prayer he announced, "We had a little pentecost at brothers . . . all were praising and glorifying God in one United Voice." The revival made an evangelist of every convert, and most turned their power on family members.

Charles Finney's revival was based on group prayer. It was a simple, urgent activity that created new hearts in hundreds of men and women, and it generated—indeed it relied upon—a sense of absolute trust and common purpose among participants. The strengthening of family ties that attended the revival cannot be overestimated. But it was in prayer meetings and evening services that evangelism spilled outside old social channels, laying the basis for a transformed and united Protestant community.

Bradford King had no patience for "Old Church Hipocrites who think more of their particular denomination than Christ Church," and his sentiments were rooted in an astonishing resolution of old difficulties. Presbyterians stopped fighting during the first few days, and peace soon extended to the other denominations. Before the first month was out, Finney marveled that "Christians of every denomination generally seemed to make common cause, and went to work with a will, to pull sinners out of the fire." The most unexpected portent came in October, when the weight of a crowded gallery spread the walls and damaged the building at First Church. Vestrymen at St. Paul's—most of them former Masons and bitter enemies of the Presbyterians—let that homeless congregation into their church. But it was in prayer meetings and formal services that the collective regeneration of a fragmented church-going community took place, for it was there that 'Christians of different denominations are seen mingled together in the sanctuary on the Sabbath, and bowing at the same altar in the social prayer meeting."

Crowded prayer meetings were held almost every night from September until early March, and each of them was managed carefully. When everyone was seated the leader read a short verse dealing with the object of prayer. Satisfied that everyone understood and could participate, he called on those closest to the spirit. These prayed aloud, and within minutes all worldly thoughts were chased from the room. (Finney knew that the chemistry of prayer worked only when everyone shared in it, and he discouraged attendance by scoffers, cranks, and the merely curious.) Soon sinners grew anxious; some of them broke into tears, and Christians came close to pray with them. Then followed the emotional displays that timid ministers had feared, but which they accepted without a whimper during the revival winter. In October Artemissia Perkins prayed with her fiancé in Brick Church. Suddenly her voice rose above the others, and over and over she prayed, "Blessed be the Name of Jesus," while her future husband, her neighbors, and people who never again could be strangers watched and participated in the awesome work. It was in hundreds of encounters such as this that the revival shattered old divisions and laid the foundation for moral community among persons who had been strangers or enemies. "I know this is all algebra to those who have never felt it," Finney explained. "But to those who have experienced the agony of wrestling, prevailing prayer, for the conversion of a soul, you may depend on it, that soul . . . appears as dear as a child is to the mother who brought it forth with pain."

At formal services this mechanism took on massive proportions. During services Christians gathered in other churches and nearby homes to pray for the evangelist's success. Sometimes crowds of people who could not find seats in the house prayed outside in the snow. Downstairs the session room was packed, and every break in the lecture was punctuated by the rise and fall of prayer.

Inside, every seat was filled. People knelt in the aisles and doorways. Finney reserved seats near the pulpit for anxious sinners—not random volunteers, but prominent citizens who had spoken with him privately. None sat on the anxious bench who was not almost certain to fall. Separated from the regenerate and from hardened sinners, their conversions became grand public spectacles. In the pulpit, Finney preached with enormous power, but with none of the excesses some people expected. He had dropped a promising legal career to enter the ministry, and his preaching demonstrated formidable courtroom skills, not cheap theatrics. True, he took examples from everyday experience and spoke in folksy, colloquial terms. (With what may have been characteristic modesty, he reminded his listeners that Jesus had done the same.) Most of his lectures lasted an hour, but it was not uncommon for a packed church to listen twice that long "without the movement of a foot." When he gestured at the room, people ducked as if he were throwing things. In describing the fall of sinners he pointed to the ceiling, and as he let his finger drop people in the rear seats stood to watch the final entry into hell. Finney spoke directly to the anxious bench in front of him, and at the close of the lecture he demanded immediate repentance and prayer. Some of Rochester's first citizens humbled themselves on the anxious bench, sweating their way into heaven surrounded by praying neighbors. It was the most spectacular of the evangelist's techniques, and the most unabashedly communal.

NEW CHRISTIANS

Charles Finney's revival created a community of militant evangelicals that would remake society and politics in Rochester. . . . The pages that follow isolate the individuals who joined churches while Finney was in town, then locate experiences that they shared and that explain why they and not others were ripe for conversion in 1830–31. Insofar as the revival can be traced to its social origins, I shall consider it traceable to those experiences.

Finney claimed to have converted "the great mass of the most influential people" in Rochester. The *Observer* agreed that new church members included most of the town's "men of wealth, talents, and influence—those who move in the highest circles of society," and church records reinforce those claims. Table 1 compares the occupational sta-

Table 1
Occupations of the New Male Admittants to Rochester Protestant Churches in the Late 1820s, and in the Revival of 1830–31 (Percentages)

	year of admission	
	1825–29 (N = 85)	1830–31 (N = 170)
businessman-professional	22	19
shopkeeper-petty proprietor	14	11
master craftsman	16	26
clerical employee	12	10
journeyman craftsman	24	22
laborer-semiskilled	13	12

Note: The 1825–29 figures are derived from the tax list and directory of 1827. Figures for the years 1830–31 are derived from the 1830 tax list and the directories of 1827 and/or 1834. To ensure that these men were in Rochester when the tax list was compiled, inclusion is limited to those who appear in the 1827 directory or the 1830 census.

tus of Finney's male converts with that of men who joined churches in the years 1825–29. (Pre-revival figures are limited to the four years surrounding the tax list of 1827. Occupations of Finney converts are derived from the 1830 assessment rolls. Thus each occupation in the table is measured within two years of the time of conversion.)

Both in the 1820s and in the revival of 1830–31, new church members came disproportionately from among businessmen, professionals, and master workmen. During the Finney revival conversions multiplied dramatically within every group. But the center of enthusiasm shifted from the stores and offices to the workshops. Indeed it is the sharp increase in conversions among master craftsmen that accounts for slight declines in every other group. Whatever the problems that prepared the ground for Finney's triumph, they were experienced most strongly by master workmen.

Table 2 begins the attempt to infer just what those problems were. The table isolates specific occupations within the business community and calculates the percentage of church members within them in 1827 and again in 1834. Increases were most spectacular among master craftsmen and manufacturers, but there were significant variations within that group. Master builders and shoemakers had made dramatic breaks with the traditional organization of work, and with customary relations between masters and journeymen. The proportions of church members among them increased 70 percent and 73 percent, respectively. Proprietors of the small indoor workshops participated in the revival, but their increase was a less impressive 51 percent. Change in the operations they controlled came more slowly. They hired relatively few journeymen, and they continued into the 1830s to incorporate many of those men into their homes.

Table 2
Percent Protestant Church Members among Selected Proprietors, 1827–34

	1827	1834	percent change
merchant (N = 73, 63)	23	33	+30
hotelkeeper (N = 14, 30)*	21	13	−38
doctor (N = 21, 28)	29	54	+46
lawyer (N = 23, 31)	22	58	+62
grocer (N = 80, 59)	9	31	+71
forwarding merchant (N = 7, 18)	14	50	+72
master builder (N = 14, 13)†	21	69	+70
master shoemaker (N = 15, 15)†	20	73	+73
small-shop proprietor (N = 20, 37)†	30	62	+52

*Includes tavernkeepers and innkeepers.

†Includes only those identified as masters through newspaper advertisements and antiquarian sources.

Among white-collar proprietors, lawyers, forwarding merchants, and grocers made the greatest gains: 62 percent, 72 percent, and 71 percent, respectively. Rochester was the principal shipping point on the Erie Canal, and most boats operating on the canal belonged to Rochester forwarders. It was their boat crews who were reputedly the rowdiest men in an unruly society, and it was the forwarders who had been the chief target of the Sabbatarian crusade. Grocers were another white-collar group with peculiarly close ties to the working class. The principal retailers of liquor, they were closely regulated by the village trust-ees. In 1832 the trustees not only doubled the price of grocery licenses but began looking into the moral qualifications of applicants. The in-creased religiosity among grocers (as well as the decline in the total number of men in that occupation) reflects that fact. Reformers had branded forwarders and grocers the supporters both of the most dan-gerous men in society and of their most dangerous habits. While they had resisted attacks on their livelihood, grocers and boat owners could not but agree to their complicity in the collapse of old social forms. Most of them remained outside the churches. But a startlingly in-creased minority joined with master workmen and cast their lots with Jesus.

With these occupations removed, the revival among white-collar proprietors was weak. Doctors and merchants had only tenuous links with the new working class, and little personal responsibility for the collapse of the late 1820s. Increases among them were 46 percent and 30 percent, respectively. Hotelkeepers in particular were divorced from contact with workingmen, for they were dependent for their liveli-hoods on the more well-to-do canal travelers. Church membership among hotelkeepers actually declined 38 percent during the revival years. (The one remaining occupation—the law—was a special case: the in-crease was 62 percent. No doubt part of the explanation lies in Finney himself, who was a former attorney and took special pride in the con-version of lawyers. But perhaps more important is the fact that many lawyers were politicians, and in the 1830s resistance to the churches was political suicide.)

With few exceptions, then, Charles Finney's revival was strongest among entrepreneurs who bore direct responsibility for disordered re-lations between classes. And they were indeed responsible. The prob-lem of social class arose in towns and cities all over the northern United States after 1820. It would be easy to dismiss it as a stage of urban-industrial growth, a product of forces that were impersonal and inevi-table. In some ways it was. But at the beginning the new relationship between master and wage earner was created by masters who pre-ferred money and privacy to the company of their workmen and the performance of old patriarchal duties. Available evidence suggests that it was precisely those masters who filled Finney's meetings.

Perhaps more than any other act, the removal of workmen from the homes of employers created an autonomous working class. Table 3 compares households headed in 1827 by proprietors who joined churches during the revival with those headed by non-church members and by men who belonged to churches before the revival. Finney's converts kept fewer workmen in their families than did other proprietors, suggesting either that they had removed many of those men or that they had never allowed them into their homes. Table 4 traces households that included "extra" adult men in 1827 over the next three years. The table is compiled from the 1830 census. That document names heads of households and identifies others by age and sex. By counting males over the age of sixteen (the age at which men were included in the 1827 directory, and thus in Table 3), we may trace the broadest outlines of household change in the years immediately preceding the revival. Most proprietors thinned their families between 1827 and 1830. But while old church members and those who stayed outside the churches removed one in four adult men, converts cut their number by more than half. Thus the analyses of occupations and of household structure point clearly to one conclusion: Finney's converts were entrepreneurs who had made more than their share of the choices that created a free-labor economy and a class-bounded society in Rochester.

Table 3
Composition of Households Headed by Proprietors in 1827, by Religious Status of Householders

householder	N	percent which included		
		kin	*boarders*	*employees*
church member in 1829	81	15	14	41
revival convert	89	8	7	33
non-church member	151	13	17	43

Table 4
Changes in the Composition of Households Headed by Proprietors, 1827–30, by Religious Status of Householders

householder*	number of males over 16 years		
	1827	*1830*	*percent change*
church member in 1829	67	48	−24
revival convert	74	31	−58
non-church member	113	80	−29

*Includes only householders who appear in both the 1827 directory and the 1830 census.

The transformation began in the workshops, but it was not contained there. For in removing workmen the converts altered their own positions within families. The relative absence of even boarders and distant kin in their homes suggests a concern with domestic privacy. And within those families housewives assumed new kinds of moral authority. The organization of prayer meetings, the pattern of family visits, and bits of evidence from church records suggest that hundreds of conversions culminated when husbands prayed with their wives. Women formed majorities of the membership of every church at every point in time. But in every church, men increased their proportion of the communicants during revivals, indicating that revivals were family experiences and that women were converting their men. In 1830–31 fully 65 percent of male converts were related to prior members of their churches (computed from surnames within congregations). Traditionalists considered Finney's practice of having women and men pray together the most dangerous of the new measures, for it implied new kinds of equality between the sexes. Indeed some harried husbands recognized the revival as subversive of their authority over their wives. A man calling himself Anticlericus complained of Finney's visit to his home:

> He *stuffed* my wife with tracts, and alarmed her fears, and nothing short of meetings, night and day, could atone for the many fold sins my poor, simple spouse had committed, and at the same time, she made the miraculous discovery, that she had been "unevenly yoked." From this unhappy period, peace, quiet, and happiness have fled from my dwelling, never, I fear, to return.

The evangelicals assigned crucial religious duties to wives and mothers. In performing those duties, women rose out of old subordinate roles and extended their moral authority within families. Finney's male converts were driven to religion because they had abdicated their roles as eighteenth-century heads of households. In the course of the revival, their wives helped to transform them into nineteenth-century husbands.

Charles Finney's revival enlarged every Protestant church, broke down sectarian boundaries, and mobilized a religious community that had at its disposal enormous economic power. Motives which determined the use of that power derived from the revival, and they were frankly millenarian.

As Rochester Protestants looked beyond their community in 1831, they saw something awesome. For news of Finney's revival had helped touch off a wave of religious enthusiasm throughout much of the northern United States. The revival moved west into Ohio and Michigan, east into Utica, Albany, and the market towns of inland New England. Even Philadelphia and New York City felt its power. Vermont's congregational churches grew by 29 percent in 1831. During the same twelve months the churches of Connecticut swelled by over a third. After scanning reports from western New York, the Presbyterian General Assembly announced in wonder that "the work has been so general and thorough, that the whole customs of society have changed." Never before had so many Americans experienced religion in so short a time. Lyman Beecher, who watched the excitement from Boston, declared that the revival of 1831 was the greatest revival of religion that the world had ever seen.

Rochester Protestants saw conversions multiply and heard of powerful revivals throughout Yankee Christendom. They saw divisions among themselves melt away, and they began to sense that the premillennial unanimity was at hand—and that they and people like them were bringing it about. They had converted their families and neighbors through prayer. Through ceaseless effort they could use the same power to convert the world. It was Finney himself who told them that "if they were united all over the world the Millennium might be brought about in three months." He did not mean that Christ was coming to Rochester. The immediate and gory millennium predicted in Revelation had no place in evangelical thinking. Utopia would be realized on earth, and it would be made by God with the active and united collaboration of His people. It was not the physical reign of Christ that Finney predicted but the reign of Christianity. The millennium would be accomplished when sober, godly men—men whose every step was guided by a living faith in Jesus—exercised power in this world. Clearly, the revival of 1831 was a turning point in the long struggle to establish that state of affairs. American Protestants knew that, and John Humphrey Noyes later recalled that "in 1831, the whole orthodox church was in a state of ebullition in regard to the Millennium." Rochester evangelicals stood at the center of that excitement.

After 1831 the goal of revivals was the christianization of the world. With that at stake, membership in a Protestant church entailed new kinds of personal commitment. Newcomers to Brick Presbyterian Church in the 1820s had agreed to obey the laws of God and of the church, to treat fellow members as brothers, and "to live as an humble Christian." Each new convert was told that "renouncing all ungodliness and every worldly lust, you give up your all, soul and body, to be the Lord's, promising to walk before him in holiness and love all the days of your life." Not easy requirements, certainly, but in essence personal and passive. With the Finney revival, the ingrown piety of the 1820s turned outward and aggressive. In 1831 Brick Church rewrote its covenant, and every member signed this evangelical manifesto:

> We [note that the singular "you" has disappeared] do now, in the presence of the Eternal God, and these witnesses, covenant to be

the Lord's. *We promise to renounce all the ways of sin, and to make it the business of our life to do good and promote the declarative glory of our heavenly Father.* We promise steadily and devoutly to attend upon the institutions and ordinances of Christ as administered in this church, and to submit ourselves to its direction and discipline, until our present relation shall be regularly dissolved. We promise to be kind and affectionate to all the members of this church, to be tender of their character, and to endeavor to the utmost of our ability, to promote their growth in grace. *We promise to make it the great business of our life to glorify God and build up the Redeemer's Kingdom in this fallen world,* and constantly to endeavor to present our bodies a living sacrifice, holy and acceptable to Him.

In that final passage, the congregation affirmed that its actions—both individually and in concert—were finally meaningful only in relation to the Coming Kingdom. Everything they did tended either to bring it closer or push it farther away.

Guiding the new activism was a revolution in ideas about human ability. The Reverend William James of Brick Church had insisted in 1828 that most men were innately sinful. Christians could not change them, but only govern their excesses through *"a system of moral regulations, founded upon the natural relations between moral beings, and having for its immediate end the happiness of the community."* We have seen, however, that certain of those "natural relations" were in disarray, and that the businessmen and master workmen who were expected to govern within them were the most active participants in the revival. Evangelical theology absolved them of responsibility by teaching that virtue and order were products not of external authority but of choices made by morally responsible individuals. Nowhere, perhaps, was this put more simply than in the Sunday schools. In the 1820s children had been taught to read and then forced to memorize huge parts of the Bible. (Thirteen-year-old Jane Wilson won a prize in 1823 when she committed a numbing 1,650 verses to memory.) After 1831 Sunday-school scholars stopped memorizing the Bible. The object now was to have them study a few verses a week and to come to an understanding of them, and thus to prepare themselves for conversion and for "an active and useful Christian life." Unregenerate persons were no longer to be disciplined by immutable authority and through fixed social relationships. They were free and redeemable moral agents, accountable for their actions, capable of accepting or rejecting God's promise. It was the duty of Christian gentlemen not to govern them and accept responsibility for their actions but to educate them and change their hearts.

William Wisner, pastor at Brick Church during these years, catalogued developments that were "indispensably necessary to the bringing of millennial glory." First, of course, was more revivals. Second, and tied directly to the first, was the return of God's people to the uncompromising personal standards of the primitive Christians and Protestant martyrs. For the public and private behavior of converts advertised what God had done for them. If a Christian drank or broke the Sabbath or cheated his customers or engaged in frivolous conversation, he weakened not only his own reputation but the awesome cause he represented. While Christian women were admonished to discourage flattery and idle talk and to bring every conversation onto the great subject, troubled businessmen were actually seen returning money to families they had cheated. Isaac Lyon, half-owner of the Rochester Woolen Mills, was seen riding a canal boat on Sunday in the fall of 1833. Immediately he was before the trustees of his church. Lyon was pardoned after writing a confession into the minutes and reading it to the full congregation. He confessed that he had broken the eighth commandment. But more serious, he admitted, was that his sin was witnessed by others who knew his standing in the church and in the community, and for whom the behavior of Isaac Lyon reflected directly on the evangelical cause. He had shamed Christ in public and given His enemies cause to celebrate.

Finney's revival had, however, centered among persons whose honesty and personal morals were beyond question before they converted. Personal piety and circumspect public behavior were at bottom means toward the furtherance of revivals. At the moment of rebirth, the question came to each of them: "Lord, what wilt thou have me do?" The answer was obvious: unite with other Christians and convert the world. The world, however, contained bad habits, people, and institutions that inhibited revivals and whose removal must precede the millennium. Among church members who had lived in Rochester in the late 1820s, the right course of action was clear. With one hand they evangelized among their own unchurched poor. With the other they waged an absolutist and savage war on strong drink.

On New Year's Eve of the revival winter, Finney's coworker Theodore Weld delivered a four-hour temperance lecture at First Presbyterian Church. Weld began by describing a huge open pit at his right hand, and thousands of the victims of drink at his left. First he isolated the most hopeless—the runaway fathers, paupers, criminals, and maniacs—and marched them into the grave. He moved higher and higher into society, until only a few well-dressed tipplers remained outside the grave. Not even these were spared. While the audience rose to its feet the most temperate drinkers, along with their wives and helpless children, were swallowed up and lost. Weld turned to the crowd and demanded that they not only abstain from drinking and encourage the reform of others but that they unite to stamp it out. They must not drink or sell liquor, rent to a grogshop, sell grain to distillers, or patronize merchants who continued to trade in ardent spirits. They must, in short, utterly disengage from the traffic in liquor and use whatever power they had to make others do the same. A packed house stood silent.

The Reverend Penney rose from his seat beside the Methodist and Baptist preachers and demanded that vendors in the audience stop selling liquor immediately. Eight or ten did so on the spot, and the wholesale grocers retired to hold a meeting of their own. The next day Elijah and Albert Smith, Baptists who owned the largest grocery and provisions warehouse in the city, rolled their stock of whiskey out onto the sidewalk. While cheering Christians and awestruck sinners looked on, they smashed the barrels and let thousands of gallons of liquid poison run out onto Exchange Street.

Within a week, Everard Peck wrote home that "the principal merchants who have traded largely in ardent spirits are about abandoning this unholy traffic & we almost hope to see this deadly poison expelled from our village." The performance of the Smith brothers was being repeated throughout Rochester. Sometimes wealthy converts walked into groceries, bought up all the liquor, and threw it away. A few grocers with a fine taste for symbolism poured their whiskey into the Canal. Even grocers who stayed outside the churches found that whiskey on their shelves was bad for business. The firm of Rossiter and Knox announced that it was discontinuing the sale of whiskey, but "not thinking it a duty to 'feed the Erie Canal' with their property, offer to sell at cost their whole stock of liquors . . ." Those who resisted were refused advertising space in some newspapers, and in denying the power of a united evangelical community they toyed with economic ruin. S. P. Needham held out for three years, but in 1834 he announced that he planned to liquidate his stock of groceries, provisions, and liquors and leave Rochester. "Church Dominancy," he explained, "has such influence over this community that no honest man can do his own business in his own way . . ."

Almost immediately, Weld's absolutist temperance pledge became a condition of conversion—the most visible symbol of individual rebirth. The teetotal pledge was only the most forceful indication of church members' willingness to use whatever power they had to coerce others into being good, or at least to deny them the means of being bad. While whiskey ran into the gutters, two other symbols of the riotous twenties disappeared. John and Joseph Christopher, both of them new Episcopalians, bought the theater next door to their hotel, closed it, and had it reopened as a livery stable. The Presbyterian Sprague brothers bought the circus building and turned it into a soap factory. Increasingly, the wicked had no place to go.

These were open and forceful attacks on the leisure activities of the new working class, something very much like class violence. But Christians waged war on sin, not workingmen. Alcohol, the circus, the theater, and other workingmen's entertainments were evil because they wasted men's time and clouded their minds and thus blocked the millennium. Evangelicals fought these evils in order to prepare society for new revivals. It was missionary work, little more. And in the winter following Finney's departure, it began to bear fruit.

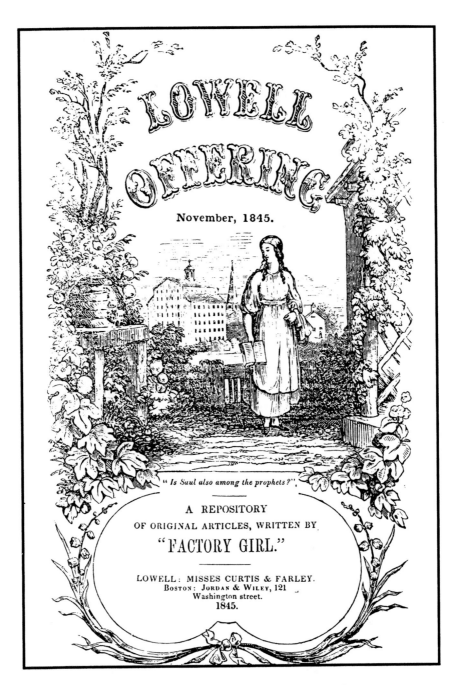

Title page from the Lowell Offering, *a journal published by the women who worked in Lowell's textile factories.*

The Early Lowell Strikes

THOMAS DUBLIN

Historians have placed the birth of America's industrial revolution in rural New England, where the spinning and weaving of textiles were first brought into mechanized factories. Many rural families of the early nineteenth century, like that of Mayo Greenleaf Patch, could no longer support themselves on the land and hence looked for work in the water-powered spinning mills of southern New England. They became the first generation of factory workers in America.

While these early mills had machines to spin the yarn mechanically, a putting-out system was employed for the weaving. Women received yarn from the mills, wove it in their homes, and returned the finished cloth. Colonial women had traditionally spun and woven at home to make cloth for their families. Now they operated their looms for piece-rate wages and produced cloth for the market.

In 1813 the first American power loom was constructed in Boston by merchant Francis Cabot Lowell and mechanic Paul Moody. Over the next decade Lowell and his merchant associates created a company town around hundreds of water-driven power looms, a development that dramatically changed the nature of women's textile work. The labor force of these power-loom factories of Lowell, as the town was named in 1826, consisted of young, single women from New England farmsteads. Whereas children and male supervisors had formed the work force of New England's early spinning mills, the power looms of Lowell were operated by the nation's first female factory labor force.

Because the mills had to be situated where water power was available, some distance inland from the seaboard urban centers, mill owners were obliged to recruit young women from the small farms and villages of New England who would both live and work in the factory town. In attracting such a labor force, however, Lowell's employers did not create the exploitative and degraded conditions of the English factory system. Instead, they designed a model community around their orderly mills, with company-run boardinghouses, churches, and cultural activities for the workers. The matrons of the boardinghouses enforced strict curfews and church attendance and reported misbehavior to the company managers. Young farm women came to this paternalistic work environment out of economic and personal motives, particularly the desire to acquire economic independence and escape the drudgery of farming and home manufacture.

The daily work life in the factory and the boardinghouse environment both created bonds of community among the young women of Lowell. In this selection, Thomas Dublin looks at how those bonds, and the women's personal attitudes and values, underlay their collective protest in the 1830s. Dublin uncovers for the reader both the unique roots of female solidarity in Lowell and the traditional values the women shared with working men who faced the new demands of industrial life. Dublin takes the Lowell strikes of 1830, a form of public protest, and links them to the individual concerns and personal expectations of the young women who spent their days in the mills.

T he nature of work and housing in early Lowell helped weld women workers together, but women as a group did not consciously array themselves against millowners or management. Solidarity grew up among women, but it was based on shared experience and culture and mutual dependence rather than upon antagonism toward employers. Mill management exercised considerable control over the lives of women workers through regulations imposed in the mills and boardinghouses, but mill employment fulfilled important needs for women, and they were generally willing to accept these regulations. As long as their expectations were met, women workers did not challenge the power and authority of the corporations. Twice in the 1830s, however, mill management took a course of action that led women workers to rebel. In February 1834 and October 1836, women workers struck to oppose first reductions in wages and then increases in the board rates charged in company housing. These events are important because they reveal the ways that women used the bonds of community forged in their daily lives to mobilize protest in times of crisis. They reveal also the way women workers drew on preindustrial values in responding to changing conditions in the mills and the way these values were transformed within an industrial setting.

THE EARLY LOWELL STRIKES   From Thomas Dublin, *Women at Work: The Transformation of Work and Community in Lowell, Massachusetts, 1826–1860* (New York: Columbia University Press, 1979). Copyright © 1979 by Thomas Dublin. Reprinted by permission of Columbia University Press.

The 1830s, the years of the first strikes in Lowell, were a period of profound unrest in the ranks of American labor. A rapid transformation of the social relations of production, particularly in the skilled urban crafts, led to a new proliferation of labor organizations. The rise of the boss manufacturer and the wholesale merchant undermined an earlier system of production based on master craftsmen, journeymen, and apprentices. The apprenticeship system had established links among the ranks of the urban working class, but increasingly an unbridgeable gulf separated employer and worker. The new urban entrepreneur was no longer an artisan but had become an employer of workers who organized the labor process and marketed the finished products. Workers responded to these developments by organizing to defend their wages, hours, and skilled positions. The period saw the rise of local trade societies within individual crafts, urban central labor organizations, or trades' unions, and national organizations that sought to promote the mutual interests of disparate local groups. The new labor organizations grew most rapidly among male workers in the artisan and building trades of the industrializing Northeast where these economic developments were first felt.

As employers sought to expand production and reduce labor costs, workers began to resist. Moving beyond the benevolent societies of an earlier era, journeymen organized trade unions whose chief concerns were wages and hours. Strikes proliferated in the mid-1830s as trade societies fought to reduce the hours of labor and increase wages in prosperous times and to maintain wage levels in periods of depression. Organized activity spilled over into the political arena as well; as workers sought to use the state to promote economic and social reform. In Boston, New York, and Philadelphia, workingmen's parties united articulate labor leaders and reform-minded merchants and professionals in campaigns aimed broadly at a democratization of economic and political life.

The growth of labor organizations on such a variety of levels—within single trades, in citywide councils, and even along national lines—is evidence of both the strength and the weakness of labor in these years. The urban trades' unions—umbrella organizations of several trade unions in a single city—grew out of the initial weakness of organizations within individual trades and the obvious need for solidarity in the face of unified employer opposition. As these citywide movements gained strength, many trades succeeded in obtaining the ten-hour working day, as in Philadelphia in 1835. But the growth of ever larger regional markets undermined the power of unions organized only at the local level. Employers facing united opposition in one city could shift production to unorganized workers elsewhere. In response, attempts were made to establish national trade unions, particularly among shoemakers and printers. Still, the strength of labor lay in its organization at the local level, and the national unions were never much more than paper organizations, which expired with the onset of depression in 1837.

Labor organizations along these lines did not develop among women textile workers in the 1830s. Several factors help to explain the differences between the responses of women operatives and male artisans in the period. Caroline Ware has emphasized the temporary nature of mill employment, arguing that "[only] as the mill population became more permanent was there any real and prolonged interest in mill conditions and any chance for effective organization." In this view, women who planned to work only a short time in the mills before marriage had little incentive to struggle to improve working conditions. One might add also that women operatives lacked the craft skills and traditions that contributed to organization among artisans in the period. Finally, they did not have the same sort of preindustrial craft work experience with which to judge factory production. They were unlikely to use their years of domestic textile production as a foil against which they would find the factory wanting. All of these factors undoubtedly inhibited the growth of permanent trade organizations among women.

Trade unions, however, are not the only mechanism through which workers can express their opposition to the demands of industrial capitalism. Women in the Lowell mills certainly were not immune from the industrial struggles raging all around them. In prosperous times workingmen complained that they were unable to arouse in operatives an opposition to the factory system. In these periods women evidently were able to fulfill their expectations and lay away enough savings to compensate for the long hours and strict regulation of textile production. Women were not entirely complacent, however. Given provocation, women workers did organize themselves, staging Lowell's first strikes in February 1834 and October 1836. The pattern of sporadic outbursts gave way in the 1840s to the growth of permanent labor organizations among women and repeated campaigns aimed at achieving the ten-hour working day. These struggles placed the Lowell women squarely within the evolving labor movement and indicated that craft traditions were not the only legitimating forces in labor protests of the period.

. . . The strikes of the 1830s, and then the Ten Hour Movement of the 1840s, are important not only because they indicate the impact of textile factories on women workers, but also because they reveal the interconnections between the experiences of women in Lowell and those of other workers throughout New England and the mid-Atlantic states. The Lowell protests were part of the larger response to the demands imposed by a maturing industrial capitalism on the working class at this time. From Lowell, Manchester, and Fall River to New York, Philadelphia, and Pittsburgh, workers organized to challenge the power and authority of employers. These struggles developed together and reinforced one another. Channels of communication and coordination developed, and workers' organizations shared tactics and strategy. Lowell operatives emulated earlier strikers, and workers in other communities, in turn, copied their actions. This coordination and imitation resulted because, even with evident differences, working men and women alike drew on certain shared traditional social and cultural values to oppose the novel demands of industrial life. Within this wider context, the Lowell struggles are most significant for what they reveal about the broader conflicts generated by the growth of industrial capitalism before the Civil War.

After a decade of rapid expansion and relative tranquility, Lowell saw its first labor protest in February 1834, when 800 women workers "turned out"—quit work—to oppose a proposed reduction in piece wages. Trouble had been brewing for two weeks since the agents of all the major firms had posted identical broadsides announcing a reduction of wages to take effect March 1. A brief chronology of the events leading up to the protest reveals the values and attitudes that prompted women workers to challenge the power and authority of mill management.

The origin of the turn-out—as the work stoppage was called—must be sought in the Boston meeting rooms of the directors of the Lowell textile firms. Faced with falling prices of textile goods, a sluggish market, and rising inventories of unsold cloth, the directors of the mills met and recommended a 25 percent wage reduction. Henry Hall, treasurer of the Lawrence, Tremont, and Suffolk companies, instructed Robert Means, resident agent at Tremont, to "act in concert with the other agents & endeavor to do what is right between the parties." The agents of all the Lowell mills subsequently met and agreed upon a reduction of half the amount initially recommended by the Boston directors. While the more distant directors pressed for greater reductions, agents in Lowell expressed concern that such action would have disastrous consequences. As William Austin, the Lawrence Company agent, wrote: "The tendency will be unfavorable to the procurement of good help in future & reduce the character of those who remain to a lower standard rendering it doubtful in my own mind whether the permanent interest of the manufacturing establishments here will be promoted by so great a reduction." The differences between the resident agents and their Boston employers remained a private matter, however, and at a subsequent meeting the agents voted to impose reductions about midway between the directors' original recommendations and their own.

The agents had good reason for concern about the reaction of women workers. Agitation in the mills began as soon as the broadsides appeared announcing the impending wage cuts. Even before agents fixed on the actual amount of the reduction, petitions circulated among the women. One agent reported to his company treasurer in Boston: "A good deal of excitement exists in all the mills, not excepting ours, in relation to the proposed reduction. Papers are in circulation, & as I am informed, extensively signed, by which the females pledge themselves to leave if the reduction is made." One such petition has survived, signed by fifty weavers at the Suffolk Company and expressing their determination to give notice and quit work if existing wage rates were not maintained. Their petition read in part:

> We the undersigned considering ourselves wronged and our priv-ileges invaded by the unjust and unreasonable oblidgment of our wages, do hereby mutually and cheerfully engage not to enter the Factory on the first of March, nor after for the purpose of work, unless the paper which causes our dissatisfaction be removed and another signed . . . purport[in]g that our wages shall be after the same rate as previous to the first of March.

The signers pledged further that if any of them later reneged she would pay five dollars to one of their number to be used for "some benevo-lent object in this Town." To mobilize support in the other mills, the Suffolk weavers sent their petition to weavers at the Appleton Com-pany, urging them to take similar action.

Women continued to hold meetings, a number convening within the mills during the dinner break. Agitation mounted, to the point where it began to disrupt the work itself. One agent, seeking to squelch the unrest before it spread, dismissed a leader. Her fellow workers rallied around her and quit work, and the turn-out had begun. Protesting op-eratives paraded through city streets, visiting the various mills and at-tempting to induce others to join in. In all, about a sixth of all women workers in Lowell turned out. The Boston *Evening Transcript* reported the procession and the mass outdoor rally that followed:

> The number soon increased to nearly *eight hundred.* A proces-sion was formed and they marched about town. . . . We are told that one of the leaders mounted a pump and made a flaming Mary Woolstonecroft [sic] speech on the rights of women and the iniq-uities of the "*monied* aristocracy," which produced a powerful effect on her auditors, and they determined "to have their own way if they died for it."

At the rally operatives endorsed a petition calling on fellow workers to "discontinue their labors until terms of reconciliation are made." The petition concluded:

> Resolved, That we will not go back into the mills to work un-less our wages are continued . . . as they have been.
> Resolved, That none of us will go back, unless they receive us all as one.
> Resolved, That if any have not money enough to carry them home they shall be supplied.

The turn-out, however, proved to be brief, and it failed to reverse the wage reductions. Turning out on a Friday, striking operatives received wages owed them on Saturday, and by the middle of the next week they had returned to work or left town. Within a week of the turn-out, mills were running near capacity.

Though short-lived, the turn-out points to the tensions evoked by the interconnections of sex and power within the mills. Operatives were, after all, *women* workers, and both strikers and mill managers were very conscious of this fact. The "Mary Woolstonecroft [sic] speech," given at the rally, linked together the causes of operatives as women and as workers. Just as the leaders of the turn-out sought to redefine woman's place, mill managers viewed the protest as decidedly unfeminine. William Austin, agent of the Lawrence Company, described the operatives' procession as an "amizonian [sic] display." He repeated his language in a letter to his company treasurer: "This afternoon we have paid off several of these Amazons & presume that they will leave town on Monday." The turn-out was particularly offensive to the mill agents because of the relationship of mutual confidence they thought they had enjoyed with their operatives. Austin probably expressed the feelings of the other agents when he wrote:

> [N]otwithstanding the friendly and disinterested advice which has been on all proper occasions communicated to the girls of the Lawrence Mills a spirit of evil omen . . . has prevailed, and overcome the judgment & discretion of too many, and this morning a general turn-out from most of the rooms has been the consequence.

Mill agents assumed an attitude of benevolent paternalism toward female operatives, and they found it particularly disturbing that women paid such little heed to their advice. Strikers were not simply unfeminine; they were ungrateful as well.

Such attitudes notwithstanding, 800 women chose to go on strike. They did so for two principal reasons. First, the wage cuts undermined the sense of dignity and social equality that was such an important element in their Yankee heritage. Second, the cuts were seen as an attack on their economic independence.

In a statement accompanying the petition circulated among operatives, the strikers expressed well their sense of themselves and their motives for protest.

UNION IS POWER

> Our present object is to have union and exertion, and we remain in possession of our unquestionable rights. We circulate this paper wishing to obtain the names of all who imbibe the spirit of our Patriotic Ancestors, who preferred privation to bondage, and parted with all that renders life desirable and even life itself to procure independence for their children. The oppressing hand of avarice

would enslave us, and to gain their object, they gravely tell us of
the pressure of the times, this we are already sensible of, and de-
plore it. If any are in want, the Ladies will be compassionate and
assist them; but we prefer to have the disposing of our charities in
our own hands; and as we are free, we would remain in possession
of what kind Providence has bestowed upon us, and remain
daughters of freemen still.

In these lines striking women workers expressed their pride and sense
of independence as "daughters of freemen." They were identifying
themselves not primarily as working women, but rather as daughters
of the propertied rural farmers. Here we see the ideological implications of the common social origins of women workers. . . .

This rural identification gave the protest strong ties to the preindustrial traditions of the striking women. They linked their action expressly to the tradition of the Revolutionary War, to the efforts of their
"Patriotic Ancestors" to secure independence from England. This identification with the traditions of revolutionary republicanism was expressed clearly in a poem that concluded their petition:

> Let oppression shrug her shoulders,
> And a haughty tyrant frown,
> And little upstart Ignorance,
> In mockery look down.
> Yet I value not the feeble threats
> Of Tories in disguise,
> While the flag of Independence
> O'er our noble nation flies.

There is no doubt who were the Whigs and who the Tories in this
particular drama.

By harking back to the Revolutionary War, women workers were
drawing on the same traditions cited by contemporary workingmen in
their trade union struggles. Seth Luther, carpenter and itinerant labor
organizer and agitator in New England, made similar allusions in his
writings:

But if *poor* men ask JUSTICE, it is a most HORRIBLE COMBINA-
TION. The Declaration of Independence was the work of a combination, and was as hateful to the TRAITORS and TORIES of those
days, as combinations among working men are now to the avari-
cious MONOPOLIST and *purse-proud* ARISTOCRAT.

Organized workingmen took the revolutionary tradition seriously. When
Lynn shoemakers published a newspaper, *The Awl*, in the mid-1840s,
they reprinted the Declaration of Independence. As Dawley has noted,
"some journeymen compared their bosses to King George, and one

proposed that workingmen assemble on Lynn Common on the Fourth of July to erect a monument to their forebears who marched to repulse the British at Concord in 1775." Fittingly enough, the great shoe-makers' strike in 1860 began on Washington's Birthday, a date chosen according to Dawley "to demonstrate that they were acting in the best traditions of the Republic." By appropriating revolutionary rhetoric, Seth Luther, the Lynn shoemakers, and Lowell women workers gave their protests legitimacy, for they became, in their own eyes at least, the direct heirs of the revolutionary tradition. For Lowell women, for in-stance, wage cuts were thus not questions of purely economic concern; they were interpreted more broadly, as attempts to "enslave" women workers, to deprive them of their independent status as "daughters of freemen."

Integral to this appropriation of the revolutionary heritage of their fathers was a clear statement of the women's sense of their own worth and dignity. As independent "daughters of freemen," they felt no def-erence toward their employers; they would certainly *not* call them their masters. Elsewhere they expressed the conviction that they were the social equals of their overseers, indeed of the millowners themselves. The wage reductions, however, struck at their assertion of equality. The cuts made it clear that the workers were subordinate to their em-ployers, or at least so millowners and agents thought, rather than equal partners in a contract binding on both parties. By turning out the women emphatically denied that they were subordinates. In returning to work the next week, they yielded to the reality that in economic terms they were no match for their corporate employers.

In point of fact the women workers *were* subordinates in Lowell's social and economic order, but they never consciously accepted this status. Their refusal to do so became evident on those occasions when the millowners exercised their power most blatantly, as in their unilat-eral decision to reduce customary piece-wage rates. This fundamental contradiction between the objective position of operatives and their consciousness of their status was at the root of the 1834 turn-out and of subsequent labor protests in Lowell before 1850. The corporations could build mills, create thousands of jobs, and recruit women to fill them. Nevertheless, they bought only their operatives' labor power, and then for only as long as the workers chose to stay. Virtually all of the women could return to their rural homes, whatever the tangible and psychic costs of such a return, and all maintained a strong sense of their own worth and dignity. The women's economic independence and their strong sense of themselves both limited the actions of management.

When women workers spoke of independence, they referred at once to independence from their families and from their employers. An ad-equate wage made them largely independent of their families back home and also allowed them to save enough out of their monthly earnings to return to their native homes whenever they so desired. But this independence was based on the relatively high level of wages in the mills. The wage cuts threatened to deny women these savings and the economic and social independence they provided, offering instead the prospect of a total dependence on mill work. No wonder, then, there was alarm that "the oppressing hand of avarice would enslave us." To be forced, out of economic necessity, into lifelong labor in the mills would indeed have seemed like slavery. The Yankee operatives spoke directly to the fear of a dependency based on impoverishment in offering to assist women workers who "have not money enough to carry them home." Wage reductions, however, offered only the *prospect* of a future dependence on mill employment. By striking, the women asserted that their economic independence and their status as "daughters of freemen" remained intact.

While the women's traditional conception of themselves as independent daughters of freemen played a crucial role in the turn-out, this factor alone would not necessarily have triggered a protest; alone it would have led women as individuals to quit work and return to their rural homes. But the turn-out was a collective action, indicating at once both the strength of women's economic motives and the importance of their sense of shared identity and purpose. They turned out in order to maintain existing wage rates and to hold onto their jobs and the economic independence they enjoyed.

The evidence of the planned, collective nature of the protest is clear. The Suffolk weavers' petition described earlier indicates that women workers initially planned to quit work en masse the day the wage cuts were to take effect. To make their pledge stick, women agreed to forfeit 5 dollars if they failed to abide by its terms. In order to secure additional support for their action, Suffolk weavers sent the petition to their counterparts at the Appleton Company and urged them to join the action. Further, leaders of the turn-out organized a run on the local savings bank, the Lowell Institution for Savings, closely allied with the textile corporations. Women withdrew their savings in order to have funds to survive during the strike and to be able to return to their rural homes. This tactic enabled the organized women to offer assistance to workers who did not have "money enough to carry them home." It also seems to have forced the corporations to provide funds to the bank to enable it to meet the demand for specie.

The extent of organization among women is most clearly revealed in the meetings they held within the mills and in the confrontation that eventually precipitated the turn-out. A remarkable letter written by a mill agent, William Austin, to his company treasurer in Boston, in the midst of the events, provides a vivid firsthand account from an interested participant. He first became concerned when he learned that workers were meeting in Spinning Room No. 1 during their dinner break. They had excluded the male watchman from their proceedings, evidently considering him an outsider. The agent described his unsuccessful efforts to dissuade the operatives from their course of action:

> It appeared that before I entered the room, they had appointed a dictatress & voted to be governed by her in all cases. This woman . . . retorted upon me with no little vehemence, & declared that there was no cause for any reduction whatever, that the causes assigned for it were without foundation in fact, that she had to pay as much for a yard of cloth as ever & that there was no truth in the assertions of the Agents.

Austin could get nowhere with his adversary, and "[p]erceiving that this woman had a great sway over the minds of the other females," he tried to persuade her to accept an "honorable discharge" and to leave the mill. She was not interested, and there Austin let matters rest as the women returned to their work. By the end of the day, however, Austin felt he had to take stronger action. This ringleader "continually had a crowd around her" which disrupted work, and Austin decided to discharge her. In response to her dismissal, "She declared that every girl in the room should leave with her, made a signal, and . . . they all marched out & few returned the ensuing morning." The Boston *Evening Transcript* confirmed Austin's account but suggested that operatives in the other Lawrence mills turned out as well. According to this source:

> On Friday evening, the young woman referred to was *dismissed* by the Agent, from her place in the mill where she worked, and on leaving the office, after receiving 'a bill of her time,' . . . waved her calash in the air as a signal to others, who were watching from the windows, when they immediately 'struck,' and assembled around her, in despite of the overseers.

Both accounts indicate that the turn-out was not simply a spontaneous outburst of enraged individuals, but rather an organized, planned protest.

The organized collective nature of the turn-out, however, did not guarantee its success. First, it mobilized only about a sixth of the female labor force, whose absence from the mills disrupted production but did not bring it to a complete halt. Anticipating the possibility of difficulties, mill agents actively sought replacements even before the turn-out. As Austin wrote on the day of the turn-out: "I have now engaged and ready to come in about two hundred girls who will come in during the ensuing month, and fifty more are offered." Even had the mills been forced to reduce production, it is unlikely that the directors would have yielded to the operatives. Given the accumulation of finished cloth unsold, there were directors who felt that it would not hurt to have the mills shut down for a period. These were not good times in which to launch the first labor struggle in Lowell's brief history.

Compounding these difficulties was the fact that mill management found the turn-out virtually incomprehensible. As one treasurer wrote to his company's agent in Lowell: "The conduct of the Female 'operatives' in yours & the neighboring mills is inexplicable unless they suppose of a *show* of resistance that the proprietors will be intimidated & induced to continue *old* prices." The disbelief expressed here stemmed as much from the fact that striking workers were females as from the novelty of their specific demands. The turn-out shocked and amazed the directors, and they took up an unyielding position in response to the women's challenge to their power and authority. With all the mill managers in Lowell acting in unison, and with agents in neighboring mill towns following suit, women found that if they wanted to work at all, they would have to accept reduced wages. Although the strike did not accomplish its immediate objectives, by demonstrating the possibility of collective action it paved the way for more successful struggles in the future.

In October 1836 women again turned out. This action was similar to the first in several respects. It, too, was a defensive action opposing a decision of management that would have reduced women's earnings—a decision to raise the price of room and board in company boardinghouses. The price increase came in response to petitions from boardinghouse keepers complaining that they could not make ends meet because of rapid inflation. The problem with management's action was that it placed the entire burden of inflation on the women workers, without increasing their piece wages accordingly. Since women generally quoted their wages exclusive of the cost of room and board, this action was viewed by women as a wage cut, not very different from that of February 1834. Further, the tactics mirrored those employed earlier. Women marched around town and held large-scale outdoor rallies to drum up support. Even the language of strike resolutions had a familiar ring: "As our fathers resisted unto blood the lordly avarice of the British ministry, so we, their daughters, never will wear the yoke which has been prepared for us." Song enlivened the protesters' march, and the lyrics recalled the earlier turn-out:

> Oh! isn't a pity, such a pretty girl as I—
> Should be sent to the factory to pine away and die?
> Oh! I cannot be a slave,
> I will not be a slave,
> For I'm so fond of liberty,
> That I cannot be a slave.

Once again the spectre of slavery was raised, clearly viewed in contrast to the economic and social independence that was the women's heritage.

Further similarities linked the two turn-outs. As in 1834 there was considerable excitement after mill management announced its decision to raise the price of board. One company treasurer expressed a concern probably shared by others: "[I] shall be anxious to know how the new rate of Board is rec[eive]d by the Ladies of Your Family. I hope there is good sense enough amongst them to see the necessity of the case." Once again women met and talked within the mills, planning their course of action. Harriet Robinson, 11 years old at this date and an active participant in the struggle, recalled events later in her reminiscences:

> I worked in a lower room, where I heard the proposed strike fully, if not vehemently, discussed; I had been an ardent listener . . . and naturally I took sides with the strikers. When the day came on which the girls were to turn out, those in the upper rooms started first, and so many of them left that our mill was at once shut down. Then, when the girls in my room stood irresolute, uncertain what to do . . . I, who began to think they would not go out, after all their talk, became impatient, and started on ahead, saying with childish bravado, "I don't care what you do, *I* am going to turn out, whether any one else does or not;" and I marched out, and was followed by the others.

This account indicates that the women actively discussed the increase in board rates and planned the turn-out, much as they had in 1834.

Despite these continuities, the differences between the two turn-outs were dramatic. First, the economic settings in February 1834 and October 1836 contrasted sharply. At the earlier date, textile sales were sluggish and a number of directors even welcomed the possibility of halting production; in 1836 sales were booming, and the mills could not recruit enough workers to meet demand. In August 1836, two months before the turn-out, one agent complained of shortages of operatives in three of his firm's mills. He wanted to shift workers from one mill to another but noted their resistance: "[It] will not meet the notions of the girls, who have a high sense of their value in the market & must be treated with corresponding delicacy and forbearance." In these prosperous times the prospects of success for the turn-out were considerably greater than they had been two and a half years earlier. In addition to the more favorable economic circumstances, this second turn-out involved a higher proportion of operatives than in 1834. Some 1,500 or 2,000 turned out in 1836, comprising between one fourth and one third of the female labor force, compared to only a sixth two years before. Moreover, the second strike lasted much longer than the first.

In 1834 operatives stayed out for only a few days; in 1836 the mills ran far below capacity for several months. Two weeks after the beginning of the 1836 turn-out, the Lawrence Company agent reported that only a fifth of striking operatives had returned to work: "The rest manifest good 'spunk' as they call it." Several days later he complained further of the impact of the continuing strike on operations in his mills: "We must be feeble for months to come as probably not less than 250 of our former scanty supply of help have left town." At the Hamilton Company about a fourth of the women workers left the mills during October, leaving the firm so short of help that management closed one of the company's three mills and shifted the remaining workers into the two still in operation.

The larger proportion of women workers taking part and the longer duration of the turn-out meant that the strikers had a much more significant impact on the operations of the mills. Estimates of the total number of participants provide one measure of this impact, but examination of individual firms may place this dimension in a clearer light. At the Lawrence Company, with a normal work force of 1,300 the agent reported that 386 women and 3 men were absent from the mills on the second day of the strike. The next day the number had increased to between 400 and 450, fully a third of all the workers, and a considerably larger proportion of women. At the neighboring Tremont Mills, between 180 and 200 were out, amounting to one half of the normal work force. Clearly the larger number of participants overall was mirrored in the experience of individual Lowell firms.

Numbers alone were only one reason for the greater impact of the turn-out. The increased organization of women workers and the greater sophistication of their tactics also played a part. To coordinate activities, women formed a Factory Girls' Association, which reached a membership of 2,500. The association organized "committees from the several corporations, to make provisions for those who have not the means to pay their board." Although the Association did not outlive the strike that gave it birth, it clearly contributed to the impact of the turn-out.

The increased organization of women was reflected in the tactics they employed. Strikers, according to one mill agent, were able to halt production to a greater extent than numbers alone could explain. He complained that although some operatives were willing to work, "it has been impossible to give employment to many who remained." He attributed the difficulty to the women's tactics:

> This was in many instances no doubt the result of calculation and contrivance. After the original turn-out they [the operatives] would assail a particular room—as for instance, all the warpers, or all the

warp spinners, or all the speeder and stretcher girls, and this would
close the mill as effectually as if all the girls in the mill had left.

Apparently giving more thought than they had earlier to the specific
tactics of the turn-out, women made a deliberate effort to shut down
the mills in order to win their demands. These tactics anticipated those
of skilled mule spinners and loom fixers in the last decades of the nineteenth century. Learning from the failure of the 1834 turn-out, and
building on the experience gained at that time, women brought a more
acute awareness of the importance of tactics to the struggle.

Mill agents were not the only contemporaries impressed by the
organization and tactics of striking operatives. A local storekeeper and
lay preacher, Aaron Lummus, expressed his amazement at the quality
of leadership among the operatives: "[It] was remarkable, that a few,
probably less than half a dozen young women, should manage this
whole affair with so much dexterity and correct judgement, that no
power, or skill, could be successfully employed against them." Lummus allied himself with the women and could clearly appreciate their
efforts in a way that mill manager adversaries could not.

The increased tactical awareness of the leadership paid off. Several
sources indicate that the striking women achieved a measure of success. According to one observer the companies rescinded the increases
in the price of room and board for operatives paid on a daily basis.
Including sparehands, spinners, and drawers, this group constituted
more than 40 percent of women workers at Hamilton Company and
probably a similar proportion in other firms. At two companies the
women seem to have been completely successful. As a mill agent wrote
in the heat of the struggle: "Merr[imack] and Boott houses have dis-
continued extra allowance to boarding houses." While this line leaves
some doubt, it does appear that the Merrimack and Boott companies
had rescinded their recent increases in board rates. These sources indicate a degree of success that was unusual for any strike—of workingmen or women—in the period.

Who were these workingwomen who dared to overstep the bounds
of female propriety to turn out when they felt their interests were challenged and their independence attacked? Available evidence suggests
that the strikers were drawn from the entire range of female mill occupations. Workingmen did not take part in significant numbers because their interests were never affected. In 1834 only the wages of
piece workers were reduced, and men working for a daily wage remained on the sidelines. In 1836 only the board rates for women were
raised. It would have made no sense for management to cut male earnings when men made up only 15 percent of the work force and such a
large proportion were employed in supervisory roles. The labor sav-

ings sought were best derived by reductions in the earnings of the vast female majority in the work force.

One textile corporation, the Appleton Company, kept a list of those workers who took part in the turn-out in February 1834. The document records the names and occupations of 125 women—about 30 percent of all females employed at Appleton at the time—who had quit work "on account of the reduction in Wages." The occupations of the strikers reveal that they were rather evenly distributed throughout the various departments of the company's mills. About 40 percent worked in the low-paying carding and spinning rooms and 60 percent in weaving and dressing, both figures approximating the proportions of women operatives typically employed in these rooms.

Strikers at the Hamilton Company in October 1836 showed a similar occupational distribution. Hamilton kept no lists explicitly identifying those who participated in the turn-out, but surviving records enable one to identify workers who left the company during that month. For several reasons it seems reasonable to consider these women strikers. First, 25 percent of women workers departed Hamilton in October, a proportion more than twice that of the months immediately preceding and following. Second, it is clear that the primary tactic employed in the turn-out was the wholesale departure of operatives who returned to their native homes. A contemporary in Lowell, a Methodist minister, Orange Scott, estimated that 2,000 women had left the city during the strike, intending to return only when their demands had been met.

As at the Appleton Company strikers at Hamilton were drawn from all ranks of the female work force. The highest paid women, those employed in the dressing room, were somewhat underrepresented, but weavers, the next ranking group, were overrepresented. On the whole, the occupations of strikers and nonstrikers were not radically different from one another. The daily earnings of the two groups reflected this fact, with strikers earning an average of $0.61 per day, and nonstrikers a slightly higher $0.63. . . .

What factors can account for the ability of women textile workers in Lowell to organize and sustain this kind of collective protest? After all, women in the mills lacked the craft traditions and scarce skills of male artisans. Further, they were not lifelong workers, supporting entire families on their earnings in the mills. Despite these dampening influences, the signal fact that stands out for Lowell in these early years is that women workers did organize two large-scale turn-outs. The conjunction of several interrelated factors best explains this reality. First, the growth of a close-knit community among women in their daily lives provided a necessary, though not sufficient, precondition of organized protest. . . . this community grew out of rich kinship and friendship networks with roots in the surrounding countryside. Work training and sharing in the mills and a shared life in company boardinghouses reinforced these bonds. A sense of sisterhood developed that functioned for women workers rather like craft solidarity among skilled male artisans. While this solidarity was a necessary precondition for organized protest, women's identification with a revolutionary republican tradition shaped their actual response to changing conditions in the mills. Viewing themselves primarily as "daughters of freemen," they saw wage cuts as attacks on their economic and social independence and responded by leaving work. Their effective solidarity then transformed individual decisions to quit into the collective response of turning out. The turn-out can thus be viewed as evidence for the continuing influence of preindustrial values and traditions that take on new meanings and serve new functions within an industrial setting.

While important in their own right for what they reveal about cultural continuity and change in early industrial capitalism, the turn-outs are also of interest because of the way they fit into the larger picture of labor protest in New England textiles in the antebellum period. They were not isolated incidents; rather they grew out of and reflected earlier strike activity and at the same time contributed to the growth and subsequent spread of labor struggle. The Lowell strikes were the largest protests of working women in the period, but they were not the first nor the last. They drew on the examples of a number of earlier textile strikes and in turn sparked protest in other mill communities.

The first strike involving women workers in New England textiles occurred in Pawtucket, Rhode Island, in May 1824, in the mills of Samuel Slater. In a period of depression, much like that a decade later, Slater found himself in an economic squeeze brought about by a decline in prices of finished cloth coupled with increases in the cost of raw cotton. To cope with these difficulties, Slater announced that beginning June 1 there would be an increase of one hour in the length of the working day and a 25 percent reduction in the piece wages of power-loom weavers. All workers felt the increase in the hours of labor, but women were particularly singled out by the wage cuts for weavers. The response of Pawtucket workers anticipated that in Lowell a decade later. An unsympathetic reporter described the initial events:

> The female weavers assembled in parliament to the number, it is stated of one hundred and two—one of the most active, and most talkative, was placed in the chair, and the meeting, it is understood, was conducted, however strange it may appear, without noise, or scarcely a single speech. The result of the meeting was a resolution to abandon their looms, unless allowed the old prices.

Unlike the Lowell turn-outs, working men and women were united at the outset. Furthermore, strikers found considerable sympathy in the larger community. In contrast to Lowell operatives Pawtucket mill-hands were generally longtime local residents with roots in Pawtucket and the surrounding towns. Nonworkers thus seem to have been drawn into the struggle. Purposeful militant crowd actions closed the mills for a time, and an instance of attempted arson may have influenced Slater. In any event by June 3 a compromise was reached, and workers returned to the mills. Slater and the striking workers were more evenly matched than management and workers in Lowell a decade later. Slater lacked the financial resources of the Boston Associates, and the mill workers enjoyed broad community support. Still, in the use of the mass meeting—dubbed a "parliament" in this account—and of the protest march, Pawtucket workers set precedents that Lowell women followed.

Dover, New Hampshire, was the scene of the first textile strike organized entirely by women workers. In December 1828 the Cocheco Manufacturing Company, one of the Waltham-Lowell type firms, introduced restrictive new regulations. These rules limited visiting in the mills, set fines for lateness, prohibited drinking, smoking, or gambling by operatives, and even banned talking by operatives while in the mills unless directly related to their work. Women workers responded with a turn-out and a mass parade about town, complete with flags and banners. Between 300 and 400 joined in, but the turn-out was short-lived and unsuccessful. Although reports on the strike are brief, it appears to have been quite similar to that in Lowell in February 1834. It had more the character of a brief demonstration than of a sustained strike.

Just as the Lowell turn-outs built on the traditions of earlier strikes, they set patterns that were to be repeated on numerous occasions thereafter. These earlier strikes were isolated affairs, but each of the Lowell turn-outs spawned further labor struggles in surrounding mill towns. These subsequent strikes occurred for two basic reasons. First, management in the smaller mill towns looked to Lowell for leadership. In January 1834 Henry Hall, treasurer of the Suffolk Company, wrote that firm's agent, instructing him to meet with other agents to determine a new schedule of wages. In that note he indicated: "The Nashua & Cocheco Companies will meet your view & probably send a 'delegate' on being notified." After the turn-out, Hall indicated that others would follow the Lowell lead: "The Jackson Co[mpany in Nashua, New Hampshire] will reduce *full* as low as your rates—they have been waiting for the Lowell Companies to set the example."

A second factor at work was the influence, both indirect and direct, of the Lowell turn-out on operatives in other mill towns. Following the brief Lowell protest in February 1834, the Cocheco Company in Dover reduced the wages of its women workers, who reacted in a predictable fashion—they turned out. They undoubtedly were aware of the Lowell events and may have been influenced by that example. In addition, several Lowell operatives may have participated in this second turn-out. A contemporary newspaper account placed a Lowell woman at the head of the protest. Furthermore, one Lowell agent wrote his company treasurer about a former operative who had gone to Nashua and was said to be stirring up trouble there. If one went to Nashua, others may have found their way to Dover. In any event, the language of Dover strike resolutions mirrored that used in Lowell only a few weeks earlier:

> We view this attempt to reduce our wages as part of a general plan of the proprietors of the different manufacturing establishments to reduce the Females in their employ to that state of dependence on them in which they openly, as they do now secretly abuse and insult them by calling them their "slaves."

Dover workers rejected the prospect of industrial slavery in no uncertain language: "However freely the epithet of 'factory slaves' may be bestowed upon us, we will never deserve it by a base and cringing submission to proud wealth or haughty insolence." Like their Lowell sisters, Dover workers lost the turn-out, but not their sense of self-respect and independence.

Similarly, events in Lowell in 1836 were repeated elsewhere. As Lowell firms increased the rate of board in company boardinghouses, others in surrounding mill towns planned to follow suit. When mill management in Chicopee, Massachusetts, copied the Lowell example at the end of October, operatives left work "*en masse.*" The outcome of this contest is unknown, but that management and workers were following the Lowell precedents cannot be doubted.

The turn-outs in Lowell and in other New England mill towns provide important evidence of the growth of a new consciousness among working women in the early mills. The first step in this process came when Yankee women chose to leave their rural homes and enter the urban, industrial world of the factory towns. In this new setting women refashioned traditional values—most notably, their view of themselves as "daughters of freemen"—and used them to justify a novel, and very untraditional, form of protest. The turn-out was itself only a tentative first effort at labor protest, and it yielded in the 1840s to a more coordinated and organized form of struggle—the Ten Hour Movement. The sporadic strikes of the 1820s and 1830s gave way to continuous and coordinated efforts throughout New England in repeated campaigns to petition for reduction of the hours of labor in the mills. Women played a leading role in this broader labor struggle, and only in this movement did the full implications of the changing consciousness of women workers become evident.

Suggestions for Further Reading

The lives of free Afro-Americans in the antebellum period have attracted much attention recently. Among the works that can be profitably consulted are Carol V. R. George, *Segregated Sabbaths: Richard Allen and the Rise of Independent Black Churches, 1760–1845** (New York, 1973); Floyd J. Miller, *The Search for a Black Nationality: Black Colonization and Emigration, 1787–1863* (Urbana, Ill., 1975); Ira Berlin, *Slaves Without Masters: The Free Negro in the Antebellum South** (New York, 1974); Leonard P. Curry, *The Free Black in Urban America, 1800–1850: The Shadow of Freedom* (Chicago, 1981); and Gary B. Nash, " 'To Arise Out of the Dust': Absalom Jones and the African Church of Philadelphia, 1785–1795," in Nash, *Race, Class, and Politics: Essays on American Colonial and Revolutionary Society** (Urbana, Ill. 1986).

Changing women's roles in the nineteenth century are the subject of much new historical inquiry. For new female roles in an industrializing work force see Hannah Josephson, *The Golden Thread: New England Mill Girls and Magnates* (New York, 1949); Caroline Ware, *Early New England Cotton Manufacturing* (Cambridge, Mass., 1931); Thomas Dublin, *Women at Work: The Transformation of Work and Community in Lowell, Massachusetts, 1826–1860* (New York, 1979); and Mary P. Ryan, *Cradle of the Middle Class: The Family in Oneida County, New York, 1790–1865* (Cambridge, Mass., 1981). Other aspects of women's life for this period an be studied in Nancy F. Cott, "Young Women in the Second Great Awakening in New England," *Feminist Studies*, 3 (1975): 15–29; Linda Kerber, "The Republic Mother: Women and the Enlightenment, an American Perspective," *American Quarterly*, 28 (1976): 187–205; Carroll Smith-Rosenberg, "The Female World of Love and Ritual: Relations between Women in Nineteenth-Century America," *Signs: A Journal of Women in Society and Culture*, 1 (1975): 1–30; Barbara Welter, "The Cult of True Womanhood, 1820–1860," *American Quarterly*, 18 (1966): 151–74; and Lee Virginia Chambers-Schiller, *Liberty a Better Husband: The Generations of 1780–1840* (New Haven, 1984).

For southern women in slaveowning families see Anne F. Scott, *The Southern Lady** (New York, 1970); Jane Turner Censer, *North*

*Available in paperback edition.

Carolina Planters and Their Children, 1800–1860 (Baton Rouge, 1984); Drew Gilpin Faust, *James Henry Hammond and the Old South: A Design for Mastery* (Baton Rouge, 1982); and Bertram Wyatt-Brown, *Southern Honor: Ethics and Behavior in the Old South* (New York, 1982).

Childbirth—and, more generally, attitudes toward sex and sex roles—can be studied further in Jane B. Donegan, *Women and Men Midwives: Medicine, Morality, and Misogyny in Early America* (Westport, Conn., 1978); G. J. Barker-Benfield, *The Horrors of the Half-Known Life: Male Attitudes Toward Women and Sexuality in Nineteenth-Century America* (New York, 1976); Nancy F. Cott, *The Bonds of Womanhood: "Woman's Sphere" in New England, 1780–1835** (New Haven, 1977); Robin M. Haller, *The Physician and Sexuality in Victorian America* (Urbana, Ill., 1974); Carroll Smith-Rosenberg, "The Hysterical Woman: Sex Roles and Role Conflict in 19th-Century America," *Social Research,* 39 (1972): 652–78, and "Puberty to Menopause: The Cycle of Femininity in Nineteenth-Century America," in Lois Banner and Mary S. Hartman, eds., *Clio's Consciousness Raised: New Perspectives on the History of Women* (New York, 1974), 22–37; and Ronald G. Walters, *Primers for Prudery: Sexual Advice to Victorian America** (Englewood Cliffs, N.J., 1974).

Much can be learned about the private lives of America's farm families in the antebellum period from Joan Jensen, *Loosening the Bonds: Midatlantic Farm Women, 1740–1840* (New Haven, 1986); and Hal S. Barron, *Those Who Stayed Behind: Rural Society in Nineteenth-Century New England* (Cambridge, Mass., 1984).

For the inner experiences of religion and participation in antebellum reform movements, the following are particularly useful: Ronald Walters, *American Reformers, 1815–1860** (New York, 1978); Barbara Epstein, *The Politics of Domesticity: Women, Evangelism, and Temperance in Nineteenth-Century America* (New York, 1981); Richard Carwardine, *Transatlantic Revivalism: Popular Evangelicalism in Britain and America, 1790–1865* (London, 1978); and Ian Tyrrell, *Sobering Up: From Temperance to Prohibition in Antebellum America* (New York, 1979).

For those who want to know more about the lives of the industrializing workforce in the antebellum era the following are recommended: Alan Dawley, *Class and Community: The Industrial Experience in Lynn** (Cambridge, Mass., 1976); Jonathan Prude, *The Coming of Industrial Order: Town and Factory Life in Rural Massachusetts, 1810–1860* (Cambridge, Mass., 1983); Bruce Laurie, *Working People of Philadelphia, 1800–1850* (Philadelphia, 1980); Anthony F. C. Wallace, *Rockdale: The Growth of an American Village in the Early Industrial Revolution** (New York, 1980); Cynthia Shelton, *The Mills of Manayunk: Early Industrialization and Social Conflict in the Philadelphia Region 1787–1837* (Baltimore, 1986); Sean Wilentz, *Chants Democratic: New York City and the Rise of the American Working Class, 1788–1850** (New York, 1984); and Christine Stansell, "The Origins of the Sweatshop: Women and Early Industrialization in New York City," in Michael H. Frisch and Daniel J. Walkowitz, eds., *Working-Class America: Essays on Labor, Community, and American Society* (Urbana, Ill., 1983).

The Expanding Nation

1840–1877

*Rice cultivation was the major sector of the low county
economy that gave rise to the task system of labor.*

Work and Culture: The Task System and the World of Lowcountry Blacks, 1700–1880

PHILIP D. MORGAN

Following the drafting of the Constitution, plantation slavery spread rapidly from the seaboard states into the rich cotton lands of the deep South. For nineteenth-century Afro-Americans as for eighteenth-century Africans, slavery was a life-draining and degrading way of life. Despite the development of a paternalistic ideology that made plantation slavery in some cases more benign in the antebellum period than in the eighteenth century, servitude remained a curse that denied blacks even the most basic human rights. Nevertheless, as was discussed in the earlier essay by Peter Wood, Afro-Americans continued to adopt strategies and act in ways to resist their enslavement and preserve a measure of autonomy. In the following piece, Philip D. Morgan writes of a more subtle aspect of resistance to the brutalizing tendencies of plantation life. This was the form of organizing labor known as the task system, which was common in the low-country region of South Carolina and Georgia from the beginning of slavery through emancipation.

The task system can be contrasted to the gang system of labor used in most of the deep South. Rather than laboring in the field from sunup to sunset, a slave who worked under the task system had to complete each day a specified job, such as hoeing or planting a certain amount of acreage. The crucial difference in this system, as Morgan points out, was that it allowed slaves some time of their own after the task was completed, and thus gave them the latitude to control at least part of the day.

Morgan argues that this central feature of low-country slave life had a profound effect on attitudes and expectations within the black community. In a system that allowed male slaves to control their own work day, Afro-Americans made time to grow and market their own crops and buy and raise their own animals, including horses. By the time of the Civil War, the task system dominated the agricultural life of the low-country South, and with emancipation the new freedmen refused to give it up, identifying it as their preferred system of labor.

W ithin the realm of slavery studies there has been a pronounced preoccupation with the external or institutional aspects of the slave system. Despite repeated clarion calls for investigations of life in the slave quarters, little scholarly attention has been directed to the domestic economy of the slaves, their work routines, their attitudes toward resource allocation, their attempts to accumulate, and their patterns of consumption. This academic shortsightedness is more easily identified than remedied. Attitudes toward work and patterns of work constitute an area of inquiry that sprawls awkwardly across academic demarcations: the subject is all too easily neglected. In addition, the genre to which this type of history is most akin, namely, labor history, often suffers from its own myopia: studies that begin by aiming to uncover the experience of workers can all too readily focus instead on management priorities. Moreover, what has been said with respect to the English farm laborer applies even more forcefully to the Afro-American slave: "No one has written his signature more plainly across the countryside; but no one has left more scanty records of his achievements."

Mindful of these difficulties and pitfalls, this article . . . attempts to bring history closer to the central concerns of ordinary people's lives—in this case, the lives of Afro-American slaves in the lowcountry region of South Carolina and Georgia. In this light, perhaps the most distinctive and central feature of lowcountry slave life was the task system. In Lewis Gray's words, "Under the task system the slave was assigned a certain amount of work for the day, and after completing the task he could use his time as he pleased," whereas under the gang system, prevalent in most Anglo-American plantation societies, "slaves were worked in groups under the control of a driver or leader . . . and the laborer was compelled to work the entire day." While previous commentators have drawn attention to the task system, few have explored how this peculiarity arose and how it structured the world of those who labored under it. In order to shed light on the first matter, I shall open three windows onto different phases in the development of this labor arrangement: its origins in the first half of the eighteenth century, its routinization during the Revolutionary era, and its full flowering by the time of the Civil War. I shall also explore the ramifications of the

WORK AND CULTURE From *William and Mary Quarterly,* vol. 39 (Oct. 1982). Reprinted by permission of the author.

task system for the slaves by analyzing its most distinctive feature so far as they were concerned: the opportunities it provided for working on their own behalf once the stipulated task had been completed. I shall argue, then, that a particular mode of labor organization and a particular domestic economy evolved simultaneously in the colonial and antebellum lowcountry.

This argument can best be secured by broadening our horizons to take in not only colonial and early national developments but also those of the antebellum and even postbellum years. On the one hand, such a strategy will show how colonial developments bore directly on nine-teenth- and even twentieth-century realities. To take a minor example, the basic task unit still current in the minds of freedmen in the 1930s will be shown to have had a precise colonial origin. On the other hand, the opportunities that the task system presented slaves can be under-stood only in the light of mid-nineteenth-century experiences. To take a more significant example, the resemblance between the experiences of some lowcountry slaves and of the protopeasants found among the slaves of certain Caribbean plantation societies emerges most clearly from a glance at the behavior of slaves and freedmen in the years sur-rounding the Civil War. In other words, to understand the evolution of the task system and its concomitant domestic economy, we shall need a telescope rather than a microscope.

The earliest, fragmentary descriptions of work practices in the low-country rice economy indicate that a prominent characteristic of the task system—a sharp division between the master's "time" and the slave's "time"—was already in place. In the first decade of the eigh-teenth century the clergy of South Carolina complained that slaves were planting "for themselves as much as will cloath and subsist them and their famil[ies]." During the investigation of a suspected slave conspir-acy in mid-century, a lowcountry planter readily acknowledged that one of his slaves had planted rice "in his own time" and could do with it as he wished. The most acute observer of early work practices, Jo-hann Bolzius, described how slaves, after "their required day's work," were "given as much land as they can handle" on which they planted corn, potatoes, tobacco, peanuts, sugar and water melons, and pump-kins and bottle pumpkins. The opportunity to grow such a wide range of provisions on readily available land owed much to the early estab-lishment and institutionalization of the daily work requirement. By mid-century the basic "task" unit had been set at a quarter of an acre. Moreover, other activities, outside of the rice field, were also tasked: in pounding the rice grain, slaves were "tasked at seven Mortars for one day," and in providing fences lowcountry slaves were expected to split 100 poles of about twelve feet in length (a daily "task" that re-mained unchanged throughout the slave era . . .). These tasks were not, of course, easily accomplished, and occasionally planters exacted even higher daily requirements; but, as Bolzius noted, the advantage to the slaves of having a daily goal was that they could, once it was met, "plant something for themselves."

A tried and tested model of labor organization—the gang system practiced on both tobacco and sugar plantations—was available when lowcountry planters discovered their own plantation staple. In fact, many of the first immigrants were from Barbados, where they must have had direct experience of operating gangs of slaves. Why did they and others decide to adopt a new system? U. B. Phillips claimed that temporary absenteeism was responsible: "The necessity of the master's moving away from his estate in the warm months, to escape the malaria, involved the adoption of some system of routine which would work with more or less automatic regularity without his own inspiring or impelling presence." However, while absenteeism may have contributed to the attractiveness of this system, it seems an insufficiently powerful agent to account for its inception. The example of Caribbean sugar production is pertinent here; if the withdrawal of an inspiring master encouraged the development of tasking, why did not sugar planters in the West Indies, where absenteeism began relatively early, adopt the system?

The absence of masters may be an unconvincing explanation for the development of a task system, but perhaps the presence of particular slaves can serve in its place. Peter H. Wood and Daniel C. Littlefield have pointed out that some black immigrants to early South Carolina were already familiar with the techniques of rice cultivation. These slaves' expertise, it might be argued, accounts for the evolution of a system that would operate more or less automatically. It has even been suggested, in this regard, that a work pattern of alternating bouts of intense labor and idleness tends to occur wherever men are to some degree in control of their own working lives (need one look any further than authors?). By displaying their own understanding of the basic requirements of rice cultivation, lowcountry slaves might have gained a measure of control over their lives, at least to the extent of determining the length of their working days. While this is an attractive argument, it is not without problems. The coastal regions that seem to have supplied a majority of slaves to early South Carolina were not rice-producing areas; lowcountry whites have left no record of valuing the knowledge of rice planting that some slaves might have displayed; and familiarity with rice planting is hardly the same as familiarity with irrigated rice culture, practiced in South Carolina from early days. Slaves undoubtedly contributed a great deal to the development of South Carolina's rice economy; but, on present evidence, it would be rash to attribute the development of a task system to their prowess, especially when that prowess went largely unrecognized and may not have been significant.

A consideration of staple-crop requirements provides the most satisfactory, if not complete, answer to the question of the system's origins. The amount of direct supervision demanded by various crops offers at least one clue to the puzzle. Unlike tobacco, which involved scrupulous care in all phases of the production cycle and was therefore best cultivated by small gangs of closely attended laborers, rice was a hardy plant, requiring a few relatively straightforward operations for its successful cultivation. The great expansion of rice culture in seventeenth-century Lombardy, for instance, was predicated not on a stable, sophisticated, and well-supervised labor force but on a pool of transient labor drawn from far afield. Nor did rice production require the strict regimentation and "semi-industrialised" production techniques that attended the cultivation of sugar and necessitated gang labor. However, the Caribbean plantation experience does offer parallels to the lowcountry rice economy: in the British West Indies, crops that required little supervision or regimentation—notably coffee and pimento—were, like rice, grown by a slave labor force organized by tasks rather than into gangs.

In addition to the degree of direct supervision required by a crop, the facility with which the laborers' output could be measured also shaped different forms of labor organization. For example, the productivity of a single coffee and pimento worker could be measured accurately and cheaply, particularly in the harvesting cycle. It was easy to weigh an individual's baskets of coffee or pimento berries, and tasking may have first developed in this stage of the respective crop cycles before being extended to other operations. Conversely, the much larger volumes involved in the cane harvest would have proved far less easy and much more expensive to measure on an individual "task" basis; not surprisingly, gang labor was employed at this and other stages of the sugar cycle. In the case of rice, it was less the harvesting and more the cultivation of the crop that lent itself to inexpensive and efficient measurement. As Phillips pointed out, drainage ditches, which were necessary in lowcountry rice cultivation, provided convenient units by which the performance of tasks could be measured. The ubiquity and long-standing history of the quarter-acre task suggest that the planting and weeding stages of the rice cycle provided the initial rationale for the task system; once tasking became firmly established, it was extended to a whole host of plantation operations.

Thus various staple-crop requirements seem to have served as the most important catalysts for the development of particular modes of labor organization. Undoubtedly other imperatives contributed to the attractiveness of one or the other labor arrangement: absenteeism and the ease with which slaves took to rice cultivation may well have encouraged a more widespread and rapid diffusion of the task system in the lowcountry than might otherwise have been the case. Moreover, once a task system had been tried, tested, and not found wanting, it could be extended to crops that were produced elsewhere by means of gang labor. In other words, once tasking became a way of life, means were found to circumvent the otherwise powerful dictates of the various staple crops.

Whatever the origins of the task system, its consequences soon became apparent. Indeed, the way in which slaves chose to spend their own "time" created unease among ruling South Carolinians. One of the earliest laws relating to slaves, enacted in 1686, prohibited the exchange of goods between slaves or between slaves and freemen without their masters' consent. A decade later, slaves were expressly forbidden from felling and carrying away timber on lands other than their masters'. In 1714 the legislature enacted its stiffest prohibition; slaves were no longer to "plant for themselves any corn, peas or rice." While this stark ban appears definitive, later legislation suggests its ineffectiveness. In 1734, for example, an act for the better regulation of patrols allowed patrollers to confiscate "all fowls and other provisions" found in the possession of "stragling negroes." That slaves produced provisions independently is further implied in a 1738 act for the licensing of hawkers and pedlars, which aimed to stamp out the illicit traffic in rice and provisions between slaves and itinerant traders. By 1751 the legislators bowed to the inevitable. By outlawing the sale of slaves' rice and corn to anybody other than their masters, they were implicitly recognizing the right of slaves to cultivate such crops. The law of 1714 had thus died a natural death.

From the evidence of plantation account books and estate records, the act of 1751 simply brought the law closer into line with social practice. In 1728 Abraham, a Ball family slave, was paid £1 10s. for providing his master with eighteen fowls, while a female slave received £8 for supplying hogs. In 1736 twenty-two Ball family slaves were paid more than £50 for supplying varying amounts of rice to their master. The extent of this trade in provisions was occasionally impressive; over the course of two years, the slaves belonging to James Hartley's estate were paid £124 for supplying 290 bushels of their corn. Henry Ravenel not only purchased his slaves' provision goods, consisting of corn, fowls, hogs, and catfish, but also their canoes, baskets, and myrtle wax.

Masters undoubtedly benefited from these exchanges while displaying their benevolence, but we should not assume that there was no bargaining, however unequal, between the parties. Henry Laurens, for example, advised one of his newly appointed overseers to "purchase of your own Negroes all [the provisions] that you know Lawfully belongs to themselves at the lowest price that they will sell it for." If a master refused to give slaves a fair price for their produce, they could take it elsewhere. One of the most persistent complaints of lowcountry planters and legislators concerned illicit trading across plantation boundaries. A slave who produced rice "in his own time" also traveled more than fifteen miles up the Cooper River to sell a barrel of his crop to his brother, who resided on another plantation. A white boatman, implicated in a slave conspiracy, openly acknowledged that he had exchanged his hog for a slave's deer skin. The records of one lowcountry estate even register payments to a neighboring planter's slaves for their seed rice. In other words, once slaves were allowed to produce provisions, they would always find ways to market them, be it to passing traders, neighboring whites, or fellow slaves.

Lowcountry slaves took the opportunity to raise a wide array of agricultural products, many of which reflected their African background. In the third decade of the eighteenth century Mark Catesby observed two African varieties of corn in the lowcountry but only among the "Plantation of *Negroes*." When William Bartram visited the lowcountry in the 1770s he noticed that the tania or tannier (a tuberous root found in the West Indies and tropical Africa) was "much cultivated and esteemed for food, particularly by the Negroes." Bernard Romans claimed that slaves had introduced the groundnut into South Carolina; by the early nineteenth century, according to David Ramsay's informants on Edisto Island, groundnuts were "planted in small patches chiefly by the negroes, for market." Romans also attributed the introduction of the "sesamen or oily grain" to lowcountry slaves; they used it, he maintained, "as a food either raw, toasted or boiled in their soups and are very fond of it, they call it *Benni*." Over one-and-a-half centuries later, a black sea islander was to be found planting what he called "bene." He used it in the same ways that his ancestors had done. Most significant, when asked where he acquired the seed, he said "his parents always had it and he was told 'Dey brung it fum Africa'." Apparently peppers were also the preserve of slaves. Knowing that his slave old Tom "plants a good deal of pepper," Elias Ball desired him to send "sum Read pepper pounded and corked up in a pint Bottle." In 1742, when Eliza Lucas sent her friend some of the same product, she referred to it, in revealing fashion, as "negroe pepper." The only tobacco grown in early eighteenth-century South Carolina belonged to the slaves. Janet Schaw was so impressed by the way in which Carolina slaves used their "little piece[s] of land" to grow vegetables, "rear hogs and poultry, sow calabashes, etc." that she thought they cultivated them "much better than their Master[s]." Furthermore, she believed that "the Negroes are the only people that seem to pay any attention to the various uses that the wild vegetables may be put to."

The cultivation and subsequent exchange of provisions allowed some slaves to claim more substantial items of property. In 1714 the South Carolina legislature denied the slaves' claim to "any stock of hogs, cattle or horses." This directive apparently fell on deaf ears, for in 1722 it became lawful to seize any hogs, boats, or canoes belonging to slaves. Moreover, this later act referred to the "great inconveniences [that] do

arise from negroes and other slaves keeping and breeding of horses";
not only were these horses (and cattle) to be seized, but the proceeds
of their sale were to be put to the support of the parish poor. The irony
of slave property sustaining white paupers was presumably lost on South
Carolina legislators but perhaps not on the slaves. Once again, legislative intentions seem to have been thwarted, for in 1740 more complaints were to be heard about those "several owners of slaves [who]
have permitted them to keep canoes, and to breed and raise horses,
neat cattle and hogs, and to traffic and barter in several parts of this
Province, for the particular and peculiar benefit of such slaves." The
most dramatic example of property ownership by a lowcountry slave
in the first half of the eighteenth century involved not horses or canoes, but men. According to a deed of manumission, a slave named
Sampson "by his Industry and the Assistance of Friends" had purchased and "procured in his owne Right and property and for his owne
Use" another Negro slave named Tom. Sampson then exchanged his
slave Tom for "fifty years of his [that is, Sampson's] Life time and
Servitude (to come)." If the task system had created the opportunities
for Sampson's "Industry" to manifest itself in this way, it truly was a
potent force.

By the late eighteenth century the task system had taken deep root
in the lowcountry. Tasks were set for almost all operations—from clearing new ground (one-eighth of an acre) to the weekly task of a pair of
sawyers (600 feet of pine or 780 feet of cypress). However, the basic
unit, a quarter-acre, was still the yardstick for virtually all rice-planting
operations. In recognition of this reality, one Georgia absentee in 1786
sent a chain "for running out the Tasks" to his plantation manager. "It
is 105 feet long," he noted, "and will save a great deal of time in Laying out the field, and do it with more exactness." Henry Ferguson, an
East Floridian who had spent seventeen years in South Carolina and
Georgia, was able to specify precisely how much land his slaves had
cleared "from the Tasks which he set to his Negroes having measured
the Ground frequently for that purpose." He added that "a Task was
a quarter of an Acre to weed p. day." Even opponents of the task
system testify to its pervasiveness. William Butler, a keen observer of
rice culture, argued in 1786 that slaves "should always be Kept in Gangs
or parcels and not scattered over a field in Tasks as is too generally
done, for while in gangs they are more immediately under the Super-
intendants Eyes, [and] of course may be much better and more immediately inspected."

The extension of the task system to the cultivation of sea island
cotton confirms the failure of Butler's advice. Since both the long- and
short-staple varieties of cotton required close attention, especially in

the tedious hoeing and thinning phases of their cultivation, they were ideal candidates for gang labor. Most upcountry South Carolina planters adopted this arrangement from the first, and sea island planters were encouraged to do the same: one lowcountry planter from Georgia advised his South Carolina colleagues that "there is no possibility of tasking Negroes" in cotton culture. However, his peers proved him wrong. By the early nineteenth century the tasking requirements of all sea island cotton operations were well established. They remained substantially unchanged throughout the nineteenth century.

Perhaps the profits being generated under the existing task system discouraged lowcountry planters from adopting gang labor, for they were not likely to restructure an arrangement that was so patently successful. In 1751 James Glen reported that South Carolina planters expected a slave to pay for himself within four to five years. Dr. Alexander Garden calculated that in 1756 planters made between £15 to £30 sterling for every slave they employed in the field, which he noted was "indeed a great deal." At that rate, a slave would pay for himself in two to three years. In 1772 a visitor to South Carolina noted that indigo planters made from £35 to £45 sterling for every able Negro; in this case, a newly purchased slave paid for himself in less than two years. The rate of return of a 200-acre rice plantation, employing forty slaves in the late colonial period, was estimated to be 25 percent, more than double the opportunity cost of capital. And although the Revolutionary war was enormously disruptive of the lowcountry economy, the 1790s were boom years for planters, as they replaced one highly profitable secondary staple (indigo) with another (sea island cotton). So profitable was this second staple that planters on Edisto Island in 1808 averaged a return of between $170 and $260 for every field hand.

Crucial to the continuing profitability of rice plantations was the wholesale transfer of production from inland to tidal swamps, a process that was well underway by the late eighteenth century. John Drayton, writing at the turn of the century, identified some of the advantages of this shift in location: "River swamp plantations, from the command of water, which at high tides can be introduced over the fields, have an undoubted preference to inland plantations; as the crop is more certain, and the work of the negroes less toilsome." Surely it was a tidewater rice plantation that a Virginian witnessed in 1780 when he observed that "after the ground is once well cleared little cultivation does the ground [need] being soft by continual moisture." In short, the development of tidewater rice culture reduced the heavy hoeing formerly required of slaves in the summer months. As might be expected, the daily task unit expanded, and squares of 150 feet (approximately a half of an acre) appeared in tidewater rice fields. The other side of this coin was the increase in heavy labor required of slaves in the winter months, for tidewater cultivation demanded an elaborate system of banks, dams, canals, and ditches. By the turn of the century, no doubt, lowcountry laborers were as familiar with the daily ditching requirement (about 600 to 700 square feet or ten compasses) as they had ever been with the quarter-acre task.

Although the precise definition of daily tasks had advantages from the slaves' point of view, the potential conflict that stereotyped tasks and their careless assignment could engender should not be underestimated. Indeed, the evidence of conflict should alert us to a battle that undoubtedly was being waged but that rarely surfaces in the historical record; namely, the constant warring between taskmaster and laborer over what constituted a fair day's work. After one such altercation between a black driver and a group of slaves, the latter took their case to their master in Charleston. When he asked them "why they could not do their Tasks as well as the rest," they answered that "their Tasks were harder." The master was sympathetic, knowing that "there is sometimes a great difference in Tasks, and Paul told me he remembered that Jimmy had a bad Task that Day. I was sorry to see poor Caesar amongst them for I knew him to be an honest, inoffensive fellow and tho't if any will do without severity, he will. I inquired his fault, & Paul told me . . . he had been 2 days in a Task." Hoeing was at issue in this dispute; on another plantation, threshing became a source of conflict. Three slaves belonging to George Austin—Liverpool, Moosa, and Dutay—"ran off early in December, for being a little chastis'd on Account of not finishing the Task of Thrashing in due time." By the early nineteenth century, a *modus vivendi* had apparently been reached on most lowcountry plantations. One South Carolina planter reckoned that the "daily task does not vary according to the arbitrary will and caprice of their owners, and although [it] is not fixed by law, it is so well settled by long usage, that upon every plantation it is the *same*. Should any owner increase the work beyond what is customary, he subjects himself to the reproach of his neighbors, and to such discontent amongst his slaves as to make them of but little use to him." The task system's requirements were hammered out just as much in conflicts with the work force as in the supposedly inevitable march of technological progress.

However onerous tasking could become for some slaves, the system at least had the virtue of allowing the slave a certain latitude to apportion his own day, to work intensively in his task and then have the balance of his time. With the institutionalization of the task system, the slave's "time" became sacrosanct. The right not to be called on once the task had been completed was duly acknowledged by lowcountry masters. One of the advantages of such a right is neatly illustrated in an incident that befell a Methodist circuit rider, Joseph Pilmore. On March 18, 1773—a Thursday—he arrived at the banks of the Santee River in the Georgetown district of South Carolina. After waiting in vain for the appearance of the regular ferry, he was met by a few Ne-groes. Presumably they told him that they "had finished their task," for that is how he explained their availability in his journal. He then hired their "time" so that he could be ferried across the river. The actual time was about three o'clock in the afternoon. Slaves could not only complete their work by mid-afternoon; they might then earn money on their own account.

In the same year that Pilmore visited the Georgetown district, an-other observer of lowcountry society, "Scotus Americanus," testified more fully to the advantages that a fully institutionalized task system presented to slaves:

> Their work is performed by a daily task, allotted by their master or overseer, which they have generally done by one or two o'clock in the afternoon, and have the rest of the day for themselves, which they spend in working in their own private fields, consisting of 5 or 6 acres of ground, allowed them by their masters, for planting of rice, corn, potatoes, tobacco, &c. for their own use and profit, of which the industrious among them make a great deal. In some plantations, they have also the liberty to raise hogs and poultry, which, with the former articles, they are to dispose of to none but their masters (this is done to prevent bad consequences) for which, in exchange, when they do not chuse money, their masters give Osnaburgs, negro cloths, caps, hats, handkerchiefs, pipes, and knives. They do not plant in their fields for subsistence, but for amusement, pleasure, and profit, their masters giving them clothes, and sufficient provisions from their granaries.

As we shall see, planting for "amusement, pleasure, and profit" con-tinued to be a prerogative of lowcountry slaves.

Pilmore and Scotus Americanus alert us to the ways in which low-country slaves continued to acquire money. It should hardly surprise us, then, that lowcountry bondmen still aspired to the ownership of more substantial items of property. In spite of the acts of 1714, 1722, and 1740, slaves remained singularly reluctant to relinquish their claims to horses. In 1772 the Charleston District Grand Jury was still objecting to "Negroes being allowed to keep horses . . . contrary to Law." In a transaction that bore a remarkable similarity to the one effected by Sampson a half-century earlier, a slave named Will showed even less regard for the law by exchanging his horses for his freedom. A witness to the exchange heard Will's master, Lewis Dutarque, say to

> old fellow Will that he had been a faithful servant to him and if he had a mind to purchase his freedom he should obtain the same by paying him three hundred pounds old currency and says he Will you have two Horses which will nearly pay me. I will allow you hundred pounds old currency for a Roan Gelding and forty five currency for your Gray for which the fellow Will readily consented

to the proposals and Mr. Dutarque took possession of the Horses and the fellow Will was to pay the Balance as soon as he could make it up. Mr. Dutarque also borrowed of the fellow Will a small Black mare which he lost and he said she was worth six Guineas and would allow him that price for her.

One begins to wonder how many horses Will possessed. Horse trading may even have been possible within the slave community, if a notice placed in a South Carolina newspaper in 1793 is any indication: "On Sunday last was apprehended by the patrol in St. George's parish, a certain negro man who calls himself *Titus* and his son about 10 year who is called *Tom*; he was trading with the negroes in that neighbourhood, and he had in his possession 2 horses . . . one poultry cart, and several articles of merchandise, consisting of stripes, linens, and handkerchiefs." Given these examples, one lowcountry master was perhaps right to be sanguine about an unsuccessful hunt that he had launched for a group of seven absentees. He was "convinced these runaways would not go far, being connected at home, and having too much property to leave."

By the middle of the nineteenth century the task system dominated agricultural life in the lowcountry. Indeed, the term so pervaded the region's agricultural terminology that its varied meanings have to be disentangled. For example, a lowcountry planter might say that he had planted "seven tasks (within one task of two acres, as a planter well knows)." At this time, a slave was expected to be able to sow two acres of rice a day; this is presumably what this planter had in mind when referring to the single task of two acres. And yet, the early eighteenth-century definition of a task as measuring one-quarter of an acre was still very much current. It was possible, therefore, to speak of seven units, measuring one-quarter of an acre each, within a larger unit measuring two acres. Similarly, a planter might say that he had penned "thirty head of cattle on a task for one week" (the "task" here refers to one-quarter of an acre); or he might mention setting a "task" of three rice barrels a day for his cooper. In other words, in common usage the term "task" not only referred to a unit of labor (a fixed or specified quantity of labor exacted from a person is the dictionary definition) but also to a unit of land measurement (almost invariably one-quarter of an acre or 105 square feet).

Slaves were completely conversant with this terminology, as the recollections of ex-slaves attest. Testifying before Southern Claims Commissioners in 1873, Peter Way knew precisely what constituted a "task" as a unit of land measurement. "Five poles make a task," he noted authoritatively, "and there is twenty-one feet in a pole." Using the term in this sense, former slaves might say that "Mr. Mallard's house was about four or five tasks from Mr. Busby's house" (about 420 or 525 feet distant), or that Sherman's troops were "about three tasks off in the woods. I could see [them] from [my] house" (about 315 feet away). When Mason Crum interviewed an old Negro woman (a former slave) in the 1930s, she told him that she owned her land "and that she had in the tract t'ree acres and a tass," by which she meant three-and-a-quarter acres. When freedmen referred to the crops that they had produced for themselves in "slavery times," they used the units acres and "tasks" interchangeably (tasks here again refer to quarter-acre plots). At the same time, ex-slaves used the term "task" to connote a unit of labor. A freedman, referring to the terms of the contract that he had signed with his employer, spoke of giving "five tasks, that is, I work five tasks for him and plant everything he has a mind to have it planted in for all the land myself and wife can cultivate." The dual meaning of the term is nowhere better illustrated than in the words of one former slave, interviewed in the 1930s, who in one and the same breath recalled "de slave [having] but two taks ob land to cultivate for se'f" (by which he meant half an acre) and "in daytime [having] to do his task" (by which he meant a quantity of labor depending on the operation at hand).

Tasking was so much a way of life in the antebellum lowcountry that virtually all crops and a whole host of plantation operations were subject to its dictates. The cultivation of corn was discussed in terms of the number of hills in a "task-row" and the number of "beds" in a task. Sea island cotton had its own task-acre as distinct from the task-acre utilized in tidewater rice culture. Even when lowcountry planters experimented with sugar cultivation in the 1820s and 1830s, they attempted to retain the notion of a task: a hundred plants, according to one authority, were to be put in a task-row and two hands could then both plant and cut a task a day. On Hopeton plantation, where sugar was grown on a large scale, task work was "resorted to whenever the nature of the work admits of it; and working in gangs as is practiced in the West Indies and the upper country, is avoided. The advantages of this system are encouragement to the labourers, by equalizing the work of each agreeably to strength, and the avoidance of watchful superintendance and incessant driving." Whether this attempt to adapt sugar cultivation to the task system contributed to the failure of lowcountry sugar production is difficult to say; but it is possible that sugar, unlike cotton, just could not be successfully grown without gang labor.

Tasking was ubiquitous in another sense: those slaves not able to benefit from the system's opportunities had to be compensated in other ways. The proposition that drivers, as a group, suffered discrimination is barely credible, but in the lowcountry, at least, such was the case. As one ex-slave recalled, "I suppose the Foreman had advantages in some respects and in others not, for he had no task-work and had no time of his own, while the other slaves had the Evenings to themselves." The son of a Georgia planter remembered that his father's driver was "obliged to oversee all day," whereas the field hands "were allowed to work in any way they chose for themselves after the tasks were done." By way of compensation, lowcountry drivers were entitled to receive a certain amount of help in tending their own crops. Thomas Mallard's driver "had the privilege of having hands to work one acre of corn and one acre of rice" on his behalf; the driver on Raymond Cay's plantation had Cay's field hands plant one acre of corn and three to five "tasks" in rice on his account. One ex-slave recalled that "drivers had the privilege of planting two or three acres of rice and some corn and having it worked by the slaves"; and, in order to dispel any misimpressions, he emphasized that "these hands worked for [the drivers] in the White people's time." Other occupational groups received different forms of compensation. A former slave plowman recalled that he "didn't work by the task but at the end of the year [his master] gave [him] 6 bushels of corn" by way of redress. A former slave carpenter recollected that "when [he] worked carpentering [his] master allowed [him] every other saturday and when [he] worked farming [his master] gave him tasks." In this man's mind, apparently, these "privileges" were about equal.

The central role of the task system in lowcountry life can best be gauged by investigating its fate immediately after emancipation. Throughout the postwar cotton South freedmen firmly rejected most of the elements of their old system of labor: from the first, gang labor was anathema. At the same time, however, freedmen in the lowcountry were tenaciously striving to retain—and even extend—the fundamentals of their former system. A Freedmen's Bureau official, resident in lowcountry Georgia in 1867, identified a basic response of the former slaves to their new work environment when he observed that they "usually stipulate to work by the task." Lowcountry freedmen even demonstrated their attachment to the task system when they rejected one element of their former slave past by refusing to do the ditching and draining so necessary in rice and sea island cotton cultivation. This work was arduous and disagreeable, of course, and since ditching was more amenable to gang labor than any other operation in lowcountry agriculture, blacks appropriately sought to avoid it at all costs. But in an 1865 petition a group of planters from Georgetown district touched on an even more compelling reason for the freedmen's refusal to perform this familiar task. They pointed out that "it is a work which, as it does not pertain to the present crop, the negroes are unwilling to perform." The recipient of this petition, Colonel Willard, was a sympathetic and sensitive observer, and his elaboration of this rationale penetrates to the heart of the issue. The freedmen's real fear, he explained, was that having prepared the ditches for the forthcoming crop, the planters would "insist on having them by the month." This arrangement would be absolutely unacceptable, because the freedmen had "been accustomed to working by the task, which has always given them leisure to cultivate land for themselves, tend their stock, and amuse themselves." If they gave way on this issue, he continued, "their privileges will go and their condition will be less to their taste than it was when they were slaves."

Precisely to avoid such a condition was the overriding imperative governing the actions of lowcountry freedmen. Once this is understood, the multifarious and fluid labor arrangements that characterized the postwar lowcountry become comprehensible. In 1865 and 1866 two basic forms of labor contract (with many individual variations) were employed in the lowlands of South Carolina and Georgia. Either the freedmen worked for a share of the crop (anywhere from one-half to three-quarters, a higher share than found elsewhere in the South), with the freedmen's share being divided among them on the basis of tasks performed, or they hired themselves for the year, with payment being made on the basis of the numbers of tasks completed (usually fifty cents a task, although payment was by no means always made in cash). Whatever the mode of reimbursement, the task was central to most early contracts.

In 1866 a third labor arrangement arose that soon became general throughout the lowcountry. Known as the "two-day" or, less frequently, "three-day" system, it simply extended the concept of task labor, for it drew an even more rigid demarcation between the planters' "time" and the laborers' "time." The Freedmen's Bureau agent for eastern Liberty County, Georgia, observed as early as February 1867 that there were in his district no freedmen working by the month and only a few for wages. Some were working for a share of the crop, but most were employed by the "two-day" system, working a third of the time on the employers' crop and receiving land to work on their own account for the remainder of the time. The agricultural census of 1880 reported that the "two-day" system was ubiquitous on the South Carolina sea islands. For ten months of the year, slaves worked two days in each week for their employers and received in return a house, fuel, and six acres of land for their own use, free of rent. Proprietors were said to dislike the system because their employees only cultivated about two acres in the owners' "time." However, the report continued, "the laborers themselves prefer this system, having four days out of the week for themselves." As a result, "they are more independent and can make any day they choose a holiday."

The reasons for the slaves' (and the freedmen's) attachment to the task system should be readily apparent, but the subject is worth a moment's extra consideration because we are in the privileged and rare position of being able to listen to the participants themselves. The most obvious advantage of the task system was the flexibility it permitted slaves in determining the length of the working day. Working from sunup to sundown was the pervasive reality for most antebellum slaves; but ex-slaves from the lowcountry recall a different reality. Richard Cummings, a former field hand, recalled that "a good active industrious man would finish his task sometimes at 12, sometimes at 1 and 2 oclock and the rest of the time was his own to use as he pleased." Scipio King, another former field hand, reckoned, as he put it, that "I could save for myself sometimes a whole day if I could do 2 tasks in a day then I had the next day to myself. Some kind of work I could do 3 tasks in a day." Exhausting as task labor undoubtedly was, its prime virtue was that it was not unremitting.

A second advantage concerned the relationship between the slaves' provisions and the planters' rations. Whatever slaves produced beyond the task was regarded as surplus to, not a substitute for, basic planter allocations of food and clothing. One former slave recalled that his master continued to dispense rations "no matter how much they [the slaves] made of their own . . . [which] they could sell . . . if they chose." July Roberts, another ex-slave, emphasized that "every week we drew our rations no matter what we raised." When one former slave claimed the loss of corn, rice, and clothing taken by Federal troops, an attempt was made to deny him his title because these represented rations and "so belonged to the master." The response of this freedman's attorneys no doubt reflected the prevailing attitude of former slaves: "It is obvious to remark that if these things had not been taken from the claimant by the army, he would have had them after 'freedom came' and were to all intents his property." Not only did slaves plant in their own time for "amusement, pleasure, and profit," they claimed the master's rations as their own to do with as they wished.

In view of these advantages, we might expect the scale and range of property owning by slaves to have assumed significant dimensions by the middle of the nineteenth century. An analysis of the settled claims submitted by former slaves to the Southern Claims Commission for loss of property to Federal troops provides the best test of this hypothesis. Taking the Liberty Country, Georgia, claimants as a sample, former field hands outnumber all other occupational groups. While most were mature adults when their property was taken, 30 percent were under the age of thirty-five. In terms of occupation and age these claimants constitute a relatively broad cross section of the slave population. Moreover, whether field hands or artisans, young or old, virtually all of them had apparently been deprived of a number of hogs, and a substantial majority listed corn, rice, and fowls among their losses. In addition, a surprising number apparently possessed horses and cows, while buggies or wagons, beehives, peanuts, fodder, syrup, butter, sugar, and tea were, if these claims are to be believed, in the hands of at least some slaves. The average cash value (in 1864 dollars) claimed by Liberty County former slaves was $357.43, with the highest claim totaling $2,290 and the lowest $49.

Some claims were spectacular. Paris James, a former slave driver, was described by a neighboring white planter as a "substantial man before the war [and] was more like a free man than any slave." James claimed, among other things, a horse, eight cows, sixteen sheep, twenty-six hogs, and a wagon. Another slave driver, according to one of his black witnesses, lived "just like a white man except his color. His credit was just as good as a white man's because he had the property to back it." Although the claims commissioners were skeptical about his alleged loss of twenty cows—as they explained, "twenty cows would make a good large dairy for a Northern farmer"—his two white and three black witnesses supported him in his claim. Other blacks were considered to be "more than usually prosperous," "pretty well off," and "hardworking and moneysaving"—unremarkable characterizations, perhaps, but surprising when the individuals were also slaves. Alexander Steele, a carpenter by trade and a former house servant of Chatham County, Georgia, submitted a claim for $2,205 based on the loss of his four horses, mule, silver watch, two cows, wagon, and large quantities of fodder, hay, and corn. He had been able to acquire these possessions by "tradeing" for himself for some thirty years; he had had "much time of [his] own" because his master "always went north" in the summer months. He took "a fancy [to] fine horses," a whim he was able to indulge when he purchased "a blooded mare," from which he raised three colts. He was resourceful enough to hide his livestock on Onslow Island when Sherman's army drew near, but some of the Federal troops secured boats and took off his prize possessions. Three white planters supported Steele in his claim; indeed, one of them recollected making an unsuccessful offer of $300 for one of Steele's colts before the war. Lewis Dutarque's Will, a horse owner of note in the late eighteenth century, had found a worthy successor in Alexander Steele.

The ownership of horses was not, however, confined to a privileged minority of slaves. Among the Liberty County claimants, almost as many ex-field hands as former drivers and skilled slaves claimed horses. This evidence supplies a context for the exchange recorded by Frederick Law Olmsted when he was being shown around the plantation of Richard J. Arnold in Bryan County, Georgia. Olmsted noticed a horse drawing a wagon of "common fieldhand negroes" and asked his host

> "[do you] usually let them have horses to go to Church?"
> "Oh no; that horse belongs to the old man."
> "Belongs to him! Why, do they own horses?"

"Oh yes; William (the House Servant) owns two, and Robert, I
believe, has three now; that was one of them he was riding."
"How do they get them?"
"Oh they buy them."

Although a few freedmen recalled that former masters had either prohibited horse ownership or confined the practice to drivers, most placed
the proportion of horse owners on any single plantation at between 15
and 20 percent. A former slave of George Washington Walthour estimated that "in all my master's plantations there were over 30 horses
owned by slaves. . . . I think come to count up there were as many as
45 that owned horses—he would let them own any thing they could if
they only did his work." Nedger Frazer, a former slave of the Reverend C. C. Jones, recalled that on one of his master's plantations (obviously Arcadia, from Frazer's description) there were forty working
hands, of whom five owned horses; and on another (obviously Mon-
tevideo) another ten hands out of fifty owned horses. This, in turn,
supplies a context for an interesting incident that occurred within the
Jones's "family" in 1857. After much soul-searching, Jones sold one of
his slave families, headed by Cassius, a field hand. A man of integrity,
Jones then forwarded Cassius the balance of his account, which
amounted to $85, a sum that included the proceeds from the sale of
Cassius's horse. Perhaps one freedman was not exaggerating when he
observed in 1873 that "there was more stock property owned by slaves
before the war than are owned now by both white and black people
together in this country."

   The spectacular claims and the widespread ownership of horses
naturally catch the eye, but even the most humdrum claim has a story
to tell. Each claim contains, for instance, a description of how property
was accumulated. The narrative of John Bacon can stand as proxy for
many such accounts: "I had a little crop to sell and bought some chick-
ens and then I bought a fine large sow and gave $10.00 for her. This
was about ten years before the war and then I raised hogs and sold
them till I bought a horse. This was about eight years before freedom.
This was a breeding mare and from this mare I raised this horse which
the Yankees took from me." This was not so much primitive as pain-
staking accumulation; no wonder one freedman referred to his former
property as his "laborment." And yet, occasionally, the mode of procurement assumed a slightly more sophisticated cast: some slaves recall
purchasing horses by installment; some hired additional labor to cultivate their crops; two slaves (a mill engineer and a stockminder) went
into partnership to raise livestock; and a driver lent out money at interest. Whatever the mode of accumulation, the ultimate source, as
identified by virtually all the ex-slaves, was the task system. As Joseph
James, a freedman, explained, "They all worked by tasks, and had a

plenty of time to work for themselves and in that way all slaves who were industrious could get around them considerable property in a short time."

By the middle of the nineteenth century, in sum, it is possible to speak of a significant internal economy operating within a more conventional lowcountry economy. According to the depositions of the freedmen, this internal economy rested on two major planks. The first concerns the degree to which some slaves engaged in stock raising. One white planter, testifying on behalf of a freedman, recalled that "a good many" slaves owned a number of animals; he then checked himself, perhaps realizing the impression that he was creating, and guardedly stated that "what I mean was they were not allowed to go generally into stock raising." And yet some slaves seem to have been doing just that. One ex-slave spoke of raising "horses to sell"; another claimed to have raised fourteen horses over a twenty-five-to-thirty-year period, most of which he had sold; and one freedwoman named some of the purchasers, all of whom were slaves, of the nine horses that she had raised. The other major foundation of this internal economy was the amount of crop production by slaves. Jeremiah Everts observed that the slaves in Chatham County, Georgia, had "as much land as they can till for their own use." The freedmen's recollections from all over the lowcountry support this statement: a number of ex-slaves reckoned that they had more than ten acres under cultivation, while four or five acres was the norm. The proprietorial attitude encouraged by this independent production is suggested in one freedman's passing comment that he worked in his "own field." Through the raising of stock and the production of provisions (together with the sale of produce from woodworking, basketmaking, hunting, and fishing), slaves were able to attract money into their internal economy. Robert W. Gibbes knew of an individual slave who received $120 for his year's crop of corn and fodder; Richard Arnold owed his slaves $500 in 1853 when Olmsted visited him. Thus, while produce and livestock were constantly being bartered by slaves—"swapping" was rife, according to the freedmen—one observer of the mid-nineteenth-century lowcountry was undoubtedly correct when he noted that "in a small way a good deal of money circulated among the negroes, both in the country and in the towns."

The autonomy of this internal economy is further indicated by the development of a highly significant practice. By the middle of the nineteenth century, if not before, slave property was not only being produced and exchanged but also inherited. The father of Joseph Bacon bequeathed him a mare and all his other children $50 each. Samuel Elliot claimed a more substantial legacy, for his father "had 20 head of cattle, about 70 head of hogs—Turkeys Geese Ducks and Chickens a Plenty—he was foreman for his master and had been raising such things for years. When he died the property was divided among his children and we continued to raise things just as he had been raising." The role of less immediate kin was also not negligible. Two freedmen recalled receiving property from their grandfathers; another inherited a sow from his cousin; and William Drayton of Beaufort County, South Carolina, noted that when his father died he "left with his oldest brother, my uncle, the means or property he left for his children," and Drayton bought a mule "by the advice of my uncle who had the means belonging to me." There were rules governing lines of descent. One female claimant emphasized that she had not inherited any of her first husband's property because she had borne him no children; rather, his son by a former marriage received the property. The ability to bequeath wealth and to link patrimony to genealogy serves to indicate the extent to which slaves created a measure of autonomy.

The property rights of slaves were recognized across proprietorial boundaries as well as across generations. Slaves even employed guardians to facilitate the transfer of property from one plantation to another. Thus when Nancy Bacon, belonging to John Baker, inherited cattle from her deceased husband who belonged to Mr. Walthour, she employed her second cousin, Andrew Stacy, a slave on the Walthour plantation, to take charge of the cattle and drive them over to her plantation. According to Stacy, Mr. Walthour "didn't object to my taking them [and] never claimed them." The way in which slave couples took advantage of their divided ownership is suggested by Diana Cummings of Chatham County, Georgia. Her husband's master, she explained, "allowed him to sell but mine didn't," so Diana marketed her crops and stock through her husband and received a part of the proceeds. On her husband's death, she received all his property for, as she put it, her "entitle" (surname) was then the same as her husband's. She had since changed it, through remarriage to Sydney Cummings, but she noted that Cummings had "no interest in [the] property [being claimed]."

By the middle of the nineteenth century the ownership of property by lowcountry slaves had become extensive and had assumed relatively sophisticated dimensions. This, in turn, gives rise to an obvious question. What significance was attached to the practice by the slaves? What was the *mentalité*, the moral economy, of this property-owning group? Certainly some freedmen spoke of "getting ahead" and of "accumulating" under slavery. Jacob Monroe, a freedman, admitted that as a slave under the task system he "could go and come when [he] pleased, work and play after [his] task was done," but he pointedly emphasized that "he chose to work." Competitiveness was also not alien to the slave quarters. One freedman recalled how the young adults on one plantation "were jealous of one another and tried to see which would get their days work done first." William Gilmore referred to the disparities in property ownership that characterized Raymond Cay's

slaves; he likened them to the "five wise and five foolish" and dispar-
aged those who "slept and slumbered the time away." Similar impressions are derived from those Northerners who came into contact with
sea island blacks in the early 1860s. B. K. Lee observed that "they are
very acquisitive indeed"; Henry Judd described their "passion for ownership of horses or some animal"; and Rufus Saxton was impressed to
find that "they regard the rights of property among themselves. If a
man has a claim upon a horse or sow he maintains his right and his
neighbours recognize it."

Acquisitiveness and respect for property had other overtones, as
Rufus Saxton's resonant phrase—"they delight in accumulating"—suggests. Display and ostentation, while not on any grand scale, of course,
seem an accurate characterization of some slaves' behavior. The ownership of horses undoubtedly had practical purposes—one freedman
explained that "some of the slaves had families a good ways off and
they used their horses to visit them. The masters said it was for their
interest to have us own horses so that we could get back home to
work." But the exhibition of status appears also to have been involved.
William Golding's ownership of a horse and saddle was proved because "he was given to riding about on Sundays." Frederick Law
Olmsted not only witnessed a head house-servant mount his horse after
church service but, in true paternalistic fashion, slip a coin to the boy
who had been holding its reins. Ex-slaves commonly justified their
ownership of a horse and wagon by their need to go to church on
Sunday. This was not just a practical matter: Leah Wilson could not
disguise the sense of status she derived from being able to drive "right
along together with our master going to church." A horse, as Edward
Philbrick observed in 1862, was more than a means of transport; it was
"a badge of power and caste." Sea island blacks had no respect for
people who could not present themselves on a horse. "They will hardly
lift their hats to a white man on foot," he noted, and viewed a "walking nigger" with contempt.

Although we find elements of display, of accumulation for its own
sake, and of "getting ahead," the *mentalité* of the slaves cannot be reduced to any one of these traits and was indeed much more. We can
uncover better the meaning and limits of such behavior by exploring,
once again, the slaves' immediate response to freedom. In terms of
their attitude toward labor, the freedmen firmly resisted the overtures
of northern reformers and proclaimed a resounding attachment to what
may be resonantly characterized as a task-orientation. Employers and
Freedmen's Bureau officials alike constantly bemoaned the impossibil-
ity of persuading the freedmen to "perform more than their allotted
tasks." In 1867 Frances Butler Leigh observed freedmen who begged
"to be allowed to go back to the old task system" when the agent of
the Freedmen's Bureau attempted to have them work by the day. "One
man," she reported, "indignantly asked Major D——what the use of

being free was, if he had to work harder than when he was a slave." Few freedmen would work a full day, a full week, "and very seldom a full month steady," complained one employer. One Northerner advocated the confiscation of the freedmen's boats so that instead of continuing in their ways of "precarious living," they might develop "habits of steady industry." The freedmen were said to work "when they please and do just as much as they please"; they then relied on hunting and fishing "to make up for what they lose in the field."

This clash between the proponents of Northeastern business methods and a laboring population wedded to an alternative work ethic reverberated throughout the postwar lowcountry. The conflict is neatly illustrated in an exchange that occurred in 1865 between Colonel Willard, a man generally sympathetic to the freedmen's plight, and two ex-slaves who were sawmill workers. Willard was approached by the harassed owner of the mill, who was unable to impress his workers with the virtues of "steady" work; they claimed, for example, at least two hours of rest during their work day. From the standpoint of a Northern businessman, Willard's argument to the two representatives of the work force was impeccable: "Laborers at the North," he pointed out, "got less wages, and worked from sunrise to sunset, this season of the year, only having an hour at noon." The freedmen's reply was equally forceful: "We want," they emphasized, "to work just as we have always worked." Willard was left to expostulate that these former slaves "have no just sense of the importance of persistent labor."

The freedmen's attitude toward the accumulation of property, much like their attitude toward work, was decisively shaped by their former experience under the task system. The argument that "the more they cultivate, the more they gain" had, as one Northern army officer discovered, no appeal. In 1868 Frances Butler Leigh made a similar discovery when she found that some freedmen refused wages and rations, preferring to "raise a little corn and sweet potatoes, and with their facilities for catching fish and oysters, and shooting wild game, they have as much to eat as they want, and now are quite satisfied with that." In short, lowcountry freedmen apparently wished to avoid an unlimited involvement in the market, favoring production for sale only within the familiar context of an assured production for subsistence. This explains, in large measure, why the freedmen would not forego their hunting and fishing activities for a greater concentration on cash crops, why they aspired to the ownership or rental of land, and why they refused to work for wages. The degree to which subsistence (in this case, hunting) formed the priorities of one freedman is captured in a brief anecdote. A special agent, who toured the lowcountry in 1878 investigating disputed claims, visited the home of Samuel Maxwell, a former slave. He was not impressed with this particular claimant's adaptation to freedom and advised him to participate more fully in the wider society. For a start, he suggested, why not raise hogs rather than dogs? To which Maxwell replied: "A pig won't help us catch coons and rabbits."

The preferences and ambitions of the freedmen reflected, above all, a desire for autonomy not only from the impersonal marketplace but also from individual whites. As one would-be employer found out in 1866, the freedmen who rejected wages and wanted to supply their own seed were expressing a fundamental desire to "be free from personal constraint." They sought, in other words, to build upon a foundation that the task system had laid, consisting of that part of a day, that plot of land, or those few animals that they, as slaves, had been able to call their own. Thus for many, if not most, lowcountry freedmen, the central priorities of subsistence and autonomy shaped whatever propensity for material accumulation and for "getting ahead" they may have had. And what these goals of subsistence and autonomy signally call to mind, of course, are nothing more than the central priorities of peasants throughout the world.

The freedman's quest for a measure of autonomy from individual whites should not be construed, however, as a desire for total disengagement from whites, particularly in the immediate postemancipation years. The moral universe of lowcountry slaves apparently contained notions of social equity and of reciprocal obligations between blacks and whites that were not jettisoned when freedom came. Henry Ravenel's slaves, for example, voluntarily presented themselves before their master in March 1865 and "said they would be willing to take a certain piece of land which they would cultivate for old Master—that they would not want a driver or overseer, but would work that faithfully for him—and that they would take another piece of land to work for their own use." Another set of plantation blacks dumbfounded their former owner in July 1865 when they told him that they now considered the land as their own; perhaps more striking, however, was their readiness to grant "Master" a portion of the crop as "a free gift from themselves." When the promise of land dimmed, the freedmen could be expected to assume a more hostile posture. While evidence of such hostility exists, some sensitive observers were still aware of a basic and continuing paradox. Thus Joseph Le Conte, writing of Liberty County, Georgia, freedmen in the 1890s, noted their refusal to be tied to whites and their rejection of wage labor based, in his view, on their ability to "live almost without work on fish, crawfish, and oysters." At the same time, however, he referred to "the kindliest feelings" existing "among the blacks . . . toward their former masters." While Le Conte may have been guilty of some self-deception, similar observations from his fellow whites suggest the reality of this paradox. Once again, this aspect of the freedmen's world view is strikingly reminiscent of a central feature of peasant life that, according to one authority, is permeated by the moral principle of reciprocity.

The significance of the particular conjunction that this article set out to explore—the conjunction between a certain mode of labor organization and a particular domestic economy—can now be assessed. From the short-run perspective of masters, this conjunction had a number of benefits. They could escape their plantations in the summer months, they were supplied with additional provisions, and their slaves were *relatively* content, or so they believed. Oliver Bostick, a Beaufort County planter, explained that he "allowed [his] slaves to own and have their property and have little crops of their own for it Encouraged them to do well and be satisfied at home." Rufus King, another lowcountry master, was satisfied that "no Negro with a well-stocked poultry house, a small crop advancing, a canoe partly finished or a few tubs unsold, all of which he calculates soon to enjoy, will ever run away." From the short-run perspective of the slaves, this conjunction increased their autonomy, allowed them to accumulate (and bequeath) wealth, fed individual initiative, sponsored collective discipline and esteem, and otherwise benefited them economically and socially. In other words, on a much reduced scale, there were lowcountry slaves who resembled the protopeasants found among Caribbean slaves. This similarity was derived from very different origins: in the lowcountry, from a particular mode of labor organization; in the Caribbean, from the need for slaves to grow most of their own food and provision the free population. There was, in short, a much wider "peasant breach in the slave mode of production" in the Caribbean than in the lowcountry.

Still, the parallel is suggestive, for in the same way that protopeasant adaptations had a comparable short-term significance for masters and slaves in both Caribbean and lowcountry, there were comparable long-term results. Wherever there were significant protopeasant activities among the slaves, there emerged after emancipation a class of people who had acquired the requisite skills that helped them escape, at least in part or temporarily, their dependence on the plantation. In the lowcountry, the course of the war, the capital requirements of its major staple crop, and the development of phosphates production go some way toward explaining the particular shape of its postwar labor history. But surely certain elements of this configuration had deeper roots, roots that without exaggeration can be traced all the way back to the early eighteenth century. The imperatives so dear to generations of lowcountry slaves achieved a measure of realization in the more distinctive features of the region's postwar labor arrangements. By 1880 the percentage of farms sharecropped in the coastal districts of South Carolina and Georgia ranked among the lowest in the South; the proportion of rural black landowners was one of the highest in the South; it is possible to speak of a "black yeomanry" in the late nineteenth-century lowcountry; and by 1880 one observer in coastal Georgia could describe how most of the Negroes in his county had "bought a small tract of land, ten acres or more [on which they made] enough rice . . . to be perfectly independent of the white man." To paraphrase Sidney Mintz, nothing else during the history of lowcountry slavery was as important as the task system and its concomitant domestic economy in making possible the freed person's adaptation to freedom without the blessings of the former masters.

Holiday processions like this were the domain of labor-ing classes in early nineteenth-century Philadelphia.

"Making Night Hideous": Christmas Revelry and Public Order in Nineteenth-Century Philadelphia

SUSAN G. DAVIS

It was not until the late nineteenth century that industrial capitalism had generally altered the organization and nature of work and working-class life. In the old commercial capitals of the northeast, pre-industrial expectations and work habits jarred against the new forms of market production well into mid-century. At the time when Lowell's mechanized factories were employing thousands of women, most urban laboring-class men and women still worked in small manufactories, in shops, or at home, figured seasonal shifts of employment into their annual work schedules and earnings, and would have found a time clock alien to their habits of labor and leisure.

While historians have studied the nature of work and relations between employers and employees in the pre-factory period, we know little about the culture of the laboring people of the pre-industrial cities. What was the culture of the streets and alleys? What types of social networks existed among urban working people? How did they spend their leisure time? These are questions that concern Susan Davis in the following essay on popular culture in Philadelphia in the nineteenth century.

Davis offers a fascinating look into the tumultuous world of Philadelphia's young laboring-class males. The youth who lived in the city's poorer districts had few securities. They drew no hard distinctions between work, leisure, and unemployment. They created a popular culture of the streets that found its most common and powerful expression in the street brawl and holiday revelry. Davis explores the activities and behavior of this working-class crowd and links the customary disguises and night activities of the young men—"masking," "shooting," "belsnickling," "rough music," "mummery", and "blackface"—to the mixture of folk traditions that had long existed in the port city. The violence and disorder that marked these street festivals, and Christ-

mas revelry in particular, held a powerful meaning for both the upper and
the lower classes of Philadelphia and hence is worthy of historians' attention.

For most of the nineteenth century respectable Philadelphians condemned Christmas as a disgrace. Philadelphia's Christmas was then an
essentially public celebration, unfolding in taverns, alleys, and squares,
and although it grew out of European festive patterns and rural customs, the festival took its shape and meaning from the city's working
class and the changing conditions of urban life. Riot and revelry, disguise and debauch gave police and property owners reason to fear the
approach of the holiday.

The history of Christmas in Philadelphia exemplifies the conflict
within and between classes over behavior in public; confrontation over
the form and enactment of the street festival was sharp and recurring.
Middle-class disapproval and hostility were recorded in reportage, ed-
itorials, ordinances, and municipal policies, while celebrants' resistance
found expression in the streets and the evolving forms of revelry. Press
accounts of holiday activities provide a unique year-by-year record, not
only of this conflict, but of working peoples' festive behavior. Moreover, the evolution of the street Christmas into an organized, sanctioned New Year's pageant—the Philadelphia Mummers Parade—
provides an example of the transformation of urban public culture in
the nineteenth century. The history of Christmas and its transformation can be examined along several dimensions: its origins in older customs and urban social life, its enactment in relation to the identities of
its creators, and the attempts to suppress it by its opponents. Critical
to its history are ethnic and class relations in the city and the special
position of urban youth.

This street festival emerged in the early nineteenth century, with
urban working-class culture in general, from the convergence of older
ways of life with unprecedented conditions. Cultural diversity distinguished Philadelphia's working people: the mingling of Germans, former slaves, Carribbeans, "native" Americans, Catholic and Protestant
Irish, and migrants from the countryside was punctuated by their often
violent clashes. Working-class heterogeneity found expression in patterns of residence, for the city's poorer districts were ethnic and racial
patchworks, and ghettoes remained few and small until late in the cen-

"MAKING NIGHT HIDEOUS"   From *American Quarterly*, 34 (Summer 1982), 185–99. Copyright 1982, American Studies Association. Reprinted by permission of the American Studies
Association and the author.

tury. Urban life was shaped by a more decisive segregation, however, as the new working-class suburbs spread out around the concentration of shops, businesses, and middle-class residences in the city center. Social life in the working-class districts grew out of the experience of labor, and although Philadelphians toiled in large workshops and mechanized factories, the lives of the majority were defined by hand labor, seasonal industry, and irregular employment. Working people blended intense labor with bouts of hard play, rejecting the rationalism and piety of their respectable neighbors and middle-class reformers. Their social life and recreation similarly combined the familiar and the new as they found leisure in commercial and customary entertainments. The most vibrant novelty, the musical theatre, spoke to an unprecedented male working-class audience, but entertainments could also be found in the tavern, dance hall, groggery, and street. The edges of town, still rural, provided livelihood and sport, both legal and illegal, complementing the free and easy, open atmosphere of the markets, amusement halls, and fairs. Thus city life in the early decades of the century was marked by the interpenetration of work and leisure, an incomplete spatial segregation of peoples and activities, and a blending of the informal and the emergent commercial.

Sacred and secular holidays were important expressions of this mixed culture, at once old- and new-fashioned. Christmas was the major punctuation of the European traditional year, and Philadelphians kept this emphasis, marking the season with relaxation and drinking, visiting and ceremony. In the first half of the nineteenth century Christmas comprised a week of amusements and celebrations such as horse races, pig chases, pigeon shoots, ox roasts, and hunting and skating parties. The thriving theatre district counted on heavy attendance at harlequinades and minstrel shows. Militia troops and clubs held balls and concerts, church women gave fairs, fire companies paraded new equipment, set fires, and brawled. Hundreds of pubs, groggeries, and cookshops treated patrons to the specialities of the season with extra liberality.

Such intense socializing was possible, in part, because the holiday fell at a time of sharp contrast between work and leisure. As December's cold deepened, the creeks and rivers froze, and the workshops, factories, and docks stood still. In this time of hardship and unemployment for working people, the line between seasonal relaxation and distress was a fine one. Desperation often combined with customary license to turn suburban lanes and central streets into scenes of beggary, drunkenness, and riot. From early in the century observers found this face of Christmas both alarming and disgraceful, a threat to public order.

Against this pattern of stepped-up socializing, disorder, and violence, two special activities took place that became the focus of outrage and suppression. "Masking" and "shooting" stood out in the street

Christmas, associated with disturbances in the city's working-class suburbs. "Shooting"—a pan-European custom—celebrated the death of the old year and "fired in" the new, although explosive noisemaking occurred on Christmas Eve as well. "Masking"—assuming a new, often inverted or paradoxical identity through disguise—reflected the varied folk-cultural backgrounds of Philadelphians. Until about 1830, "belsnickling," a type of masking that involved disguised adults visiting houses to query children about their conduct, was popular in the city, an importation from the German-speaking countryside. Another form of disguised house-visit, masking (sometimes called mumming), became common after the 1820s. Costumed processions from door to door, with or without the performance of a folk play, were familiar to immigrants from the British Isles and the coastal South.

The record of a new kind of masking and shooting began in the 1830s, when descriptions of Christmas Eve processions of young men started to appear in newspapers. Though they were often in costume, these processions were different from rural German and British Isles traditions. Unlike the single, inquisitorial belsnickle, who was known to the families who let him in, these young men roved in bands, stopping at taverns and brawling on street corners. And although they paraded in their own neighborhoods, probably visiting the houses of friends and relatives, they also marched from the suburbs to sport in the city's crowded thoroughfares.

Observers found new names for these urban maskers: "fantasticals" and "callithumpians" designated their distinct but overlapping themes of disguise. Callithumpians made charivari-like rough music, taking the conventions of marching bands and fife and drum corps and turning them inside out. Dressed in burlesque, they mocked real music with cracked pots, cowbells, kitchen utensils, bent horns, cow horns, fake trumpets, and the whole folk repertoire of homemade and pretend instruments.

The fantasticals flew even further into antisense. In extravagant parody of the militia, they marched in drill form, bearing mock weapons and pseudo-military names. Appearing in both city and outlying towns, fantasticals drew their identities from real events and from the minstrel stage, mingling "Santa Ana's Cavalry" with the "Strut-Some Guards." Accounts of a mock-militia parade held in Easton, in early January, 1834, give the fullest description of fantastical dress and behavior. Led by a "Colonel" mounted on a jackass, one hundred men dressed as soldiers, with huge hats and weapons, wearing paintbrushes, hogs ears, and tobacco plugs for epaulettes and strings of bones and fish around their necks, conducted elaborate sham manoeuvres. They were accompanied by a callithumpian band made up of "Indians, hunters, Falstaffs, Jim Crows and nondescripts," wearing tent-sized hats and ballooning trousers. The exaggeration and inversion of military ceremony at play in this parody, as well as the theatrical borrowings, served as common devices of city maskers.

Though remarkable, such fantastical and callithumpian processions were not highly framed or specialized performances. On the contrary, noise and disguise, the two enduring and basic motifs of the festival, found endless repetition and myriad forms in the crowd's "rude revelry" of gun firing, drum beating, bell ringing, and simpler disguises.

Costumes were spare and dramatic, varying within a narrow range of imagery. Occasionally a lone belsnickle—half-demon, half-man—turned out. But in contrast to older, rural themes of semihuman disguise, Philadelphians commonly impersonated kinds of people, in conventionalized but differing interpretations of racial and national types. "Red Indians," "Chinamen," "Dutchmen" (standing both for German-speaking farmers and later, German immigrants), and rural New Englanders—"Brother Jonathans"—all appeared. But the most familiar disguises treated very familiar people: women and blacks. Wearing women's clothing was an easy transformation and popular, although arrests for transvestism brought stiff fines. Dressing as a woman could be as simple as filching a sister's dress or as elaborate as an impersonation of Jenny Lind or "Mrs. Langtry."

Blackface was a popular theme in the street Christmas from the 1830s. Here, as with the stereotyped images mentioned above, there was an intimate connection to performances in city theatres and their most successful form, the Negro minstrel show. "Jim Crow" began to march in parades and processions almost immediately after his debut in 1832. Like transvestism, blacking-up was quick and cheap, but could sustain elaboration into a stage character or a marching minstrel troupe. Female clothing often combined with blackface to make an "Aunt Sally," a double inversion of race and sex.

Though masks and disguises varied, the real identities of the holiday revelers stood clear: the Christmas and New Year's crowds were always described as young and male. Year after year the newspapers railled against the "drunken men and boys in the streets," the "half-grown boys," "the young rioters," "the inebriated young men," the "groups of hobbledehoys," and "black sheep" "who made night hideous with Galathumpian doings." Similarly, those arrested for masking and shooting and worse were uniformly young and male. The facts of youth and maleness illuminate the specific meanings of the festival for participants and observers, for the noisy, often violent crowds were not anomalous or extraordinary. Revelry crystalized the city's year-round youth problem. In a period of rapidly increasing industrialization, and before universal public education, the breakdown of the apprenticeship system and the decline of craft skills meant that young men were a severely underemployed group. Youthful criminals caused anxiety in all parts of the city, but the notorious gangs were only the most visible aspect of male street life. Most boys and young men diverted themselves less violently than the "Killers" and "Stingers"; still, their ever-present "destructionism," petty gambling, and hanging out annoyed gentle citizens, reminding them that the city seemed to corrupt youth.

In the street Christmas, rowdy youth culture reached its apotheosis; concern over riotous holiday nights was constant from the 1830s on. The editor of the *Chronicle* complained that on Christmas Eve, 1833, ". . . riot, noise and uproar prevailed, uncontrolled and uninterrupted in many of our central and most orderly streets. Gangs of boys howled as if possessed by the demon of disorder." In 1844 the *Ledger's* New Year's editorial deplored the "riotous spirit raging" in the streets and declared that "our city has almost daily been the theatre of disorders which practically nullify civil government." The mid-1840s were especially uproarious, but tumult and commotion seemed ominous for decades.

Anxieties over youth and holiday crowds came together in outrage over the volunteer fire companies, who contributed heavily to the ceremonial and rowdy aspects of Christmas week and set the tone of the wild night. Key institutions of working-class peer culture, these all-male fraternities reflected ethnic and ideological splits among workers, as well as local rivalries over gang territory and fire-fighting prerogatives. The volunteers' love of parades, costumes, and machinery was surpassed only by their enthusiasm for fighting; by the 1840s firemen ranked as leading incendiaries and rioters in a city well known for violent upheavals. During Christmas week, firemen filled the theatre of the streets with their horse races, promenade dances, fantastical troupes, and less benign celebrations.

Many firemen and other "rowdies" lived in the new suburbs, where on holiday nights they created masquerades and uproars. In 1845 the *Public Ledger* remarked of Southwark's brawls, "the people who live in this region are demons." But as fantasticals and callithumpians, young men sought their largest audiences in the main business and theatre district, Chestnut between Fourth and Broad, where playgoers and promenaders thronged to view shop-window illuminations. The sense of threat, then, turned in part on the influx of carousers into the city's respectable heart; many of those arrested downtown for masking began their sport in Spring Garden, the Liberties, Passyunk, or Moyamensing.

Observers understood from suburban residence and demeanor the revelers' membership in the growing, heavily foreign-born, and poor stratum of the working class. There is, however, little information about the nativity of the crowds, and as noted above, masking customs would have been familiar to many of the city's natives and immigrants. Just as they came from all areas of the city, so the maskers likely sprang from different national backgrounds. Neither were the crowds all white, despite the mocking convention of blackface, for blacks made fantastical parades and played music in the streets as well. One of the first clear descriptions of a Christmas procession reports the attack on a black fife and drum corps by a white gang. Given the size of the city's black population, its concentration near the center, and the steady influx of blacks from the coastal South where slaves developed distinct mumming traditions, it is likely that Afro-Americans contributed much to the shape of Christmas revelry.

These, then, were the revelers: young men from the city's poorer districts, ethically and racially diverse, invading the respectable and propertied downtown. Fantasticals and callithumpians, highly visible because of their costumes and antics, became the focus of uneasiness and the objects of attempts to suppress the wearing of disguise. Maskers' own customs also led to notoriety and outrage. For instance, a favored callithumpian sport was collecting free drinks in neighborhood taverns. But if treats were ungenerous or refused, rough musicians were likely to retaliate. Crossing neighborhood boundaries probably provoked more fights than did stingy proprietors, and tavern owners seem to have preferred the noise of maskers to interference by authorities. In 1854 watchmen who tried to stop a callithumpian performance at William Myers's tavern found themselves mobbed by the band, the clientele, and the owner.

A New Year's Eve murder in 1857 illustrates the involvement of gangs and the night's use for the expression of ethnic antipathy. Witnesses to the stabbing death of Andrew Beiche, a young German, described his attack by a group of fantasticals. Calling themselves the "Ruggers" and sporting blackened faces, white robes, and plumes, the fantasticals followed Beiche's serenading party, beating them with wooden swords, fence stakes, and brickbats. References at the inquest to the Ruggers' code words, headquarters, and activities make it clear that they were one of the city's numerous gangs. Maskers and undisguised gangs fought each other, or joined up to attack "outsiders" and immigrants. White assaults on blacks, mobbings of black churches, battles between white and black gangs, and attacks on the watch were venerable holiday traditions.

Nighttime violence could be still more capricious: shootings and knifings erupted from disputes between maskers, and accidents were common, as when firing out the old year resulted in chance shootings of bystanders. The holidays seemed to offer endless possibilities for crime, violence, arson, riot, and misadventure.

The street Christmas held different and antagonistic meanings for those who created it and those who opposed it, meanings and interpretations located in the social identities of the maskers, in their disguises, and in their violent, disorderly behavior. For the boys and young men, "making night hideous" was a condensed statement made to and about three groups of people: themselves, their social superiors, and those they saw as outsiders or inferiors. For the young of the working class, the custom of masquerading forged and perpetuated group identity in particular neighborhoods or for particular gangs. Dressing up together, carousing and collecting free drinks, and finding and thrashing common enemies all created sensations of solidarity. At the same time, those denied power, recognition, and adult status because of their class and in particular because of their weak position in the city's economy could for once take over the respectable central district. In streets lined with the shops and residences of businessmen, the world turned upside down as maskers forced the most decried features of their peer culture on the entire city. The young men created a giant exemplary display of noise, intemperance, and riot, and they seem to have delighted in the outrage they caused.

Disguise expressed the point of view of working-class youth: in the patterned and selective transformation of identity, they discussed local social relations, outlining and emphasizing differences between kinds of people. The street Christmas shared this central motif—the delineation of the traits of inferiors—with much of nineteenth-century popular culture. But the racial and ethnic stereotypes that preoccupied maskers did not spring from an abstract repertoire; they reflected immediate conflicts and complexities in local and national life. Germans, whether rural or urban newcomers, were an important group in Philadelphia and the objects of joking and hostility in daily life, on stage, and in broadsheets. Chinese people were only a little removed, presented as subhuman idiots in newspapers and on the minstrel stage from San Francisco to Philadelphia. News of Indian removals and wars circulated constantly; Indian plays and later Wild West shows served as staple Christmas entertainments. The rural hick or "Brother Jonathan" strode the stage for most of the century, and Philadelphians witnessed his idiosyncracies in comic publications, the press, and at first hand.

But the group closest to home was the Negro, whose inferiority was delineated, celebrated, and reproduced in print and in the popular theatre. Young white men who dressed as blacks did not merely borrow imagery from commercial culture, they created a kind of localized commentary on central tensions in Philadelphia neighborhoods. From the early nineteenth century blacks competed with working-class whites for jobs and resources, achieving before the Civil War a position of relative strength in a few unskilled occupations and all-black guilds. Blacks were barely tolerable to whites when they acted like slaves: since the eighteenth century they had been permitted to hold festive dances in Potter's Field. But as the black population in the central city and Southwark grew in the 1830s and 1840s, black attempts at full social and political participation drew mockery, abuse, and violence from the majority of their white neighbors.

Christmas impersonations, like minstrel shows, mocked urban blacks' attempts to "act white"; that is, to participate equally in city life. But the homemade masquerades were unique in that they were not performed for commercial consumption, but as part of an informal means of creating group unity. In derogatory repetition of familiar images, popular ideas moved easily between stage and street and were enacted by neighbors for neighbors. On the other hand, masking made an ambiguous statement about race despite its violent mocking tone, for blackface found use as a way to play with racial identity, important in a city where black inferiority was taken for granted yet segregation was incomplete. John Szwed has described processes of moving back and forth across racial and cultural boundaries, involving the use of gesture, specific behaviors, voice, dialect, and other linguistic features. Such play, often the preserve of youth, paradoxically accomplishes learning and absorption of "alien" culture. Theatricals are only heightened examples of this play with socially constructed boundaries between kinds of people. Part of Christmas's delight was the liberty to "act black," all the more enjoyable because maskers could count on a safe return to their real identities.

The popularity of transvestism at Christmas is more difficult to explain, if only because we know so little about the lives of Philadelphia's working women. But the festival, like carnivals elsewhere, expressed vivid male/female, home/street oppositions. The heavily male tavern life and fighting mystique of peer culture opposed a respectable world of home, marriage, and family, so that in an era of absolute male supremacy in public life, sexual inversion made a strikingly complete identity transformation. Perhaps sexual boundary-crossing voiced anxiety about the definition of sex roles, for women's new activities as industrial workers and their involvement in evangelical religion, temperance, trade unions, abolitionism, and feminism all seemed worthy of derision and violence from men.

Mockery and parody could also aim upward: the fantastical take-offs of militia drills appeared in Philadelphia at the same time that the city's artisans organized against the unequal and oppressive compulsory militia system. This antiauthority strain continued in later impersonations of policemen, dog-catchers, and even mounted policemen, all municipal innovations resented in working-class neighborhoods.

Inferiority, then, was the street Christmas's subject, and masking, inequality's spare but complete enactment. Revelry took for its text acceptance of the fundamental divisions on which the republic of equals rested and asserted the right of the white male to take what was his— jobs, education, a limited measure of political power—by force, if necessary. This margin of privilege was reconstructed daily in laws, informal practices, and by riot, so that it is not surprising to find masquerades shaded into violence against blacks and immigrants, and rioters disguised as blacks and women at times other than Christmas. Playful and serious assertions of power, maskings and mobbings marked proximate points along a continuum of antagonistic expression.

The racial and ethnic antagonisms within the working class served middle-class interests, fragmenting the potential for class-wide labor and political organization. Not one of the public complaints against masking objected to the strands of mocking supremacism it contained, but as the century progressed fear of the festival's form and tone increased. Arrests, stiff fines for masking and shooting, denunciations in the press, and attempts to keep crowds from forming expressed the mingled annoyance and anxiety with which middle-class Philadelphians viewed "the Christmas disgrace."

Gentle citizens felt rankled by more than noise. The "young black sheep of the community" were the group the authorities could least control, and imprecations hurled by the press—"rag-tag," "loafers," "vagrants"—reveal recognition of and uneasiness about youth's unemployment and the distress of winter. Precisely because of the year-round boisterousness of working-class youth, the street Christmas made the worst fears of the respectable seem about to come true. When the street Christmas was called a threat to property, authorities proved especially sensitive to complaints from downtown storekeepers. So the watch made forays into the suburbs to quell masking and shooting, but from early on concentrated their efforts on Eighth and Chestnut Streets.

The deepest threat loomed for moral and symbolic order, as defined by center city residents. Christmas focussed uneasiness through the lens of concern over youth, but at the same time that outrage over rowdyism swelled, the middle class was attaching its own new meanings to the festival. By the 1840s Christmas was becoming the apotheosis of middle-class ideals of childhood and family. Though still a holy day for the pious, affluent people now sought the day's meaning in the cozy, innocent delights of gift-giving, stocking-filling, and a family dinner celebrated at the altar of the hearth. The new icon of the holiday press—jolly, doting Santa Claus—barely resembled his country cousin, the whip-cracking belsnickle. This is not to argue that working-class families enjoyed no domestic Christmas; however, the elaboration and commercialization of this domestic holiday were accomplished largely by popular magazines, especially women's magazines, speaking to a newly prosperous and growing urban middle class.

The street Christmas collided with this celebration of private sentiment, throwing the disparity between middle-class expectations for behavior in public and anxieties about working-class youth into sharp relief. Hopes that the lower orders would raise themselves through temperance, piety, and self-denial (hopes held by some among the working class as well) found contradiction in the defiant rudeness of the festival. Most ironically, the exposition of irrationality unfolded on the holiest night of the pious year, openly, freely, and in public. Despite its critics' denunciations, it annually grew more disreputable.

In the 1860s, with the exception of the war years, the crowds of revelers swelled and their music grew rougher. Chestnut Street from Eighth to Independence Hall was "completely blockaded," and the firing of guns and blowing of trumpets incessant. Now the street Christmas reached a turning point: in the past masking and shooting had been tolerated when they could not be prevented, but the consolidation of the city's watches into a central police force in 1854 meant that all neighborhoods now experienced a more consistent presence of authority. Disorder could be met, at least in theory, in a concerted and forceful way. Thus, as the Christmas disgrace reached a new peak, the city government could begin a campaign to establish control over the holiday streets. Christmas Eve now saw the theatre district lined with hundreds of armed, uniformed men stationed in front of the shops. Proclamations forbidding masking, guns, and horns were issued from year to year, and "reasonable restraints" resulted in hundreds of arrests annually, mostly for drunkenness. These attempts at suppression continued into the 1870s, but none worked. Instead of withering away, processions of fantasticals and callithumpians became more numerous, and the themes of noise-making and disguise persisted with resilience. In years when the city issued bans on "the horn nuisance," crowds of boys turned out ringing bells. When the little tin horns sold by hawkers were prohibited, men and boys blew brass trumpets, fog horns, rams horns—anything not made of tin.

Pressure from above did shift the location, forms, and interpretations of the festival. Massed police kept celebrants out of the business district and closer to home in the suburbs, until masqueraders, long active in all parts of town and even in Camden, began to be thought of as "belonging" to the southern wards. But the most important and symbolic effect of organized crowd control was to shift the theatre of disorder from holy Christmas Eve to secular New Year's Eve and eventually to New Year's Day. New Year's had always been a nonreligious if less well-loved holiday, and seemed less susceptible to defilement than the night of Christ's birth.

At the same time, attitudes toward a more restricted range of festive activities softened. In 1880, describing a scene on Chestnut Street, the *Inquirer* commented that although fantasticals created pandemonium with their mock weapons and voices, ". . . it is the prerogative of New Years that as long as the people do not violently break the peace, they can be as noisy and jolly as they will." Why was condescending tolerance possible after decades of complaint, contempt, and suppression? It was the growing tendency of the maskers to organize themselves into clubs and to give coordinated performances that proved decisive in forcing the city's acceptance of modified mummery. While early fantasticals and callithumpians had gathered spontaneously among age cohorts, by the mid-1880s Philadelphia maskers participated in New Year's social clubs. A few "Socials" were active year after year under the same names, prefiguring the famous twentieth-century string bands and comic clubs. Socials with money to spend paraded in "fancy dress," yet themes of racial and sexual parody persisted. These more elaborate marches earned approval from commentators who distinguished between the "tasteful" and the "crude," and between mock musicians and troupes with hired brass bands.

The beginnings of the organized clubs and the stepped-up efforts at crowd control coincided with the city's victory in 1871 in its long battle to bring the volunteer fire departments under municipal authority. There is some evidence that the social functions of the fire companies flowed into the activities of the New Year's clubs, a shift from one heavily invested all-male institution to another. The socials retained the volunteers' names and ties to firemen in other cities, and behaved much as the hose and engine crews had done, parading, giving dances, and brawling. Women participated in auxiliaries, sewing banners and costumes. The cycle of ceremony and social exchange remained dense and busy.

Masking gradually became a very different kind of activity. In the eighties, participation shifted toward family involvement, often across generations, and families identified with particular clubs. In club life, maskers adapted and modified the older forms of revelry, following the general tendency toward more organized urban recreations. As a result, revelry shifted away from the domain of rowdy youth. Though working-class youth and gangs still prompted anxiety, the noisy strains of youth culture receded from the festival's core. Mummery now tended to become—and could become—more "creditable." Costumes became flashy and elaborate; "furs, feathers, bullion and embroidery" appeared in the crowds. Formally making a masquerade more of a performance and less a wild revel provided one way of being in control of being out of control. With increasing elaboration, structure, and consciousness of form the wild night was becoming a parade, and the disgrace could be recast into an appropriate and rational part of the city's self-image.

Most important, the clubs gave the city authorities a flexible means of control over maskers' performances. In 1884 the mayor issued permits, making the leader of each troupe responsible for the actions of all its members. By requiring maskers to carry permits and present them like licenses, the city assured that mummery took place not in the face of authority but under its sponsorship. This authority maskers accepted to a degree, by desisting from impersonating local politicians and policemen, and by further organizing and differentiating themselves from the crowd. When merchants offered prizes for the best troups and costumes, the shift in public meaning was assured—the disgrace transformed into an entertaining custom. All that remained was to shift the theatre of disorders from the night to the day.

Still, the transformation of the wild night into an official tradition did not take place in one year or even over one decade. In 1883–84 several large clubs and fife and drum corps applied for the first permits. Yet of 190 applications more than 140 were filed by individuals and unnamed persons, and many of these, the *Inquirer* remarked, were boys. Requests were "respectfully submitted" for "a few friends [to have] a sociable time," for "six private citizens to maskerade [sic]," and "for blakin' up as colored men to serenade a few friends. " Though tortuous callithumpian notes still prevailed over brass bands, large associations did the main streets, decked out in spangles and satins, their clowns in blackface at the rear. But as the *Inquirer* commented, the majority of masquerades took place on a "cheap and shabby scale"; that is, they were homemade and neighborhood oriented.

As a result of pressures and counter pressures, the rude street festival had been changed and contained, yet it expanded into a formal parade. In 1900 the Mummers Parade, as observers now called it, received the city's official sanction and sponsorship. Although arbiters of culture occasionally offered suggestions for making the parade more "artistic," the clubs retained control of their performances' content and good relations prevailed between Mummers and officials until the 1960s. Except for regulations prohibiting the impersonation of local politicians, content was self-regulated, or rather, Mummers' and official notions of parade-worthy topics did not diverge significantly.

In the parade, a selective and distilled statement of working-class culture and point of view found institutionalized, public expression. One segment of the city's working class, a mostly white, self-organizing portion, wrested for itself and was allowed to gain an important medium of communication. Enmeshed in a complex binding of kin, neighborhood, and ethnic ties, the new parade linked working-class recreation and social life to commerce, advertising, and more recently, to tourism. But in the process of transformation, the possibility of the wild night as a means to explore alternate interpretations and orderings of society—a possibility that flickered and threatened in the nineteenth century—was foreclosed. Thus it is no surprise to find that while the parade has remained a stoutly working-class activity, black participation in the festival withered away after 1900. Official sanction alone did not diffuse revelry's rowdy threat and redirect its social commentary. The ideology celebrated in the street Christmas—Jacksonian masculinity, white supremacy—saturated the challenge to order implied in the explosion of youth culture. Along with other new features of popular culture, the street Christmas delineated inferiors, foreigners, and social "others," and this aspect of revelry, never challenged by authorities, persists most vibrantly today. It was not inevitable that the Mummers Parade become a joyful elaboration of the primacy of racial and sexual divisions and loyalties over other social values and larger class interests, but this was the result of the process of organization, incorporation, and control. Decisively changed was the social definition of what might be enacted in public.

Promoters of education perceived public schools as the
route to morality and stability for America's working
class children.

The Abolition of Beverly High School

MICHAEL B. KATZ

In March 1860, two years after it opened its doors, Beverly High School in Beverly, Massachusetts, was closed by a vote of the town's citizens. This was not an event of national importance, or even of great significance in the history of education. The controversy over the survival of the local public high school, however, brings into focus the tensions and conflicts that divided the inhabitants of an industrializing community. Michael Katz uses Beverly as a case study to explore how educational reform and economic change touched the lives and relationships of individuals in mid-nineteenth-century communities. Using a variety of sources, he traces the steps that led up to the divided vote over the high school's existence.

Beverly was a single-industry town. Long before industrialization, shoemaking had formed the base of the town's economy. By mid-century, however, shoemaking was being transformed from a mechanics' craft into a factory industry. While businessmen promoted the growth of industry and urbanization, shoemakers and their families found that the community's economic development did not improve their livelihoods or the nature of their work.

The clash over Beverly High School was bound up with the opposing views of business interests and working people over the social consequences of industrialization. Those who perceived progress in industrial development backed the public high school as an institution that would educate the working classes. Those who opposed it were hostile to urban growth and the development of manufacturing. Katz underscores the importance of the fact that the vote over abolishing the high school occurred amidst a large strike by the town's shoemakers. What can this case study of one community tell us about the nature of educational reform and social change in industrializing communities? In what ways were communities like Beverly changing after mid-century?

At the Beverly town meeting in March 1860, clerk John I. Baker called the roll of the eligible voters on a motion of Joseph Thissell to abolish the two-year-old high school, redistribute the money already appropriated among the school districts, and challenge in the supreme court the state law requiring towns of a certain size to maintain a high school. Numerous citizens, unable to make up their minds, stayed silent when Baker called their names. But 392 did vote, 143 against the motion to abolish, 249 in its favor. Contrary to the myth that views public secondary education as the fulfillment of working-class aspirations, the Beverly vote revealed the social and financial leaders of the town, not the least affluent citizens, as the firmest supporters of the high school.

Beverly was not an important town, and the abolition of its high school was not, in itself, of significance for the development of American education. However, the vote is of first-rate importance because it suggests answers to critical and largely unanswered questions concerning mid-nineteenth century educational reform. Heretofore assertions about the supporters and opponents of educational innovation and generalizations about the conflict involved in the reform process have been based on strikingly little empirical evidence. The Beverly incident provides concrete data about the dynamics of the reform process.

Analysis of these data suggests specific answers to the basic questions of who supported and who opposed reform and what sorts of conflicts arose. Although Beverly was in some ways unique, developments in the town, as we shall see, represented a particularly explicit manifestation of the problems inherent in the impact of technological progress upon ante-bellum communities; and consequently the abolition of the high school poses questions of relevance to an understanding of the relationship between educational innovation and social progress throughout the state.

Because the high school issue was so important within Beverly, clerk Baker, most unusually, recorded the name of each individual who voted and the nature of his vote. Tax books and the manuscript census of 1860 furnish information about the residence, occupation, wealth, age, and number of dependents of 343 of the 392 voters. . . . First of all, consider the people who opposed abolition of the high school. Most of them lived in the two most populous, dense, and centrally located districts, the Grammar and the South. Supporters included those in the most prestigious occupations: 17 of the 19 professionals and public em-

THE ABOLITION OF BEVERLY HIGH SCHOOL   From Michael B. Katz, *The Irony of Early School Reform: Educational Innovation in Mid-Nineteenth Century Massachusetts* (Cambridge: Harvard University Press, 1968). Reprinted by permission of the author.

ployees, 8 of the 9 sea captains and master mariners, and all 4 "gentle-men." The vote of the businessmen was less decisive, but a significant majority of this heterogeneous category, including everything from wealthy merchant to shopkeeper, were among the supporters of the high school. Moreover, most of the businessmen who lived in the Grammar and South districts supported the high school as did most of the wealthiest ones. Throughout the town the vote of the artisans was split, but those who lived in the Grammar and South districts and those with children generally favored the high school. The wealth of the town was clearly on the side of the high school. Those who opposed aboli-tion had an average personal estate, real estate, and total estate much higher than those who favored it. Of those in the top category for each kind of valuation, over $5,000, high school supporters predominated. Sixteen of 26 with real estate in this category, 18 of 24 with personal estate, and 33 of 49 with total estate were among those who stood out against the abolition of the high school.

Most of the men who favored abolition lived in the outlying dis-tricts, which were sparsely populated. The Cove district, where only 5 out of 57 voters supported the high school, was the only district un-touched by the railroad. Moreover, those in the least prestigious occu-pational categories were as solidly opposed to the high school as the prominent were in favor. Voting to abolish were 37 of the 44 farmers, 80 of the 109 shoemakers, 21 of the 24 mariners and fishermen, and all 10 laborers. The businessmen who opposed the high school generally had less wealth than the ones who supported it, and more lived in the outlying districts. As for the artisans, fewer of the ones who voted for abolition had children of school age than did those who supported the high school. Indeed, dependency was an important characteristic. Of 171 voters with no children of school age, 120 voted to abolish the high school. However, no significant differences existed between groups of voters in number of children of high school age or in number of teen-age children attending school. Finally, the people who voted to abolish the high school were the least wealthy on every measure. Not only that, but the distribution of the wealth they did have was different. Whereas those who supported the high school generally had an estate balanced fairly evenly between real and personal property, those who voted for abolition had more valuable real than personal holdings. That is, opposition to the high school came not only from the least wealthy but also from those whose holdings in land and buildings exceeded their personal property.

None of these characteristics, of course, is truly independent of the others. Yet there were two sorts of dominant groupings in the vote on the high school issue. First of all, people with no school-age children were protesting the continuation of an institution that increased their tax bill. Beyond this was a clear social division that encompassed many, though not all, the voters. Those in prestigious occupations and those most wealthy were supporting an innovating addition to the educational system, even though they were the ones who would pay the highest taxes. Opposition came from the working class: fishermen, farmers, shoemakers, and laborers. These groups were almost as unanimously opposed to the high school as the former were in favor. A third important element was the business and artisan groups among which few differences in wealth could be discerned. In fact, it was again the wealthier businessmen, who would be more highly taxed, who voted more often for the high school. For the business and artisan groups, concerns other than taxation probably were important. The association between vote and residence provides a clue here since these people were engaged in retail work; they were dependent upon their neighbors for a livelihood, and it is reasonable to infer that both the prejudices of their neighborhood and the desire to avoid offending customers were relevant factors in their vote.

Still, we must ask, were there other reasons for these more middle-class townsmen to support the high school? Indeed, the explanation of the vote to abolish Beverly High School is far from clear. Opposition did not come from vested interests, and it came only partly from the traditional bane of educational innovators, parsimonious people with no children of school age. Why did the wealthy and prestigious favor a high school? Why did the working class oppose? . . . To begin the inquiry, a closer look at an individual supporter of Beverly High School helps refine our questions.

One of the most prominent high school promoters in Beverly was Robert Rantoul, Sr. His son, Robert Rantoul, was the famous Democratic senator who helped found the Free Soil Party and whose early, tragic death evoked an ode from Whittier. Rantoul, Sr., was one of the first citizens of both Beverly and Massachusetts. Born in 1778 in Salem, Rantoul was the son of a Scottish immigrant drowned at sea when his son was still quite young. In spite of severe financial difficulties Rantoul attended, successively, a dame school, a private writing school, the town grammar school, and, occasionally, a Latin school. At the age of fourteen he left school and was apprenticed to a doctor-apothecary. Rantoul, a quick learner, was soon managing the shop; and his successful experience enabled him to raise the money to buy a vacant apothecary shop in Beverly when he was but seventeen and a half years old. Rantoul continued his success as an apothecary and began his rise to eminence as a local merchant. Most likely with an eye toward his political future, Rantoul by himself studied law and learned enough to practice and to become a local judge. He signified his arrival at the top of Beverly society by providing his son with one of the most prestigious educations Massachusetts could offer. Robert Rantoul, Jr., attended Phillips Andover Academy and upon graduation in 1820 entered

Harvard College. Another sign of Rantoul's social arrival was his prominent position in important town financial ventures. He was founder of the Marine Insurance Company in Beverly and an active director of the local bank. These activities, as well as a legacy including a complete set of *Hunt's Merchants Magazine*, indicate that Rantoul was a promoter. The extent of Rantoul's holdings and his involvement with commercial life and industrial development are revealed by his estate. Rantoul left $16,350 in real estate and $28,326.45 in personal estate. His stock holdings were distributed among railroads, steam cotton mills, turnpikes, banks, and insurance companies. The uncollected debts he left indicate that he was also a moneylender, and the bequeathed rents on a number of properties show that he was likewise a realtor.

Rantoul's public speeches and private writings offer no clue that he was a promoter; rather they are designed, it would seem deliberately, to present a rather different impression. To Rantoul no value deserved more attention than social unity; nothing was more repugnant than communal conflict. Throughout his speeches and his autobiography runs a real longing for a truly unified society, which he locates somewhere in the past. When Rantoul lectured on "economy" at the Lyceum in 1835, he stressed that he would say "nothing to encourage that miserable spirit of envy and jealousy, which finds its highest gratification in planting and fostering the most bitter feelings of opposition and hatred between those in the different classes into which society is divided." Instead, he stressed "mutual dependence." Elsewhere he commented with nostalgic regret on the demise of voluntary fire fighting, which had provided a "favorable influence upon the mass of the community, provoking a generous desire to aid one another by personal efforts and sacrifices." Unfortunately, the termination of voluntary fire fighting represented one phase of a misguided "lessening of sympathy for our fellow beings." Similarly, the high point in the history of Beverly, according to Rantoul, was the united community action in response to an 1832 cholera threat, united action that would not have been possible, he lamented, a few years later.

Other observers noted the earlier social unity in Beverly. Historian Joseph Ober saw harmony as a product of kinship and portrayed Beverly as a large family, almost a clan. Throughout generations the people of Beverly "had contentedly tilled the soil and ploughed the sea, leaving their ancestral homes only to participate in the business affairs of the town or when summoned by the imperative calls of war." Intermarriage had united the people in the different sections of the town, and they "were individually members of one and the same great family; their interests and their traditions were identical." Edwin Stone, another historian, noted in 1842 that lawyers in Beverly found it impossible to make a living by fees alone. A "distinguished member of the Essex bar," he wrote, had remarked "as a singular fact in his experience, that during a practice of nearly forty years, he had never known a native of Beverly convicted of any heinous crime."

To Ober, the destroyer of the happy family was the summer boarder, whose arrival with the railroad around 1840 introduced a "new element" into the town. As for Stone's comments on the law-abiding nature of Beverly citizens: among the seventy-nine arrests in the town during 1864, one was for murder, seventeen were for assault, eighteen for larceny, one for keeping a "disorderly house," and two for "night walking." Two, likewise, were of "stubborn children"; four were for adultery. In 1863 the newspaper reported with horror that one Stackpole, an example of the "fast young men" who infested the town, had killed his sister and attempted to murder his parents. Nor were the recent immigrants always placid, as indicated by the town paper's disgusted account of the stabbing of one Irishman by another on Water Street.

Rantoul perceptively connected the demise of social unity with the changes that were overtaking the commonwealth and the town of Beverly. "The introduction of shoemaking as a general employment" had "gradually changed the habits, manners and morals of the mass—from a fishing, sea-faring and farming population" into "a manufacturing population in the main." Farming, Rantoul told a local audience, was better than trade as an occupation. In itself mercantile life, the distribution of products and luxuries over a wider area, was a fine activity; but, unfortunately, trade had some unlovely aspects: "too many mean artifices and tricks, too much overreaching and even gross atrocious frauds, and a reckless sacrifice of health, morals, comfort and of the vast number of lives . . ." On the whole then, agriculture provided a better life than trading. Massachusetts soil was not the most fertile, but "labor, intelligently and skillfully applied in the cultivation of the ground," offered an "ample reward." No farmer could grow as rich as a merchant or a manufacturer; there was no hope of sudden or spectacular accumulation; but an "active and industrious" man would obtain a "comfortable subsistence" and have a bit left over. And how much superior was the idyllic life on the farm to the uncertainties and questionable morality of trade. It was unfortunate that the country had suffered already from the "large and disproportionate number . . . withdrawn from the laborious and productive classes in rural life, to engage in the unproductive pursuits of trade . . ." Thus spoke Robert Rantoul, merchant, lawyer, promoter: a man who never was a farmer, who grew up in a city, who directed a bank, who sent neither son nor grandson to a farm, who subscribed faithfully to that agent of the mercantile spirit, *Hunt's Merchants Magazine*.

In 1854 Robert Rantoul formally retired from town affairs. But three years later he returned to the annual spring town meeting. One purpose, claimed the aging patriarch, was to bid farewell and thanks to the townspeople; the other was to speak in favor of the proposed town high school. In his nearly completed autobiography Rantoul commented, "This subject I deem to be very important and have come to speak and vote in favor of such a school. I spoke at some length but by the result of the vote with very little effect as there was a large majority against the measure." Yet, some citizens drew up an indictment against the town for not complying with the state law requiring towns of its size to have a high school. This action precipitated another town meeting. Again Rantoul attended; this, however, was the last time. By his side were his grandsons, who also argued for the high school. One grandson was Robert S. Rantoul, a lawyer, later president of the Essex Institute. In his papers exist the fragments of a speech listing citations of court cases, which were apparently chosen to show the town that the law was clearly on the side of the state. Surely, he must have told the townspeople, they would lose the ensuing legal battle if they persisted in their defiance. The high school, started in 1858, was abolished in 1860; by then Rantoul was dead, but one of those who stood out against its destruction was the wealthy druggist, William Endicott, one of the grandsons who had been at Rantoul's side in 1857.

Why did Rantoul support a high school? Is there a relation between his activities as a promoter, his longing for social harmony, his disingenuous or incongruous remarks on the virtues of farm life and his activity on behalf of education, especially a high school? Rantoul left no direct answers to these questions, but his perception of his society and the values he extolled were representative of leading schoolmen and high school promoters throughout the state. . . .

Recall that in Beverly the citizens of least wealth and least occupational prestige successfully opposed the high school. Recall, too, that the high school was strongly supported by those at the other end of the social and economic scale. The supporters used arguments similar to those expounded by high school promoters around the state. The opponents were, to understate the case, less vocal, at least in print. The least affluent citizens of Beverly recorded their opposition to the high school in votes, not in words. No record of their reasons for opposing the persuasive rhetoric of promoters exists. Yet good reasons for opposition can be inferred from a consideration of their social and economic situation. The abolition of Beverly high school occurred amidst the greatest social crisis in the history of the town. In the same week that they voted four to one to abolish the high school, the shoemakers of Beverly, the dominant occupational group in the town, went on strike, and so did thousands of other shoemakers in Essex County. The walk-out by Essex County shoemakers in 1860 was the largest strike in the United States before the Civil War.

Beverly had been a small and homogeneous community until the advent of the railroad in 1840. From the 1840's through the mid-1850's a number of manufacturing enterprises started in the town. The industries were of various types, and it seemed as though Beverly would turn into a small but diversified manufacturing center. During the depression of 1857, however, many of the new, small industries with little capital failed, never to revive. Equally good harbors and better facilities for manufacturing, such as water power for mills, existed elsewhere in Massachusetts. Only for the shoe industry, which it could supply with many skilled workers, did Beverly provide an attractive outlet for capital. . . .

As Beverly developed into a one-industry town it experienced the grave social consequences that accompanied the transformation of shoemaking. It was in the 1850's and 1860's that shoemaking became mechanized. Factory production replaced the skilled craftsman. Technological change hit shoemakers with the impact of modern day automation. With the introduction of machines the number of shoes manufactured per shoemaker rose rapidly, and the increased output soon exceeded the demands of the market. As apprenticeship ceased to be necessary, manufacturers hired unskilled, untrained workers who swelled the ranks of shoemakers to overflowing. Overproduction and a plethora of workmen produced a crisis in the industry, and the price of shoes declined drastically. In this situation, manufacturers introduced a sizable pay cut, and the shoemakers struck.

The shoemakers of Beverly left no written records, and the timid town newspaper tried to pretend that the strike did not exist. To find the attitude of the strikers one must turn to Lynn newspapers. In both places shoemaking dominated the economy, and it is reasonable to assume that within the same county technological developments were closely paralleled from town to town. Moreover, within the area that serviced the Boston market prices would be similar. One can assume that the attitude of the Lynn shoemakers was shared by the hundreds of their colleagues who struck in Beverly, and it is the attitude of the strikers that is important, because this reveals the social gulf that widened with industrialization and contributed to the abolition of Beverly high school.

Articles in pro-strike papers stressed other than strictly economic grievances. One writer proclaimed to the mechanics of Lynn that "those occupying a position in society different from yours . . . have wantonly and ill-advisedly insulted all that is manly in your breasts"; and in a very real sense the strike was about manliness, about the preservation of honor. Another writer delineated the grievances of the strikers: the tensions and opinions engendered by the strike were "the unerring indications of a social wrong, felt to be such by the whole community, yet so interwoven with our social condition that its reform has become the most perplexing problem of the age." The "wrong" was the increase in both the inequality of the distribution of wealth and the loss of independence by the artisans. "Great fortunes" were being concentrated "under the control of a few manufacturers" in Lynn while "hundreds of workmen" were "gradually crowded from the in-dependent positions they formerly occupied." Shoemakers, noted the writer, were "men of more or less means." In fact, as a group they probably owned more property than the manufacturers; clearly this was no strike of a proletariat. But shoemakers were being compelled to re-linquish "the luxuries, next the conveniences, and finally the necessar-ies of life."

Two consequences stemmed from the deterioration in their posi-tion: while the country became richer, the shoemakers became poorer; and they were progressively unable to take advantage of the new ed-ucational and communal facilities being introduced. "We have better streets, better schools, and more wholesome sanitary regulations," one article declared, "but we do not get an education commensurate with the increase of our facilities." Children were being "removed from school two or three years too early," and an alarming "number of young men and women" were sinking "into early graves." Why? The writer re-jected the thesis that shoemakers removed children from school through cupidity: For every parent who took a boy of thirteen from school for selfish reasons, a hundred did so from necessity. "The parent finds the expenses of his household constantly increasing, while the wages of his labor are steadily diminishing," and he has no choice but to submit to that which he considers a wrong to his family. But in the wonderful, inventive nineteenth century, "to say that such a thing is either right or necessary, is a libel upon the age." The promise of industrialization was being betrayed; "the benefits resulting from a proper division of labor and the application of machinery [were] monopolized by the few, instead of being diffused in just proportions." The author stressed, in his conclusion, not the drop in wages, but the tendency "plainly to break down the independence of the laborer, and to abridge the var-ious sources of his social enjoyment."

The protest of the shoemakers was an agonized remonstrance against the loss of personal and financial independence, and indeed, of a whole way of life. One old shoemaker, according to the editor of the pro-strike paper, perfectly summed up the issue of the strike in a single phrase: "Once it was *honorable* to labor, now it is a disgrace." The great Essex County shoe strike was a last protest against the modern world of the machine and factory. To a certain extent the shoemakers shared the ambivalence of educational promoters. They saw the promise of a better life in the machine and in the process of social change occurring around them. Yet they, especially, felt the hard consequences of mechanization, and it is likely that they swiftly became less ambivalent, that in their minds the machine became tarnished to an extent never shared by promoters like the Rantouls. . . .

Thus, the shoemakers who voted against Beverly High School had a rather different orientation from the Rantouls. . . . For the core of opposition to Beverly High School the future was not promising. The shoemakers were the propertied, once moderately comfortable and independent group whose life was being altered by technological development. For the shoemaker the past, certainly, was better than the ominous future. And it was an urban-industrial future, precisely, that the high school was supposed to promote. In Beverly, Rufus Putnam among others had spread the doctrine, prevalent also throughout the state, that the high school would promote economic development. If this were true, if the shoemaker accepted the logic of the educational promoter, then the last institution he would want to establish would be a public high school. Moreover, to property owners whose incomes had been reduced, as many shoemakers' were, any proposal that would raise taxes would hardly be appealing. Besides, to what avail was the democratic argument . . . ? The high school might be there, but, as the shoemaker in Lynn pointed out, modern economic conditions were so hard that children were forced to begin work precisely at the age when they could benefit from a high school.

Farmers, too, probably would be moved by some of these arguments. For them the advance of industrial society offered little but a lure to their children. As Rantoul observed, more and more boys were leaving the parental farm for the city. The decided weighting of high school opponents' property toward real estate rather than personal estate symbolized their roots in a community being torn apart by the forces backed by the supporters. The high school issue brought into focus the different orientations toward social development within a nineteenth century New England town.

At the time of the high school vote the shoemakers in particular were hostile to the representatives of the manufacturing and commercial interests, who had lowered wages. Yet the tradition of machine breaking and direct physical assault, prominent in other countries, did not spread to America in this period. In voting to abolish the high school, a favorite innovation of their antagonists, the shoemakers had an opportunity to vent their anger in a perfectly legal way. The shoemakers, it has been argued, and most likely other groups of little wealth as well, were hardly enthusiastic about the social and economic alteration taking place around them. But industrialization is a diffuse antagonist; it is hard to assault directly. The high school, explicitly billed as the harbinger of manufacturing and urban growth, was a convenient issue to attack.

For three reasons, then, the Beverly citizens voted to abolish the high school: first, people, those without children especially, protested the raising of taxes; second, the least affluent citizens felt that the high school would not benefit their children; third, they were hostile both to the wealthy leaders of the town and to the onset of industrialism. The educational promoters, who were by and large the wealthy and prominent citizens, failed to preserve the high school because they advanced arguments unacceptable to the less prosperous citizens and because they overestimated their own powers of leadership. The supporters based their pro–high school arguments on mobility and economic growth; what they failed to see was that their own values were not shared by the entire community. The promoters who stressed mobility and wealth as products of education appealed to exactly the wrong values in terms of an outlook skeptical of progress. A strike was some evidence of social division. More subtle, but more devastating, was the community leaders' failure to perceive the weakness in their own rhetoric and the limits of their prestige and power. Their probable assumption that the rest of the town would docilely follow their advice was rudely disproven. In the first week of May 1860, the shoemakers of Beverly staged a dual revolt against these communal leaders. They struck, literally, at the source of their income, and they rejected their favorite educational innovation.

The underlying cause of both the establishment and abolition of Beverly High School was the shifting economic base and the consequent social division in both the town and the state. It was to keep pace with these changes that promoters urged an extended educational system; it was to assure opportunity for the individual within an altered economy that the high school was argued; it was to reunite a splintering community that a high school was necessary. The unraveling of the social fabric that accompanied the growth of a manufacturing economy heightened the distance between the members of the community; it produced the decaying economic position of craftsmen and became the source of the antagonisms that finally erupted in the great shoe strike and the abolition of the high school.

How typical was the Beverly experience? Can we generalize from it about educational controversy throughout the state of Massachusetts? The geographic location of Beverly on the coast and its dependence upon one industry are factors that make it somewhat distinctive. Nevertheless, the underlying causes of communal dissension, the impact of the introduction of manufacturing upon society, occurred throughout the state, often with more swiftness than in Beverly. Attitudes toward social change were shared by educational reformers throughout Massachusetts. Everywhere the high school was urged for the same reasons. The problems raised by industrialism, too, were similar. Not only the large body of shoemakers but the hand-loom weavers and other craftsmen were affected adversely by the coming of the factory and machine. The tensions that erupted in Beverly were inherent throughout most of the towns in the commonwealth. Because of a conjunction of circumstances they became particularly visible in Beverly in March 1860. The events in Beverly formed one of those moments that illuminate for the historian widespread smoldering controversies. The nature of the controversy in Beverly, moreover, suggests that the identification of antagonists by older historians was essentially correct. In spite of the predictable and continuing parsimony of childless taxpayers and the mixed reaction of certain middling social groups, two distinct clusters of antagonists emerge: prominent, prestigious leaders and a working class. But the antagonists' attitudes defined by older historians must be reversed: the Beverly experience reveals that one dynamic of educational controversy was the attempt of social leaders to impose innovation upon a reluctant working class.

Predictably, the high schools forced upon reluctant towns met many problems. During the first few years after the founding of a high school committees usually reported euphorically on the achievements of the new institution, but after a time difficulties generally arose. By itself, separation from younger children failed to make the older ones more obedient, and discipline was frequently a serious problem within the high school. Attendance and tardiness were two issues related to the problem of discipline. Indeed, irregular attendance and truancy were the most persistent and common complaints of school committees, and, in some towns, the worst offenders were high school students.

School communities were virtually obsessed with the problems of punctual and regular attendance. It is not unreasonable to assume that these concerns were based on real problems. However, the concern with time and reliability implies that schools were to serve the new society in part by producing those habits particularly needed in the work force and in an urban population. A writer in the *Massachusetts Teacher* asserted:

> That the habit of prompt action in the performance of the duty required of the boy, by the teacher at school, becomes in the man of business confirmed; thus system and order characterize the employment of the day laborer. He must begin each half day with as much promptness as he drops his tools at the close of it; and he must meet every appointment and order during the hours of the day with no less precision. It is in this way that regularity and economy of time have become characteristic of our community, as appears in the running 'on time' of long trains on our great network of railways; the strict regulations of all large manufacturing establishments; as well as the daily arrangements of our school duties . . . Thus, what has been instilled in the mind of the pupil, as a principle, becomes thoroughly recognized by the man as of the first importance in the transaction of business.

Indeed, the problem of transforming agrarian habits in which precision and promptness are less emphasized into the traits necessary to conduct city life and large scale manufacturing is characteristic of urbanizing and industrializing societies. Without regular and prompt attention neither the city and factory nor the school can function adequately. Industrialists explicitly recognized that the school served as a means of disciplining the work force. This was patently, sometimes even crudely, clear in the responses that Mann and Boutwell received in 1841 and 1859 to circulars questioning manufacturers on the value they saw in educated labor. Two examples make this evident. From Lowell in 1841 H. Bartlett, who had "been engaged, for nearly ten years, in manufacturing, and . . . had the constant charge of from 400 to 900 persons," replied in part: "I have never considered mere knowledge . . . as the only advantage derived from a good Common School education." Workers with more education possessed "a higher and better state of morals, [were] more orderly and respectful in their deportment, and more ready to comply with the wholesome and necessary regulations of an establishment." Perhaps most important, "in times of agitation, on account of some change in regulations or wages, I have always looked to the most intelligent, best educated and the most moral for support." On the other hand, "the ignorant and uneducated I have generally found the most turbulent and troublesome, acting under the impulse of excited passion and jealousy." Similarly, in 1859 William B. Whiting, who had entered a cotton mill at the age of eleven and had, over a thirty-year period, worked his way upward, wrote that the educated always try, "by diligence and a willing acquiescence in necessary regulations, to merit the good opinion of their employers and the community"; they "secure . . . by the same means, the respect and confidence of their fellows," and "oftentimes exert a conservative influence in periods of excitement of great value pecuniarily and morally." The educated, in short, were seen as company men.

Some school communities also had a problem rather different from irregular attendance. Many parents applied steady pressure to the committees to lower the entrance requirements for high schools, thus threatening the standards of the new schools. Parents mobilized personal influence and pressure against the committees; in sociological terms they were emphasizing ascribed rather than achieved qualities, and it was precisely this emphasis that schoolmen were trying to eliminate from the educational system. Likewise, complaints about the unfair advantages academies offered children of the wealthy and complaints about the hiring of unqualified friends and relatives as teachers were protests against rewards based on ascription rather than achievement. The ideal school system was graded, promotions were equally open to all solely on the basis of merit, teachers were hired for their professional qualifications; this ideal school system reflected a belief that status based on achievement should pervade society. In a rural, agricultural society labor is divided within the family; for the most part jobs require little special skills and formal training; responsibility is based largely on age; the social hierarchy rests mainly on custom; and few pressures force an alteration of traditional attitudes. In such a society ascription forms a relatively powerful criterion for the assignment of status. Industrialization, on the other hand, dissolves the traditional social fabric; many tasks become highly specialized and technical competence becomes of paramount importance. To cope adequately with its business an industrial, urban society must award relative priority to achieved rather than ascribed qualities. Achievement is of course a fundamental criterion for reward in democratic theory, but the stress on achievement in this period is particularly significant. The transition of the state from an agricultural-commercial to an industrial economy required a corresponding shift in the basis of social valuation. By trying to institutionalize achieved status through public education and to indoctrinate parents with its virtues, schoolmen again were facilitating economic change through the transformation of social attitudes.

The virtues that education promoters attached to schooling apparently did not appeal to the people as much as they had hoped. In the mid-sixties school committees were still complaining of a parental apathy that resisted the efforts and achievements of educational reformers. The Groton school committee, for one, virtually confessed failure. Public interest in education had not increased, and how the school could be maintained without this enthusiasm and support was uncertain.

In fact, the high school was failing to serve the community in the ways its advocates had predicted. Promoters had emphasized that the high school would promote social mobility, unify and civilize communities, awaken and sustain a community-wide interest in education, and raise the value of real estate. In reality, the high school did none of these things: the statistical analysis, the facts of high school attendance, the developments in Beverly and Groton, and the complaints of schoolmen all make this clear. Only a minority of the children in a community, and those mainly from the more well-to-do sectors, attended the high school. The high school could not serve as a means of boosting many poor children up the economic ladder.

The high school was, however, relevant to the mobility of middle-class children. For middle-class boys the high school probably served as both a means of status maintenance and an entree into the business world. Information in school registers has been found concerning thirteen boys who left Somerville High School between 1856 and 1860. Of these, eight became clerks, two entered business, and three became apprentices. For all but one of the apprentices the jobs represented an occupation different from that of their fathers, who with the exception of three businessmen were artisans and farmers. These seven, sons of artisans and farmers, very likely saw the high school as a way of helping to retain a middle-class status at a time when mechanization and other economic alterations made the future of their fathers' occupations less secure. They may have hoped, as well, that through business they could rise above the social level of their parents.

The high school also had obvious uses for middle-class girls, and substantially more girls than boys attended. The high schools usually offered preparation for teaching; and teaching was undoubtedly the most attractive vocational goal for the middle-class girl who wanted to earn some money because all the other occupations populated by large numbers of females were manual, arduous, and decidedly lower-class. According to the state census of 1865, the largest number of employed females, 27,393, were domestics; next came operatives (meaning factory workers), 20,152; third came teachers, 6,050. Other groups of more than one thousand females were, in order of size, seamstresses, shoe workers, tailoresses, dressmakers, straw and palm leaf workers, milliners, laundresses, nurses, and clerks. The middle-class girl who wanted to work at something respectable had little choice; teaching it almost had to be. For girls who had no intention of becoming gainfully employed the high school must have offered a relatively painless way of passing the time until they came of marrying age.

Thus, the fable that the high school served the entire community was naturally attractive to middle-class parents because it justified having the entire community support an institution most useful to the middle-class. Through the high school they could spread among the population at large the burden of educating their children. The ideology of communal benefit served wealthy groups well too. Prosperous parents, owners of successful businesses for instance, may have been moved by the same concerns as the Boston merchants. For them the high school would provide a fine way of occupying their sons during the years of adolescence when an extended apprenticeship was no longer necessary. Moreover, the most articulate spokesmen for high schools, often also economic promoters, were deeply ambivalent toward the society for which they were responsible; and they sought innovations that would simultaneously promote economic growth and prevent the consequences that industrialism had brought in other societies, especially England. The high school was an ideal innovation because it would allegedly serve both these ends. Promoters' attachment to this ideology gave them a good psychic reason for avoiding a confrontation with the actual facts of high school attendance and with the impact of a drive for educational innovation upon a community. To have admitted the disparity between theory and actuality would have raised too many haunting questions, too many doubts about the real nature of the promoters' own impact upon society.

To recognize that the high school did not meet its goals, to suggest the functions that it did in fact serve is not to explain *why* it failed or where reform went wrong. Obviously, the ideology of reform was confused, since it simultaneously advocated and damned urban, industrial society. The two sides of the ideology offered a set of highly incompatible goals. Nevertheless, reformers might have argued that it was the obstacles within old towns rather than the incompatibility of their goals that had frustrated their efforts. If only they could have a chance to build a system from scratch, then they might produce the small city on a hill of which American communal leaders had dreamed since the seventeenth century. The opportunity of constructing a school system in a new town would provide a test case for the viability of reform theory.

*Richmond, Virginia, in 1856, the scene of a widespread
bread riot during the Civil War.*

Harlots or Heroines? A New Look at the Richmond Bread Riot

MICHAEL B. CHESSON

The Civil War drastically altered the normal circumstances of daily life in the South, where most of the fighting took place. Between 700,000 and 800,000 southern men left families and farms to fight with the Confederate army and navy. As a consequence, large numbers of yeoman families who lost husbands and fathers to the military slipped for the first time into the ranks of the dependent poor. Destitute of able-bodied men and unable to subsist in rural areas, thousands of women and children streamed into the southern cities. Along with war refugees and camp followers they swelled the urban populations. Richmond, which became the administrative center of the Confederacy, saw its population increase two and a half times during the war.

In the first year of the war the North attempted to choke the Confederacy into submission with a naval blockade of southern ports. That strategy effectively created shortages of such common foodstuffs as salt, sugar, and coffee. Speculators and "forestallers" made matters worse by hoarding supplies and waiting for prices to be driven up by the artificial scarcity. Shortages and speculation led to runaway inflation, which increased prices for the basic necessities by 7,000 percent during the war.

In view of government inaction and spiraling prices, it is not surprising that wartime consumers in southern towns and cities regularly turned to violence to secure the basic necessities of life. These protests commonly took the form of bread or food riots. In the next selection, Michael Chesson writes about one of the largest and best organized bread riots of the war, fomented by women in the capital city of Richmond on April 2, 1863. By analyzing this traditional form of civilian violence, Chesson provides a fascinating look at the conditions of daily life in wartime Richmond. He seeks answers to what caused the riot, who participated, what the official response was, and what was significant about this women's riot in the Confederate capital. This one episode during the Civil War makes clear that wartime existence was no more glorious on the home front than in the front lines.

April 1, 1863, occurred in Richmond what is commonly called the 'bread riot'. . . . The incidents of this remarkable affair have never yet been written up in truly historical style, though they deserve to be. . . ."

"It remains for the historian or some one gifted in examining and weighing testimony to sift a clear and connected account of the mass of contradictory evidence."

So wrote the editors of the Richmond *Dispatch* in 1888 of the wartime disturbance, also known as the Holy Thursday or "woman's riot," which had occurred in the Confederate capital twenty-five years before. As if to illustrate the difficulty of writing accurately about this colorful Civil War episode, the careful editors of nineteenth-century Richmond's largest paper erred twice in placing the riot on April Fools' Day, an all too appropriate date. It actually took place on 2 April 1863, the day following the city elections. Newspaper editors were getting the date wrong as early as the next year, when the *Sentinel* of 1 March 1864 referred to the riot "on May last." . . .

[The historian] Emory Thomas has called the Richmond incident "the best case study of the results of Southern food supply problems" and suggested that it and various other food disturbances had a larger importance. But the bread riot has usually been treated as merely a dramatic, or even comic event, a sort of Civil War gate porter's scene, and certainly a useful interlude in summaries of military and political events. Bruce Catton felt that the bread riot "meant nothing in particular." This casual attitude may explain why so many errors have been made in writing about it. Perhaps the bread riot should not be so lightly dismissed. It may be worth a careful reexamination, even though it does not feature posturing generals and charging troops, but merely a crowd of protesting women.

The riot in Richmond was only one, albeit the largest and most important, of more than a dozen similar food riots that occurred in cities and towns throughout the South. Ironically, there is general agreement about the causes of the riot. It has usually been attributed to wartime inflation and a lack of adequate food supplies at fair prices. Extensive military operations around Richmond in the previous year

HARLOTS OR HEROINES?   From *Virginia Magazine of History and Biography*, vol. 92 (April 1984). Reprinted by permission of the Virginia Historical Society.

had disrupted agricultural production, yet the city's swollen population needed even more food. In order to supply Confederate armies,
commissary agents often impressed the provisions that farmers sent to
Richmond's markets during the winter of 1862–63. Fearing seizure by
the government without compensation at fair market value, some
growers withheld their meat and produce. The greater demand for food
pushed up the price of what little was available, leading to hoarding
and speculation. It became increasingly difficult to buy sufficient amounts
of food with Confederate money. The salaries of most Richmonders
did not keep pace with inflation. Many women with men in the army
were struggling to support families on one income, if indeed they were
fortunate enough to have jobs. During 19–21 March 1863, Richmond
received at least a foot of snow, not the nine inches found in most
accounts. It quickly melted, making roads already damaged by heavy
military use impassable and adding another obstacle for farmers and
hucksters trying to reach the city markets. Local observers like Robert
Garlick Hill Kean and John B. Jones noted signs of famine in the following week.

That a bread riot followed this series of events should surprise no
one, and the above account would seem a plausible explanation of the
event. Yet it does not explain why the riot took place when it did, for
similar circumstances prevailed in Richmond throughout the war and
conditions worsened after 1863. Nor does it explain why there was no
repetition of the riot.

There are other reasons for the mob that April morning, some of
them major, some merely further irritants to a disgruntled population.
On 13 March 1863, there was an explosion at the Confederate ordnance
laboratory, in which sixty-nine were killed, sixty-two of them women,
mostly of the poorest working class. At least one possible widower
from this accident, Bennet G. Burley, was charged with rioting, two
weeks before the body of Mrs. Martha A. Burley was finally found in
a millrace. At the end of March the city waterworks broke down because of a flood from melting snow that damaged the pumps. Much of
the city's working class, accustomed to public hydrants, was now dependent on an ancient well in Capitol Square or on the river itself at
great inconvenience to themselves.

The riot should be placed in the larger context of social conditions
in wartime Richmond. What happened on the day of 2 April 1863 was
not very much different from what took place on a smaller and less
organized scale almost every night of the war. Crime of all kinds increased with the unprecedented growth of the city's population. Bur-
glaries and other robberies were commonplace. On the day of the riot
the Richmond *Sentinel* reported the recovery of goods stolen from the
store of Samuel C. Greenhow several days earlier, including 625 pounds
of bacon, 77 pounds of sugar, 85 pounds of tea, 48 pounds of coffee,

and a box of candles, a cargo that any rioter would have proudly claimed. A month later, again at night, the store of J. B. Watkins was robbed of $500 in groceries, a trifling sum in wartime prices, but the comment of the *Sentinel*'s editor is significant: "The frequency of these robberies renders extreme caution necessary on the part of the citizens, for the police of the city seem powerless to prevent their recurrence." In fact, the day police force of eleven officers and a seventy-two-man night watch were hardly adequate for a city whose population has been variously estimated, but which was almost certainly well above 100,000, several times larger than it had been in 1860.

The bread riot was only the most open and obvious sign up to that point of the breakdown of social stability, restraints, and law enforcement. Young women were reported more than once stealing flowers from Confederate graves in the spring of 1863. Rock battles between rival gangs of boys were common in Shockoe Valley, in Capitol Square, and on the city's streets; occasionally adult pedestrians were injured by flying stones. Under the circumstances, the absence of beggars, noted on several occasions by J. B. Jones, is remarkable.

The issue of beggars is related to the extent of poverty in Richmond, the degree to which the authorities had sought to relieve hunger, and the psychology of many who were on the edge of something they were too polite to call starvation. Petulant statements were made after the riot by President Jefferson Davis, Gov. John Letcher, Mayor Joseph Mayo, members of the common council, William Willis, Jr., president of the Richmond Young Men's Christian Association, and the editors of the *Examiner* to the effect that there was sufficient food in the city to supply the needy, that is, the deserving poor. Indeed, the city had appropriated funds for such aid, and only part of it had been used at the time of the riot. Officials apparently had difficulty understanding the reluctance of those in need to rely on charity, just as modern historians have failed in understanding the mentality of people, unaccustomed to a welfare system, who would riot but were too proud to beg. Many rioters wanted only to be able to purchase adequate amounts of food at reasonable prices. Unable to do that, they seized not only food but many other items during the riot, but they had no desire for government handouts until the dole became their only alternative. The dishonest stole what they wanted, before and after the riot, as well as during it; those who had never before had to rely on charity resisted begging, whether from individuals or institutions.

The exact timing of the Richmond bread riot, as distinct from other causes, is probably related to disturbances elsewhere in the Confederacy. Historians have long recognized that similar food riots occurred in other Southern cities, before and after Richmond. Douglas O. Tice, in the best extant article on the subject, is notable for emphasizing the sequence of a series of similar events in the two weeks before the Richmond riot. A food riot occurred in Atlanta on 16 March 1863, followed by a flour riot in Salisbury, North Carolina, 18 March, on one of the main rail links between Virginia and the lower South. There was trouble in Mobile on 25 March and at High Point, and possibly in the vicinity of Raleigh, in North Carolina about the same time. In Petersburg, minutes away from Richmond by train, there was a bread riot on 1 April. Most of these events had been reported in local papers. On 4 April the *Examiner* referred to several of them and to its earlier accounts in its famous description of the riot. On 27 March the paper had reported the flour riot in Salisbury, with words of approval for soldiers' wives who had raided speculators there. The paper's favorable treatment of the Tar Heel women may well have encouraged those in Richmond, as suggested by Tice.

But the *Examiner*'s explanation of the event closest to home, whether inspired by the Davis government or not . . ., was that Northern agitators had made their way to Richmond after causing disturbances further south. In one sense, this outside agitator theory is absurd, and no evidence has been found to support it by scholars like James Ford Rhodes and others. But wartime Richmond had become a city of strangers and camp followers, some with criminal intent. Many were war refugees, including farm families displaced from their homes and unused to city life under the best of conditions. Others were workers from the Federal armory at Harpers Ferry, who with their families had sought jobs at the new Confederate armory in Richmond. Such people found reasons enough to riot without being agents of the Union. And some of them, true to the pattern of European riots described by George Rudé, knew of the disturbances elsewhere, just as did Jefferson Davis. By their own testimony, a number of the women who were arrested for rioting thought their actions quasi-legal, justified by circumstances. Rioters in every time and place, from the food riots in France to the political riots of Great Britain and the impressment riots of Jack Tar in colonial America, as well as those of our own more recent past, have felt the same way.

The *Examiner*'s portrayal of the rioters as "highway robbers . . . and a mob of idlers" recalls the "idle rogues" of seventeenth-century England and Virginia. There is just enough truth in this colorful picture to make it credible, if only because the *Examiner* drew it so often. Its editors managed to combine class prejudice with ethnic, sectional, and sexist slurs in describing the rioters as criminals, prostitutes, Yankees, and foreigners, who were also physically unappealing as women. Ideally, scholars will learn as much as they can about the participants in a historical event. Social and quantitative historians, using the manuscript census, tax records, city directories, and other sources, will carefully attempt to define and to identify a group that is representative of a larger population. But this admirable technique is somewhat more difficult to use when studying "the crowd in history." The historian cannot always be certain that the police have arrested a representative sample of a mob. Something like the ideal may have happened in the far larger draft riots in New York City a few months later, but in Richmond, as in many riots, it was probably the leaders, the greedy, the unlucky, and the slow-of-foot who were apprehended. A good deal is known about a few of the leaders; the *Examiner* and eventually other papers reported at least some details about many of the several dozens who were arrested. Unfortunately, it is impossible to conclude much about the proportion or the representativeness of this sample because the size of the crowd that rioted on 2 April is simply not known.

Hundreds of women participated in the bread riot, perhaps more than a thousand. Most descriptions of the mob contain only very general remarks as to its size and fail to distinguish between actual looters and spectators. However, war clerk J. B. Jones, who witnessed the beginning of the event (those who claimed to have seen it all are not to be trusted) and who later testified at a hearing, wrote in his diary that the mob began with a few hundred women and boys and grew to "more than a thousand" upon leaving Capitol Square for the business district. Dr. J. W. Anderson recalled in 1888 that the women were followed by about one thousand male spectators, and there is considerable evidence that both groups increased in size. The cautious James Ford Rhodes, whose account may still be the best brief sketch available, was probably correct when he concluded that "considerably more than a thousand took part in the riot."

Since the women split up into groups and attacked different stores on the same or even several streets simultaneously, the perspective of witnesses was limited by what they observed on one street or from inside a single store. A clerk in the shoe store of James Knotts reported that most of the looters were men (males did take the lead at some stores in breaking through doors and windows), but a witness to the attack on John T. Hicks's shoe store said the mob there consisted of at least five hundred women and very few men. Each man reported the portion of the mob and riot that he had observed.

Sketchy news of the event reached Catherine Edmonston in Halifax County, North Carolina, by 10 April, almost certainly from a copy of the *Examiner* of 4 April. She concluded "that the riot in Richmond was more serious than we supposed, 20000 persons being assembled in the streets." While this figure probably reflects rumor and exaggeration, it could be literally true. Writing to his sister Nettie on 3 April, Confederate private Hal Tutwiler described the scene. The young soldier thought that "there were fully 5000 persons on Cary st., if not more, besides that many more on Main & Broad."

Because of his military experience, Tutwiler may have been able to estimate crowd sizes better than most civilians. Such crowds would not have been impossible, given the swollen population of wartime Richmond. Various other accounts describe the streets filled with people. But a few officials and merchants and the small forces of police and of the Public Guard could hardly have suppressed an active mob of thousands. Tutwiler, Edmonston, and others simply failed to separate actual rioters from bystanders. Yet it seems that Richmond papers, to the extent that they reported the event at all, minimized the number of women looters and downplayed the role of men who helped them.

The bread riot clearly was not a spontaneous event. The women of Richmond planned a protest of some kind, if not the incident that eventually occurred. A meeting attended by Mary Jackson, Martha Fergusson (alias Jamison), and other leaders took place in the Belvidere Hill Baptist Church on Church Street, just south of the penitentiary, on the evening before the bread riot (not the same morning as is sometimes stated). The church was on Oregon Hill, a western, working-class suburb, and close to the street where Mary Jackson lived in 1860, before moving to a small farm several miles further west of the city. Many of the rioters came from Oregon Hill, the adjacent neighborhoods of Sydney and Penitentiary Bottom, and Sheep Hill at the end of Leigh Street. They were all west end neighborhoods. At the meeting on the eve of the riot, the women decided they would demand food from the governor and would take it by force from the merchants if their requests were not satisfied. They were told to bring axes and hatchets to accomplish their mission.

The sun rose about six the day of the riot. Confederate ordnance chief Josiah Gorgas described it as a "very fair" day. According to a fellow huckster, Robert F. Redford, Mary Jackson arrived in the early morning at her usual place of business, the Second or New Market, at Sixth and Marshall streets, just north of Broad. While there she was observed with weapons, including an unloaded pistol loaned to her by one of the men in the market and a knife that she used to cut meat. She told both James P. Tyler, clerk of the market, and Augustus A. Hughes as well as policemen Washington A. Griffin and William N. Kelley that the women would demonstrate and seize food. These men warned her but apparently did not believe that she was serious. Their testimony and that of J. B. Jones indicate that Mayor Joseph Mayo also knew of the protest in advance, but he denied any prior knowledge both at the hearings in his own police court and in statements to the newspapers. Other testimony and the recollections published later in the Richmond *Dispatch* show that many in the city had heard rumors of some kind of demonstration.

About eight that morning Jackson left the Second Market, followed by other women as she crossed Broad Street on her way to Capitol Square. Women and boys from various parts of the city, including the western suburbs and working-class neighborhoods in the east end such as Rocketts and Port Mayo, gathered in the square about the same time. They were joined by women from the counties around Richmond. The crowd congregated at Crawford's equestrian statue of George Washington in the northwestern section of Capitol Square. Here the group was seen by several men on their way to work. At perhaps 8:30 A.M. a delegation that included Mary Johnson, a "highly respectable" woman of about sixty, and Martha Fergusson, from Penitentiary Bottom, approached the Governor's Mansion a few hundred feet to the east, passing behind the State Capitol. Demanding "bread or blood" (a slogan used in Mobile and elsewhere), the women talked not to the governor but to his aide, Col. S. Bassett French, who denied their requests and told them that Letcher was already at work in the Capitol. Some of the women returned to the crowd at the monument, but Fergusson testified that she had sought the governor in the Capitol, lost her way inside the building, and emerged to find him addressing the women. Accounts differ as to whether Letcher spoke from the Capitol or the base of the monument.

Unsatisfied with the governor's response, the crowd of women surged out of the western gates of Capitol Square onto Ninth Street around nine. They were armed not only with axes and hatchets but with "rusty old horse pistols, . . . clubs, . . . knives, and many carried bayonets in their belts, and specimens of those huge old home-made knives with which our soldiers were wont to load themselves down in the first part of the war," recalled Dr. Anderson. In eerie silence they marched down the steep grade on Ninth to Main, gathering supporters along the way, and trailed by a crowd of curious and incredulous men. Maj. John Warwick Daniel recalled that he was standing in the middle of Main Street when it suddenly filled with women entering from side streets. The crowd continued to Cary between Twelfth and Thirteenth, impressing carts and wagons as they walked.

Two large wholesale houses in Shockoe Slip were the first to be looted. One belonged to the firm of Pollard and Walker, the other to Tyler and Son. Robert S. Pollard had been a clerk for grocer Austin E. Moore on Cary Street as recently as 1860, but had entered a partnership with Joshua Walker, a commission merchant whose store was nearby. It was at Pollard and Walker's that Mary Johnson, "a toothless old woman with a most determined phis," broke through the door with an axe and carried off five hundred pounds of bacon valued at $500. She was assisted by young Virgil Jones, also seen using an axe, who stole $600 of ham and bacon. Another widow, the middle-aged Frances Kelly, stole $100 of bacon. The store was thoroughly sacked by other rioters.

At 134 Cary Street, the firm of Tyler and Son also caught the full force of the mob's first assault, though the building at the time was being used as a government warehouse. The partners eventually claimed

$6,468 in damages from the city, a claim that the common council refused to honor on the advice of the city attorney, as it did in all such cases with one exception.

Next to Tyler and Son was the shoe store of John T. Hicks, who claimed $13,530 in damages from the city, also rejected. Observers said that after the successful attack on this store most rioters were wearing shoes from Hicks's shop. The crowd proceeded methodically down the south side of Cary, looting each store in order and loading the stolen goods into horse-drawn vehicles that were driven away by women from the crowd. Only a few of the surprised merchants had sufficient courage or reacted quickly enough to resist the mob. Austin Moore's grocery was a few doors below Thirteenth and the Columbian Block. He defended his store with a drawn revolver against a crowd of three to four hundred men and women. S. C. Tardy and James T. Williams at Thirteenth and Cary shuttered their windows and barricaded their doors in time to deter the looters.

The first official on the scene was probably "Old Joe" Mayo, sixty-eight and mayor since 1853. He stood on a stool or some other improvised platform and read the riot act from a statute book, though he was ignored by the women who rushed around him. Some of the looters continued down Cary, breaking into a Confederate commissary and into another government warehouse between Mayo's Bridge at Pearl (Fourteenth) and the Old Market at Seventeenth. A large group ran up Thirteenth to Main and down that street to the shoe store of James Knotts at 52 Main Street. Knotts was cleaned out of his stock, as was about half the inventory of I. Marcuse, a Jewish merchant whose store was adjacent. The looting of other stores continued down Main Street past the Old Market, at least as far as Eighteenth Street, before the crowd swung around onto Franklin and headed back up the hill. Part of the mob had earlier left Main at Fourteenth for Franklin.

It was on Main Street that the mob first met general resistance from merchants, many of them retailers of luxury items, who had been alerted by the disturbance on Cary. It was also on lower Main Street and Franklin that the crowd entered a German and Jewish quarter reputed to be a center for profiteers, or "speculators." Major Daniel remembered that "certain people down there were credited with great wealth. It was said that they had made barrels of money out of the Confederacy, and the female Communists went at them without a qualm of conscience." Among the merchants in this area was the widow Minna Schweitzer.

Governor Letcher is generally credited with calling out the Public Guard, a state force which dated back to the aftermath of Gabriel's Insurrection. It had been established during the term of Gov. James Monroe to guard the Capitol and Capitol Square and the state (now Confederate) armory and penitentiary in the western part of the city. It is ironic, considering the charges made about the Yankee, ethnic, and foreign composition of the mob, that as shown by the 1860 census 24 percent of the men in the Public Guard were foreign-born and another 17 percent were born outside Virginia, generally in northern states. At the head of the Public Guard was Lt. Edward Scott Gay, the company's acting commander and a rather hard-bitten character. The repeated references in virtually every source to a company of troops under the command of Gay are conclusive evidence that it was the Public Guard and not the City Battalion that ended the riot. A number of accounts including some of the earliest refer to the Public Guard as "the city battalion." (The latter force was commanded by Lt. Col. Wyatt M. Elliott and was the Twenty-fifth Battalion of Virginia Volunteers, Local Defense Troops. It marched down the streets the day after the riot, dispersing crowds that had gathered.) The men of the Public Guard came down Ninth Street following the same route the women had taken. Led by Gay they wheeled left into Main Street and pursued the rioters. It is unlikely that the guard arrived in time to meet the rioters on Cary, but some sort of confrontation may have taken place on Main. Gay and about twenty of his men double-timed down the street after the looters. Some of the rioters ran up Fourteenth to Franklin, while other women continued to the Old Market at Seventeenth and turned up that street to Franklin. When the troops reached the corner of Seventeenth and Franklin, people could be seen running in every direction. One group continued west on Franklin for several blocks, apparently halting somewhere between Fourteenth and Tenth streets.

In the twenty-five years between the riot and the three retrospective articles about it that appeared in the Richmond *Dispatch*, attitudes toward the rioters softened somewhat. As the cult of the Lost Cause flourished, there was a growing solidarity among Richmonders who had been through the war and a realization that some, not all of them military veterans, had suffered more than others.

The chief controversy generated by the series of articles was whether President Jefferson Davis or Gov. John Letcher had dispersed the mob by dramatically ordering the Public Guard under Lieutenant Gay to open fire on the crowd if it did not leave the street in five minutes. Davis, or Letcher, is portrayed as standing on a rice barrel, a dry goods box, or a wagon, warning the crowd, and then eyeing a pocket watch while the guard loaded its weapons and the mob slowly dispersed. While most modern secondary sources give the credit for issuing the order to Davis, a trend dating back at least to Varina Howell Davis's memorial volumes, Governor Letcher has had his defenders. The bulk of contemporary evidence, including an account in the New York *Herald,* the Tutwiler letter, J. B. Jones, Judith McGuire, Frank Moore, Sally A. Brock Putnam, and others, gives the credit to the governor, as do the later accounts of Sarah Agnes Rice Pryor and Ernest Taylor Walthall. Jones and Pryor describe Davis giving a separate speech that was kind and gentle, even sad, with no threat of lethal force. Both men apparently spoke to portions of the crowd at different times and places and were observed separately by different witnesses.

Of the sixteen separate accounts (one anonymous) published in the three *Dispatch* articles, five give Letcher the prominent role, as did the editors. Four of five witnesses who supported Letcher specifically declared that the governor had dispersed the mob with a five-minute warning, but differ as to whether or not the Public Guard was actually on the scene when he spoke to the looters, as well as to the location of his speech. S. Bassett French, hardly a disinterested witness, defended his former superior, but so did two merchants who had had stores in the area, George L. Herring at 56 Main (next door to the shops of Knotts and Marcuse) and James T. Williams at Thirteenth and Cary (Shockoe Slip near Pollard and Walker and John T. Hicks). Unfortunately, they did not agree on whether Letcher spoke on Cary or Main. The majority of the accounts that mention Letcher speaking, a total of five, place him on Main somewhere between Thirteenth and Fifteenth. Two have him speaking on Franklin, either at the Old Market, or between it and the Exchange Hotel at Fourteenth. Only one account, that of Williams, places him on Cary.

President Davis is described as speaking to the mob in eight of the accounts. Six versions describe him giving a quiet, moving, but non-threatening speech, but at various times and locations. Davis is said to have spoken to the crowd at Thirteenth and Cary, just after the sacking of Tyler and Son early in the riot; a little later, on Main between Tenth and Eleventh in front of the Post Office; behind the Post Office at its northwest corner at Tenth and Bank; further east at the corner of Governor and Franklin; and on Franklin, just to the east of the Exchange Hotel at Fourteenth Street.

Only two accounts credit Davis with giving the mob a five-minute warning and telling Gay to have his men load their weapons. Major Daniel, "the lame lion of Lynchburg," a leading politician and spokesman for the Lost Cause, was supposedly overheard by a New York reporter on a train in 1878 praising the role that Davis played in the riot. The newspaperman wrote down what he had heard as soon as he could. This version, which had been denied by Letcher when previously published, was reprinted in 1888. The other Davis defender was Polk Miller, a prominent druggist and member of the Richmond establishment. It seems probable that some people wanted to give Davis all the glory for dispersing the mob, once he had become the honored ex-president of a defeated nation. But in the days and years immediately after the event, accounts credited Governor Letcher for breaking up the bread riot with the Public Guard, and this seems most credible from the evidence.

Mayor Mayo was certainly on the scene, though apparently to little effect. Several other men besides Davis, Letcher, and Mayo spoke to the mob at various times and places, adding to the confusion of the event and later memories of it. Some of these lesser known individuals may or may not have resembled one of the famous trio. Some of the witnesses who later gave their recollections had never before seen one or more of the three leaders, and may thus have been mistaken in their subsequent identifications.

Catholic Bishop John McGill was called upon by the civil authorities, as was the case with Archbishop John Hughes during the New York draft riots, presumably because both prelates would calm the ethnic looters from their flocks. William P. Munford, head of the Union relief committee, a quasi-official group that worked with private charities and supplemented the city's own welfare activities, got in a furniture wagon at Twelfth and Cary to read a message from Letcher and to appeal to the mob to desist, promising food would be provided. Gabriel Johnson, an elderly man with long white hair and beard who worked as an auctioneer at Tardy and Williams on Cary, addressed the crowd from the front of the store after the proprietors had barricaded themselves within. Dr. Anderson claimed that neither Davis nor Letcher was on the scene when Lieutenant Gay and the Public Guard scattered the mob. J. J. Gilleswater said that Davis had spoken at Fourteenth and Franklin, but that it was Gay who had given a seven-minute warning to disperse. Other accounts have Gay speaking with tears running down his cheeks. Col. John B. Baldwin, a leading Virginia politician, spoke to the mob somewhere on Main from a dry goods box and is also credited with defending a store near the Old Market. William Taylor, a justice of the peace for Jefferson Ward, acting at the request of the president of the common council, read the riot act at Eighteenth and Franklin from a dry goods box. . . .

The Richmond police did not prevent the riot from starting and do not seem to have been particularly effective in suppressing it. During the first minutes of looting on Cary, neither soldiers nor police were in sight according to Major Daniel. An old merchant, James Sinton, who had a soap and candle works at Eighteenth and Franklin, recalled that "from the time the mob started down Main Street from the St. Charles Hotel [northeast corner of Fifteenth or Wall] there was not an officer, civil or military, who interfered or attempted to stay the progress of the mob, although they passed the First police-station [rear of Old Market at Seventeenth, between Main and Franklin]. The only attempt was by the owners of the stores, which in most cases proved unavailing." One explanation of this account would be that Letcher had already confronted the mob above Fifteenth, with the guard merely pursuing them in Sinton's area; another is that Letcher and the guard did not meet the mob until Franklin Street somewhere west of the Old Market.

Dr. Anderson remembered a woman huckster who mounted a cart loaded with bacon, candles, and other goods and drove away.

> She had scarcely gone one hundred yards from the crowd and turned
> a corner when a policeman, emerging like a big spider from his

ambush, pounced upon her and her commissary supplies and captured the whole concern without the firing of a gun. The cart and contents thus left standing without a proprietor soon attracted attention and a new-comer coolly took possession, but no sooner had she gathered up the reins for a start than forth came the inevitable policeman and she followed her predecessor to the cage.

Most of the rioters who were caught in the act of looting were apprehended by merchants aided by prominent citizens, and not by the police. Their arrests generally came after the riot was over, or at least when an individual's active participation had ended. Thus John Jones, a pop-eyed, redheaded man of forty, was arrested while standing guard over a pile of hats, shoes, coffee, and bacon. Some of the goods were identified and claimed by John Hicks and by Tyler and Son, but the coffee could not be traced back to a particular store. A number of women were arrested riding away on vehicles loaded with stolen goods or walking home from the scene of the looting. Other women and several couples who were merchants themselves were charged with receiving or possessing stolen goods. The tardy nature of many of the arrests made it difficult to prove that individuals had actually stolen the goods in question, and in some cases it was impossible to learn their origin if not still in a marked store container.

Although there was physical violence, including windows and doors broken and a few instances of merchants and bystanders struck or even knocked down or policemen assaulted or threatened with weapons, there were only three cases of bloodshed noted. None can be substantiated, but at least two have the ring of truth. There is mention in a New York paper of a merchant who struck a woman rioter and was then wounded in the shoulder by a shot from a revolver. Walthall remembered the blood dripping from an axe that had been used to strike "Mr. Tyler," one of several merchants by the name. And Private Tutwiler wrote that

> one woman knocked out a pane of glass out of a shop window, of which the door was fastened, & put her arm in to steal something, but the shopman cut all four of her fingers off. . . . It was the most horrible sight I ever saw.

There are no other allusions to actual bloodshed, and the three above are not corroborated by legal records or newspaper accounts.

The Richmond bread riot was over by eleven in the downtown area, approximately two hours after the women left Capitol Square for the business district. There are a few references to looting on Broad Street at the peak of the riot, but the center of activity appears to have been on Cary and then Main with the final looting on Franklin. Rioters with stolen goods disappeared into alleys and side streets and attempted to evade the police on their way home. Those unencumbered by loot, or with concealable items, mingled with the crowd of spectators. About 11:00 A.M., on Franklin near the Post Office, Robert Redford saw Mary Jackson for the first time since her departure from the Second Market. At her hearing, a woman testified that around noon Jackson came back to her house to retrieve a knife that she had left before the riot began. About the same time, probably as she was heading home, Mary Jackson was finally arrested, at First and Broad. She had just led a crowd of women who broke into a store three blocks east. The policeman who arrested her found a knife wrapped in paper. Her odyssey had ended just a few blocks from where it began.

Mary Jackson and Minerva Meredith have always been the most popular with writers on the bread riot, because the two women are conveniently identifiable leaders. The 1860 directory and census show that Jackson, thirty-four, lived with her husband Elisha, thirty-one and a painter, on Pine Street between Plank Road and Elmwood in Sydney. Though illiterate, Mr. Jackson owned $700 in real and $100 in personal property and claimed $7,000 in real estate when he tried to bail his wife in 1863. In 1850, when he was apparently living within the city limits, he had even owned an eighteen-year-old male slave. Mary Jackson worked as a huckster in the Second Market for seven years before the riot. The couple had four children, three sons and a daughter, in 1860. The oldest boy apparently enlisted or was drafted into the army, and Mary made repeated efforts through J. B. Jones to secure his discharge. Much negative evidence, including the allegation that she herself speculated in beef, and some favorable testimony were presented at her initial hearing in Mayor Mayo's police court. Bail was denied. Jackson ultimately may have been convicted only of a misdemeanor, if that, for it could not be proven that she had actually stolen anything. Her goals appear to have been political rather than material. Her part in organizing and leading the women in the early stages of the riot was clear, yet one witness recalled that she had lost control of her followers by the time they left Capitol Square. But another observer remembered that she had led the attack on John C. Page's shoe store at 93 Main near Fourteenth midway through the riot, and she was arrested on Broad after leading another assault on a store at the end of the riot. . . .

The name usually linked with [Jackson's] is Minerva Meredith's. Described as six feet tall, rawboned, muscular, and forty years old, she was accused and convicted of robbing Henry Myers, the steward of the city hospital, of a wagonload of beef that he had bought for his patients. He was subsequently reimbursed by the common council for 310 pounds of beef valued at $295, the only victim to be compensated by the city. Although two witnesses testified that Meredith's sister (or possibly daughter) Anne had robbed Myers of the beef, Minerva insisted that it was she who was responsible, perhaps in an effort to protect her younger relation. Myers said that he knew Minerva and that when he told her the meat was intended for his smallpox patients, she walked away, but that two other women jumped on the wagon and drove it off. As a butcher's apprentice, Minerva probably knew Mary Jackson. She was bailed on a misdemeanor charge the Tuesday after the riot. A month later she was tried and found guilty by a circuit court jury and fined the maximum $100. Judge John A. Meredith gave Minerva Meredith only half the permissible sentence, six months in jail, perhaps because her petition for a pardon from the governor had been endorsed by Mayor Mayo. She seems to have been punished as much for being a leader of the riot and for being a conspicuous individual, as for any guilt in the theft of beef. . . .

Of the rioters who have been identified, more came from the western part of the city and the suburbs beyond than from any other area. A strong case can be made for a connection between some of these individuals because they lived so close together. Martha Goode and Sarah Wright, both of Sheep Hill, were arrested together for rioting. Martha, twenty-four, and her husband Oscar, thirty-one, an ornamental sign painter, were natives of Virginia. A positive identification of Sarah Wright is more difficult, but perhaps the most likely candidate is a young woman of seventeen or eighteen who was living with her parents in 1860 in the westernmost part of Monroe, the ward closest to Sheep Hill. Her father and both her brothers were painters, indicating a possible link with the Jacksons and Goodes.

Martha A. Cardona appears on the census page preceding Goode, in the western district of Henrico. A native of Virginia, thirty-four and illiterate, Martha lived with her husband Francis Cardona, thirty-eight, a carpenter born in Spain. He is listed in the 1860 city directory as Frank Cardona, cabinetmaker, with a house on Oregon Hill near the Pine Street Baptist Church. The family's location poses a problem, as the directory listing contradicts their proximity to the Goode household of Sheep Hill on the census, unless the Cardonas lived in two different neighborhoods at the time the census was taken and when the directory was compiled. The difficulty of using the census for locating individuals is that by the time of the riot, three years later, some of them could have moved, particularly as housing rents within the city rose dramatically during the war.

A short distance west of Cardona and Goode in Henrico County lived two male rioters. Alexander Jennings was an upholsterer's apprentice of nineteen in 1860, who lived with his mother Elizabeth, possessed of $6,000 in real and $22,000 in personal property. Both were Virginia natives. Jennings was eventually acquitted of looting James Knotts's store. Apparently, the merchant had asked him to hand out small items such as needles to the mob of women who had already demolished the shop windows. But the merchant was knocked down and stunned by the rioters, and after recovering, he had Jennings arrested, not remembering that he had told him to distribute goods to the women. The testimony of store clerks and other witnesses was contradictory, but the mayor was satisfied that Jennings had been mistakenly arrested. His testimony against Dr. Thomas Palmer may also have helped him in his case.

Lawrence Martin's name appears on the census two pages after that of Jennings. Born in Ireland, he was a twelve-year-old orphan when arrested for rioting in 1863. On the 1860 census he appeared in western Henrico in the household of Brien Martin, thirty-eight, an Irish carpenter, who apparently was a widower with six children ranging from eighteen to six.

Martha Fergusson, alias Jamison, lived closer to the city and had been involved in the riot from the beginning. Her neighborhood was Penitentiary Bottom, a poor district around the prison where convicts deposited street sweepings. Two barrels of flour, several hams, and a barrel from Tyler and Son with traces of butter were found at her home. After giving damaging testimony against her associate Mary Jackson, Fergusson received a fine of only $10 and a day in jail, possibly as a reward for testifying and because she claimed to have four children at home. But no woman by either name fitting these characteristics has been found in the census or been confirmed by a directory listing.

In addition to the accused rioters, most of whom were not convicted, there were several caught up in the arrests who were not as directly involved. Andrew J. Hawkins was a foreman at the Confederate shoe shop, R. G. Mason, a distiller, placed him in the mob around George W. Gretter's store on lower Main Street, where he was seen encouraging a crowd of women to break in. W. T. Trueman confirmed Mason's testimony and had called the policeman who arrested Hawkins. Two unidentified witnesses, one Irish and one German, also saw Hawkins at the spot in midday and heard him express approval of the riot and sympathy for the women. Yet Hawkins won his freedom with an alibi from his supervisor that he had been on the job until noon, after the riot was over. J. J. Hawkins, a shoemaker, is listed in the 1860 directory, but no "A. J."; however, in 1870 Andrew J. Hawkins is listed as a city policeman. Tice has found evidence that Hawkins was a member of the Belvidere Hill Baptist Church, where the demonstration was planned, and that he lived in the Oregon Hill neighborhood where many of the rioters resided.

Oregon Hill was also the home of James and Martha Marshall, one of three couples involved in the riot. The Marshalls were illiterate and natives of Virginia. James Marshall had only $100 in personal property in 1860, when he was a member of the Public Guard. He and Martha had three children at this time. By 1863 he was forty-four and worked in his shoe shop on Oregon Hill. A merchant and two policemen went to their home the afternoon of the riot and asked Marshall if any stolen goods had been brought there. He denied it, but the police and merchant were acting on a tip. A search revealed a shoulder of bacon, butter, two hats, and candles. Martha Marshall ran and hid in the outhouse during the search, but finally admitted that the items were her share of a wagon load of goods that had been sent over to Oregon Hill from downtown and divided among the women rioters in the neighborhood. James Marshall was indicted for rioting but found not guilty. His wife, thirty-seven, was found guilty, fined $5.00 and court costs, and given a thirty-day jail sentence.

A second couple, William and Frances (or Sarah) Farrand, both from North Carolina, had a store downtown on Fourteenth Street at Mayo's Bridge, close to the scene of the first looting. Both were charged with receipt of stolen items. Shoes and assorted dry goods were found in their shop, but the Farrands denied any knowledge that the articles had been stolen, and charges appear to have been dropped.

The Farrands may have been involved with several boy rioters who brought them stolen items. John Hopkins was so charged after he was identified by the couple. Hopkins protested that he had bought the goods from another boy, "little Johnny Camp." The outcome of the boys' cases as rioters is unknown, but Camp was in trouble again for petty crime in 1864. Morgan S. Burns, another boy, was among the first rioters arrested. He was ten and had been born in New York of Irish parents. His father of the same name, aged thirty-seven, worked as a tailor. Like Johnny Camp, young Burns was again in trouble in early 1864 for stealing gold.

The third couple, Isaac and Caroline (Mary) Jacobs, had a store on Main Street in the looted area. They were charged with receipt of stolen goods that had been brought to their shop by a trio of women, at least one of whom was from the east end. A policeman testified that he had gone to their store, which Mrs. Jacobs refused to open, claiming that her husband had locked it and taken the only key. Under threat of a search warrant, she opened the shop, where a large quantity of shirts, hats, shoes, calico, candles, brooms, and bacon were found hidden behind the counter. Mrs. Jacobs at first said that the goods had been left by a stranger, but she later identified her as Mrs. Mildred Imry, an employee. Further testimony by a young clerk in the store revealed that the three women (Imry, along with Martha Smith and Jeanette Williams) had brought goods in Mr. Jacobs's absence and that they often left items. The latter two women have not been identified, but Mildred Imry, alias Melinda Emory, is probably the Mrs. M. Imary listed as a grocer at Twenty-third and Main streets in the 1860 directory, and as Mildred Imray, widow of James P., boarding in Fulton in 1870. Both addresses were in the east end. Mrs. Jacobs and two of the other women were charged with misdemeanors. Mr. Jacobs successively posted bail of $1,000; $3,500; and then a $500 peace bond for his wife, stating that he owned "a large store and niggers." As charges against the three other women were eventually dropped, it seems unlikely that Mrs. Jacobs could have been convicted of receiving stolen goods.

Women known to have come from the east end neighborhood of Rocketts include Margaret Pomfrey, discussed below, and a Mrs. Jordan and Mrs. Enroughty, both from Rocketts "Old Field." Jordan has not been identified. Enroughty was referred to in the newspapers as Anne, Harriet, and Sarah and cannot be positively identified either, as the directories and census for eastern Henrico and the easternmost city ward (Jefferson) list six different women with those names. Elizabeth Goode, another Rocketts rioter, may be an illiterate woman of twenty-eight who appears on the census for eastern Henrico with a thirty-five-year-old husband, Isaac, an illiterate laborer. But another woman of twenty-seven with the same name is on the same page of the census.

Mrs. Barbara Idoll, a redheaded, pregnant German, was a tent-maker earning twenty-five dollars a week. Her husband owned a house and lot in Rocketts. A jury acquitted her of rioting. The 1860 census lists "Barbary" Idle, thirty-two, living in eastern Henrico with Frederick, thirty-nine, a carpenter, and their two-year-old son; both parents were born in Germany.

Mrs. Sarah W. Champion lived below Rocketts with her husband and three children and was indicted for assaulting James Knotts and stealing shoes, slippers, and candles. Bail was refused and she was sent on to be tried in the hustings court, but was acquitted the following June. James Champion, a laborer of forty and a native of North Carolina like his wife, appears on the 1860 census in the eastern district of Henrico. His wife, Sarah, thirty-five, had five children, all born in Virginia except the eldest.

The only girl arrested as a rioter was Melissa Jane Palmeter, fourteen, who had supported herself as a thief and prostitute for the previous two years, according to the unfriendly account in the *Examiner*. She was the only rioter so described individually. Melissa Jane was arrested leaving the scene of the riot on a wagon loaded with stolen articles. Like so many whose arrests were reported, her fate is unknown because of missing court records, nor is she again mentioned as a rioter in the papers. However, she was soon at liberty, for in September she was before the hustings court, charged with robbing a soldier of $190. The 1860 census reveals that she was then nine and living with her mother, Elizabeth Palmeter, a forty-year-old seamstress. Both were natives of Virginia. While the mother was credited with no real or personal property, their neighborhood on South Fifth Street in Madison Ward was not a poor one.

No case more clearly illustrates the fact that some kind of protest scheduled for 2 April was planned in advance and that some of the participants were at least moderately well off than that of Mrs. Margaret Adeline Pomfrey. Her story also indicates that not all of the women rioters were prostitutes, Yankees, or foreign-born. A Virginia native, Mrs. Pomfrey lived in New Kent County, almost due east of Richmond. The county courthouse was approximately 11.5 miles from the city limits. Though her farm appears west of the courthouse on large-scale Civil War maps, and thus closer to the city, the distance by road from her farm to the capital was probably twice as far. Yet Pomfrey, who also owned a house and land in the Port Mayo area of Rocketts and who had lived there at various times, testified that she was in the city on Thursday expressly for the purpose of taking part in a demonstration. She apparently returned to New Kent immediately after the riot, because a city policeman had to be sent out to her farm to arrest her and bring her back to the mayor's court.

On 18 April she was charged with rioting and stealing bacon from Pollard and Walker. Robert S. Pollard said that he recognized her while other women were looting his store and asked, " 'Is it possible . . . that you are robbing me too?' " According to the indignant merchant, she replied that " 'she was obliged to do it,' " and left with his bacon. Her statement may have reflected her own conviction, needs, or perhaps fear that she would be "mobbed" herself, a fate said to be in readiness for women who did not participate, according to Martha Fergusson.

In her defense Mrs. Pomfrey stated that she had been shoved into the store by the mob as she was walking by it, but the mayor rejected this excuse. Said Mayo: " 'Nothing more clearly proves the character of that "bread riot" than that you, owning a farm and negroes in the county of New Kent, should be engaged in it.' " The census of 1860, the slave census, and New Kent County real and personal property tax books, confirm the mayor's charge. Mrs. Pomfrey did indeed own three tracts of land totaling 127.5 acres, as well as a small number of slaves during the 1850s and early 1860s. Mayo required Pomfrey to post bail to appear for trial on a misdemeanor charge before circuit court judge John Meredith. Before she left, Margaret Pomfrey insisted, " 'I heard they were going to distribute provisions to the ladies, that's why I came up to town that morning.' " Presumably she spent the night at her home in Port Mayo, just beyond the city limits, for it would have been difficult to leave New Kent early enough to arrive in time to join in the riot.

The New Kent farmer was found guilty in May, fined $50, and given a thirty-day jail sentence, despite the testimony of two women who said that she had left the county for fear of the Yankees and that she was seen leaving the city on the day of the riot with no goods in her possession. A New Kent neighbor, Dr. J. C. Vaiden, himself a slaveowner whose farm appears on contemporary maps, testified that he knew Mrs. Pomfrey in the county as " 'a woman of some property in land and negroes, and [who] bore a fair character.' " A Civil War historian might ask if this woman, not of the planter class but hardly a poor white, kept a diary, like more famous members of her sex. If she did, the entry for 2 April 1863 might read, "Went to Richmond. Had a riot."

Surely if Margaret Pomfrey knew that something was planned for Holy Thursday and could make her way to the capital from New Kent, women much closer to the city were even more likely to have known about and been present for the event. An exhaustive search of the census and tax records for the entire area of several counties around Richmond might turn up a few more of the arrested but as yet unidentified rioters, though few of the known details confirm their presence.

What might appear to be a double standard of justice seems to have been applied in the cases of a number of women rioters, some of whom were young, attractive, well-dressed, and with fair reputations, as compared with another group who were older and in many cases widows or the wives or mothers of Confederate soldiers.

For example, Mrs. Mary Woodward, eighteen and recently married but whose husband was "away in the country" (not the army), was bailed by her wealthy mother-in-law, Louisa Woodward, and was described by reporters as "genteel looking" and "pretty and handsomely dressed." She was arrested on a furniture wagon loaded with two barrels of flour, a barrel of soap, and eighteen pieces of bacon. Her companion in crime was a Mrs. Wesley, who was described as "old and hard featured" and who stated that she was "from the country." The case against Mrs. Wesley, who forthrightly admitted her guilt, was continued, and her fate is unknown. Mary Woodward was quickly released, on account of "sickness." She was eventually represented by attorney John S. Caskie, later a judge, who was the son of a wealthy tobacco merchant, John Caskie, and nephew of the recorder in the police court and hustings court member James K. Caskie. Despite the testimony of arresting officer Morris that Mary Woodward had struck him and had drawn a pistol when he stopped the wagon, she was discharged less than a week after the riot.

Other examples of favorable treatment given to accused women who possessed the right attributes include that of Kate Ammons, bailed on 3 April, even though she had taken the name Elizabeth, belonging to another local woman. She was described as "handsome and handsomely dressed" and as "a very good looking young woman." She was arrested with shoes, suspenders, and red cloth, but said the items had been given to her (a common defense) by a soldier. A number of character witnesses testified for her. In mid-May a circuit court jury was unable to agree on a verdict, and she was discharged until the next term. Final disposition of Kate Ammons's case is unknown, but there is no evidence that she had an attorney.

Nor did Miss Laura Gordon of Oregon Hill, eighteen, have counsel. She was said to be "a young lady of some means" and "neatly dressed." Despite the fact that police found stolen goods in her home, a number of witnesses appeared in her defense. In early May she was found guilty in the circuit court of rioting and fined $25. After the verdict was pronounced, she took laudanum in the courtroom and collapsed. She was held in nominal custody, and a month later Judge Meredith reduced her thirty-day jail sentence to four hours. She then burst into tears and could not be consoled.

Middle-aged and elderly women, even if nicely dressed and able to afford an attorney, did not escape so lightly. Mrs. Mary Johnson, often confused even in contemporary accounts with Mary Jackson, had gone to the Governor's Mansion and later led the mob that broke into Pollard and Walker. Attorneys Ratcliffe and Johnson ably defended her, according to newspaper accounts, but the evidence against their client was too strong. Indicted for a felony in May, she was tried in Judge William H. Lyons's hustings court in October 1863. She was found guilty of a felony and sentenced to five years in the Virginia State Penitentiary, the only one of the women rioters to be so convicted and sentenced. She had a married daughter living in Richmond and a son in Lee's army.

The widow Frances Kelley was indicted for breaking into Pollard and Walker with Johnson, but the indictment was returned by the hustings court on a technicality and the charge was dropped. She was charged and bailed again, but fled to Lynchburg where she was found by her bondsman in January 1864 under an assumed name. Kelley was brought back to Richmond, tried and convicted by a hustings court jury that gave her one year in the penitentiary, "this news being received by the prisoner with an outburst of grief pitiable to behold." Her attorney, George D. Wooten, fortified with a stack of law books, had cited Exodus 22:22, "Ye shall not afflict any widow," in his closing argument. Judge Lyons decided that the articles she had stolen were worth less than twenty dollars and instructed the jury that it could find the prisoner guilty of the lesser charge of petty larceny. The jury reconsidered its verdict and gave Mrs. Kelley thirty days in jail.

One convicted rioter was represented not by a lawyer but by her physician. Mary (or Lucy) Duke was indicted by the grand jury for rioting. She had been seen waving a Colt's Navy revolver while looting Minna Schweitzer's store. In May she was found guilty, fined $100, and sentenced to six months in jail. A month later her teenage son filed a petition with Governor Letcher, asking for a pardon of her remaining sentence, since she had four children and a husband in Lee's army. The son himself had served in the Irish battalion under Jackson as a drummer for a year, and now supported his sisters (ten, seven, and two) as a newsboy. In a separate letter Mary Duke's own doctor and the physician at the city jail certified her "delicate health with a decided tendency to pulmonary consumption." Thomas U. Dudley, long-time city sergeant, reported that she had paid her $100 fine for a misdemeanor conviction and her court costs. On 1 July 1863, citing all these factors in her case, Governor Letcher ordered Mrs. Duke discharged.

Anna Bell claimed to have three children at home. She testified that she was involved in the riot only to the extent of trying to keep one of her sons out of it, but the ubiquitous Charles H. Wynne, who testified against many of the rioters, said that she had "threatened to blow his brains out if he interfered" with her looting of Mr. Ezekiel's store on Main Street. Anna Bell was eventually convicted of a misdemeanor and fined seventy-five dollars, with thirty days in the city jail.

Only twelve women are known to have been convicted of any charge, and only one (Johnson) of a felony. Three of the twelve, and at least six women in all, had lawyers, including Johnson, Kelley, and Pomfrey, who were convicted, and Jacobs, Woodward, and Jackson (possibly), who were not. There does not seem to be a correlation between verdicts and whether a woman was represented by counsel. All six were in serious trouble and probably felt that they needed lawyers. It may or may not be significant that in a group of women who were said to come from the bottom of society, at least six from a group of forty-odd could afford attorneys. There does seem to be a relationship between youth and attractiveness and dismissal of charges, acquittal, or reduced sentences for those women possessing the desired characteristics.

Stiffer sentences also were handed down to male rioters. At least four men were sentenced to the penitentiary after being convicted of felonies and two for misdemeanors from a total group of suspects considerably smaller in number than the women who were initially accused. Four of the six convicted men had attorneys. In one of the felony cases an attorney was able to get his client's guilty verdict set aside after he had been sentenced to a year in the penitentiary. A second trial resulted in acquittal. In two misdemeanor cases the lawyers won new trials and charges were dropped.

The case of Thomas Samanni, Jr., one of the four men convicted of felonies, illustrates several important aspects of the riot, including anti-Semitism in wartime Richmond, hostility to immigrants in a city that had been a stronghold of the Know-Nothings, and motivation of the rioters—whether they were acting out of impoverishment, opportunism, or outright criminality. Samanni's chief victim was the widowed Jewish merchant Minna Schweitzer, whose store he ransacked. Though a native of Richmond, he was the son of a Corsican immigrant who had amassed a fortune of $40,000 in real and $4,500 in personal property. At the time of the riot the younger Samanni had already been involved in several forgeries. He was indicted for making a riot and for destroying and stealing the goods of Mrs. Schweitzer, including 200 yards of homespun cotton goods, 4 hats, pieces of calico, pairs of men's boots and shoes, a large quantity of handkerchiefs, stockings, gloves, socks, pants, coats, shirts, combs, and 300 yards of sheeting, all valued at $1,000. Samanni was found guilty and sentenced to two years in the penitentiary.

The involvement of military personnel in the riot is shown by several cases. That of Virgil Jones also illustrates the difficulty of identifying individuals with several first names or aliases and the same or similar common last names. George, Orvell, or Virgil Jones, twenty-four, had been a member of the Public Guard, but he had been discharged from the company three months earlier for trying to bribe a guard at the Confederate lithograph works to steal treasury notes. He had also married recently. Jones was found guilty of breaking into Pollard and Walker, of threatening the merchants, and of stealing 500 pounds of bacon. An officer, a sergeant, and two other members of the guard gave damaging testimony against him, as did Martin Meredith Lipscomb, a prosperous bricklayer and later one of Richmond's leading scalawags. Jones was sentenced to three years in the penitentiary. Yet thirty of his former comrades signed a petition to Governor Letcher, asking for a new trial, avowing the innocence of Jones, and pledging $115 for his defense costs and the support of his pregnant wife. Aided by his attorneys, Jones filed his own petition with the governor, which was also signed by his wife's former employer, John Dooley, a wealthy hat manufacturer and Confederate veteran.

The most human document in the case is the appeal of the expectant wife:

> Richmond July 1st 1863
>
> To his excellency Gover Letcher of Va.
>
> Sir if you were convinced of the innocence of my husband as my self I know that you would pardone him immediately if you will examine the record you will find the indictment altogether wrong. . . . I know that he is inocent and has done nothing to deserve the punishment that is put up on him. I know my self that I met him that morning as I was coming from the clothing Depot on the other side of the street just as they were in the act of breaking in the store. he told me not to stop but keep on home. said he thought it was a disgraceful thing so I can safely say my self that he is not guilty of the charge that is Against him if he had done any crime to go to the penitentiary for I would not mind it so much. but to be sent there for nothing, it allmost breaks my heart he is so young and if he is sent there it will ruin him forever. Where if you will pardon him it will make him a better man. it will teach him a lesson that he will never forget. he has been in jail ever since the

2nd day of April and I have been by myself all the time. I have no one to stay with me and I expect to become a mother in a few weeks . . . and oh govr to save him self and his wife and child from shame and disgrace I entreat you to pardon my husband. . . . I have said all to you that I think is necessary. I know that you have the power to save him . . . and leave it with you to decide . . . if you send him there you destroy my happiness and make me miserable for life . . . and oh Gov. I beg and entreat you to pardon him is the Prayer of his heart broken Wife.

MARY E. JONES

The unfortunate young husband did not win a pardon and went to the penitentiary.

William J. Lusk helped Thomas Samanni break into Minna Schweitzer's store and also played a prominent role in looting James Knotts's shoe store, where he broke through a window, climbed inside, and then helped women into the shop. He was caught, being among the last to leave, and violently resisted arrest. After being subdued, he declared that he was an infirm patient at Winder Hospital. Lusk was fined $100 and given a year's sentence, though it is not clear whether he spent it in the city jail or penitentiary. His widow Anna was supporting herself as a milliner in 1870.

Robert W. McKinney was a soldier in the Nineteenth Battalion of Virginia Heavy Artillery. McKinney was seen in a crowd around the Old Market that was dispersed by a policeman. The same officer found him a few minutes later on Franklin Street, urging a crowd of women to tear down the "cage," a venerable structure used to hold prisoners, and to take what they wanted from the stores—and he would help them. Arrested by the policeman, who said that McKinney was intoxicated at the time, the prisoner in his own defense said that he was so drunk on Thursday he could not remember anything that had happened. His punishment, if any, is unknown.

Benjamin Slemper, a young German and a substitute member of the Public Guard, pled guilty to the charge of breaking into Knotts's store and of stealing boots and shoes. He received a sentence of three years eight months in the penitentiary.

One indication of the seriousness with which the authorities regarded the bread riot is their tension after it was over. Perhaps the last of the nonrioters to be arrested were a Mrs. Lane of Henrico County and Mrs. Isabella Ould, an Englishwoman. They were standing on the front steps of the City Hall facing Capitol Square as the first day of hearings in the riot cases was ending in the mayor's police court. Other bystanders heard the two women expressing sympathy for the rioters, approving their actions, and stating that they, too, would like calico dresses. They were promptly arrested by the shocked men around them and brought before a furious Joseph Mayo, who charged both with incendiary language. They were eventually discharged, but Mr. Ould at first had to post a $500 peace bond for his wife and was warned that her alien status did not protect her.

Word of the riot spread quickly, despite the Confederate government's attempt to censor news over the telegraph and in the city's papers, which was further evidence of official nervousness. By eleven that morning word had reached Danville on the wire that a mob of three hundred women and five to ten thousand men had roamed the capital, sacked the principal stores, and had eventually been put down by the military with heavy loss of life. Such exaggerations were supplemented by passengers on trains coming from Richmond. Business halted in Danville, and morale there and along the route of the Richmond and Danville Railroad plummeted. As early as 4 April the *Examiner* commented on the stories in both Danville and Lynchburg papers, citing their "flaming accounts of a thief-and-harlot riot" with "thousands engaged in it." The editors described such reports (similar to the *Examiner*'s own) as "the work of exaggeration" best left to the Yankees.

The Yankees may have first learned of the bread riot, as was feared by the *Examiner*, from recently exchanged Union prisoners of war, some of whom could have actually witnessed the event from inside Libby (at Twentieth and Cary) and other downtown prisons. On 3 April, the day after the riot, 329 prisoners were sent downriver to City Point for exchange and transportation to Fort Monroe. By 18 April the *Examiner* reprinted a story from the New York *Herald* about bread riots in Richmond and other southern cities. On 23 April the paper reprinted another account from the *Herald* of 11 April, purporting to be a report of a recent refugee from the city.

The refugee's story in the *Herald* as reprinted ended on an ironic note.

> The authorities are much exercised over it [the riot], and the greatest vigilance is enjoined upon the police force. The leading men of the city attempted to circulate the report that the women were "Irish and Yankee hags" [an exact quote from the *Examiner* itself] endeavoring to mislead the public concerning the amount of loyal sentiment in the city, but miserably failed.

This account, allowing for some distortion to please northern readers, is one of the first to give a sympathetic view of the rioters, quite at odds with that in the *Examiner*, which actually succeeded in setting the tone for most later secondary sources. The anti-Davis paper began extensive coverage of the riot on 3 April, ignoring the government's request for suppression of the news. The more cooperative Richmond *Enquirer* commented on the needs of the poor the day after the riot, followed with a short story about it on 4 April, and gradually increased its coverage of the hearings and trials that followed. The *Sentinel*, *Dispatch*, and *Whig* followed similar policies.

Though the size of the mob cannot be stated exactly, for reasons discussed above, it is strange that less than a score of stores were reported as sacked, though a few others were besieged unsuccessfully. Some were completely stripped of goods, while others had their stocks severely depleted. The relatively limited damage could mean that the actual number of looters was small. The riot itself lasted only about two hours. Of the hundreds of retail and wholesale establishments in the city, the few that were reported as being broken into might represent those that were popularly perceived as belonging to the "extortioners" and "speculators" so often railed against by J. B. Jones. To the extent that this was a factor in the mob's choice of targets, the riot can be said to have been purposeful and not aimlessly violent, as has often been shown to be the case in such incidents. Some merchants, such as Napthali and Rebecca Ezekiel, Isaac Marcuse, and Minna Schweitzer, were probably singled out because of their religion. But anti-Semitism was not the sole motive; several notable gentile houses were sacked. Another possible explanation for the limited damage is that very little of it was reported. Only a few merchants filed claims with the city, and the brief initial newspaper accounts may have overlooked many of the damaged stores. Yet given the small police force, the slowness with which the authorities responded, and the size of the crowd of rioters and spectators, the damage could have been much more extensive. That it was not is because some merchants had earlier warning, reacted more quickly, or were better prepared to withstand the fury of a mob than the riot's victims. . . .

The merchants who suffered losses to the mob included some who were certainly prosperous in 1860 and still in business three years later. Judged by new partnerships and status, some of them had improved their positions during the war. A number were of military age, but had not volunteered for service, and had somehow escaped conscription as late as April 1863. They may not have been profiteers, but certainly it might be said of some of them that they "prospered during the war," a trenchant phrase in years to come in the South. It seems likely that these merchants were symbols to the rioters of a conflict that had become a "rich man's war, and a poor man's (and woman's) fight." In the evacuation fire of 2–3 April 1865, virtually all of the stores plundered in 1863 were destroyed.

The question that remains to be answered is whether or not the Richmond bread riot was important, and if so, what ways was it significant? The event does seem to indicate an ominous breakdown in Confederate supply lines. A month before Chancellorsville, three months before Vicksburg and Gettysburg, food could not be transported in sufficient quantities to the capital so as to ensure reasonable prices in the city markets. And yet the riot was not repeated until exactly two years later, when a mob that helped spread the evacuation fire made the bread rioters seem like respectable citizens. Despite worsening conditions, the incident did not recur until the final collapse because of an improved municipal welfare system and because the determination of the authorities to suppress further riots, with regular troops and artillery if necessary, was clearly expressed.

The riot of 2 April was not an isolated event in Richmond. Sullen crowds gathered the next morning but were quickly dispersed. On 4 April with more trouble expected, Capt. Peter G. Coghlan, keeper of the state armory, wrote to Governor Letcher, citing his experience with mobs in Europe. He requested permission to order two mountain howitzers from Lynchburg, since "they will run easily on the streets. . . . They will be easily, very easily drawn, being light." Coghlan said he could get ammunition from the same town. In a postscript he thoughtfully added that "if it should unhappily be the case that it be necessary to use the guns . . . if you give charge of them to me I promise to use them with effect."

Union prisoners on Belle Isle lived under the mouths of cannon placed there to intimidate them. Following the bread riot, cannon were indeed placed on the streets of Richmond to overawe the capital's civilian population. One witness in 1888 recalled cannon on Main Street between Fourteenth and Fifteenth pointing west in the direction from which the mob had come. Such extreme measures were apparently necessary. There were widespread rumors that yet another riot was planned for Friday night, 10 April, and troops under Maj. Gen. Arnold Elzey, commander of the Department of Richmond, were ordered into the city to reinforce those of provost marshal Gen. John Winder. Elzey had previously informed Gen. James Longstreet on 6 April that it would not be possible to provide certain troops for field duty because of "the continually threatened riots in Richmond." Given the fact that the bread riot and its aftermath had some effect on the movements of the Army of Northern Virginia, however slight, the event would seem to have some military importance. Observers in 1863 (and 1888) also speculated darkly about what would have happened had the Public Guard fired on women and children whose male relatives filled the ranks of the army around the city. Certainly the riot seems to be evidence of a breakdown of order, morale, and discipline in the Confederate capital of the kind that eventually crippled the South. The actions of officials during and after the riot also indicate a high degree of alarm.

The Richmond disturbance seems to have been one part, albeit a major one, of a larger pattern of food riots that occurred in the South, primarily in the spring of 1863 but also in the spring and fall of 1864. The spreading pattern of outbreaks in 1863 is similar to the violence in a number of Northern cities that followed the massive draft riots in

New York, but it even more closely resembles the food riot patterns traced in France by George Rudé, along with similar events in England. . . .

The Richmond bread riot, finally, has something to say to historians of a masculine era that has long been dominated by military scholarship. The same thing was said to the authorities in 1863. Upperclass young ladies like Lucy Parke Chamberlayne and her friend Sally Grattan, in "Angels Retreat," their Confederate Treasury Department office at Fourth and Broad, "worked on tranquilly" when they heard of the riot downtown. But many Richmond women, some of whom were quite respectable and solidly middleclass and some who were admittedly less genteel, were not acting within their traditional roles. This surprising behavior appeared throughout the Confederacy but most embarrassingly in its capital. Men at the time did not know what to make of such behavior. Nor do they now. Wives and mothers who demonstrate in the streets and openly defy civil and military authorities hardly conform to traditional definitions of patriotism or feminism. The official solution to this quandary, and one adopted by far too many historians, was to ridicule, insult, or ignore the female protesters. The women of 1863 were neither harlots nor heroines, but simply individual human beings whose lives had been blighted by war. Their cries still echo down the streets of Richmond and a dozen other southern towns. Historians would do well to listen to them.

*A family portrait, in the midst of the arduous journey
to the west.*

"Ladies Have the Hardest Time, That Emigrate by Land"

JULIE ROY JEFFREY

As twentieth-century Americans living in the automotive age we think of ourselves as a geographically mobile people. The American family, it is said, is perpetually on the move. Job transfers, searches for new careers, and just plain wanderlust seem woven into our social fabric. Little do we realize that in the nineteenth century rootlessness was also epidemic in America, so much so that everyday life for thousands of families each year centered on breaking up a homestead, taking to the trail, and resettling in a distant location.

Daily life was far more affected by these relocations in the pre-automotive age because of the time they required and the conditions under which the trip was made. The transcontinental railroad was not completed until 1869, so most westward-moving Americans went by boat and wagon across the roadless plains and mountains. It was a trip that lasted not days but months. So much time elapsed that all the phases of life—birth, maturation, marriage, and death—were likely to occur at some point as a wagon caravan threaded its way from the East or the Midwest to the Rockies and the Pacific Coast.

The following selection by Julie Roy Jeffrey explores the trauma of the overland odyssey. The author is particularly concerned with the effect of the journey on how women thought about themselves. She argues that of necessity women began to take up men's work on the overland trail, though the reverse was much less frequent. Like women in the American Revolution, who were obliged to take up new tasks and assume new responsibilities, these women of the caravans shucked the cult of domesticity on the westward-moving frontier. Whether this alteration of sex roles produced a lasting change in women's attitudes and self-images after the destination was reached is another question, to which Jeffrey constructs an interesting answer.

Many years after her overland journey to California in 1860 Southern-born Lavinia Porter found the experience as vivid in her mind "as . . . yesterday's events." The trip, she observed, had been difficult, so difficult that it was still "a constant source of wonder to me how we [women] were able to endure it." That she and so many other women survived the months of hardship suggested to Porter that her sex shared some important characteristics. "An American woman well born and bred," she wrote, "is endowed with the courage of her brave pioneer ancestors, and no matter what the environment she can adapt herself to all situations, even to the perilous trip across the western half of this great continent, ever ready to wander over paths which women reared in other countries would fear to follow."

Porter's choice of courage and adaptability as the traits characterizing American pioneer women suggests that emigration forced women to modify normal behavioral patterns. As she realized, the frontier, which for most women began as soon as they left home and friends, challenged conventional sex roles and accepted modes of behavior. During the five- or six-month ordeal on the Overland Trail to California and Oregon, thousands of women challenged domestic stereotypes by assuming male responsibilities and undertaking men's work. In extreme cases, when husbands became ill or died, women took charge of the whole venture of moving west. Just as women performed men's work, so too, at least occasionally, did men find themselves doing tasks which society defined as women's. The lines of differentiation between the sexes, theoretically and often actually so clear in a culturally established setting, blurred. The months on the trail offered women a taste of a West which could disrupt cultural arrangements between the sexes and question sexual ideology. It was an opportunity for women to question, to modify, even to challenge established stereotypes. Yet few women did so; most did not find it easy to throw off accustomed ways of thinking even when forced into new ways of behaving. Possibly the polarization of sex roles which cast women into the role of the dependent, if superior, sex made it psychologically difficult to create sexual alternatives even when the environment seemed favorable. More likely, the trail experience suggests that women found comfort and personal reinforcement in their own sphere and were reluctant to abandon it altogether, no matter what stresses and tensions existed within it, no matter how far short of its standards women's conduct was.

It is, of course, difficult to generalize about women's responses to the trail experience since so few left any evidence of their passage at

"LADIES HAVE THE HARDEST TIME"   From Julie Roy Jeffrey, *Frontier Women: The Trans-Mississippi West, 1840–1880* (New York: Hill and Wang, 1979). Copyright © 1979 by Julie Roy Jeffrey. Reprinted by permission of Farrar, Straus and Giroux, Inc.

all. As one emigrant pointed out, "Pioneer women were quite too busy in making history to write it." The majority of women as well as men lacked the time and perhaps the skills to keep a diary or journal. Those who did keep accounts of their trip probably agreed with Elizabeth Geer, an Indiana woman, who observed, "I could have written a great deal more if I had had the opportunity. Sometimes I would not get the chance to write for two or three days, and then would have to rise in the night when my babe and all hands were asleep, light a candle and write." Reminiscences written years after the trip supplement travel journals, but these must be used cautiously, since time often cast a rosy glow over events on the trail. Still, we may know more about pioneer women taking the overland routes west than we know about them before or after. Since the long journey was a major event, quite different from the three or four shorter moves many had made to other frontiers, women kept diaries or reminisced about it.

Then, too, men kept diaries about this significant adventure which also reveal information about women during the months of enforced and intimate interaction. For many men and women the trail saga constituted their only contribution to the historical record of the westward movement and, in fact, the only record of their own lives.

Their journals, which focused on the five to six months of travel, first along the valley of the Platte River, then through the South Pass to destinations in California or Oregon, described the most popular but not the only means of reaching the Far West. It was possible, if costly, to sail from East Coast or Gulf ports to Central America, cross by land, and then continue by ship to final destinations in the West, or to go by sea around Cape Horn. During the first year of the gold rush, about 40,000 of the 100,000 fortune seekers chose ships. But the majority always went by land. Between 1841 and 1867, the years of heaviest traffic on the trails, 350,000 took the overland route to California and Oregon; others traveled part of the way by trail. So heavy was the traffic that parts of the trail resembled a highway several miles wide. With the completion of the transcontinental railroad in 1869, traffic gradually declined, although wagons crossing the South Pass were reported as late as 1895.

During the decades of the eighteen forties, fifties, and sixties, the basic pioneer pattern diverged from the familiar one of moving from one area to the adjoining frontier to emigration to the Far West. Those who could afford to do so crossed half a continent to a destination two thousand miles from starting points like Independence, Missouri. The relative neglect of frontier close at hand was due to a number of factors. The depression of the late thirties and early forties hit the recently settled Mississippi Valley hard. The financial calamity was accompanied by bad weather, floods, and disease. Influenza, plague, chills, malaria, and yellow fever helped make the area uninviting, while propaganda from the West Coast painted the frontier there in rosy col-ors. California was the land of eternal spring and endless fertility, while Oregon possessed rich soil and peaceful natives. In any case, land directly to the West was still Indian country, closed to settlement, and considered unsuitable for farming. It was not until the seventies that pioneers pushed eagerly out onto the prairies of Minnesota, the Dakotas, Nebraska, and Kansas, and in the eighties that they moved to the chancy, arid frontier sweeping from the Dakotas and Montana on the north to Texas to the south. Finally, the trek to the Far West was clearly possible as emigrants in the early forties, testing the overland route, proved. In 1843 the first mass migration, helped by the return of good times, set out for Oregon. Each year thereafter saw more emigrants selling out and starting on their way to the coast. In 1847 the Mormons opened their own trail cross the prairies. Eventually Salt Lake City would become a resting point for many of the emigrants headed for California.

Most of those who passed over the trail were young and often traveled with their immediate families or relatives. With the exception of the emigration of 1841 and the years during the height of the gold rush (1849–51), families rather than single people dominated the trail. In the forties, for example, approximately 50 percent of the emigrants were adult men, the other half women and children. After the excitement about California gold died down, the family pattern reappeared. Geographically, emigrants tended to come from rural and small-town backgrounds in the Midwest and upper South, although some hailed from the urban East or the newer cities of the Midwest. Many had moved several times before, however, often as children. The 1850 census of the Oregon Territory, revealing a cross-section of those who had emigrated, showed that almost half the adult men came originally from the East Coast, with only 11 percent born west of the Mississippi; most of the "native" Missourians were children of parents born elsewhere. The general composition of emigration, then, suggested a movement of families, many of whom had roots in the East.

Economically, emigrants were neither very rich nor very poor. Though family situations differed, all emigrants had to be financially solid enough to raise the substantial amount of cash necessary for the trip. Guidebooks estimated that emigration for four would come to over $600, although the sale of wagons and cattle at the trip's end might reduce final costs to $220. (A trip around the Horn was estimated at $600 per person.) Even those pushing out onto adjacent frontier land in the seventies and eighties required capital. Thousands began farming on the plains with *less* than $500, but the risks of doing so were high. Obviously emigration was not an option for the poor.

Women diarists, few when compared to the total number of women going west, seem representative of the mainstream overland migration. Most had lived most recently on Midwestern farms or in small towns there, though a few came directly from the East. Despite earlier moves to frontier settings (from Vermont to Indiana to Iowa to Oregon, for example), they were middle class in attitude and well acquainted with ideas of woman's sphere. It is, of course, true that there were other kinds of women on the trail, less obviously acculturated. Lavinia Porter, a Southern emigrant, described the rough and uncouth pioneers from Texas, Arkansas, and southwestern Missouri, the men blasphemers, the women "fitting mates for the men." She was not the only one to be disgusted with these emigrants, who, leaving little in the way of written records, cannot defend themselves. The trail experience may have differed by class or regional background, though how significant these differences were is impossible to determine. What we do know is what literate women thought and felt on the weary road west.

Their thoughts and emotions in the months preceding departure are, however, usually hidden. Most often their diaries start with the journey's beginning. Yet most must have suspected the arduous nature of the trip from their reading of guides and newspaper accounts. Folk music reinforced the theme of hardship. "The ladies have the hardest time, that emigrate by land, / For when they cook with buffalo wood, they often burn a hand; / And then they jaw their husbands round, get mad and spill the tea, / And wish the Lord, they'd be taken down with a turn of the dia-a-ree."

Since emigration meant months of hard living, one wonders what motivated women to go west at all. Were they just dragged unwillingly by their men or did they participate in the decision? If they contributed to the decision, what were their reasons for doing so? Though the sources are meager, they do suggest some answers to these questions.

The major impulse behind emigrating appears to have been economic. To one Ohio woman, "going to the far west seemed like the entrance to a new world, one of freedom, happiness and prosperity," while a Southern woman candidly admitted the "imprudent financial speculations" and embarrassments which led to her family's decision. The West was a land of promise, though whether the promise was one of land, gold, or professional opportunity partly depended on the destination. An important secondary factor involved health and climate. "We were bound to search for a healthier and milder clime than Illinois," one emigrant woman explained, "to spend the remainder of our days . . . I do not in the least regret leaving the sickness and cold, sand piles and lakes . . . behind and am looking forward to the time to arrive when we may all get settled safely at the place of our destination." Other women focused specifically on their own health and their hopes for its improvement.

Men were, of course, expected to "make decisions," especially about economic matters, and the evidence suggests a pattern in which men brought up the subject of emigrating. Some women were taken by surprise, for, as one said, "the thought of becoming a pioneer's wife had never entered my mind." But this did not mean that women were passive spectators. Their style was to respond, to influence, even to argue. Certainly, there were enough women participating effectively in the decision-making process to pass into Western folklore. A popular folk song, variously entitled the "Wisconsin Emigrant," the "Kentucky Song" or the "California Emigrant," suggests the extent of female influence. In it, a farmer suffering hard times at home decides to go west. His wife, reluctant to emigrate, unwilling to accept his initial decision, offers one reason after another to change his mind. All fails until she points out, "Remember, that land of delight / Is surrounded by Indians who murder by night. / Your house they will plunder and burn to the ground, / While your wife and your children lie murdered around." Her appeal succeeds, and her husband gives up his scheme, confessing, "I never had thought of your dying before . . . you, my dear wife, are more precious than all." Other evidence corroborates female power to affect decision-making. Since the trip's success usually hinged on the participation of all family members, a wife's stubbornness could block her husband's plans. "All my father could do," wrote one woman, "was to read every item of California news he could get and talk . . . for my mother would not be persuaded to undertake such a journey." Interestingly enough, this reluctant pioneer changed her mind only when her daughters and their husbands decided to emigrate for reasons of health. Even so, she insisted that their home be kept "unencumbered to return to in case we should not like California." The frequency with which marriage and emigration coincided suggests another facet of power. Whatever ideology had to say about the necessity of female submission, women felt free to disrupt male emigration projects and, because of the cooperative nature of pioneering or their single state, had bargaining powers. Of course, opposition to male schemes did not necessarily constitute a departure from female norms. Women, blessed with superior insight, had been told to direct and to influence their less sensitive husbands. The line between obstinacy and duty might well become blurred.

Others who shuddered at the idea of undertaking a "long and perilous journey" did not openly oppose their husbands. Their timid behavior reflected the standard interpretations of woman's nature at the same time that it highlighted an attempt to live up to the expected norms. For many women apparently forced themselves to acquiesce to the "dictates of duty." "My dear mother" did not oppose my father, wrote one daughter. "She tried to put down her fears for the perilous undertaking." Striving to act as a good wife, Abbey Fulkerath began her journal with these telling words: "Agreeable to the wish of my husband I left all my relatives . . . although it proved a hard task to leave them but still harder to leave my children buried in Milton graveyard but such is our lot on earth we are divided." There is no hint of resistance to her husband's plans.

But not all woman were reluctant emigrants. Those who thought emigration "a romantic wedding trip," or who thought like Lydia Rudd— who wrote in her journal one May day in 1852, "With good courage and not one sigh of regret I mounted my pony"—were positive about the move west. Their support for emigration reveals that, despite an ideology assigning men the responsibility for making economic decisions, women also participated in decision-making and shared men's opportunism. "We had nothing to lose, and we might gain a fortune," one woman wrote, hardly sounding the disinterested female. The dream of easy circumstances often attracted women as strongly as it did men, even leading one woman to conceal her pregnancy and to suppress her fears about her health so that she could go west that year.

Lying at the heart of women's interest in the economics of emigration were contradictions in the concept of domesticity. Women, unsullied by material interests, were supposed to find fulfillment at home. Yet, their ability to do so depended in some measure upon their husbands' economic success. Though ideology might proclaim that home was home, no matter how humble, most women knew better. Women wanted to live in easy circumstances in their own homes. All this took money. "Disinterested" women, therefore, were necessarily interested in economic questions, and in emigration if it seemed to offer a way of acquiring the resources needed for comfortable domesticity.

The vision of family life so central to domestic ideals also encouraged a positive female response to emigration. Mary Jane Hayden's explanation of the family decision to emigrate is revealing. When she learned her husband was contemplating a journey to California alone, Mary Jane told him she had resolved to go, too. "We were married," she said, "to *live together* . . . and I am willing to go with you . . . and under these circumstances *you have no right to go* where I cannot, and if you do, you need never return for I shall look upon you as dead." By insisting upon accompanying their husbands, women like Hayden showed how firmly they believed in the family and how determined they were that their husbands accept familial responsibilities. Letting a man go west alone, unless it were only to prepare a homesite, was a risky venture at best, even if the rationale was that of improving family finances. Women's magazines condemned gold fever because it unhinged men, making them feel "free as a bird" as they flew from "many a cheerful fireside . . . many a happy home." This "fearful curse" destroyed families and, in the end, the gold seekers themselves. Abandoning wives, children, and home meant "no fond arms wherein to rest . . . [a] cold brow as life fled!" So it was hardly surprising women willingly accompanied their husbands. "Where he could go I could," remarked one Missouri woman, while another pointed out, "It is the females that can improve your condition and make a home, and them alone."

Since the family provided meaning for women's lives and the basis for self-esteem, women might well wish to cooperate with emigration plans. How many were enthusiastic, how many reluctant, is unclear, since sources so rarely discuss the pre-trip scene. But those that do show a range of responses and suggest the need to avoid characterizing all women as reluctant emigrants. Of course, other factors also led to positive attitudes. The adventure and romance of emigration was appealing for some; a few mentioned their affection for their husbands. "I was very fond of my husband," recalled one, "and was nearly brokenhearted at the thought of the separation."

Missionary wives were a decidedly eager group of pioneers. To them the West was the means of realizing a religious vocation. This pattern of female commitment to religious work in the West became evident in the 1830's, when the first women participated in the short-lived attempt to convert Oregon's Indians. Early conversion experiences persuaded numerous single women that they must devote their lives to Christ. Since missionary societies generally frowned upon sending single women out into the mission field, however, they were relegated to teaching and good works at home unless they could find husbands. More often than one might expect, men who needed wives as assistant missionaries turned up; hasty proposals and marriages resulted. Although women might view such a marriage as part of a divine plan, the appearance of potential husbands was not entirely due to chance or God. Women like Almira David did pray "earnestly for some person who it appeared I was dependent on for going," but a network of friends and acquaintances often helped prayers come true. An Ithaca minister's letter to the mission board reveals the process of matchmaking at work. "A word in reference to their engagement and marriage," the pastor wrote. " 'Tis true their acquaintance had been very short—of but two or three weeks. . . . But Mr. Gray came well recommended to the Rev. Samuel Parker, thro' whom he became acquainted with Miss Dix." Nor were the women themselves unresourceful. One young woman, who at twenty-six was considered an old maid, albeit one with a missionary enthusiasm, attended the General Conference of Congregationalists in Bangor, Maine. There she met a young man sharing her devotion to missionary work who, in turn, wondered whether "possibly his prayers were being answered in the person of this lady." After corresponding, the two married and set out for Oregon in 1856. Since Eastern missionary societies sent over 2,600 men to the West by mid-century, the number of enthusiastic wives was substantial.

In an April entry of his 1853 trail journal, Henry Allyn observed, "Miss Martha Wood wishes to go with us and we conclude to take her." Allyn's entry noted an unusual event on the trail, the single woman moving west without the protection of family or friends. Their motives are usually hidden. There are tantalizing references such as the one in the Bradley diary to "four lewd females" on the trail and occasional comments about young women moving west to join bachelor brothers. But certainly, whether they hoped to support themselves, find husbands, or just have adventures in the West, these women decided for themselves.

The motives of one group of single women—teachers—for going west are clearer. Like female missionaries, these women saw themselves as part of a national effort to save the West for Protestantism and civilization. Catherine Beecher's educational campaign, initiated in 1845 with her book *The Duty of American Women to Their Country*, helped to organize hundreds of these women to go west to teach. A group, formed at the Mt. Vernon Congregational Church in Boston in 1846, defined its goal as sending "competent female teachers, of unquestioned piety, belonging to the Congregational Churches in New England," to the West. Although sectarian aims were apparent, the group also recognized that it could provide "a merciful provision for hundreds of well-educated Christian young women, whose sex forbids their adventuring as their brothers do, and yet who, if such a Society will encourage them, and send them forth, may go cheerfully and understandingly right to the best spot for them in all that wide region." Acting as an agency for single teachers, the group sent 109 women west before merging in 1854 with the Board of National Popular Education, founded by Beecher in 1847. The board not only acted as an agency but also gave prospective teachers some job training. Although the religious mission was strong, the organization was nonsectarian. By 1858 it had sent over a hundred women across the Mississippi who, in turn, often found jobs for friends. The organization's work was publicized through magazines like *Godey's Lady's Book* and served as an informal stimulus for other women to leave home for a Western schoolroom.

The records of the Board of National Popular Education contain revealing applications from prospective teachers. Of course, no application was entirely candid; applicants provided the kind of information the board wanted to read. Candidates had to describe conversion experiences, for example, and to place their goals within a religious framework. So Augusta Allan told the board, "I humbly trust that I have sought, and experienced this change [conversion], and that my motives in going West, are a desire to benefit others, and to be benefited myself." Like Allan, most women said they wanted to be useful in a region they described as religiously and culturally destitute. But the women gave a variety of other reasons for wishing to go west which reveal not only their own situation but their expectations. Many of them were already teaching, and thought the frontier might provide more opportunity and even more money. They frankly acknowledged their financial needs. "Being dependent upon my own exertions," wrote Betsey Brownell, "I feel it necessary also to look at the subject, in another light, which I think is not inconsistent with the spirit of doing good." These applications reveal how industrialization was affecting single women in the East. No longer economically essential within their families, unmarried women found themselves in a hazardous world offering them few means of support beyond factory work, domestic service, and teaching. Teaching was the most respectable and offered means for independence; teaching in the West might be an improvement.

Women also spoke of their desire for a better climate and hinted at health problems. Some told the board of a long-time interest in emigration, for the lure of adventure could play a part for women just as it did for men. As one candidate explained, she was interested in the welfare of others, but she was also driven by the "love of adventure and desire to be acquainted with the manners and customs of the inhabitants of more distant parts." Taken together, these applications indicate that these unmarried working women had a variety of positive reasons for undertaking the journey west, ranging from the need to support themselves to the desire to see the world.

What evidence there is on women's motivation and involvement in planning the trip west, then, suggests the danger of viewing women solely as reluctant pioneers. This did not mean that they would not experience a sense of loss at leaving family and friends behind. Both sexes did. But it warns against describing women as passive victims of men's choices rather than as active participants in the process of emigration.

No matter how the decision to go west was reached, no matter how great or small a part women played in it, leave-taking was a traumatic experience. Weeks of activity preceded the day of departure and for some concealed the reality of leaving itself. Women were busy sewing, making dresses, sunbonnets, tents, wagon covers, and seeing their friends. As women attended to these female chores, men disposed of the homestead, either selling or renting it, and acquired the stock, wagons, and supplies the guides said were necessary. Finally, the moment came for farewells. Leave-taking occurred at home, or friends and relatives accompanied the emigrants for a day's journey. The occasion was usually a solemn and sad one as both the emigrants and the stay-at-homes contemplated the implications of the departure. "On the evening before [starting], the whole family, including my mother, were gathered together in the parlor, looking as if we were all going to our graves the next morning," one woman wrote. "There we sat in such gloom, that I could not endure it any longer, and I arose and announced that we would retire for the night, and that we would not start tomorrow morning, not until everybody could feel more cheerful."

Some diaries poignantly describe the tears shed by men and women alike as they set out. Others have terse, yet equally revealing, entries, like the one written by Amelia Knight, "STARTED FROM HOME." The very brevity conveys the emotion of the scene. Men and women both experienced a sense of loss. For the women, however, though emigration symbolized a means of realizing the domestic sphere, it also ripped away some of its supporting framework. True, the immediate and sometimes not so immediate family might remain intact when groups of relations and friends traveled west together. And equally true was the fact that women were socialized to expect the experience of losing family and friends when they married and moved away from mother, sisters, and friends. But this did not make it any easier to leave the current home with its familiar objects and rituals, with its groups of female companions and relatives who had contributed so much to one another's emotional life. And this move, unlike earlier moves to nearby frontiers, would separate friends by vast distances. It represented what well might be a permanent break. No wonder a deep sense of loss pervades the records. In her journal, Lodisa Frizzell asked herself, "Who is there that does not recollect their first night when started on a long journey, the wellknown voices of our friends still ring in our ears, the parting kiss feels still warm upon our lips, and that last separating word *Farewell!* sinks deeply into the heart. It may be the last we ever hear from some or all of them, and to those who start . . . there can be no more solemn scene of parting only at death." That women so often compared leave-taking to death was at once a realistic assessment that it was "not at all probable that we ever will meet again on this side of the dark river," as well as a symbolic recognition that the emotional void was like death itself. As for what lay ahead, it was "so far away and vague, that it seemed very unreal" to many of the women at the outset of the journey. What was real was what was behind.

Women's diaries, more than men's, tended to focus on the friends at home. An early entry in Anne Booth's journal suggests many others. "Nothing can atone for the loss of society of friends." The trip was hard enough, women wrote, without having "our hearts torn by the loss of dear ones." Although their marriage might be an affectionate one, a husband did not usually compensate for the loss of female friends. Men, too, of course, missed old companions, but Asahel Munger's reaction to his wife's grief typifies the male point of view. "This day has been rather long and lonesome to E," he wrote. "She thought much of home—friends—prospects—& present condition. I tried to have her get above these things." Men did not dwell on absent friends in their journals; women did. Perhaps the long hours women spent sitting in wagons while men herded cattle, forded rivers, and drove wagons encouraged them to reminisce about absent friends.

Most women, however, did try to "get above these things." As they catalogued each sign of the passing of civilization, women coped with their sense of desolation by reproducing aspects of the world they had left behind. Thus, women arranged their wagons, writing in their journals of the little conveniences they had fixed, the pockets in the wagon's green cloth lining which held "looking-glasses, combs, brushes, and so on," the rag carpet to keep the floor of the tent snug at night, the bedding, sleeping, and dressing arrangements. As one woman explained, she was busy making "our home" comfortable so that there would be little time "for that dreaded disease, 'home-sickness.' " Another hoped to maintain some continuity by dressing as neatly on the trip as she might at home, in a blue traveling dress with white collar and cuffs rather than homespun, linsey-woolsey or calico.

These attempts to reproduce the rudiments of a home setting and to perpetuate a sense of the familiar, though they might appear trivial, were not. Publicists of domesticity had encouraged women to believe that the physical arrangements of their homes exerted a powerful influence over their families. The makeshifts of the journey were an unconscious way of asserting female power and reassuring women of their sexual identity. And, of course, the objects symbolized an entire way of life temporarily in abeyance. When her husband grumbled about the quantity of her baggage, Lucy Cooke revealed how vital her knick-knacks were. Fearing that she would have to discard some of her luggage, she confessed, "I had a cry about it . . . as I seemed to have parted with near everything I valued."

Although Cooke's husband promised to stop complaining about belongings which provided so much comfort for her, other women would find it difficult to maintain symbolic ties with home life and the female world. The woman who started out in a traveling dress with clean collar and cuffs soon found she had to abandon it for clothes she originally had refused to wear. Indeed, changes in clothing hinted at the social disruption the frontier could cause women. By 1852, some women on the trail were wearing the bloomer costume, finding the "short skirt and pantletts" a "very appropriate dress for a trip like this." Although bloomers were practical, the costume, espoused by feminists as dress for liberated women, carried a radical sexual and political message and was, in the words of one magazine, "ridiculous and indecent." So one woman who had brought bloomers with her found she lacked the "courage" to wear them and vowed, "I would never wear them as long as my other two dresses last." Women bickered over the pros and cons of the costume. Supporters accused women in dresses of being vain and preoccupied with appearance, while they, in turn, replied that bloomers led to male gossip. Said one opponent, "She had never found her dress to be the least inconvenient . . . she could walk as much in her long dress as she *wanted to, or was proper for a woman* among so many men."

At the beginning of the trip, however, there were only hints of a disruption of "propriety" as both sexes attempted to maintain the comforting division of labor based on the concept of distinct sexual spheres. Generally men drove the wagons, repaired them, hunted, ferried the cattle and wagons across rivers, and stood guard at night, while women were responsible for the children, meals, and family washing.

"Felt very tired indeed—went to bed early," wrote Ellen Tompkins Adams in a typical journal entry. The refrain of constant fatigue occurs over and over again in women's diaries. On the trail women's work was difficult and exhausting. Maternal duties were taxing. Some women were in the last stages of pregnancy on the trip, although few of them mentioned it in their journals. Apparently pregnancy was a subject discussed among friends but not on paper (even in letters to female relatives, women approached the subject indirectly by talking about making baby clothes) until the baby had been safely delivered. Once the baby was born there was little time to regain strength. A day or so of rest before the trip resumed was about the most any new mother could expect. Some recovered quickly and resumed their chores, but for others childbirth proved a nightmare. "Her sufferings were so great," wrote one woman of her sister, "that she does not remember anything for quite a space along there. It all seems like a jumble of jolting wagon, crying baby, dust, sagebrush and the never ceasing pain."

Child care was complicated by traveling. Although older children often walked and herded loose cattle, mothers had to supervise their small children in the wagon all day. It must have been almost impossible to keep children good-tempered in cramped quarters; accidents were an ever-present possibility. Diaries refer to children falling out of wagons, under wagons, miraculously escaping harm, breaking limbs or even being killed in accidents. Their more careful older brothers and sisters caused concern by wandering or riding off or lagging behind and disappearing. Children of all ages came down with fevers, diarrhea, even cholera, and became fretful in a lurching, hot, and uncomfortable wagon. It is not surprising that journals often mentioned children as frightened, weeping, or disagreeable, but that mothers characterized their children in this way did not mean that they were necessarily unfeeling or that they did not accept conventional sentimentalized views of children. Hovering behind many of their comments lay the very real fear of a loved child's death, of leaving a "little body in that strange country for the Indians to dig up or wild beasts to devour." Part of women's exhaustion was psychological.

Preparing meals was also a challenge. Morning and evening cooking took place over campfires or camp stoves in all weather. "Unpleasant as it is, I have been cooking beans and stewing fruit and baking bread," noted one women on a blowy, rainy day. Clothes were reduced to tatters "from coming into frequent contact with the camp fire," and occasionally serious accidents occurred. "Her dress caught fire from the stove," Mary Fisher observed, "and before it could be extinguished it was nearly burned off her." This she considered *almost* a bad accident.

Despite these trying conditions, women were satisfied when they carried out their traditional tasks successfully. As one woman observed, she suspected the other women "engaged in helping to cook supper . . . all enjoyed it heartily, as I did." In some trains, men had been hired to do the cooking. But rather than enjoying their freedom, privileged women in those trains often reported that they wished to take over the cooking, either because "the boys kept everything so dirty," or "because we liked it." When women did the cooking, one explained, the meals were more regular, less wasteful, and tasty. She could also have added that when women cooked it was more like home.

In numerous other ways women sought to continue their familiar round of activities during the early and relatively easy months of travel through the Platte River Valley. The journals noted the times when they cared for the sick and the dying of their own company and when they visited other trains in their efforts to help out. As at home, they sustained one another in the familiar rituals of birth and death. "Late in the afternoon a group of women stood watching Mrs. Wilson's little babe as it breathed its last," wrote one woman describing an important moment of emotional support. And women made efforts to maintain the remnants of their female network on a daily rather than just an emergency basis. They reached out to construct new support groups for the journey. "During the day," Catherine Haun, an emigrant from Iowa, explained, "we womenfolk visited from wagon to wagon or congenial friends spent an hour walking, ever westward, and talking over our home life back in 'the states'; telling of the loved ones left behind; voicing our hopes for the future . . . and even whispering a little friendly gossip of emigrant life." As women exchanged recipes, as they knitted and crocheted, they were keeping themselves "in the practice of female occupations and diversions." The journals indicate the feelings of satisfaction women felt when they visited, cooked together, or went swimming, and their frustration when "the plain fact of the matter is, *we have no time for sociability.*"

But as the trip wore on, and the rolling prairies receded and gave way to harsh deserts and mountains, it became clear that women would be unable to keep the world they valued intact. Knickknacks, treasured belongings were cast aside in an effort to lighten the wagons and quicken the pace so that provisions and animals would survive until the journey's end. Female friendships were broken off as companies separated.

When friends parted, women wept. "We had become so attached to each other having travelled so far together, and being dependent on each other in times of danger and accidents," explained one woman, while another, facing separation from her sister because of their husbands' "first class row," confessed that her sister "did not feel that she would ever be happy again." Troubling, too, was the prospect of being without the comforting company of other women. Ellen Adams, who nursed a sick woman in her train, finally had to leave the invalid and her husband behind at an army barracks. "I felt very badly to come away as there are no women at the Fort," she reported, evidently thinking the presence of soldiers and husband hardly compensated for the loss of female companionship.

Ultimately, even standard chores became unfamiliar and unfeminine. Cooking not only reduced women's clothes to rags and tatters but also forced women to take on jobs at which a lady would blush. As cooks, women found meal preparation often included gathering fuel. Since firewood was scarce on the trail, buffalo dung, called "chips," served for cooking. Some women saw the dung as the practical solution to the fuel problem. Others found gathering the chips demeaning and indelicate. "This caused many ladies to act very cross and many were the rude phrases uttered, far more humiliating to refined ears than any mention of the material used for fuel could have been," observed one of the pragmatists from Missouri. Some of the women wore gloves to avoid touching the dung, although eventually "most of them . . . discarded their gloves," and accepted unpleasant reality. Using the chips to cook food was another problem. "Mother thought at first she could not do that," recalled one daughter, and though, as always, her mother compromised, "she was never reconciled to that kind of fire, and never liked to think of those experiences afterwards."

Familiar patterns disintegrated under the trip's strain, and even the comforting sense of the flow of time vanished. Most striking was the disappearance of the Sabbath, which had become by mid-century a symbol of women's religious and moral authority. Initially many women had hoped to use the day for worship and rest. Parties lucky enough to have both a preacher and leaders who considered layovers no threat to the train's pace observed the Sabbath. But often the need to find water and food for the cattle, the need to make mileage, made traveling on the Sabbath necessary, especially as the months passed. Women had to agree, but confided in their journals that they were unhappy with the situation. Traveling "does not seem pleasant," on the Sabbath, wrote one, while another felt that the waters of the river her company had forded "seemed to reproach us."

Even when the caravan broke the journey to observe a day of rest, women found they had few moments for meditation or relaxation. "I was obliged to do many things I was very loth to do on the Sabbath,"

Esther Hanna revealed in her diary. Pennsylvania had been different. Baking, washing, mending, sewing all continued, Sabbath or no, while men had a break from their activities. Men, one sympathetic woman explained, needed "physical rest, so they lolled around in the tents and on their blankets spread on the grass, or under the wagons out of the sunshine, seeming to realize that the 'Sabbath was made for men' . . . [Yet] women, who had only been anxious spectators of their arduous work [during the week], and not being weary in body, could not fully appreciate physical rest." Whether men deserved the rest or not, "Does not seem like Sunday at all today—have been obliged to work nearly all day" was a constant refrain tired women echoed. The truth was, one sadly reflected, it was just impossible to have a real Sabbath on the trail. "And today is Sunday again. O what Sundays. There is nothing that seems like the Sabbath."

As civilization receded, some of the ways in which women thought about themselves changed. Domesticity suggested true women were feminine and attractive. However unlikely the attainment of this ideal, it shaped women's views of themselves and served as a normative goal. But it was a losing battle to be concerned about appearances on the frontier, and most women stopped thinking in these terms altogether. "As the days lengthened into weeks, our self-respect suffered somewhat in the matter of clothes," wrote one, who described her skirt as "a piece of wide fringe hanging from belt to hem." Another explained, "We were so worn out that we were not particular how we were dressed but presented a mixture of fashions." Only after the trip was nearly over did Luzena Wilson suddenly realize how thoroughly she had forgotten the female norms she had observed in Missouri. As her party drew near to its destination, a man dressed in a clean white shirt came out to meet the travelers. The sight of someone in respectable clothes jolted Wilson and, as she recalled, "revived in me the languishing spark of womanly vanity." Realizing how she looked in her ragged sunbonnet, tattered skirts, "worn off in rags above my ankles," her face sunburnt, her hands "brown and hard," and, of course, gloveless, she shrank modestly away from the man's observation. By the end of the journey, Lavinia Porter agreed, "I doubt whether any of us could have been recognized."

"Getting tough, I can tell you," Mary Warner noted in her diary, after describing driving one of the wagons. If some familiar norms were forgotten, new ones were useful. For it was just as well if women got tough. As the trip progressed, women continued to be responsible for washing, cooking, and caring for children. But under the strain of travel, of parties splitting and hired hands quitting, women also took on jobs once clearly defined as male. They pitched tents, loaded and unloaded wagons, drove them, yoked the cattle. Some even drove stray cattle on horseback, and one surprised man noted "a couple of ladies" galloping

full speed ahead after the beasts. Another disapprovingly noted that
ladies even rode astride, "the greatest curiosity I have seen yet." Women
whose husbands became sick or died on the trail, of course, assumed
all the responsibilities for the family's survival and welfare, unless they
were lucky enough to fall under the protection of another man. For
many travelers, the line dividing the actual activities of men and women
blurred and, in some cases, disappeared.

As women did men's work, men did women's. Single men shifted
for themselves, but even married men sometimes helped with the
washing and, when their wives were sick or out of humor, did the
cooking. Some women suggested that helpfulness was a regional characteristic. As one wrote in her journal, she was lucky to have a Yankee
for a husband, "so am well waited on." But another pioneering wife,
from the South, felt that male courtesy and sharing was rare. "Men on
the plains . . . were not so accommodating nor so ready to serve or
wait upon women as they were in more civilized communities." If men
helped with female work from time to time, this did not mean they did
it regularly. Most of the disintegration of work roles affected women.
A man assuming female responsibilities was doing a favor. A women
doing a male job was doing what was necessary.

Because of the many unavoidable difficulties of the journey and the
exhausting grind of steady work, most women automatically cooper-
ated with shifting requirements. There seemed to be no alternative. But
some women welcomed the expansion of the female sphere. Rebecca
Ketcham, a single woman from New York traveling west with friends,
reported her riding adventures with glee. Others wrote that they enjoyed driving wagons and were proud of their ability to handle animals. They noted incidents which they felt revealed courage and skill.
Some went so far as to adopt the symbol of masculinity, the gun. "I
keep close to my gun and dog," commented one woman from Illinois.

But even when women seemed to enjoy their new responsibilities,
few speculated on the significance of their actions or capitalized on
their increased importance within the family. For most women found
the trip neither exhilarating nor liberating. Far from welcoming the expansion of the female sphere, a few specifically found fault with it.
"There were occasional angry debates while various burdens were being
adjusted," noted one diarist. "Warner says I am cross for the first time,"
wrote a young wife. "Well none of the women think it their duty to
help the cook, and he is cross if he doesn't get help, and of course he
gets tired also." Women complained to their journals and to each other
more about their fatigue, the monotony of the daily routine, the dirt
and dust, than they did about their unaccustomed duties, but the point
was the same. "This gy[p]sy life is anything but agreeable." "It is impossible to keep anything clean, and it is with difficulty that you do
what . . . you have to do." The meaning of this catalogue of griev-

ances is captured in a typical passage in the journal of a woman who had already moved once from Ohio to Iowa. "Oh dear," she confessed, "I do so want to get there it is now almost four months since we have slept in a house. If I could only be set down at home with all the folks I think there would be some talking as well as resting." Women hoped not to expand their domestic sphere but to recapture it.

Women's cultural values were also revealed when they came into contact with Mormons and Indians during the trip. Unable to see Mormons as the persecuted defenders of religious freedom or Indians as either noble savages or the victims of white civilization, women perceived both as threats to domestic culture. Only when the Indian or Mormon seemed to conform to their own standards did the women have anything positive to say. Thus, they admired Salt Lake City, a stopping-off point for California emigrants, for its beautiful plan, its cozy, snug homes, its prosperous and bustling air. Observant women approved of Indian mothers who made children's bonnets, or who dressed neatly and presented a "clean and wholesome . . . appearance," and even Indian men who seemed to be noble warriors and "well behaved."

But more often than not, women saw the similarities between their own culture and Mormon or Indian culture as superficial. Underneath it all, Margaret Hecox reflected, Indians were "just Indians." "I doubt if the savage instinct can ever be eradicated from the wild man's breast." Disgustedly, women recorded that Indians were thieves and beggars, little recognizing how their own civilization had contributed to the disintegration of Indian society. Indians were habitually described as filthy, lazy, dishonest, and harsh to women. As for the Mormons, the female writers found the men "very hard looking" and the women ugly. In the eyes of the overland emigrant woman, the two groups represented the collapse of civilized life and a negation of familial values.

Underlying the observations ran a fear of sex uncontrolled by all the conventions of nineteenth-century society. Women constantly commented on and obviously closely observed the nakedness of Indian men, who were "guiltless of clothing . . . very many . . . in the state of our first parents before they committed their first sin." Indians' sexuality was clearly suggested by many popular captivity accounts with their female victims who recollected savages whipping their "almost naked" bodies. Readers could easily imagine what other foul acts Indians perpetrated upon the "almost naked" female form. The actions of men seemed to reinforce the idea that they lusted after white women's bodies. A number of women recounted episodes in which Indian men tried to trade ponies for white women. The women's response was one of stark fear. Some described hiding in wagons to avoid the savage's flattery. Others became the butt of their husbands' sense of humor. One revealed that her husband pretended to strike a bargain with an Indian, his wife for two ponies. The Indian, little realizing the joke, generously offered three, "then he took hold of my shawl to make me understand to get out. About this time I got frightened and really was so hysterical, began to cry."

If the intentions of Indians seemed clear to these diarists, so too were the polygamous practices of the Mormons. Women writers assumed polygamy exploited women sexually without giving them anything in return. "These demons marry some girls at ten years of age," wrote one horrified observer who emphasized that the demons often took on "a mother and her daughters and marry them all." To get "only one third or perhaps one twentieth share of a man" was hardly worth the hard work Mormon men expected of their wives. Indeed, Mormon wives were "all . . . a poor heart broken and deluded lot and are made slaves to the will of these hellish beings who call themselves men. . . . They have not so much liberty as common slaves in the south." The fear of sexual license and the conviction that women in the other culture were men's slaves suggests the confidence these women had in their own values and social place as well as their fear of change.

These confrontations with an alien world and the hardships of travel which increased so dramatically during the second part of the trip caused women, at times, to feel fearful and bitter. Under stress, some women turned against their husbands and blamed them for the whole unhappy undertaking. "I felt as though myself and little ones were at the mercy of a madman," Mary Powers reflected, while Margaret Hecox, who had retreated into the family's wagon with her children as the rest of the party watched an Indian war dance, agreed. "I wondered what had possessed my husband, anyway, that he should have thought of bringing us away out through this God-forsaken country. I feared that we all were to be scalped or taken prisoners before morning." After a moving description of her younger brother's sickness and death, Ada Millington tersely observed, "Ma thinks if we had been 'at home he needn't have died.' "

Despite her bitter thoughts, it apparently did not occur to Margaret Hecox to confront her husband. Nor did Mary Powers, who noted in her reminiscences, "I said nothing." The ways in which women handled their frustrations most often testifies to their attempts to live up to norms of female behavior, at least in front of their men. Lavinia Porter confessed she often cried, wished herself at home, and then returned to chores with an air of assumed cheerfulness. For others, keeping journals must have served as a legitimate release of tension and as a place for cataloguing grievances. "This journey is tiresome . . . it is perilous, the deaths of many testify, and the heart has a thousand misgivings, and the mind is tortured with anxiety," explained one weary woman in her journal. Women also expressed their grievances to one another. "Husband is scolding and hurrying all hands (and the cook), and Almira says she wished she was at home, and I say ditto." And occasionally all the women gathered together to share their feelings. "The female portion of our little train are almost discouraged," observed one writer. "We sat by moonlight and discussed matters till near 11 o'clock."

On August 3, 1854, Mary Burrell wrote, "Worse than all, stuck my nose in where I had no business." Though she did not reveal what she had done, the entry suggests that though women most often seem to have tried to keep their place, they did not always succeed. Nor were men more successful. Both sexes indulged in disagreeable and petty behavior. "All out of humor" noted one woman, while another revealed she had hardly expected "to see so much selfishness and bad temper." "Being jolly when you are so tired yourself is no picknick," observed one woman still well enough socialized to feel it was her duty to cheer the "tired and cross" men. Men admitted in their journals to "heavy hearts," quarrels, complaints, and described shockingly inappropriate masculine behavior. John Minto told of coming across a father of four, "lying on his back upon a rock, taking the rain in his face, seemingly given up all thought of manly struggle." The cry of Indians sent some of the men of another train scurrying to hide in the wagons, courage fast forgotten. Vignettes of inept husbands unable to control their wives' behavior suggested how hollow were the claims of some to male authority.

It is not surprising that given the difficulties of the journey social restraints occasionally broke down and frustrations, usually controlled, exploded. As tension built up in one party, the observant Rebecca Ketcham noted how the behavior of all her fellow travelers changed. "It does seem as though we might have everything pleasant, but is all the other way. Mr. Gray [the captain] scolds when he is around, and when he is away the rest scold and find fault with him." As time passed, Rebecca detailed how the women finally stopped complaining to each other, abandoned all sense of woman's place, and "talked pretty plain [to Mr. Gray] me more so than ever. I don't know how he liked it, but I cannot help it." Other examples of what could be called female insubordination crop up in the diaries: women refusing to cook, women refusing to camp at the assigned spot, a few trying to bring the trip to an end altogether. One set flames to the family wagon; another beat her husband with a horsewhip. These were the extreme, but subtle resistance was, no doubt, more common and also less likely to be recorded. Lavinia Porter, who disapproved of her husband's barrel of whiskey, described what she did. Sure that complaints or reasoning would fall on deaf ears, she resorted to indirection, certainly a part of the female style. "I patiently bided my time, and one day when no one was around," she proudly recounted later, "I quietly loosened . . . the barrel . . . and by nightfall there was nothing left."

A 250-pound woman berated and abused her husband, "charging him with bringing his wife and children out into the God-forsaken country to starve and die"; she was, however, the exception and Lavinia Porter probably more typical. But neither open insubordination nor indirect resistance apparently resulted in any clear rethinking of the female role or of the relations between the sexes. Rather, women struck out blindly, angry at the tedium of the trip and the prolonged disruption of their female world. They were, perhaps, too tired to do otherwise. And as the journey neared its end, there seemed less and less need to rethink as women's thoughts turned more and more to the future and the reestablishment of their world, now so sharply contrasted with life on the trail. What had initially been vague now loomed close. "I am very weary of this journey, weary of myself and all around me," wrote one woman in late August. "I long for the quiet of home where I can be at peace once more."

The journals and reminiscences show the rich variety of responses women pioneers had to the overland experience. They noted the cheerful and lively moments as well as those of suffering and death. Many testified to the new and strong ties they had formed with one another, a good beginning for a new life. "I feel that the good friends we have made on the journey more than make up for the hardship," noted one woman. The trip had been a mixed experience. But now it was time to start anew. At the end of her journey, one woman wrote this artless poem which captures so much of the response of women to emigration.

> Day after day
> We wend our way; Through sage and sand,
> In hope to find,
> To please our mind,
> A home in a happy land.

Suggestions for Further Reading

For contrasting views of antebellum slave life the student can probe John Blassingame, *The Slave Community: Plantation Life in the Ante-Bellum South** (New York, 1972); Eugene D. Genovese, *Roll, Jordan, Roll: The World the Slaves Made** (New York, 1974); Herbert G. Gutman, *The Black Family in Slavery and Freedom** (New York, 1976); and Lawrence W. Levine, *Black Culture and Black Consciousness: Afro-American Folk Thought from Slavery to Freedom* (New York, 1977). Also valuable are Kenneth Stampp, *The Peculiar Institution: Slavery in the Ante-Bellum South** (New York, 1956); Vincent Harding, *There Is a River: The Black Struggle for Freedom in America* (New York, 1981); George P. Rawick, *From Sundown to Sunup: The Making of the Black Community* (Westport, Conn., 1972); Nathan Huggins, *Black Odyssey: The Afro-American Experience in Slavery** (New York, 1978); and Charles Joyner, *Down by the Riverside: A South Carolina Slave Community* (Urbana, Ill., 1984).

Education, transmitted through either formal institutions or the daily experience of living, was woven into everyone's life. For a conceptual discussion of this see Bernard Bailyn, *Education in the Forming of American Society** (Chapel Hill, N.C., 1964). On rearing children in the antebellum period see Bernard Wishy, *The Child and the Republic: The Dawn of Modern American Child Culture* (Philadelphia, 1967). For secondary education the inquiring student can turn to Andrew Gulliford, *America's Country Schools* (Washington, D.C., 1984); Carl F. Kaestle, *Pillars of the Republic: Common Schools and American Society, 1780–1860* (New York, 1983); Stanley K. Schultz, *The Culture Factory: Boston Public Schools, 1789–1860* (New York, 1973); Wayne E. Fuller, *The Old Country School: The History of Rural Education in the Middle West* (Chicago, 1982); and David Nasaw, *Schooled to Order: A Social History of Public Schooling in the United States* (New York, 1979).

The western frontier experience, for both old-stock Americans and immigrants, is well described in Richard A. Bartlett, *The New Country: A Social History of the American Frontier, 1776–1890** (New York, 1974); Everett Dick, *The Sod-House Frontier, 1854–1890* (New

*Available in paperback edition.

458

York, 1937); Merle Curti, *The Making of an American Community: A Case Study of Democracy in a Frontier County** (Stanford, Cal., 1959); Rodman W. Paul, *Mining Frontiers of the Far West, 1848–1880** (New York, 1963); Johnny Faragher and Christine Stansell, "Women and Their Families on the Overland Trail to California and Oregon, 1842–1867," *Feminist Studies*, 2 (1975): 150–66; Sandra L. Myres, ed., *Ho for California!* (San Marino, Cal., 1980) and *Westering Women and the Frontier Experience, 1800–1915* (Albuquerque, N.M., 1982); and Lillian Schlissel, *Women's Diaries of the Westward Journey* (New York, 1982). Complementing these studies are the poignant novels of frontier life, such as Willa Cather, *My Antonia** (Boston, 1926); Hamlin Garland, *A Son of the Middle Border** (New York, 1917) and *A Daughter of the Middle Border** (New York, 1921).

For the eastern immigrant experience in the nineteenth century, the inquiring student can begin with Oscar Handlin, *Boston's Immigrants, 1790–1865: A Study in Acculturation** (Cambridge, Mass., 1941); Robert Ernst, *Immigrant Life in New York City, 1825–1863* (New York, 1949); Barbara M. Solomon, *Ancestors and Immigrants: A Changing New England Tradition* (Cambridge, Mass., 1956); and Maldwyn Jones, *Destination America* (New York, 1976).

The experience of Americans during the Civil War can be probed in George W. Smith and Charles Judah, eds., *Life in the North during the Civil War: A Source History* (Albuquerque, N.M., 1966); Bell Wiley, *The Life of Billy Yankee: The Common Soldier of the Union* (Indianapolis, 1952) and *Southern Negroes, 1861–1865** (New Haven, 1938); Frank Owsley, *Plain Folk of the Old South* (Baton Rouge, 1949); Mary E. Massey, *Ersatz in the Confederacy* (Columbia, S.C., 1952); Charles W. Ramsdell, *Behind the Lines in the Southern Confederacy* (Baton Rouge, 1944); and Peter Levine, "Draft Evasion in the North during the Civil War, 1863–1865," *Journal of American History*, 67 (1981): 816–34.

B 8
C 9
D 0
E 1
F 2
G 3
H 4
I
J 5

CPSIA information can be obtained
at www.ICGtesting.com
Printed in the USA
FFOW01n1905131115
18616FF

9 780534 142490